Poverty, Poverty Alleviation and Social Disadvantage:

Analysis, Case Studies and Policies

Poverty, Poverty Alleviation and Social Disadvantage:

Analysis, Case Studies and Policies

VOLUME - I

CLEM TISDELL

SERIALS PUBLICATIONS
NEW DELHI (INDIA)

First Published - 2007

ISBN: 978-81-8387-111-2

Published by

SERIALS PUBLICATIONS
4830/24, Prahlad Street, Ansari Road
Darya Ganj, New Delhi-110002 (India)
Phone : 23245225. Fax : 91-11-23272135
E-mail: serials@satyam.net.in

CONTENTS

PREFACE

Economics is mainly concerned with the problem of reducing scarcity by improving the management of society's available resources. Because poverty involves severe scarcity of commodities, it ought to be one of central concern of economics. Nevertheless, poverty is not just an economic matter–it also involves other dimensions such as social, cultural and institutional elements. Therefore, it is appropriate that contributions to this book, *Poverty, Poverty Alleviation and Social Disadvantage,* are from both economists and non-economists. This is especially appropriate because poverty usually entails social disadvantage. Furthermore, a reduction in social disadvantage is often a prerequisite for reducing the incidence of poverty among particular social groups and vice versa.

Although the economic wealth of the world has increased greatly in recent times, overcoming poverty still remains a pressing issue, particularly (but not exclusively) in the developing world. In its declaration for the second millennium, the United Nations identified the need to overcome poverty (and its associated ills) as the most important goal for the 21st century.

The main, but not the exclusive, focus of this book is on the study of poverty and poverty alleviation in developing countries, as well as policies for alleviating or for averting the occurrence of poverty and social disadvantage.

Contributors come from many different parts of the world and present diverse perspectives on poverty, poverty alleviation and social disadvantage. I wish to thank all contributors for the time and effort that they have put into preparing their contributions. All papers have been subject to review.

This book has its genesis in contacts that were established at the 86th Annual Conference of the Indian Economic Association (IEA) held in Kolhapur, Maharashta, India when I gave the Keynote Address on poverty and poverty alleviation at the invitation of Professor Raj Kumar Sen, the then President of the IEA. It was also there that Mr. S.K. Jha of Serials Publication made contact with me and requested me to edit a book on economic globalisation. This book entitled *Globalisation and World Economic Policies: Effects and Policy Responses of Nations and their Groupings*, was published by Serials Publications in 2005. This led to a subsequent request from Mr. Jha to consider a further edited book with Serials. With further encouragement from Mr. Vijay Kumar of Serials Publications, this has resulted in the present work, which he wanted to consist of three volumes. At the time, I was also editing a special issue of the *Indian Development Review (IDR)* focusing on poverty and poverty alleviation. Consequently, I requested that at least some of the relevant articles from this special issue of the *IDR* be incorporated in this larger work. To this, Mr. Kumar agreed.

I appreciate the enthusiasm of Serials Publications for publishing this work and their professional approach to its production. I thank Genivieve Larsen for assisting with initial correspondence involved in the planning of this book, Evelyn Smart and Adeline Edwards for adjusting and formatting manuscripts, and Dr. Glyn Edwards for assistance with the editing of the contributions. I am grateful to the School of Economics at The University of Queensland for its support and use of facilities. I also appreciate the support of Mariel, my wife, for this project.

I hope this book will improve our understanding of the reasons for the occurrence of poverty and provide new insights into the effectiveness of policies to address it. In addition, it should provide new perspectives on social disadvantages and policies to reduce these. Social disadvantage and poverty are often interrelated. A feature of this book is that its coverage of concepts, policies and analysis is strengthened by case studies and empiricism.

Clem Tisdell
Brisbane
Australia

LIST OF CONTRIBUTORS

Clem Tisdell, Professor Emeritus, School of Economics, The University of Queensland, Brisbane, 4072, Australia.

Raj Kumar Sen, Professor of Economics, Rabindra Bharati University, 'Asutosh Dham' 35. Bipin Mitra Lane, Kolkata, 700004, India.

Ratan Lal Basu, Reader in Economics, Bhairab Ganguly College, Kolkata, India.

Tariq Saiful Islam, Department of Economics, Rajshahi University, Rajshahi 6205, Bangladesh.

Md Abdul Wadud, Corresponding author, is also at the above address. Email: wadud68@yahoo.com.

Qamarullah Bin Tariq Islam, Previously Centre for Policy Dialogue, Dhaka, Bangladesh.

Peter Warr, John Crawford Professor of Agricultural Economics and Director, Poverty Research Centre, Division of Economics, Research School of Pacific and Asian Studies, Australian National University, Canberra, ACT 2601, Australia.

Joe Remenyi, Associate Professor, International and Community Development, Deakin University, Pigdons Road, Geelong Victoria, 3217, Australia.

Max Kelly, Lecturer, International and Community Development, Deakin University, Pigdons Road, Geelong Victoria, 3217, Australia.

Kam Ki Tang, Senior Lecturer, School of Economics, The University of Queensland, Brisbane, 4072 Australia.

D.S. Prasada Rao, Professor, School of Economics and Director, Centre for Efficiency and Productivity Analysis, The University of Queensland, Brisbane, 4072 Australia.

Elisabetta Magnani, School of Economics, The University of New South Wales, Sydney, NSW 2052, Australia.

Anu Rammohan, Discipline of Economics, School of Economics and Political Science, The University of Sydney, 2006, NSW, Australia.

Habibullah Khan, Associate Professor of Economics, Universitas 21Global, 5 Shenton Way, 01-01 UIC Building, Singapore-068808.

Jeremy B. Williams, Associate Professor of e-learning, Universitas 21 Global, 5 Shenton Way, 01-01 UIC Building, Singapore-068808.

Sheela Rai, Lecturer, West Bengal National University of Juridical Sciences, Kolkata, India.

Anis Chowdhury, Professor of Economics, School of Economics & Finance, University of Western Sydney, Campbelltown Campus, Locked Bag 1797, Penrith South DC, NSW 1797, Australia.

S.A.R. Bilgrami, Professor Economics (retired) Jamia Millia Islamia, New Delhi-25.

Suchitra Krishna Kumar, Professor, Dayanandasagar Institute of Management and Information Technology, Shavige Malleshwara Hills, Kumaraswamy Layour, Bangalore-560078, Karnataka, India.

B.P. Vani, (Mrs). Assistant Professor, Institute for Social and Economic Change, Nagarbhavi, Bangalore-560072, Karnataka, India.

M. Ramanjaneyulu, Professor of Economics, Department of Economics, Jnanabharathi, Bangalore University, Bangalore-560056, India.

M.S. Gupta, Department of Commerce, R.K Dwarika College (Magadh University), Patna, Bihar/India, Mailing Address: 4C Konark Residency, Road No. 12, Rajendra Nagar, Patna-800016 (Bihar).

S.K. Dhage, Reader and Head of Department, Department of Economics, Baburaoji Gholap College, Sangavi, Pune-411027 India.

Praduman Kumar, Former Professor (Agriculture Economics), Indian Agricultural Research Institute, New Delhi, India and Consultant, Policy Economics and Social Science Discipline, WorldFish Centre, Penang, Malaysia.

Madan M. Dey, Regional Director, World Fish Centre, Penang, Malaysia.

Sukhpal Singh, Associate Professor, Centre for Management in Agriculture (CMA), Indian Institute of Management, Ahmedabad–380015, Gujarat, India.

J. Nirmala, Reader in Economics, Sarah Tucker College, Tirunelveli, Tamilnada, India.

Dhulasi Birundha, Professor and Head of Department of Economics, Madurai Kamaraj University Madurai, Tamil Nadu, India.

Siddhartha Sarkar, Faculty, Department of Commerce, Dinhata College, Dinhata 736135, Cooch Behar, West Bengal, India.

PART - I
General Issues

1

POVERTY, POVERTY ALLEVIATION, AND SOCIAL DISADVANTAGE: AN OVERVIEW

Clem Tisdell

Introduction

Despite the considerable improvements in living standards globally in the last century or so, and even though unprecedented advances in technology have occurred, millions of people still remain in poverty, mostly, but not entirely, in low income countries. The exact number is imprecise and varies according to the way in which poverty is measured. Nevertheless, even when the poverty line is set very low, at a level so low that there can be no quibble about whether individuals below it are in poverty, globally millions remain in poverty.

It was estimated that about 1.2 billion people in 2005 in the developing world were below the international poverty line of US$1 per day (World Bank, 2005). This meant that almost 1 in 4 persons in the developing world (24 per cent) were below the poverty line. Most poor people in this group are unable to meet their basic food requirements of 2100 calories per day. Using this indicator of poverty, 815 million people (over 16 per cent of individuals) in the developing world were estimated to be hungry (UNDP, 2005). Even allowing for the fact that these figures are approximations, there is no doubt that poverty and ills associated with it, such as hunger and malnutrition, adversely affect millions of people globally.

The reasons why so many people remain in poverty are varied, and show variations regionally depending, for example, on cultural factors. Several essays in this book identify factors that contribute to the occurrence of poverty, provide evidence on the extent of and trends in poverty in different parts of the world, and examine measures of the magnitude of poverty and social disadvantage. Others describe and assess public policies that have been adopted to reduce the incidence of poverty. Several essays consider social disadvantages that many contribute to impoverishment such as, lack of access to education, lack of relevant language and other cultural skills of migrants arriving in a new country, or discrimination on the basis of race, caste or membership of particular social groups.

The purpose of this chapter is to first of all provide an overview of concepts of poverty and social disadvantage and touch on some policy issues involving positive policy discrimination in favour of the poor and the socially disadvantaged. Then general sources of and reasons for the existence of poverty are considered and welfare arguments (that is, arguments involving social philosophy) for assisting or not assisting the poor are discussed. Subsequently, the organization of the book and the broad coverage of its contributions are outlined and general results that emerge from its contributions are indicated.

Concepts of Poverty and Social Disadvantage

There are many different views about what constitutes poverty. *The Macquarie Dictionary* (Delbridge, 1988) gives several meanings for the term poverty, the first being "the condition of being poor with respect to money, goods or means of subsistence". This definition, however, leaves open the question of how 'poor' is to be judged. This dictionary also points out that one may speak of poverty in relation to other attributes, e.g. poverty of ideas, poverty of soil. Very often economic poverty is associated with poor education, poor health, poor housing and so on.

From an economics viewpoint, (absolute) poverty involves extreme or considerable scarcity of commodities. Because of their economic deprivation, individuals in poverty often have great difficulty in satisfying their basic needs for survival, and lack the economic means to develop their capabilities, for example, by becoming well-educated and their children suffer as well.

There are, of course, different degrees of poverty or economic deprivation. At the one extreme is a situation in which individuals and families have barely enough economic resources for their survival. Millions of people globally still experience absolute poverty of this type. They are barely able to obtain enough economic resources for their physical existence.

However, it is also possible for individuals or families to be categorised as poor by a society if they have insufficient economic means to afford a minimum socially acceptable standard of living. This acceptable standard is usually higher in wealthier nations than in poorer ones and one would also expect this standard to be raised in poorer countries as they develop economically. This socially determined measure of poverty tends to be imprecise because there do not seem to be clear rules as to how it should be derived from the sentiments of individuals in a community.

Furthermore, we should also note that in any society in which income is unequally distributed, some will have less income than others. The less well-off can be considered to be comparatively or relatively poor although none of these individuals may be in absolute poverty, or even socially very deprived in their living standards. One would need to study the distribution of income carefully to determine the extent to which those on lower incomes (for example, have a per capita income less than 50 per cent of the median income of a nation) are in absolute poverty or economically deprived.

The poverty line, based on the minimum consumption of 2100 calories a day, can be regarded as a physical subsistence measure of poverty. Those who are unable to reach this level have a high risk of not having a long life. A now widely used measure of the presence of poverty is whether an individual's daily consumption per head is less than the purchasing power equivalent of US$1 per day is low but includes some social influences. It was determined as being representative of poverty lines widely used in low-income countries (Deaton, 2001).

As indicated above, a variety of uni-dimensional poverty lines have or are being used of which the US$1 per day figure is one. Another used, for example, by the Food and Agricultural Organization (FAO) is an energy food-intake of 2100 calories per day. Various national governments also determine national poverty lines based on levels of income or expenditure they decide to be appropriate. The United Nations has also developed a poverty line of US$2 based on purchasing power per family (PPP), and one of US$10 (PPP) per day. The percentage or proportion of a population below a specified poverty line is the head-count ratio of the incidence of poverty. It is one of the most widely used indicators of the occurrence of poverty. However, it does not indicate the depth or severity of poverty and it is sensitive to the choice of the variable and the level used to designate the poverty line.

Commonly used indicators of the severity of the occurrence of poverty are the Poverty Gap Index and the Squared Poverty Gap Index. The Poverty Gap Index (PGI) is equal to unity minus the average extent to which the variable measuring poverty falls below the poverty line when this is expressed as a proportion of the poverty line.

$$\text{Thus: } PGI = 1 - y/z$$

where y is the average amount by which the relevant variable affecting welfare e.g. income, calories of food-intake, falls below the poverty line, z.

This measure assumes that the loss in well-being of an individual is proportionate to the amount by which the relevant variable, for example income or caloric food-intake falls below the poverty line. On the other hand, the Squared Poverty Index ensures that the larger is the shortfall relative to the poverty line in the indicator of poverty being used, the greater is the proportionate weight given to it. This is consistent with the view that a reduction in the welfare is likely to occur at an increasing rate the greater is the extent of deprivation. Further information about these indices are available in some United Nation's Publications, see, for example, United Nations Division for Sustainable Development (2004).

Multidimensional indicators of human well-being and poverty have become increasingly popular with agencies of the United Nations. They are usually used for comparative purposes and are expressed as indices. As a rule, they incorporate variables that are consequences of poverty.

Consequential effects of poverty and measured by such factors as life expectancy, incidence of under weight children, extent of education (knowledge) and so on are used by the United Nations to provide measures of poverty and differences in well-being of individuals and groups (for details see UNDP 2005). For example, a Human Poverty Index (HPI), of which there are now two forms, HPI-1 and HPI-2, is often used to provide a crude macro-measure at the regional or national level of the extent of poverty and is frequently used for comparative purposes. The Human Development Index (HDI), is employed widely as an indicator of comparative economic well-being of groups. The Gender Development Index (GDI) adjusts HDI to allow for estimated differences in the well-being of males and females whereas the Gender Employment Index (GEI) purports to portray the relative social power of males and females. For comparative purposes all of these indices can be used to indicate relative socio-economic disadvantage or advantage.

Although their use varies from contribution to contribution, all of these concepts of poverty and social disadvantage are applied in this book. Nevertheless, all these measures are subject to limitations. For example, if we measure the frequency of poverty by its consequences, we may find that its consequences are not well correlated with the presence of poverty. Deaton (2001, p. 136) states, for example, that "health and literacy measures should not be regarded as measures for income. We do not have a reliable link between income and non-income measures of poverty that would allow us to infer the former from the latter." Furthermore, Deaton (2001) warns that much of the official data used to study trends in the incidence of poverty and economic growth are of poor quality and subject to biases. Therefore, caution is required in interpreting results based on the available data.

The two human development indices of UNDP most closely monitoring poverty are the Human Poverty Index-1 (HPI-1) and the Human Poverty Index-2 (HPI-2). UNDP regards HPI-1 as relevant to developing countries and HPI-2 to be applicable to a group of higher income countries, that is, most OECD countries (UNDP, 2005). Both are measures of human deprivation but they must be regarded as relatively crude indicators of the incidence of poverty.

HPI-1 is based on a formula which takes into account;

(1) the probability of not surviving to age 40,

(2) the incidence of adult functional illiteracy,

(3) the percentage of the population below an income poverty line defined as 50 per cent of the median level of household disposable income, and

(4) the rate of long-term unemployment defined as the percentage of the population unemployed for 12 months or more.

Both in the case of HPI-1 and HPI-2, UNDP (2005) claims that the independent variables taken into account are indicative of the extent to which humans lack longevity, lack knowledge and fail to have a decent standard of living. All these factors are correlates of poverty. However, in the case of HPI-2, UNDP adds the variable long-term unemployment because it is believed to be associated with social exclusion. This seems to reflect an increasing multi-dimensional approach to identifying poverty.

These human poverty indices are relative measures of the occurrence of poverty. They identify occurrence of poverty indirectly by its correlates, and should be interpreted cautiously. The fact that they yield definite numbers may surround them with a false air of accuracy. This may also disguise the fact that the indices incorporate value judgements as a result of their weights and the selection of relevant variables. The choice of variables for the indices is, in many cases, also based on administrative convenience and data availability rather than sound academic argument. Nevertheless, these means are particularly valuable in keeping issues involving poverty and social disadvantage in the spotlight globally.

Policies to Overcome Poverty and Social Disadvantage

In principle, poverty might be eliminated by promoting sustainable economic growth provided its benefits flow through to the poor or, in the absence of significant economic growth, by redistributing income or economic opportunities in favour of the poor. This however, requires that those who are better-off have sufficient margin to make this practical. Alternatively, a combination of economic growth and redistribution of income and economic opportunities may be used to alleviate poverty.

Mahatma Gandhi was of the view that by uplifting the deprived in society, the whole society would benefit. As several contributions in this book illustrate, the caste-system in India is still a barrier to uplifting the deprived. Mahatma Gandhi was courageous in his opposition to the rigidities and inequalities associated with the system. He led by personal example in his opposition to these aspects, particularly in an attempt to improve the lot of the 'Untouchables', Harijans (Fischer, 1954, 107-124). However, given that caste distinctions have long been embedded in Hindu traditions, (Fischer, 1954, pp. 110-111) bringing about a change in Indian social attitudes is not easy to achieve. According to Husain (1961, p. 37), "In the ideal society of Gandhi, where every individual has the same intrinsic value, social equality will naturally be added to political equality. There will be no distinction of caste or class in the sense of regarding some people as higher than or superior to, others on account of their birth or occupation." In addition, Gandhi was strongly in favour of economic equality (Husain, 1961, p. 39). Gandhi stated: "True economics never militates against the highest ethical standard... True economics....stands for social justice, it promotes the good of all equally, including the weakest, and it is indispensable for a decent life." (Gandhi, *Harijan* 9 October, 1937 quoted in Husain, 1961, p. 39).

Mahatma Gandhi believed that in order to assist the most disadvantaged in India, positive discrimination in their favour would be required. Therefore, after its Independence, India reserved several positions in the public source for those belonging to scheduled castes and scheduled tribes. It was hoped that, in due course, positive discrimination in favour of such disadvantaged groups would no longer be necessary. However, more than 55 years after India's Independence, this system still remains in India and caste divisions still affect economic and social inequality.

Unfortunately, those who are intended to benefit from positive discrimination are often not its beneficiaries. In India, those who are eligible for reserved positions often have to pay officials bribes to obtain these positions. That becomes a possibility when the demand for such positions exceeds the supply at the prevailing public service salary. Because of their need to pay bribes, those eligible for reserved positions may end up with little economic benefit.

This is illustrated in Figure 1. There the curve marked DD represents the demand for labour of a disadvantaged group, e.g. caste or tribe, and the curve SS represents the supply of such labour. The demand and supply curve may reflect social taboos or the employment possibilities of this labour. In competitive conditions, market equilibrium would be established at E, with L of the labour

Figure 1
Reserving places for the employment of the disadvantaged in the public service, as in India, may bring them little or no financial advantage. Competition may result in all their potential economic benefits being lost due to bribe-taking by public officials.

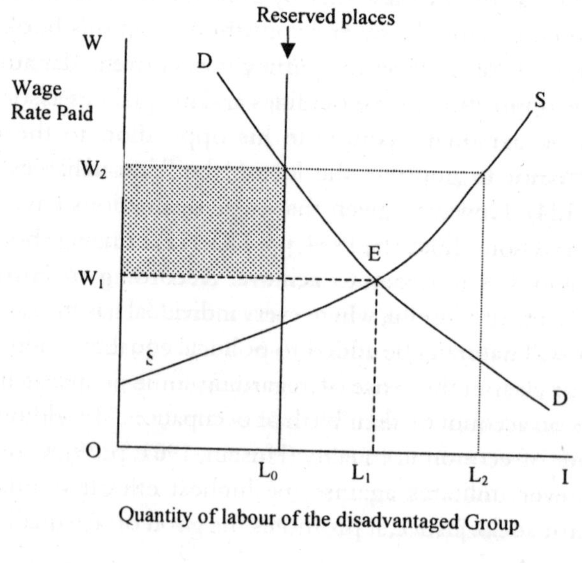

of this group employed at a wage rate of W_1. But suppose that employment equivalent to L_0 is reserved for members of this disadvantaged group in the public service where they are paid a wage rate of W_2. At this wage rate, L_2 of this disadvantaged group would like to be employed. So the supply of L_2 exceeds the demand in the public service of L_0. Members of the disadvantaged group would be willing to pay a bribe of up to $W_2 - W_1$ to be employed in a reserved position. Thus, dishonest public servants responsible for the hiring of labour are able to extract a total amount in bribes from the disadvantaged group equal to the area of the dotted rectangle. Consequently, the disadvantaged group is left with no financial benefit from this arrangement.

Prejudice and social taboos artificially depress the demand for the employment of those who are subject to social discrimination. They reduce their job choices and their bargaining power. Furthermore, this can reduce the economic incentive of disadvantaged groups to invest in improving of their social capital, such as their education. Limited job opportunities are likely to depress the returns on their investment in social capital. Low levels of investment in education by disadvantaged groups, and in some cases, females can be a reflection of their limited job prospects compared to others with the same level of education. Overcoming social prejudice and gaining social acceptability matter when it comes to eliminating poverty and social disadvantage.

Correlates of Poverty and Philosophical Attributes to Poverty

Many different factors can be associated with the occurrence of poverty, several of which are outlined by the World Bank (2001, Ch. 2). Societies are often poor because they have few natural resources or their natural resources are of poor quality, or they may be short on physical capital and human capital and may also lack adequate social capital. Furthermore, they may have little access to technologies and methods able to enhance economic productivity.

Individuals or households may be in poverty because they are deprived socially of resources and other entitlements relative to others.

Individuals can also experience poverty due to physical or mental impairment, sickness and so on. They may also fall into poverty due to natural disasters, damages caused by war or similar events.

In many countries, households headed by females are often in poverty. Some individuals or households may become poor as a result of profligate behaviour or their inability to manage their own financial affairs.

The ostensible reason why individuals or households fall into poverty often leads to moral judgements. For instance, a distinction has, at least in the past, been made between the deserving and the undeserving poor–the deserving poor being those worthy of assistance and the undeserving poor being those not worthy of help. In general, most societies are sympathetic to the plight of those who fall into poverty due to no apparent fault of their own, but very often not to those who are thought to have been the cause of their poverty. However, whether or not individuals should be blamed for falling into poverty is difficult to determine objectively, and some take the moral position that individuals in need should be helped no matter how they came to be needy.

The extent to which the conditions of individuals is a result of their own determination or of pre-determined events is a contentious philosophical issue. John Rawls (1971) appears to believe that an individual's economic fortune is largely predetermined by external events. He, therefore, argues that justice requires incomes be equally distributed unless equality is to the advantage of all. This has often been used by environmentalists to argue that current economic growth and developments should be such as to make future generations no less well off than present generations. In particular, Rawls' theory of justice implies that it would be immoral for present generations to impoverish future generations by pursuing unsustainable economic development. The issues involved are complex. However, it is apparent that poverty not only involves current interpersonal distributional matters but intergenerational ones as well.

The Geographic Location of Poverty

Whether or not the United Nations' poverty line of US$1 per day or the presence of hunger as indicated by those not able to obtain a minimum energy intake of 2100 calories per day is used to identify the presence of absolute poverty, the ranking of the incidence of poverty by major regions of the world is much the same. The incidence is highest in Sub-Saharan Africa, followed by South Asia, then East Asia and Latin America and the Caribbean. The general pattern is clear from Table 1. The entries for the incidence of poverty as measured by the poverty line of US$1 per day and the incidence of hunger can be seen to have almost perfect rank correlation.

Although the incidence of absolute poverty is highest in Sub-Saharan Africa, this is not the region of the world with the greatest number of people in poverty. There are more people in food poverty in India than in Sub-Saharan Africa. For every individual in food poverty in Africa, about 2.5 persons are in food poverty in the Asia-Pacific Region. Approximately, two-thirds of the world's poor are located in the Asia-Pacific region and a quarter in Sub-Saharan Africa if the food intake being of 2100 calories per day is used as the determinant. The numbers of those in poverty on this basis and their geographic location are indicated in Table 2.

Although most persons with inadequate food-intake live in developing countries, not all are in these countries. It is estimated that in 2001 to 2003, 852 million persons had insufficient food to obtain an energy intake of 2100 calories daily. Of these, 28 million lived in transitional countries, 9 million in developed countries and 815 million in developing countries (UN Millennium Project Task Force on Hunger, 2005).

Table 1
The Incidence of Poverty (%) by Developing Regions of the World based on the UN Poverty Line of US$1 per day and the Ability to Obtain a Food Energy Intake of 2100 Calories per day

Region	*% of population on less than US$1 per day in 2004*	*% of population unable to obtain 2100 calories of food intake 2001-03*
Sub-Sahara Africa	44.0	31
South Asia	31.2	21
CIS Asia	–	20
East Asia	14.1	12
South East Asia	7.3	12
Oceania	7.3	12
Latin America and Caribbean	8.9	10
Western Asia	–	9
N. Africa and W. Asia	2.4	–
North Africa	–	4
Transitional Economiesof SE Europe	1.8	
CIS	2.5	–
CIS, Europe	–	3

Source: Derived from data on pp. 4-5 of United Nations (2006) The Millennium Goals Report 2006.

Table 2
Numbers in Poverty and their Regional Location as Indicated by Insufficient Food Caloric Intake in the Period 2001-2003

Place	*Numbers in Millions*	%
India	225	27.5
China	140	17.1
Other Asia and Pacific	156	19.0 (a)
Asia-Pacific	521	63.8
Sub-Saharan Africa	204	25.0
Latin America and the Caribbean	53	6.5
Near East and North Africa	39	4.8
	817(b)	**100.0**(a)

Notes: (a) Due to rounding figures do not tally exactly.
(b) Because of rounding, these figures add to 817 but the total in the absence of rounding is actually 815.

Source: Data derived from Figure 2.1 of UN Millennium Project Task Force on Hunger (2005).

Of course, aggregate figures for regions conceal significant differences between social groups within regions and between geographical areas within regions. Contributions in this book help to reveal a number of differences both in higher income countries, such as Australia, and in developing countries, such as India.

It is very difficult, probably impossible, to capture all dimensions of poverty and social disadvantage in a single measure. This is probably one reason why the United Nations has developed multiple measures of the occurrence of poverty and a variety of indicators of human welfare. These are mostly aggregate indicators. Often the welfare indicators are estimated as a weighted average of several variables. It should, however, be kept in mind that their values are sensitive to the relative weights used and to decisions about the variables included. Particularly the first aspect and to some extent the second, involve value judgements.

In recent years, UNDP has been using two Human Poverty Indices, HPI-1 for developing countries and HPI-2 for higher income countries. However, these are not measures of the incidence of absolute poverty but are primarily measures of relative economic and social deprivation or inadequacy. For example, the variables taken into account in measuring HPI-2 for a country are:

1. the probability of an individual at birth not surviving to age 60;
2. the percentage of people lacking functional literary skills;
3. the percentage of the labour force experiencing long-term unemployment; and
4. the percentage of the population below 50 per cent of the median per capita income level (UNDP, 2005).

In general, a low life expectancy, lack of literacy and long-term unemployment are usually associated with the presence of human poverty. The percentage of the population below 50 per cent of the median income in a country is a measure of relative economic deprivation or relative impoverishment rather than absolute impoverishment. If, however, the median income level in a country is low, it is also possible those with an income of less than 50 per cent of it will experience absolute poverty. This indicator can also be regarded as a primitive measure of income inequality. Statistical data reveal that Sweden, Norway, Finland and the Netherlands have the lowest Human Poverty Index (HPI-2) and Australia, the United Kingdom, Ireland and the United States the highest (if the countries with the highest Human Development Indices are considered (Wikipedia, 2006a). The data are summarised in Table 3.

The countries with a low HPI-2 are characterised by a low percentage of relatively income-deprived individuals, and the presence of much higher functional literacy skills in their population. The United States is characterised by a comparatively low life expectancy rate, a relatively high rate of functional illiteracy, and a relatively large percentage of income-deprived individuals. On the other hand, its rate of long-term unemployment appears to be quite low. The degree of functional illiteracy and of income inequality as measured by the percentage of the income-deprived is also high for Australia, the United Kingdom and Ireland. The reasons for these high rates of illiteracy are unclear but they may in part be related to immigration. The high degree of relative poverty (as measured by the entries in the last column of Table 3) compared to that in Nordic countries and in the Netherlands may be due to the political retreat of Australia, the U.K., Ireland and the U.S.A. from the ideal of a Welfare State and their increased reliance on market-based economic liberalism as a policy guide. In the case of the U.S.A., it seems particularly worrying that one in eight newborn individuals are not expected to survive to 60 years of age. Thus, it is apparent that economic and social deprivation is not just an issue for developing countries.

Table 3
The Ranking, Values for HPI-2 and the Magnitudes of its Components for the Four Nations with the Lowest HPI-2 and the Four with the Highest HPI-2 Amongst 17 Higher Income Countries

Rank	*Country*	*HPI-2*	*Probability of not surviving to 60 (%)*	*Illiteracy (%)*	*L.I.T Unemploy-ment (%)*	*Population below 50% of median income (%)*
1	Sweden	6.5	7.3	7.5	1.1	6.6
2	Norway	7.2	8.3	8.5	0.2	6.9
3	Finland	8.4	10.2	10.4	2.4	5.4
4	Netherlands	8.4	8.7	10.5	1.6	8.1
14	Australia	10.9	8.8	17.0	1.4	14.3
15	U.K.	14.8	8.9	21.8	1.3	12.5
16	Ireland	15.3	9.3	22.6	3.2	12.3
17	USA	15.8	12.6	20.7	0.3	17.0

Notes: (a) These 17 nations are from the group of 21 nations with the highest HDI's as listed in the UNDP (2003) *Human Development Report.* Information was not available for four of these 21 countries.

Source: Based on date quoted in Wikipedia (2006a) derived from UNDP (2003) *World Development Report.*

The Organization of the Book and Further Discussion

This book has been divided into nine parts. Part I (this part) deals with general issues involving poverty and social disadvantage. Part II focuses on broad features and trends in poverty and social disadvantage in India, whereas Part III consists of regional and case studies of poverty in India. Part IV continues to focus on South Asia but the contributions deal mainly with India's neighbours, such as Bangladesh, Nepal and Sri Lanka; or the India situation in comparison to that of its neighbours.

Part V examines poverty and social disadvantage in Central Asia and in China. Central Asian economies are in a state of early transition to market economies whereas the economic transition of China is well advanced. Southeast Asian countries such as Indonesia, Laos, Malaysia, Singapore and Vietnam are given attention in Part VI.

Sub-Saharan Africa has a high incidence of poverty. Case studies for Sub-Saharan Africa are contained in Part VII. Studies for Europe, Australia and Brazil are contained in Part VIII and followed in Part IX by those for the Pacific Islands, mainly Fiji.

The relative degree of coverage of this book by regions in terms of case studies broadly reflects the proportion of individuals globally estimated to be in absolute poverty (see Table 2). The majority of the contributions relate to Asia, particularly India, and Sub-Saharan Africa.

The contributions are diverse and the viewpoints expressed are varied. For example, some authors doubt whether it is possible to quantify the extent and incidence of poverty and social disadvantage satisfactorily, whereas others seem quite content to rely on quantification.

Certainly it is difficult to quantify the extent and incidence of poverty satisfactorily, and it is often stated to be multidimensional. This may be one of the reasons why a variety of measures of poverty are now being used. It is necessary, however, to be clear in each case about what is being measured and what is not being measured. There is also a danger if the number of measures of poverty continue to proliferate that the public will become thoroughly confused about what is being measured. Furthermore, the method of measuring a particular indicator is also sometimes altered and this may lead to confusion a far as trends in poverty are concerned.

Signs of confusion are apparent from the description of the Human Development Index (HDI) given in Wikipedia, the free encyclopaedia. It describes HDI as "a comparative measure of poverty, literacy, education, life expectancy..... It is a standard means of measuring well-being...." (Wikipedia, 2006b). But it is a poor measure of well-being because it does not take account of leisure-time, nor psychological stress and so on. Furthermore, it is hardly a very informative indicator of the extent and incidence of poverty because it does not take into account the frequency distribution of the variables (life expectancy, the adult literacy rate, school enrolment and GNP for example) on which it is based.

While the United Nations' Human Poverty Indices are more focused on poverty measurement, they also rely on national or regional aggregates or averages. Many of the case studies in this book make an important contribution by getting closer to poverty at its grassroots and suggest alternative ways to view poverty and gauge social disadvantage.

REFERENCES

Deaton, A. (2001), "Counting the World's Poor: Problems and Possible Solutions". *The World Bank Research Observer* 16(2), 125-147.

Delbridge, A. (1981), *The Macquarie Dictionary*, Macquarie Library Pty. Ltd., St. Leonard's, NSW, Australia.

Fischer, L. (1954), *Gandhi: His Life and Message for the World.* Mentor Books, New York.

Husein, S.A. (1961), *The Way of Gandhi and Nahev.* Asia Publishing House, London.

Rawls, J. (1971), *A Theory of Justice.* Harvard University Press, Cambridge, M.A.

UNDP (2003) *Human Development Report 2003*, New York.

UNDP (2005) *Human Development Report 2005*, New York.

UN Millennium Project Task Force on Hunger (2005), *Halving Hunger: It can be done.* Earthscan, London, U.K. and Sterling, V.A., U.S.A.

United Nations Division of Sustainable Development (2004) "Combating Poverty". http://www.un.org./esa/sustdev/natinfo/indicators/indisa/english/chapter.htm (Accessed 15/9/2006).

United Nations (2006), *The Millennium Goals Development Goals Report 2006*, New York.

Wikipedia (2006a), "Human Poverty Index" http://en.wikipedia.org/wiki/Human_Poverty_Index (Accessed 8/9/2006).

Wikipedia (2006b), "Human Development Index" http://en.wikipedia.org/wiki/Human_Development_Index (Accessed 8/9/2006).

World Bank (2001) *World Development Report 2000/2001: Attacking Poverty*, Oxford University Press, New York.

World Bank (2005) World Development Indicators 2005. http//devdata.worldbank.org/wdi2005/cover.htr.

2

THE LIMITATIONS OF NATIONAL POVERTY LINES AND A CASE STUDY FOR INDIA

Raj Kumar Sen

Introduction

The objectives of this article are to show that:

(a) as poverty is not uniformly distributed either among the developing countries of the world or among the different regions of a single poverty-affected country, it is difficult to appreciate the acuteness of nation-specific poverty or the appropriateness of the poverty alleviation programmes by people belonging to non-poor countries, who are usually the donors to help the poor countries;

(b) the adoption of national poverty line is often not comparable with other country-specific poverty lines and/or international poverty lines due to difference in methodologies and assumptions involved in the construction of such poverty lines;

(c) over time, due to changes in methodologies and assumptions and also due to changes in poverty perceptions, it becomes also difficult to compare the secular changes in poverty within the same country;

(d) the effectiveness of poverty alleviation policies also is seriously limited due to adoption of a single poverty line which (i) divides artificially the people into two income groups only, poor and non-poor (while actually there are many) neglecting the distribution of income in these two groups, (ii) implicitly encourages the authorities to help the people at the margin only to maximize the numerical success of the poverty alleviation measures (which are often in paucity of funds) and consequently leaves the poorest of the poor untouched frustrating the basic target of such strategies, and (iii) conceals the regional features in large heterogeneous countries through the law of average, and all these call for sub-regional and multi-stage poverty lines:

(e) with ever-increasing inequality among the countries and the current craze about globalization, the national poverty lines are losing their relevance to international poverty lines;

(f) in many countries, expenditures on state-sponsored poverty alleviation programmes often lead to wastages and leakages and only a small part reaches the target group and under present LPG (Liberalisation, Privatisation, Globalisation) strategies, the governments are urged to stop such wasteful expenditures and depend on the market-driven growth only as growth is considered as the surest antidote to poverty, while it is clear that the trickle-down theory of benefits has failed almost everywhere in the absence of any thrust on redistribution of income; and

(g) the onslaught of ever-changing technologies prevents on the other hand the creation of productive employment with appropriate technologies, which only can reduce poverty in such countries permanently.

All these points are analysed in the context of India, which is, as per the recorded history, the habitat of a large number of poor for the last couple of centuries or more and it is a country where the national leaders were very much aware of the urgent need for poverty amelioration through appropriate strategies even before India's independence in 1947. This is further important for the developing poverty-stricken economies because while India has adopted poverty alleviation strategies since the early stages of her economic planning (to be specific, since her 4th Plan which started in 1969), she could not control poverty till now and almost a quarter of her billion plus population still reel under poverty as defined officially (which we shall see later is a misnomer and is quite close to subsistence level of expenditure).

This chapter is organized in eight sections of which the first seven show the various aspects (as mentioned above) of the limitations of a single poverty line as experienced by the low-income developing countries in general and India in particular. The last section contains the concluding remarks and policy suggestions.

The Uneven Distribution of Poverty

While poverty has long recognized by international authorities such as the World Bank and others as an important problem to tackle, this problem is never distributed in an even manner among the different regions/countries of the world nor is it so within a country or region which is known to be poverty-stricken. Thus, while there are pockets of poverty even within rich and prosperous countries/regions, we find that among the continents of the globe, poverty is rampant only in Asia and Africa, and not in Europe, Australia and the Americas. As per the estimates of the *World Development Report 1990* (devoted to the analysis of *poverty*), more than one billion people in the developing countries are living in poverty and are struggling to survive on less than $370 a year (roughly $1 per day). Among them nearly half (46.4%) live in South Asia which accounted for only 29.7% of the world's population. Unfortunately, the situation did not improve much even a decade later. The *World Development Report* 2000-01(dealing with the analysis of *Attacking Poverty*) has repeated the same story–"of the world's 6 billion people, 2.8 billion—almost half—live on less than $2 a day, and 1.2 billion—a fifth—live on less than $1 a day, with 44% living in South Asia." This shows that even in Asia and Africa, all countries are not poor. Thus, while poverty is most acute or intense in Sub-Saharan Africa, poverty is most extensive and the numbers in poverty are greater in South Asia, mainly consisting of the countries like India, Bangladesh and Pakistan. Not only that, the marginal decline in poverty share of this region has been eaten up by its high rate of population growth, and the number of poor people in this region increased during the decade from 474 million to 522 million. Spatially also, the poor are found to be concentrated in rural areas with high population densities (e.g., in the Indian Gangetic Plain and in Java of Indonesia) and in resource-poor areas (e.g., Andean Highlands, Sahel etc.).Groupwise, women, the aged and children suffer disproportionately from the burden of poverty indicated by their inadequate supply of inputs (e.g., health care, education, nutrition etc.) on which the quality of life depends. The ethnic groups and minorities in different countries (e.g., indigenous people in Mexico, Peru etc. and the scheduled castes and tribes in India) usually bear a heavy burden of poverty. Many of the poor are found to dwell in areas suffering from environmental degradation which has resulted chiefly from expanding population pressure and adverse effects of traditional growth strategies. All these are usually concealed in the national poverty lines based on averages (Sen 1991).

If we focus on India only, which has the dubious distinction of being the country which is the habitat of the largest number of poor in the world (320 million in 1993-94, a number remaining almost constant since 1973-74 and 260 million in 1999-00 as per estimates of Planning Commission, Govt. of India, a figure which is controversial due to change in survey methodology which we shall discuss later), then also we observe that in 1993, out of the 30+ States and Union Territories constituting India, more than 50% of the poor are concentrated in 5 states only, viz., Bihar, Orissa, Uttar Pradesh, (U.P.), West Bengal, (W.B.) and Rajasthan. This concentration increased from 46% in 1973-74. This increasing level of concentration was also associated with a rise in the incidence of poverty in those states in this period from 21.42 to 32.77% (Sen 2001). According to another estimate, if we add to this list Assam and Madhya Pradesh (M.P.), and exclude Rajasthan, the rural poverty share of these six states increased from 68.8% in 1993-94 to 74.4% in 1999-00. Again, 54.4% of India's rural poor live in three states only, i.e., Bihar, U.P. and M.P. in 1999-2000 (Dev 2005).

Due to the spatial unevenness in the distribution of poverty throughout the world (among the continents, countries or regions), it becomes extremely difficult for the non-poor regions/communities/countries to appreciate the tragedy of their unfortunate neighbours, be they within the same country, or in a different one. It is quite natural that such countries often fail to realize why the poor countries are so slow in their poverty alleviation process inspite of their adoption of various poverty eradication programmes for quite some time, many of which are funded by grants from rich donor countries. No one can blame the people of such donor countries if they feel that all such funding are nothing but a waste and they are made to bear a burden which does not yield any fruitful result for the poor countries.

Comparability Problems with the National Poverty Lines

As the distribution of the per capita GDP among the countries of the world is not only unequal but also the inequality is increasing over time, it is quite natural that the country-specific national poverty lines used to find out the number of poor in respective countries will often not be comparable due to differences in methodologies and assumptions involved in the construction of such national poverty lines. For the same reasons, it is also not possible to compare such lines with the international poverty lines adopted by the international agencies to rank countries according to their poverty levels and to decide upon the priority among the countries for releasing the sanctioned funds earmarked for poverty alleviation programmes. For instance, while the Head Count Ratio is used in India for poverty measurement, many other countries follow the Poverty Gap methodology for this purpose. It is strange to note that though the use of a very crude, traditional and non-discriminatory Head Count Ratio is widely criticized as it cannot fulfil the two basic axioms required for the use of poverty line, viz, the monotonicity axiom (i.e., given other things, a reduction in income of a person below the poverty line must increase the poverty measure) and the transfer axiom (i.e., given other things a pure transfer of income from a person below the poverty line to anyone who is richer, must increase the measure), yet in India, the use of this method is still continuing.

Further, all the vigorous and illuminating debates on Indian poverty have by passed this fundamental limitation of the used poverty line (Sen 1988). It would have been better if this poverty line construction methodology had been improved with the help of available suggestions. Reference may be made in this context to the P-index of Amartya Sen (Sen 1983) which on the one hand satisfies not only both the desired axioms mentioned above but also three additional axioms as required by the norms of relative equity, ordinal rank weights, monotonic welfare and normalized poverty value and on the other, combines in a unique way the two most widely used measures of poverty and a measure of inequality. One great advantage of this index is that it has been possible to estimate it with the available data for the Indian economy. There was also an attempt (Sen 1977) to combine the National Sample Survey(NSS) expenditure classes into three conventional high, middle and low expenditure groups and derive an index 'E' of inequality on the basis of relative inter-group differences of real consumption expenditure.

Consider the use of the International Poverty Line of $1 a day or the upper poverty line $2 a day as prepared by the World Bank. It attempts to hold the real value of the poverty line constant between countries. The WDR (*World Development Report)* 2000-01 admits that "international comparisons of poverty data entail both conceptual and practical problems. Different countries have different definitions of poverty and consistent comparisons between countries based on the same definition can be difficult. National poverty lines tend to have greater purchasing power in rich countries, where more generous standards are used than in poor countries." In 1990, national poverty lines of 33 countries were converted into 1985 PPP prices, and the most typical line among the low-income economies for which poverty lines were available was selected. In 1999, the same lines were converted into 1993 PPP prices, and the new line of $1.08 a day was obtained as the median of the 10 lowest poverty lines. The upper poverty line was calculated by doubling the amount of the lower poverty line reflecting poverty lines more commonly used in lower-middle-income countries. However, these international poverty lines are useful only as indicators of global progress, and not for assessing the national level or to guide national policy and programme formulation. But at least these lines can provide an idea about the extent of difference between the national and international perceptions of poverty. Thus, for India while in 2000, 26.3% are below poverty according to national poverty line, it shoots up to 86.2% if the desideratum is the $2 a day international poverty line.

For large federal and heterogeneous countries like India, it becomes urgent to construct state/region specific poverty lines also along with the national poverty line to obtain a realistic picture about the poverty scenario. This is further necessary when, as noted in the previous section, poverty is unevenly distributed in the country. In fact, in India, only after the acceptance of the recommendations of the Expert Group appointed by the Planning Commission made in 1993 after considerable delay, the state-specific poverty lines along with national poverty line came into existence and on the basis of availability of National Sample Survey's (NSS) quinquennial reports, these became available for the years 1973-74, 1977-78, 1983, 1987-88 and 1993-94 and later extended to 1999-2000 (Dutt and Sundharam 2006). Naturally, there were no official estimates for state-level poverty lines before 1973 and consequently the earlier poverty alleviation schemes could not take into account the differential nature of the magnitude of poverty in India. However, this improvement of the methodology for the measurement of poverty did not change the practice of using a single poverty line for a state, despite (see the first section) the uneven distribution of poverty among the different districts/regions of the state itself. Moreover, the 1999-2000 NSS survey is criticised due to its change in survey methodology from a 30-day reference period used in earlier surveys to a combination of 7,30 and 365 days reference periods. It appears that the results are not comparable to those from previous NSS rounds (Sen 2000).

The Comparability Problem over Time for a Single National Poverty Line

It is further observed that specially for time series data on poverty ratios such values are not strictly comparable over time due to factors like changes in methodology for defining poverty, changes in the perception of relative poverty with growing income and also rising inequality in the distribution of income and wealth, changes in the assumptions made during the construction of poverty line due to changes in the economic and sociological scenario of the society at different levels of development, increasing integration with the international societies in this era of globalization making national poverty lines less relevant, inadequate reflection of the rural-urban differential of the standard of living in the difference between rural and urban poverty lines, and similar other factors.

If we look at the evolution of the methodology of the poverty line in India, we come across to an interesting story of changing concepts making comparisons over time really difficult. Thus, the 4th Plan used the 'minimum desirable consumption standard'. On the basis of initial recommendations, this was Rs. 20 per person per month at 1960-61 prices which was developed later as the national poverty line. It was converted to Rs. 40.60 at 1972-73 prices for the purpose of the 4th Plan through price adjustments. The 6th Plan defined it as per the Report of the Task Force on Projection of Minimum Needs and Effective Consumption Demand in a modified way. In 1979-80, it was as Rs. 76 for rural areas and Rs. 88 for urban areas. The 7th Plan used an 'updated version of poverty line' based on 6th Plan calculations and estimated it to be Rs. 107 and Rs. 122 for rural and urban areas respectively at 1984-85 prices. With these, the 7th Finance Commission added, in 1970-71, the concept of the Augmented Poverty Line by adding to the private consumer expenditure norm an estimate of public expenditure. The estimates of poverty have been officially revised since 1973-74 on the basis of the modified methodology suggested by the Expert Group of the Planning Commission in 1993 which actually proved that the previous projections of poverty reduction in India were overestimates in most of the cases. It introduced for the first time the use of both national and state-specific poverty lines in India. The 9th Plan used the concept of 'poverty gap' and also the 'squared poverty gap' concept of the World Bank to measure the severity of poverty. However, this Plan was implemented in a period when the economic reforms process initiated in 1991 was in full form which advocated the withdrawal of the state from different economic spheres of the economy and the utility of the centralized planning itself was under question in a system which aimed at putting the market mechanism in the driver's seat. In any case, there was emphasis in this Plan on state-specific poverty lines and also on urban poverty which were lacking to some extent in the earlier Plans though there was no move towards eliminating the limitations associated with the use of a single poverty line (Sen 1998).

Efficacy of Poverty Alleviation Policies with a Single Poverty Line

The adoption of a single poverty line is seriously misleading in the context of the pursuing of poverty alleviation policies at different operational levels (e.g., for a federal country, at central, state, district or village/town levels) for several reasons. This single line divides the population into two groups only, viz., poor and non-poor, while both poor and non-poor groups need to be considered at much more disaggregated levels. Thus, we have already the usual classification for the non-poor group as rich, higher middle income, middle income and lower middle income groups. The inequality among the rich is no less pronounced than in other income classes (in fact, many consider it as quite high) and in order to reduce social tension between the various income classes, many sociologists prescribe a 1:6 ratio to exist between the highest and lowest income levels. In fact, during Indian independence, the Father of Nation, M.K. Gandhi suggested that the upper limit of the yearly salary for an Indian should be Rs. 500 only (at that time, about US$100). However, for the purpose of this present chapter, we are not considering the income inequality aspect among the rich though this may exert an important influence on the allocation of resources and production structure of any economy and lead to intolerance in low income economies like India. Similarly, the poor also is never a homogenous group. We always consider people, besides being poor, also as very poor or ultra-poor, to borrow the term from World Bank (those who are reckoned at or below 75% of the expenditure poverty line), and destitute. Besides, we have also the concepts of absolute poverty and relative poverty. The use of a single poverty line always neglects these important differences among the poor, which are not only real, but also leads to misunderstanding due to this neglect. Thus in India, the national poverty line officially used, shows that in 2000, the share of population lying below poverty line was 26.3%. This means that the remaining 63.7% people are not poor and the poor becomes a minority.

India being the largest democracy in the world, it is quite natural that the interests of the poor will not receive due attention where decisions are made by majority rule. In this way, by concealing the intra-class differences among the rich and poor classes, the single national poverty line is serving the interest of the rich class as a whole and consequently the artificially aggregated poor class has to suffer. In India, the poor are already powerless and non-vocal and concentrated largely in the rural areas thus lying outside the zone given the main attention of the media, policymakers and the ruling elite. The situation would not have been so bad, had the income distribution in these two aggregated groups been given due place and importance in the analysis.

With a bit of hindsight, we find that the origin of the concept of the poverty line as used in India, lies in the idea of a 'starvation line' based on the consumption of at least 2300 calories per person per day as mooted by Boyd-Örr, the first Director General of FAO, in 1945. On this basis, the Planning Commission of India tried to work out in 1962 the money value of consumption necessary to maintain a 'minimum level of living' so that the 'body and soul may be kept together'. It should be noted that this concept of minimum required expenditure is based on single cut-off line and this has played an important role in the efficiency and adequacy of poverty alleviation measures adopted in India. Though later this concept was converted into that of a 'poverty line', it was actually a 'subsistence line'. This means that the current poverty line concept is not only misleading but also a misnomer as it placed the expenditure level of the poor at an exceptionally low level. It officially put a large number of people above the so-called poverty level though in reality they should have been placed below it. Moreover, while fixing the minimum level of expenditure, it was then assumed that free primary education and basic medical facilities are available to the society, but gradually they became either non-existent or qualitatively unacceptable. But these features were never reflected in the later revisions of the poverty line concept.

The other area where the single poverty line leads to unsatisfactory results almost without exception is the targeted number of poor to be uplifted above the poverty line through poverty alleviation measures within a fixed period of time. This has been recognized by the World Bank in its WDR 2000/01 (p. 18) as 'policymakers seeking to make the largest possible impact on the head-count measure (used to calculate the single national poverty line) might be tempted to direct their poverty alleviation resources to those closest to the poverty line (and therefore least poor)'. On the other hand, this problem can be largely bypassed when the poverty measure takes into account the distance of poor people from the poverty line(the poverty gap measure) and the degree of income inequality among poor people (the squared poverty gap measure). Otherwise, the problem will be really acute when the resources are scarce for poverty alleviation programmes (which is a grave reality for low-income developing countries). At the same time there is the urgency of reducing the maximum number of persons in poverty within minimum time. In such cases, the authorities will invariably try to enable the maximum number of poor people existing just below the poverty line to cross the line by any means, including even exploiting the people who are still poorer or adopting unsustainable and/or unrealistic measures. It also goes entirely against the Gandhian principle of '*antyodaya*' i.e., the uplifting of the economically weakest person/section in the society which is naturally a necessary condition for the other principle of '*sarbodaya*' i.e., the uplifting of all (Sen 1997). It goes without saying that in a country like India where the corruption level is quite high, such situations are bound to frustrate the poverty alleviation measures. In fact, one of the former Prime Ministers of India had to comment that only 14% of the money earmarked for such measures actually reached the targeted people.

Finally, the use of a single poverty line conceals the regional and intra-class variations among the poor through the law of averages and consequently, poverty alleviation policies are often misdirected and mismanaged leading to misallocation and misappropriation of scarce resources. Naturally in large low-income countries this calls for the introduction of sub-regional and multi-stage poverty lines. In fact, during the 1990s, India introduced state-specific poverty lines (see section two) after following a single national poverty line for nearly two decades. In large countries, like India, where diversity is the rule rather than exception, a poverty line based on a uniform calorie consumption norm cannot be used due to widely divergent consumption habits of different people living in the same country (eg, in India, tribals, hill people, forest dwellers, South Indians etc.).

Globalization and National Poverty Lines

Historically, it is observed that the inter-country per capita income inequality in real terms (i.e., in terms of constant US dollars) has increased continuously over the last three or four centuries at an increasing rate. Furthermore, this rate has accelerated since the adoption of the strategy of globalization throughout the world, specially after the fall of the Soviet Union in the mid-1980s. The ever increasing enhancement of the communication system, which has reduced the world into a global village, is demonstrating the standard of living being enjoyed by the rich and the poor across the international boundaries and the enlarging gulf of difference between such standards is instantaneously perceived by everybody. Another important aspect of globalization is the integration of the different regions of the world economically and also in setting up a process of convergence in living standards enjoyed by different people in different lands. Naturally in this context, the international poverty line becomes more relevant, meaningful and policy-wise useful compared with the individual country-specific national poverty lines. The international poverty line is also upwardly revised on average, more quickly than the national poverty lines of the poor countries, for the simple reason of a faster growth of per capita GNP in absolute terms in high income countries compared with that of the low income ones inspite of their higher rate of income growth. This also shows the hollowness of the claims of poor countries about the so-called success in the reduction of their country-specific poverty levels by using their respective national poverty lines.

Another negative role of the use of the single poverty line in poverty removal programmes is that it conceals from the public the presence of rapidly expanding income inequality among the persons lying above this line. This has become further relevant under the current globalization process which accentuates the pace of growing inequality. We usually forget the feeling of deprivation by the less well-off section of the population (who are not officially poor) due to the demonstration effect of the growing affluence and conspicuous consumption of the rich who are very few in number but strong trend-setters in the economic aspirations of the society. Unless the overall inequality in the income distribution can be reduced to a tolerable level (varying among societies), the adherence to a unique poverty line may lead to an increase in social tension rather than reduce it. The consumption dualism (Sen 1983) prevailing in each income-decile requires to be minimized as far as possible in order to minimize the aggregate loss of social welfare. It is this consumption dualism which makes the incidence of poverty highly intolerable and gives rise to black money. A set of decile wise poverty lines may serve our purposes more effectively than a single line in the perspective of a long-term strategy for poverty removal in the foreseeable future.

Poverty, State, Market and Economic Reforms

Poverty is usually conceived as an instance of market failure and consequently the state is required to intervene to help the poor through various poverty alleviation programmes. While many felt in the 1950s and 1960s that economic growth is the surest antidote to poverty as the additional income created through income growth was expected to trickle down to the lowest income decile and uplift the poor, such expectations did not materialize in many low income developing economies including India. This failure of trickle-down of benefit strategy in India, led to the adoption of state-aided direct methods for attacking poverty in the 1970s which initially proved to be effective in reducing the poverty level, but its efficacy came under doubt considering the huge wastages and leakages associated with such schemes included in these direct methods. With the fall of the erstwhile USSR in 1985, the role of the state in the economy came under criticism and reliance was placed on the market mechanism and the state gradually started to withdraw itself from various economic activities. But this dependence on the market advocated in the process of economic reforms started in India since 1991, again restored the failed strategy of trickle down theory of benefits into action through maximization of the rate of growth of national income.

The economic reforms in India, after the experience of 15 years, are found to be more helpful to the richer states/regions leading to a more difficult situation for the poorer states/regions/sections of the population due to withdrawal of state subsidies and lack of investment in the agriculture sector. Naturally, the poverty scenario of different states was affected differently and though every Indian union budget after the initiation of economic reforms aimed at poverty reduction, yet there are controversies about the level of poverty reduction (Sen 2004). This is due to the adoption of various anti-poor policies like reduction of subsidies, the withdrawal of state sectors from the provision of public goods and social services, the throwing different sectors of the economy open to foreign competition and preventing labour from reaping the benefits of globalization by restrictions on the international movement of labour. In this situation it is difficult to believe that a high rate of growth will automatically lead to a rapid reduction of poverty (Sen 2005). It may be mentioned, in this context, that the divergent impacts on poverty reduction in different Indian states are known through the application of state-specific poverty lines in the post-reform period, which was not possible in the pre-reform days.

Tyranny of Technology and Poverty-Stricken Countries

The last century has seen an unprecedented progress of technology and this has resulted in enormous material prosperity in the world and established the fact beyond doubt that knowledge is the ultimate source of power. But as this spread and invention of technology was solely concentrated in the high-income industrialized countries of the world, it led to a further division between the rich North and poor South to an extent which was never experienced earlier by the humanity. The change of technology became so fast in the closing decades of the 20th century that the developing countries can hardly dream of meeting the challenge of the ever-changing technology. In particular to the poor of the poorer countries, the situation appears to resemble a tyranny of technology and this leads to a sharp division between the rich and poor in the same society of such a magnitude that nobody can expect to bridge the widening gap. In this context, the single poverty line looses its relevance due to the rapidly emerging consumption pluralism from a state of consumption dualism in the poor countries. Thus in India, people talk about 'shining' India having 20% of its population rich or with middle incomes (mostly living in urban areas) and 80% of its people poor, mostly living in rural *Bharat*, (the ancient name of India). The former enjoy all the new benefits and comforts from the most modern technology while the other devoid of these are being crushed under the burden of both absolute and relative poverty.

Conclusions

To conclude: while correct estimates of poverty are extremely important for rapid reduction of poverty in an economy, the whole exercise is often futile due to, among many other factors, the use or misuse of a single national poverty line for the various reasons elaborated in the previous sections. To some extent, this can be said for the uniform international poverty line also inspite of its updating. The problems arising out of the use of a single poverty line is more serious in large democratic federal heterogeneous low-income economies like India and these have become really acute in the context of growing inequalities under the present globalization process. While India has adopted state-specific poverty lines along with the national poverty line, she is yet far away from the use of multi-stage and multi-regional poverty norms. In fact, barring the suggestion of decile-wise poverty lines by Bhatty (1974), economists have not generally considered this alternative seriously. The application of the Head-Count Ratio in computing poverty line needs to be immediately replaced by poverty gap and/or squared poverty gap measures. The Indian consumption calorie specific poverty norm needs to be adjusted according to the needs of the region/community. The current Indian poverty line is in fact a misnomer as it is close to the subsistence line and needs to be upgraded to reflect the real situation. On the other hand, under the present globalization process, it will be better if the international poverty line is used in place of national poverty lines as national poverty lines are gradually losing their relevance. To follow our own arguments, it may be suggested that just as the Human Development Report uses two types of Human Poverty Index separately for the rich and poor countries, the International Poverty Line also may be constructed differently for these two group of countries to demonstrate the world poverty scenario in its true perspective.

REFERENCES

Bhatty, I.Z. (1974), 'Inequality and Poverty in Rural India'. In Srinivasan, T.N. and P.K. Bardhan (eds): *Poverty and Income Distribution in India.* Calcutta, India.

Dev, S. Mahendra (2005), 'Regional Disparities in Poverty and Malnutrition'. Paper presented in the National Seminar on *Accelerated Economic Growth and Regional Balance.* Sept. 16-18, 2005. Indian Economic Association, Institute for Studies in Industrial Development and Institute for Human Development. New Delhi, India.

Datt, Ruddar and K.P.M. Sundharam (2006). *Indian Economy.* 53rd edition. S. Chand & Co. Ltd, New Delhi, India.

Sen, A.K. (1983), *Choice, Welfare and Measurement.* Chapter on 'An Ordinal Approach to Measurement'. Oxford University Press, Delhi, India.

Sen, Abhijit (2000), 'Estimates of Consumer Expenditure and its Distribution: Statistical Priorities after NSS 55th Round'. *Economic and Political Weekly,* December 16, Mumbai, India.

Sen, Raj Kumar (1977), 'Our Level of Living during the Plans'. *Indian Economic Journal,* Vol. 25, No. 2, Bombay, India.

Sen, Raj Kumar (1983), 'The Unsanctioned Economy and Consumption Dualism'. In Monga, G.S. and V.J. Sanctis (eds): *The Unsanctioned Economy.* Himalaya Publishing House, Bombay, India.

Sen, Raj Kumar (1988), 'Poverty Line and Poverty Removal in India'. *Economic Growth and Social Change.* September, New Delhi.

Sen, Raj Kumar (1991), 'Development and Poverty Alleviation with reference to India: A Quest for Policies'. In Roy, K.C. *et al.* (eds): *Economic Development of Poor Countries.* International Institute for Development Studies (IIDS).Calcutta, India.

Sen, Raj Kumar (1997), 'Level of Living and Gandhian Economic Theory'. *International Journal of Social Economics.* Vol. 24, Nos. 7/8/9. (Essays in Honour of Clement Allan Tisdell, Part III). Bradford, England.

Sen, Raj Kumar (1998), 'Poverty in India and Approach to the Ninth Plan'. *Occasional Papers,* Vol. VI. Economics Dept., Rabindra Bharati University, Calcutta, India.

Sen, Raj Kumar (2001), 'State Level Poverty in India: 1973-1994', In Brahmananda, P.R. and V.R. Panchamukhi (eds.) *Development Experience in the Indian Economy: Inter-State Perspectives.* Bookwell, Delhi, India.

Sen, Raj Kumar (2004), 'Economic Reforms and the Poor: A Looking Back to Indian Budgets'. *Occasional Papers.* Vol. XII. Economics Dept., Rabindra Bharati University, Kolkata, India.

Sen, Raj Kumar (2005), 'Pro-Poor Growth Strategies in India.' In Achha, L.L. (ed): *New Dimensions in Indian Economic Growth and Social Change.* Centre for Indian Economy and Business Studies, New Delhi, India.

World Bank (1990), *World Development Report 1990: Poverty.* Washington D.C.

World Bank (2000), *World Development Report 2000-01: Attacking Poverty.* Washington D.C.

3

IS POVERTY AN ETHICAL QUESTION?

Ratan Lal Basu

Introduction

Any observant visitor venturing through the congested cosmopolis of Kolkata cannot but be bewildered by the striking contrast in the juxtaposition of dazzling riches and loathsome poverty, posh dwelling houses and stinking slums, and the fine blending of gorgeously attired patricians and bare bodied, semi-naked or shabbily dressed commoners in the unending stream of commuters. A thoughtful person would immediately visualize a perfect replica, a miniature model of the global scenario checkered with scintillating opulence and suffocating indigence. He might even be overwhelmed by the sudden zooming in of the ghastly reality (as if in a Hitchcock horror film), the inner story of our glorious civilization, the haunting shadows of poverty, deprivation and oppression lurking behind the hallmarks of human civilization–the lofty Pyramids, the invincible Chinese Wall, the exquisite Taj Mahal, the magnificent architectures and technological marvels.

The strange revelation may turn a conscientious economist irrational–in a momentary lapse, he may slip out of his well protected intellectual confines and inadvertently step into the forbidden arena of emotion and ethical paradigms which cannot be taken care of by theories and the analytical tools he has been brought up with. Why irrational? Suppose we reverse the premises of our reasoning so that what seems rational in the conventional sense turns out irrational and the other way round! What if we put forward the queer proposition that poverty is out and out an ethical question? No doubt, this would directly land us amidst the conflict between the positivist and ethical (may be loosely termed normative) approach to the analysis of poverty.

In modern economic literature the subterranean influence of positivist psychosis (which springs from 'logical empiricism') very often makes the economist hesitant to explore the ethical aspect of poverty. Positivism, in a way, asserts that scientific statements are empirically verifiable while ethical value judgements are not. Thus this approach conceives of a fact/value dichotomy. A variant of the same doctrine, the concept of non-cognitivism, holds that ethical values are cognitively meaningless, i.e., they are neither true nor false, because they are not amenable to any method of verification. Now this attack on moral and ethical value judgements by the old positivists on the ground that the ethical propositions are untenable as they are not open to test may also make many propositions in pure science meaningless. In fact, many of the propositions of which the theories of pure science are composed could not survive the demand that each single proposition must, at least in principle, be open to empirical test. (Putnam 1993).

The obsession with the concept of non-cognitivism has long subsided but it has been revived in the new form of relativism which asserts that ethical statements cannot be true or false non-perspectively. This new version of the old theory holds that values are projected and not discovered in this world. The proponents of this view opine that scientific theories are non-perspective and pertain to absolute truth. On the other hand, ethical or moral propositions are only relatively true (*Ibid*).

But in this new form also, the positivist doctrine turns out to be self defeating. In reality, theories of pure science never converge to any absolute truth. Each discovery in pure science cannot but be only a relative truth as it is conditioned by the perceptive capability of human brain and sense organs. We can never know the being or the essence underlying any phenomenon. (Sartre 1972). Modern physics provides many examples of such ambiguity, e.g. wave-particle duality, duality between classical and quantum mechanics, Heisenberg's Uncertainty Principle, time-space perspectivism of Einstein.[1]

In fact, from whatever angle we look into the question of poverty, factual or ethical, we cannot escape the exigencies of perspectivism. Even the most liberal and broader concept involves the question of relativism, the standpoint of human race (and its material and cultural advance), an infinitesimal phenomenon created by the random process in Nature. So nothing is good or bad or significant unless we judge it from the standpoint of the human race alone. Existence or non-existence of the human race has the same connotation judged from the impartial standpoint of Nature. Suppose we are appreciating successful treatment of a disease by antibiotic drugs. This is good from the standpoint of the human race, but not so from the standpoint of the bacteria killed, as there is no conceivable reason why Nature should be partial to a specific living being, viz. human race. Blind Nature is not likely to bother about whether a man is killed by the bacteria or bacteria are killed by medical devices. So, whenever we talk about anything good or bad, right or wrong, we simply make our judgement from human perspective. In the same way, all branches of science are our creation, the way we try to perceive or explain natural phenomena. Physics, chemistry, zoology, biology all these nomenclature are linguistic expressions of human beings to look at Nature from some specific angle. Nature has no such subject division or nomenclature.

Both ethical values and so-called facts discovered in pure sciences have the same source, human perceptive faculty. Thus, there is very little justification for shelving aside the ethical approach towards analysis of poverty on the ground of relativism and concentrate only on the materialistic aspects of poverty.

Now it is high time we try a meaningful definition of the all important term 'poverty'.

The term poverty may be interpreted in both an absolute and relative sense. In the narrow sense, absolute poverty refers to the lack of basic amenities for sustenance of life without any reference to the relative economic position of the person concerned vis-à-vis other persons in the society he resides in. Relative poverty, on the other hand, is concerned with inequality of income distribution and refers to the relative position of the person in comparison to richer counterparts.

These two concepts, in this narrow sense, may or may not be interdependent. In a very primitive economy, absolute poverty may exist without any existence of income inequality, e.g., in the 'primitive communism' referred to by Marx and Engels. On the other hand, in a highly developed country, high income inequality may exist without the existence of absolute poverty in its narrow interpretation. We use the term 'narrow' because the very definition of absolute poverty may itself change with rising income in a society. This is so because the concept of 'minimum subsistence' is likely to change with the increasing opulence of a society. No wonder, an income level considered the critical level for defining absolute poverty in the USA may appear far above the average middle class income in an LDC like India. Absolute poverty has in fact both physical and psychological dimensions and here it becomes difficult to segregate absolute poverty from income inequality. Thus the question of poverty turns out to be a highly complex phenomenon unlikely to be amenable to treatment with oversimplified terminologies and definitions.

Leaving aside the definitions and linguistic juggleries, it can hardly be denied that absolute poverty in the LDCs has in recent decades assumed a serious dimension in sheer physical terms and has posed a threat to the lives of millions of people residing in these countries. On the other hand, relative poverty as well as absolute poverty (even if in purely psychological sense) has been the basic source of social tensions in many a developed country. In the global context, poverty among nations has been widening, nullifying all the predictions of meticulously constructed growth models emphasizing 'convergence theories'. So far as the LDCs are concerned, low per capita income combined with extreme income inequality have forced these nations to the precipice of disaster.

Under this situation, it may be worthwhile to look into the basic causes of poverty of all varieties. Is it purely a question of lack of economic development or otherwise inadequate care to the question of redistributive policies or none of them? There is no denying that absolute poverty in primitive societies may be explained by man's limited power to manipulate Nature (and the underlying causes like limited scientific knowledge, primitive technologies and, therefore, limited productive capabilities). But the same logic cannot be applied for societies which are capable of generating surplus value. The reasons for absolute poverty which has been a faithful companion of inequality ever since the emergence of private property and economic surplus, is to be sought elsewhere. In fact, all conventional approaches towards this question have always been by-passing the basic cause.

The development of productive power and knowledge to have command over Nature through agricultural practices changed the situation that existed in the very primitive societies and clan lives. In course of time, productive forces, through man's increasing command over Nature, went on snowballing and at present material production has assumed a spectacular dimension by means of the trinity of science, technology and industrial innovation. Unfortunately, human society is still being pestered with the nagging problem of poverty. Both opulence and poverty have been marching steadily onwards with the latter taking the leading role.

The problem of poverty and private property emerged in this world as perfect twins. Prior to emergence of private property, poverty had very little association with social injustice. Poverty arose simply because of lack of material means of sustenance and it was equally applicable for all the members of primitive communities or clans. But with the advancement of methods of production and emergence of surplus value, it was no longer 'poverty for all' but poverty for the property-less majority and riches for the property owning minority living on surplus values generated by the poor majority–poverty thus got associated with social injustice. Paucity of material means was no longer the basic cause of poverty but the cause lay deep in human psychosis–insatiable greed and resultant leanings of the propertied minority to perpetrate exploitation of the property-less majority. Ownership or non-ownership of property also sprang from a basic vice, the cunning and unethical manoeuvre of the minority to grab all means of production.

Karl Marx could, to some extent, recognize this basic cause, but erroneously fell into the same trap and sought the solution of the problem through material advancement alone. He failed to recognize that class division, inequality, exploitation and the resultant poverty spring from a deeper cause, the baser and unethical leanings in human nature (which exist side by side with nobler aspects in all human beings, barring a few exceptions).

Among the Marxists, Mao Zedong of China could anticipate this danger and endeavoured through the 'Cultural Revolution' to prevent the Communist Party of China from turning into a new instrument of exploitation (like communist parties in all other countries). However, the way he visualized the basic causes of this degeneration of the Communist Party and the Socialist State had nothing to do with the inner vices of human nature. He simply looked at the problem from the standpoint of 'class struggle'. So ultimately this so-called Cultural Revolution degenerated into a simple power struggle within the Communist Party of China, and in its termination, left the Chinese economy and society in utter chaos and doldrums.

Long before the emergence of Marxian concepts, Adam Smith could identify the basic psychic nature of human beings that are responsible for poverty amidst plenty. But he could not suggest any meaningful way out of the vicious circle–the intricately interwoven forces of baser human sentiments strengthening one another to give the unethical entity perpetuity.

As regards the basis of human nature, most scientific analysis is to be found in Sânkhya, one of the six major philosophies that sprang from Vedic world outlook. But it is questionable how far it is practicable to translate the Sānkhya-based process into reality to bring about an exploitation-free, poverty-free world.

Before going into these intricate questions, let us first have a glimpse of the conventional poverty concepts and the suggested means for their solution. So we start with modern definitions of poverty. The plan of the rest of the article is depicted below.

- Conventional Poverty Concepts
- Marx and Genesis of Poverty
- Adam Smith and Moral Sentiments
- Sânkhya Concepts
- Sen-Haq-Drèze Approach
- Conclusion

Conventional Poverty Concepts

Topics directly or indirectly associated with poverty have taken a lion's share in modern economic literature as the phenomenon of poverty has posed the most serious challenge to development efforts in the new millennium. Sources of many other serious maladies are rooted in this primeval malady. So far as the majority of the population of the world are concerned, the question of absolute poverty has justifiably been considered as the primary issue, although attention has also been drawn to the question of inequality, both intra-nation and inter-nation.

At present, the most pressing problem of the Third World countries comprising the overwhelming majority of the world's population, has been the precarious situation generated by appalling absolute poverty and, therefore, at least on the theoretical plain, the major concern of economic policies of the government of each of these countries has been to devise appropriate and fruitful means to grapple with the problem of absolute poverty. The question has also been a matter of deep concern for the developed countries, but for completely different reasons. The Continuation of abject poverty in the Third World countries is likely to generate enough provocation for these countries to opt for communistic uprisings. Moreover, poverty in the LDCs leading to lack of effective demand delimits the global market of the multinational corporations of the developed countries.

Now as we turn to the question of removal of poverty, we immediately come up against the tricky question of quantitative measurement, without which it is hardly possible to frame any realistic target-oriented poverty removal policy. To this end the crudest approach considers income as the criterion of defining poverty and attempts to measure poverty by the Head Count Ratio (HCR). In this measure, at first the minimum income necessary for provision of subsistence requirements is determined. This threshold income is called the poverty line. At the next step, data on the number of persons with income below this critical level are collected. At the final stage this figure is expressed as a percentage of the total population of the country under consideration.

The most perturbing question in connection with the HCR is the ambiguity in identifying the critical income level pertaining to the poverty line. The critical poverty line income differs from country to country depending on the variability of per capita income, structure of national income, ethnic and cultural factors that make a world of difference in the concept of subsistence requirement. Generally the poverty line income for a poor country is less than that for a relatively opulent country.

Not withstanding these inter-country differences, the World Bank has defined a general poverty line for the world as an income of U.S. $1 per person per day at purchasing power parity. Although this may enable the World Bank to have a rough idea about overall poverty in the world, for policy framing of the LDCs, the standard may seem too high and for the highly developed nations, too low. The Third World countries afflicted with abject poverty are compelled to set a much lower margin of income for the poverty line and devise policies to raise the incomes of the poor in relation to this critical level. For example, the official poverty line in India, based on minimum calorie requirements for sustenance of life, is much below this World Bank standard.

Apart from this conceptual limitation, the HCR has also revealed limitations from the policy standpoint as the measure fails to quantify the income gap of the poor from the poverty line. Thus, it does not provide any guideline as to the magnitude of the total income gap to be covered if a country wants to remove poverty of a targeted segment of the poor. Moreover, this measure is also a poor instrument of inter-country comparison of poverty.

The poverty gap measures have been devised to take into account the income-shortfall of the poor from the poverty line. There have been innumerable indices of this category devised to take into account specific aspects of poverty gap. The details of all these measures and the mathematical formulas are irrelevant for this study[2]. Amartya Sen has criticized the income-based poverty measures as they fail to take account of deprivations in terms of basic amenities of life (literacy, healthcare, safe drinking water, pollution-free atmosphere). So, he has defined poverty indices based on these aspects of human living, popularly known as capability-based indices (Sen, Amartya 1984, 1993). In this connection, the Human Poverty indices of UNDP are worth mentioning. (UNDP, HDR 2003, pp. 342-43). Sen's approach will be taken up in a subsequent section.

Inequality

In modern economic literature, attention has also been drawn to various aspects of relative poverty or inequality both in terms of income and in terms of basic amenities. The common statistical measure to quantify inequality is the Gini coefficient derived from the Lorenz curve[3].

All surveys to quantify inequality in terms of this approach have revealed widespread inequality in terms of income, basic amenities and human development in most of the countries (irrespective of the level of economic development). Research works have also revealed wide differences in the degree of inequality in various regions of the same country. If we look into the world scenario and compare different nations on the basis of per capita income and the Human Development Index, wide disparities among nations would become apparent. Time series data from the *World Development Report* and *The Human Development Report* reveal widening disparities among nations over time, negating all the nicely constructed growth models indicating convergence.

Poverty Removal Measures in LDCs

So far as the LDCs are concerned, inequality and low levels of development have combined to assign such a grave significance to absolute poverty that poverty removal has been the most crucial policy issue for all sensible governments, especially in the LDCs. The two major theoretical approaches in this direction are:

(i) Trickledown Approach
(ii) Direct Approach

The distinctions between these two approaches may be clarified with examples from India.

At the initial stage of planning in India it was expected that economic growth would automatically trickle down to remove the intensity of poverty at the lower strata of income. But this did not materialize as most of the fruits of planned economic development had been cornered by the well to do minority magnifying the intensity of poverty and inequality. So since the Fifth Five-Year Plan (1974-79), the 'trickledown approach' was abandoned and emphasis was laid on direct poverty removal measures. Since then innumerable special poverty removal programmes (like IRDP, SFDA, ILDDPAP, TADP, MNP) have been undertaken to grapple with appalling poverty in India. (Hiraway 1986, Kumar 1993).

No doubt, this direct attack on poverty has produced some positive results, but they have been quite inadequate considering the magnitude of poverty in this highly populated country. (World Bank 1997, 1998, 1999, Muqtada 1990).

Since the 1990s it has been emphasized that a combination of growth and direct programmes would be the best measure for poverty removal in India. (Hanumantha Rao 1992). Other Third World countries are likely to have similar experiences. This has been in perfect harmony with the guidelines of the international institutions like the UNO, IMF and the World Bank. This is obvious from the exhortations in all the recent issues of the *World Development Report*, the *Human Development Report* and all other publications by the world bodies. But are these going to attack the poison tree at its very roots and destroy it?

Before going further into this issue, let us have a glimpse of the excellent account of the genesis of poverty provided by Karl Marx and Frederick Engels.

Marx and Genesis of Poverty

Marxian theory of the historical process of development of the human society gives an excellent account of the genesis of poverty and inequality. From an economic standpoint Marx divides the process of the development of human society till his time into four major stages: primitive communism, slave society, feudalism and capitalism. He predicts that capitalism would be replaced by socialism, which again will ultimately dissolve into communism, a classless stateless society.

At the first stage, during primitive communism, poverty in the modern sense did not exist (poverty in the modern sense is meaningful only when its opposite, viz. opulence, exists). It was simply limitation of amenities, applicable to all members of a clan, because of limited knowledge to explore natural resources to meet human demand. These clan societies were characterized by equality. To quote:

> "The household was communistic, comprising several, and often many, families. Whatever was produced and used in common was common property: the house, the garden, the long boat." (Engels 1884, Ch. IX, P. 155)

Man-nature conflict gradually led to improvement in methods of production– man gradually having more and more command over Nature with its increasing knowledge. With the acceleration of this process, by increasing the social division of labour, surplus over and above consumption requirements started emerging. And at the same time human values pertaining to fellow feeling and equality started degenerating into slavery–oppression of one class of people by another. To quote:

> "The increase of production in all branches–cattle breeding, agriculture, domestic handicrafts–enabled human labour power to produce more than was necessary for its maintenance. At the same time, it increased the amount of work that daily fell to the lot of every member of the gens or household community or single family. The addition of more labour power became desirable. This was furnished by war; captives were made slaves. Under the given general historical conditions, the first great social division of labour, by increasing the productivity of labour, that is, wealth, and

> enlarging the field of production, necessarily carried slavery in its wake. Out of the first great social division of labour arose the first great division of society into two classes: masters and slaves, exploiters and exploited." (*Ibid.* p. 157).

> "The continued increase of production and with it the increased productivity of labour enhanced the value of human labour power. Slavery, which had been a nascent and sporadic factor in the preceding stage, now became an essential part of the social system." (*Ibid.* p. 159)

> "The distinction between rich and poor was added to that between freemen and slaves–with the new division of labour came a new division of society into classes." (*Ibid.* p. 160)

With the emergence of money as the most convenient medium of exchange and the emergence of the parasitic merchant class, the process of property ownership and accumulation of wealth by a few and the consequent poverty and inequality were further crystallized. To quote:

> "Here a class appears for the first time which, without taking any part in production, captures the management of production as a whole and economically subjugates the producers to its rule; a class that makes itself the indispensable intermediary between any two producers and exploits them both." (*Ibid.* p. 162)

> "The commodity of commodities, which conceals within itself all other commodities, was discovered; the charm that can transform itself at will into anything desirable and desired. Whoever possessed it ruled the world of production; and who had it above all others? The merchants." (*Ibid.* p. 163)

> "Besides wealth in commodities and slaves, besides money wealth, wealth in the form of land came into being." (*Ibid.* p. 163)

Continued material progress, made possible by man's increasing command over Nature, ultimately paved the way for the Industrial Revolution, which ushered in the capitalistic or bourgeois society. Capitalism enhanced the pace of materialistic development but at the same time it facilitated more ruthless exploitation of the labour class turning them into proletariats. To quote:

> "With slavery, which reached its fullest development in civilization, came the first great split of society into an exploiting and an exploited class. This split has continued during the whole period of civilization. Slavery was the first form of exploitation, peculiar to the world of antiquity; it was followed by serfdom in the Middle Ages, and by wage labour in modern times. These are three great forms of servitude, characteristic of the three great epochs of civilization; open and latterly, disguised slavery, are its steady companions." (*Ibid.* p. 172)

> "The bourgeoisie, during its rule of scarce one hundred years, has created more massive and more colossal productive forces than have all preceding generations together. Subjection of Nature's forces to man, machinery, application of chemistry to industry and agriculture, steam navigation, railways, electric telegraphs, clearing of whole continents for cultivation, canalization of rivers, whole population conjured

> out of the ground–what earlier century had even a presentiment that such productive forces slumbered in the lap of social labour?" (Marx and Engels 1948, Ch. 1, p. 48)
>
> "In proportion as the bourgeoisie, i.e., capital, is developed, in the same proportion is the proletariat, the modern working class, developed–a class of labourers, who live only so long as they find work, and who find work only so long as their labour increases capital. These labourers, who must sell themselves piecemeal, are a commodity, like every other article of commerce, and are consequently exposed to all the vicissitudes of competition, to all the fluctuations of the market." (*Ibid.* Ch.1, p. 51)

Now as regards the cause of oppression, exploitation, and increasing poverty and inequality along with material progress Marx and Engels held class society and the institution of private property responsible. But because of either superficial observation or obsession with some specific motive, they failed to visualize that these are but manifestations of some deeper cause inherent in human nature. They, in fact, identified the effect as the cause and lapsed into the tautological fallacy. They also invented the concept of class struggle as the sole cause of the transformation of human society from one stage to another and also found in it the ultimate means of resolving the problem. To quote:

> "The history of all hitherto existing society is the history of class struggles."

Freeman and slave, patrician and plebeian, lord and serf, guild-master and journeyman, in a word, oppressor and oppressed, stood in constant opposition to one another, carried on an uninterrupted, now hidden, now open fight, a fight that each time ended, either in a revolutionary re-constitution of society at large, or in the common ruin of the contending classes." (*Ibid.* Ch. 1, pp. 40-41)

> "The modern bourgeois society that has sprouted from the ruins of feudal society has not done away with class antagonisms. It has but established new classes, new conditions of oppression, new forms of struggle in place of the old ones." (*Ibid.* Ch.1, p. 41)

Marx insisted on overthrowing the existing State Machinery with the help of the weapon of 'class struggle', and replacing it by the rule of the proletariat class, the immediate task of which would be to abolish private property. To quote:

> "The immediate aim of the Communists is the same as that of all the other proletarian parties; formation of the proletariat into a class, overthrow of the bourgeois supremacy, conquest of power by the proletariat." (*Ibid.* Ch. 2, p. 62).
>
> "In this sense, the theory of the Communists may be summed up in the single sentence: Abolition of private property." (*Ibid.* Ch. 2, p. 63)

The class struggle would continue and ultimately end up in a classless, stateless, family-less society of eternal bliss. To quote:

> "The bourgeois family will vanish as a matter of course when its complement vanishes, and both will vanish with the vanishing of capital." (*Ibid.* Ch. 2, p. 68)

> "The state, then, has not existed from all eternity. There have been societies that did without it, that had no idea of the state and state power. At a certain stage of economic development, which was necessarily bound up with the split of society into classes, the state became a necessity owing to this split. We are now rapidly approaching a stage in the development of production at which the existence of these classes not only will have ceased to be a necessity, but will become a positive hindrance to production. They will fall as inevitably as they arose at an earlier stage. Along with them the state will inevitably fall. Society, which will reorganize production on the basis of a free and equal association of the producers, will put the whole machinery of state where it will then belong: into the museum of antiquities, by the side of the spinning-wheel and the bronze axe." (Engels, *op. cit.* p. 170)

Marx and Engels strongly asserted that their concepts had been derived from historical facts rather than invention. To quote:

> "The theoretical conclusions of the Communists are in no way based on ideas or principles that have been invented, or discovered, by this or that would-be universal reformer."

They merely express, in general terms, actual relations springing from an existing class struggle, from a historical movement going on under our very eyes." (Marx and Engels *op. cit.* Ch. 2, p. 62).

The conviction of Marx and Engels that class struggle had played the crucial role in every qualitative transition of human society in the past is hardly convincing–it is neither supported by historical facts nor can it be substantiated by any logically consistent theory. So is also the prediction of a stateless-classless society. Moreover their apparently factual stages of development were based mainly on the observations of the economic history of some developed European countries, especially, the United Kingdom. These stages are difficult to find in Asiatic countries like India, China etc. Now think of the so-called proletarian philosophy. The depth of knowledge and introspection required to grasp the essence of the Marxian world outlook can hardly be found among the wage-earning class. Thus it is simply a world outlook invented by the speculative faculty of a highly intelligent and well read middleclass intellectual like Karl Marx who claimed it to be springing from the historical experience of the labour class. Nothing could be more ludicrous than this.

Ironically, the Socialistic States, which were conceived as a means to do away with social injustice, ultimately degenerated into another instrument of human slavery (Fast 1957, Solzhenitsyn 1969, 1971, 1985). Ultimately, most of the oppressive socialist regimes collapsed during late 1980s and early 1990s[4].

Marx failed to realize (because of either superficial observation or a myopic view or parochial obsessions) that causes of poverty, inequality, exploitation and similar maladies do not lie in private property, family relations, the state or any other visible phenomenon as such, but it lies deep in human nature, in the unethical sentiments like greed, pride, jealousy. So, eradication of the maladies, if at all possible, is to be accomplished by some process that would reduce the prevalence of these basic vices in the human mind. There has been a misconception (which mainly sprang from the over enthusiastic observations of western authors like Joan Robinson[5]) that Mao Zedong's Cultural Revolution was such a process of moral transformation. But any deep observation of the Cultural Revolution would reveal that the Maoist method was simply the shibboleth of class struggle. We shall take up the issue once again below.

Adam Smith and Moral Sentiments

Adam Smith, the father of modern economic thought (although officially a professor of 'Moral Philosophy'), is the most misunderstood and misinterpreted among the eighteenth century intellectuals. It was Thomas Carlyle who first identified the science of economics by the pejorative term 'dismal science'. It is held, not only by common people but also by eminent economists like J.K. Galbraith, that Carlyle's conviction was provoked by the dismal 'stationary state' of Ricardo-Malthus interpretation of the classical theory of economic development. (Galbraith 1977, p. 35; Oser and Brue 1988, p. 91).

But Carlyle's vehement attack on the science of economics had nothing to do with Ricardo or Malthus. It came out of two reasons:

1. Carlyle's crusade against anti-slavery campaigns and
2. Misunderstanding/misinterpretation of Smithian economics.

In 1843, Carlyle described preaching of the existing science of economics as 'Gospel of Mammon' (Carlyle 1843) and it sprang from a misinterpretation of Smithian admiration for the division of labour and capitalistic initiative as the motive force behind progress of human society Carlyle rightly criticized the capitalistic exploitation of labour, turning the labourers into inhuman robots. Here Carlyle misunderstood Smith who had never appreciated these unethical aspects of capitalism. However, the inherent reason for Carlyle's hatred of economics became clear only in 1849 when he wrote his anti-Negro and pro-racialist essay in Fraser's Magazine (Carlyle 1849, Vol. 11). Here he first described economics as 'dismal science' as it considered that whites and Negroes are not inherently different and both are simply human beings[6]. John Stuart Mill makes it clear that it was Adam Smith who was the principal target of attack by Carlyle as equality of all races and theory of 'supply and demand' were first unequivocally enunciated by him. (Mill 1850, Persky 1990).

The assertion that all men are basically the same can be traced back to Adam Smith's *Wealth of Nations.* To quote:

> "The difference of natural talents in different men is, in reality, much less than we are aware of; and the very different genius which appears to distinguish men of different professions, when grown up to maturity, is not upon many occasions so much the cause, as the effect of the division of labour. The difference between the

> most dissimilar characters, between a philosopher and a common street porter, for example, seems to arise not so much from nature as from habit, custom, and education. When they came into the world, and for the first six or eight years of their existence, they were, perhaps, very much alike, and neither their parents nor play-fellows could perceive any remarkable difference. About that age, or soon after, they come to be employed in very different occupations. The difference of talents comes then to be taken notice of, and widens by degrees, till at last the vanity of the philosopher is willing to acknowledge scarce any resemblance." (Smith 1976, Book I Ch. 2, p. 120)

Most probably the criticisms of Smithian economics by the followers of Carlyle like William Morris (Morris 1884) and John Ruskin (Ruskin 1905, pp. 25-6), sprang simply from misinterpretation. Unfortunately, the misconception and misinterpretation of the *Wealth of Nations* of Adam Smith had been carried forward to the future generations of thinkers. In this connection a funny rhyme by the Canadian economist and humourist Stephen Butler Leacock is worth quoting:

> "Adam, Adam, Adam Smith,
> Listen what I charge you with!
> Don't you say
> In the class one day
> That Selfishness was bound to pay?

Of all doctrines that was the Pith" (Leacock 1936, p.75; also quoted in Sen, Amartya 1987, p. 21).

This misinterpretation of the Smithian view (that pursuance of self interest by each and every one is going to bring about equilibrium in a *laissez faire* system) arises from the study of the *Wealth of Nations* in isolation. Smith was basically a moralist and never advocated self seeking as the true goal of human life. (Basu 2000).

In fact, the critiques of Smith have done great injustice to the "Father of Modern Economics" by depicting him as a staunch advocate of unrestricted capitalism. If we look deeply into the basics of the Smithian world outlook, it would be clear that the above view is simply a superficial understanding of Smith. So let us have a cursory glance at the Smithian world outlook.

From the study of the progress of the Industrial Revolution, Smith could realize that the ultimate progress of human society depends on the development of industry (and, therefore, the initiatives of the capitalists), which is free from natural limitations unlike agriculture, and where division of labour can be raised to a much higher level than in agriculture. But Smith was hardly satisfied with the social role of the private sector industrialists and merchants (the capitalists) and the undesirable outcomes brought about by free market capitalism. Most of the allegations against Smith by his critiques are based on the conviction that he was a staunch advocate of the capitalistic system and had moral support for the selfish behaviour of economic agents that made possible the spectacular material progress under a capitalistic system. If examined closely it would become clear how unfounded their allegations are.

For Smithian views regarding the capitalists, let us examine the following excerpts:

1. "The interest of the dealers, however, in any particular branch of trade or manufactures, is always in some respects different from, and even opposite to, that of the public." (Smith 1776, Book I Ch. IX, conclusion, p. 358)
2. "To widen the market and to narrow the competition is always the interest of the dealers. To widen the market may frequently be agreeable enough to the interest of the public; but to narrow the competition must always be against it, and can serve only to enable the dealers, by raising their profits above what they naturally would be, to levy, for their own benefit, an absurd tax upon the rest of their fellow citizen." (Ibid. p. 358)
3. "The proposal of any new law or regulation of commerce which comes from this order ought always to be listened to with great precaution, and ought never to be adopted till after having been long and carefully examined, not only with the most scrupulous, but with the most suspicious attention. It comes from an order of men whose interest is never exactly the same with that of the public, who have generally an interest to deceive and even to oppress the public, and who accordingly have upon many occasions, both deceived and oppressed it." (Ibid. p. 358-59)

From the above excerpts it is quite clear that Smith had no illusion that the spectacular material progress brought about by the unrestrained activities of the capitalists would be an unmixed blessing for the human race as a whole. Apart from historical evidences, Smith put forward a theoretical justification too. On the basis of Smith's philosophical masterpiece, '*The Theory of Moral Sentiments*' the basic sentiments of man can be broadly divided into two opposite categories: self interest and fellow feeling. All the major sentiments belonging to either of these two categories are assumed by Smith to be endowed to man by Nature. To quote:

> "The great division of our affections is into the selfish and the benevolent." (Smith 1759, VII. II. 4)

All human ethics belong to the second category of the Smithian sentiments viz. 'fellow feeling'. Material progress is brought about mainly by the motive of improving one's own condition (a motive belonging to the self interest category) and in its full manifestation it becomes the dominant sentiment. To quote:

> "It is this which first prompted them to cultivate the ground, to build houses, to found cities and commonwealths, and to invent and improve all the sciences and arts which ennoble and embellish human life, which have entirely changed the whole face of the globe, have turned the rude forests of nature into agreeable and fertile plains, and made the trackless and barren ocean a new fund of subsistence and the

great highroad of communication to the different nations of the earth" (Ibid. IV. I.10) but "….is the cause of all the tumult and bustle, all the rapine and injustice which avarice and ambition have introduced into this world." (Ibid. I.III. 23)

Capitalistic systems open up endless opportunities for material advancement of traders and industrialists and in their reckless drive towards achieving higher and higher gains, all ethical sentiments, fellow feeling and human values are bound to be swept away unless restrained by some outside force. As regards this outside force, Smith argues that all our notions of moral and ethical senses which as such are helpless in a conflict with self interest may be made effective by converting them into positive laws. The important steps in this regard as described by Smith are:

> "It is thus the general rules of morality are formed. They are ultimately founded upon experience of what, in particular instances, our moral faculties, our natural sense of merit and propriety, approve or disapprove of. We do not *originally* approve or condemn particular actions because, upon examination, they appear to be agreeable or consistent with a general rule. The general rule, on the contrary, is formed by finding from experience that all actions of a certain kind, or circumstanced in a certain manner, are approved or disapproved of." (Ibid. III.I.95)

The general rules of morality can be effective only if they are framed into positive laws of justice. To quote:

> "As the violation of justice is what men will never submit to from one another, the public magistrate is under the necessity of employing the power of the commonwealth to enforce the practice of this virtue." (Ibid. VII.IV. 36)

These laws of justice can be framed also to restrain the harmful activities of the 'dealers' (the Smithian term meaning the capitalists and merchants). Smith was by no means an advocate of the '*laissez faire*' doctrine and he, in fact, was in favour of imposing state regulations on the 'class' whose interest, he unequivocally considered, was always opposite to that of the public. This is an effort, though in embryonic form, towards devising an alternative to the free market capitalism. But here he is confronted with an insurmountable obstacle. To quote:

> "From the beginning of the reign of Elizabeth too, the English legislature has been peculiarly attentive to the interests of commerce and manufactures." (Smith, *op. cit.* Book 3, Ch. 4, p. 517)

Smith was not probably aware that this was quite a natural outcome as the economically dominant class (in this case the capitalist class) also controls the legal system and the government. So how can the government impose 'laws of justice' to restrain the capitalist class and thereby make them work in conformity with the interests of the public? It becomes clear that Smith could not devise a way out of the vicious circle, the capitalist-politician nexus. Notwithstanding his incapability to suggest a realistic way out, Smith's contribution is invaluable as he could correctly identify the inner cause of poverty, inequality and other maladies that inexorably accompany material progress–the baser human sentiment of 'self-interest'.

Once again we are confronted with a stark reality–the apparently indelible primeval vice residing in the innermost recesses of human psychosis and ascribing perpetuity to poverty and inequality. Should we be so pessimistic? Can't we find any way out? Let us examine the matter and endeavour to trace out the very root of the evil. This directly takes us to the ancient Indian Sânkhya approach to the basic causes of human misery.

Sānkhya Concepts

The ancient Indian view of human nature is most clearly presented in the Sānkhya philosophy[7] according to which human consciousness is a part of the material manifestation of Nature and it is the combination of three modes, viz. *satva*, *rajasa* and *tamasa*, endowed by Nature[8]. All these basic modes combine in different degrees to assign different characteristics to different individuals. If isolated in the abstract, unmixed *satva* pertains to goodness and virtue, *rajasa* to passion and insatiable desire and *tamasa* to darkness of mind, obsession and inertia. All our mental and intellectual faculties originate from these three basic modes. (Ballantyne 1885: Sānkhya Aphorisms: I.61, I.125-27, I.141, II. 27).

The creator is omnipresent and *nirguna* (having no attribute). But human beings are *saguna* (having specific attributes) which are of three kinds: *tāmasika* (dominated by '*tamasa*' mode), *rājasika* (dominated by '*rajasa*' mode) and *sātvika* (dominated by '*satva*' mode). *Sātvika* people are characterized by nobler qualities (like abstinence, self-sacrifice, love, philanthropy, mercy, self-confidence, diligence, composure) whereas *rājasika* and *tāmasika* people possess various combinations of baser qualities (like greed, envy, hatred, anger, selfishness, lust, idleness, cruelty, pride) (Basu 2001).

The sacred Hindu scripture Gītā describes in detail the various aspects of these basic attributes (*Telang* 1882: Gītā: 14.05-09, 14.11-13, 14.16, 14.17, 17.12, 17.18, 17.19 -22, 18.20-39).

Nature fetters the eternal individual soul to the body by the three modes viz. *satva*, *rajasa* and *tamasa*.

A *sātvika* person is free from egotism, seeks knowledge of self and the eternal, performs duties unselfishly and without attachment (i.e. without desiring rewards or fruits of the activities and being unperturbed by success or failure), is full of resolve and enthusiasm.

A *rājasika* person is activated by material desires (for wealth, power, sensual pleasures etc.) and is attached to his works (too much concerned with the fruits of work), is full of greed and selfishness, egotism, restlessness and excitement over the results of his works. He may undertake austerity, acts of sacrifice and charity, but only to get something in return (revenue, power, social positions etc.) and to show off. He cannot distinguish between righteousness and unrighteousness, and right and wrong action.

A *tāmasika* person is full of inertia leading to ignorance, delusion, slowness of mind, carelessness, laziness, inactivity, excessive sleep, vulgarity, malice etc. He performs sacrifices only as a mechanistic ritual, observes austerity with foolish stubbornness, with self-torture or for harming others, and undertakes charity without paying respect to the receiver. His head is full of irrational and baseless knowledge, fear, grief, despair, and he undertakes action out of delusion, disregarding his abilities and loss or injury to others. He is always depressed and procrastinating. He accepts unrighteousness as righteousness and thinks everything to be that which it is not. V.R. Panchamukhi has given a simplified account of these characteristics of the three classes of people (Panchamukhi 2000).

Now let us take up another concept from ancient Sanskrit texts, viz. the concept of *ripu*. In general *ripu* means enemy. These *ripus* in Hindu philosophy are excesses of some basic instincts or reflexes of human mind or intellect. The basic instincts are necessary for our material existence. So, as such they are not enemies. But for beneficial effects they must be balanced and kept under the control of the mind. If they are in excess, they become our enemies or *ripus* and result in disastrous effects both for us and for the society as a whole. The western scholars often mistakenly translate *ripu* as sin. But *ripus* are not sins, rather reasons for sins or vices. There are six *ripus*: *kāma* (desire for material pleasure/sexual desire/lust), *krodha* (anger), *lobha* (greed), *moha* (infatuation/attachment/obsession), *mada* (pride/vanity/arrogance), *mātsarya* (jealousy/envy).

The basic instincts, pertaining to the *ripus*, can be used for good or bad, but by themselves they are neutral. Sexual desire is normal and good, but sexual obsession is harmful. Controlled anger is also a necessary element that makes us human—without it we cannot have respectability. Greed is a form of desire—it can be an insatiable foolish desire or positive desire that can be used as an incentive for progress. Likewise, vanity and pride are necessary for self respect and envy can foster healthy competition. If the basic instincts are kept under control, they are always beneficial, but if they get the better of us, they turn into enemies and ruin us in the short or long run.

Gītā considers kāma (in the wider sense it means the desire for worldly pleasures), *krodha* (anger) and *lobha* (greed) the most serious among the *ripus* *(op. cit.)*

"Lust, anger, and greed are the three gates of hell leading to the downfall (or bondage) of the individual. Therefore, one must learn to give up these three." (*Gītā*: 16.21, *op. cit.*)

Gītā describes how *ripus* originate from the perverted attachment to worldly pleasures and lead one on to the path of destruction *(op. cit.)*

"One develops attachment to sense objects by thinking about sense objects. Desire for sense objects comes from attachment to sense objects, and anger comes from unfulfilled desires." (*Gītā*: 2.62, *op. cit.*)

"Delusion or wild idea arises from anger. The mind is bewildered by delusion. Reasoning is destroyed when the mind is bewildered. One falls down from the right path when reasoning is destroyed." (*Gītā*: 2.63, *op. cit.*)

"A disciplined person, enjoying sense objects with senses that are under control and free from attachments and aversions, attains tranquility." (*Gītā*: 2.64, *op. cit.*)

The *ripus* take various major forms under different modes.

For *sātvika* persons they are fully controlled and turn out benign–they reside in such a person in perfect harmony with ethical living. To him *kāma*, in the narrow sense, gets sublimated by love and associated with the birth of children, and in the wider sense it turns into a desire for knowledge and wisdom; *krodha* becomes reserved demeanor that inspires respect in the honest persons, and awe in the miscreants, *lobha* turns into hankering for getting access to the unknown eternal being; *mada* turns into dignity, confidence and self-respect; *moha* turns into strict adherence to ethical and righteous living; *mātsarya* (jealousy) gets converted into love, fellow feeling and philanthropy.

For a *rājasika* person, *kāma* in the narrow sense takes the form of preoccupation with sensual pleasure, and in the wider sense it leads to an insatiable craving for power and wealth (by just or unjust means); *krodha* takes the form of secret planning and conspiracy for taking reprisals; *lobha* gets associated with achieving all sorts of.material pleasures, power, fame etc.; *moha* makes him always pre-occupied with the fruits of his works and activities; *mada* and *mātsarya* goad him to desperate and restless activity in order to supercede all his superiors.

For a *tāmasika* person *kāma* is associated with perverse and brutal sexual desire, forceful violation of the opposite sex, incest and unnatural sex behaviour. His *krodha* is blind and destructive, both for others and for himself; his *lobha* centers on all conceivable dirty and shabby pleasures–addictions to drugs, alcohol etc. For him, *mada* leads to false vanity and day-dreaming; *moha* is full of superstitions, baseless knowledge and inactivity; *mātsarya* burns his soul and goads him to inflict harm to others.

Now let us come down to the relevance of the above concepts for a modern society. Although it is very difficult to isolate persons on the basis of the three modes, as in most of the persons the three modes remain intermixed. Still we may try a broad classification. In a modern society, on the whole, capitalists and businessmen belong to the *rājasika* category, whereas persons living in luxury on unearned income (rent income, interest income etc.) belong to the *tāmasika* category. The labourers and all sorts of poor people belong to the *tāmasika* category, but for a different reason than that for the rent earning class. For them it is because of abject poverty, oppression, illiteracy and the resultant hopelessness and fatalism. They are in that state because of the opulence of the capitalists and rent-earning class. Here the poverty removal measures and human resource development endeavours become relevant. Without lifting these persons out of the morass of abject poverty, it is not possible to enable them to move on to higher modes. But to this end the first and foremost task would be to infuse some *sātvika* qualities to the business class. As such, in a capitalist system, *sātvika* values cannot flourish among the capitalists and businessmen. This mode may naturally manifest only among the educated and thoughtful persons in the middle class. *Sātvika* persons are visible in all sorts of religious and philanthropic organizations–among fathers of churches, Hindu *swāmījis* and *sanyāsīs*, Buddhist monks, Muslim *sufis* and *fakirs*, but they are mostly preoccupied with the religious world and , therefore, not directly relevant for our purpose.

In modern literature approaches to the analysis and removal of poverty have been initiated by educated intellectuals belonging to the middle class. Most noteworthy among them are Amartya Sen, Mehabub Ul Haq and Jean Drèze. Let us take a brief glimpse of their efforts and analyze the efficacy and sustainability of these efforts in the light of our analysis of human nature.

Sen-Haq-Drèze Approach

In recent years, Amartya Sen's contributions have assigned a new dimension to the 'economics of poverty', especially its ethical aspects. Sen's major contributions in revitalizing the non-conventional economic thought have been remarkable. He gave a new lease of life to normative économics then languishing under 'Arrow's Impossibility' theorem (Arrow 1951, Sen, Amartya 1970). He also played an important role in reviving the development economics (moribund under the onslaught of aggressive neo-classicism, reemerging with renewed vigour with the up tide of the process of globalization) by redefining economic development in terms of entitlements and capabilities[9] (Sen, Amartya 1984) and freedom (Sen, Amartya 2000). To quote:

> "The process of economic development can be seen as a process of expanding the capabilities of people. Given the functional relation between entitlements of persons over goods and their capabilities, a useful–though derivative–characterization of economic development is in terms of expansion of entitlements." (Sen, Amartya 1984, p. 497)

Capabilities depend, besides exchange entitlement, on provision of public goods (market failure results in no private supply)–health, education, longevity, a pollution-free environment, safe drinking water etc.

> "But when it comes to health, or education, or social equality, or self respect, or freedom from social harassment, income is miles off the target." (Ibid. pp. 499-500)

Mahabub Ul Haq's remarkable contribution was in the arena of human development. He was the pioneer of the quantitative measurement of human development (Haq 1997). The Human Development Indices published by the UNDP are constructed on the basis of ideas originally conceived by Haq.

In some of his major works, Sen and his followers have brought to the fore the role of state policy and public action in preventing the acute manifestation of poverty, viz. famine (Drèze and Sen 1989; Drèze, Sen and Hussain 1995; Sen, Amartya 1981). Their general observation in this regard is that many famines occurring in India during the British period (including the horrible Bengal Famine of 1943) and elsewhere in the modern age were mainly due to 'Entitlement-Failure' and negative state policy and/or lack of political will.

Sen appreciates the role of the present government of India in tackling famines by suitable public action and appropriate policies. In this regard he emphasizes the role of freedom of mass media and public opinion in a democratic polity as in independent India (which is absent in 'centrally-controlled' states like China). To quote:

> "The distinction between the 'collaborative' and 'adversarial' roles of the public has some relevance to this dichotomy between the advantages of political commitment vis-à-vis those of political pluralism. While a leadership committed to radical social change can often inspire more public collaboration, having a committed leadership is not adequate for–and may even be hostile to–the exercise of the adversarial role of the public. Since both the roles have value in combating deprivation, it is natural to look for the possibility of combining the advantages of committed leadership with those of pluralist tolerance. Whether such combinations are possible, especially in the circumstances that rule in most developing countries, remains a challenging question. There is no reason, in principle, why a political system that allows, encourages and helps the public to be active (both adversarially as well as collaboratively) cannot also lead to governments that provide bold initiatives and inspiring leadership. But it is obvious that in practice the actual possibilities are much constrained by social, political and economic circumstances, and the 'ideal combinations' are hard to realize, as the history of the world has shown again and again." (Drèze and Sen 1989, pp. 278-79).

Sen, however, admits that socialist China has a better record so far as tackling chronic poverty is concerned. To quote:

> "On the other hand, there is no such relief for the third of the Indian rural population who go to bed hungry every night and who lead a life ravaged by regular deprivation. The quiet presence of non acute, endemic hunger leads to no newspaper turmoil, no political agitation, no riots in the Indian Parliament. The system takes it in its stride." (Sen, Amartya 1984, p. 500)

> "Finally, it is important to note that the protection that the Indian poor get from the active news distribution system and powerful opposition parties has very severe limits. The deprivation has to be dramatic to be 'newsworthy' and politically exploitable. .... The Indian political system may prevent famines but, unlike the Chinese system, it seems unable to deal effectively with endemic malnutrition. In a normal year when things are running smooth, both in India and China, the Indian poor is in a much more deprived general state than his or her Chinese counterpart." (Ibid. P. 503)

Now, Sen hints at the possibility of combining the advantages of these two contrasting political systems. To quote:

> "Whether the disparate advantages of the contrasting systems can be effectively combined is a challenging issue of political economy that requires attention. Much is at stake." (Ibid. p. 504)

In this connection it would be worthwhile to look into the merits of various major forms of political systems as regards ensuring social justice by minimizing poverty, inequality and deprivation. Here the main contenders are centrally controlled systems (Dictatorship, Monarchy and Socialism) and Democracy.

Dictatorship: Historical experience of oppressive aspects of all forms of non-socialist dictatorial regimes (in the past and at present) has unraveled their overwhelmingly *râjasika-tâmasika* essence[10]. So we rule out this form.

Monarchy: Ancient Indian texts (especially Manusmriti and Arthaúâstra of Kautilya[11]) have laid down detailed rules and procedures to make an ideal king. (Basu 2005a) Unfortunately, in the recorded history, except Aœoka (Thapar 1961; Sastri 1967, pp. 201-48; Kosambi 1981, pp. 157-65), there is no evidence of the existence of another ideal king. The great Greek philosopher Plato conceived of a Philosopher King, (*Plato* 1901, PP. 215-40). As regards his concept of 'Philosopher King' Immanuel Kant made an interesting comment. To quote:

> "That 'kings will philosophize or philosophers become kings,' is not to be expected. Nor indeed is it to be desired, because the possession of power inevitably corrupts the free judgment of reason. But kings or king-like nations, who govern themselves according to laws of equality, should not allow the philosophers as a class to disappear, or to be silenced; rather should they be allowed to speak forth their maxims publicly. Nay, this is even indispensable to both for the mutual enlightenment of their functions. Nor should this process of communicating enlightenment be jealously regarded as a kind of Propagandism, because as a class the philosophers are by their nature incapable of combining into political clubs and factions." (Kant 1795, Second Supplement: Secret Article Relating to Perpetual Peace). Plato later on abandoned this idea after a bitter experience[12]. So monarchy is ruled out.

Socialism: Like the Indian concept of Ideal King or Plato's Philosopher King, socialism is also a utopian concept and at the same time *sātvika* in intention. It differs in one respect–unlike the former two concepts the means to achieve its goal is the *tāmasika* 'class struggle'. This is the basic reason that compelled the USSR, the first and the most powerful socialist state, to revert back to a capitalistic path (Basu 1999). In connection with socialism Mao Zedong's Cultural Revolution deserves special mention as this exemplifies Mao's 'relentless efforts to save socialism.

Mao and the Cultural Revolution: The ideal of socialism, although utopian and based on *tāmasika* means, is *sātvika* in its goal–to abolish the *rājasika* (and the raison-d'être of all poverty, inequality and exploitation) capitalistic system along with its *rājasika* culture and world outlook. Indefatigable Mao endeavoured to prevent China from going the Soviet way, although he, too, ultimately failed because of his wrongly chosen means, viz. the Marxist concept of class struggle.

Nonetheless, it would be a grave injustice to Mao if we fail to appreciate his historical contribution as one of the greatest warriors against exploitation and injustice. So it is worthwhile to have a look at Mao's experience in the course of two dramatic episodes in modern Chinese history, viz. the Great Leap Forward (GLF) and the Cultural Revolution (CR).

With some abstraction the main players in these two interrelated episodes may be interpreted in the light of the Sānkhya principles in the following manner:

Mao Zedong: *Sātvika* in essence.

Deng Xiaoping, Liu Shaoqui, and the Premier Zhou Enlai: Defeatist and *tāmasika* in essence.

Jiang Qing, Mao's wife and Lin Biao, the Defence Minister: Power mongering and *rājasika* in essence.

Red Guards: *Tāmasika* in essence

The following developments prompted Mao to hastily resort to the CR:

> Mao wanted to adopt radical Marxist policies in order to pave the way for a rapid transition of the Chinese economy from a semi-feudal condition to socialism. The Second Five-Year Plan (1958-63) was chosen as the starting point of the GLF. Mao, notwithstanding his noble intentions, failed to realize that his methods would not work in a country still dominated by *tāmasika* and *rājasika* masses, government officials and members of the communist party. The inevitable consequence was miserable failure leading to economic disaster and the death of millions of people by famine[13]. Liu Shaoqi, Deng Xiaoping and Zhou Enlai got disillusioned with socialism and opted for Soviet type State-Capitalism. Mao was held responsible for the disaster and he resigned from the position of head of the state (although retained the position of Party Chairmanship). Because of his honesty and dedication, he was still the most revered politician among the masses. So Mao opted to root out the bourgeois world outlook (which, he rightly identified as the major cause of failure of the GLF) with the help of the masses and apparently radical socialists like Jiang Qing, Lin Biao, Chen Boda and Kang Seng. So he planned to launch the so-called CR. He, however, had been obsessed with the wrong notion about the students, peasants and the factory labourers, who were *tāmasika* in essence. He also failed to judge the characters of Jiang Qing and Lin Biao.

Moreover, the declared means of the CR, for the removal of the capitalistic or bourgeois elements from power in the communist party and the government, was the *tāmasika* class struggle. The following extracts from Mao's directives are evidence of this approach of the CR. (Mao: *Selected Works*, Vol. IX).

1. "The old Social Democrats in the past decades, and modern revisionists in the past dozen years or so. . . have formed a group of anti-communist, anti-people, and counter-revolutionary elements against whom we are waging a life-and-death struggle. There is no equality between us and them. Therefore, the fight against them is a fight for our preservation and their extinction. The

relationship between us and them can never be one of equality; it is a relationship of one class oppressing another—i.e. proletarian dictatorship over the bourgeoisie. The day when the people are happy will be the day when the counter-revolutionaries begin their misery."

2. "The basic contradiction the great proletarian Cultural Revolution is trying to resolve is the one between the proletariat and the bourgeoisie, between the proletarian and bourgeois roads. The main point of the movement is to struggle against the capitalist roaders in authority in the party."

To fight the opponents Mao wanted to rely on the students and the masses who could be easily moved by emotional and idealistic preaching. Red Guards (formed mainly with the emotional students) were directed to attack Mao's opponents. To quote:

> "The revolutionary red guards and revolutionary student organizations must form a grand alliance. As long as they are revolutionary mass organizations, they must form a great alliance according to revolutionary principles." (Ibid.)

Mao also realized that without control over the military force it would not be possible to combat and corner the opponents. To win the support of the military force, especially the Peoples Liberation Army (PLA) he forged an alliance with Lin Biao, the Defence Minister with the assurance that he would be the successor of Mao. Mao issued the following guidelines for Lin Biao:

> "You must dispatch troops to support the broad left-wing revolutionary masses. Later on, whenever true revolutionaries need support from the PLA, you should do likewise. The so called 'non-interference' is untrue. [The PLA] has been involved for some time. I think on this matter you should issue new orders; the old ones should be cancelled." (Ibid.)

Now as regards the first and foremost task of the pro-CR student-mass-army alliance, Mao issued the directive:

> "Bombard The Headquarters–My First Big-Character Poster." (Ibid.)

The consequences of the CR were simply devastating–chaos, anarchy, civil war, arson, looting, wanton damage of property and productive resources, killings and all other conceivable manifestations of *tamasa*. The CR left China in a condition experienced by a land gripped under a horrible cyclone. In course of the turbulent incidents, there was shuffling and reshuffling of power from one leader to another. It turned out to be a power struggle between two radical groups led respectively by Lin Biao and Jiang Qing. With the supremacy of the latter group, Chen Boda, a follower of Lin, was arrested and killed and Lin was killed in a plane crash while fleeing China in 1971. But then the wind took a reverse turn, now against the remaining radicals led by Jiang Qing. Mao died and then Jang Qing, the last supporter of the CR, was arrested in 1976. The CR came to an abrupt end leaving China in shambles. (Barnouin and Yuchanggen 1993, Chen 1975, Domes 1973,

Joseph et. al. (eds.) 1991, Lee 1978, Tang 1986) [For chronology of the CR see the Appendix to this chapter.]

Democracy: Now we are left with democracy, which, from the standpoint of human freedom, is the best conceivable form of government. We have already touched upon Amartya Sen's views about the role of public opinion and the mass media in ensuring positive changes in the society. We also rest our ultimate hope on this form of government. But the present state of democracy in the world and the global trends are not at all encouraging. The Neoclassical view, based on 'perfect competition' and '*laissez faire*' doctrine and playing the ideological basis of economic policies in the modern democratic countries till the early twentieth century, revealed its serious vulnerability during the 'Great Depression' of the 1930s. Keynesian economics emerging out of the bitter experiences of the Great Depression led to an abandonment of the *laissez faire* doctrine permitting state-intervention in the free-market economies, although to a limited scale. In the newly independent democratic countries like India during the post-war era, pervasive state-intervention in the form of comprehensive planning, control of the private enterprises, the pioneering role of the state sector in strategic fields, price control, public distribution systems for food and mass consumption commodities etc., became necessary both to break through the vicious circle of backwardness and to ensure social justice. But because of the *rājasika* and *tāmasika* contents of the political parties and the government officials, both planning and public sector enterprises in these so-called 'mixed economies' came up against serious hurdles.

Under these conditions, during the late 20th century, there was strong opinion among economists for revival of the free-market economy, completely devoid of state-interventions (Friedman 1980). In the meantime debacles of the socialist countries and planned mixed economies prepared grounds for the revival of Neoclassicism. The process of reversal got momentum with the spectacular communication revolution and ultimately the so called era of 'globalization' emerged.

With this backdrop let us look into the efficacy of the democracies in ensuring social justice with progressive reduction in poverty, inequality and deprivations in the new era.

We have already mentioned that Amartya Sen has strongly appreciated the role of public opinion and free mass media in ensuring social justice in the democratic countries. In this context Sen, however, failed to realize that unless the masses and the media men are made free from *tāmasika* and *rājasika* obsessions, they cannot play the cherished roles. Moreover, the politicians and political parties in the democratic countries are but characters of the puppet-show–the operators are the capitalists, nowadays, the *rājasika* multinational corporations (MNCs), whose sole mission is to shackle the entire world into slavery. Within the LDCs, the politicians (who themselves are slaves of the capitalists) thrive on slavery of the *tāmasika* masses. This is the democratic world we are living in. In fact, whenever we speak of freedom of the press and public opinion in the democratic countries one may pose the question: what roles did the mass media and public opinion play in a democratic country like the USA to prevent bombing in Vietnam during the 1960s and in Afghanistan and Iraq in recent times? The heinous role of the Central Intelligence Agency and the Neo-imperialistic policy of the democratic USA (*Ali* 2000, 2003; Coll 2001) are enough to make the most optimistic spokesmen of democracy disillusioned.

True democracy could be restored in individual countries and in the world as a whole only if it is possible to inculcate *sātvika* values among the common men and also the capitalists. Unless the capitalists are purified, they would never permit the slaves to acquire *sātvika* values and be free from their clutches. But here we are confronted with a serious problem–it is not possible to effectively inspire the common people with *sātvika* values unless the *rājsika* character of the capitalists is moderated, which appears impossible as the capitalists would encounter a "Prisoner's Dilemma" situation here. If all capitalists are imbibed with *sātvika* values, it is well and good, but if not, then the adherents of *sātvika* values would be rooted out by the existing *rājasika* counterparts.

We are in all praise for the Sen-Haque-Drèze approach for poverty alleviation. But we also emphasize that this is but a palliative and would never remove the deep seated cause lying in human nature. On the contrary, this may make the deprived dependent on outside help and thereby get further submerged in *tamasa*. Long ago, Rabindranath had warned against this attitude of helping the common people. At the same time he suggested how *sātvika* values could be inculcated among the masses. To quote:

> "For this reason, the most urgent necessity in our country is not to place begging bowls at their hands, but to make them confident of their own strength, to make them realize that a man united with others is a complete entity, an alienated individual is but a fragment." (Tagore 1986)

Conclusion

In course of the above analysis we have endeavoured to bring to the fore the fact that the basic cause of poverty and inequality lies within human psychosis itself, the interplay of two baser modes of living, viz. *rajasa* and *tamasa*. The *rājasika* people fulfill their insatiable greed by keeping the *tāmasika* majority in perpetual slavery. This is the root cause of poverty ever since the emergence of private property. The history of human civilization since then has been characterized by this dualism–the *rājasika* slave-owners and the *tāmasika* slaves, the *rājasika* feudal lords (or equivalent classes) and the *tāmasika* cultivators, the *rājasika* merchants/capitalists and the *tāmasika* wage earners, *rājasika* leaders of the communist party and the *tāmasika* common people.

In the era of globalization, the *rājasika* MNCs have gradually been enslaving the population of the entire world, by forcing them to be in *tāmasika* state. Their global investment policies, sales efforts (through advertisement), work culture that is designed to make the employees thoughtless robots, all are directed to this goal.

In connection with the question of way out, we have come to the conclusion that remedial measures, if at all possible, could be undertaken only in a democratic form of government. Unfortunately, modern democratic governments are run by politicians who are simply the privileged slaves of the capitalists headed by the MNCs. So far as the common people are concerned, poverty of the majority is itself a hindrance to inculcating *sātvika* values among them. So the foremost task is to contain the *rājasika* capitalists by infusing *sātvika* values among them. But under the present circumstances, it appears to be a very difficult, if not a completely impossible task.

Still we may go on trying and trying, like Mao's 'Foolish Old Man'[14]. We may fail, but in future someone may achieve success. So we reiterate–let us try and try again:

> "You have right over doing your duty only, but no control or claim over the results. The fruits of work should not be your motive, and you should never be inactive[15]." (Telang 1882: Gītā: 2.47).

NOTES

1. For various measures of inequality and the problems associated with them see Sen, Amartya 1973, 1982.
2. For details see EPW Research Foundation 1993; Sen, Amartya 1981; Sinha and Sen, Raj Kumar (eds.) 2000, pp. 193-265.
3. See Powell and Craseman 1961 and Edington 1930.
4. The Socialist Regimes collapsed in Bulgaria, Czechoslovakia, Hungary, Poland and Romania in 1989, in Albania, East Germany and Yugoslavia in 1990 and in Russia (then USSR) at the end of 1991. Surprisingly this corresponded exactly with the predictions made by George Orwell long ago (Orwell 1949).
5. Robinson, Joan, (1970) *The Cultural Revolution in China.* Middlesex: Penguin Books.
6. In connection with labour shortages in factories in the West Indies as a consequence of abolition of slavery, Carlyle opined that black men are born to be slaves–so they should be compelled to work as slaves. He wrote about those who argued that the forces of supply and demand rather than physical coercion should regulate the labour market that: "the Social Science ... which finds the secret of this Universe in supply and demand and reduces the duty of human governors to that of letting men alone ... is a dreary, desolate, and indeed quite abject and distressing one; what we might call ... the dismal science." (Carlyle 1849, Vol. 11 P. 177)
7. There are six Vedic philosophies: Nyāya, Vaiśeshika, Sānkhya, Yoga, Pūrva-Mīmāmsā, Vedānta. (Sen, K.M. 1961, pp. 78-85)

8. In many English versions, *sātva* is translated as goodness, *rajasa* as passion and *tamasa* as ignorance. But these renderings hardly convey the actual connotations of these terms–in fact there are no equivalent terms in the English language as the concepts are new to the western world. So it would be judicious to incorporate these words directly into the English vocabulary.
9. "Entitlement refers to the set of alternative commodity bundles that a person can command in a society using the totality of rights and opportunities that he or she faces............ On the basis of this entitlement, a person can acquire some capabilities, i.e. the ability to do this or that (e.g. be well nourished), and fail to acquire some other capabilities." (Sen, Amartya 1984, p. 497)
10. See Black 1986, Fitch and Lowenthal (eds.) 1986 for the heinous roles of dictatorial regimes in Latin America; Amitav Ghosh's novel, *The Glass Palace* (Ghosh 2001), portrays a vivid account of the oppressive dictatorial regime in Myanmar (Burma).
11. See Manusmriti: Chapter 7, pages: 30-49, 58, 79, 142-47, 221-26 (*Sacred Books of the East*, Vol. XXV, edited by F. Max Müller, Oxford Clarendon Press, 1888) and Arthaúâstra of Kautilya: Book I: Ch 5/7-17; Ch 6/1-10; Ch 7/1-8; Ch 9/6-25; Ch 19/9-11 (Kangle 1986).
12. According to the Greek author Diogenes Laertius, Plato received an invitation from Dionysius, the king of Syracuse to turn his kingdom into Utopia and Plato readily accepted the invitation. But when Plato suggested that the king either to become a philosopher himself or to relinquish power for some philosopher in order to make his kingdom a utopia, the king got infuriated with Plato and sold him as a slave. Fortunately Plato's disciple Anniceris appeared in time as a rescuer by repurchasing Plato from the slave trader. This disillusioned Plato. (Laertius 2001, Book 3, XIV-XVIII) However, it is difficult to prove the authenticity of this story–Laertius had Herodotus-like reputation of mixing facts with fantasy.
13. See [http://www.historylearningsite.co.uk/great_leap_forward.htm].
14. "There is an ancient Chinese fable called The Foolish Old Man Who Removed Mountains. It tells of an old man who lived in northern China long, long ago and was known as the Foolish Old Man of North Mountain. His house faced south and beyond his doorway stood the two great peaks, Taihang and Wangwu, obstructing the way. He called his sons, and hoe in hand they began to dig up these mountains with great determination. Another graybeard, known as the Wise Old Man, saw them and said derisively, 'How silly of you to do this! It is quite impossible for you few to dig up those two huge mountains.' The Foolish Old Man replied, 'When I die, my sons will carry on; when they die, there will be my grandsons, and then their sons and grandsons, and so on to infinity. High as they are, the mountains cannot grow any higher and with every bit we dig, they will be that much lower. Why can't we clear them away?' Having refuted the Wise Old Man's wrong view, he went on digging every day, unshaken in his conviction. God was moved by this, and he sent down two angels, who carried the mountains away on their backs." Mao's concluding speech at the Seventh National Congress of the Communist Party of China, 11.6.1945 (*Mao*, selected works, Vol. III).
15. "Karmanyebādhikāraste mā faleshu kadāchana.
Mā karmafalaheturbhumā te sangohstvakarmani"

BIBLIOGRAPHY AND REFERENCES

Ali, Tariq (2000), *Masters of the Universe: NATO's Balkan Crusade*, Verso.

Ali, Tariq (2003), *Bush in Babylon*, Verso.

Arrow, K.J. (1951), *Social Choice and Individual Values*, New York, Wiley 1963.

Ballantyne, James R. (translator) (1885), *Sānkhya Aphorisms of Kapila*, London, Trübner & Co.

Barnouin, Barbara and Yu Changgen (1993), *Ten Years of Turbulence*, London, Kegan Paul International.

Basu, Ratan Lal (1998), "Adam Smith and Socialism" in R.K. Sen (ed.): *Market Capitalism and Socialism*, Calcutta, The New Book Stall.

Basu, Ratan Lal (1999), "Material Progress and Ethics: a Pilgrimage Through Time" in *The Culture Mandala* (The Bulletin of the Center for East-West Cultural and Economic Studies, Bond University, Australia), Vol. 4, No. 1, December 1999-January 2000. [http://www.international-relations.com].

Basu, Ratan Lal (2000), "Magnificent Men in Quest of Ethics" in A.K. Sinha & R.K. Sen (eds.): *Economics of Amartya Sen*, New Delhi, Deep & Deep Publications Pvt. Ltd.

Basu, Ratan Lal (2005), "Why the Human Development Index Does not Measure up to Ancient Indian Standards" in *The Culture Mandala* (The Bulletin of the Center for East-West Cultural and Economic Studies, Bond University, Australia), Vol. 6, No. 2, January 2005. [http://www.international-relations.com].

Basu, Ratan Lal (2005a), "Human Development Part 2: Ancient Kingship, Modern Politicians and the Problem of Corruption in India" in *The Culture Mandala* (The Bulletin of the Center for East-West Cultural and Economic Studies, Bond University, Australia), Vol. 7, No. 1, December 2005. [http://www.international-relations.com].

Black, Jan Knippers (1986), *Sentinels of Empire: The United States and Latin American Militarism*, New York, Greenwood Press.

Carlyle, Thomas (1849) "Occasional Discourse on the Negro Question" in H.D. Traill (ed.) *Collected Works of Thomas Carlyle*, Volume 11, PP. 171-210, London, Chapman and Hall, 1896-99.

Carlyle, Thomas [1843] (1949) *Past and Present*, London, J.M. Dent & Sons.

Chen, Jac (1975), *Inside the Cultural Revolution*, New York, MacMillan.

Coll, Steve (2001), *Ghost Wars: The Secret History of the CIA, Afghanistan, and bin Laden, from the Soviet Invasion to September 10, 2001*, USA, Penguin Group.

Domes, Jurgen (1973), *The Internal Politics of China 1949-72*, New York, Praeger.

Drèze, Jean and Sen, Amartya (1989), *Hunger and Public Action*, New Delhi, Oxford India Paperbacks 1999.

Drèze, Jean, Sen, Amartya and Hussain, Athar (eds.) (1995), *The Political Economy of Hunger*, New Delhi, Oxford India Paperbacks 1999.

Economic and Political Weekly (EPW) Research Foundation (1993), "Poverty Levels in India: Norms, Estimates and Trends", Bombay, *EPW*, Vol. XXVIII, No. 38, August 31.

Edington A.S. (1930), *The Mathematical Theory of Relativity*, New York, Cambridge University Press.

Engels, Frederick (1884), *The Origin of the Family, Private Property and the State*, Moscow, Progress Publishers 1972.

Fast, Howard (1957), *The Naked God; the Writer and the Communist Party*, New York, Praeger.

Fitch, J. Samuel and Abraham F. Lowenthal (eds.) (1986), *Armies and Politics in Latin America*, New York, Holmes & Meier.

Friedman, Milton and Rose (1980), *Free to Choose*, London, Penguin.

Galbraith, John Kenneth (1977), *The Age of Uncertainty*, Boston, Houghton Mifflin.

Ghosh, Amitav (2001), *The Glass Palace*, Harper Collins.

Hanumantha, Rao, C.H. (1992), "Integrating Poverty Alleviation Programmes with Development Strategies", Bombay, *Economic and Political Weekly*, Vol. XXVII, No. 48, November 28.

Haq, Mahbub Ul (1997), *Human Development in South-Asia*, New Delhi, Oxford University Press.

Hiraway, Indira (1986), *Abolition of Poverty in India*, New Delhi, Vikas Publishing House.

Joseph, William et al. (eds.) (1991), *New Perspectives on the Cultural Revolution*, Cambridge, MA, Harvard University Press.

Kangle, R.P. (1986), *Kautilîya Arthaúâstra*, Part-II [English translation], Delhi, Motilal Banarasidass.

Kant, Immanuel (1795): "Perpetual Peace", in *Kant's Principles of Politics, including his essay on Perpetual Peace, A Contribution to Political Science,* trans. W. Hastie, Edinburgh, Clark 1891.

Kosambi, D.D. (1981), *The Culture and Civilization of Ancient India*, New Delhi, Vikas Publishing House.

Kumar, T. Krishna (1993), "Measure of Poverty Suited to Design and Evaluate Poverty Alleviation Programmes", Bombay, *Economic and Political Weekly*, Vol. XXVIII, No. 52, December 25.

Laertius, Diogenes (2001), *Lives of Eminent Philosophers*, Vol. I, translated by R.D. Hicks, Harvard University Press.

Leacock, Stephen (1936), *Hellements of Hickonomics in Hiccoughs of Verse Done in our Social Planning Mill*, New York, Dodd, Mead & Co.

Lee, Hongyong (1978), *The Politics of the Chinese Cultural Revolution*, Berkeley, CA, University of California Press.

Mao Zedong: *Selected Works* Vol. III & IX [http://www.marxists.org/reference/archive/mao/selected-works/volume-9/index.htm].

Marx and Engels (1848), *Manifesto of the Communist Party*, Moscow, Progress Publishers 1975.

Mill, J. S. (1850), "The Negro Question" Jean O'Grady and John M. Robson (eds.) *Collected Works of John Stuart Mill*, Volume 21, U.K., Rouledge 1991.

Morris, William (1884), 'Art and Labour', in Le Mire, E. (ed.) *Unpublished Lectures of William Morris*, Detroit, Wayne State University Press 1969.

Muqtada, M. (1990), *The Elusive Target: An Evaluation of Target Group Approaches to Employment Creation in Rural Asia*, ILO.

Orwell, George (1949), *Nineteen Eighty-Four*, London, Secker & Warburg.

Oser, J., and S. Brue. (1988), *The Evolution of Economic Thought*, Fourth edition, San Diego, Harcourt Brace Jovanovich.

Panchamukhi, V. R. (2000), *Indian Classical Thoughts on Economic Development and Management*, New Delhi, Bookwell Publishers.

Persky. J. (1990), "A Dismal Romantic", *Journal of Economic Perspectives*, Volume 4, PP. 165-72.

Plato (1901), *The Republic*, edited and translated by Benjamin Jowett, New York, P. F. Collier & Son.

Powell, J.L. and Craseman, B. (1961), *Quantum Mechanics*, New Delhi, Oxford & IBH Publishing Co.

Putnam, Hilary (1993), "Objectivity and Science-Ethics Distinction" in Martha C. Nussbaum and Amartya Sen (eds.) *The Quality of Life*, New Delhi, Oxford India Paperbacks 1999.

Ruskin, John (1905), 'Unto This Last'. In Cook, E.T. and A. Wedderburn (eds) *The Works of John Ruskin*, Vol. XVII, London: George Allen. PP. 25-6.

Sartre, Jean Paul (1972), *Being and Nothingness*, translated by H.E. Barnes, New York, Washington Square Press.

Sastri, K.A. Nilakanta (ed.) (1967), *Age of the Nandas and Mauryas*, Delhi, Motilal Banarasidass.

Sen, K.M. (1961), *Hinduism*, Penguin Books.

Sen, Amartya (1970), *Collective Choice and Social Welfare*, Amsterdam, North-Holland 1979.

Sen, Amartya (1973), *On Economic Inequality*, New Delhi, Oxford India Paperbacks 1999.

Sen, Amartya (1981), *Poverty and Famines*, New Delhi, Oxford India Paperbacks 1999.

Sen, Amartya (1982), *Choice, Welfare and Measurement*, New Delhi, Oxford India Paperbacks 1999.

Sen, Amartya (1984), *Resources, Values and Development*, New Delhi, Oxford India Paperbacks 1999.

Sen, Amartya (1987), *On Ethics and Economics*, U.K., Basil Blackwell.

Sen, Amartya (1993), "Capability and Well-Being" in Martha C. Nussbaum and Amartya Sen (eds.) *The Quality of Life*, New Delhi, Oxford India Paperbacks 1999.

Sen, Amartya (2000), *Development as Freedom*, New Delhi, Oxford India Paperbacks.

Sinha, Ajit Kumar and Sen, Raj Kumar (eds.) (2000) *Economics of Amartya Sen*, New Delhi, Deep and Deep Publications Pvt. Ltd.

Smith, Adam (1759), *The Theory of Moral Sentiments*, London, A. Millar, Sixth edition, 1790.

Smith Adam (1776), *Wealth of Nations*, Penguin Series (Pelican Classics), Edited by Andrew Skinner, 1977.

Solzhenitsyn, Alexander (1969), *The Cancer Ward*, translated by Nicholas Bethell & David Burg, London, Bodley Head.

Solzhenitsyn, Alexander (1971), *One Day in the Life of Ivan Denisovich*, translated by Ralph Parker, Penguin Books.

Solzhenitsyn, Alexander (1985), *The Gulag Archipelago*, 1918-1956: *an Experiment in Literary Investigation*, translated by Thomas P. Whitney and Harry Willetts, New York, Harper & Row.

Tagore, Rabindranath (1986), "Samabaya Nîti", in *Rabindra Rachanavali*, 125th Anniversary Edition, Vol. 14, P. 313, Calcutta, Visva-Bharati Publishers (translated from Bengali by the author of this article).

Tang, Tsou (1986), *The Cultural Revolution and post-Mao reforms: a historical perspective*, Chicago, University of Chicago Press.

Telang, Kâshinâth Trimbak (translator) (1882), "The Bhagavad Gītā", *The Sacred Books of the East*, Vol. 8, Oxford, Clarendon Press.

Thapar, Romila (1961), *Asoka and the Decline of the Mauryas*, New Delhi, Oxford University Press.

UNDP: *Human Development Report*, Various Issues.

World Bank: *World Development Report*, Various issues.

World Bank (1997) *India: Achievements and Challenges in Reducing Poverty.*

World Bank (1998) *Reducing Poverty in India: Options for More Effective Public Services.*

World Bank (1999) *Reducing Poverty in India: Options for More Effective Public Services.*

APPENDIX

A Chronology of the Cultural Revolution in China

May 1966: Concept of Cultural Revolution (CR) in Communist Party newspaper.

August 1966: Mao officially launched CR-formed the Red Guards to combat his opponents in the Communist Party.

October 1966: At a mass meeting in Tiananmen Square Mao called for the Red Guards to destroy the four olds: old ideas, old behaviour etc.

Fall 1966: Mao closed schools and called for the formation of the Red Guards to challenge party officials. Officials, intellectuals and people in positions of power and influence were attacked verbally and physically by the Red Guards. Mao left Beijing, leaving Liu Shaoqi and other top leaders to handle the social turmoil. Mao later returned to Beijing after a much publicized swim in the Chang Jiang (Yangtze River). Mao deemed Liu Shaoqi a counter revolutionary. Later Liu's wife was publicly humiliated at a mass meeting. She and Liu were arrested and imprisoned. Liu was beaten and tortured to death.

January 1967: Red Guards overthrew the existing provincial party committee officials and replaced them with radicals.

February 1967: Party officials called for an end to the CR but Mao continued to support it.

July 1967: Red Guards attacked the political leadership of the city of Wuhan and full fledged civil war ensued. Zhou Enlai personally interceded to resolve the crisis by restraining the Red Guards.

Summer 1967: Fight among rival factions of the Red Guards ensued and Mao ultimately ordered Lin Biao to use the Army to bring order to the Red Guard movement.

1968: The disorders caused by the CR resulted in 12% decline in industrial production in 1968 compared to 1966. The Army took control of government offices, schools and factories. Millions of young people were sent to the countryside to 'learn from the peasants'.

April 1969: Border clashes with the USSR–declaration of Martial Law by Lin Biao who was declared the official successor of Mao. Mao opted for open talks with the USA to combat the Soviet threat.

1970-71: Jiang Qin's group started opposing Lin as successor of Mao.

August 1971: Chen Boda, a supporter of Lin, was arrested and killed.

September 1971: Lin Biao was killed in a plane crash in Mongolia attempting to flee China. He was accused of plotting to kidnap and kill Mao and take control of China himself.

Late 1971–Mid 1973: Mao had a stroke and Chou, cancer.

February 1972: Richard Nixon, the US President, visited China. The Shanghai Communiqué defining China-US friendship was issued.

Early 1973: Deng was rehabilitated.

Mid 1973–Mid 1974: Jiang Qing's group once again became dominant in the government.

July 1974: Mao shifted support to Zhou and Deng.

Fall 1974: Mao shifted back support to Jiang Qing. Deng was formally removed from power.

January 1976: Zhou died.

February 1976: Hua Guofeng was appointed acting Premier.

September 1976: Mao died. Hua was made party Chairman.

October 1976: Armed forces arrested Jiang Qing and her group–the so-called 'Gang of Four'.

July 1977: Cultural Revolution ended and Deng emerged as the paramount leader of China.

Later the 'Gang of Four' was tried and Jiang Qing was imprisoned in 1981. She committed suicide in prison in 1991.

4

INEQUALITY IN DISTRIBUTION OF WORLD INCOME, RESULTING INDEBTEDNESS, AND SUGGESTIONS FOR INCOME REDISTRIBUTION

Tariq Saiful Islam, Md. Abdul Wadud and Qamarullah Bin Tariq Islam

Introduction

There are several objectives of this paper. These are to describe and analyze inequality in distribution of world income, to obtain an estimate of equalizing income transfer, to study indebtedness resulting from inequality, and to suggest some income transfer that can be both feasible and effective.

Income distribution is analyzed in tabular form as well as in terms of the Lorenz curve and the Gini coefficient. We then use the Pietra ratio to estimate the amount of income transfer that brings about equalization. There are several consequences of unequal distribution of income, but we focus on the indebtedness of the poorer countries. At the end of the paper, we make a specific suggestion of income transfer from the high to the low-income countries. We believe this will bring tangible benefits to the recipients.

A key aspect of this paper is our endeavour to obtain an estimate of income transfer from the debt-free to the debt-ridden nations. Although we were able to obtain only a rough estimate, it is unlikely that any other estimate will be startlingly different from ours.

Inequality in World Income

In order to have a clear picture of inequality in world income, we divide the countries of the world into three categories–low-income countries having per capita income of less than \$1000, middle-income countries having per capita income of \$1000 to less than \$3000 and high-income countries having per capita income of \$3000 and more. This categorization is ours and differs from other categorization used elsewhere. Table 1 contains data on distribution of world income between high, middle and low-income countries. All our estimates are expressed in US dollars.

We obtained data from the World Bank source, *World Development Indicators* (WDI). Although there are about 195 countries in the world, due to missing data of some countries, we were able to collect data for only 150 countries. So, 'our world' consists of 150 countries. The countries that had to be left out were mostly small countries.

Table 1
Distribution of World Income between High, Middle and Low-income Countries, 2003

Classification	*GDP in Trillion*	*Share of World GDP (%)*	*Population in Billion*	*Percentage of World Population*
Low-income (Below US$1000)	1.1762	3.28	2.317	38.16
Middle Income (US$ 1000 – less US$3000)	3.1603	8.82	2.224	36.63
High Income (US$3000 and Above)	31.5012	87.90	1.53	25.20
Total	35.8377	100	6.071	100

Source: The World Bank, World Development Indicators 2005 (online version)

High-income countries having only 25 per cent of world population have 87.9 per cent of world GDP. Middle-income countries with 36.63 per cent of world population generated only 8.82 per cent of world GDP. Low-income countries, which have separately 38.16 per cent of world population, can muster only 3.28 per cent of the world GDP. Low and middle income countries having 74.8 per cent population have only 12.10 per cent of the world GDP. In short, 25 per cent of the world's population has 88 per cent of the world's GDP and the rest, 75 per cent are left with only 12 per cent of the world's GDP. This inequality is seen in Table 1.

Figure 1
Distribution of GDP in 2003 (in percentages)

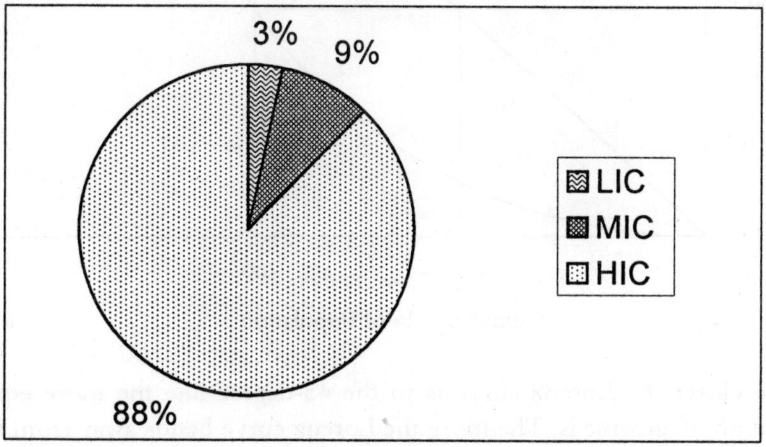

Figure 1 dramatically displays the skinny share of world income of the low- and middle-income countries.

Measurement of Inequality of the World's Income: Use of the Lorenz Curve and the Gini Coefficient

The inequality in distribution of world income can be formally demonstrated by the Lorenz curve. A quantitative estimate of inequality can be obtained by the Gini coefficient. These are described below.

The Lorenz Curve

The Lorenz curve shows inequality of income distribution. This is given in Figure 2. The cumulative percentage of population is shown along the horizontal axis whilst the cumulative percentage of income is plotted along the vertical axis.

The 45 degree line shows the situation when there is an even distribution of income, that is, for example, 30 per cent of the population earn 30 per cent of the income and 60 per cent of the households earn 60 per cent of the income and so on. This is the egalitarian line and shows absolute equality.

Figure 2
The Lorenz Curve

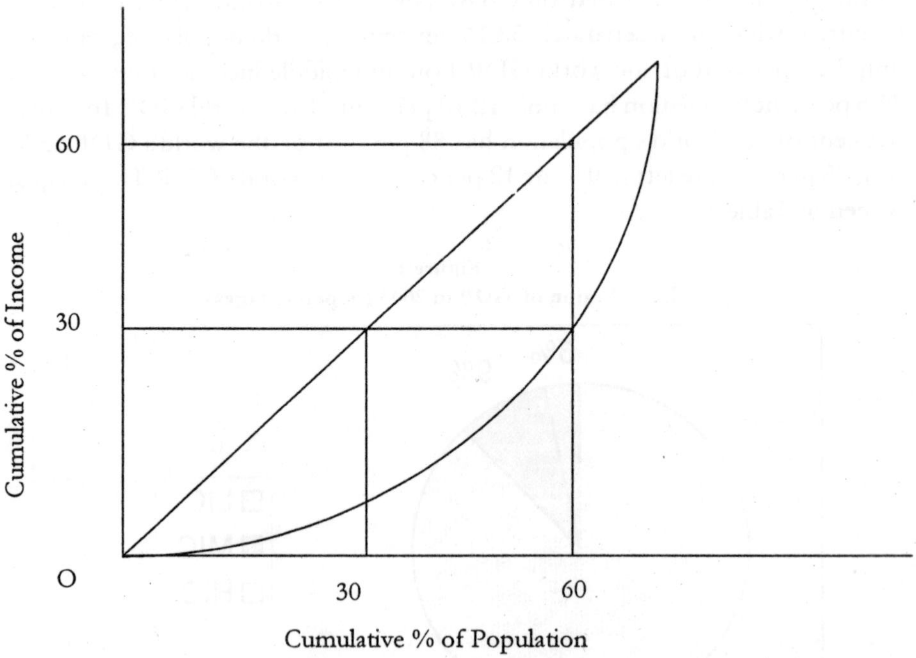

The closer the Lorenz curve is to the 45-degree line the more equal the distribution of income is. The more the Lorenz curve bends away from the 45-degree line of absolute equality, the less equal is the distribution of income. In reality, no country exhibits a totally equitable distribution of income.

A Derived Lorenz Curve for the World

A Lorenz curve based on distribution of income (GDP) of 150 countries that we considered has been drawn and is given in Figure 3. The glaring inequality is manifested in the fat space between the line of equality and the Lorenz curve.

Figure 3
A Lorenz Curve for the World

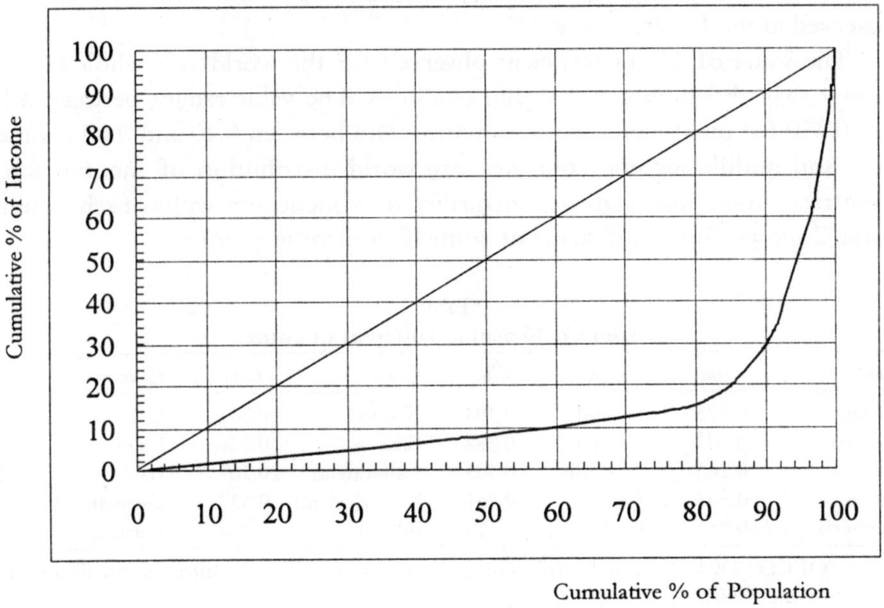

The Gini Coefficient

The Lorenz curve gives us an indication of inequality in the income distribution. A measure that quantifies this maldistribution is called the Gini coefficient.

The value of the Gini coefficient can be estimated by considering the area between the Lorenz Curve and the 45-degree equality line. This area is divided by the entire area below the 45-degree line (which is always exactly one half). The quotient is known as the Gini coefficient, which provides a measure of inequality.

An Estimate of the Gini Coefficient for the World

The Gini coefficient has been estimated using data of 150 countries that we considered. We use the formula derived by Pyatt et al. (1980) and applied by Lerman and Yitzhaki (1984), Garner (1993), and Yitzhaki (1994). Their formula can be written as:

$$\text{Gini coefficient, G} = \frac{2\,Cov\,(y, r_y)}{n\,\bar{y}}$$

where $Cov\ (y, r_y)$ is covariance between y and r_y. Here y is any variable and r_y are ranks of all individuals according to y, n is total number of individuals and $\bar{y}$ is the mean value of y.

Treating nations as individuals, the estimated value of the Gini coefficient for the whole world is found to be 0.8821. Since the value of the Gini coefficient ranges between 0 (no inequality) and 1.00 (perfect inequality), the estimated value of 0.8821 indicates very high degree of inequality and confirms the great inequality observed in the Lorenz curve.

The value of Gini coefficient observed for the world as a whole is much greater than those observed within countries. The value ranges between 0.225 and 0.350 for most high-income countries and between 0.40 and 0.60 for most low- and middle-income countries. So, world distribution of income across countries shows much greater inequality than inequality within each country. Table 2 shows Gini coefficients of some high-income countries.

Table 2
Gini Coefficient in Different Countries

Country	*Gini*	*Country*	*Gini*	*Country*	*Gini*	*Country*	*Gini*
Denmark	0.225	Ireland	0.304	Norway	0.261	U.S.	0.337
Canada	0.301	Austria	0.252	U.K.	0.326	France	0.273
Sweden	0.243	Australia	0.305	Switzerland	0.267	Italy	0.347
Spain	0.303	Finland	0.261	New Zealand	0.337	Germany	0.277
Netherlands	0.251	Japan	0.314	Belgium	0.272	Portugal	0.356

Source: OECD (2004), Income Distribution and Poverty in OECD Countries in the Second Half of the 1990s.

Equalizing Income Redistribution: The Pietra Ratio

The Pietra ratio, which is also known as the Robin Hood Index, indicates the amount of income that needs to be taken from the more affluent and given to the less affluent countries in order to achieve an equal distribution. The Robin Hood Index is shown in Figure 4.

The Robin Hood Index is equivalent to the maximum vertical distance between the Lorenz curve and the line of equal income. The value of the measure approximates the share of total income that has to be transferred from countries above the mean to those below the mean to achieve equality in the distribution of income.

Works based on the Gini coefficient have attempted to provide different redistribution schemes for more egalitarian distribution of the income. One such measure is the Schutz-coefficient (Schutz, 1951; Lambert, 1993), also referred to as Pietra-ratio (Kondor, 1971), maximum equalization percentage (Kondor, 1975) or Robin Hood Index (Kennedy, Kawachi, and Prothrow-Stith, 1996) in the income distribution literature. The Schutz-coefficient can be interpreted as the percentage

Figure 4
The Robin Hood Index

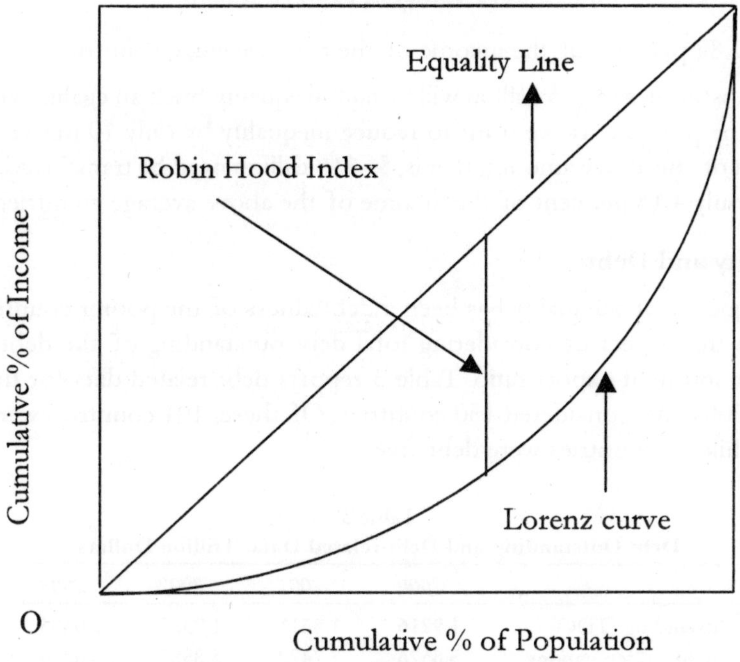

of total income that needs transferring from the group of countries with above average incomes to the group with below average incomes in order to reach equality. It is defined as half the relative mean deviation (Kondor, 1971):

$$S = \frac{1}{2n}\frac{\sum|y_i - \bar{y}|}{\bar{y}}$$

where *S* denotes the Schutz-coefficient, *y* is income, is mean of income and *n* is the number of samples. The estimated Schutz-coefficient is

$$S = 0.577696$$

In order to obtain the total amount that has to be transferred, it is necessary to multiply the average per capita income of the richer countries by their population and then multiply the whole thing by the Schutz-coefficient that is, 0.577696. The average per capita income for the upper income group is $ 23013.65 and the total population of the group is 991 millions. So the total amount that needs to be transferred, given by T, comes to

T = (Average per capita income
of the above average income) × (total population of the above average countries) × (estimated Schutz-coefficient)

= 23013.65 × 991 × 0.577696

= 13175440 million dollars, that is, $13.175 trillion.

This is 41.82 per cent of the income of the above average countries.

A transfer of $13.175 trillion will bring full equality. Such an egalitarian action may not be possible. If we want to reduce inequality by only 10 per cent, then one tenth of the above amount, that is, $1.318 trillion need be transferred. This is equal to only 4.18 per cent of the income of the above average countries.

Inequality and Debt

A consequence of inequality has been indebtedness of the poorer countries. We deal with this aspect by considering total debt outstanding of the debt-ridden countries and debt-export ratio. Table 3 reports debt related data for the years 2000 to 2004. We considered 150 countries. Of these, 101 countries were debt-ridden while 49 countries were debt-free.

Table 3
Debt Outstanding and Debt-related Data, Trillion Dollars

	2000	*2001*	*2002*	*2003*	*2004*
Total debt outstanding (TDO)	1.9216	1.8811	1.9389	2.0685	2.1797
GDP of the debt-ridden nations (GDP-DRN)	5.6526	5.7472	5.8580	6.6210	7.7325
(TDO/GDP-DRN)× 100	33.9944	32.7301	33.0975	31.2410	28.1894
GDP of the Debt free nations (GDP-DFN)	25.2844	24.9557	26.0249	29.2162	32.2864
(GDP-DRN/GDP-DFN) × 100	22.3562	23.0296	22.5093	22.6621	23.9497
(TDO/GDP-DFN) × 100	7.5999	7.5376	7.4500	7.0799	6.7513
(TDO/World GDP) × 100	6.2113	6.1267	6.0812	5.7718	5.4468
World GDP	30.9371	30.7029	31.8830	35.8373	40.0189

Source: The World Bank, World Development Indicators 2005 (online version).

Several important things emerge from Table 3. In the year 2003, which we take as the point of reference, total debt outstanding of all debt-ridden countries stood at $2.01 trillion. This is a huge amount and constituted 31.24 per cent of total GDP of the debt-ridden countries. Let us make a comparison with the debt-free nations. GDP of the debt-free nations stood at $29.22 trillion. GDP of the debt-ridden nations was only 22.6 per cent of the GDP of the debt-free nations, yet the debt-ridden countries had total debt outstanding that was nearly one-third of their GDP.

It is seen that the total GDP of all debt-ridden countries stood at $6.6210 trillion in 2003 (see Figure 5). In the same year, total debt outstanding of all indebted countries amounted to $ 2.0685 trillion. This means that the total burden of debt was a massive 31.24 per cent of total GDP.

Figure 5
GDP of the Debt-ridden and Debt-free countries in 2003 (in trillions)

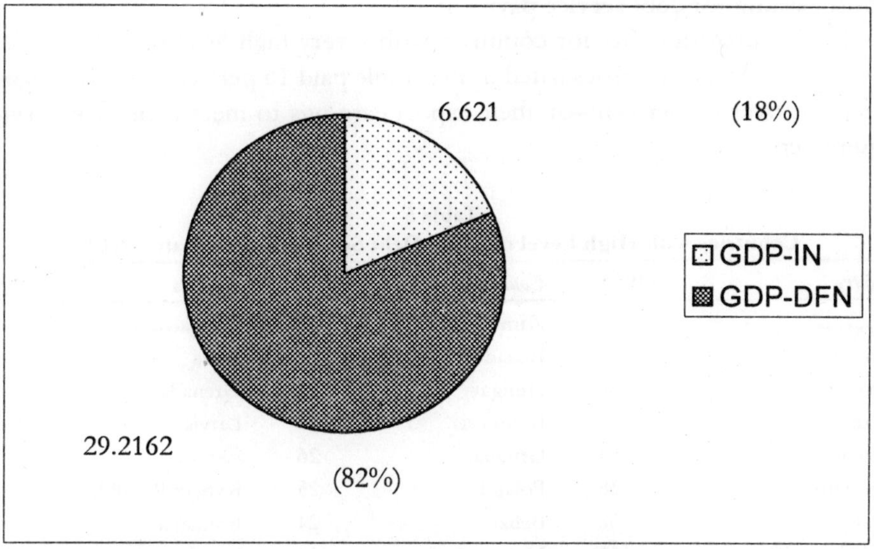

Although total debt stood at $2.0685 trillion in 2003 which considering total GDP of the debt-ridden countries appears quite large, the figure may look different when compared with the total GDP of the debt free nations, which stood at $29.2162 trillion. The total debt is only 7.08 per cent of the total GDP of the debt-free nations. This means that a transfer of 7.08 per cent of income of the debt-free to the debt-ridden nations would wipe out the whole outstanding debt of all the debt-ridden nations.

Debt Service-Export Ratio

The debt-ridden countries have to pay back the principal amount as well as interest for the loans that they have taken. Economists often compare this burden by estimating the ratio of debt service and export.

Table 4
Debt Service-Export Ratio

Number of debt-ridden countries*	101
Average DS/X**	15.12%
Maximum	68%
Minimum	1%

Note: *Out of 150 countries that we could consider. ** Unweighted average of 101 countries.
Source: The World Bank, World Development Indicators 2005 (online version)

A summary of debt service-export ratio in different countries is presented in Table 4. A total number of 101 countries out of 150 that we could consider were found to be debt-ridden. Average debt service-export ratio (DS/X) was found to be 15.12 per cent. Some countries had to pay a very high percentage of their export earning for debt service payment.

Table 5 provides data for countries with a very high level of debt service-export ratio. All 38 countries listed in this Table paid 16 per cent or above–some as high as over 60 per cent–of their export earnings to meet their debt service requirement.

Table 5
Countries with High Level of Total Debt Service-Export Ratio, 2003

Country	*DS/X*	*Country*	*DS/X*	*Country*	*DS/X*
Lithuania	68	Zambia	30	Uzbekistan	21
Burundi	66	Ecuador	28	India	19
Lebanon	66	Hungary	28	Grenada	18
Brazil	64	Indonesia	26	Latvia	18
Colombia	44	Uruguay	26	Estonia	17
Argentina	38	Poland	25	Kyrgyz Republic	17
Turkey	38	Belize	24	Romania	17
Kazakhstan	35	Morocco	24	Jamaica	16
St. Kitts and Nevis	35	Peru	22	Jordan	16
Mongolia	32	Philippines	22	Kenya	16
Sao Tome and Principe	31	Bolivia	21	Pakistan	16
Chile	30	Croatia	21	Thailand	16
Venezuela, RB	30	Mexico	21		

Source: The World Bank, World Development Indicators 2005 (online version).

It is known that most of the developing countries have balance of payment deficits, so the little amount that they earn through export is very valuable to them. But they end up paying considerable amount out of this hard earned money as debt services. The result is that their problem intensifies and external value of their money continues to fall with far reaching adverse consequences. And there is no sign that this process is going to be reversed in the near future.

On Income Transfer

We were unable to directly obtain data on transfer of income from the debt-free to the debt-ridden countries of the world. In order to obtain an estimate of income transfer in a particular year, 2003, we deduct total debt outstanding of 2002 from total debt outstanding of 2003, as given in Table 6. This is equal to \$0.1296 trillion, which is total debt for that year. Assuming that grants constitute 10 per cent of total debt, a plausible assumption, total amount of grant comes to \$0.01296 trillion. This is equal to 0.0444 per cent of the total GDP of the debt-free nations. This means that only 1/25 th of 1.00 per cent of total GDP of the debt free nations was transferred to the debt-ridden countries in 2003.

Table 6
An Estimate of Income Transfer in 2003, Trillion Dollars

1.	Total debt outstanding in 2003	2.0685
2.	Total debt outstanding in 2002	1.9389
3.	Total debt in 2003: (1) – (2)	0.1296
4.	Total grant in 2003 (10 % of (3))	0.0129
5.	Grant–GDP ratio of debt free nations (%)	0.0444

Throughout this exercise we have observed how little is needed to bring about major changes. We found that a 7 per cent of income from the rich to the debt-ridden countries can wipe out their total debt outstanding (Table 3). Such a transfer may appear to be too much to ask for. Even if only 10 per cent of the total debt is wiped out, the rich countries need to transfer only 0.7 per cent of their income.

How Large (or Small) is Estimated Total Transfer of $0.0129 Trillion

The Stockholm International Peace Research Institute said on June 12, 2006 that world military spending reached $1.118 trillion in 2005 or $173 for every person on Earth (AFP report, *Daily Star*, June 12, 2006). The U.S. is responsible for 48 per cent of the world total, that is, $0.5366 trillion.

The world military expenditure for 2005 was $1.118 trillion. Hence, the transfer of income in 2003 is only 1.15 per cent of world military expenditure of 2005. The U.S.'s military expenditure was $0.5366 trillion in 2005. Thus total income transfer, which was $ 0.0129 trillion, was only 2.40 per cent of the U.S. military expenditure. Said in another way, the world was spending 86.67 times on military expenditure than on income transfer to the debt-ridden countries. The U.S. alone was spending about 42 times more on military expenditure than world transfer of income to the debt-ridden countries.

A Specific Recommendation for Income Transfer

We recommend a yearly transfer of 1.00 per cent of income from the high to the low-income countries. This amounts to $0.315 trillion (Table 1). The recommendation is based on the reasoning that while this transfer will not in any way adversely affect the debt-free nations-a 1.00 per cent transfer should never do–it can bring great relief to low-income countries whose income will go up by as much as 27 per cent. This transfer should be made in a principled way, on a regular basis and subject to certain conditions like democracy, human rights, good governance and support for anti-terrorism measures that the recipient countries should fulfill. This definitely will bring tangible changes in their economic plight.

We have not proposed any income transfer to the middle-income countries, which could command only 8.82 per cent of the world GDP although 36.6 per cent of world population live in these countries. It appears that if the high income group having 88.00 per cent of world's income could make a 5.00 per cent transfer to the middle- and low-income countries, most of their economic problems would be solved.

Conclusion

The resources of the world have not been distributed among the countries in an efficient manner but have been mostly the result of many historical factors. So, the richer countries have a responsibility to the poorer countries and the poorer countries can justifiably lay claim for at least a small slice of income of the richer countries. In this paper, we have tried to suggest an income transfer that can bring about a fairly radical change in the conditions of the low-income countries.

Writing this paper has been both fascinating and sad. Fascinating, because we obtained some startling results. Sad because we found the world divided into two parts—one part with 25 per cent of world's population having 88.00 per cent of world's GDP and the other part having 75 per cent of world population able to generate only 12 per cent of world's GDP. So, our world is a world of glaring inequality.

In this age of loud claim about cooperation and foreign aid the actual resource transfer that was taking place was found to be very small. If the richer countries, most of which are also advanced, would address this issue urgently, if they could gather enough courage to make a small but regular transfer of income like the one we suggested to the poorer nations, then we will have a better world to live in.

REFERENCES

Garner, T.I. (1993), Consumer's Expenditure and Gini Inequality–An Analysis based on Decomposition of the Gini Coefficient, *Review of Economics and Statistics*, 75, 1, 134-138.

Kennedy B.P., Kawachi I., Prothrow-Stith D. (1996), Income Distribution and Mortality: Cross Sectional Ecological Study of the Robin Hood Index in the United States, *British Medical Journal*, 312, 1004-7.

Kondor, Y. (1971), An Old-New Measure of Income Inequality, *Econometrica*, 39, 6, 1041-2.

Kondor, Y. (1975), Value Judgments Implied by the Use of Various Measures of Income Inequality, *Review of Income and Wealth*; 21, 3, 309-21.

Lambert, P. (1993), *The Distribution and Redistribution of Income: A Mathematical Analysis*, 2nd Edition, Manchester University Press, Manchester.

Lerman, R.I. and S. Yitzhaki (1984), A Note on the Calculation of the Gini Index, *Economics Letters*, 15, 363-368.

Pyatt, G., C.N. Chen and J. Fei (1980), The Distribution of Income by Factor Components, *Quarterly Journal of Economics*, 95, 451-473.

Schutz, RR. (1951), On the Measurement of Income Inequality, *American Economic Review*, 41, 107-22.

The Daily Star, June 12, 2006.

The World Bank, World Development Indicators 2005, Online Version.

Yitzhaki, S. (1994), Economic Distance and Overlapping of Distributions, *Journal of Econometrics*, 61, 147-159.

5

AN ASSESSMENT OF THE UN'S MILLENNIUM DEVELOPMENT GOALS AND ITS MILLENNIUM DECLARATION

Clem Tisdell

Introduction

In September 2000, the General Assembly of the United Nations adopted the United Nations Millennium Declaration. This specifies a set of 'fundamental values' which the General Assembly accepted as being important to pursue in the twenty-first century. In order to work towards the realization of these values, the General Assembly agreed that it would make special efforts in relation to:

1. Peace, security and disarmament.
2. Development and poverty eradication.
3. Protecting our common environment.
4. Human rights, democracy and good governance.
5. Protecting the vulnerable.
6. Meeting the special needs of Africa.
7. Strengthening the United Nations.

Its Millennium Development Goals (MDGs) are mainly specified under the section of the Declaration dealing with development and poverty eradication. This section also specifies targets that should be met, mainly by 2015, in pursuing these goals.

Considerable attention has been given by UN administrators and by scholars about whether these targets are likely to be met. The general consensus seems to be that this is more unlikely, particularly in the case of Africa (Sahn and Stifel, 2003; World Bank 2004). The World Bank (2004, p.xvii) is somewhat pessimistic about the prospects for achieving the MDGs and states that there is a need to scale up action, significantly and quickly.

The *Global Monitoring Report 2004* of the World Bank (2004, p.xvii) states:

> "On current trends, most Millennium Development Goals (MDGs) will not be met by most countries. The income poverty goal is likely to be achieved at the global level, but Africa will fall well short. For the human development goals, the risks are much more pervasive across the regions. Likely shortfalls are especially serious with respect to the health and related environmental goals–child and maternal mortality, access to safe drinking water and basic sanitation. Few, if any, regions will achieve the mortality goals."

The purpose of this article is not so much to discuss why the MDGs are not being met and the extent of the possible shortfall in meeting these (addressed for example in UNDP 2005 a,b) but to consider the adequacy of the United Nations Millennium Declaration itself and within this, to examine the specification of the MDGs and their associated targets. I shall, first of all, consider the values and principles espoused in the UN Millennium Declaration and aims not normally listed as part of the MDGs, and the focus on the MDGs before providing a concluding assessment.

The Values Espoused in the UN Millennium Declaration

Six fundamental values are identified in Article 6 of the UN Millennium Declaration. It is necessary to repeat the statement of these fully here in order to appreciate their meaning and discuss them adequately. The remaining part of the Millennium Declaration specifies objectives and targets that are believed to be necessary to realize these values. They can be regarded as lower order goals that need to be pursued to achieve the higher order goals or values.

The following are the fundamental values specified in the UN Millennium Declaration:

- "**Freedom**. Men and women have the right to live their lives and raise their children in dignity, free from hunger and from the fear of violence, oppression or injustice. Democratic and participatory governance based on the will of the people best assures these rights.
- **Equality**. No individual and no nation must be denied the opportunity to benefit from development. The equal rights and opportunities of women and men must be assured.
- **Solidarity**. Global challenges must be managed in a way that distributes the costs and burdens fairly, in accordance with basic principles of equity and social justice. Those who suffer or who benefit least deserve help from those who benefit most.
- **Tolerance**. Human beings must respect one other, in all their diversity of belief, culture and language. Differences within and between societies should be neither feared nor repressed, but cherished as a precious asset of humanity. A culture of peace and dialogue among all civilizations should be actively promoted.

- **Respect for nature**. Prudence must be shown in the management of all living species and natural resources, in accordance with the precepts of sustainable development. Only in this way can the immeasurable riches provided to us by nature be preserved and passed on to our descendants. The current unsustainable patterns of production and consumption must be changed in the interest of our future welfare and that of our descendants.
- **Shared responsibility**. Responsibility for managing worldwide economic and social development, as well as threats to international peace and security, must be shared among the nations of the world and should be exercised multilaterally. As the most universal and most representative organization in the world, the United Nations must play the central role."

While one might agree in general with all of these values, their closer examination suggests that they are to some extent rhetorical and incompletely defined. Furthermore, there is no hint that it may be impossible to achieve all these fundamental goals or values simultaneously. Nevertheless, these values do seem admirable and are intended to reduce social and economic inequality globally. Let us consider some possible problems in satisfying the fundamental values.

One can agree with the freedom objectives of the Millennium Declaration in principle. However, it is not clear that democratic and participatory governance based on the will of the people will always assure that the rights of individuals are respected. The United States is widely regarded as a strong democracy with participatory governance but the Bush Administration has not applied the fundamental principle of *habeas corpus* in the case of prisoners in Guantanemo Bay in Cuba held as 'enemy combatants'[1]. Some nations still continue as one-party states but consider themselves to be democratic, and maintain that they have participatory governance. Are they really democratic?

Regarding equality, it would of course be nice if everyone and every nation could benefit from development. But this could happen and gross inequality could still emerge because those who are already better off gain much more than those who are worse off. There is also the possibility that the desired level of growth of all nations will not be sustainable environmentally (Tisdell, 2001) and will conflict with the goal involving respect for nature. There is no hint of such a conflict in the Declaration nor any indication about how such conflict is to be resolved. The objective of promoting gender equality seems more straightforward. The solidarity value has to do with the distribution of costs and burdens of meeting global challenges. In general, it implies that the better off should help those who are less well off. The extent to which this should be done is not indicated but it is an important social principle that those who are better off should assist the disadvantaged. Nevertheless, views differ about what is socially just and equitable as far as economic distribution is concerned. Divergant views exist about the principles of social justice and equality (Rawls, 1971; Tisdell, Ch. 6, 1993). For example, Rawls (1971) argues that income should be distributed equally between individuals unless inequality is in the interests of all, but others disagree.

Tolerance also seems a desirable value but there are limits to how much tolerance is desirable and about what we ought to be tolerant of. Clearly, for example, one should not be tolerant of genocide, child abuse and so on. To what extent should one be tolerant of the denial of civil rights of individuals? Could one be held responsible for human abuse in certain circumstances by failing to take any action? The UN Declaration provides no guidance in this regard.

Again in principle, one can agree with the view that there should be respect for nature. The Declaration mentions, however, that this respect should be exercised in accordance with "the precepts of sustainable development". This advice is not straightforward because different concepts of sustainable development exist. Most are centred on the meeting of human needs and wants. In that regard, they are anthropocentric, and pay little attention to the rights of other species to exist independently of human wishes. The Declaration, however, does state that present patterns of economic production and consumption are unsustainable and must be changed in the interest of future generations. Nevertheless, as more and more nations seek to foster their economic growth and as higher income nations continue to pursue ever continuing economic growth, there are few signs that patterns of resource-use are being radically altered to sustain economic development. For example, global emissions of greenhouse gases continue to rise substantially and no end to this process appears to be in sight, despite the Kyoto Protocol. Furthermore, the declaration provides no specific guidance on how economic production and consumption should be altered in order to achieve economic sustainability. and so as take adequate account of the needs of future generations.

The Declaration's vision of global responsibility for meeting worldwide economic, social and security challenges and the view that this should be coupled with multilateral action, seems desirable. However, many nation states still continue to act unilaterally, or in concert with a few supporting nations, when it suits their own self-interest. The attack on Saddam Hussein's Government in Iraq led by the United States is a relatively recent example of international action that lacked complete multilateral support.

Objectives of the Millennium Declaration other than the MDGs

Adam Smith (1776) pointed out that peace, order and good government are prerequisites for the creation of national wealth. Many of the objectives of the UN Millennium Declaration not usually listed amongst the MDGs are concerned with the securing of peace, order and good government globally. Without these objectives being satisfied, it will be difficult, if not impossible, to meet the MDGs, particularly in countries ravaged by war, armed conflict and civil unrest. Iraq has in recent times experienced all these traumas, and Nepal and parts of Sudan have, for example suffered from insurgence and civil unrest.

The UN Millennium Declaration lists a number of objectives that the UN would like to pursue to promote peace, security and disarmament. Progress on some of these fronts has been slow. One of the objectives, for instance, is "to strive for the elimination of weapons of mass destruction, particularly nuclear weapons..." Many major powers, including the United States and Great Britain, appear to have been unwilling to reduce their stock of nuclear weapons, and proliferation of nuclear weapons capability seems to be occurring, with Iran and North Korea being cited as potential producers of nuclear weapons.

The pursuit of human rights, democracy and good government is seen as important[2]. The UN Declaration states (Article 24): "We will spare no effort to promote democracy and strengthen the rule of law, as well as respect for all internationally recognized human rights and fundamental freedoms, including the right to development."

It can be observed that the rule of appropriate laws and good governance are important to promote economic development. However, there are differences of opinion about whether democracy and what forms of democracy are most conducive to economic development. It is possible that different forms of political institutions may make for the social stability of nations at different times in their history or evolution. Therefore, prescribing democracy for all nations irrespective of their culture and social traditions and their evolutionary stage may be misguided. Furthermore, democracy alone does not ensure respect for human rights.

Protecting the vulnerable, meeting the special needs of Africa and strengthening the United Nations are also recognized as important in the UN Declaration. Regarding the strengthening of the United Nations, no radical suggestions for reforming world governance are made. For example, the possibility of moving away from national states as the sole means of representation in the UN is not considered. In fact, the approach in the Declaration is to reinforce state-based government representation. For example, in Section 31, an aim is said to be "to strengthen further cooperation between the United Nations and National Parliaments through their world organization, the Inter-Parliamentary Union..." Should there be representation of regional bodies such as the European Parliament on the UN? Is there a case for direct election of some members of the UN? Should the UN evolve towards a world parliament in this millennium? These are difficult questions but requirements for global governance have moved on in the 50 years or so since the creation of the United Nations.

On the other hand, greater emphasis than in earlier times is also put in the Declaration on the involvement of non-government entities in the programme of the United Nations. In Section 30 of the Declaration, it is stated that it is desirable:

> "To give greater opportunities to the private sector, non-governmental organizations and civil society, in general, to contribute to the realization of the organization's goals and programmes."

This appears to be a step towards involvement of bodies or agencies other than the representatives of national governments in the affairs of the UN, even if not in the General Assembly.

The UN's institutional apparatus and its functioning are currently locked into a system involving representation of national governments. It is difficult (almost impossible) for it to escape from this constraint, because its funding depends on financial contributions by national governments. It displays path-dependence and it has become a platform for pursuing national ambitions. Possibly there is a need in this millennium for the United Nation's General Assembly to involve some members that are not representatives of national governments and for the UN to have some sources of funding independent of the financial contributions of individual nations.

Clearly there is a need for a better system of global governance, not just improved governance at the national level.

The Millennium Development Goals and Targets

As a step towards satisfying the fundamental values outlined in the Millennium Declaration, eight MDGs are stated. In order to make these goals more concrete and to monitor whether they are being achieved, eighteen targets for their realization are specified. This specification is at least the usual practice of UN administrators who appear to have taken some liberties in interpreting the Declaration. Table 1 contains a relatively comprehensive statement of goals and targets as envisaged by UN administrators monitoring progress in meeting the MDGs.

Different summaries of the MDGs produced by different UN bodies often emphasize or leave out some targets. This may be due to the needs of brevity and decisions about what aspects of the MDGs will interest different audiences. For example, the United Nations Department of Public Information issued in October, 2002, the summary of MDGs given in Table 2. In relation to the environmental sustainability goal, it chose to concentrate on only one feature-access to safe water and sanitation. It did not mention the principle of sustainable development. This suggests increasing emphasis on human needs and less on ecological concerns compared to the 1990s as typified by the UN Summit on Sustainable Development held in Rio de Janeiro in 1992.

The UN sees the MDGs as a useful means of co-ordinating the efforts of the agencies of the UN. The UN Department of Public Information (2002, p1) states:

> "The MDGs provide a framework for the entire UN system to work coherently together towards a common end. The UN Development Group (UNDG) will help

Table 1
UN Millennium Development Goals and Targets as stated by the World Bank.

Goal 1		**Eradicate Extreme Poverty and Hunger**
	Target 1	Halve, between 1990 and 2015, the proportion of people whose income is less than $1 a day
	Target 2	Halve, between 1990 and 2015, the proportion of people who suffer from hunger.
Goal 2		**Achieve Universal Primary Education**
	Target 3	Ensure that by 2015, children everywhere, boys and girls alike, will be able to complete a full course of primary schooling.
Goal 3		**Promote Gender Equality and Empower Women**
	Target 4	Eliminate gender disparity in primary and secondary education, preferably by 2005, and at all levels of education no later than 2015.
Goal 4		**Reduce Child Mortality**
	Target 5	Reduce by two-thirds, between 1990 and 2015, the under-five mortality rate.
Goal 5		**Improve Maternal Health**
	Target 6	Reduce by three-quarters, between 1990 and 2015, the maternal mortality ratio.
Goal 6		**Combat HIV/AIDS, Malaria and other Diseases**
	Target 7	Have halted by 2015 and begun to reverse the spread of HIV/AIDS
	Target 8	Have halted by 2015 and begun to reverse the incidence of malaria and other major diseases.
Goal 7		**Ensure Environmental Sustainability**
	Target 9	Integrate the principles of sustainable development into country policies and programs and reverse the loss of environmental resources.
	Target 10	Halve by 2015 the proportion of people without sustainable access to safe drinking water and basic sanitation.
	Target 11	Have achieved a significant improvement by 2020 in the lives of at least 100 million slum dwellers.
Goal 8		**Develop a Global Partnership for Development**
	Target 12	Develop further an open, rule-based, predictable, non-discriminatory trading and financial system (including a commitment to good governance, development, and poverty reduction, nationally and internationally).
	Target 13	Address the special needs of the least developed countries (including tariff- and quota-free access for exports of the least developed countries: enhanced debt relief for heavily indebted poor countries and cancellation of official bilateral debt; and more generous official development assistance for countries committed to reducing poverty).
	Target 14	Address the special needs of landlocked countries and small island developing states (through the Programme of Action for the Sustainable Development of Small Island Developing States and the outcome of the 22nd special session of the General Assembly).
	Target 15	Deal comprehensively with the debt problems of developing countries through national and international measures to make debt sustainable in the long term.
	Target 16	In cooperation with developing countries, develop and implement strategies for decent and productive work for youth.
	Target 17	In cooperation with pharmaceutical companies, provide access to affordable, essential drugs in developing countries.
	Target 18	In cooperation with the private sector, make available the benefits of new technologies, especially information and communication.

Source: World Bank, 2004, p.xxii

Table 2
Millennium Development goals to be achieved by 2015 according to UN Department of Public Information

- HALVE EXTREME POVERTY AND HUNGER

  1.2 billion people still live on less than $1 a day. But 43 countries, with more than 60 per cent of the world's people, have already met or are on track to meet the goal of cutting hunger in half by 2015.
- ACHIEVE UNIVERSAL PRIMARY EDUCATION

  113 million children do not attend school, but this goal is within reach; India, for example, should have 95 per cent of its children in school by 2005.
- EMPOWER WOMEN AND PROMOTE EQUALITY BETWEEN WOMEN AND MEN

  Two-thirds of the world's illiterates are women, and 80 per cent of its refugees are women and children. Since the 1997 Microcredit Summit, progress has been made in reaching and empowering poor women, nearly 19 million in 2000 alone.
- REDUCE UNDER-FIVE MORTALITY BY TWO-THIRDS

  11 million young children die every year, but that number is down from 15 million in 1980.
- REDUCE MATERNAL MORTALITY BY THREE-QUARTERS

  In the developing world, the risk of dying in childbirth is one in 48. But virtually all countries now have safe motherhood programmes and are poised for progress.
- REVERSE THE SPREAD OF DISEASES, ESPECIALLY HIV/AIDS AND MALARIA

  Killer diseases have erased a generation of development gains. Countries like Brazil, Senegal, Thailand and Uganda have shown that we can stop HIV in its tracks.
- ENSURE ENVIRONMENTAL SUSTAINABILITY

  More than one billion people still lack access to safe drinking water; however, during the 1990's nearly one billion people gained access to safe water and as many to sanitation.
- CREATE A GLOBAL PARTNERSHIP FOR DEVELOPMENT, WITH TARGETS FOR AID, TRADE AND DEBT RELIEF

  Too many developing countries are spending more on debt service than on social services. New aid commitments made in the first half of 2002 alone, though, will reach an additional $12 billion per year by 2006.

Source: United Nations Department of Public Information (2002).

> ensure that the MDGs remain at the centre of those efforts. On the ground in virtually every developing country, the UN is uniquely positioned to advocate for change, connect countries to knowledge and resources and help coordinate broader efforts at the country level."

There is evidence to indicate that the UN agencies do take account of the MDGs in their decision-making but since the weights to be placed on the various goals are not specified, the framework they establish is relatively open-ended.

The UN has encouraged individual countries to set their own priorities taking account of the MDGs and has been active in persuading and assisting countries to monitor their progress towards meeting the MDGs. The UN is also playing a major role in monitoring regional and global progress towards meeting the MDGs.

Discussion of the MDGs and Targets

The fact that several of the MDGs and targets are relatively specific is useful for monitoring purposes. In practice however, they are also subject to interpretation and to variation. For example, the UN Millennium Declaration does not mention the base year against which progress in meeting the millennium targets should be judged. At first sight, because the Declaration was adapted in 2000, one would imagine that 2000 would be the base year against which to judge progress in meeting the millennium targets. In fact, 1990 has been set as the base. Because some countries, particularly in Asia, such as populous China, made substantial progress in reducing their incidence of poverty in the 1990s, it means that on a global scale, significant progress had already been made by 2000 towards meeting the MDGs poverty reduction target.

On the other hand, those countries making little progress in reducing poverty in the 1990s, such as many Sub-Saharan African countries had greater hurdles to overcome to meet the MDGs, and effectively a shorter time-period in which to meet the MDG targets. The use of the retrospective base year 1990 introduces distortions into the monitoring of progress towards meeting the MDGs. Furthermore, none of the progress is reducing the incidence of poverty and meeting other targets in the decade prior to the UN Millennium Declaration can be ascribed to it. It seems anomalous that progress in meeting goals in this millennium should be judged in relation to the situation in 1990 rather than 2000. It should be kept in mind that this may produce distortions in the levels of achievement in this millennium and exaggerate some recorded achievements.

The nature and size of the bias arising from the use of 1990 rather than 2000 as a base for meeting the MDGs is evident from the following statement in the World Bank's *Global Monitoring Report 2004*. It indicates that within about 4 years of the UN Millennium Declaration, the poverty reduction goal was virtually met globally.

> "At the global level, the world will likely meet the first goal of halving income poverty between 1990 and 2015, thanks to stronger economic growth spurred by improvements in policies–especially in China and India, the world's two most populous countries. With current trends, most regions will achieve or come close to achieving the goal. East Asia has already met it. However, Sub-Saharan Africa is seriously off track; just eight countries, representing about 15 per cent of the regional population, will likely achieve the goal. Within other regions that will likely meet the goal at the aggregate level, a number of countries will not. Low-income countries under stress (LICUS), about half of which are in Africa, are especially at risk of falling far short. The trends are broadly similar with respect to the target of halving the proportion of people who suffer from hunger, also part of Goal 1. The target will likely be met at the global level, but Sub-Saharan Africa and a number of countries in other regions will likely fall short." (World Bank, 2004, p. 2)

Doubts have also been raised about the adequacy of some of the socio-economic indicators adopted in specifying MDG targets. For example, it has been suggested that the criterion of less than $1 per day as a measure of extreme poverty, needs to be higher in parts of the world which experience considerable coldness during the year. This is because heating is essential for survival in these regions. In some countries, shortcomings in statistical information may also make it difficult to measure actual progress towards meeting the goals.

As mentioned above, no specific weighting is put on the individual MDGs. However, it is possible that the order in which the individual MDGs are mentioned in the UN Millennium Declaration is indicative of their relative importance. In that case, eradication of extreme poverty and hunger would have top priority. But achievement of many of the other goals, such as attaining universal primary education is not independent of reducing the incidence of extreme poverty; a reduction in the incidence of poverty should assist poor families to send their children to school. Furthermore, child mortality is likely to fall and national health to improve as poverty is reduced.

Nevertheless, it cannot be assumed that all MDGs are entirely consistent. For example, the goal of environmental sustainability may be imperilled if economic growth is stressed as the only way to achieve the MDGs. There is still a strong tendency to see economic growth as the key to attaining the MDGs. It is true that most countries experiencing significant economic growth have made progress in achieving the most of the MDG objectives and those that have failed to obtain economic growth have retrogressed in this regard.

Yet we cannot be sure of the sustainability of continuing economic growth, particularly on a global scale. For example, greenhouse gas emissions continue to rise as a result of global economic growth. Predicted climate change and sea-level rises could make it difficult to sustain economic growth. Furthermore, depletion of natural resource stocks as a result of economic growth could eventually limit economic growth (Tisdell, 2005, Ch.11). The fact that this has not occurred yet does not mean that the problem can never arise. Hence, a cautious approach is required in assessing the desirability of economic growth as a means for attaining the MDGs.

There is a difference of views amongst economists about whether economic growth driven by man-made capital formation (that is investment in man-made physical capital) provides a suitable bequest to future generations. It involves the conversion of natural resources to man-made goods and may degrade the environment. Therefore, the cost of it is likely to be a reduced environmental and natural resource stock. There are concerns amongst ecological economists that this conversion could become an obstacle to future economic growth and productivity and could consequently impoverish future generations if carried too far (Tisdell, 2005, Ch. 11).

This group of economists would suggest that economic growth ought to be subject to constraints on the economic use of the natural environment and resources. On the other hand, the more orthodox economic view is that man-made capital formation provides a suitable bequest to future generations, and constraints on natural resource-use are unnecessary, (Tisdell, 2005, Ch. 11). Supporters of this optimistic view believe that scientific and technological progress will be adequate to overcome natural-resource shortages and environmental problems that may emerge as a result of continuing economic growth. This progress may be sufficient for some time to come but is necessarily based on faith in the ability of science to provide the needed solutions and a belief that socioeconomic systems will always function in a manner that ensures the necessary flow of invention and innovations are sustained. This optimistic view was forcefully stated by Frederick Engels (1959) in criticizing the theory of Malthus Engels claimed that nothing was impossible to science in raising food productivity and therefore, he rejected the view of Malthus that there could be a population problem. These optimistic views about technological progress are, for example, discussed in Tisdell (1981, Section 1.7).

Concluding Comments

The UN Millennium Declaration and associated MDGs outline a global vision and state objectives for achieving this vision. On the whole, the goals that the Declaration expresses are positive and desirable but not without limitations as is pointed out in this article. For example, one detects a naïve view that democracy can be expected to result in good governance and protection of human rights. Unfortunately, it does not always do this. The consequences of political systems are much more complex.

The UN's monitoring of progress towards achieving the MDGs helps to assure that political consideration of these goals is not lost sight of. However, as pointed out in this article, it seems anomalous that progress in achieving the MDGs is measured in relation to the situation in 1990 not 2000. Furthermore, achievement of the goals continues to be hampered by political instability and wars in several parts of the world.

Furthermore, monitoring of the UN of progress by individual countries in meeting their MDGs as well as its assessment in formulating their MDGs should help their achievement of their MDGs. On the other hand, this assistance by the UN may also be regarded by some nations as an intrusion on their national sovereignty and to some extent a costly exercise. While the UN brings some resources to engage in this administrative exercise, it also makes use of the scarce resources of the public service in the countries involved in undertaking its missions. The UN's assistance is not entirely costless to the recipient nation. In addition, taking into account the theories of Niskanen (1971), we should not dismiss the possibility that some of the actions of the UN are motivated by the selfish interests of its bureaucracies which on occasions may complement the interest of national bureaucracies. The institutional structure and performance of UN bodies should not be beyond criticism. Hopefully, on the other hand, the self-interest of the UN's bureaucracies may mostly serve a wider social interest than their own.

The pursuit of the MDGs is seen as a way to help achieve the fundamental values outlined in the UN Millennium Declaration. These goals certainly highlight the plight of the disadvantaged both by countries, regions and globally. The UN's actions have ensured that the needs of the disadvantaged are not lost sight of at these various geographical levels. Without the vision of the UN, worldwide policies for assisting the disadvantaged would be less co-ordinated and most likely would have a lower priority than at present. The UN's initiative has assisted many countries in formulating development goals. These may not have been articulated, or may have been poorly specified, in the absence of the UN's MDGs[3].

While the World Bank (2004, p. 13) reported that there are signs that official development assistance to less developed countries is rising, having previously fallen, it also warns that the statistics could be, to some extent, deceptive. It states:

> "While aid volumes are rising again, there is some concern that much of the increase may be dominated by strategic considerations-the war on terrorism, conflict and reconstruction in Afghanistan and Iraq. Large amounts have recently been committed for these purposes, but it is unclear whether all of these commitments represent an increase in total aid or are in part a reallocation of aid from other countries. In the period ahead, it will be important to ensure that development aid is not crowded out by aid influenced by such strategic objectives." (World Bank, 2004, p. 13)

The UN Millennium Declaration only provides limited guidance about actions that should be taken to achieve the MDGs. Its main purpose is to specify a vision rather than to outline means to realize this vision. It has been left to bodies such as the World Bank and the IMF to formulate policies that may enable this vision to be achieved. Policies, such as those outlined by the World Bank (2004), favour liberal economic policies and advocate institutional reform in developing countries to improve their governance. However, institutional change is difficult to engineer and institutions cannot be altered quickly because cultural embeddedness is a barrier to change, as for example, seems to be underlined by recent experiences in the Solomon Islands and in East Timor.

It is interesting to note that the World Bank (2004, p.11) not only supports liberalization of international trade in goods and services and capital flows but also of migration. The geographical location and structure of some countries and their available resources are so poor that there is little prospect of free trade and capital movements alone eliminating their current economic disadvantage. In such cases, international migration provides the best prospect for increasing the economic welfare of their residents. Some small island countries in the South Pacific may, for example, be in this situation (Tisdell, 1990, Ch.10; 2007).

NOTES

1. More information about *habeas corpus* may be found, for example in *Wikipedia*, the Free Encyclopaedia. This states (2006, p. 4) that during the War on Terrorism *habeas corpus* is suspended by the US for persons declared to be enemy combatants. More

specifically, "The September 18, 2001 Presidential Military Order gives the President of the United States the power to declare anyone suspected of connection to terrorists or terrorism, as an enemy combatant. As such, that person can be held indefinitely, without charges being filed against him or her, without a court hearing, nor is this person entitled to a legal consultant."

2. It has been claimed that democracy promotes economic growth but empirical evidence provides conflicting results (Sirowy and Inkelos, 1990; Przeworski and Limongi, 1993). The hypothesis is unproven (Chand and Tisdell, 2006, p. 42).
3. Kumar and Prasad (2006) argue, for example, that poverty would have been given much less attention by the Government of Fiji in the absence of the UN's MDGs.

REFERENCES

Adam Smith (1776), *The Wealth of Nations*. Republished 1910 by J.M. Dent & Sons, London.

Cland, B. and Tisdell, C. (2006), Institutions, *Economic Performance and Sustainable Development: A Case Study of the Fiji Islands*. Nova Science Publishers, New York.

Engels, F. (1959), Outlines of a Critique of Political Economy. In K. Marx, *Economic and Philosophic Manuscripts of 1844*. Foreign Languages Publishing House, Moscow.

Kumar, S. and Prasad, B. (2006), Poverty in Fiji: Analysis, Trends, and causes. *Indian Development Review*. Forthcoming.

Niskenen, W. (1971), *Bureaucracy and Representive Government*. Aldine, Chicago.

Przeworski, A. and Limongi, F. (1993), Political Regimes and Economic Growth. *Journal of Economic Perspectives* 7, 51-69.

Rawls, J.R. (1971), *A Theory of Justice*. Harvard University Press, Cambridge, Mass.

Sahn, D.E. and Stifel, D.C. (2003), Progress towards the Millennium Develpmental Goals in Africa. *World Development* 31, 23-52.

Sirowy, L. and Inkelas, A. (1990), The Effects of Democracy on Economic Growth and Inequality: a review. *Studies in Comparative International Development* 25, 126-157.

Tisdell, C.A. (1981), *Science and Technology Policy: Priorities of Governments*. Chapman and Hall, London.

Tisdell, C.A. (1990), *Natural Resources, Growth and Development*. Praeger, New York.

Tisdell, C.A. (1993), *Economic Development in the Context of China*. Macmillan, London and St. Martin's Press, New York.

Tisdell, C.A. (2001), Globalisation and Sustainability: Environmental Kuznets curve and the WTO. *Ecological Economics* 39, 185-196.

Tisdell, C.A. (2005), *Economics of Environmental Conservation*, 2nd edition. Edward Elgar, Cheltenham, UK and Northampton, MA, USA.

Tisdell, C. (2007), Globalisation and the Future of Small Isolated Nations, Particularly in the Pacific. In B. Prasad and K.C. Roy (eds). *Development Problems of Pacific Island States*. Nova Science Publishers, New York. In Press.

United Nations Department of Public Information (2002), The Millennium Development Goals and the United Nations Role. Fact Sheet, October. New York.

UNDP (2005a), UN Millennium Project, 2005. *Investing in Development: A Practical Plan to Achieve the Millennium Development Goals. Overview.* UNDP, New York.

UNDP (2005b), UN Millennium Project, 2005. *Investing in Development: A Practical Plan to Achieve the Millennium Development Goals.* Earthscan, London and Sterling, VA.

Wikipedia (2006), 'Habeas Corpus'. http://en.wikipedia.org/wiki/Habeas_corpus (Accessed 7 May 2006).

World Bank (2004), *Global Monitoring Report 2004.* World Bank, Washington, DC.

6

HOW DO INFRASTRUCTURE PROJECTS BENEFIT THE POOR?

Peter Warr

Introduction

Developing countries spend roughly a fifth of their total public investment budgets on infrastructure, also referred to as 'social overhead capital'. This buys facilities for transport, power, sanitation, communication, and water for domestic use, industrial use and irrigation. Multilateral and bilateral development agencies also invest heavily in public infrastructure projects such as roads, telecommunication facilities, electricity services and irrigation. These investments are intended to deliver benefits to households in the form of improved incomes and thus higher levels of consumption of the goods and services that households desire. They are also intended to facilitate access to public services such as educational and health facilities. Social objectives like the Millennium Development Goals (MDGs) are therefore potentially served by these outcomes.

It is generally necessary that public institutions participate in some way in the provision of this form of investment. This necessity arises from two overlapping features shared by these forms of social overhead capital. First, the tend to exhibit economies of scale. This implies that when they are provided on an exclusively private basis, *monopolies* tend to result Second, infrastructure facilities tend to be quasi-public or partially public goods. When goods of this kind are provided by the,private sector. they are normally *under-provided.* The under-provision arises because of the difficulty of capturing the benefits privately. Much of the benefit spills over to people other than the investor. Because private sector investors are unable to capture the benefits that the investments generate, they may invest little or nothing in forms of infrastructure which generate large social returns-rural roads provide a good example. Hence, the case for some form of public provision. But purely public provision is often inefficient and in any case the public sector is

---

Note: Chapter marked with will be reprints from the special issue of the Indian Development Review.

commonly short of capital for investment. Various forms of public and private partnership have therefore been used in the attempt to achieve the efficiencies and access to capital available from private participation while avoiding the monopolistic pricing and/or under-provision that purely private provision tends to produce.

There is considerable evidence that public investments in infrastructure do indeed deliver substantial benefits to private households. The evidence generally takes the form of statistical studies which show a relationship between the availability of public infrastructure and desired social outcomes. The latter include household incomes, household expenditures on goods and services and (less commonly) broader social outcomes such as health standards or educational attainment. The existence of evidence of this kind should surprise no one. Although some investments turn out to be unproductive, the overall importance of public infrastructure facilities for public welfare is obvious and becomes painfully so when natural or man-made disasters destroy these assets. Great hardship invariably results. But how are the benefits from public infrastructure actually attained? What are the transmission mechanisms through which improved infrastructure delivers benefits to private households? That is the focus of this paper. The discussion is partly theoretical, partly a review of previous empirical studies.

From Infrastructure to welfare: Mechanisms of Transmission

A simple theoretical framework is developed below for thinking about the channels through which infrastructure development affects welfare at the household level. This framework is summarized in Figure 1. There are three components to the diagram. The upper section focuses on the way infrastructure impacts on household incomes. The lower right section focuses on the way infrastructure influences access to public services and the lower left section on the way infrastructure affects household expenditures. Since most, but not all, countries measure poverty incidence by looking at expenditures, the connection between infrastructure and poverty reduction comes through this channel. Each of these three components of the diagram is reviewed in subsequent sections. First, we summarize the major categories of infrastructure spending.

Four forms of Infrastructure are Distinguished

Transport infrastructure

New roads, upgraded roads, and the maintenance of existing roads are the principal examples, where 'roads' are defined to include associated bridges. The effect of providing or improving roads is to reduce transport costs. The effects can be profound[1]. Reducing transport costs raises the net return producers can obtain for their products and reduces the costs to them of consumer goods and inputs

Figure 1
How Infrastructure Projects Affect Households?

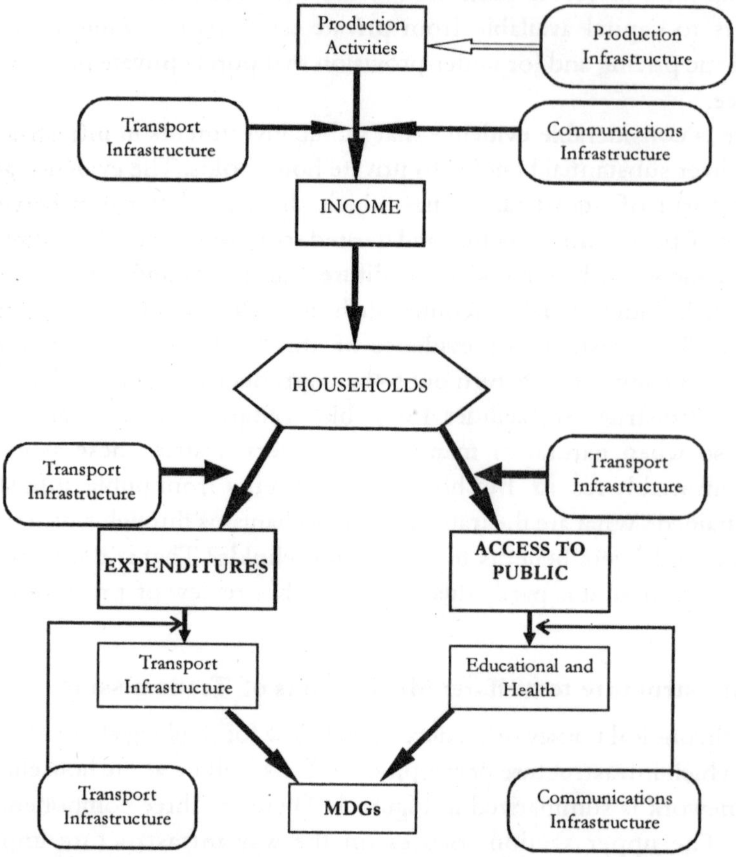

used in production. In a tropical or mountainous environment, existing roads may be impassible altogether during the extended rainy periods of the year. During other times, the poor quality of the roads may still result in transport costs which virtually preclude production for the market. Many countries with previously highly restrictive policies with regard to market participation have undertaken market-friendly reforms which remove prohibitions on market-oriented economic activity. But the effect of these reforms can be seriously blunted for communities facing very high transport costs, such as those in isolated rural areas. To be effective, the reforms must be accompanied by something more costly than simply removing restrictions on market activity–investment in the transport infrastructure that can make participation in the market feasible.

Production Infrastructure

This includes infrastructure facilities intended to contribute directly to production. Examples include irrigation facilities, electricity facilities servicing private firms and some communication facilities. The benefits generated take the form of enhanced productivity of land and labour in the areas immediately serviced by the infrastructure, but not elsewhere.

Electricity Infrastructure

By linking a community to the electricity supply network, cost reducing technologies and communications facilities are made accessible. The use of electricity-based consumer goods is also made feasible. This form of infrastructure is therefore complementary with private expenditure on electrical consumer and producer goods.

Communications Infrastructure

Participation in the market requires information. Telephone networks facilitate this. The poor state of the telephone networks in many countries has partly been ameliorated by new mobile telephone technology, which is capable of bringing communications capabilities to otherwise isolated communities more cheaply than by extending the land line system. What is required is to extend the network of transmitters and ensuring that competitive conditions prevail in the provision of mobile phone services, preventing the development of private monopolies.

New Facilities versus Maintenance

In the case of each of the above forms of infrastructure investment, there is often an over-emphasis on provision of new facilities at the expense of maintaining *existing* infrastructure. If infrastructure investments are not maintained, their value can be lost quickly. Rural roads in tropical areas provide a good example. Conventions of government accounting can be an obstacle in this regard. In public sector accounts, new facilities are called investment or development expenditures, while maintenance tends to be classified as recurrent expenditure. It is much easier to obtain outside assistance for new 'development' expenditures. They tend to be politically more attractive within the country as well. But maintenance, along with other forms of 'recurrent' expenditure, tends to be left to the resources of the government, even though the latter might be quite insufficient for the purpose.

The fungibility of public funds sometimes reduces the force of this point. If the public sector would otherwise have invested in say, new roads, then when an external agency provides the funding for these roads funds are freed up for use elsewhere. These alternative uses of funds can include maintenance of existing roads. It follows that even though the external agency provides no direct funding for maintenance, its funding for new investment nevertheless makes resources available for other uses, including maintenance. However, when the recipient government is so short of revenue that little or no spending on new roads would have occurred in the absence of the external funding, this argument does not apply.

A frequent reality is that new infrastructure facilities are funded even while existing facilities deteriorate to the point where they are unusable for lack of maintenance. For this reason, expenditures on maintenance can be much more cost-effective than construction of new facilities. From an economic point of view, maintenance of existing roads, dams, electricity networks and so forth is investment in exactly the same sense as the construction of new facilities. It is a sacrifice of current income for the sake of the future productivity of an asset. Maintenance of existing infrastructure deserves the same priority as new investment. But since this form of expenditure has often been neglected in the past, because of funding constraints, its marginal value is greater.

Infrastructure and Incomes: Distributional Issues

The top section of Figure 1 focuses on the way that infrastructure development affects household incomes. The most obvious channel is that production infrastructure contributes directly to the productivity of privately owned assets. Irrigation projects raise the productivity of land and labour. Electricity supplies make possible the operation of light manufacturing and communication facilities and make it possible to obtain the inputs needed for these activities. Once the output is produced, transport and communications infrastructure facilitate its sale.

It is obvious that production infrastructure such as transport, electricity and communications facilities all contribute to the generation of household incomes. But how? Since households derive their incomes primarily from the ownership of productive assets, including their own labour, land and capital, public infrastructure must operate on incomes by raising the returns to these factors of production. But different households own very different combinations of labour, land and capital. The way that infrastructure affects the returns to these factors thus has important implications for the distributional impact of these infrastructure investments. A recent study (see Box 1) by Jacoby (2000) provides an insightful analysis of the mechanisms involved, in the context of rural Nepal.

Jacoby's results imply that rural road improvement is an effective measure of reducing absolute poverty incidence but not an effective way of reducing income inequality. The benefits tend to be spread widely across the income distribution and the effect on inequality is very small. These general findings are common in the analysis of the distributional impact of public infrastructure. The effects of this form of investment generally do not discriminate strongly in favor of poor groups, relative to others, or *vice versa*. However, it is important to note that the poor are not excluded from the benefits of infrastructure investment. It cannot be said that these investments benefit only the rich.

Box 1. Distributional effects of rural roads in Nepal

Jacoby (2000) studies the effects of rural roads in Nepal using household survey data. He examines the relationship between incomes and distance from the market and decomposes this difference into a return to land and a return to labour. The effect of reduced distance from the market, measured in transport cost, is divided into these two major components and this information is then used to analyse the effects of improved roads at the household level. The economic story underlying this statistical analysis is an assumed production function in which output depends on inputs of land, labour and purchased inputs like fertilizer. Improved roads reduce the price farmers must pay for inputs like fertilizer and raise the price, net of transport cost, that they receive for their output. Under the assumptions made, the increased value of output made possible by the new roads will result in increased returns to land and labour. But in what proportions?

To the extent that new roads raise the productivity of land, then if land prices are determined similarly to other economic assets, the increased income earning capacity of land will be capitalized in the form of increased land prices. On the other hand, to the extent that the productivity of labour is increased, the real return to labour will rise. The difference between the two may be quite important. If the main effect is to increase land prices, the beneficiaries will be land owners, who are not necessarily the poor. But if the real wages of unskilled labour rise, the beneficiaries will indeed be among the poorest people because for them, their labour is their principle asset. The question posed by Jacoby is therefore the magnitude of these two effects, how this depends on distance from the market, and how this translates into incomes at the household level. Jacoby's analysis, therefore, provides a way of studying the distributional impact of infrastructure improvement.

Jacoby's results confirm that both real land prices and real wages are raised by road development. The net effect is slightly progressive with respect to income, meaning that households with lower real incomes initially, who tend on average to be furthest from the markets, receive the largest proportional income gain from improved roads.

Infrastructure and access to Public Services: Benefit Incidence Analysis

A common approach to studying the way that projects affect households at different levels of income is known as *benefit incidence analysis.* Despite its name, this approach does not focus at all on the benefit that households actually derive from the projects. Rather, it studies the *cost* to the government of providing the facilities concerned, and how this cost may be allocated across household groups. These studies are thus best regarded not as analyses of the full impact of public expenditures but rather as studies of access to public services, indicated on the lower right hand side of Figure 1.

There are three components to such studies.

(i) **Unit costs:** The first step is to determine the unit (average) costs of delivering the infrastructure concerned. In the case of roads, for example, this means the cost per kilometer of a particular kind of road in a particular kind of terrain.

(ii) **Participation rates**: The second step is to assess the degree to which households in different income (or expenditure) categories receive the services of these publicly provided facilities. This is by far the most demanding of the three steps. This step is greatly facilitated when available household income and expenditure surveys include questions on access to infrastructure services.

(iii) **Assignment of costs to income groups** (or expenditure groups): The third, and least demanding of the three steps uses the results of steps (i) and (ii) to assign the value of the government services provided to income groups, focusing in particular on the poor. The calculation of the value of services delivered is important only when aggregating across different kinds of expenditures, say roads and electricity services.

Benefit incidence analysis is not especially new. Two World Bank studies, by Meerman (1979) on Malaysia and Selowsky (1979) on Colombia, were early influential applications of the methodology. These studies look at a wider set of public expenditures than just infrastructure, but each considers public infrastructure specifically. A frequent finding is that infrastructure has little distributional impact. All broad social groups obtain access to these facilities, regardless of incomes.

A partial exception to these findings was a study of expenditure incidence for Thailand, by Sussangkarn and Patmasiriwat (1999) (see Box 2). This study found that the distributional impact of transport infrastructure was directly related to income. The authors suggest that in a middle income country like Thailand, improved road infrastructure generates additional benefits, mainly to those households possessing private automobiles. Improved roads shorten travel time for them, but do less for those reliant on public transport. Obviously, those owning cars tend to be the better off. When roads are very poor, especially rural roads, those using public transport benefit from road improvement as well.

It is important to recognize that while these studies are capable of generating useful information on access to the facilities funded by public spending, they do not necessarily identify the reasons for these effects. For example, suppose it is found that poorer groups obtain little benefit from irrigation investment. The details of the study may provide clues as to why this is happening, but in itself the finding does not tell us what needs to be done to address any problem which might be revealed by its conclusions. These may lie in the distribution of land ownership, the placement of irrigation schemes, or exclusion of some groups from irrigation associations. It should not be assumed that all forms of infrastructure investment should necessarily benefit the poor, but if benefit incidence studies can help find the reasons why the poor do not benefit, and these reasons are capable of being corrected, these findings can be of great value.

Box 2: Benefit incidence in Thailand: Transportation Infrastructure

An especially comprehensive and ambitious study of the distributional incidence of both government expenditures and taxes was recently conducted for Thailand by the Thailand Development Research Institute (Sussangkarn and Patmasitiwat 1999). The most interesting feature of the study is its comprehensiveness: it attempts to apply a similar framework to describe the distributional effects of both government expenditures and taxes. In the case of expenditures, it applies the standard benefit incidence analysis methods to study the impact of education, public health, agriculture and transportation infrastructure spending. Some of their results, which relate to 1994, are summarized below.

Thailand: Results of Regressions of Expenditure Benefit Against Household Income

Types of expenditures	*Coefficient*	*Significance Level: P–value*	*Elasticity with respect to income*
Total	0.048	0.000	0.41
Education	0.014	0.008	0.33
Health care	0.000	0.011	0.02
Agriculture	-0.002	0.009	-0.09
Transportation	0.035	0.000	1.09

Source: Warr (2003), based on data in Chalongphob Sussangkarn and Direk Patmasitiwat (1999).

Except for agricultural and health expenditures, groups with higher incomes tended to receive higher benefits from public spending. In the case of agricultural and health expenditures the estimated benefits were independent of incomes. For education expenditures, the elasticity of benefit received with respect to income was less than unity, meaning that as incomes rise, say, by 10 per cent, the benefit received rises by less than 10 per cent. For transportation infrastructure, the elasticity was about 1. The benefits received rise roughly in proportion to income.

These results need to be interpreted in conjunction with the S-P study's corresponding estimates of the distributional burden of taxes, which of course pay for the above expenditures. The implied estimate of the elasticity of tax burden with respect to income was 1.05, almost the same as the above elasticity of benefit from transport infrastructure with respect to income. Combining these two sets of estimates, the net effect of raising taxes to finance transport infrastructure spending is similar across households of different incomes; the net effect of raising taxes to finance these infrastructure investments neither favours nor discriminates against the poor, relative to other income groups.

Infrastructure and Expenditures: Effects on the Poor

Most countries measure poverty incidence by means of household expenditures. Infrastructure investments affect poverty through two central channels. First, they affect incomes, as discussed above. Second, they affect the prices of goods the poor purchase and thus the real value of the goods and services which can be purchased from a given level of income. Of these two channels, the first is generally, but not always the more important.

A focus on poverty leads naturally to efforts to ensure that investment does indeed reach the poor. The World Bank's 1994 assessment, contained in its 1994 *World Development Report* is seemingly pessimistic about the prospects for doing this: "Although the relationship between infrastructure and poverty is pivotal, infrastructure is nevertheless a blunt instrument for intervening directly on behalf of the poor" (p. 80). What this seemingly self-contradictory statement means is that infrastructure development in itself does not necessarily produce benefits which are *targeted* towards the poor, relative to other groups. Indeed, this is the finding of most of the empirical studies reviewed here. The benefits of public infrastructure provision are generally widely spread across the income distribution. But, especially in the poorest countries, their value to all major groups, including the poor, may be so large that significant effects on poverty can be achieved from this form of investment. Furthermore, so long as the benefits are not skewed away from the poor, the fact that poor people make up a significant proportion of the population implies that they are large recipients of the benefits from such investment.

Issues which affect the distributional impact of infrastructure development include the distribution of productive assets within the affected population, because this affects the capacity to take advantage of public infrastructure. Other factors include, in the case of domestically financed projects, the way it is financed, meaning the distributional effects of the taxes which pay for it, and the regional distribution of the infrastructure investments. Within regions, the distributional effects of infrastructure development tend to be minor, but there is a big difference between providing improved infrastructure in poorer and richer regions. The main distributional effect is thus between regions. Of course, regional targeting is not an end in itself-allocating infrastructure to poorer regions is effective in assisting the people of that region only if it is productive.

Targeting the Poor: Two Kinds of Error

The mechanisms available for targeting infrastructure expenditures towards the poor are very imperfect. Suppose the government attempts to direct expenditures to a particular social group–in this case the poor. Two kinds of errors are possible, as summarized in Figure 2. The areas labeled B and D correspond to these two kinds of error. They are analogous to the Type I and Type II errors of statistical theory.

Type I error (Area B: under-coverage) – people who need improved access fail to receive it.

Type II error (Area D: leakage) – people who do not need improved access do receive it.

Figure 2
Poverty Targeting: Two Kinds of Error

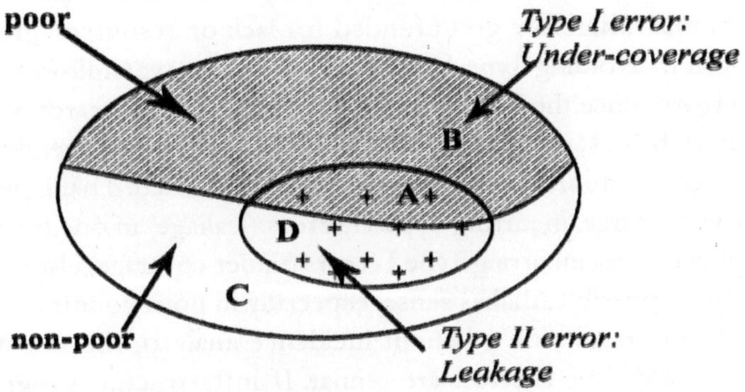

Receiving access

A Target group receiving access-*no error*
B Target group not receiving access-*Type I error: under-coverage*
C Non-target group no receiving access-*no error*
D Non-target group receiving access-*Type II error: leakage*

There is a trade-off between these two kinds of error. In order to minimize, say, Type I error (under-coverage), more widespread provision of improved infrastructure (say, roads) throughout the country might be attempted. The consequence is that some areas where infrastructure was already adequate and which did not need the increased expenditure, nevertheless receive it. Errors of Type II (leakage) will inevitably result, implying some wastage of public revenues, given the objective of targeting the poor. Conversely, in order to minimize Type II errors, stricter criteria might be applied for the assessment of areas eligible for say, improved roads, giving preference to poorer areas. Type II errors might be lessened but more errors of Type I (under-coverage) will occur, because many poor households might actually be present in areas which are non-poor on average.

Attitudes to these two kinds of error seem to differ across countries. One hypothesis that seems plausible is that social attitudes to these two kinds of error change systematically as societies become richer. In particular, the willingness to tolerate more Type II error (leakage), in order to reduce Type I error (under-coverage) seemingly increases as the society becomes wealthier.

An interesting study by Cornia and Stewart (1995) recognizes the distinction between these two kinds of error involved in targeting and applies it to several developing country case studies of the effects of public spending. Their discussion implies that when developing countries give greater emphasis to avoiding Type-II errors (leakage) relative to Type-I errors (under-coverage), they are somehow misguided or irrational in doing so. But this criticism seemingly misses an important point. Very poor countries typically have great difficulty in raising public revenues. It seems reasonable that where public revenues are very scarce, and where many worthy expenditures must therefore go unfunded for lack of resources, greater emphasis will be given to avoiding Type-II errors in all public expenditures than to avoiding Type I errors. Since the former imply the waste of these scarce public revenues, they occur at the cost of other, more productive forms of expenditure. When revenue is wasted in one area, something else goes unfunded. That is, when public revenues are very scarce, incurring Type II errors (leakage) in one form of expenditure necessarily implies incurring Type I errors (under-coverage) elsewhere. Avoiding leakage, where possible, makes sense, especially in poor countries.

When looking at the results of a benefit incidence analysis, the statistical implications of Type I and Type II errors are similar. If infrastructure programs are targeted, say, by incomes per person, then if these errors were very small there would be a strong negative relationship between the benefits received per person from these expenditures and incomes per person. The larger the errors, whether of Type I or of Type II, the weaker will be this negative relationship.

In a study of 'poverty related' expenditures identified by Thailand's Bureau of the Budget, Warr and Sarntisart (2005) used data on the allocation of these expenditures among Thailand's 76 provinces. Infrastructure was one of six such categories of 'poverty related' expenditures[2]. Thailand's provinces vary widely in income per person and the official estimates of poverty incidence. The authors studied the relationship between the provincial allocation of these expenditures per person and poverty incidence at the provincial level. They also examined the relationship between provincial expenditures per person and income per person. They hypothesized that if being 'poverty related' meant that these expenditures were targeted towards the poor, then a positive relationship between infrastructure expenditure per person and poverty incidence should exist. That is, provinces with higher poverty incidence should have more expenditure per person. Similarly, a negative relationship should exist between provincial spending on infrastructure per person and provincial income per person[3].

The results indicated that the relationship between provincial spending per person and poverty had the predicted sign, but the estimated coefficient was not significantly different from zero. Similarly, the estimated coefficient for income per person had the expected negative sign but was again not significant. Spending at the provincial level on infrastructure was not significantly related to poverty incidence or to income per person. While these results do not indicate the presence of significant poverty targeting, they do contradict the claim sometimes expressed that richer areas are favored in the allocation of infrastructure spending. No such effect was found. The effect that was significant was that of population size. Smaller provinces receive more spending per person.

The Interaction between Infrastructure and other Factors

Studies of the return to infrastructure projects have a consistent feature. They tend to indicate implausibly large estimates of the rate of return to infrastructure investments. Several examples are cited in World Bank (1994). Rates of return of 20 per cent per annum are common and some studies indicate rates of return as high as 60 per cent (World Bank 1994, p. 15). These rates of return are simply not plausible. A clue to the possible source of these puzzling results is provided by a case study of rural roads in Laos (Warr 2005). When the relationship between road development and incomes or expenditure is studied directly, a very strong relationship is found, implying very high rates of return, and this is typical of the findings found in the literature. But when allowance is made for other variables which also differ between households which have access to improved roads and those which do not, this very strong relationship weakens considerably.

These 'other' variables are factors which tend to enhance the value of roads. For example, the presence of local market places, schools and health facilities within a reasonable distance makes a big difference to the benefits in income, education and health terms which result from improved roads. The road is much more useful if it makes it possible to reach facilities which are actually present, but which would otherwise before be difficult to utilize. If these facilities are not present within a reasonable distance the value of the road is much less. The presence of these other variables tends to be correlated with the existence of improved roads, so looking in isolation at the relationship between improved roads and the benefits seemingly derived is misleading. It misses the contribution of the other supporting infrastructure which is correlated with the roads and wrongly attributes all the benefit derived to the road itself. When multiple regression methods are employed, allowing for the contribution of these other factors, this bias is removed.

Figure 3 illustrates this crucial point. The return to improved infrastructure, by itself, might not be high. The potential benefits depend on the coexistence of other things: supporting facilities such as local schools, health clinics and market facilities, along with a policy environment which recognizes the importance of health and education systems, reflected in adequate resources for local teachers and health professionals and which permits the effective functioning of markets, including international as well as domestic markets.

For example, for the poor farmers of northern Laos, the crucial form of market access is to the northeast provinces of Thailand. These are much closer, geographically, than the urban markets of the Vientiane region of central Laos. Improving roads within northern Laos without improving border access to the markets of northeastern Thailand would not be helpful. Conversely, improving border access without improving the road system of northern Laos would assist Lao farmers within easy reach of the Thai border crossing points but exclude the

Figure 3
The Interaction between Infrastructure, Supporting Facilities and Policy

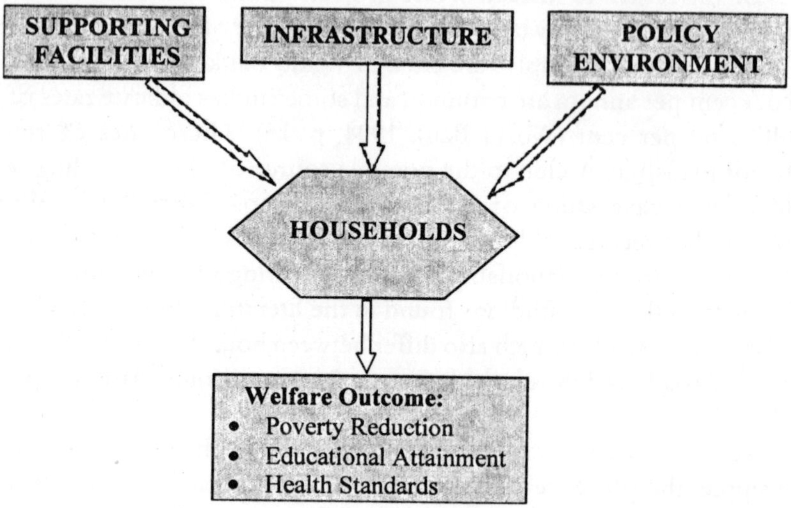

great mass of Lao farmers of this area who are not close to the border and for whom road access is currently very limited.

The key point is that improving infrastructure is an important part of the development effort but if this is all that is done the returns might not be high. Other factors must also be present–supporting facilities and an appropriate policy environment. These factors interact. When they are addressed together, the returns can be very high indeed.

Conclusions

This paper has focused on the mechanisms through which infrastructure investments benefit households. It emphasizes three channels. First, it raises household incomes by raising the productivity of the resources owned by the household. For example, production infrastructure like irrigation does this by providing inputs which are directly complementary with the resources own by the household. Transport infrastructure like roads does it by reducing transport costs to and from markets. This raises the net returns farm households can obtain for their goods and reduces the cost to them of the inputs they need to purchase. Transport infrastructure may also facilitate direct employment of household members outside the household, thus raising the return to their labour directly[4].

The distributional element of these increases in incomes depends on the distribution of resource ownership among households and on the magnitude of the productivity improvements that occur in these resources. In the important case of transport infrastructure, the empirical evidence is far from conclusive, but suggests that the effects tend to be distributionally neutral[5]. This means that all major income groups are affected similarly. Transport infrastructure thus tends to reduce absolute poverty, without significant effects on inequality. Within regions, infrastructure projects are not a particularly good candidate for poverty targeting, because all major income groups tend to benefit. Between regions, there is greater scope for targeting, by directing the benefits towards poorer regions. Poorer regions can benefit from this practice, provided the infrastructure they receive is actually productive, given their circumstances.

The second channel of effects is through access to public services such as education and health facilities. The infrastructure reduces the cost of reaching these facilities, in the case of roads, or improved information about them, in the case of communications facilities. The possibility of benefits of this kind depends on the coexistence of educational and health facilities within reach of the household. The final source of benefit is that infrastructure improves access to final consumer goods and by reducing transport costs, makes them more affordable. Electricity infrastructure makes it possible for the household to use a wide range of consumer goods otherwise unavailable to them.

Negative effects of infrastructure provision can be important. As road access to remote areas improves, negative environmental outcomes such as deforestation, caused by increased commercial logging and/or land clearing for agriculture may increase. The flow of drugs may increase, although the capacity of governments to suppress the production of drugs may also be improved. Trafficking in women and children may be facilitated. Finally, the spread of HIV/AIDS may increase. These potential negative effects raise the importance of governance. Achieving the demonstrated social benefits from improving infrastructure while avoiding or at least minimizing the negative effects is a challenge to governance throughout the developing world.

NOTES

1. Not all of these economic effects are necessarily positive. Improved transport may generate losers. For example, small village shopkeepers may lose from new competition from outside sources made cheaper by lowered transport costs. The lower the ability of such local suppliers to adjust their resource allocation to meet changing circumstances, the greater the likelihood of negative economic effects of this kind.
2. The others are 'Poor and Low Income People Projects', 'Agriculture and Natural Resources Projects', 'Health and Social Welfare Projects', 'Education and Traning Projects', and 'Others'. Between 2000 and 2002 total expenditures on the 'Infrastructure Projects' were about 21 per cent of total expenditures on these six 'Poverty Related' categories.
3. The analysis described above relates to the flows of public expenditure rather than to the stocks of capital that they create. A further complication which should be acknowledged is that public investment in one province could have spillover effects on neighbouring provinces.

4. Lanjouw (1999) shows the importance of this in the case of Ecuador.
5. It should be noted that the distributional component of the possible negative effects mentioned in endnote 1 is ignored in most available empirical studies.

REFERENCES

Cornia, Giovanni and Frances Stewart (1995), 'Two Errors of Targeting' in Dominique van de Walle and Kimberly Nead (eds.) *Public Spending and the Poor: Theory and Evidence*, Baltimore: Johns Hopkins University Press, 350-386.

Gibson, John and Scott Rozelle (2003), 'Poverty and Access to Roads in Papua New Guinea', *Economic Development and Cultural Change* 52 (1), October, 151-185.

Hammer, Jeffrey, Ijaz Nabi and James Cercone (1995), 'Distributional Impact of Social Sector Expenditures in Malaysia', in Dominique van de Walle and Kimberly Nead (eds.) *Public Spending and the Poor: Theory and Evidence*, Baltimore: Johns Hopkins University Press, 521-554.

Howe, John and Peter Richards (eds) (1984), *Rural Roads and Poverty Alleviation,* London: Intermediate Technology Publications.

Jacoby, Hanan G. (2000), 'Access to Markets and the Benefits of Rural Roads', *Economic Journal,* 110 July 717-37.

Lanjouw, Peter (1999), 'Rural Nonagricultural Employment and Poverty in Ecuador', *Economic Development and Cultural Change* 48 (1), October, 91-122.

Meerman, Jacob (1979), *Public Expenditure in Malaysia: Who Benefits and Why?* New York: Oxford University Press for the World Bank.

Selowsky, Marcelo (1979), *Who Benefits from Public Expenditures? A Case Study of Colombia*, New York: Oxford University Press for the World Bank.

Srinivasan, T.N. (1986), 'The Costs and Benefits of Being a Small, Remote, Island, Landlocked or Ministate Economy' *World Bank Research Observer* 1 (2) July, 205-218.

Sussangkarn, Chalongphob and Direk Patmasiriwat (1999), *Characteristics of the Distribution the Tax Burden and Expenditure Benefits: Thailand,* Thailand Development Research Institute, Bangkok, Preliminary report submitted to Fiscal Policy Office, Ministry of Finance, revised version, December. (in Thai).

Van de Walle, Dominique (1996), 'Infrastructure and Poverty in Vietnam', *Living Standards Measurement Study Working Paper* 121, World Bank Policy Research Department, Washington, DC.

Van de Walle, Dominique (2002), 'Choosing Rural Road Investments to Help Reduce Poverty'. *World Development,* 30 (4), April, 575-89.

Van de Walle, Dominique (1995), 'Incidence and Targeting: An Overview of Implications for Research and Policy', in Dominique van de Walle and Kimberly Nead (eds.) *Public Spending and the Poor: Theory and Evidence,* Baltimore: Johns Hopkins University Press, 585-619.

Van de Walle, Dominique and Kimberly Nead (eds) (1995), *Public Spending and the Poor: Theory and Evidence,* Baltimore: Johns Hopkins University Press.

Warr, Peter (2003), 'Fiscal Policies and Poverty Incidence: The Case of Thailand', *Asian Economic Journal,* 17 (1), February, 1-23.

Warr, Peter (2005), 'Road Development and Poverty Reduction: The Case of Lao. PDR', Asian Development Bank Institute, Discussion Paper 25, February. Available at *http://www.adbi.org/discussion/2005/02/23/897.roads.poverty.laopdr/* (accessed 5 May 2006).

Warr, Peter and Isra Sarntisart (2005), 'Poverty Targeting in Thailand', in John Weiss (ed.) *Poverty Targeting in Asia,* Cheltenham, UK: Edward Elgar, 2005, 186-218.

World Bank (1994), *World Development Report 1994: Infrastructure for Development,* New York: Oxford University Press.

7

OWN-POVERTY EVALUATION NETWORK AN *OPEN* APPROACH TO POVERTY ASSESSMENT AND MONITORING FOR SUSTAINABLE PRO-POOR DEVELOPMENT

Joe Remenyi and Max Kelly

Introduction

The contemporary rhetoric of development is dominated by the view that development has to be pro-poor. But, to be pro-poor it is first necessary to have a consensus on (i) how the poor are to be identified, (ii) how the incidence of poverty is to be measured, and (iii) how the impact of poverty-reduction interventions is to be monitored. In this paper, we argue that pro-poor development, as it is currently managed, does not give priority to the interests, the voice, and lived experiences of the people for whom poverty is a day-to-day reality. To ensure that development really is pro-poor we argue for the use of management strategies, to fulfil these three aspects of pro-poor, development, that are more inclusive of targeted poor individuals and households than is the case using most extant approaches to poverty mapping and impact assessment.

We argue that the *OPEN* approach to pro-poor development, using *self* evaluation of 'own-poverty', assessed by one's peers, provides a more robust and responsive approach to measurement of the incidence of poverty than the alternatives. The intensive involvement of poor people in the *OPEN* approach leads to more effective poverty targeting and greater accuracy and timeliness of intervention impact evaluation. *OPEN* is, therefore, more pro-poor, more culturally, socially and institutionally consistent with the requirements of sustainable development, and more cost-effective than less inclusive, externally managed top-down strategies of poverty mapping, consultant dominated design and administration of pro-poor poverty interventions, and independent project impact assessment.

About *OPEN*

OPEN involves the engagement of poor people, using participatory, group-based methods of data collection and analysis, in the consensual measurement of the most important ways in which *they* experience poverty and changes in the incidence of *their* poverty over time. The focus of *OPEN* is 'own poverty' 'evaluation' by a 'network' of poor people who are known to one another. *OPEN* results in self-assessed measures of poverty, with data collected in a comparative context relative to the 'own poverty' of one's neighbours and fellow villagers or slum dwellers. Hence, *OPEN* produces an assessment of the incidence of poverty that is 'evaluated' personally, but vetted by a network of peers and local leaders.

OPEN engages communities not only in the participatory assessment of poverty, but also through capacity building within the community to enable ongoing ownership over the development process–relevant to local priorities and conditions and allowing much more focused targeting of development interventions, under a policy framework informed by the needs and priorities of individuals and communities. *OPEN* combines the consensual or democratic approach to poverty analysis[1] with participatory processes, giving rise to improved opportunities for locally managed pro-poor development and locally managed poverty reduction project monitoring and impact assessment.

OPEN is founded on beneficiary-led consensual self assessment, with the key purpose being to develop locally relevant 'levels' of poverty (poor, poorer, poorest), locally determined indicators of poverty, and community wisdom on how the impact of poverty reduction interventions can be monitored and evaluated. The measurement of poverty is a complex and contested area. Econometric measurements of a unitary model of the household, depending on an indicator identified as a proxy of poverty, placing people above or below an arbitrarily devised poverty line has little meaning to those outside the circle of development policy-makers, academic institutions and professional development consultants. The 'objective' poverty-line approach has, therefore, attracted a wide spectrum of criticism from a number of quarters[2], yet it remains an important part of poverty analysis in development planning and impact assessment. The pro-poor approach, in contrast, has been associated more with concepts of poverty that are "multidimensional phenomenon, with a strong locally specific character"[3], yet even the typical pro-poor approach is tied to the limitations of an externally defined income-based proxy for poverty.[4]

The *OPEN* approach to poverty mapping and poverty monitoring, shares with pro-poor development planning a commitment to poverty as a multidimensional phenomenon, with strong situation-specific characteristics. *OPEN* does not, however, suffer the limitations that come from slavish dependence on a unitary, externally imposed proxy for the incidence of poverty.

In this chapter we examine ways in which *OPEN* is different from received practices and the reasons why *OPEN* ought to be a mainstream approach for poverty analysis, progress monitoring and impact evaluation.

OPEN in Practice

Examples of the *OPEN* approach to pro-poor development are not commonplace, but in the development literature there is a concentration of examples dealing with community based natural resource management, capacity building for more effective Water User Associations and Participatory Irrigation Management, and the multi-sector approach to locally managed Pro-Poor Development Planning.[5]

In 2000, the ADB (Asian Development Bank), at the request and in partnership with Chinese authorities, funded a technical assistance pilot project (TA3610) to identify a more effective strategy for village development planning and poverty reduction. The results of that exercise were reported in ADB 2002. I was the so called 'methodology and poverty expert' on the team of eight, led by Professor Li from the China Agriculture University, that undertook the assignment and which resulted in *OPEN* as the recommended framework.

The essential elements of the TA361 project were a series of field-based participatory action research and poverty assessments with poor villagers to explore (i) what poverty meant to them; (ii) how they believed poverty needs to be measured; (iii) their views on the key causes of their poverty that need to be overcome if escape from poverty is to be possible; and (iv) their views on the sorts of poverty reduction interventions that they believe would be effective and practicable. The results of these participatory explorations with villagers across several northern provinces in China has lead to significant reforms in the way in which village poverty reduction is planned and implemented across almost the whole of China.

In addressing what poverty meant to them, villagers consistently stressed the fact that even though there are several types of poverty, overwhelmingly poverty means 'having no money', especially when you need it most. Access to money, whether borrowed or otherwise, provides the means by which one can do something to relieve the immediate and the long-term effects and causes of poverty, be this livelihood poverty, infrastructure and environmental poverty or human resource poverty.

The importance given to cash-flow, (i.e., access to money) is not surprising, but it is crucial to know because of what it says to the policy maker and the pro-poor development planner. It highlights that it is cash flow not income that is critical. The difference is important and all too often ignored in income-based poverty line assessment of the incidence of poverty. Cash flow and income overlap, but as far as the poor are concerned, for example, 'cash-for-work is preferred over food for work'. For similar reasons, TA3610 found that poor communities hunger for public assistance projects, whether in the form of infrastructure upgrades, welfare payments or paid employment, that inject additional liquidity into their liquidity starved local economies.

The priority that poor villagers involved in TA3610 gave to cash flow does not mean that they were unaware of the importance of factors that contribute to the productivity of their farms, their households, their village economies or the access they have to the broader economy. Quite the opposite is the case. After a lengthy period of consultation and replication across literally hundreds of villages, TA3610 was able to report that in assessing their own poverty, a pattern of consistent responses could be identified. This pattern consisted of three primary types of poverty, the incidence of which could be mapped or measured using eight simple and well understood indicators. These three types of poverty and eight indicators are summarized in Table 1.

Table 1
Types of Poverty and Associated Indicators Identified by Poor Villagers in China

Types of Poverty: *1. Livelihood*	*2. Infrastructure/Environment*	*3. Human Resource*
Indicators:		
(1.1) Average cash income per person per year	(2.1) % With easy access to potable water	(3.1) % drop-out from primary education
(1.2) Average grain production per person per year	(2.2) % Households with reliable electricity	(3.2) % women with a significant health problem during the year
(1.3) % of households with poor quality housing	(2.3) % Villages with an all weather access road	

A close examination of Table 1 soon reveals the valuable insights that these indicators provide development planners into the root causes of poverty. For example, indicator 3.2 highlights the importance that villagers place on women's health issues as a factor determining the incidence of household poverty. The result also confirms the view that poverty is not gender neutral. Similarly, access to a reliable electricity supply not only influences the income generation opportunities open to poor villagers, but it also has an important bearing on the quality of their daily lives. Further comments on these results can be found in Remenyi and Li (2004).

Poverty mapping is, of course, only one part of pro-poor development planning. Another part is the identification of the poverty reduction interventions that might be incorporated into public assistance. Here too, TA3610 revealed some important outcome of the *OPEN* approach. Field work in China for TA3610 included the construction of an 'opportunity matrix'. This involved a set of general community based brainstorming sessions that asked three key questions: (i) what can the village do to reduce household poverty, through their own efforts, if they had permission to do so?; (ii) what activities or investments would the village like to make if modest levels of external assistance and expertise were to be available?; and (iii) what do the villagers dream about as sources of village and household prosperity, but which they do not think possible without substantial external inputs? The animated and excited responses that villagers gave to their discussion of these three questions were as a joy to behold.

Needless to say, the opportunity matrices arising out of these village consultations also gave rise to a pattern. This pattern has given rise to a reasonably stable menu of village development options that local officials in China now use as a short-cut to village development planning. The typical village development menu is replete with proposals for infrastructure upgrades, farmer-skills development, village health centre improvements, improved school facilities, and non-farm enterprise development support activities. Moreover, the methods used to upgrade local roads, schools, drinking water facilities, etc., favour cash-for-work methods, while other components of the development menu are concentrated on increasing village productivity and paid employment opportunities.

Reluctance to be *OPEN*

Despite the strong demonstration effect of projects like TA3610 and other *OPEN* based approaches to pro-poor development interventions, the consensual methods underlying *OPEN* are not as commonly applied in community development as they deserve to be. This is in part because the received wisdom is that poverty is not about how people 'feel' about their socio-economic, cultural and political situation, but about how people live. The increasing popularity of Participatory Poverty Assessment (PPA) to describe and quantify how people live notwithstanding, there remains a significant degree of skepticism among development researchers and practitioners of the ability of poor people to understand, accurately describe and correctly analyze the reasons for their plight based on self-assessment. Subjective poverty ranking by poor respondents excepted, best practice in well-planned PPA exercises is to firmly and clearly guide participating poor households, if not to simply tell them, which indicators will be used to measure the incidence of poverty in their community. Consequently, most studies of poverty and analysis of the root causes of poverty are heavily influenced by researchers who are not poor, have never been poor and have little to loose if their investigation is flawed or the results erroneous.[6]

Traditional impact assessment incorporating monitoring and evaluation also tend to be top down, externally implemented, primarily meeting the needs of donors. The *OPEN* philosophy of placing poor people squarely at the centre of the process of defining, understanding, measuring poverty and in identifying priorities to tackle poverty reduction also requires a strong commitment to ongoing, and in depth analysis of the impact of development interventions, both intended and unintended. This holistic assessment of the diverse consequences of development interventions builds on the consensual self assessment principles of *OPEN*. Participatory Impact Assessment and Participatory Monitoring and

Evaluation can provide a platform for this kind of self-assessment, however can also be much more strongly oriented to instrumentalist, extractive approaches. The key is the linking of the three aspects of pro poor development ((i) how the poor are to be identified, (ii) how the incidence of poverty is to be measured, and (iii) how the impact of poverty reduction interventions is to be monitored) utilizing the consensual self-assessment approach of *OPEN*. This provides robust and responsive characteristics for pro poor development, as identified through the example of TA3610 above. *OPEN* does this by integrating poor people into the research process, facilitating the ability of poor people to contribute their expert knowledge of poverty into the data collection, data analysis and project management processes. *OPEN* enables poor people to participate in the design, implementation and monitoring activities associated with pro-poor project interventions, thus strengthening the probability that the primary beneficiaries will be the poor communities targeted.

The Importance of Participation in Poverty Assessment

The principal causes of poverty can be debated without end. However, the weight of evidence, from innumerable participatory poverty assessments, social investigations of what it means to be poor, and a long list of situation specific research reports on poverty, points consistently to the view that the primary cause of poverty is the powerlessness of vulnerable people in the face of natural and systemic socio-economic, institutional and political forces.[7]

Understanding what poverty can mean to different actors is crucial to the study of poverty and poverty alleviation strategies. It is also important to our argument in support of the *OPEN* approach to pro-poor development. Central to this understanding is the notion of poverty as an absolute and a relative concept. The poor are very aware of this distinction, as any person who has conducted a village wealth ranking will attest. *OPEN* also assists in our understanding of the distinction between indicators and causes of poverty[8], how people become poor, and why they stay poor. It is only relatively recently that poverty researchers have discovered the importance of coming to understand the unique problems of the 'near-poor', who so easily slide back into poverty if their climb out of poverty has not generated for them a sufficiently substantial asset base, in contrast to the chronic poor. *OPEN* is also an heuristically powerful means by which to investigate the importance of material depravation as an indicator of poverty versus broader (and deeper) notions of poverty encompassing concepts such as inequality, insecurity, or deprivation of other non material factors.[9] The experience of development practitioners working to strengthen WUAs, for example, also appears to show that *OPEN* enables poor farmers and their households to acknowledge in a meaningful way that the meaning, measurement and abolition of poverty are as much political decisions as they are technical decisions influencing both policy and practice.[10]

The study of poverty can be divided into studies that identify how people become poor and studies that explore why people stay poor. The distinction is fundamental, if too often ignored. Participatory approaches to poverty have shown that the more important of the two approaches to the study of poverty is the latter; ie, why do poor people stay poor.[11] Though there is always a migration of individuals above the poverty line and a flow of back-sliders, the vast majority of poor people are not newly poor or even among the 'near' poor. The poverty pyramid is dominated by people who have been poor for some time, possibly the whole of their lives.[12] The challenge for policy makers and development professionals committed to poverty reduction is to identify ways in which these chronic poor can be assisted in their efforts to escape from the mire of poverty that holds them trapped.

Poverty reduction planning and programming invariably begins by an attempt to identify poor individuals/households/communities to be targeted. The criteria used to do this targeting are typically based on the selection of objective measures commonly held to reflect the incidence of poverty. For simplicity, let us call this the *objective approach* to poverty mapping. The most common of these measures is income; usually income per person or income per household. The income measure may be supplemented by a range of social development indicators, each of which is, in effect, a proxy for income. Nutritional intake per person, months of food stress endured, participation in education, quality of housing available, and spending on health or other basic needs are each a function of income available. Often these income measures are set beside environmental indicators of poverty, reflecting the view that isolation, distance from a reliable source of potable water, or local vulnerability to natural disasters are also the source of factors that impoverish individuals, households or even entire regions.

While a great deal of constructive insight into poverty has been derived from the *objective approach* to poverty mapping, and recognizing that even objective poverty measures include some level of subjectivity there is every reason to believe that the results will not lead policy-makers and poverty-reduction project staff to choose optimal strategies for poverty reduction, unless by serendipity. This is so because the *objective approach* may or may not lead to poverty-reduction interventions that address the constraints and problems that are really important to poor people. The *OPEN* approach to poverty-reduction planning overcomes this defect by adopting a *subjective approach,* allowing poor people to identify the key indicators of poverty that best describes and measures their experience of poverty. *OPEN* begins, therefore, with a set of participatory exercises that allow poor communities to select the indicators most relevant to their poverty. Subsequent steps allow these same communities to explore what it is that they feel is needed to realize improvements in the quality of their lives. Adopting this approach incorporates notions of democratic legitimacy that measures of poverty identified by 'independent experts can not attain.[13] Differences in objective and subjective approaches to poverty measures are amply demonstrated by current literature.[14] Aligning policy for pro poor growth with the measures of poverty intervention generated using *OPEN* will produce pro-poor development plans that are locally relevant and situationally appropriate.

Participatory studies of poverty have shown that there is no justification for approaches to poverty reduction that are based on the view that 'the poor are poor because it is their own fault': ie. because they are lazy, irrationally resistant to change, lacking in marketable skills or motivation, itinerant and not worthy of trust. The rare individual who voluntarily takes on a vow of poverty excepted, participatory analysis of poverty has unequivocally revealed that poor people are highly motivated to escape from poverty. These same PPA (participatory poverty analysis) studies show that the chronic poor are frustrated by the obstacles to escape from poverty that causes their poverty to persist, motivation and hard work notwithstanding. Poor people lack money and the opportunity to benefit from the productivity that their ability to work ought to generate. The overwhelmingly positive response of poor householders to the relief that microfinance providers bring to the liquidity and financial intermediation constraints that are the bane of the poor is clear evidence of this.[15]

Participatory poverty analysis has also taught us that poverty can be understood more broadly to cover non-material issues, in particular issues of powerlessness, and marginalization. Although we are firmly in the area of subjective and relative measures of poverty it is important to make explicit the issue of non homogeneity of the poor. As a prime example, poverty is not gender neutral.[16] Not only do women and children dominate the ranks of the poor, but female-headed households dominate the ranks of the hard-core poor, the frail, disabled and the ill excepted. Acknowledging the complexities introduced by the bounded realities of the very poor and marginalized, in particular women, Noble et al. (2004) argue solidly that "careful and methodologically sound qualitative work should help remove some of the difficulties associated with bounded realities." [17]

Welfare is an appropriate response to the needs of the old, the disabled and the ill. Welfare is not, however, an appropriate response to the needs of the able-bodied poor, whether from female-headed households or otherwise, who seek a sustainable and personally managed solution to their poverty. It is this group of poor people, the able bodied but vulnerable poor, who find it most difficult to participate effectively in modern markets for labour, finance, know-how and the sale of final products to consumers.[18] Modern factors of production and product markets have evolved to meet the needs of those with the financial strength to participate in commercial transactions. Typically this means that the poor are excluded because they do not have the means that entitles them to be a player.[19] Even in simple barter-based labour markets, the structures that have evolved to facilitate labour contracting are structures that are suited to the employment of individuals who are adult and able to respond at a moment's notice to casual work opportunities. The burdens of child care and home duties, often in cultural contexts that discriminate against open participation by females in the commercial sector, create constraints to the realization of higher levels of income generation by those who are not adult or unable to abandon all at short notice. In the poorest households, it is not uncommon to find that a key cause of chronic poverty is the shortage of able-bodied labour, capable of participating in productive subsistence or wage labour. It is these very complexities that need to be addressed.

OPEN Processes in Poverty Reduction Planning and Implementation

It is not our purpose here to go into great detail about the *OPEN* methodology. This has been described elsewhere[20]. Suffice it to say here that a substantial body of practical experience is accumulating on community managed poverty reduction interventions, including the important role that locally managed natural-resource (typically water) user associations are playing in the revitalization of economic activity in poor communities. The volume of published literature on these projects is thin, but it cannot be doubted that they are demonstrating the practicality and effectiveness of self-managed and monitored pro-poor development.

OPEN is a process. It must be a process because in consulting with local poor communities one is inexorably drawn to deal with the consequences of limited local capacity for modern forms of project management. *OPEN* does, therefore, lead to the incorporation of community based human resource development investments, if only to facilitate the ability of local community representatives to fulfil the on-going reporting requirements of the typical project cycle. Similarly, local management of the flow of funds needed to ensure that planned activities are implemented may require training of local people in simple book-keeping, budgeting and financial reporting. In the case of natural resource user associations, the level of training in strategic goal setting, demand management, pricing policy formulation and impact monitoring can be quite demanding and time consuming.

OPEN is a process that draws veracity and viability from its reliance on the role that networking plays in harnessing the discipline of peer review. As one goes from household to household or village to village, the own-poverty assessments and views on appropriate indicators to measure poverty are subject to the scrutiny of neighbours and local community leaders. This review process gives rise to three important outcomes. First, the own-poverty assessments will produce results that can be examined for patterns that reveal key constraints and obstacles to self-help based escape paths from poverty. These patterns can form an important basis on which to conduct further discussion with local people about the reasons why, for example, the productivity of cropping or animal husbandry is so low; children do not attend school; the incidence of health problems is seasonal. Second, the indicators of poverty chosen by poor households provide development planners with a unique insight into what local people believe are core causes of their poverty. By addressing these causes, be they the prevalence of water or soil based health problems, the lack of markets at which to sell local produce, or the absence of financial institutions willing to provide the poor with the financial services they need to take up economic opportunities, pro-poor development planning can be relevant, timely and effectively targeted at the intended beneficiaries. Third, the local community is given the basis and the ability to monitor movements in the poverty indicators that they have chosen. The experience of Water User Associations the world over has illustrated the importance of this factor as a source of motivation and local pride.

NOTES

1. Noble et al. 2004
2. See escecially Du Toit 2005, Norton et al. 2001, Moore et al. 1998, Maxwell 1999
3. Norton et al. 2001, p. 6.
4. See, for example, the World Bank's Word Development Report 2000-2001, Attacking Poverty and the multi-agency report of 2005, Operationalising Pro-Poor Growth.
5. See, for example, ADB 2002, INPIM 2004, Mangahas, 1995, Remenyi and Li 2004, Peter 2004, Taylor and Plummer 2004.
6. Contrast Chambers 1995, Grosh and Glewwe 2000, Stiglitz 2002, Streeten 1998, UNDP 2000, World Bank 1990
7. See Sen 1976, 1981, 1983 and 1992, plus World Bank 2000-2001
8. Moore et al. 1998
9. Moore et al. 1998
10. Noble et al., 2004
11. Multiple references to the study of chronic poverty including Aliber 2003, Balisacan and Fujisaki 1999, Callan, Nolan and Whelan 1993, Chambers 1995, Collier and Dollar 2000, Dasgupta 1993, DeRose, Messer and Millman 1998, Bradshaw and Sainsbury 2000, Moore et al. 1998,
12. On the poverty pyramid see Remenyi 1991, Remenyi 2000, and Remenyi and Li 2004
13. Noble et al. 2004
14. See for example Carletto and Zezza 2006
15. Jain 1996, Todd 1996, Rutherford 2001, etc
16. See Chant 1997, plus other gender studies of poverty
17. Noble et al. 2004, page 16.
18. There are a number of surveys of poor households that illustrate the problem. See in particular Bittman and Goodin 1998, Pyatt and Ward 1999, Grosh and Glewwe 2000, World Bank 'voices of the poor', Cornia, Jolly and Stewart 1988, Lipton and Ravallion 1995, etc.

19. It is useful to consider this point in the way in which thinking on poverty has evolved in the Nobel Prize winning work on poverty by Sen 1976, 1981, 1983, and 1992.
20. See Li, et al., 2002, Remenyi 2005, Remenyi, , 2006.

REFERENCES

ADB (2002), Preparing a Methodology for Development Planning in Poverty Alleviation under the New Poverty Strategy of PRC, TA 3610–PRC, July http://www.adb.org/Documents/Reports/Consultant/TA3610_PRC_Final_Report.pdf

Aliber, Michael (2003), Chronic Poverty in South Africa: Incidence, Causes and Policies, *World Development*, 31 (3), 473-491.

Balisacan, A.M. and S. Fujisaki (1999), eds., *Causes of Poverty: Myths, Facts and Policies*, University of Philippines Press, Manila.

Bittman M. and R.E. Goodin (1998), An Equivalence Scale for Time. SPRC Discussion Paper No. 85. Kensington: Social Policy Research Centre, University of New South Wales, Kensignton, NSW.

Bradshaw, J. and R. Sainsbury (2000), eds., *Experiencing Poverty*, Ashgate, Aldershot.

Callan, T., B. Nolan and C.T. Whelan (1993), Resources, Deprivation and the Measurement of Poverty, *Journal of Social Policy*, 22 (2), 141-172.

Carletto, G. and A. Zezza (2006), Being Poor, Feeling Poorer: Combining Objective and Subjective Measures of Welfare in Albania, *The Journal of Development Studies*, 42(5), 739-760.

Chambers, R. (1995), Poverty and Livelihoods: Whose Reality Counts?. *IDS Discussion Paper* 347, IDS, Sussex, Brighton.

Chant, Sylvia (1997), Women Headed Households: Poorest of the Poor?, *IDS Bulletin* 28 (3), 26-48.

Collier, Paul and David Dollar (2000), Can the World Cut Poverty in Half?, Working Paper 2403, World Bank, Washington, DC.

Cornia, G.A., R. Jolly and F. Stewart (1988), eds., *Adjustment with a Human Face*, Clarendon Press, Oxford.

Dasgupta, P. (1993), *An Enquiry into Well-being and Destitution*, Clarendon Press, Oxford.

DeRose, L., E. Messer and S. Millman (1998), *Who's Hungry? And How do we Know? Food Shortage, Poverty and Deprivation*, UNU, Tokyo.

du Toit, A. (2005), Poverty Measurement Blues: Some Reflections on the Space for understanding 'Chronic' and 'Structural' Poverty in South Africa Working Paper 55. Manchester: IDPM/Chronic Poverty Research Centre (CPRC).

Grosh, M. and P. Glewwe (2000), eds., *Designing Household Survey Questionnaires for Developing Countries: Lessons from 15 Years of the Living Standard Measurement Study*, World Bank, Washington, DC.

INPIM (2004), *PIM and Monitoring*, International Network on Participatory Irrigation Management, Washington DC.

Jain, P.S. (1996), Managing Credit for the Rural Poor: Lessons from the Grameen Bank, *World Development* 24 (1), 79-89.

Lipton, M. and M. Ravallion (1995), Poverty and Policy, in Behrman, J. and T.N. Srinivasan 1995, eds., *Handbook of Development Economics*, 2553-2607, Elsevier, Amsterdam.

Maxwell, S. (1999), The Meaning and Measurement of Poverty, ODI Poverty Briefing No. 3. Overseas Development Insititute, UK.

Mangahas, M. (1995), Self-rated Poverty in the Philippines 1981-92, *International Journal of Public Opinion*, 7 (1), p. 40-55.

Moore, M., M. Choudhary and N. Singh (1998), How Can We Know What They Want? Understanding Local Perceptions of Poverty and Ill-being in Asia, Worksing Paper 80, IDS, Susses, Brighton.

Norton, A., B. Bird, K. Brock, M. Kakande and C. Turk (2001), *A Rough Guide to PPAs: Participatory Poverty Assessment, an introduction to theory and practice*, Overseas Development Institute, UK.

Noble, M., Ratcliffe, A. and Wright, G. (2004), Conceptualising, defining and measuring Poverty in South Africa: an Argument for a Consensual Approach, Centre for the Analysis of South African Social Policy, Oxford University.

Pyatt, F.G. and M. Ward (1999), eds., *Identifying the Poor*, IOS Press, Amsterdam.

Peter, R.J. (2004), PIM-Lessons from International Experience, Paper presented at the Workshop on "PIM-Pathways to Progress" Organized by the Asian Development Bank, Hanoi, Vietnam, March 31-April 2, 2004.

Remenyi, J.V. (1991), *Where Credit is Due: A Study of Credit Based Income Generation Programmes for the Poor in Developing Countries*, Intermediate Technology Publications, London.

Remenyi, Joe (2000), 'Transition into Poverty: The Mongolian Experience, 1989-95', in Henke, Holger and Ian Boxill, eds., 2000, *The End of the 'Asian Model?*, John Benjamins, Amsterdam, 109-127.

Remenyi, Joe (2006), Participatory Village Poverty Reduction Planning and Index Based Poverty Mapping in China, forthcoming in Brock, K, 2006, *Springs of Participation*, IDS, Sussex.

Remenyi, Joe, with Li Xiaoyun, Li Zhou, Liu, Yanli, Liu Yonggong, Wang Sibin, and Zhang Chuntai (2002), CPAP, A Methodology for Participatory Development Planning for Poverty Reduction in China, Asian Development Bank, TA3610-PRC, October, Beijing.

Remenyi, J. and X Li (2004), 'Towards Sustainable Village Poverty Reduction? The Development of the CPAP Approach', in Taylor, J. and J. Plummer, eds., *Community Participation in China: Issues and Processes for Capacity Building*, pp. 269-306, Earthscan for DFID, London.

Rutherford, S. (2000), *The Poor and Their Money*, Oxford University Press, New Delhi.

Sen, A. (1976), Poverty: An Original Approach to Measurement, *Econometrica* 44, 219-232.

Sen, A. (1981), *Poverty and Famines: An Essay on Entitlement and Deprivation*, Clarendon Press, Oxford.

Sen, A. (1983), Poor Relatively Speaking, *Oxford Economic Papers* 35 (2), 153-169.

Sen, A. (1992), *Inequality Re-examined*, Oxford University Press, New York.

Social Weather Station 2006, http://www.sws.org

Stiglitz, J.E. (2002), Globalism's Discontents, *The American Prospect*, Winter, 16-21.

Streeten, P. (1998), Beyond the Six Veils: Conceptualising and Measuring Poverty, *Journal of International Affairs* 52 (1), p. 1-31.

Taylor, J. and J. Plummer (2004), eds., *Capacity Building in China*, DFID, London.

Todd, H. (1996), *Women at the Center: Grameen Bank Borrowers After One Decade.* Dhaka: University Press Ltd.

UNDP (2000), *Overcoming Human Poverty*, UNDP, New York.

World Bank (1990), *World Development Report: Poverty*, Oxford UP, New York.

World Bank, 2000-2001, *World Development Report: Attacking Poverty*, Oxford UP, New York.

World Bank et. al. (2005), Pro-poor Growth in the 1990s: Lessons and Insights from 14 Countries, Report of the Operationalising Pro-Poor Growth Research Program, World Bank, Washington, DC.

8

MEASURING SOCIAL DISADVANTAGE WITH AVOIDABLE MORTALITY RISKS

Kam Ki Tang and D.S. Prasada Rao

Introduction

In order to assess the prevalence of social discrimination and the effectiveness of policy intervention aiming at its eradication, it is necessary first to have good measures of social discrimination. Mortality has long played a crucial role in the assessment of social exclusion.[1] For example, empirical evidence shows that a disproportionate share of ill-health and premature mortality is borne by the socially disadvantaged (Braveman, Krieger and Lynch 2000).

There is strong methodological foundation placing mortality prominently in the measurement of social disadvantage. Firstly, mortality is perhaps the simplest summary measure of health status, which is an important component of human capital (means of achievement) and wellbeing (purpose of achievement). Secondly, as a single measure of wellbeing, mortality rates provide a better measure of well-being than wealth, because wealth is useless without the capability to enjoy it and death strikes at the heart of this capability (Sen 1995). Thirdly, mortality is strongly related to the capacity to meet certain basic but essential physiological needs, including nutrition, basic education, health, sanitation, water, shelter, and safety (Hicks and Steeten 1979). As a result, a mortality rate can be considered a composite measure of adequacy of access to basic social provisions.

Despite the universal acceptance of mortality as a social welfare indicator, it is not without its own problems. The first problem is that mortality does not include non-fatal health outcomes. There has been effort to incorporate morbidity and disability into mortality measures. A lot of progress has been achieved in this area, as indicated by the development of a large array of more comprehensive health indicators, including disability-adjusted life expectancy (DALE), disability-adjusted life years (DALYs), disability-free life expectancy (DFLE), active life-expectancy (ALE), quality-adjusted life expectancy (QALE), years of healthy life

(YHL), and healthy life years (HLY).[2] In comparison, the progress in dealing with the second problem has been limited until very recently.

The second problem is that not all mortalities have the same welfare implications. Mortalities can be classified at the simplest into avoidable and unavoidable. Obvious examples of avoidable deaths include deaths due to violence or starvation. In comparison, what constitutes unavoidable deaths is less obvious. For instance, the Centers for Disease Control and Prevention of the United States (CDC 1986) classify deaths caused by violence, starvation, consumption of tobacco, obesity, alcohol consumption, toxicants, illicit use of drugs, and vehicle accidents as preventable. However, this classification method identifies only the most obvious causes of avoidable deaths and therefore implicitly assumes that deaths caused by other factors are unavoidable. This method can be quite problematic when handling disease-related deaths. On the one hand, even for incurable diseases, it is still possible to take measures to avoid infection in the first place. On the other hand, even for illnesses against which effective treatments have been developed, there are chances that some patients cannot survive them due to their own peculiar health conditions. How such deaths can be classified as being either unavoidable or avoidable is not a straightforward issue. Notwithstanding the difficulties in classifying the nature of death, the fact that human beings are mortal is the strongest evidence that some mortality risks are unavoidable.

Separating avoidable and unavoidable mortality has important policy implications. If a death is unavoidable, then by definition it can not be prevented from happening by means available to humanity. In other words, unavoidable deaths are not related to socio-economic factors and are beyond policy intervention. As a result, for mortality to be a meaningful indicator of social discrimination, it is essential to separate unavoidable morality from avoidable mortality.

In review of the limitation of the classification method, Tang, Chin and Rao (2006) have recently developed a new method to tackle this problem. This method identifies a death as either avoidable or unavoidable based on the *probability* that each scenario arises, rather than the actual cause of death and, therefore, can circumvent the aforementioned problems of the classification method. The method requires data from standardized life tables across a large number of countries or populations. Such dataset was not available until the recent release of world mortality data by the World Health Organization (WHO) for 191 countries in the year 2000 (World Health Organization 2002).

In the next section, we explain how this new method can be used to separate mortality into avoidable and unavoidable mortalities. In the following two sections, we show how to improve existing mortality-based wellbeing measures using the concept of avoidable and unavoidable mortality risks. Subsequently, we modify life expectancy at birth so that the resulting measure can be used to examine gender bias in a society. We then modify age-at-death and use the resulting estimates to study inequalities between gender and ethnic groups in the United States and New Zealand. The last section offers some concluding remarks.

Reference Distribution Representing Unavoidable Mortality Risks

The Okinawa prefecture of Japan is renowned for longevity. For instance, Okinawa has 39.5 centenarians per 10,000 people, compared to 14.1 for Japan as a whole. However, a study by Moriguchi et al. (2004) shows the longevity of Okinawan has a lot more to do with life style than with genes. They find that Japanese immigrants from Okinawa living in Brazil face a higher mortality risk from cardiovascular diseases and have a shorter mean life expectancy compared with their counterparts living in Okinawa. The higher mortality risks of Okinawa immigrants in Brazil were due to their change of diet to a lower intake of fish and a higher intake of meat. The study concludes that the effect of lifestyle on longevity can be large enough to modulate the expression of genes.

The essence of the Okinawan study is that mortality risks are not static, they can be reduced by improving resource availability, especially those related to health, nutrition and safety. Here resource is broadly defined, including financial resources and non-financial resources such as human capital, institutions, environment, and technology. Therefore, a country that allocates more resources to a particular population group will result in a lower mortality rate for that group. However, even with the best resources that are feasible at a point in time, some mortality risks cannot be completely eliminated, such as those related to chance and genes. Those risks are considered as unavoidable or natural morality risks. Unavoidable mortality risks are expected to differ with age and gender, and change with time, due to technological progress and environmental changes. For example, there are reports that some recently developed drugs have successfully extended the life span of cancer patients (Arnst 2005). Consequently, if we can picture a hypothetical country that has the lowest conditional probability of dying (probability that a person aged x at the last birthday dies during the year) for each age-gender groups amongst all countries, this country can then be considered as being free from avoidable mortality risks for a given state of technology and resources that are available at the time of measurement. This country is labeled "the reference country." Tang et al. (2006) propose a data envelopment method to construct the mortality profile of this hypothetical reference country. The method is briefly explained below. Details of the method and robustness tests are provided in their study.

The mortality distribution of the reference country, by age and gender, is constructed by enveloping the observed mortality distributions of all the countries included in the study. A number of assumptions are made in the process:

(a) avoidable and unavoidable mortality risks are uncorrelated;

(b) mortality risks, avoidable and unavoidable, are age and gender specific, and time variant; and

(c) unavoidable mortality risks for different age-gender groups at a given point of time are invariant across countries or communities.

Suppose the conditional probability that a person of age x dies before reaching the next birthday is equal to q_x. Therefore, if q_x is plotted against x, then $q_x = 1$ for a sufficiently large value of X i.e., a person must die eventually.

In Figure 1, the conditional probabilities of dying for three countries are plotted. The curves for Countries 1 and 2 do not cross each other. For any given age, the conditional probability of dying is lower in Country 1 than in Country 2. Therefore, Country 1's mortality distribution displays first order stochastic dominance over that of Country 2. This implies that a person in Country 1 is better off than in Country 2 in terms of longevity. On the contrary, the curves for Countries 1 and 3 cross each other as indicated. This means that those of ages below x are better off in Country 1, while those above x are better off in Country 3. In this case, neither country's distribution displays first order stochastic dominance over the other, and it is necessary to examine second order stochastic dominance. However, if a hypothetical country has the conditional probability of dying plotted against age equal to the envelopment of Countries 1 and 3 from *below*, then this country's distribution will, by construction, display first order stochastic dominance over all the three countries. This envelopment concept is used to construct the reference distribution of unavoidable mortality risks.

Suppose there are K countries (in the present study, $K = 191$). The conditional probability that a person in country k who survives to age x will die before reaching the next birthday is denoted by q_{xk}. Let $\tilde{q}_x$ be the conditional probability of dying for a person in the reference country who survives to age x.

Figure 1
Conditional Probability of Death at Age x

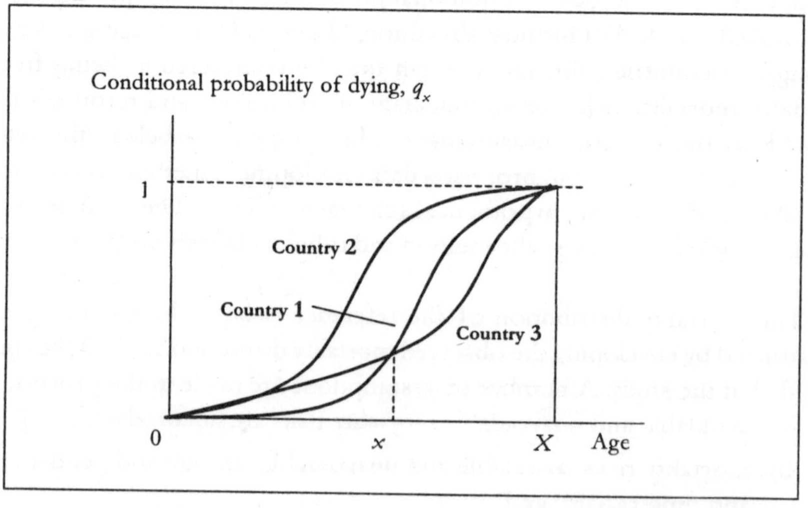

Then, $\tilde{q}_x$ is defined as

$$\tilde{q}_x = \begin{cases} \min\{q_{xk}, k = 1,2,...,K\} & x < X \\ 1 & x = X \end{cases} \qquad (1)$$

To allow for gender differences in natural mortality risks, the construction of the reference country mortality profile is undertaken separately for females and males. Once the reference country mortality profile is constructed, life expectancy for a person in each age group of the reference country can be calculated based on the probabilities of death given by equation using standard life table methods (see Tang et al., 2006 for details). By construction, the reference country has the lowest conditional probability of dying for all ages and, thus, the highest life expectancy amongst all countries.

The proposed method is applied to the life tables of 191 countries in the year 2000 compiled by WHO (2002). This dataset covers all member countries

Table 1
Mortality Profile of the Reference Country: Male Population

Age[1]	*Country*[2]	*Conditional probability of dying*[3]	*Life expectancy*[4]
0	Singapore	0.00373	79.36
1	Sweden	0.00052	78.66
5	Malta	0.00037	74.70
10	Estonia	0.00054	69.72
15	Iceland	0.00164	64.76
20	Malta	0.00239	59.86
25	San Marino	0.00300	55.00
30	San Marino	0.00319	50.16
35	San Marino	0.00399	45.31
40	San Marino	0.00648	40.48
45	Iceland	0.00915	35.73
50	Iceland	0.01735	31.04
55	Sweden	0.03091	26.54
60	Sweden	0.05292	22.31
65	Switzerland	0.08612	18.41
70	Monaco	0.12906	14.91
75	Monaco	0.18951	11.75
80	Monaco	0.31792	8.92
85	Brunei Darussalam	0.43098	6.91
90	Brunei Darussalam	0.52386	5.25
95	Brunei Darussalam	0.67937	3.82
100	Brunei Darussalam	1	2.69

Notes: 1. The column shows the lower bound of the age group.
2. The column shows the probability of a person dying before reaching the next age bracket.
3. The column shows the country that determines the envelopment for a given age group.
4. The column shows life expectancy at different age groups, thus, life expectancy at age zero is the life expectancy at birth.

of WHO and essentially whole of the world population. The mortality risk profiles for the male and female populations in the reference country are shown in Table 1 and Table 2, respectively. The second column of the tables indicates the country that has the lowest mortality risk for a given age group among the 191 countries in the dataset and, thus, contributes to the identification of mortality risks associated with the reference country. The data envelopment method has identified a mixture of countries from various regions around the world. Countries contributing to the profile of reference populations are quite different for male and female populations. It, therefore, supports the need to construct gender-based reference mortality risk profiles. Furthermore, the fact that countries contributing to the reference country belong to different continents indicates that ethnicity and race are not dominant factors in determining unavoidable mortality risks.

Table 2
Mortality Profile of the Reference Country: Female Population

Age	*Country*	*Conditional probability of dying*	*Life expectancy*
0	Sweden	0.00282	85.55
1	Sweden	0.00046	84.79
5	Slovenia	0.00019	80.83
10	Cyprus	0.00039	75.84
15	Denmark	0.00092	70.87
20	Israel	0.00100	65.94
25	Sweden	0.00128	61.00
30	Sweden	0.00140	56.07
35	Malta	0.00235	51.15
40	San Marino	0.00349	46.26
45	San Marino	0.00558	41.42
50	San Marino	0.00747	36.64
55	Andorra	0.01307	31.89
60	Andorra	0.02177	27.28
65	Japan	0.03440	22.83
70	Japan	0.05825	18.56
75	Monaco	0.10224	14.55
80	Japan	0.20225	10.92
85	Monaco	0.31431	8.06
90	Antigua and Barbuda	0.48322	5.61
95	Grenada	0.66230	3.98
100	Grenada	1	2.86

Notes: as for Table 1.

If a country has adequate resources and uses them as effectively as the reference country in reducing avoidable mortality risks for a particular age-gender group, then this group's mortality risks would be the same as their counterparts in the reference country. That is, the group will have no, or negligible, avoidable mortality risks. However, if the country provides inadequate resources for the group or uses available resources less effectively than the reference country, the group will have higher mortality risks than the risks observed in the reference country. The difference between the actual and reference country mortality risks is defined as the *avoidable mortality risk*. In the following sections, we apply the concepts of avoidable and unavoidable mortality risks to improve on some existing mortality-based wellbeing measures so that the resulting measures can be used to assess social disadvantage.

Life Expectancy Index

There are a number of mortality-based wellbeing measures amongst which life expectancy at birth (abbreviated as "life expectancy" hereafter) is perhaps the most commonly used social indicator. However, if we want to measure whether a gender is socially disadvantaged, directly comparing male and female life expectancies can be misleading. This is because males and females face different natural mortality risks at different ages due to biological differences. For instance, Tabutin and Willems (1998) find that male children in the age group 1 to 4 are more vulnerable to death than female children of the same age group due to the slower development of their lungs. On the other hand, mortality risks associated with pregnancy simply does not exist for male adults. In what follows, we develop a modified life expectancy measure that adjusts for the biological differences between men and women, so that any socio-economic differences between the two genders can be readily revealed.

Since life expectancy of females and males in the reference country are determined only by unavoidable risks, it can be used as a benchmark to measure the impact of socio-economic factors on life expectancy of any given country. Hence, we can defined the life expectancy index (LEI) as

$$\varepsilon_k^g = e_k^g / \tilde{e}^g ; g = f, m \tag{2}$$

where $\tilde{e}^g$ is the life expectancy of gender g of the reference country and e_k^g is the life expectancy of gender g in country k.

Since $\tilde{e}^g$ is the maximum life expectancy for gender g, ε_k^g measures the degree to which the gender group has achieved its full potential. It should be noticed that LEI is bounded between zero and one. If ε_k^g is equal to 0.7, this means that the life expectancy of gender g in country k is 30 per cent lower than its reference country counterpart, and it could potentially be improved if better resources are provided to the group.

For the country as a whole, the LEI is given by

$$\varepsilon_k = \sum_g (n_k^g / n_k)\, \varepsilon_k^g \tag{3}$$

where n_k^g is the actual population of gender g in country k and $n_k = \sum_g n_k^g$ is the total population.

By normalizing life expectancy of a country with that of the reference country, LEI has essentially controlled for natural mortality risks. As a result, LEI for the two genders are now commensurable and, thus, can be used to measure gender bias. Hence we define the ratio of gender specific LEI for country k as

$$R_k = \frac{\text{LEI for males}}{\text{LEI for females}} = \frac{\varepsilon_k^m}{\varepsilon_k^f} = \frac{e_k^m / \tilde{e}^m}{e_k^f / \tilde{e}^f} \tag{4}$$

The value of R_k is bounded below by zero but unbounded above. If there is no gender bias in the society, R_k will equal to one. On the other hand, the more the socio-economic environment is against females (males), the closer R_k is to infinity (zero).

Figure 2 shows the value of the ratio of gender specific LEI against the average LEI for the whole population for 191 countries in the year 2000. It can be seen that the vast majority of the countries with relatively low LEI (and mostly low income) witness higher inequality against females. On the other hand, for countries with relatively high LEI, inequalities against males and females are equally prevalent.

The ten countries in which females are most disadvantaged are (in descending order): Nepal (R_k = 109), Namibia, Botswana, Maldives, Lesotho, Zambia, Bangladesh, Pakistan, Zimbabwe and Burundi (R_k = 106). Out of these countries,

Figure 2
Ratio of Gender Specific LEI Against LEI at Country Level

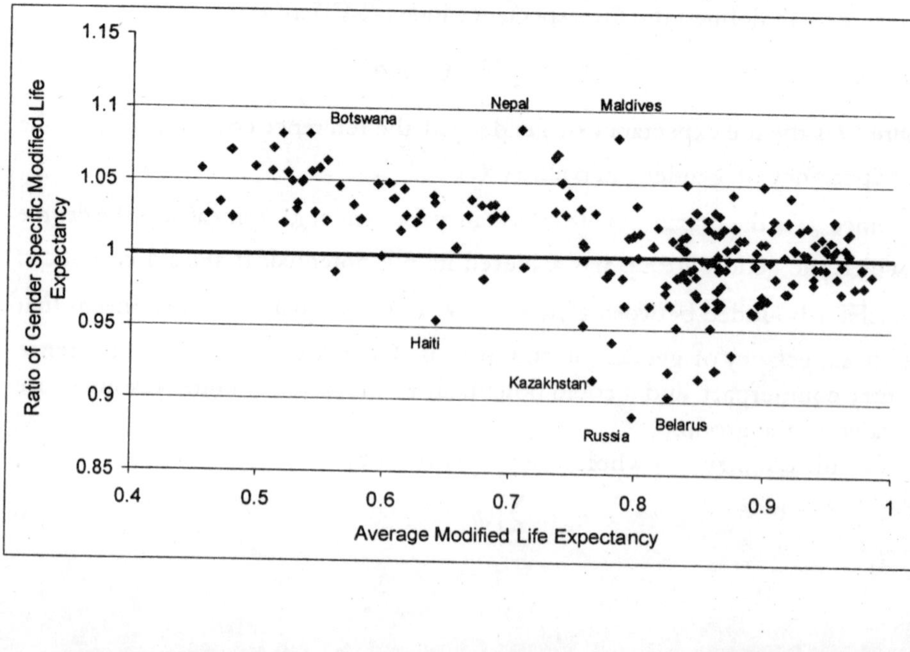

six are African countries and the remaining four are South Asian countries. The figures imply that, for instance, were there no biological differences, a male infant in Nepal would be expected to live 10 per cent longer than a female infant. Lack of equal access to education is one of main reasons why females are socially disadvantaged in Nepal. According to the 2001 Census of the country, adult (+15) literacy rate for females is equal to 34.6 per cent, only a little bit more than half of the 62.2 per cent for males.

The ten countries in which males are most disadvantaged are (in a descending order): the Russian Federation (R_k = 0.89), Belarus, Kazakhstan, Latvia, Ukraine, Estonia, Lithuania, Kyrgyzstan, Hungary, and Albania (R_k = 0.95). Among the ten countries, three countries that are Central Asian countries while the remaining seven are Eastern European Countries. The disadvantaged position of males in these countries is closely related to the collapse of the communist regimes in the late 1990s. The collapse of the communism led to the shrinking of the state sector and army, and the associated employment opportunities and social identities. In this changing social, political and economic landscape, men are hit particularly hard because Russia is a patriarchal country where men are traditionally expected to shoulder the financial burden of their families. Alcoholism has become an escape route for many unemployed males. Moreover, alcohol abuse is often associated with other problems, such as drug addiction, smoking, poor nutrition and, particularly, violence, which also attribute to the deteriorating life expectancy of Russian males. The results presented here suggest that the ratio of gender specific LEI reflects the social disadvantage associated with different gender and socio-economic groups.

Modified Age-at-death

The concepts of avoidable and unavoidable morality risks are very versatile and, in principle, can be used in modifying any mortality-based wellbeing measures. In this section, we illustrate how these concepts can be used to modify another commonly used mortality-based wellbeing measure, viz. age-at-death. Age-at-death is used mostly to identify the impacts of specific fatal causes, such as influenza. Le Grand (1987; 1989) first used the dispersion of age-at-death as a measure of health inequality. The basic premise is that a person's length-of-life or age-at-death is closely related to the person's health and socio-economic conditions.

Suppose the age-at-death is denoted by x, and the number of deaths at age x for gender g in country k is denoted by D^g_{xk}. Then for gender g as a group, the average age-at-death is given by

$$x^g_k = \sum_x x\,(D^g_{xk} / D^g_k) \tag{5}$$

where $D^g_k = \sum_x D^g_{xk}$ is the total number of the deaths of gender g in country k.

Similar, for the country as a whole, the average age-at-death in country k is given by

$$x_k = \sum_g x_k^g (D_k^g / D_k) \tag{6}$$

where $D_k = \sum_g D_k^g$ is the population size of country k.

A greater average age-at-death implies a higher average length-of-life for those who die in a given year and, therefore, is unambiguously reflecting greater welfare, *ceteris paribus*. However, directly using age-at-death as a well-being measure has two problems.

Firstly, since age-at-death covers only a small portion of the population–those who died in the year of survey, it is not necessarily a good representation of the whole population, especially those who have survived that particular year. This issue can be addressed by using the stationary population associated with a given distribution of mortality risks. The stationary population of a country is constructed by repeatedly subjecting the population to the same age-gender specific mortality rate profiles as observed in the year of survey until the demographic structure becomes static. At the same time, the number of births is standardized to 100,000. The number of deaths for each age-gender group in the stationary population, by definition, will remain unchanged over time. Therefore, the population of deaths associated with the stationary population provides the expected number of deaths associated with the population.

Secondly, since death which is unavoidable is beyond the control of humanity and, therefore, the age at which an unavoidable death occurs has no welfare implication. Therefore, avoidable and unavoidable deaths should be distinguished in the construction of the age-at-death measure. This can be achieved by making use of the mortality profile constructed for the reference countries. The reference country's mortality profile is used here as a benchmark to measure natural mortality risks. Since natural mortality risks are, by assumption, invariant across countries, we can compute the number of avoidable deaths for each age and gender groups. The difference between the number of deaths and the number of unavoidable deaths is therefore equal to the number of avoidable deaths. This procedure is formalized in the following.

The number of deaths of age and gender in a stationary population k, $d_{xk}^g = m_{xk}^g q_{xk}^g$, is observable, where m_{xk}^g is the stationary population size of the age group and q_{xk}^g is its conditional probability of dying. Suppose the number of unavoidable deaths for the group is equal to u_{xk}^g. This number is not directly observable but can be imputed from $u_{xk}^g = m_{xk}^g \tilde{q}_x^g$, where $\tilde{q}_x^g$ is the conditional probability of dying for the same age-gender group in the reference country, which is, by assumption, free of avoidable mortality risks.

Hence, we can express the number of avoidable deaths for the group, a^g_{xk}, as

$$\begin{aligned} a^g_{xk} &= \text{observed deaths–unavoidable deaths} \\ &= d^g_{xk} - u^g_{xk} \\ &= m^g_{xk}\, q^g_{xk} - m^g_{xk}\, \tilde{q}^g_x \\ &= m^g_{xk}\, q^g_{xk}(1 - \tilde{q}^g_x / q^g_{xk}) \\ &= d^g_{xk}(1 - \tilde{q}^g_x / q^g_{xk}) \end{aligned} \tag{7}$$

where $\tilde{q}^g_x / q^g_{xk}$ is the probability that an observed death is unavoidable. Therefore, the closer is q^g_{xk} to $\tilde{q}^g_x$, the larger is the number of unavoidable deaths for a given total number of deaths and, thus, the smaller is the number of avoidable deaths.

If the gender group in country has a smaller proportion of avoidable deaths in the total deaths, i.e. a^g_k / d^g_k, it indicates that the group has better socio-economic conditions that limit avoidable deaths. Therefore, a larger value of $(1 - a^g_k / d^g_k)$ is an indication of better wellbeing for the group. Furthermore, for those who die of avoidable causes, the higher their age-at-death, the better off they are. Therefore, a higher value of the average age-at-death of the avoidable deaths for the group, i.e. $x^g_k = \sum_x x(a^g_{xk} / a^g_k)$, is an indication of better well-being as well. These two can thus be combined to give a comprehensive measure of well-being.

Hence we define the modified average age-at-death (MAAD) for gender *g* in country *k* as

$$\begin{aligned} \textit{Modified } x^g_k &= y^g_k \\ &= (1 - a^g_k / d^g_k) x^g_k \\ &= (1 - a^g_k / d^g_k) \sum_x x(a^g_{xk} / a^g_k) \end{aligned} \tag{8}$$

For the country as a whole, MAAD is given by

$$\begin{aligned} \textit{Modified } x_k &= y_k \\ &= \sum_g y^g_k (d^g_k / d_k) \\ &= \sum_g 0.5\, y^g_k \end{aligned} \tag{9}$$

where $d^g_k / d_k = 0.5$ because the total number of deaths for both genders are fixed at 100,000 for the stationary population.

By applying to both genders, we can obtain two gender-specific MAAD measures. These two measures are commensurable because the natural differences in mortality risks between genders have been accounted for using the reference country's mortality profile as a benchmark. As a result, the ratio of these two measures, i.e. y_k^m / y_k^f, can be used as an indicator of gender bias. If $y_k^m / y_k^f > 1$, there is gender bias against females, and vice versa.

Moreover, if we have mortality profiles of individual races, we can also apply equation to each of the racial populations, and use the resulting estimates to measure inequalities between races. Mortality gaps between races and between genders have been considered important as they potentially reflect class inequality, health care disparity, and discrimination (e.g. see Cooper 2002; Nazroo 1998). In this aspect, previous studies show that income alone fails to reveal inequality between different races or ethnic groups. In particular, the New Zealand Census-Mortality Study (NZCMS)[3] shows that, for those who were 25 to 77 year old during the 1990s, the death rate of high income Maoris was 2.25 times that of high income non-Maoris,[4] and 1.5 times that of low income non-Maoris. Also there was substantial variation between males and females. The death rate of high income Maori females was 20 per cent higher than that of Maori males. These results clearly indicate that mortality can reveal "hidden" social discrimination that is not disclosed by income comparison. However, as discussed at length previously, direct comparisons of mortality rates between genders could be misleading due to differences in natural mortality risks. In this aspect, the method explained above provides a different tool from life expectancy to examine racial and gender inequalities using mortality data. As an illustration, we apply the methods to the life tables of Maoris and non-Maoris in the New Zealand, and Blacks and Whites in the United States. The life tables of Moaris and non-Maoris are obtained from the New Zealand Statistical Department for the year 2000-2002. The life tables for American Blacks and Whites for the year 2000 are obtained from the Centers for Disease Control and Prevention (CDC).

The results are summarized in Table 3. The Table shows estimates of MAAD for Maori and non-Maori males and females, and Black and White males and females, respectively. A number of findings are worth noting.

Firstly, in both countries there is significant racial inequality. In New Zealand, the MAAD of Maoris is less than half that of non-Maoris and this is true for both males and females. In the United States, the MAAD of Blacks is about two-thirds that of Whites, even though the value for females is somewhat higher than that of males.

Secondly, in comparing MAAD across two socially disadvantaged groups, viz., Maoris and Blacks, we can see that while Maoris males are not far behind Black males, Maori females are significantly worse off than their Black counterparts. This means that Maori female group is the most socially disadvantaged group amongst the eight race-gender groups.

Thirdly, non-Maoris fare substantially better than the Whites, especially for the males. The MAAD of non-Maori males is over 25 per cent higher than that of White males, while the MAAD of non-Maori females is over 15 per cent higher than that of their White counterparts. This means that non-Maori male group is the most socially advantaged group amongst the eight race-gender groups.

Table 3
MAAD for Maoris and non-Maoris, and Blacks and Whiles

Countries	*Race*	*Modified Average Age-at-Death*			
		Male	*Female*	*Both*	*Male/Female*
New Zealand	Maori	32.0	27.7	30.0	1.16
	Non-Maori	65.1	58.5	62.0	1.11
	Maori/Non-Maori	0.49	0.47	0.48	1.04
United States	Black	32.9	35.5	34.4	0.93
	White	51.9	50.0	51.5	1.04
	Black/White	0.63	0.71	0.67	0.89

Fourthly, in relative terms, gender bias is substantially smaller than racial bias. The figures in the first column on the left hand side of the table show the extent of gender bias across different race groups. In New Zealand, the MAAD of Maori males is about 15 per cent higher than their female counterparts, while that of non-Maori males is about 10 per cent higher than their female counterparts. In the United States, Black males have a MAAD which is 7 per cent lower than that of Black females, making it the only male group that is worse off than their female counterparts. For White males and females, the difference in MAAD is only about 4 per cent in favour of males.

Overall, we observe that social disadvantage is more prevalent along the racial dimension than along the gender dimension. Nevertheless, within each race, especially the minority, there is still a substantial gender bias, typically against females. These results imply that a female in a minority group normally faces double impediments in advancing their well-being.

Conclusion

Social discrimination can take place in many different dimensions, including access to education, access to health services, access to livable environment, nutrition, employment opportunity, work payment, protection against violence, freedom of speech, and right for political participation. Due to its multidimensional nature, quantifying social discrimination is a challenging issue confronted by all stakeholders who endeavor to identify socially disadvantaged groups, to prevent practices of social discrimination, and to eradicate social exclusion. Income or consumption, while useful, can only capture at most a few of the dimensions aforementioned. Morality is arguably the most comprehensive single measure of wellbeing. So it is not surprising that mortality has long been used in policymaking process for development. For instance, one of the United Nations' Millennium Development Goals is to reduce the mortality rate amongst children under five by two-thirds by 2015.

With the prominence of mortality statistics in policy setting, improvement in their measurement could have significant impact. In this chapter, we present a few of the latest developments in the use of mortality statistics for measuring wellbeing. We reviewed the data envelopment methodology on life tables to construct age and gender specific profiles of unavoidable morality risks. The constructed unavoidable morality risk profile allows us to separate avoidable and unavoidable mortality risks for each age, gender or even race group for individual countries. The separation of avoidable and unavoidable mortality risks has important implication to studies of social disadvantage. As biological factors give rise to natural differences in morality risks between people of different ages and genders, observed mortality rates of different age-gender group are not directly commensurable. Most importantly, the observed mortality gaps between different age-gender groups are not necessarily a good indicator of their socio-economic disparities. Hence the constructed unavoidable mortality risk profile provides a benchmark to control for natural mortality risk differentials between genders and between age groups.

As an illustration, we applied the concepts of avoidable and unavoidable morality risks to modify two mortality-based well-being measures: life expectancy at birth and age-at-death. The applications of the unavoidable mortality risk profile in the modification of these two measures are quite distinct, demonstrating the versatility of the concepts of avoidable and unavoidable mortality risks. The modified life expectancy measure successfully identified groups of countries in which either males or females are socially deprived. While the construction of the unavoidable mortality risks used national data, the concepts of avoidable and unavoidable mortality risks are applicable to sub-national populations. We used the modified age-at-death concept to measure inequality between Maoris and non-Maoris in New Zealand, and between Black and White populations in the United States. The modified average age-at-death measure successfully revealed the socially disadvantaged position of Maoris, especially the females. The results call for specific attention to the welfare of indigenous girls and women in a society, as they typically face discrimination not only in the wider community, but also in their own ethnic circle.

NOTES

1. The terms social disadvantage, social discrimination and social exclusion are used interchangeably in this chapter.
2. For a review of various health indicators, see Murray et al. (2002), Murray, Salomon & Mathers (2000) and Murray (1996).
3. For details of the study and associated publications, go to http://www.wnmeds.ac.nz/academic/dph/research/HIRP/nzcms/index.html.
4. Pacific people were excluded from the non-Maoris group. But Asian and Europeans were included.

REFERENCES

Arnst, C 2005, 'Biotech, Finally', *Business Week*, June 13 2005.

Braveman, P., Krieger, N. and Lynch, J. (2000), 'Health Inequalities and Social Inequalities in Health. Feedback', *Bulletin of World Health Organization*, Vol. 78, No. 2, pp. 232-3.

CDC (1986), 'Premature Mortality in the United States: Public Health Issues in the Use of Years of Potential Life Lost', *MMWR Supplements*, Vol. 35, No. 2S, pp. 1s-11s.

Cooper, H. (2002), 'Investigating Socio-economic Explanations for Gender and Ethnic Inequalities in Health', *Social Science & Medicine*, Vol. 54, No. 5, pp. 693-706.

Hicks, N. and Steeten, P. (1979), 'Indicators of Development: the Search for a basic Needs Yardstick', *World Development*, Vol. 7, No. 6, pp. 567-80.

Le Grand, J. (1987), 'Inequality in Health: Some International Comparisons', *European Economic Review*, Vol. 31, No. 1, pp. 182-91.

—— (1989), 'An International Comparison of Distributions of Ages-at-death', in J. Fox (ed.), *Health Inequalities in European Countries*, Gower, Aldershort, pp. 75-91.

Moriguchi, E.H., Moriguchi, Y. and Yamori, Y. (2004), 'Impact of Diet on the Cardiovascular Risk Profile of Japanese Immigrants Living in Brazil: Contributions of World Health Organization Cardiac and Monalisa Studies', *Clincial and Experimental Pharmacology and Physiology*, Vol. 31, pp. S5-S7.

Murray, C.J.L. (1996), 'Rethinking DALYs', in C.J.L. Murray & A.D. Lopez (eds.), *The Global Burden of Disease*, Harvard University Press, Cambridge, Mass. Vol. 1, pp. 1-98.

Murray, C.J.L., Salomon, J.A. and Mathers, C. (2000), 'A Critical Examination of Summary Measures of Population Health', *Bulletin of World Health Organization*, Vol. 78, No. 8, pp. 981-94.

Murray, C.J.L., Salomon, J.A., Mathers, C.D., et al. (eds.) (2002), *Summary Measures of Population Health*, World Health Organization, Geneva.

Nazroo, J.Y. (1998), 'Genetic, Cultural or Socio-economic Vulnerability? Explaining Ethnic Inequalities in Health', *Sociology of Health and Illness*, Vol. 20, No. 5, pp. 710-30.

Sen, A. (1995), *Mortality as an Indicator of Economic Success and Failure*, Innocenti Lectures, Istituto degli Innocenti, Florence.

Tabutin, D. and Willems, M. (1998), 'Differential Mortality by Sex from Birth to Adolescence: The Historical Experience of the West (1750-1930)', in *Too Young to Die: Genes or Gender?*, United Nations, Dept. of Economic and Social Affairs, Population Division, New York.

Tang, K.K., Chin, J.T.C. and Rao, D.S.P. (2006), 'Avoidable Mortality Risks and Measurement of Wellbeing and Inequality', *MRG Working Paper #9, University of Queensland.*

World Health Organization (2002), *World Mortality in 2000: Life Tables for 191 Countries*, World Health Organization, Geneva.

9

POPULATION AGEING AND INTRA-HOUSEHOLD RESOURCE REDISTRIBUTION IN THE ASIAN-PACIFIC REGION

Elisabetta Magnani and Anu Rammohan

Introduction

The dramatic shift in age structure that many low and middle income countries in the Asian-Pacific region will experience over the next thirty years was set in motion by a decline in fertility levels and falling death rates in the early 1970s. These changes in the age structure and the consequent population ageing are affecting economic and social aspects of life, including financial security, employment, living arrangements, and health care. As fertility rates decline and life expectancy increases, countries across the developing world face the prospect of rapidly ageing populations, combined with lagging or non-existent social safety nets.

The debate on population ageing in developed countries has a long history and provides important comparisons for the current discussion in developing countries, where the immediacy of the ageing problem stems from the much faster pace of ageing. However, our understanding of ageing in a developing economy, in the absence of universal health care, and labour market opportunities for the elderly is limited. A lack of formal universal social security systems makes population ageing in less developed countries a major demographic issue of public, political and scientific concern. Not surprisingly, most governments of Asian countries are interested in preserving the family-oriented support system in some form. By doing so they hope to avoid the costs and problems associated with the extensive formal support measures common in the West. However, little is known about the issues surrounding the intra-household resource allocation that ageing involves.

While there is a large literature from developed countries on the effect of population ageing on the demand for health and pensions, few studies from developing countries have examined the link between ageing, health and labour supply decisions by the elderly and the younger household members. Also, the literature has often overlooked the manner in which population ageing in low and middle income countries stresses the traditional coping mechanisms available to the elderly, primarily in the form of household female resources.

The historical changes in the demographic characteristics of countries may be interpreted as a transition from a regime of high birth and death rates to one where they are both low. The *Demographic Transition Theory* (Notestein, 1948, 1953; Thompson, 1929), describes three stages of a socio-economic transition that countries go through during the course of development. Stage I is characterised by high death rates, and only those societies with high birth rates survive. Population growth rates are low during this period due to high birth and death rates. In Stage II, there is a fall in mortality due to factors such as improvements in public health, better sanitation, control of diseases and so on. Since birth rates are high relative to death rates there is an increase in population growth rates. In the final stage, population growth rates fall as birth rates eventually decline to levels close to death rates. A longer pattern of historical change reveals that while the transition to lower fertility and mortality is already complete in Western Europe, North America, New Zealand, Australia and East Asia, this is not the case in Indonesia.

Furthermore, the risk environment in developing countries is very different from developed countries, both due to a lack of well-functioning markets and also because of the high dependence on the agricultural sector, where variability in income is high. Finally, the challenge of population ageing is further compounded by the absence of a universal health care system. This is further exacerbated during periods of economic and financial distress. This has led to a greater reliance on informal sources of old-age support.

In this article, we review the demographic trends in population ageing and the support mechanisms available to the elderly by focusing on the South-East Asian region, and Indonesia in particular. Indonesia is a particularly interesting economy to study these issues for numerous reasons. First, population censuses since the early 1970s show rising education levels, delayed marriage and increasing workforce participation among Indonesian women, particularly in Java and Bali. Second, family relationships in Indonesia, while still modelled by a strong patriarchal principle and, at times, by an upsurge of religious extremism, are changing considerably, due to the speed of economic growth as well as more subtle processes of cultural change (Hugo, 1996). Third, rapid population ageing has become a major demographic preoccupation in Indonesia in the twenty-first century.

The article is set out as follows. In the next section, we review the recent trends in population ageing in South-East Asia. In this section, we report macro data on the demographic trends that are occurring in South-East Asia. This is followed by a section where we examine various macroeconomic effects of ageing. In particular, this section will focus on population ageing in Indonesia and its effects on savings, debt and exposure to financial risk. We further analyse the relationship between ageing and economic growth. Population ageing however has implications not just for the domestic economy but also affects international migration. In the subsequent section, we discuss the interrelationship between population ageing and labour market response. The macroeconomic effects of population ageing, however, have been well-researched. Although the middle-income developing countries of Asia experienced rapid economic growth in the 1980s and 1990s, there was no attempt to establish a universal social safety net. This has resulted in family networks being seen as the principal source of old age security for the elderly. Despite high levels of labour force participation among the elderly, coresidence with adult children remains the principal source of income support for the elderly. Hence, in Section 5 we review these trends and present results from the large *Indonesian Family Life Survey* (IFLS3) conducted in 2000 and finally we conclude in Section 6.

Demographic Change in the Asia Pacific Region: A Review of Trends

It is important to put the issue of population ageing in low and middle income countries in context. Although countries in Europe, North America and East Asia have passed through Stage III of the demographic transition, with both fertility and mortality rates declining, the demographic transition currently happening in South-East Asia is particularly significant. This is because it is occurring at a faster pace and within a context of changes in national institutions and values, rapid social and economic development. Further, social safety nets in developing countries are far smaller than in developed economies. In 1996, the average expenditure on social insurance as a fraction of GDP in countries with below-median per capita income was 6.8 per cent; whereas the corresponding figure in above-median countries was 18.5 per cent (ILO, 2003). This is why the prospect of financing the health and retirement of large numbers of people is likely to impose a strain, both on public health resources, and on the household's financial resources and time. This issue is particulariy significant in the Indonesian context as only about 10% of all Indonesians (both workers and their spouses) have some form of pension coverage (ILO, 2003).

In Table 1 data are reported on the broad trends observed in elderly dependency ratio in Asia in 2005. In Asia, the largest decline in the population aged under 15 has been in East Asia, where in Japan, Hong Kong and Macau, the population aged below 15 represents barely 16 per cent of the population. In South Korea and China, the world's most populated country, the proportion of the population under 15 years is less than a quarter of the population. These figures are indicative of the falling fertility rates over the last two decades. They, however, raise important questions on the funding of the retirement needs of a rapidly ageing and longer living population.

All these Asian countries are experiencing falling fertility rates and longer life expectancies, however, the magnitude and intensity of these changes vary. For example, the elderly dependency ratio (as measured by the population aged 60 and above as a proportion of the working age population) is highest in East Asia. As Table 1 shows, the elderly dependency ratio in Japan, Korea, China and Hong Kong are well above those in the South-East and South Asian region. This is followed by countries in the South-East Asian region (Singapore and Thailand followed by Indonesia). Hence, although population ageing does not appear to be an urgent problem in Indonesia, increases in life expectancies combined with falling fertility levels and a lack of universal social safety nets dramatically compound this problem. Furthermore, income levels in these South East Asian countries are far below those in western countries at a similar stage in their demographic transition.

Table 1
Population Ageing in Asia

	Under 15	*Aged 60 years and above*		*Working age population*	*Elderly dependency ratio*
		Female	*Male*		
South Asia					
Bangladesh	35	6	5	54	0.20
Bhutan	38	7	7	48	0.29
India	32	9	7	52	0.31
Maldives	41	5	5	49	0.20
Myanmar	29	8	7	56	0.27
Nepal	39	6	5	50	0.22
Pakistan	38	6	6	50	0.24
Sri Lanka	24	12	10	54	0.41
South-East Asia					
Brunei Darussalam	30	4	5	61	0.15
Cambodia	37	7	4	52	0.21
Indonesia	28	9	8	55	0.31
Lao People's Democratic Republic	41	6	5	48	0.23
Malaysia	32	7	7	54	0.26
Philippines	35	7	6	52	0.25
Singapore	20	13	11	56	0.43
Thailand	24	11	10	55	0.38
Timor-Leste	41	5	5	49	0.20
Vietnam	30	8	7	55	0.27
East Asia					
China (1)	21	12	10	57	0.39
Hong Kong SAR	14	15	16	55	0.56
Macao SAR	16	11	10	63	0.33
Japan	14	29	24	33	1.61
Mongolia	30	6	5	59	0.19
Republic of Korea	19	16	12	53	0.53

Source: United Nations (2002)

In particular, Indonesia is experiencing rapid demographic changes with falling fertility rates, rise in life expectancy and a shrinking labour force. In Indonesia birth and death rates fluctuated considerably until the mid-1970s. From 1975 however, there has been a significant decline in both birth and death rates. The large decline in total fertility rates over the period 1972-77, also coincides with a period during which per capita GDP increased. A study by Gertler and Molyneaux (1994) finds that 75 per cent of the fertility decline between 1982-1987, is attributable to an increase in contraceptive use, induced primarily through economic development, improved education and economic opportunities for women.

Over the last two decades, the average number of children born per woman has declined from 4.1 in 1980 to 2.5 in 2000. At the same time, life expectancy has increased from 56 to 67 years (UNDP, 2005). It is expected that the rapid ageing of the population will induce a drop in the overall number of labour force participants. Moreover, the Indonesian population aged 65 years and older is expected to rise dramatically over the next few decades, from 9.3 million in 2000 to 46.9 million in 2050, representing about 20% of the Indonesian population (Edwards, 2003).

However, the issue of population ageing is compounded by poverty among the aged. According to figures from the Asian Development Bank, approximately 16.5 per cent of the elderly aged 65 and older are living below the poverty line of which 9.5 per cent are considered to be chronically poor and 7 per cent are transient poor (ADB, 2004; Arifianto, 2005). Inadequate earnings and savings and a lack of pension coverage makes them particularly vulnerable to poverty.

Macroeconomic Effects of Population Ageing

As outlined in the previous section, the Asia Pacific region is demographically extremely diverse (Hull, 1997). This underlying diversity produces a sizeable range of variation in both fertility and mortality rates as well as in the fraction of the population above 60 and in the dependency ratios. For example, already in 1995, Indonesia showed low to moderate mortality and low to moderate fertility, indicating that it is approaching the third phase of the demographic transition, while many other countries in the region still experience moderate to high fertility rates and low mortality rates. However, it is well-accepted that no Asian country will avoid a substantial ageing of its population sometime during the twenty-first century. In fact, there are good reasons to expect that the demographic composition of Asia Pacific countries, particularly in South-East Asia, will closely resemble in 2150 the Japanese demographic structure in 2000. For most countries in the region, demographers expect an almost inevitable decline in the size of the population, which is already observed in Japan. These trends are clearly marked in the case of Indonesia as the following table illustrates.

Table 2
Demographic Trends in Indonesia: 1950-2050

	1950	*1975*	*2000*	*2025*	*2050*
Proportion of older people (60+)	6.2	5.3	7.6	12.8	22.4
Proportion of young people (0-14)	39.2	41.4	30.8	23.0	19.9
Proportion of working age population (15-59)	54.6	53.3	61.6	64.2	57.7
Total dependency ratio	75.8	80.6	55.2	45.7	57.1
Old age dependency ratio	6.9	5.9	7.5	12.2	25.8
Median age	20.0	19.1	24.6	33.0	38.0
Life expectancy (years) at birth	37.5	52.7	67.3	73.9	77.4

Source: United Nations, "World Population Ageing 1950-2050", Population Division, Department of Economics and Social Affairs (2002)

The literature has often considered the impact of population ageing on the total dependency ratio, which is defined as the population aged 0-14 plus the population aged 65 and over divided by the population aged 15-64. In most cases in the Asia Pacific region we observe a V-shaped transition in the total dependency ratio: when fertility decline starts the size of the population aged 0-14 drops, but the elderly dependency ratio, the population aged 65 and plus divided by the population aged 15-64 will start to increase 40-50 years later. Not surprisingly population ageing can be seen as the counterpart of the "population bonus" that countries such as Japan for example observed with the fall in fertility between 1950 and 1990.

The Macroeconomic Consequences of the Demographic Transition

The trends discussed above are likely to affect significantly the macroeconomics of many countries in the region. In Table 3, we report 3-year averages for saving rates, investments, GDP growth as well as major fiscal indicators of the Indonesian public finance.

Table 3
Indonesia major Economic Indicators: 3-years Averages 2000-02

Labour force participation (65+)	*Domestic savings/ GDP*	*Investment/ GDP*	*GDP growth rate*	*Fiscal deficit/ GDP*	*Public expenditure on Health/GDP*
39.8[(a)]	24.3	16.3	4.4	1.1	0.7

Source: International Monetary Fund "World Development Indicators", World Economic Outlook, 2004.

By significantly affecting the size and the age composition of the population, ageing will lead to important changes in labour force participation, in productivity and economic growth. It will be a significant factor underlying the decline in household savings. The demographic shift is also likely to have a sizeable impact on the government budget position by affecting expenses such as health and pensions. It is these likely macro aspects of the demographic transition that this section aims to illustrate.

Ageing, Private Savings and Public Savings

An increasing total dependency ratio will rapidly produce a drop in the household saving rates. This has been emphasized by a number of studies that rely on a variety of models for their prediction including the life-cycle model (Kelley and Schmidt, 1996) and an open economy Ramsey model (Guest and McDonald, 1999; Guest and McDonald, 2004). The life cycle model would emphasize the inter-generational differences in saving rates, high and positive for the working age group, low and even negative for the older group. The Ramsey model in general emphasizes the negative impact of a low support ratio, the ratio of employment to total population, on productivity. In general, a low support ratio (a high dependency ratio) reduces the "first demographic dividend" (Bloom *et al.*, 2002) as it reduces the ability of the working age group to generate extra wealth that can be used to finance consumption in a later phase of life.

Inter-temporal optimization models such as the one explored in Guest and McDonald (2004) emphasize a general rule prescribing *optimal* saving rates in the face of population ageing: savings fall in anticipation of decreasing dependency ratios and rise in anticipation of high dependency ratios. This prepares a country for the subsequent periods of low support ratios, during which the optimal rate of savings falls. The "second demographic dividend" arises to the extent that consumers and policy makers are forward-looking and respond effectively to the demographic changes that are coming. Mason (2005) and Guest and McDonald (2004) among others, point out that consumption in the future can be maintained only through accumulation of wealth in the present to allow for productivity enhancing capital deepening technological change that is able to boost growth in output per worker. Such wealth can take different forms of course. One possibility is that the old rely on transfers from public pension schemes and welfare programs. Otherwise they can rely on transfers from children and extended family. Another possibility is that individuals accumulate capital during their working life and they support themselves during retirement years. Although Mason (2005) provides productivity projections for a small number of countries only, it is expected that in the period (2000-2050) the productivity effect in Japan will drop to only 0.2 per cent per year.

It is then clear that an increase in the old-age dependency ratio substantially affects fiscal policy decisions. Government expenses in crucial budget components such as medical insurance benefits and public pension schemes will rapidly increase. The other dimensions of the government budgetary situation, namely tax revenues, are also likely to be affected by the demographic change. In fact, the drop in the working age population is likely to reduce the tax base of the future by potentially reducing the average productivity levels of those still working (Guest and McDonald, 2004). Many Asian countries are currently experiencing large (and chronic) fiscal imbalances. Table 3 illustrates that Indonesia in not an exception. However, it is important to put the Indonesian case in perspective. For example, a comparison of the government budget positions in a group of Asian countries illustrates that the Indonesian fiscal deficit over GDP of 1.1 per cent is a more solid fiscal situation than the 9.7 per cent of India, or the 5.4 per cent of Thailand or even the 4.0 per cent of the Philippines (Mohan, 2004).

Overall national savings are affected by their two components, namely private savings and public savings. Predictions of the effect of population ageing on national savings conclude that the weakened budgetary position of governments facing demographic transitions such as the Indonesian one will in general be unable to contrast the drop in private savings. Thus, for example, Chun (2005) evaluates the effects of population ageing on Korean national savings. Using a life-cycle model, he finds that the combination of low private savings and the government budgetary imbalance will substantially reduce national savings. The ultimate effect of the demographic shift on the current account will depend on the sign and size of the change in domestic investment relative to the decline in savings.

Demographic Shift and its Impact on Private Investments, Foreign Debt and Exposure to Financial Risk

Less known and certainly more overlooked is the impact of the demographic transition on investments despite the well acknowledged fact that investments are likely to endogenously respond to changes in economic fundamentals. There are various channels though which population changes can affect investment, primarily the size and skill of the labour force and the potentially resulting skill shortage. These factors can play together determining a rather complex response of investments to the demographic shift.

It is worth commenting on the likely impact of population ageing on the interest rate and the wage rate as they are likely to impact on profitability and so on investments. A shrinking of the labour force may induce a rise in the wage rate. This combined with higher interest rate due to the drop in domestic savings may negatively affect investments as these factors reduce the perceived profitability of any investment plan. The potential labour shortage produced by the rapid ageing of the labour force can have an opposing effect on investment as it may induce labour saving technological change.

Obviously if the decline in savings outweighs the decline in investment or investments increase due to the demographic shift, a country will experience a large current account deficit. Although the effect of population ageing on the external balance is of great interest to policy maker, at this stage the existing simulations are unable to reach a consensus (e.g., Masson and Tryon, 1990; Williamson and Higgins, 2001). However, it is generally accepted that the decline in the national savings projected for many Asian countries, can produce sizeable levels of foreign debt. It is the short term component of foreign debt that is often argued to be a potential cause of currency crises. In the case of Indonesia, the economy that was so dramatically affected by the financial crisis of the late 1990s, there is a sound expectation that policy makers would look at such a risk with deep apprehension.

Pension Programs in Indonesia

Public pension programs in Indonesia are limited to employees in the public sector and in particular, the *Jamsostek* program for private sector workers in the formal sector and the *Taspen* program for current and retired civil servants and their families are the two largest programs (Arifianto, 2005). However, the rate of participation in the pension system continues to be very low, with less than a fifth of the work force and less than one-third of the formal sector. In 1995 approximately 12 million workers had access to formal pension plans, of which about 8 million are members of the mandatory Jamsostek program, which has a defined contribution plan with modest rates of contributions. The remaining four million are covered by a civil service program (Leechor, 1996).

However, due to its small amount of benefits and limited coverage, the Jamsostek scheme was unsuccessful in protecting many poor retirees during the 1997-98 economic crisis. According to Leechor's (1996) estimates, the total amount of pension received by a *Jamsostek* recipient at retirement is only valued at about 7% of their final basic salary after 35 years of active work. International Labour Office (ILO) figures show on average a Jamsostek pension only amounts to 5.5 months of their basic salary or 8.5 months of the current minimum wage (UMR) (ILO 2003: 90).

In recognition of these shortcomings, the Indonesian Government has responded by proposing a new social security scheme that intends to provide benefits to the entire Indonesian population. Arifianto (2005) argues that while it is too early to provide an assessment of the likely impact of this new social pension program on the elderly, there are several problems with it. In particular he argues that the program does not take into account the rapid ageing of Indonesians in the near future, which could put additional fiscal strain to the government, and ignores the potential for poor governance and management.

Ageing and Growth

The East Asia and Pacific region has a formidable record of economic achievement in the last half century as celebrated recently by Takatoshi Kato, Deputy Managing Director at the International Monetary Fund in 2004. Not surprisingly he cites ageing as one of the major trends that are likely to affect economic growth in East Asia over the medium term. Several studies have pointed out that a large fraction of the growth rates observed in East Asia in the last decades may well be due to the high savings and investments derived from the first stage of the demographic transition, the one dominated by the drop in fertility rates and the consequent drop in young age dependency ratios (Mason, 1988). Table 4 summarizes the Indonesian growth performance in the period 1990-95.

Table 4
Indonesia's Main Economic Growth Indicators

GDP per capita 1995 (US$)	*GPD per capita growth rate 1990-1995*	*Life expectancy at birth (in years) 1990-1995*	*Total fertility rate per woman 1990-1995*
2,495	6.12	62.6	2.9

Source: See Table 1 in Kannan Navaneetham (2002).

The previous discussion strongly suggests that there is a wide agreement on the fact that demographic shift will impact on savings. As the young becomes adults in working age and the larger cohort of adults ages, the rise in the old age dependency ratio will worsen the income growth opportunities. In other words, many Asian miracle economies will experience the necessary counterpart of the first demographic dividend, the "gift" of large GDP growth rates observed during the 1970s and 1980s. In the case of Indonesia the "window of opportunity" for economic growth starts around 1975 and ends in 2025 (Navaneetham, 2002). So, while it is perceived that Indonesia has great potential for improving its economic growth record for a few more years, it is also acknowledged that this opportunity will soon reduce. Navaneetham performs regression analysis on per capita GDP growth for a number of East Asian countries between 1960 and 1990 including Indonesia. He finds that the growth of total population has in the main a statistically insignificant impact on economic growth. It is interesting to note that this study along with other studies on the relationship between demographic shift and GDP growth, finds mixed results about the impact of the share of the population 65 and plus on economic growth (Bloom and Williamson, 1997). Shimasawa and Hosoyama, (2004) use an overlapping generation model calibrated to fit actual economic parameters of five large Asian economies. Their study reports a dramatic finding: according to them, population ageing's effects on savings, capital accumulation and public finances will lead to the end of Asia's high economic growth rates.

It is of course of concern that ageing is a widespread phenomenon in the Asian region as slower growth in the advanced economies of Japan, Korea and Hong Kong could mean weaker demand for exports from other countries in the region. The decline in the saving rates in these economies could also translate into more contained flows of investment capital into low and middle income countries in the region. It is not surprising that the focus on economists' attention in assessing the growth impact of population ageing is on the labour market response, particularly in terms of migration, labour supply and productivity.

Global Dimensions of the Demographic Shift: the Case of International Migration

One of the effects of the demographic shift is the shrinking of the population and the labour force, their rapid ageing and the dropping of the population growth rates. Already there is evidence that the population growth rate in Indonesia will go from 2.2 per cent in 1975-80 to 0.3 in 2045-50 (Mohan, 2004). However it is important to keep in mind that the ageing of the populations in the Asia-Pacific region occurs in a context of population ageing in other higher income countries. The global aspect of the demographic shift is often downplayed in favor of a more nation-centered analysis, but it is important to appreciate that the scale and intensity of the impact of ageing on savings, investments and economic growth are directly affected by the global dimension of these phenomena. This is particularly evident when we consider the impact of the demographic shift on international migration.

Table 5
Main East and South-East Asian Labour Exporting Countries: Percentage of Overseas Workers Deployed to Middle East and Asian Destinations, 1980–94

Country of origin and region of destination	*1980*	*1986*	*1990*	*1994*
Philippines				
Middle East	84	73	65	54
Asia	11	22	27	36
Indonesia				
Middle East	74	83	72	60
Asia	8	4	39	36
Thailand				
Middle East	97	87	43	10
Asia	3	12	47	89

Source: Hugo G., in "International Migration in the Asia-Pacific Region: Emerging Trends and Issues, page 85, in *International Migration Prospects and Policies in a Global Market* (2004).

International migration is a component of population growth. A simple flow approach to demographic change outlines that $r = n + m$, where r is the annual rate of growth of the population, n is the rate of natural increase, and m is the net migration rate. International migration is often cited as a possible solution to the booming fiscal burden caused by the demographic shift in mature economies. According to many, migration would alleviate the negative impact of population ageing by adding young workers to an aged workforce in wealthy countries and by generating continuous flows of remittances from migrant workers in low and middle income countries. For many countries in the Asia Pacific region that are undergoing rapid demographic transition, as fertility begins to fall the reliance on international migration inflows may increase (Zlotnik, 2004). For the major labour-exporting countries in the Asian region (Hugo, 1997)—Bangladesh, India, Indonesia, Pakistan, Philippines, Thailand—this may involve a dramatic change in international migration trends. The table below illustrates the percentage of overseas workers deployed to Middle East and Asian destinations by major labour exporting countries.

Table 6 shows the distribution of foreign workers in Taiwan, Indonesia and Malaysia by employment sector.

Table 6
Employment Sector of foreign workers in Taiwan and Malaysia and from Indonesia

Industrial sector	*Taiwan 1994*	*Indonesia 1989–94*	*Malaysia 1991*
Agriculture/Plantation(%)	0.8	22.5	45.8
Manufacturing	68.6	0.0	3.4
Construction	21.6	0.1	26.6
Social/Personal Services	8.9	60.7	19.1
Transport	0.0	13.9	0.0
Other	0.1	3.8	5.1
Total (*N*)	199,553	642,268	1,200,920

Source: Hugo (1995); Stahl and PECC-HRD Task Force (1996).

It is remarkable that a significant 60.7 per cent of foreign workers are employed in social and personal services in Indonesia, the industry that is rapidly growing under the pressures exercised by population ageing. In this respect the often celebrated ability of international migration to produce a win-win situation may underestimate the demand for young workers induced by the rapid ageing of the population in traditionally sending nations such as Indonesia.

Population Ageing and Labour Market Response

A large fraction of the economic growth that took place in the last fifty years in the Asian region can be attributed to the availability of a large young workforce (Bloom and Williamson, 1997). However, undoubtedly in the twenty-first century, the labour force will grow slowly and will continue to age. The case of Indonesia clarifies the situation many other countries in the region face.

Table 7
Indonesian Trends in Labour force Participation: 1950-2050

	1950	*1975*	*2000*	*2025*	*2050*
Proportion of working age population (15-59)	54.6	53.3	61.6	64.2	57.7
Labour force participation (65+)	58.2	47.0	39.8	35.2	30.8

Source: United Nations, "World Population Ageing 1950-2050", Population Division, Department of Economics and Social Affairs, 2002.

The first trend is towards a smaller proportion of the population in working age (15-59), which is consistent with the ageing of the large cohort of youth that supported Indonesian economic growth in the 1970s and 1980s. The second trend is towards lower labour force participation among the older group of the labour force, a trend that, although common to many other countries in both the rich world and in low and middle income groups, is mostly driven by the rapid ageing of this Indonesian population group. Table 8 outlines the workforce participations of male and female groups of individuals at different levels of ageing in Indonesia. Table 8 shows a general and rather expected trend in decreasing participation as age progresses for both males and females, although workforce participation of older females has increased over time.

Table 8
Indonesian Labour Force Participation Rates (%) by Sex and Age, 1971-95

	1971		*1980*		*1990*		*1995*	
	Males	*Females*	*Males*	*Females*	*Males*	*Females*	*Males*	*Females*
25-44	94.2	39.9	94.3	40.5	96.7	49.0	97.7	51.8
45-49	93.4	45.9	94.1	46.8	96.8	53.9	97.4	55.8
50-54	90.6	43.5	90.0	44.3	94.2	51.6	94.8	53.4
55-59	86.0	40.5	84.6	40.8	89.3	48.1	87.3	48.4
60-64	79.3	35.2	76.7	32.9	80.5	40.3	79.3	38.4
65+	62.9	24.5	53.4	19.0	59.3	23.5	56.5	30.7

Source: Hugo Graeme, (2000), table 16.8, page 311.

Thus although Indonesia shares with other Asian countries the unusually large participation rates among the elderly, the combination of these trends clearly points to the need to boost the ability of labour markets to absorb the working age population. Not surprisingly, female labour force participation is perceived as insufficient to cope with the effect of the demographic shift on the labour markets. In the years to come more policy attention will be devoted to individual choice in terms of labour force participation, employment and hours. It is worth then to shift to a more microeconomic focus to understand what the future might be.

Microeconomic Effects of Population Ageing Focus on Indonesia

Despite rapid economic growth in the 1980s and 1990s in Indonesia, much of the government spending on social services was on health and education, and families and communities were expected to provide the bulk of 'social insurance' (Sumarto et al., 2004). This family-oriented support system for the elderly has been actively encouraged by governments in many Asian countries (Chan, 1999; Knodel, 1999).

In the Indonesian context, although there was some subsidized health care and a compulsory social security program for formal sector employees, there was no formal universal safety net program until 1998. Furthermore, the focus of these programs was on the traditionally poor as well as the newly poor (Sumarto et al., 2004), but they did not specifically target the elderly.

Although the adverse macroeconomic effects of population ageing are well explored in the literature (Bloom et al., 2000), its consequences at the household level, is generally overlooked. A direct consequence of population ageing is its impact on the health care system. In developing country environments, due to a lack of universal social safety nets, the household typically acts as an informal source of old-age security (Cameron and Cobb-Clarke, 2006). Although physical support in the event of illness is generally provided by spouses of the elderly, the situation for women is somewhat more difficult. This is because while traditionally men tend to marry younger women, social support for men comes from their spouses. Women however, tend to rely more on the extended family system, and adult children in particular, as they are more likely to be widowed (Chang, 1992).

Family Support Systems for Elderly in Asia

Co-residence between older parents and at least one adult child is a central feature of the familial support system of developing countries, and in Asia in particular (Asis et al., 1995; Bongaarts and Zimmer 2001; DaVanzo and Chan 1994; Hermalin et al., 1996; Kim and Choe 1992; Knodel et al., 1999; Natividad and Cruz 1997). Furthermore, income from adult children remains a key source of support for elderly in the Philippines, Thailand, Taiwan and Singapore (Hermalin, 2000). Studies from China (Chen and Silverstein, 2000; Zimmer and Kwong, 2003), further show that the size of these benefits from children is considerable, with one-third to one-half of all elderly receiving some financial support from family members, mainly adult children.

However, researchers such as Hugo (1996) have raised concerns on this traditional reliance on family-based support systems at a time of rapid demographic and economic changes in the region. In particular, falling fertility levels, rising life expectancies combined with changing family structures and migration of adult children in search of economic opportunities is likely to impose a strain on this traditional means of old-age support for the elderly.

This *intra-household* intergenerational effect of population ageing however, remains a less researched issue. For example, Cameron and Cobb-Clarke (2006) point out that, despite the importance of research on intergenerational economic relationships, particularly in the context of a rapid ageing of the population in low and middle income countries, little is known about the nature of such relationships in developing economies (Cameron and Cobb-Clarke, 2006). Although the literature on intra-household resource allocation from Indonesia has examined the impact of unemployment shocks on household's health and education expenditure (Frankenberg et al., 1999), consumption smoothing due to illness (Gertler et al., 2001; Gertler and Gruber, 2002), they do not specifically focus on the elderly. Recent studies by Cameron and Cobb-Clarke (2006) and Cai et al., (2005), study old-age security and the role of intergenerational transfers in the absence of a public safety nets for Indonesia and China respectively.

In particular, several questions remain-what is the role of informal social security mechanisms such as the family and social networks in mitigating the negative effects of age-related functional decrements in elderly household members? What is the effect on the labour supply of household members (particularly women) due to the presence of elderly household members and changes in their health status? Does the household's reallocation of time and resources due to the presence of elderly impact upon the welfare of younger household members?

These issues are particularly important because female labour force participation in the formal labour force has increased substantially over the last two decades in most Asian countries. This type of engagement with the labour market may be incompatible with aged care. Population ageing at the household level therefore imposes greater constraints on the labour market participation of women who are traditionally the main carers of young and old dependents. Besides financial support, many of the elderly will also need help in their daily lives due to their frailty. Hence, future generations of working adults face a greater burden of support for their elderly parents.

Furthermore, deterioration in the health status of elderly members in the household could have adverse effects on female labour market participation, and the household's allocation of time and resources to other household members. Alternatively, older household members may provide informal child care, which facilitates greater female labour force participation. Studies from Taiwan and the Philippines show that grandparents often provide care for grandchildren (Natividad and Cruz, 1997; Hermalin, 2002), and in the case of the Philippines according to Natividad and Cruz's (1997) study, nearly 93 per cent of grandparents regularly care for their grandchildren.

However, this traditional relationship between the elderly and their adult children is likely to be affected due to the economic growth and the greater reliance on the urban sector to provide jobs. In particular, rural-urban migration by adult children is also likely to have implications for the availability of traditional support mechanisms for the elderly (Caldwell, 1982; Knodel et al, 2000). For example, Cruz and Obcena's (1991) study from the Philippines shows high levels of migration among females, which will reduce the availability of potential care-givers for the elderly. On the other hand, Giles and Mu (2005) find that in rural China, the ill health of elderly parents imposes restrictions on the likelihood of migration of younger adults. However, having other adult siblings who may be potential care-givers, reduces the impact on the probability of employment. They conclude that the availability of health insurance and pensions can improve the welfare of both the elderly and the adult children.

Under these circumstances and due to the widespread lack of comprehensive and universal formal retirement income maintenance schemes in the region, employment among older persons continues to be an important factor in financial security. Indeed, this is a pattern that is commonly observed in many developing countries (Ofstedal et al., 2003).

However, the interplay between development and demographic transition is challenging as development brings changes in the labour market that can differently affect the position of older persons (Magnani, 2006). For example, while employment in the informal and rural sectors makes employment and training opportunities for the elderly limited, technological improvements, better nutrition and other factors have weakened the traditional association between age and functional disabilities. Furthermore, as van Eeuwijk's (2002) study shows, one of the challenges facing the elderly in Indonesian cities is the greater uncertainty that they face both socially and economically. For example, kinship obligations are gradually breaking down, we similarly see uncertainty with regard to financial support and simultaneously, there has been an increase in communicable diseases due to changing socio-economic conditions. His study finds evidence of greater vulnerability, particularly among elderly unmarried women and childless widows.

This is a trend observed in Abikusno (2002) as well using Indonesian data, where older men are typically married, whereas older women are mostly divorced. Further while elderly men are generally heads of the household, elderly women are more likely to be spouses or parents in the household. These factors combined with the lower education levels among elderly women increases the likelihood of economic vulnerability in their old age.

The greater economic vulnerability of women relative to men is also supported in a study by CELADE (2002). They report that in the sample of Latin American countries (16 urban and 10 rural), for which data is available, with the exception of one country, older men were more likely to be recipients of pensions and other forms of retirement income. This probably reflects their greater labour force participation. However, interestingly in a study of 5 Asian countries, Chan et al (2002) find no gender differences in economic well-being with the exception of Vietnam. Below we describe data on socio-economic characteristics and living arrangements of the elderly drawing on a large cross sectional dataset from Indonesia.

Socioeconomic Characteristics and Living Arrangements of Indonesian Elderly

The Indonesia Family Life Survey (IFLS) is a continuing longitudinal socioeconomic survey, which contains a rich set of information on health, labour market behaviour, demographic and financial aspects. The IFLS3 conducted in 2000 is a random sample survey, covering thirteen provinces where 83 per cent of the population resides. However, it is broadly representative of the Indonesian population.

Table 9
Socio-economic Characteristics of Elderly in Indonesia: Sample Survey

	Total	*Age 18-59*	*Age 60-69*	*Age 70+*
N (Sample 3130)	23,335	20,391	1,820	1,124
Rural/urban				
Rural	0.4215	0.4077	0.5236	0.5587
Region				
Sumatra	0.2012	0.2009	0.1813	0.1993
Java (excl. Jakarta)	0.4974	0.4921	0.5599	0.5854
Jakarta	0.0926	0.0965	0.0698	0.0391
Bali	0.0478	0.0493	0.0440	0.0445
Other outer islands	0.1609	0.1613	0.1451	0.1317
Sex and marital status				
Female	0.5259	0.5258	0.5495	0.5116
Married	0.6473	0.7239	0.6709	0.5249
Separated/divorced	0.0255	0.0264	0.0440	0.0311
Widowed	0.0648	0.0327	0.2808	0.4395
Education				
Primary school	0.3899	0.4087	0.4418	0.3790
Junior high school	0.1645	0.1584	0.0654	0.0498
Senior high school	0.2359	0.2394	0.0593	0.0240
College	0.0792	0.0978	0.0203	0.0027
Labour market status				
Working	0.6667	0.7250	0.6192	0.4244
Normal hours per week	41.7720	42.8371	36.0053	32.2239
Normal weeks per year	40.4963	40.7669	42.7120	43.0771
Gross yearly net income (Rp. million)	5.9473	6.5140	3.5675	2.9060
Health status				
Very healthy	0.0777	0.0820	0.0335	0.0196
Somewhat healthy	0.7809	0.7914	0.7049	0.6584
Somewhat unhealthy	0.1254	0.1111	0.2456	0.2927
Very unhealthy	0.002	0.0011	0.0077	0.0116
ADL10	9.3597	9.5665	8.2366	6.7899
Household characteristics				
Household size	6.1247	6.1287	5.8764	5.3710
Household head age	47.5018	45.3411	61.4448	66.7866

Note: Fraction of a present proportion of the samples.
Source: IFLS- 3 (2000), authors' calculations

In Table 9, we present socio-economic characteristics for the elderly in Indonesia. In terms of geographical characteristics, as can be seen from this table, more than half the elderly population lives in rural areas, with Java having the largest proportion of elderly population. In terms of education, the elderly tend to be less educated than their younger cohorts. At all levels of education, we observe lower levels of educational attainment among the elderly in the 70+ age group than in any other age category. However, it is interesting that labour force participation among the elderly is reasonably high with nearly 43 per cent of the elderly aged 70 years and above reporting working up to 32 hours per week. This is consistent with the studies of both van Eeuwijk (2002) and Cameron and Cobb-Clarke (2006), where they report high levels of labour force participation among the elderly in Indonesia.

With regards to economic characteristics, not surprisingly the elderly tend to be poorer than their younger cohorts. For example, although the elderly aged 70 years and above, work approximately 9 fewer hours a week compared to working adults in the 18-59 age category, their yearly income is less than half that of the adults in the prime working age group. In terms of marital characteristics, just over 52 per cent of the oldest elderly (aged 70 and above) are currently married, this figure is substantially higher for those aged between 60 to 69 years. However, widowhood is also more common among the elderly aged over 70 with nearly 44 per cent being widowed, relative to 28 per cent in the 60-69 age group.

The oldest elderly are also much more likely to be disabled in not being able to perform the 10 'Activities of Daily Livings' (ADLs). The ADL is a count of the number of ADL activities that the respondent is limited to due to illness. Ten ADLs are included in the analysis and each of these carry an equal weight. They include the following daily activities: (i) to carry a heavy load for 20 meters; (ii) to walk for 5 kilometers; (iii) to walk for 1 kilometre; (iv) to bow, squat, kneel; (v) to sweep the house floor yard; (vi) to draw a pail of water from a well; (vii) to stand up from sitting on the floor without help; (viii) to stand up from sitting position in a chair without help; (ix) to go to the bathroom without help; (x) to dress without help. For each activity an indicator variable takes on a value of 1 if the individual can perform the activity without difficulty and zero if the individual cannot perform it. ADL is the sum of all the positive indicator variables. From Table 9 we find that elderly respondents were able to perform less than 7 of these ADLS without difficulty. This is consistent with an increase in functional disabilities that ageing brings about.

From Table 10, we observe that there are approximately 1 per cent more females than males aged 60 and above, and this trend of having more females relative to males persists in all age-groups over the ages of 40. Further, it is interesting that although currently the Indonesian population is relatively young with approximately 60 per cent of the population aged under 39 years, the working age population aged between 20-59 years represents approximately half the population.

Of the 2944 older Indonesians in our data set aged 60 and above, we observe that over three-quarters are either household heads or their spouses. Regarding the living arrangements of the elderly, Table 11 shows that around 11 per cent of the elderly lived alone (and another 15 per cent only with their spouses). However, co-residence with biological children and with other family members was the dominant living arrangement among the elderly. These figures are indicative of the strong role played by family members and children in particular in providing old-age security for the elderly.

Table 10
Indonesian Population by Age and Sex: Sample Survey

	Full sample N = *49217*	*Males* N = *24044*	*Females* N = *25173*
Age category	% of total	% of males	% of females
0-9	18.87	19.69	18.09
10-19	21.19	21.26	21.12
20-29	21.46	21.35	21.56
30-39	14.04	14.22	13.87
40-49	9.92	9.91	9.92
50-59	6.38	6.18	6.58
60+	8.15	7.40	8.86
60-69	4.61	4.20	5.01
70-79	2.52	2.32	2.70
80+	1.02	0.088	1.16

Source: IFLS 2000, authors' calculations.

Table 11
Living Arrangements of Elderly Aged 60 and above: Indonesian Sample

N	*2,944*
	%
Is the household head	60
Is the spouse of household head	19
Living alone	11
Living with spouse only	15
Living with spouse and other	26
Living with no spouse and other	48
Living with biological children	37

Source: IFLS 2000, authors' calculations.

Conclusion

In this article, we reviewed the demographic ageing happening in South-East Asian region and in Indonesia in particular. All the countries in Asia are faced with major demographic changes such as falling fertility rates, longer life expectancies and an absence of a universal social safety net. However, the intensity of these changes varies in different countries. The demographic transition occurring in this region is going to have a profound impact both because of the speed at which it is occurring and also because it is happening in a background of lower relative incomes and a greater reliance on family-based support networks.

However, although macroeconomic aspects of the demographic transition in Asia are well-researched, there is limited research on intra-household resource allocation and in particular the strain imposed on coresident household members due to population ageing and the resultant demand for care.

Indonesia is not yet facing the same crisis of an ageing population as some of the East Asian countries, such as Japan, face. However, there are several issues that are of immediate concern. In particular, Indonesian elderly do not have the same access to universal social safety nets that the elderly in rich countries have. The two large pension programs in Indonesia are restricted to private workers in the formal sector and civil servants. Further, the low benefits form these programs, along with their restricted coverage implies that the elderly in Indonesia rely on their own labour income or on family networks for old-age security. However, falling fertility rates, increasing life expectancy and an increase in the labour force participation of females is likely to put a strain on these traditional means of old age support.

REFERENCES

Arifianto, A. (2005), "Social Security Reform in Indonesia: A Critical Analysis", mimeo, SMERU.

Asian Development Bank (2004), *Inception Report for the Indonesian Sustainable Social Protection Project*, Jakarta.

Asis, M., Milagros B., Lita D., John K. and Kalyani M. (1995), "Living Arrangements in four Asian Countries: A Comparative Perspective", *Journal of Cross-Cultural Gerontology*, Vol. 10, pp. 145–162.

Bloom, D.E. and Williamson J.G. (1997), "Demographic Transition and Economic Miracles in Emerging Asia", NBER Working paper #6268.

Bloom, D.E., Canning D. and Malaney P. (2000), "Population Dynamics and Economic Growth in Asia", In Chu, C.Y.C. and Lee, R. (ed.), "Population and Economic Change in Asia", *Population and Development Review*, Supplement to Vol. 26, pp. 257-290.

Bloom, D.E., Canning, D. and Sevilla, J. (2002), *The Demographic Dividend: A New Perspective on the Economic Consequences of Population Change*, Santa Monica, Ca: Rand Corporation.

Bongaarts, J. and Zachary, Z. (2001), "Living Arrangements of Older Adults in the Developing World: An analysis of DHS Household Surveys," Policy Research Division Working Paper No. 148, New York: Population Council.

Cai F., Giles, J. and Xin M. (2005), "How Well Do Children Insure Parents Against Low Retirement Income? An Analysis Using Survey Data from Urban China", mimeo.

Cameron, L. and Cobb-Clarke, D. (2006), "Do Coresidency with Financial Transfers From Children Reduce the Need for elderly Parents to Work in Developing Countries?", forthcoming *Journal of Population Economics.*

Centro Latinamericano y Caribeno de Demografia (CELADE), (2002), "Los Adultos Mayores en America Latina y El caribe: Datos e Indicadores", Santiago de Chile: CELADE.

Chan, A. (1999), "The Social and Economic Consequences of Ageing in Asia: An Introduction", *Southeast Asian Journal of Social Sciences*, Vol. 27, issue 2, pp. 1-8.

Chang, T.P. (1992), "Implications of Changing Family Structures on Old-Age Support in the ESCAP Regions", *Asia-Pacific Population Journal*, Vol. 7, Issue 2, pp. 49-66.

Chen, X. and Silverstein, M. (2000), "Intergenerational Social Support and the Psychological Well-Being of Older Parents in China", *Research on Aging*, Vol. 22, issue 1. pp. 43-65.

Chun, Y.J. (2005), "Population Aging, Fiscal Policies, and National Saving: Prediction for Korean Economy", Department of Economics, University of Incheon.

Cruz, T. and Angelito, O. (1991), "Future Directions for Ageing Policy in Philippines", In "Population Ageing in Asia", Asian Population Studies Series No. 108 (Bangkok, ESCAP), pp. 54-60.

DaVanzo, J. and Angelique C. (1994), "Living Arrangements of Older Malaysians: Who co-resides with their Adult Children?" *Demography*, Vol. 31, Issue 1, pp. 95–113.

Edwards, C. (2003), "Asia's Population over the Next 50 Years: Implications for Business and Government", Paper presented at the Center for Strategic and International Studies Seminar, Jakarta, Indonesia.

Ettner, S. (1996), "The Opportunity Cost of Elder Care", *Journal of Human Resources*, Vol. 31, Issue 1, pp. 189-205.

Ettner, S. (1995), "The Impact of Parent Care on Female Labor Supply Decisions", *Demography*, Vol. 32, Issue 1, pp. 63-80.

Frankenberg, E., Beegle, K., Thomas, D. and Suriastini, W. (1999), "Health, Education, and the Economic Crisis in Indonesia", mimeo, RAND Corporation.

Giles, J, and Mu, R. (2005), "Elder Parent Health and the Migration Decision of Adult Children: Evidence from Rural China", mimeo, Department of Economics, Michigan State University.

Gertler, P.J. and Molyneaux, J.W. (1994), "How Economic Development and Family Planning Programs Combined to Reduce Indonesian Fertility", *Demography*, Vol. 31 Issue 1, pp. 33-63.

Gertler, P., Levine, D. and Moretti E. (2001), "Do Microfinance Programs Help Families Insure Consumption Against Illness?", mimeo, Department of Economics, UCLA.

Gertler, P. and Gruber, J. (2002), "Insuring Consumption Against Illness", *American Economic Review*, Vol. 92, pp. 51-70.

Guest, R.S. and McDonald, I.M. (1999), "An Evaluation of the Saving, Investment and Current Account Balances of Five ASEAN Countries", *Journal of Asian Economics*, Vol. 10, pp. 445-64.

Guest, R.S. and McDonald, I.M. (2004), "Demographic Transition and Optimal Saving in Four Asian Countries", *Economic Analysis and Policy*, Vol. 34, Issue 1, pp. 1-13.

Hermalin, A.I., Ofstedal, M.B. and Chang, M. (1996), "Types of Supports for the Aged and their Providers in Taiwan," In Hareven, T.K. (ed.) *Aging and Generational Relations Over the Life Course: A Historical and Cross-Cultural Perspective*, New York: Walter de Gruyter, pp. 400–437.

Hermalin, A. (ed.) (2002), *The Well-Being of the Elderly in Asia*, Ann Arbor: University of Michigan Press.

Hugo, G.(1992), "Ageing in Indonesia: A Neglected Area of Policy Concern". In Phillips DR. (ed.) *Ageing in East and South-East Asia*, London: Edward Arnold, pp. 207-230.

Hugo, G. (1995), "Labour Export from Indonesia: An Overview", ASEAN Economic Bulletin Vol. 12, Issue 2, pp. 275–98.

Hugo, G. (1996), "Over to the Next Century: Continuities and Discontinuities", *In Added Years of Life in Asia*, Asian Population Studies Series No. 141 (Bangkok, ESCAP), pp. 179-206.

Hugo G. (1997), "Migration and Mobilisation in Asia: An Overview", Paper prepared at the Conference on Asian Immigration and Racism in Canada, Institute of Asian Research, University of British Columbia, Canada.

Hugo, G. (2000), "Lansia—Elderly people in Indonesia at the turn of the Century" In Phillips, D.R. (ed.), *"Ageing in the Asia-Pacific Region: Issues, Policies, and Future Trends"*, Routledge, London.

Hugo, G. (2004), "International Migration in the Asia-Pacific Region: Emerging Trends and Issues", In Massey, D.S. and Taylor, J.E. (ed.) *International Migration Prospects and Policies in a Global Market*, Routledge, London. pp. 77-103.

Hull, T.H. (1997), "The Setting: Demographic Mosaic of the Asia Pacific Region–issues Defining the Future", *Asia Pacific Viewpoint*, Vol. 38, Issue 3, pp. 197-99.

International Labour Office (ILO) (2003), *Social Security and Coverage for All: Restructuring the Social Security Scheme in Indonesia–Issues and Options*, International Labor Organization, Jakarta.

International Monetary Fund (2004), "World Development Indicators", World Economic Outlook.

Kelley, A. and Schmidt, R.M. (1996), "Savings, Dependency and Development", *Journal of Population Economics*, Vol. 9, pp. 365-386.

Kim, I.K. and Choe., E.H. (1992), "Support Exchange Patterns of the Elderly in the Republic of Korea", *Asia-Pacific Population Journal*, Vol. 7, Issue 3, pp. 89–104.

Knodel, J. (1999), "The Demography of Asian Ageing: Past Accomplishments and Future Challenges", *Asia-Pacific Population Journal*, Vol. 14, Issue 4, pp. 39-56.

Knodel, J., Chanpen S. and Berit I. (1999), "Studying the living Arrangements of the Elderly: Lessons from a quasi-qualitative case study approach in Thailand," *Journal of Cross-Cultural Gerontology*, Vol. 14, Issue 3, pp. 197–220.

Leechor, C. (1996), "Key Options for Reforming Indonesia's Pension System", Policy Research Working Paper 1677, The World Bank.

Magnani, E. (2006), "Technological Change and Older Workers' Training", Paper presented at the 2005 JEPA-COE conference in Kobe, Japan.

Mason, A. (1988), "Savings, Economic Growth and Demographic Change", *Population and Development Review*, Vol. 14, pp. 113-144.

Masson, P.R. and Tryon, R.W. (1990), "Macroeconomic effects of Projected Population Ageing in Industrial Countries", International Monetary Fund Staff Papers, Vol. 37, No. 3, pp. 453-85.

Mohan R. (2004), "Fiscal Challenges of Population Ageing: The Asian Experience", Available online: http://www.kansascityfed.org/PUBLICAT/SYMPOS/2004/pdf/Mohan2004.pdf.

Natividad, J. and Cruz, G. (1997), "Patterns in Living Arrangements and Familial Support for the Elderly in the Philippines", *Asia-Pacific Population Journal*, Vol. 12, Issue 4, pp. 17-34.

Navaneetham K. (2002), "Age Structural Transition and Economic Growth: Evidence from South and South-East Asia", Asian MetaCentre Research Paper Series No. 7, Asian MetaCentre for Population and Sustainable Development Analysis.

Notestein, F. (1948), "Summary of the Demographic Background of Problems in Undeveloped Areas", *Milbank Memorial Fund Quarterly* Vol. 26.

Notestein, F. (1953), "Economic Problems of Population Change" In *Proceedings of the 8th International Conference of Agricultural Economists,* Oxford University Press, Oxford.

Nugroho, A. (2002), "Sociocultural Aspects of the Aged: A case study in Indonesia", *Asia Pacific Journal of Clinical Nutrition,* Vol. 11, Issue 3, pp. S348–S350.

Knodel, J. (1999), "The Demography of Asian Ageing: Past Accomplishments and Future Challenges", *Asia-Pacific Population Journal,* Vol. 14, Issue 4, pp. 39-56.

Ofstedal, M.B., Erin R. and John K. (2003), "Gender Differences in Economic Support and Well-being of Older Asians", Population Studies Center Research Report 03-350, Ann Arbor, University of Michigan.

Shimasawa M. and Hosoyama H. (2004), "Economic Implications of an Ageing Population: the case of five Asian Economies", mimeo.

Stahl, C.W. and PECC-HRD Task Force (1996), "International Labour Migration and the East Asian APEC/PECC Economies: Trends, Issues and Policies", Paper presented at PECC Human Resource Development Task Force Meeting, Brunei.

Sumarto, S., Suryahadi, A. and Winefrida, W. (2004), "Assessing the Impact of Indonesian Social Safety Net Programs on Household Welfare and Poverty Dynamics", Working paper, The SMERU Research Institute.

Thompson, W.S. (1929), "Population", *American Journal of Sociology,* Vol. 34, pp. 959-975.

Takatoshi K. (2004), "Can the East Asian Miracle Persist?", A Speech by The Deputy Managing Director of IMF, Available online: http://www.imf.org/external/np/speeches/2004/120204.htm

United Nations, (2002), "World Population Ageing 1950-2050", Population Division, Department of Economics and Social Affairs.

United Nations Development Programme (2005), *Human Development Report: International Cooperation at a Crossroads: Aid, Trade and Security in an Unequal World,* Oxford and New York: Oxford University Press.

Van Eeuwijk, P. (2002), "Ageing and Health in Urban Indonesia", *Urban Health and Development Bulletin,* Vol. 5, No. 3 and 4, pp. 25-31.

Williamson, J. and Higgins, M. (1996), "Asian Savings, Investments, and Foreign Capital Dependence: The Role of Demography", In Bloom, D. and Sachs, J. (ed.) *Emerging Asia,* Background Paper for the Asian Development Bank.

Williamson J.G. and Higgins, M. (2001), "The Accumulation and Demographic Connection in East Asia", In Mason, A (ed.) *Population Change and Economic Development in East Asia: Challenges Met, Opportunities Seized,* Stanford: Stanford University Press, pp. 123-54.

Zimmer, Z. and Kwong, J. (2003), "Family Size and Support of Older Adults in Urban and Rural China: Current Effects and Future Implications", *Demography,* Vol. 40, Issue 1, pp. 23-44.

Zlotnik H. (2004), "Population Growth and International Migration" In Massey, D.S. and Taylor, J.E. (ed.) *International Migration Prospects and Policies in a Global Market,* Oxford University Press, New York, pp. 15-34.

10

POVERTY ALLEVIATION THROUGH ACCESS TO EDUCATION: CAN E-LEARNING DELIVER?

Habibullah Khan and Jeremy B. Williams

Introduction

Education to alleviate poverty

Despite the inherent difficulties in quantifying the real contribution of education to Gross Domestic Product (GDP) or other national income aggregates, it has always been considered a powerful instrument for reducing poverty and inequality through productivity enhancement which is, of course, a key ingredient for the maintenance of economic growth. The relationship between education and poverty is quite clear; educated people have higher earning potential and are better able to improve the quality of their lives, which means they are less likely to be marginalised within society at large. Education empowers a person and it helps them to become more proactive, gain control over their lives, and to broaden the range of available options (UNESCO 1997). Education is recognised as a basic human right and it is closely linked to virtually all dimensions of development-economic, social, and human. It is also a key factor in improving the quality of governance that has a significant impact on national income.

Since women and children are more likely to be poor and malnourished and less likely to receive medical services, clean water, sanitation, and other benefits, education for women has been particularly emphasised for reducing overall poverty. Expanding girls' education, for example, has a positive effect on fertility, infant mortality, nutrition, and enrolment rates of the next generation. Keeping children in school, meanwhile, is a well-recognised strategy for reducing child labour. Educating this section of the populace means they have easier access to important information about disease (for example, HIV/AIDS) prevention and other public health issues. An educated woman is capable of taking better care of the children and has easier access to formal sector employment, social security and other benefits. It is no surprise, therefore that empowerment of women through the promotion of gender equality and eliminating gender disparities in primary and secondary education is a key to poverty reduction; a message forcefully conveyed in the World Development Report 2000-01 (World Bank, 2001).

While the provision of basic education up to primary level is still considered vital for the reduction of poverty, there has been a slight change of emphasis of late in that it is now increasingly recognised that the second of the eight Millennium Development Goals (MDGs)—"universal primary education"—cannot be achieved without higher education. Until now, the conventional wisdom has been to highlight the role of higher education as a driver of economic growth in developed countries, but view it as a luxury good in developing countries. The new, emergent view is that-far from being a luxury-higher education is essential for poverty reduction; the argument resting on the complementary roles of primary, secondary, and tertiary education where the neglect of higher education means providing primary education without training teachers, without developing locally relevant curricula, and without equipping the principals and ministry of education officials with solid management and governance skills. Higher education provides fundamental expertise to all sectors of society and the economy and this is why it must be a part of any realistic poverty reduction strategy.

A recent report published by the United Nations Millennium Project Task Force (Juma and Lee, 2005), has emphasised that science, technology, and innovation have helped to lessen poverty and hunger and drive economic growth in much of South-East Asia. The report suggests that these same factors must be at the forefront, therefore, of all policies designed to achieve the MDGs. The report goes on to state that there is no way that the world can succeed in the eradication of poverty if the developing world is not a part of knowledge creation, its dissemination and its utilisation to promote innovation. Similar conclusions were drawn by the World Bank in its publication Constructing Knowledge Societies (World Bank, 2002b), and more recently, by Nobel Laureate, Jeffrey Sachs, in his much acclaimed book, The End of Poverty, (Sachs, 2005).

Education in the knowledge economy

The implication of this new train of thought for developing nations is that their focus has to be much more on the process of economic development. In the past, this has been less of an issue. For example, while development of productive capacity in an industrial economy requires relatively fixed factors of production, progression to knowledge economy status is not as straightforward. The contribution of human resource development is of critical importance, and as a number of contemporary researchers have observed (e.g Chen and Dahlman, 2004), it is not just a question of identifying the changes in the work that people do, the growth of the service sector, and the creation and use of new technologies. To bring about change one has to focus on the link between the aspirations and abilities of the workforce and the human resource requirements of the knowledge economy.

External forces are certainly playing their part, and globalisation has created intense competition between nations which, in turn, has spawned the widespread commercialisation of educational services (particularly in the developed world). Increasingly, knowledge is considered the engine of growth and countries are doing their best to increase the "value-add" from their investments in human capital. Significant changes have occurred in the labour market as a consequence, and larger numbers of workers are requiring higher levels of skills and training. Interestingly, there is a growing demand for continuing education (lifelong learning) in order to update knowledge and skills on a regular basis because of the short "shelf life" of knowledge.

Reflecting this change in the durability of knowledge, there has been something of a paradigm shift in the process of learning. Given the tremendous growth in its production and distribution, information is much more readily available. What this means is that the learning of facts has become less important. Of growing importance, on the other hand, is the ability to learn in an autonomous manner; the emphasis being placed on information-seeking, analysis, the ability to reason, and problem-solving rather than memorising specific information. Another trend is for learners to acquire several qualifications from multiple institutions in parallel or sequentially in order to raise their profiles in a highly competitive labour market.

E-Learning as a Vehicle for Extending Access to Education

It is useful to identify the factors with the potential to broaden the human capital base in a country by making its acquisition cheaper and easier. This is where e-learning makes a significant contribution. E-learning is typically web-based and not location-bound. In an online environment, students are not required to physically attend university; the university comes to them. Students thus save on time and travel costs. Also, the cost of online education is a fraction of traditional 'brick-and-mortar' education. A curriculum, once created, can be offered electronically, not just to hundreds of locally-based students, but to tens of thousands around the world. Although there is additional expenditure on IT infrastructure maintenance, training and technical support, the online mode of delivery might lead to as much as 60% cost savings compared to standard classroom training, as shown by some estimates (see Kejak and Ortmann, 2003, p. 3).

More importantly, e-learning eliminates the human capital 'bootstrapping problem' that arises in many developing countries (including the transitional ones). Since these countries lack educators with sufficient expertise, local teachers will have to learn the requisite skills before they can deliver education themselves and that is a time-consuming process. E-learning eliminates this problem by guaranteeing 'just-in-time' training of a superior quality that is literally (and metaphorically) at people's fingertips. Recent studies (World Bank, 2003b; Chen and Dahlman, 2004) therefore suggest that government spending on IT infrastructure is likely to improve the performance of the economy through the increase in access to e-learning.

These developments suggest that there needs to be a re-examination of what constitutes the 'optimal' level of education in developing countries. There are solid grounds now for arguing that it can be extended to post-secondary or even tertiary as both the social and private costs of education will diminish drastically vis-à-vis the benefits of education. Critically, of course, this assumes government policies ensure that coordination problems do not hinder the process of e-learning initiatives at various levels, private as well as public. Considering the inherent 'public good' characteristics of e-learning, governments need to create appropriate incentives for private investors so that they can recoup costs of creating knowledge and earn a fair rate of return.

The above factors weigh heavily in favour of widespread adoption of electronic modes of organisation and delivery of educational services. The fiscal crisis faced by many countries, the rise in the cost of higher education in industrialised countries, and the growing demand for higher education in the less developed world all make it necessary to find more cost-effective alternatives to face-to-face (F2F) education. Although the issue of the "digital divide" still remains a concern, the World Bank believes that widespread adoption of Information and Communication Technologies (ICTs) and e-learning have the potential to help meet the MDGs that includes the eradication of extreme poverty. Indeed, the Bank has, since 1998, overseen a distance learning program called "The Global Development Learning Network (GDLN)" which offers a number of knowledge services such as courses, seminars, training programs, and policy dialogues to client countries of the Bank. This initiative has been found to be more cost-effective than F2F methods without any reduction in the quality of learning outcomes and the Bank aims to expand the network in future.

While it may be clear from the foregoing discussion that e-learning has - in the macro sense - strong economic advantages including cost and flexibility and access which meet the needs of the developing world, the question still remains as to the form of e-learning that would be most appropriate for the developing world as part of a poverty-reduction strategy.

To examine this question, we concentrate more on outcomes than process, taking an economic rather than an educational approach. At the risk of being accused of economic determinism, our goal, simply, is to focus on education that is operative and relevant to a knowledge economy. This is not to dismiss knowledge for knowledge's sake, but to emphasise that when a country is burdened with grinding poverty, swift and effective action is required to produce the desired results in as short a time as possible. To participate in the knowledge economy one must have the means to create, acquire, and utilise knowledge whether it is through machines, organisations or the ways in which people think and act. If e-learning can be shaped to provide this means, then there is an opportunity for individuals and organisations to strengthen labour market responsiveness, to develop human capabilities through education and training more consistently, and to foster knowledge foresight, co-ordination and networking.

The remainder of this paper is organised as follows. A brief overview of the problem of poverty and its relationship with education is presented in the next section. Subsequent sections discuss the role of the ICT revolution in poverty alleviation, changes that globalisation has brought in terms of the educational needs of the labour force, a new education policy for poverty reduction that also incorporates best practices for e-learning, And a summary and conclusions are presented.

Education and Poverty Alleviation: What Economists Say?

The World Bank reports that of the world's six billion people, 2.8 billion (or nearly half of world population) live on less than US$2 a day, and 1.2 billion (or a fifth of world population) live on US$1 a day. The figure of US$1 per day is considered a poverty line for defining 'absolute' poverty and 44% of the absolute poor people live in South Asia. Although this is purely an income-based poverty concept, it provides an easy way of estimating the extent of poverty in a country, it is - on occasion-considered a too narrow and unsatisfactory definition from a policy perspective. The World Bank, for example, suggests that poverty includes powerlessness, voicelessness, vulnerability, and fear (World Bank, 2001), factors for which there are no readily available metrics. The Nobel Laureate, Amartya Sen, meanwhile, describes poverty using what he refers to as the "capability" approach which implies an absence of freedom to participate in economic life leading to a deprivation in the range of things people can do, and the knowledge and skills needed to act independently for productivity or personal welfare consumption (Sen, 1999). Other broad definitions of poverty include deprivations from political participation, education, and information needed to participate in the wider society at the local, national or global level. We have no argument with these definitions of poverty, and acknowledge that they will more accurately describe the impact of poverty in all its manifestations. Our position, simply, is that even if poverty is viewed in the narrow sense of insufficient income (be it US$1 or US$2 a day), it is still a pretty sound indicator of deprivation of the basic necessities of life (i.e. food, shelter, primary education, and minimum healthcare facilities).

Economists have-for a very long time-stressed that education has a significant role to play in poverty reduction in various ways. A positive link between an income-based poverty concept and education can be found in the process of economic growth. Education can directly reduce poverty through the contribution that productivity enhancement makes to economic growth, and indirectly in the way it helps to alleviate poverty though its positive spill-over effects (externalities) on society more broadly. Adam Smith, who is often referred to as the founding father of the economics discipline, strongly advocated that government actively support education, two-and-a-quarter-centuries ago, on the grounds that education makes people (that includes the labour force) more sophisticated and progressive, which he deemed essential for the smooth functioning of an economy:

> "The more they are instructed, the less liable they are to the delusions of enthusiasm and superstition, which, among ignorant nations, frequently occasion the most dreadful disorders. An instructed and intelligent people, besides, are always more decent and orderly than an ignorant and stupid one. They feel themselves, each individually, more respectable, and more likely to obtain respect of their lawful superiors, and they are, therefore, more disposed to respect those superiors. They are more disposed to examine, and more capable of seeing through, the interested complaints of faction and sedition, and they are, upon that account, less apt to be misled into any wanton or unnecessary opposition to the measures of government." (Smith, 1776, p. 309)

In more recent times, however, a theoretical debate has raged over the contribution of education to economic growth. There has been widespread agreement that investment in education by an individual will generate a solid return on that person's investment, but-in the macro sense there is no strict causal relationship. In short, there are plenty of examples of countries spending similar amounts on education but deliver disparate rates of economic growth.

The 'neoclassical' growth model propounded by Robert Solow in the mid-1950s (Solow, 1956; 1957), asserted that the influence of education and human capital can only be studied through their impact on technological progress, which was assumed to be 'exogenous' in the model. According to this theory it is argued that as technology improves, the efficiency and productivity of labour increases (or technology is 'labour augmenting'). Improvement in technology, meanwhile, can be seen in the mechanical sense (new machines or computers) or in terms of human capital (education and skills development).

Modern economists have attempted to explicitly demonstrate how education and human capital can expedite the process of growth in their 'growth models'. Robert Lucas, for example, in his 'endogenous' growth model used education as the critical variable that generates technical progress in an economy (Lucas, 1988). He shows that education and the creation of human capital are responsible for both the differences in labour productivity and the differences in overall levels of technology that can be observed from the real world data.

Mankiw, Romer, and Weil (1992) in their "augmented Solow model", explicitly introduced human capital (measured by enrolment levels for secondary education in each country) into the production function and found that such a model explains the observed economic growth much better than the simple two-sector Solow model. Meanwhile, in a study of sources of economic growth, Denison (1985) calculated that for the period 1929-82 over one-quarter of the average annual rate of increase of 1.48 per cent in US national output per employed person was due mainly to improvements in the level of education of the workforce (1985, p. 113). Many other empirical studies (see Sala-i-Martin, 1997) have tried to analyse the broad characteristics of economic growth. Although most of them confirm the expected positive relationship between education and economic growth, the statistical strength of the relationship is often relatively modest. This, it is believed, is mainly due to difficulties in accurately measuring the quantity and quality of education across a large number of countries.

These modest contributions to the research literature on the relationship between education and growth (and thereby poverty reduction) were given a boost in the mid-1990s, however, following the publication of the World Bank's East Asian Miracle report (World Bank, 1993). In this report, the spectacular economic success of East Asia during the 1970s and 1980s was attributed, in large part, to investment in education and human capital. This was most notable in the economies of Singapore, Hong Kong, the Republic of Korea, and Taiwan. The study found that improvement in primary education was a very powerful explanatory variable for East Asian economic growth, but the report also noted that:

> "In nearly all the rapidly growing East Asian economies, the growth and transformation of systems of education and training during the past three decades has been dramatic. The quantity of education children received increased at the same time that the quality of schooling, and of training in the home, markedly improved, Today, the cognitive skill levels of secondary school graduates in some East Asian economies are comparable to, or higher than, those of graduates in high-income economies." (World Bank, 1993, p. 43)

Krugman (1994) famously challenged the durability of the East Asian 'model' and, analysing the role of education in the context of the Solow model, he argued that education can at best help economic growth temporarily as human capital investment like any other physical capital investment in the model is subject to diminishing returns. The rapid economic growth, he said was more to do with 'perspiration' (use of more inputs) than 'inspiration' (innovations).

At the time of writing, Krugman was probably right. Our contention is that things are different in the knowledge economy. Investment in education (rather than plant and machinery, for example) becomes the more sensible option. Furthermore, as the World Bank noted in its Constructing Knowledge Societies report (World Bank, 2002), 'tertiary education is necessary for the creation, dissemination, and application of knowledge and for building technical and professional capacity' and, if nothing is done about this, "developing and transition countries are at risk of being further marginalised in a highly competitive world economy because their tertiary education systems are not adequately prepared to capitalise on the creation and use of knowledge" (p. 36).

The Changing Global Economy and the Implications for Education

Three interrelated factors have reshaped the global economy in recent years. First, there is 'globalisation'; the complex process of integration of capital, technology, and information across national boundaries that has led to intense competition between firms as well as countries in a global economy. Second, the character of economic development is changing such that countries are becoming increasingly dependent on their ability to acquire and apply new 'knowledge' (technical or otherwise)—a trend that is accelerating with globalisation. Finally, there is the phenomenal progress in science and technology that has produced a worldwide ICT revolution leading to a dramatic reduction in barriers to information access and communication among people, institutions, and countries.

Globalisation

Although globalisation is a historical process, it has gained new momentum in the past three decades. The end of the Cold War, the development needs of the transitional economies, financial and trade reforms in the developing countries, the ICT revolution, and rapid productivity growth in the global economy all played a key role in accelerating the pace of internationalisation. While some people see this evolution as a major source of opportunities for trade and investment, others fear the dangers of high interdependency and volatility such as the risk of transferring financial crises from one country to another country. But whether one likes it or not, globalisation is likely to stay and every individual, firm, country is likely to be affected by it.

So what are the implications of this rapidly changing global economy for education? As the forces of globalisation become stronger, the need for education and human capital investment will likely rise even further, as efficiency is the most critical factor for economic success in the face of rising competition. Indeed, it is not just education per se but the quality of education that remains paramount if one is to get ahead in this competitive struggle.

The World Bank reports that globalisation has increased the returns to education in many countries, particularly at primary levels, enabling them to invest more in their children (World Bank, 2002a). The report claims that the "new globalisers" like China and India have had significant reductions in poverty in the past twenty years due to relatively stronger integration with the rest of the world. It also reveals that many developing countries representing as many as two billion people saw increasing poverty as they failed to integrate with the world, and cautions that these countries are likely to be 'marginalised' if appropriate measures are not taken. The report then proposes an "agenda for action" that includes creation of a strong investment climate and delivery of quality education and health services in order to reap the benefits of globalisation.

The Changing Character of Economic Development

The chances of marginalisation for poor countries are significantly enhanced by the fact that economic growth is becoming increasingly linked to a nation's ability to acquire and apply knowledge. Whereas once it was all about the transformation of raw materials drawing on a stock of cheap labour, in the knowledge economy it is about how information is created, acquired, transmitted, and used more effectively by individuals, enterprises, organisations, and communities to promote economic and social development (World Bank Institute, 2001). It is estimated, for example, that firms devote roughly one-third of their investment to knowledge-based intangibles such as training, research and development, patents, licensing, designing, and marketing. (Salmi, 2000, p. 4)

The advent of the knowledge economy will clearly transform the pattern of the demand for labour throughout the world, with quite profound implications for education and training. Where new technologies have been introduced, demand for high-skilled workers, particularly high-skilled ICT workers, has increased. At the same time, demand for low-skilled workers has declined and is likely to decline further. With a view to preparing workers for the knowledge economy, a new model of education is emerging; often referred to as 'lifelong learning'. Lifelong learning, as the name implies, is continuous learning throughout one's entire life, from childhood to retirement. According to a World Bank report (World Bank, 2003a), lifelong learning includes (1) formal education and training that is recognised by the national education system leading to approved certificates; (2) Non-formal education and training such as apprenticeships and on-the-job training, including structured programs that are not formally recognised by the national system; and (3) informal education and training that includes unstructured learning that can take place almost anywhere including home, community, or workplace.

The ICT Revolution

The 2005 UN Report entitled "Innovation: Applying Knowledge in Development" points out that science, technology, and innovation have helped to lessen poverty and hunger and drive economic growth in much of South-East Asia (Juma and Lee, 2005). It also says: "Today's economic circumstances make higher education a more compelling need in developing countries than it has ever been. Key factors in this change include increased demand for higher education due to improved access to schooling, pressing local and national concerns that require advanced knowledge to address, and a global economy that favours participants with high-technological expertise." (p. 89) The report adds that universities, polytechnics and vocational institutes in developing countries have immense potential to promote technological development by updating their curricula, training their faculty, and encouraging more women into science and engineering courses. The report receives strong endorsement from Jeffrey Sachs in the foreword and indeed he, himself, advocates the increased application of science and technology for poverty reduction in his recent book. He states that "a special effort of world science, led by global scientific research centres of governments, academia, and industry, must commit specifically to addressing the unmet challenges of the poor. Public funding, private philanthropies, and not-for-profit foundations will have to back these commitments, precisely because market forces alone will not suffice." (Sachs, 2005, p. 367)

A major scientific innovation that has helped the growth of knowledge economies are the ICTs that have revolutionised the capacity to store, transmit, access, and use information. Rapid progress in electronics, telecommunications, and satellite technology has resulted in the virtual abolition of physical distance by making communication and transmission of information markedly cheaper. For example, a World Bank paper (Salmi, 2000) claims that a phone call from New York to London that used to cost the equivalent of US$300 per minute in 1940, now costs around only 5 cents per minute. In 1985, the cost of sending 45 million bits of information per second over one kilometer of optical fiber was close to US$100 but in 1997, it was possible to send 45,000 million bits per second at a cost of just 0.05 cents. (Salmi 2000, p. 5)

Many other studies support such claims and demonstrate that the ICT revolution has, indeed, made significant positive contributions to economic growth by raising overall labour productivity (see Oliner and Sichel (2000) and Chen and Dahlman (2004), for example). It should not be altogether surprising, therefore, that the World Bank has become a strong advocate of the use of ICTs for poverty reduction, funding various ICT projects in developing countries that specifically target groups affected by poverty. (see World Bank, 2003b)

An important consequence of this information revolution is the diminished importance of traditional learning methods. The practice of learning facts and basic data is fast becoming obsolete. The learning process now needs to focus on the capacity to find, access, and apply knowledge to problem-solving. In this new paradigm, primacy is given to information literacy, analysis, and the ability to reason rather than to memorise specific information that quickly loses currency. Competencies such as creative thinking, the ability to work collaboratively in teams, and the capacity to adjust to change are the new skills in high demand. People are now required to learn in an autonomous manner at any age, and this they might do by enrolling on several programs simultaneously at institutions in different locations, at home, or while travelling. In short, education is no longer something that someone does for part of their life; it has become a way of life. The only non-negotiable in all of this is internet connectivity.

The Scope of E-learning

The electronic mode of organisation and delivery of educational services, commonly referred to as 'e-learning', has responded to the needs of today's labour market and its educational requirements. E-learning is internet-based and physical or geographical location are immaterial for the reception of such services. In an e-learning environment—which is largely asynchronous students are not required to attend an educational institution at a particular time; the institution comes to them. Students can learn anytime, anywhere and at their own pace, thus saving on time and travel costs. Also, the cost of online education is a fraction of traditional 'brick-and-mortar' education. For example, the cost of producing a graduate from the UK Open University is about one-third of that at a regular university (Salmi, 2000, p. 16). A curriculum, once created, can be offered electronically not just to a few hundred locally-based students but to tens of thousands of students around the world. Although there is additional expenditure on IT infrastructure maintenance, training and technical support, the online mode of instruction can generate substantial cost savings. UNESCO and the World Bank have reported that in the world's ten biggest distance education institutions the majority of which are in the less developed world—the cost of education per student is, on average, about one-third the cost at traditional institutions in the same country. (Harris, 2004, p. 22)

E-learning is highly appropriate for poverty groups and can help those who are usually deprived of education or other social services. It can provide education to populations in rural areas without schools, women facing social or cultural barriers that limit their access to educational institutions, socially disadvantaged groups that include minorities who are usually marginalised, and students with disabilities. It is estimated that nearly 80% of the world's disabled population of 500 million people lives in developing countries and their disability compounds the problems they face as poor citizens. The World Bank has funded various e-learning initiatives in developing countries (such as Turkey, Brazil, Afghanistan, Peru and Kenya) with a view to providing computer literacy to all teachers and students, influencing public opinion on gender equality, increasing economic opportunities for women, and enhancing women's ability to know their rights and participate in decision-making. (World Bank, 2003b)

Another area where e-learning can make a significant contribution is in teacher training. This has a direct bearing on worldwide poverty reduction as trained teachers are required for enhancing the quality of education and for meeting the MDG educational targets. A developing country can draw on teachers with superior knowledge from advanced countries rather than local teachers who first have to learn the requisite skills before they can train others. E-learning is thus capable of resolving the so-called 'bootstrapping' problem that makes it very unlikely that poor and transitional economies can catch up to be at the frontiers of knowledge (Kejak and Ortmann 2003).

Although the problem of the 'digital divide' still concerns many, the World Bank believes that "the debate in the 1990s over choosing between ICT and other development imperatives has now shifted from one of tradeoffs to one of complementarity." (World Bank, 2003b, p. 7) In fact, large-scale adoption of IT and e-learning has the capacity to transform the digital divide into 'digital dividends' by bringing in the marginalised and socially disadvantaged sections of the population to productive economic activities when they might otherwise have been left out.

The Global Development Learning Network (GDLN), a training initiative set up by the World Bank Institute, aims to provide a wide range of cost-effective ICT tools for connecting policymakers and development practitioners across the world, enabling them to share ideas and to integrate global experiences into country-level initiatives. This is likely to have a significant positive impact on worldwide poverty reduction, as envisaged by Jim Wolfensohn, President of the World Bank, when he made the following statement in June 1998: "As we look at the challenges of poverty, it is very clear that money alone is not what is needed. We need colleagues who can learn and share experience with each other. Distance learning, obviously is the tool that will enable this and benefit us all." (cited in Foley, 2003)

Today, the GDLN has over 60 centres around the world and more than 30,000 people participate in GDLN activities every year. Dialogues and learning exchanges among developing countries have become a common practice, with countries in Africa, Asia, and Latin America sharing experiences about education reforms, sustainable development, HIV prevention, community participation, gender equality, and other poverty-related issues. Significantly, GDLN activities (seminars, training workshops, policy dialogues) are more cost-effective than face-to-face methods (without compromising learning outcomes), and the Bank aims to expand the network in the future.

Other international initiatives that have been undertaken to maximise the potential benefits of the ICT revolution for poverty alleviation include 'E-learning Africa 2006' and 'One Laptop per Child (OLPC)' (a Media Lab of MIT project that received strong UN endorsement). This latter initiative, in particular, ties in with the widely held view by contemporary economists that a one-time increase in the rate of human capital accumulation by improvement in the economy's ICT infrastructure (rather than the total stock of resources devoted to RandD and human capital) can stimulate economic growth with significant positive effects on human poverty. The so-called East Asian miracle economies, for example, experienced high growth rates accompanied by significant poverty reduction due, in part, to accelerated investment in information technology and human capital development in the 1980s. (Chen and Kee, 2005)

The Optimal Level of Education: A Model

It is not just education but the even distribution of educational benefits among a country's socioeconomic groups, in both rural and urban areas, that is required for poverty reduction. This was a central theme in the World Bank publication, The Quality of Growth, (World Bank, 2000), in which it was argued that the main asset of the poor is human capital. It follows, therefore, that successful poverty eradication requires full and proper development of this asset through equitable educational programs. Public expenditure on education and generous educational subsidies, says the Bank, if they do not benefit the poor, will lead to undesirable outcomes and should therefore be discouraged. Similar views have been expressed by other economists (see, for example, Todaro and Smith, 2005, Chapter 8); the prevailing inegalitarian educational systems in many developing countries are being blamed for their poor economic performance.

The absence of socially broad-based education systems in the developing world has led to a conceptualisation of an optimal level of education which does not extend beyond the primary school level (see, for example, Psacharopoulos, 1994; and Ram, 1996). The rationale advanced by development economists is that, considering social and private benefits and costs of education, beyond primary level, marginal social costs exceed marginal social benefits. This means that additional public investment in the secondary and tertiary education sectors will yield a negative net social rate of return. As opportunities for e-learning become increasingly available then theoretically, at least, the equilibrium level of educational provision should be at a higher level in terms of years spent in the education system; the point of optimality (where net social benefits are maximised) perhaps extending to the tertiary level.

Figure 1
The Optimal Level of Education under E-Learning and F_2F Learning

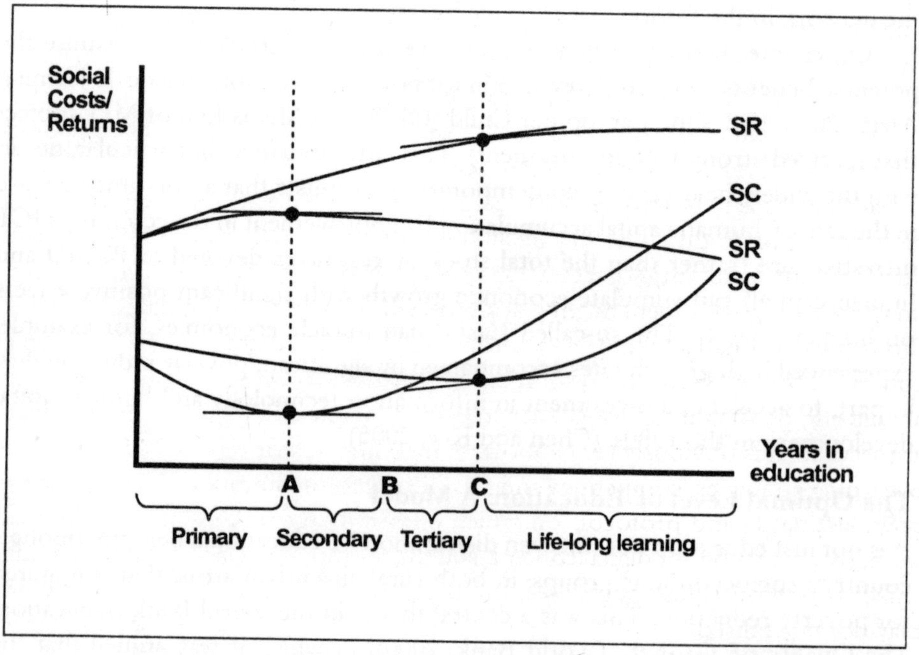

Figure 1 illustrates the optimal levels of education under two different scenarios; traditional 'brick-and-mortar' education versus online education or e-learning. In the case of traditional education, the social cost curve (SC) shows a slow rate of growth for early years of schooling (basic education) and then a much more rapid growth for higher levels of education (indicating higher marginal social costs for post-primary education). This is because of the expensive capital and recurrent costs of higher education and the fact that much post-secondary education in developing countries is heavily subsidised.

The social cost curve (SC') for e-learning, on the other hand, is much flatter on the assumption that the marginal cost of education - using the various ICTs - will fall rapidly. An online course may be quite expensive to develop but, as it is potentially deliverable to millions of students at very little extra cost, unit cost has the potential to fall over a large output range (in this case, the quantity of hours spent in education). The assumption of a higher initial cost for IT infrastructure for e-learning (compared to that for traditional education) is illustrated by the SC' curve starting higher up the vertical axis in Figure 1.

The social benefits or social return curve (SR) for the traditional educational model rises sharply at first, reflecting the improved levels of productivity (particularly in the primary production sector) that result from basic education, and then begins to taper off with additional years of schooling. By contrast, the social return curve for e-learning (SR') shows an upward trend, illustrating the benefits associated with this paradigm shift in education. With continuous lifelong learning, it is theoretically possible for this curve to maintain a positive slope. The SR' curve also starts at a higher initial level on the vertical axis and remains always above the SR curve, reflecting the assumption that the employment of ICTs is likely to produce higher rates of productivity.

If this theoretical justification for the optimal level of education being around the tertiary level is accepted, then the policy implications are self-evident. E-learning needs to be strongly supported by government; it just remains a question of how best to do this. One way of getting around the high initial cost of course development is to forge partnerships with the private sector or with foreign universities. A government might play the role of a 'catalyst' by providing sufficient funds for the construction of an appropriate IT infrastructure, and in the event a country does not have the resources, international cooperation and assistance should also be sought to finance such initiatives. Where public-private partnerships are secured, it is obviously very important that there are clear policy guidelines on e-learning strategies, competitive and flexible telecommunication pricing policies, open standards and protocols on which e-learning model are built, intellectual property protection for digital content, and the promotion of an IT culture among citizens. Without these guidelines, the theoretically optimal level of education may not be realised.

Summary and Conclusions

In an era where knowledge is the key to economic success, education has never been so important. In the case of developing economies, it is particularly critical because the 'knowledge gap' between rich and poor countries will almost certainly widen, causing less developed countries to become further marginalised. It is the firm belief of the authors of this paper that the only solution open to developing countries is e-learning. Other alternatives are simply too costly.

E-learning is a viable option largely because of the ICT revolution which has provided the tools for easy access to quality education at an affordable price. This ease of accessibility means that it is possible for educational programs to target groups most affected by poverty including the low-income population living in rural and inaccessible areas, women facing cultural and religious barriers, the physically disabled and handicapped, and other marginalised segments of the community. Employment of ICTs serves to raise the general level of productivity, thereby contributing to the economic growth which is essential for poverty reduction but, equally important, is the opportunity that ICTs provide in terms of access to higher levels of education. Once considered largely the preserve of the rich countries (and a luxury in poor countries), it now makes economic sense from a societal point of view to provide secondary and tertiary education.

E-learning is ideally suited to the needs of different socioeconomic groups within developing countries. With increasingly dynamic labour market conditions, it provides the wealthier working population with the most pragmatic way of upgrading their skills and knowledge without interrupting their jobs and day-to-day lives, and for the poor and marginalised it provides the means to develop their human capital (the only asset they have). E-learning is accessible from virtually anywhere, substantially cheaper (one-third of the cost of traditional education), and the quality is likely to be higher if provision is through international partnerships. The alternative is for the poor country governments to continue investing their scarce resources in curriculum development and teacher training programs and inevitably running up against the 'bootstrapping problem' and its attendant delays in implementation and economic inefficiencies. Adoption of e-learning at all levels can eliminate these problems by providing 'just-in-time' education to all sections of the community at an affordable price.

On the basis of these arguments, the authors believe there is a convincing case for a challenge to the conventional wisdom on what constitutes the optimal level of education in developing countries. As we have argued here, there are fairly compelling theoretical grounds for suggesting that the optimal level may now extend up to the tertiary level. Under these circumstances, governments need to shape policies accordingly. One such approach is through international cooperation in the field of e-learning-something strongly endorsed by international agencies not least because an electronically interconnected world makes this so much easier. The main challenge for developing country governments is the provision of a robust IT infrastructure and associated socio-legal framework that will ensure best practice delivery of e-learning.

REFERENCES

Chen, D.H.C. and Dahlman, C.J. (2004), *Knowledge and Development:* A Cross-Section Approach, World Bank Policy Research Working Paper 3366, August.

Chen, D.H.C. and Kee, H.L. (2005), *A Model on Knowledge and Endogenous Growth,* World Bank Policy Research Working Paper 3539, March.

Denison, E.F. (1985), *Trends in American Economic Growth,* 1929-82, Washington D.C.: Brookings Institution.

Harris, R.W. (2004), *Information and Communication Technologies for Poverty Reduction,* Kuala Lumpur: UNDP-APDIP.

Juma, C. and Y.C. Lee (2005), *Innovation: Applying Knowledge in Development,* United Nations Millennium Project Task Force, London and Sterling, VA: Earthscan.

Kejak, M. and Ortmann, A. (2003), *E-learning: A Way to Solve the Human Capital Bootstrapping Problem in Transitional Economies in Central Europe,* Research paper funded by World Bank's Global Development Network. Available online: http://home.cerge.cuni.cz/ortmann/Papers/23paperkejort.pdf (Accessed 31 May 2006).

Foley, M. (2003), The Global Development Learning Network: a World Bank initiative in distance learning for development, in Moore, M.G. and Anderson, W.G. (eds), *Handbook of Distance Education,* Portland, OR: Lawrence Erlbaum.

Krugman, P. (1994), The myth of Asia's economic miracle, *Foreign Affairs,* Vol. 73, No. 6, pp. 62-78.

Lucas, R.E. (1988), On the mechanics of economic development, *Journal of Monetary Economics,* Vol. 22, pp. 3-42.

Mankiw, N.G., Romer, D. and Weil, D. (1992), A Contribution to Empirics of Economic Growth, *Quarterly Journal of Economics,* Vol. 107, pp. 407-438.

Oliner, S.D. and Sichel, D.E. (2000), The Resurgence of Growth in the Late 1990s: is Information Technology the Story? *Journal of Economic Perspectives,* Vol. 14, No. 4, pp. 3-22.

Psacharopoulos, G. (1994), Returns to Investment in Education: A Global update, *World Development,* Vol. 22, pp. 1325-1343.

Ram, Rati (1996), Level of Development and Rates of Return to Schooling: Some Estimates from Multicountry Data, *Economic Development and Cultural Change,* Vol. 44, pp. 839-857.

Sachs, Jeffrey (2005), The End of Poverty: *How We Can Make It Happen In Our Lifetime,* New York: Penguin Books.

Sala-i-Martin, X.X. (1997), I Just Ran Two Million Regressions, *American Economic Review,* Vol. 87, No. 2, pp. 178-183.

Salmi, J. (2000), *Tertiary Education in the Twenty-First Century: Challenges and Opportunities,* The World Bank, LCSHD Paper Series No. 62. Available online: http://wbln0018.worldbank.org (Accessed 31 May 2006).

Sen, Amartya (1999), *Development as Freedom,* New York: Anchor Books.

Smith, A. (1776), *An Enquiry into the Nature and Causes of the Wealth of Nations,* Vol. 2, Chicago: University of Chicago Press.

Solow, R. (1956), A Contribution to the Theory of Economic Growth, *Quarterly Journal of Economics,* Vol. 70, pp. 65-94.

Solow, R. (1957), Technical Change and Aggregate Production Function, *Review of Economics and Statistics,* Vol. 39, pp. 312-320.

Todaro, M.P. and Smith, S.C. (2005), *Economic Development,* London: Pearson Education.

UNESCO (1997), *Adult Education in a Polarizing World,* Paris: UNESCO.

World Bank (1993), *The East Asian Miracle,* New York: Oxford University Press.

World Bank (2000), *The Quality of Growth,* New York: Oxford University Press.

World Bank (2001), *World Development Report* 2000-01: Attacking Poverty, Washington, D.C.: World Bank.

World Bank (2002a), *Globalization, Growth and Poverty:* Building an Inclusive World Economy, Washington, D.C.: World Bank.

World Bank (2002b), *Constructing Knowledge Societies: New Challenges for Tertiary Education,* Washington, D.C.: World Bank.

World Bank (2003a). *Lifelong Learning in the Global Knowledge Economy: Challenges for Developing Countries,* Washington, D.C.: World Bank.

World Bank (2003b), ICT and MDGs: *A World Bank Group Perspective.* Available online: http://info.worldbank.org/ict/WSIS/docs/mdg_Complete.pdf (Accessed 31 May 2006).

World Bank Institute (2001), *Korea and the Knowledge-based Economy,* Washington, D.C.: World Bank.

11

WTO AND DEVELOPING COUNTRIES: ARE COUNTRIES, SUCH AS INDIA, DISADVANTAGED?

Sheela Rai

Introduction

In his celebrated work, 'The Wealth of Nations,' Adam Smith advised never to attempt to make at home what it will cost more to make than to buy. Successive generations of economists have supported and refined Smith's argument contending that "if a foreign country can supply us with commodity cheaper than we ourselves can make it, better buy it from them with some part of the produce of our own industry, employed in a way in which we have some advantage."[1] This is known as the concept of comparative advantage on which the principle of free trade rests. Economists contend that a decentralised market system that allows producers and consumers the freedom to choose according to market prices will provide the most efficient allocation of the scarce resources, and this will result in a gain in real national income. Under free trade, comparative advantage dictates that a country should exchange what it can produce most efficiently for what others can produce more efficiently. Even if a country could produce every commodity well (absolute advantage), it would still gain by specialising in its better products (comparative advantage). An economist does not admit to many exceptions to free trade. They arise only when domestic markets fail to allocate resources efficiently or non-economic objectives receive priority. Equal application of market economic principles to all firms is considered to be the backbone of free trade.[2] Free trade, however, does not mean unfair trade.

Trade is unfair when two players in the market are not at an equal level. This can be either because the exports are subsidised or dumped or because two countries that are trading partners are not at an equal level of development and this adversely affects their competitive and negotiating skills. Free trade in such a case results in unfair trade because the lesser-developed country is bound to welcome imports at the cost of its own economy, industry and the livelihood of its citizens. What should be the strategy of the less developed country in such a case, keeping in mind the history of colonialism and protectionism in the now developed countries?

The paper explores the place of the developing countries in the world trading system under the GATT and now the WTO and argues that the developing countries should effectively use the available trade policy instruments to their advantage. This calls for firstly, the development and utilisation of good negotiating skills to put across their point of view and secondly, prudent use of protective measures to safeguard their own citizens from falling into impoverishment and despair giving rise to economic, social and political problems.

The paper is in two parts. The first part discusses the role and place of developing countries in the history of the GATT and the WTO and highlights that the rule-based trading regime has necessitated the developing countries to be more and more assertive in order to extricate it time and again from power bases. The second part advocates a prudent use of protective measures by developing countries to enable them to protect their industry and competition in the market and allow them to pursue their social policy goals. The theme in Part II is illustrated by antidumping cases in India.

Free Trade: Developing Countries[3] in the GATT and WTO

Movement Towards Free Trade

Protectionist measures taken in reaction to the Great Depression in the 1930s were considered to be one of the major reasons for precipitating World War II. When World War II was in progress the Allies, especially the United States and the United Kingdom, agreed to devise a system for international regulation of exchange flows, international loans and international trade that would complement the upcoming United Nations' effort in generating international interdependence and co-operation. In short, the so-called Bretton Woods institutions (IMF, World Bank and ITO) were to help in burying the 19th century European politics of the balance of power. That one of the three institutions, the ITO, did not come into force shows that countries were equally zealous in protecting their sovereignty and national interests in the movement towards international co-operation. With the failure of ITO, what remained was the GATT 1947.

When the GATT was negotiated and signed in 1947 many developing countries were either still fighting for freedom from colonial rule or, as in the case of India, had got their freedom only recently. The GATT had 23 original signatories of which 10 were developing countries. India had got its freedom in that year only and immediately joined the GATT as a free country. Developing countries continued to be in the minority until the late 1960s. By May 1970, 52 of the 77 GATT contracting parties could be classified as developing countries. The proportion of developing countries has continued to increase, and developing countries now constitute a large majority of the WTO Membership.[4]

While developing countries were never a tiny minority (even in the 1960s), their number did not do much to turn the benefits of world trade in their favour. However, this fact was always realised. The GATT Ministerial Decision in November 1957 cited the failure of the trade of less developed countries to develop as rapidly as that of industrialised countries as a major problem. The result of this decision was the Haberler Report which supported the perception that the export earnings of developing countries were not satisfactory. In late 1961, Uruguay filed a legal complaint against virtually the entire developed-country membership, listing 576 restrictions that allegedly nullified and impaired Uruguayan exports. This litigation, which ended inconclusively in three panel reports, highlighted the shabby treatment of developing countries.[5] The United Nations Conference on Trade and Development (UNCTAD) came into existence in 1964. The formation of UNCTAD had major influence on the GATT. It led the GATT to accept, in principle, that the US principle of reciprocity in trade concessions creates an unfair trading regime for the less developed countries. The Contracting Parties adopted two decisions which, in principle, modified the requirement of reciprocity in trade negotiations.

Part IV of GATT

In 1965, the contracting parties adopted Part IV of the GATT. Part IV of the GATT labelled as 'Trade and Development' stated:

1. The contracting parties,
   (a) recalling that the basic objectives of this Agreement include the raising of standards of living and the progressive development of the economies of all contracting parties, and considering that the attainment of these objectives is particularly urgent for less-developed contracting parties;
   (b) considering that export earnings of the less developed contracting parties can play a vital part in their economic development and that the extent of this contribution depends on the prices paid by the less-developed contracting parties for essential imports, the volume of their exports, and the prices received for these exports;
   (c) noting, that there is wide gap between standards of living in less developed countries and in other countries; and
   (d) the developed contracting parties do not expect reciprocity for commitments made by them in trade negotiations top reduce or remove tariffs and other barriers to the trade of less-developed contracting parties.

Developing countries for long had contended that the obligations under Part IV are binding. The developed countries have been arguing otherwise. However, in the ongoing negotiations on the Doha Development Agenda, the Members in the Hong Kong Ministerial Meeting agreed on a less than full reciprocity principle for developing countries in the case of non-agricultural market access. However, how effective this would be would depend on the two formulas for tariff reduction that are yet to be finalised. This was achieved due to an assertive and, at times, an aggressive negotiating strategy adopted by the developing countries who put up a joint front led by India and Brazil.

Generalised System of Preferences

In 1971, the GATT adopted two waivers for types of preferences to favour developing countries: (1) a set-aside of the MFN obligation to permit a "generalised system of preferences"; and (2) permission for developing countries to exchange tariff preferences among themselves. In 1979, during the Tokyo Round negotiations, both waivers were made permanent through the so-called Enabling Clause.

The generalised system of preferences continues. However, the Appellate Body has held that a developed country while giving tariff preferences need not extend it to all developing countries.[6] It can choose among the developing countries provided the choice is made on the basis of criterion laid down in advance. The decision opens up the possibility for the developed countries to lay down any criterion for differentiation, for example, labour standards, nuclear disarmament etc. which would work as potential non-tariff barriers against preferential treatment in the future.

Special and Differential Treatment of Developing Countries

Another concession which the developing countries usually get on paper is special and differential treatment. While most of the agreements of the WTO state in the preamble the need to take into account the special position of the developing countries, none of them provides any substantial concession. Most of the concessions were in the nature of providing extended time for implementation. Most of these concessions are now over so far as the developing countries are concerned.

Protection against Developing Country Exports

While the GATT was signed in 1947 with the expectation of ushering in an era of free trade and the developing countries were now and then goaded to open up their markets, the developed countries usually took care to protect their sensitive sectors. For this reason, textiles and agriculture became an exception to GATT disciplines.

Textiles

When, in the beginning of 1960s, the textile industries of some developed countries faced problems in the face of competition from imports, these countries did not resort to the safeguards provision of Article XIX.[7] The reason was that safeguard provision under Article XIX has to be taken on the MFN basis, something which the importing developed countries wanted to avoid because this would have included some less developed countries also. The result was that a special arrangement in the textile sector was introduced as an instrument for restraining the imports from specific countries; in actual practice, it was used to restrain developed countries' imports from developing countries. The special arrangement was based on the argument that the developing countries were exporting cheap textile products and the textile industries of the developed countries needed time to adjust or phase out. However, this never happened and the textile industries of the developed countries got used to this support mechanism.[8] Earlier there had been a Short-Term Agreement and a Long-Term Agreement covering cotton textiles and clothing. In 1973, a comprehensive agreement in this sector was worked out. Formally, it was called the Arrangement Regarding International Trade in Textiles. Its coverage was expanded to include fibres other than cotton, viz. wool and synthetic fibres. Hence it was popularly called the Multi-Fibre Arrangement (MFA). The MFA provided a special framework for restraints on imports. Within this frame, restraints were worked out in bilateral agreements between an exporting country and importing country. And under certain situations, even unilateral restraints on imports could be imposed. This arrangement was extended almost every four years thereafter and there was further expansion of its coverage to include silk-blends, vegetable fibres, etc.[9] With the coming into force of the WTO the MFA was reincarnated as the Agreement on Textiles and Clothing which came to an end in January 2005.

However, it is still a matter of speculation as to how much market access the developing countries like India who had a comparative advantage in the sector, would get in the developed country markets. In the face of the increasing threat of non-tariff barriers, countries like India have not much to hope for especially, when in about more than 40 years, the world production scenario has changed and many new players have entered the market as a result of the old quota system. The example of the quota system in textiles is a clear example that world trade often has not been guided by the principle of comparative advantage. It has been, usually, the power dynamics that have prevented the developing countries from taking advantage of the sectors where they have a comparative advantage.

Agriculture

By the end of the nineteenth century the protectionist measures in agriculture had become increasingly prevalent. One of the causes of this was the steady expansion of American production and the resulting fall in world prices. While some nations tried to adjust, for example, the Dutch became more specialised in livestock-others including France, Germany, and Austria-Hungary, reacted by protecting existing producers and subsidising exports if domestic output exceeded consumption. During the inter-war period agricultural protection and domestic market regulation increased further. After World War II, farmers and agricultural ministries in OECD countries exempted agriculture from key GATT disciplines and Multilateral Trade Negotiations. The US led the way with its request for waiver in 1955. With the creation of the EEC and its Common Agricultural Policy (CAP) in 1957, European countries also insisted on special treatment for this sector.[10]

In the Uruguay Round negotiations, agriculture was a major contentious issue. During the Uruguay Round the developing countries wanted to bring agriculture, which, like textiles, was an exception under the GATT regime, under the generally applicable trade rules. They wanted the agricultural subsidies to be subjected to the disciplines of the Agreement on Subsidies applicable in the case of other goods. By this time different opinions were prevailing among the developed world itself. As a result, what we got was a separate Agreement on Agriculture and the developed countries undertook to phase out their subsidies, especially their export subsidies.

However, after 10 years of the establishment of the WTO regime the developed countries stated that the undertaking under the Agreement of Agriculture was only recommendatory and not binding. The heavily subsidised agricultural sector of the developed countries is not only a barrier to exports from developing countries it is also a legal recognition of predatory pricing and dumping. According to the Institute for Agriculture and Trade Policy (IATP), the US has been dumping cotton in international markets since 1990. The difference between the selling price and the cost of production, which amounts to predatory pricing ranged from 32 per cent to 47 per cent between 1990 and 2003, touching 63 per cent and 65 per cent in 2001 and 2002 respectively.[11] This enormous dumping has depressed the prices of cotton in the international markets and consequently, impaired the livelihoods of millions of farmers across West and Central Africa. Since 2001, when the fall in cotton prices became very evident, Africa has been losing on an average US$ 441 million a year because of the distorted cotton trade. Since 2003, the West and Central African producers have suffered export losses of about US$ 382 million According to a study done by Oxfam, the US government provided subsidies worth US$ 490 million between 1995 and 2003. Due to these generous subsidies, Riceland, a US-based agribusiness firm, has been exporting rice to 75 countries. Further, these subsidies made the US the third largest exporter of rice in 2003, after Thailand and Vietnam, although producing rice in the US is almost two times costlier than it is in Thailand and Vietnam.[12]

Developing countries that are pressurised to bring down their tariffs would be facing a situation where their markets are flooded with heavily subsidised and dumped imports. Around 200 farmers have committed suicide in India even without facing the full repercussions of the new trade regime based on the so-called rules of free and fair trade. However, after an aggressive stand taken by the developing countries in the Cancun Ministerial conference, the developed countries have agreed in the Hong Kong Ministerial to phase out their export subsidies to agricultural products by the year 2013. This was also achieved because of a joint front and aggressive negotiating strategy adopted by the developing countries.

Protection in the Rule-Based System of the WTO

The WTO came into being as a single undertaking and ushered in the era of a legally enforceable trade regime with its compulsory and binding dispute settlement system. The legally enforceable trade regime establishing a rule-based system is considered to be favourable to the developing countries who would otherwise be the loser to the developed countries in the bargaining process in bilateral negotiations. However, this rule-based system has not always played fair with the developing countries. The judicial activism of the Appellate Body has not only legalised many non-tariff barriers[13] but has also increased the opportunity for many others.[14] In the face of such a situation many contend that, when the rules themselves are not fair, then a binding rule-based system cannot be fair. Hence, we need to devise ways whereby the concerns of the developing countries are given deference in the dispute settlement system. Supporters of this line of thinking advocate adoption of the National Deference principle whereby a permissible interpretation of a WTO provision given by a developing country would be accepted by the Dispute Settlement Body.[15]

The above shows that adoption of a proper negotiating strategy and keeping a joint front has helped the developing countries in extracting some concessions which were otherwise not available to them. The developing countries were earlier preoccupied with a defensive posture to safeguard their sovereignty which was always hooted down as bad economics. Demands for major concessions in return for concessions are yielding better results, even though late. Learning from their experience of the Uruguay Round the developing countries successfully blocked the way for the inclusion of the three of the four Singapore issues in the Doha Development Agenda. The result of this success is availability of bargaining power in the future round of negotiations.

The Uruguay Round which culminated with the establishment of the WTO, introduced many new issues like services, investment and intellectual property rights, despite strong opposition from the developing countries. However, at the insistence of the United States many new trade issues like services and some non-trade issues like protection of intellectual property rights, were negotiated and adopted by the Members into binding agreements. In the bargaining process, the developing countries were able to secure the phasing out of the textile quota at the cost of the health of their citizens and some rules on the use of protective measures like safeguard measures. Developing countries have always been apprehensive of the indiscriminate use of these protective measures against their limited exports. However, as this paper suggests, these protective measures should be and indeed they have become an important trade and economic strategy for the developing countries.

Unfair Trade Practice: Prudent Use of a Protective Clause. A Case Study of India

The second line of action which the developing countries need to pursue, and which they are doing, is to adopt a prudent policy for the use of protective measures. This is explained using illustrations of antidumping measures taken by India.

Antidumping Measures in India

An antidumping law was introduced by Canada in the year 1903. Soon thereafter New Zealand in 1905, Australia in 1906 and the Union of South Africa in 1914 came up with legislations that empowered them to take antidumping measures. Thereafter, Section 801 of the American Revenue Act of 1916 was enacted which prohibited predatory dumping. Antidumping duties were, therefore, originated by the developed countries to protect their domestic markets against low-priced imports. Until the 1980s, the United States, Australia, Canada and the EC were the main users of the antidumping duties. Based on a tabulation of cases by the United States General Accounting Office, from 1980 to 1989, the GATT had a total of 1,456 new antidumping cases reported to it, and the aforementioned countries were responsible for starting 95% of them. However, although developing countries hardly initiated antidumping complaints during this period, they were the main targets of antidumping actions. Therefore, from the beginning the developing countries supported multilateral efforts to regulate antidumping actions, even though there were some basic disagreements between them and the developed countries. However, lately, the developing countries have become the major users of antidumping measures[15] with India now the leading user of antidumping measures.

The liberal use of antidumping measures by India is usually criticised on the ground that Indian industries, accustomed to protection from competition, have found a new shelter against competition in antidumping measures. Indeed, the present writer herself had cautioned in an earlier paper[16] that, in India, most of the cases were being initiated by the industries that were monopolies and hence, there was a danger that antidumping measures might be used for anticompetitive purposes. However, in view of the later developments and comparative study, I find that there is no need for much anxiety. Antidumping measures become necessary not only to protect domestic industry which is adjusting itself to the liberalised regime[17] but they are also needed to protect competition and consumer interests. My contention is based on two arguments:

1. The Indian market is threatened by unprecedented aggressive pricing.
2. A comparative study of the use of antidumping measures by other countries, especially the developed countries, shows that India is not abusing antidumping measures because they are protecting their industry even in face of much less danger.

The number of cases initiated in a year is not a very reliable basis for branding a country as protectionist. If we do a comparative study of the use of antidumping measures by India and other developed countries, we find that antidumping measures have been taken by those countries in much less serious situations. For this purpose, I have done a comparative study of 15 cases - 10 Indian (Table 1) and 5 EU cases (Table 2). These cases have been picked at random with no particular order or method applied in their selection.

A survey of these cases shows that the Indian market is faced with a precarious situation. Dumping margins are as high as 290%, 693% and 1069%! On the other hand, the EU has taken antidumping measures with a dumping margin of 13.1%, 24.8%, 48.5%, 4.6% 3.4% etc. It is not contended that these dumping margins are insignificant or that India has not taken antidumping measure at these margins. The contention here is that the EU is not faced with the situation where dumping margins are going up to 1069%. In such a situation it is not justified to say that India is using antidumping measures as a protectionist device. The extraordinarily high dumping margin shows a strategy of aggressive pricing by companies marketing their products in India and the vulnerable position of Indian markets and Indian companies. Another important discovery in this study is that most of the companies alleged to be dumping have not cooperated with the investigating authorities. One or two companies that have cooperated have been found not to be dumping. This is another indication of the strategy of the foreign companies dumping in India. They did not offer any defence since they knew that they had been indulging in unfair trade practice of a type which it was difficult to defend.

It can be questioned by critics of antidumping measures in India whether the calculation of a dumping margin by India was fair? In most of these cases, a constructed normal value and an export price were adopted. Secondly, we should not forget the fact that both the EU and the USA have maintained the system of zeroing which inflates the dumping margin and has been ruled to be WTO inconsistent by the Appellate Body.[18]

Now if we examine the extent of injury suffered by the domestic industry, we see that in the European Union loss of market share of 2%, 3% or 4% has been considered to be a material injury. On the other hand, in India, loss of market share has been about 10 to11%. No doubt, in some cases market share has increased. However, with regard to profitability, we find that, in some cases Indian industry has been compelled to sell below the cost of production. In most of the cases where domestic industry has been able to maintain its market share or to increase the same, it has been at the cost of significant price depression which has sometimes led to sales below the cost of production.

Thus, on a comparative basis, if we analyse India's use of antidumping measures vis-a-vis a developed region, we cannot say that India is abusing the antidumping measures to protect its industry which was, for long, shielded from competition. If a developed region needs to use antidumping measures, when its

Table 1
Indian Antidumping Cases

	Name of the case	*Domestic Industry (DI) constitution*	*Dumping Margin*	*Injury (Loss of market share (MS)*	*Injury (Loss of Profit)*	*Others*
1.	AD investigation concerning (HFRM) from China PR. (12/1/98) (1999)	4 (5th company neither supported nor opposed)	76%	Increase in volume of sales.	Decline in sales realisation from Rs. 51 per kg. To Rs. 35 per Kg.	No cooperation or response from the exporters
2.	AD Invest. of Hexamine from Iran (14/352002 DGAD) (2005)	4 (all supported the petition)	43.91%	MS in terms of import increased from 9.27% to 30.82% share in demand of DI declined from 45.34% to 33.59%	While cost of production increased from 100 to 125, selling price increased to 106 which shows negative returns.	1. Violation of price undertaking 2. No cooperation or response from the exporters
3.	AD Invest. of Green Veneer Tape from Chinese Taipei 14/50/2002 DGAD (2003)	One	135%	From 32.08% to 27.72%. Increase in imports from –12.16 to 203.13%	Price suppression/ depression of DI products	1. domestic industry a new company with market share of 25 to 30%. 2. No information support from exporters.
4.	Non-Brass Flashlight from China PR14/27/ 2002 DGAD (2003)	Petitioner company produced 77% of domestic production	693% (NBMFL2 cell small, 468% (NBMFL 2cell large), 798% 3 cell large)	From 63.46% to 26.54% Increase in imports from 13.48% to 62.12%	Resulted in significant price depression for the domestic industry	1. Only one exporter cooperated who was found not to be dumping
5.	Aniline from EU 21/1/2000 DGAD (2001)	3 companies	166.7%	Increased from 86.8% to 92.1% Increase in imports from dumped sources from 4.3% to 98.4%	DI forced to sell at less than cost of production	Only two exporters responded who claimed not to have exported Aniline to India. Other exporters did not respond.

	Name of the case	Domestic Industry (DI) constitution	Dumping Margin	Injury (Loss of market share (MS)	Injury (Loss of Profit)	Others
6.	Measuring tapes from China PR 14/31/2002 DGAD (2003)	2 companies constituting 90% of the production	1069% (steel tape) 148% (Fibre glass tape)	From 67.73% to 52.9% Dumped imports increased from10.83% to 28.15%	Selling Price below the cost of production	No information from exporters.
7.	Methylene Chloride from EU South Africa and Singapore 17/1/2001/DGAD (2003)	3 companies	85.32% & 55.75% (EU); 99.92% SA; 62.42% Singapore;	From 69.51% to55.66%, increase in dumped imports from 9.41% to 25.33%	Decline in domestic price by 18%	Some companies contended that they do not export. Those who responded the information they provided were found to be grossly inadequate.
8.	Vitrified Porcelain Tiles from China PR and UAE37/1/2001 DGAD	3 companies constituted only 60% of production	13.27% & 99% for UAE 290% for China PR	Imports acquired 3.66% of MS (total demand) in one year.	DI as a whole had negative return on investments.	Imports from UAE and China rose from nil (as per cent of total imports) in 1998-99 to about 71% in 1999-2000
9.	Toluene Di-Isocyanate from Chinese Taipei, EU, USA, Japan, Korea RP	One	5.5%, 20.46%, 61.75%, 16.52%, 16.11%, 63.42%	DI gained Market share and MS for dumped imports decreased.	No significant price undercutting	No Injury finding
10.	Trimethoprim from China	6 companies producing the product in India.	92.09%	MS for dumped Imports increased from 0.5% to 9.96%. Share of DI fell from 99.4% to 90%	DI selling below cost of production	1. No response from exporters. 2. China and India major producers of Trimethoprim in the world.

industry is faced comparatively with much less threat, there is no reason why a developing country, like India when faced with such aggressive dumping and comparatively more injury, should not protect its much more vulnerable industry.

Table 2
Antidumping Cases Decided in the European Union

	Name of case	*Dumping Margin*	*Loss in Market Share for domestic industry and increase in dumped imports*	*Loss/gain in profits for domestic industry*
1.	Cotton Type Bed Linen from Pakistan	13.1%	From 20.8% to 18.9%	Average price increased from EUR 13.3 to EUR 14.2 over the period considered covering high & low value products. Dropped from 7.7% in 1999 to 4.4% in Investigation Period i.e.by 42%
2.	Large Rainbow Trout from Norway and Faeroe Islands	24.8% Norway; 54.5%,30%,42.6% Faeroe Islands	Decrease in MS of DI from 25.9% to 21.7%. Increase of MS of Dumped imports by 13%.	Sales price of community industry undercut in the range between 7.3% to 28.4% Profitability decreased from 8.6% to 0.5%
3.	Bicycles from Vietnam & China PR	48.5% China PR; 15.8% Vietnam	Increased from 0.73% to 4.07% China; 1.77% to 8.70% Vietnam. MS of DI declined from 67% to 51%	Decrease in sales price by 2% Increase in profit only by 32%
4.	Barium Carbonate from China PR	3.4%, 4.6%, 31.7%	MS of DI loss of about 10%	Selling price reduced by 14%.
5.	Certain Castings from China PR	47.8%	MS of DI 3.8%. Increase in MS for dumped imports 10.1%	Profits declined by 18%

A value-based argument can be made that if a particular country or region is abusing the antidumping measures, it does not mean that we should follow its example. However, we should not forget that trade or free trade is not a categorical imperative of Kant, which should be promoted as a good or value in itself. We trade because we derive certain benefits from it. If free trade starts hurting us then we do not need it. We do not want to promote trade at the cost of the life and livelihood of Indian people. We want trade in a way and to the extent that it helps in promoting a good life for the Indian people and increases the competitive edge of Indian industry. A timely and judicious use of protective measures helps in ensuring that trade is fair and beneficial to all. That India is not making injudicious use of antidumping measures is proven by the fact that the Indian market is faced with aggressive pricing and Indian use of antidumping measures is no more protective than use by other developed countries that are our trading partners.

Competition

There has been debate since the beginning of antidumping measures about the conflict between antidumping measures and the principles of competition policy. This conflict is summed up by saying that antidumping measures protect competitors while competition law and policy protect competition. Antidumping measures are protective measures that are imposed against what is stated to be unfair trade practice. Opponents of antidumping measures contend that the use of dumping is a type of price discrimination between markets, which is a normal commercial practice. Opponents contend that by antidumping measures small inefficient groups of producers are protected at the cost of consumers who are large in number. According to the opponents, even if the exporter is indulging in unfair trade practice, it is the consumers of the exporting country who are suffering and there is no case to support antidumping measures by the importing country whose consumers are being benefited by cheaper products in the market.

Economists have enumerated various causes of dumping. Supporters of anti-dumping policies argue that anti-dumping is a justifiable attempt by importing country governments to offset the market access restrictions existing in an exporting firm's home country market and that underlie the ability of such firms to dump. Such restrictions may consist of import barriers preventing arbitrage, but may also reflect the non-existence or non-enforcement of competition law by the exporting country. Thus, the US had claimed that lax Japanese antitrust enforcement permits Japanese firms to collude, raise prices, and use part of the resulting rents to cross subsidise (dump) products sold on foreign markets.[19] Viner developed the original theoretical rationale for anti-dumping law. He argued that anti-dumping may be needed to protect domestic consumers from predatory dumping.

Let us analyse the claims of proponents and opponents of antidumping measures with reference to the Indian position. Here the contention of the writer is that antidumping measures are an important tool of competition policy of the country and help to maintain competition in market situations which would not be covered by the competition law of the country.

As pointed out above, the Indian market is again faced with a precarious position. It is faced with aggressive and predatory pricing especially by Chinese companies. Most of these companies are non-market and are sometimes subsidised by the Chinese government. Out of the 145 cases reported by the Indian Ministry of Commerce on its website in which a final finding is made, 54 cases include the Peoples Republic of China. These companies indulge in aggressive pricing which is an indicator of predatory intent. This can also be noted that of the ten Indian cases discussed above, 5 of the cases involve China. If Indian industries are left to the mercy of the markets which are distorted and or being captured by companies temporarily indulging in aggressive pricing, then not only the Indian companies would be wiped out of the market but the Indian consumers would be left at the mercy of these foreign companies who later would surely increase the prices and recoup their earlier losses by overcharging the consumers later. That I am not talking of a hypothetical situation and that dumping is used for anticompetitive purposes can be explained with the help of the vitamin cartel case.

The Vitamin Case[20]

The international vitamin cartel operated from 1990 to 1999 and involved producers located in Canada, Germany, Japan, Switzerland and the United States. The cartel, especially the Vitamin C cartel, had its root in the scientific discovery regarding the importance of vitamin C in preventing heart diseases. The true nature of heart disease as a simple vitamin C deficiency was recognized in the late 1940s and early 1950s.[21] According to the Matthias Rath website[22] this cartel was formed after Dr. Rath briefed the heads of these pharmaceutical/vitamin manufacturers about the true nature and cause of heart disease. Dr. Rath claims that after he provided them with proof that cardiovascular disease is essentially a Vitamin C deficiency disease, these companies began to organize the now infamous cartel. According to Dr. Rath, he originally approached the presidents of these companies thinking that he might encourage their vitamin C production and help him inform the public. Rath was shocked to see that they did the opposite. In order to preserve the higher profit margins of other divisions, e.g. the cholesterol-lowering drug divisions, says Rath, the head of the major companies instead conspired to raise the prices of vitamins. According to Rath, this price fixing was to discourage the use of vitamins, in favour of cholesterol-lowering medications, and to increase profits should the truth about heart disease become widely known.[23]

The conspiracy lasted from January 1990 to February 1999 and affected the vitamins most commonly used as nutritional supplements or to enrich human food and animal feed, merely vitamins A, B2, B5, C, E, and Beta Carotene. Vitamin premixes, which are used to enrich breakfast cereals and numerous other processed foods were also affected by the conspiracy.

> Every year round August or September, the senior executives from the world's largest producers of vitamins would gather clandestinely for a few days at a European hotel or an executive's home for what called the "top-notch meeting" and other the "summit conference" to plan "the budget for Vitamin Inc.," [t]he meetings set production quotas, prices and distribution for vitamin ingredients that were used to enrich products in every refrigerator and kitchen cabinet in America, from morning supplemental pills to enriched milk and orange juice, fortified breakfast cereals, breads, butters and meats. The global markets for such vitamins as A, B2 (riboflavin), B5, C

> E and Beta Carotene would be divided among the participants to the half per centage point. A few months later the budget would be reviewed by midlevel executives to make sure everything was working as planned, or it would be adjusted to reflect corporate profits and world wide demand.[24]

The culprits were made to pay large fines in the United States, the EU, Australia, Brazil and Japan. While India did not take any action against the culprits for violation of competition law, the same firms started dumping various vitamins in India after the cartel was busted. The dominant producer of vitamins in India has taken over the subsidiary of one of the pharmaceutical companies involved in the cartel. The dominant producer although never petitioned for violation of competition law, did file an antidumping petition in which it succeeded, with the Antidumping Authority averring that protection of competitors is necessary to protect competition in the market as it provides more choice to consumers.

There is no doubt that the dominant Indian producer is using antidumping measures to protect him from losing his competitive edge in the Indian market. When the prices are raised it can be argued that Indian consumers are hurt. But to look at the other side of the story, there is only one main producer of vitamins in India. If that producer collapses, would Indian consumers benefit when left in the hands of companies that have been guilty of an infamous cartel? Won't the same companies again raise the prices when the market is at their mercy? In these situations one is forced to conclude that protection of competitors is necessary to protect competition.

Moreover, it is not only the Indian companies that are benefited by antidumping measures. Antidumping measures help other foreign companies to explore the market who would otherwise be shy of entering the market in the face of dumped prices. This is concluded in the article "Extent of Protection via Antidumping Law: a Case Study of Vitamin C Industry in India".[25] The writers have discovered that antidumping is very effective in restricting imports from the countries that are named to be dumping. However, there was also strong evidence of trade diversion; imports were diverted away from the named source country to the non-named countries. Moreover, after the imposition of antidumping duties on the named countries there was an influx of new entrants. Countries that were not supplying vitamin C to India earlier had now become an important source of imports.

Thus, antidumping measures ensure the entry of other and new entrants to the market. To put it the other way round, dumping can be used in a particular market, not only against the domestic industry, but also as an entry barrier against other foreign firms. Thus, antidumping measures are an important tool to protect competition in the market, especially in the market of developing countries which are in the process of liberalisation and whose vulnerable industries might collapse in the face of unfair trade practices leaving both the market and the consumers at the mercy handful of companies.

Consumer Interest

In most of the cases decided in India, consumers have defended the foreign companies as favourable to their interests. However, the vitamin case shows that a handful of companies can successfully jeopardise the consumers' life and interest by indulging in anticompetitive practices. Dumping can be one such anticompetitive practice with much less loss to the company indulging in it.

Moreover, we need to be careful about who these consumers are. In most of the cases, consumers are user industries. In some of these cases, the dumped goods are of inferior quality. In such a situation, while the user industries might benefit from it, the ultimate consumer might be the loser and the Indian and other industries who are selling better quality products are naturally the losers because they can never compete with inferior quality dumped goods on price. In the case of vitrified porcelain tiles from China PR and UAE, the major exporter M/s. RAK Ceramics from UAE themselves admitted that they supply 3rd and 4th quality tiles to India. Thus, while the Builders Association of India, the user industry, supported the exporting firms, its view cannot necessarily be taken to be representative of Indian consumers' interest.

Social Justice

The classical theories of liberalism and capitalism advocated a police state. In a police state, the job of the government is limited to the maintenance of peace and order and defending the state against foreign aggression. The rest was expected to be left to the individuals. This is Nozick's minimal state.[26] The individual was neither to be hindered nor interfered with by the state in the pursuit of his legitimate goals, displaying the best of his abilities, nor was he supposed to be supported by the state if he could not fend for himself. The fittest was to survive. In the political sphere application of this theory ensured civil and political freedom to individuals and in economic sphere application of this theory meant a free market economy powered by capitalism and competition. However, the application of this theory in practical life brought about such stark inequalities in the lives of people which could not always be supported on the basis of the Darwinian theory of survival of the fittest. Society has always been divided into haves and have-nots. As such, individuals belonging to the latter group were not in an equal position with the individuals of the former group, therefore competition between these two individuals was not considered fair.

Marxism was a reaction to this theory. Marxism envisioned a classless and stateless society. However, in the meantime, unless society got completely adapted to the classless world, there was to be dictatorship of the proletariat in a socialist state. Socialism collapsed because the endeavour was said to be unrealistic and normal people started suffocating under the political and economic laws imposed from above.

Liberalism on the other hand, gave birth to the idea of democracy. However, liberalism/capitalism and democracy are the antitheses of each other, surviving, in most cases, together. Democracy does not function on the basis of survival of the fittest. Democracy functions on the principle of majority rule. People do not choose their representatives as an umpire that would allow the best to win. People choose their representatives to further their interests in the law-making and in enunciating and implementing the policies of the government. As such, most of the democratic governments try to balance conflicting interests because they represent conflicting interests.

The tussle between individuals and society yielded within the democratic system a synthesis of the two extreme views on individuals and the society or state. The foremost exponent of this synthesis is John Rawls who tried to harmonise individual liberty with equal distribution.[27] Rawls' theory of justice consists of two principles:

First Principle: Each person is to have an equal right to the most extensive total system of equal basic liberties compatible with a similar system of liberty for all.

Second Principle: Social and economic inequalities are to be arranged so that they are both:

(a) to the greatest benefit of the least advantaged, consistent with the just savings principles, and

(b) attached to offices and positions open to all under conditions of fair equality of opportunity.

However, social justice, which also like socialism is a hat that has lost its shape and is defined in various ways and can best be expressed in following terms:[28]

> [A] just society must be concerned for the goodness of its members' lives, and not merely of their equality, though in a more limited way than beneficence implies. A just society must protect each member from being injured or interfered with by others, and it must not, by omission or commission, itself inflict evil upon any of them, deprive them of goods which they might otherwise gain by their own efforts, or restrict their liberty – except so far as is necessary for their protection or the achievement of equality. Although we are speaking of the *just* society and, not of the *good* society, its concern with the goodness of the lives of its members need not be considered merely negative and protective. It seems reasonable to assign to the just society a more positive interest (though one which falls short of beneficence) by saying that it must, so far as possible, provide equally, the conditions under which its members can, by their own efforts (alone or in voluntary associations), achieve the best lives of which they are capable. This means that the society must at least maintain some minimum standard of living, education, and society for all its members.

A state, especially a democratic state is under an obligation to provide its citizens with a reasonable means of survival. Hence a political and legal view on antidumping would be different from the general economic view. Economists generally take a utilitarian view of welfare that is the greatest good of the greatest number. However, the political and legal view would emphasise more the distributive element, which takes into account, as far as possible the interests of each individual. Hence the argument that dumping benefits consumers and consequently benefits a country because consumers are more in number would not appeal to a legal mind which is involved with the rights of each individual. Hence, for a lawyer and a political person, antidumping measures are an important tool to ensure that employees and companies giving employment to several citizens survive because their survival ensures the survival of those dependent on them. The right to employment has been bestowed by the Indian state on its citizens in a privatised era. Therefore, it is clear that the Indian Government cannot provide employment to millions of Indian nor is it in a position to give them an unemployment allowance. What it can do is to see that Indian companies employing these people are not wiped away because of unfair trade practices by foreign companies which in the long run would not benefit the consumers either.

Conclusion

The purpose of this paper was to re-emphasise an often stated fact that the present rules for free trade are not fair, both because they try to put at an equal level countries that are not at an equal level, and also because the stronger parties to these trade agreements do not always play by the rules. The theory of comparative advantage has never worked in sectors where developing countries could be the gainers whether it was textiles or the movement of natural persons. However, since these rules are the result of negotiations, the developing countries should work out an effective and hard bargaining stand based on hard facts and sound economics. On the other hand, the developing countries should also effectively and prudently, use the available trade measures to protect their national interest. The democratic governments today are caught in a strange dilemma. While they are accountable for their international obligations and cannot afford to remain aloof in the era of globalisation, they also have to ensure that justice is done to their people back at home. Justice in national constitutions and national policy is not evaluated in terms of GNP and BOP but in terms of each individual's right to certain social and economic amenities. To attain this, while developing countries should participate and take advantage of the global trade regime, they should cautiously evaluate the impact of each trade measure adopted by their trading partners and should also make proper use of the available trade remedies and measures to ensure that so-called free trade is not supported at the cost of their citizens' welfare.

NOTES

1. Adam Smith, *An Inquiry into the Nature and Causes of the Wealth of Nations* (Glasgow ed. 1976), Book IV, Ch. III.

2. Sheela Rai, *Recognition and Regulation of Antidumping Measures under GATT/WTO* (Eastern Book Company, Lucknow 2004).
3. It is difficult to define developing countries. The World Bank uses a classification system to differentiate between countries based on income. So-called developing countries are divided into low-income economies ($755 or less per captia in 2000) and middle-income economies (between $756 and $ 9,265 per captia). The latter group is divided into lower middle income economies (between $756 and $2995 per captia) and upper middle income economies (between $2,995 and $ 9265 per captia). Many upper middle income economies also are called newly industrialised economies or countries. The fourth group is high-income economies, primarily members of the OECD, with incomes of $9,266 or more per captia. The term developing country is not defined in the WTO Agreement nor was it defined in the GATT regime. As a result, developing country designation is made on an ad hoc basis and primarily through self-selection. The WTO Agreement does, however, provide a reference for "least developed" countries, namely, those recognised as such by the United Nations. The term developing country is vague because (1) there is a lack of international consensus; and (2) the term is used for different purposes in various international contexts. At the conclusion of the Uruguay, Round the US and the EU declared that they would not consider certain countries such as Singapore, Hong Kong and South Korea, to be developing countries. Both the US and the EU adopted their own definitions of developing countries for the purposes of their national preference programme. Mitsuo Matsushita et al, *The World Trade Organisation: Law Practice and Policy* (Oxford University Press, 2003), 375.
4. Mitsuo Matsushita et al; *The World Trade Organisation: Law Practice and Policy* (Oxford University Press, Oxford 2003), 375.
5. Ibid. 376.
6. *European Communities-Conditions for the Granting of Tariff Preferences to Developing Countries* WT/DS246/AB/R adopted on 7 April, 2004.
7. B.L. Das, *The World Trade Organisation: A Guide to the Framework for International Trade* (Earthworm Books Pvt. Ltd.,Chennai 1999), 257.
8. Ibid.
9. Ibid. 358.
10. Bernard Hoekman and Michel M. Kostecki, *The Political Economy of the World Trading System: The WTO and Beyond* (Oxford University Press, New York 2001), 209.
11. Institute of Agriculture and Trade Policy (IATP), United States Dumping on World Markets, <http:// www.tradeobservatory.org/library.cfm?refID=48538>Cited in Prabhash Ranjan, "Agriculture and NAMA Negotiations: Searching for the landing Zone" Working Paper-4 (Centre for Trade and Development 2006), 2.
12. Oxfam, Kicking Down the Door, <http:// www. Maketradefair.com/en/assets/english/kickingreport.pdf.> cited in Prabhash Ranjan, "Agriculture and NAMA Negotiations: Searching for the landing Zone" Working Paper-4 (Centre for Trade and Development 2006), 2.
13. *United States-Import Prohibition of Certain Shrimp and Shrimp Products*, WT/DS58/AB/R asopted on 12 October 1998.

14. *European Communities-Measures Affecting Asbestos and Asbestos Containing Products.* WT/DS135/AB/R adopted on 12 March 2001.
15. While in the eighties, more than 80% of the cases were initiated by the four traditional AD users, recent years have seen developing countries become increasingly active. Thus, for example, in 1998, South Africa initiated 41 proceedings, India 30, Brazil 16 and Mexico 10. In 1998 the four traditional users were responsible for only 34% of all initiations. The main targets of world-wide anti-dumping action in that same year were China (23 cases), Korea (22 cases) and the EC 7 Member States (42 cases). Of the 225 cases initiated during 1998, 143 targeted developing countries. A study examining the use of anti-dumping over the period 1987-1997 concludes, among others, that:"...developing countries now initiate about half of the total number of anti-dumping cases, and some of them employ anti-dumping more actively than most of the developed country users." Jorge Miranda, Raul A. Torres and Mario Ruiz, "The International Use of Antidumping: 1987-1997", *Journal of World Trade* 32(5): 5-71, 1998.
16. Sheela Rai, "Determination of Injury: A Study of Antidumping Cases in India" *SEBI & Corporate Laws,* Vol. 39 part 5, p. 75.
17. Jorge Miranda, Raul A. Torres and Mario Ruiz, "The International Use of Antidumping: 1987-1997", *Journal of World Trade* 32 (5): 5-71, 1998.
18. *European Communities–Anti-Dumping Duties on Imports of Cotton-Type Bed Linen from India* ("*EC–Bed Linen*"), WT/DS141/AB/R, adopted 1 March 2001.
19. Gunnar Niles and Adriaan ten Kate, "Trusting Antitrust to Dump Antidumping: Abolishing Antidumping in Free Trade Agreements Without Replacing it with Competition Law", *Journal of World Trade,* 29.
20. Rai, Sheela "Protection of Competition Through Antidumping Law: A Case Study of Vitamin Industry in India", to be published in *Journal of World Trade* (2006).
21. Linus Pauling and Matthias Rath, "A Unified Theory of Human Cardiovascular Disease Leading the Way to the Abolition of This Disease as a Cause for Human Mortality", See:http://www.orthomed.org/links/papers/rathpau.htm.
22. http://www.rath.nl/mr-publishing-internet/books/network/health_system/usa/busting_cartell.htm. See also Owen R. Fonorow, "Who Among us Has the Power to Routiney Plant Fake Health-Science "News" Reports in the Mass Media"(2001); http://www.internetwks.com/owen/fakenews.htm.
23. Dr. Matthias Rath website:*See*:http://www.drrath.com/mr-publishing-internet/network/health_system/uk.
24. Stephen Labaton and David Barboza, "U.S. Outlines How Makers of Vitamins Fixed Global Prices, http://www.econ.ucsb.edu/~tedb/eep/news/vitpfix.mon.txt.
25. Sumeet Gulati et al; and published in *the Journal of World Trade* 39(5): 925-936, 2005.
26. Nozick, R., *Anarchy, State and Utopia* (1974) Blackwell, Oxford.
27. Rawls, J.R., *A Theory of Justice* (Harvard University Press, Cambridge, Mass., 1971)
28. Frankena, William K., "The Concept of Social Justice" In Peter Vallentyne (ed.) *Equality and Justice* Vol. 1 *Justice in General* (Routledge, New York/London) p. 21.

12

POVERTY, POLITICAL FAILURE, AND THE USE OF OPEN-ACCESS RESOURCES IN DEVELOPING COUNTRIES

Clem Tisdell

Introduction

Open-access resources are resources which anyone is free to use without payment and the use of which is not subject to social or communal control. They have sometimes been described as common property resources (Gordon, 1954; Plourde, 1971). But nowadays this term is usually reserved to identify resources that are used subject to communal regulation or control (Tietenberg, 2003, pp. 70-72, Bromley, 1991; Ostrom, 1990).

In practice, different types of property rights in natural resources form continuous rather than discrete patterns. For example, if we consider only open-access property and common property subject to communal rules, a spectrum of possibilities such as that illustrated in Figure 1 may arise. At the one extreme, is complete open-access. At the other is common property, the use of which is subject to complete communal control. In between are cases in which the use of natural resources is subject to varying degrees of communal control. For example, located just to the right of the left hand side of this spectrum in Figure 1 may be

Figure 1
The Extent of Communal Control of the use of Shared Resources May form a Continuous Spectrum

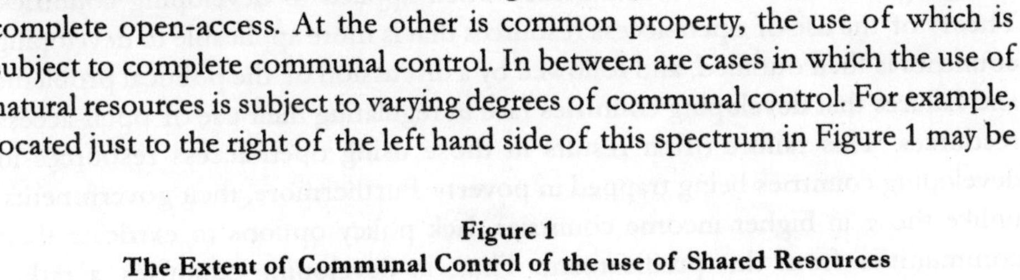

Note: Chapter marked with will be reprints from the special issue of the Indian Development Review.

cases where open-access is restricted to those in a village, area, or region near a natural resource that is being used. For example, only villagers from an adjacent village may be allowed access to adjoining inshore coastal resources, and for them complete open access may exist. The economic consequences of such a form of property rights, however, may become similar to the extreme open-access case, particularly if the comparative number able to use the resources is large.

Open access to many natural resources occurs in developing countries. Open-access is frequent in the capture fisheries, particularly in the artisinal fisheries, in developing countries. The analysis in this paper will focus on fisheries but the analysis also has applications to the use of other open-access resources. There is a high incidence of poverty of artisinal fishermen in developing countries and generally of families who rely on the use of open-access resources for their livelihood. This article explores why this is so, and considers why governments in developing nations fail to avert the occurrence of poverty that arises from the over exploitation of open-access resources and their helplessness in rectifying this poverty situation when it arises.

It will be argued that in developed countries, open-access to the use of natural resources does not as a rule result in poverty but that it usually does so in developing countries. Furthermore, governments in developed countries find it easier to adopt policies to reduce over exploitation of open-access natural resources than those of developing countries which may have little or no leeway to intervene so that communities escape the poverty trap arising from the over-exploitation of open-access natural resources.

The paper is developed by first outlining relevant features of the economic theory of the use of open-access resources as proposed by Western economists. It highlights limitations of this theory when applied to developing countries. Theory of the use of open-access resources that is more applicable to developing countries is then outlined, and followed by a discussion of the political problems and failures that developing countries face in regulating their use of open-access resources. This failure often results in those using open-access resources in developing countries being trapped in poverty. Furthermore, their governments, unlike those in higher income countries, lack policy options to extricate their communities from this predicament. Thus, in developing countries, a rather hopeless economic situation can emerge for those whose livelihood depends on the utilisation of open-access resources.

Features of the Standard Economic Theory of Use of Open-Access Resources

The standard economic theory of the utilisation of open-access resources assumes an economy with a well developed market system, and its exponents appear to suppose implicitly that the system has most of the features of a developed economy. The theory assumes an economy in which labour is fully employed and mobile and normally perfect competition is supposed. Thus, labour employed in an open-access industry will not have an income less than the highest income it can earn elsewhere which in developed countries is well above subsistence level.

Consequently, in studying the use of open-access resources, economists from higher income countries have not focused on poverty aspects. Rather, their attention has been on resource misallocation associated with the use of open-access resources. Although this misallocation reduces the level of aggregate economic production, it is not likely to be a source of poverty in developed countries because labour is relatively mobile and few resources involve open-access. The main concern of Western economists has been that when open access to resources occurs a Paretian optimum is not achieved and a Kaldor-Hicks (Paretian) economic improvement is possible. This implies that all could, in principle, be better off if the use of resources could be reorganised.

The focus of this theory can be illustrated by Figure 2. It is supposed that perfect competition prevails and the price of the product being harvested is independent of the amount of the harvest in the region under consideration. Let us assume that the product being harvested is fish, although the theory is applicable to any biological open-access resource. In Figure 2, line AC represents the value of the average product of labour harvesting fish and line AE is its corresponding

Figure 2
An Illustration of an Economic Inefficiency Occurring in the use of an Open-Access Resource in a Market Economy

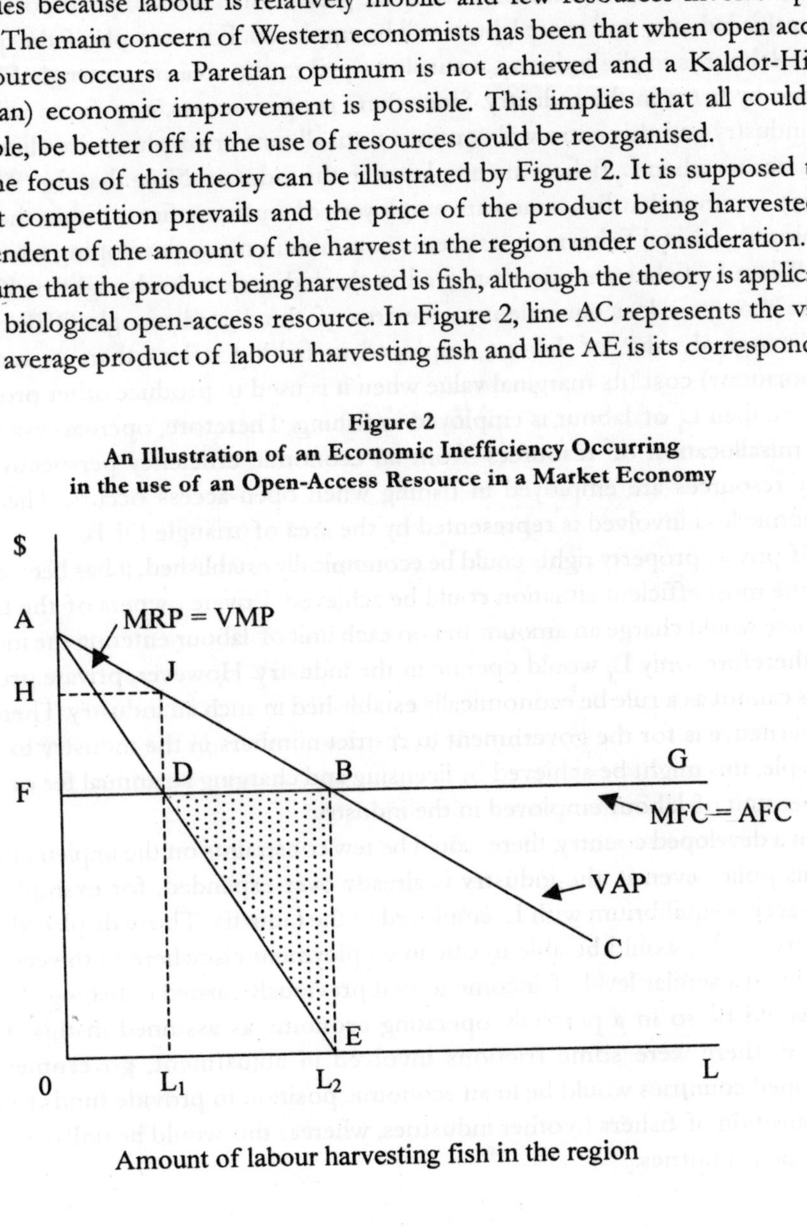

marginal revenue product curve. Line FG represents the marginal factor cost of labour. Under perfect competition, it is the marginal value of labour if labour is used elsewhere in the economy. The value of production in the economy will only be maximised if the marginal value of labour in fishing in this region is equal to its marginal factor cost, which also represents its marginal value when used elsewhere in the economy. Note that although labour is mentioned as the only input into the fish catch, the theory also applies if it is assumed that each unit of labour requires the use of complementary resources in fixed proportions.

If businesses in the industry can make greater than normal profit, others will enter this industry and more labour will be employed. For example, if the quantity L_1 of labour is in the industry, a surplus equal to the area of rectangle FDJH is earned by firms in the industry. Since there is open-access, new firms will enter the industry and this entry will continue until all rent or surpluses are eliminated. This occurs when L_2 fishers are employed in the industry. Note that the 'Western' theory assumes that fishermen are employees of business firms rather than self-employed artisinal fishermen, as seems common in many developing countries.

When L_2 fisherman are employed in the industry, a deadweight or Kaldor-Hicks economic loss equivalent to the area of the dotted triangle DEB occurs. The marginal value of labour employed in fishing is less than its marginal (opportunity) cost (its marginal value when it is used to produce other products) if more than L_1 of labour is employed in fishing. Therefore, open-access results in a misallocation of resources–from an economic efficiency perspective, too many resources are employed in fishing when open-access occurs. The social economic loss involved is represented by the area of triangle DEB.

If private property rights could be economically established, it has been argued that the most efficient situation could be achieved. Private owners of the fishery resource would charge an amount FH on each unit of labour entering the industry and therefore, only L_1 would operate in the industry. However, private property rights cannot as a rule be economically established in such an industry. Therefore, an alternative is for the government to restrict numbers in the industry to L_1. In principle, this might be achieved by licensing and charging an annual fee or tax of FH per unit of labour employed in the industry.

In a developed country, there would be few constraints on the implementation of this policy even if the industry is already over-expanded, for example, is in open-access equilibrium with L_2 employed in the industry. Those displaced in the industry, L_1–L_2, would be able to obtain employment elsewhere in the economy and obtain a similar level of income to that previously earned in fishing. At least, this would be so in a perfectly operating economy as assumed in this theory. Even if there were some frictions involved in adjustment, governments in developed countries would be in an economic position to provide funds to assist the transition of fishers to other industries, whereas this would be unlikely in less developed countries.

Of course, the above is not the only type of economic inefficiency that can arise when there is open-access to resources. Another shortcoming is the failure of those in an open-access industry to take into account marginal user costs. Consequently, resources may be used in the present which would be more valuable socially if conserved for the future. This and other types of economic efficiency that arise when there is open-access to resources are discussed, for example, in Tisdell (2002, Ch. 8; 2005, Ch. 6).

In developed countries such economic inefficiencies do not result in poverty because labour is assumed to be mobile, wages in those countries are above subsistence level, and few industries involve open-access. But in developing countries, wages are low and those displaced from use of open-access resources are hard-pressed to find employment elsewhere. In developing countries, incomes of those involved in open-access activities may fall to subsistence level and their governments may find it difficult or impossible to rectify the situation. Let us analyse this matter.

The Open-Access Problem in Developing Countries and the Presence of a Poverty Trap

In many developing countries, utilisation of open-access resources provides an economic opportunity for the employment of individuals who do not own significant amounts of private resources, and who are unable to find employment working for others. In the theory outlined here, it will be assumed that open-access resources are utilised directly by individuals mainly for subsistence purposes and that if income from their use is above subsistence level, this attracts others to exploit these open-access resources. Entry continues until incomes fall to subsistence level. This may occur because entrants are attracted from elsewhere in the economy, or because the Malthusian theory of population growth applies, that is, the population of those utilising the open-access resources increases when incomes are above subsistence level.

The theory can be illustrated by Figure 3. Let β represent the subsistence level of per capita income which is assumed to be a poverty level of income. This may be also interpreted as the income level per family, needed for subsistence, assuming that available labour per family is proportional to family size and that the population supported is in proportion to the numbers working in the open-access industry. The line $y = \beta L$ represents the total output needed to supply a subsistence level of income for all engaged in the harvesting of the open-access resource which, for simplicity, we suppose is the stock of fish. The government would like to have a per capita income level for fishermen of an amount a indicated by the slope of line OC in Figure 3. The curve marked OABF (which is often assumed to be a quadratic function) represents the relationship between the total harvest of fish and the number of fishers.

If initially income per fisher exceeds the subsistence level, β, for example is at α, numbers engaged in fishing increase and do so until incomes fall to subsistence level. In this case, the open-access equilibrium will be at E and L_4 fishers will be employed in fishing. This is an excessive number in relation to the target income per fisher of α. It is L_4-L_3 more than required for the desired result, which corresponds to point C. However, of course, even C is not economically optimal because it involves more effort than is compatible with achieving maximum sustainable yield. This occurs at point B and involves the employment of L_2 fishers, assuming that each fishes or works a 'standard' number of hours. However, the government may not have the ability to regulate effort in the industry to achieve this result or may not have sufficient knowledge to identify this maximum.

The issues can be most easily analysed by considering per unit curves that correspond to those on Figure 3. These are shown in Figure 4 supposing that the production function is a quadratic. Line ABE represents the average product from fishing and line AMN is its corresponding marginal product line. OF represents the subsistence level of income and OH represents the target level of per capita income. The equilibrium occurs at point D if open-access prevails, and per capita income is β which is below the target level of α.

Figure 3
In Developing Countries Open-access to Resources is Likely to Result in an Equilibrium Where users of the Resources only earn a Subsistence Level of Income that Corresponds to Point E in this case

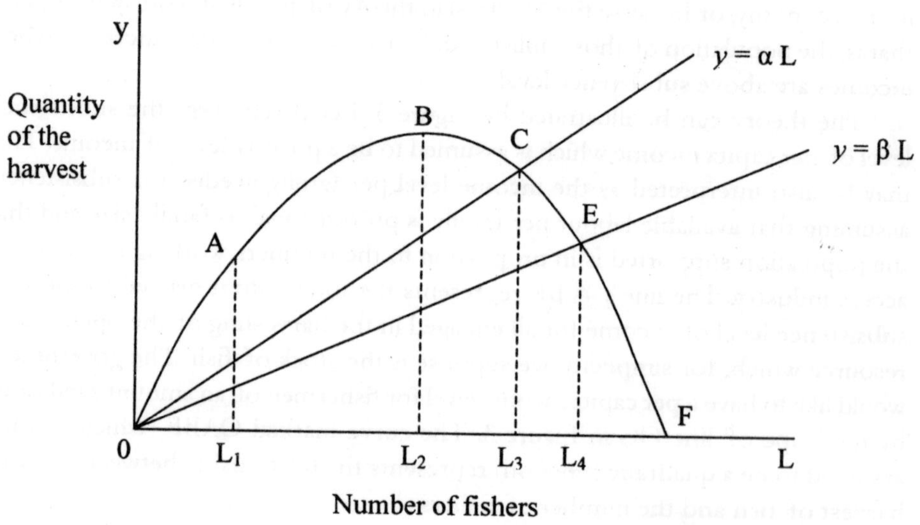

Figure 4
Long-run Relationships between Marginal Product and Average Product as a Function of Fishing Effort

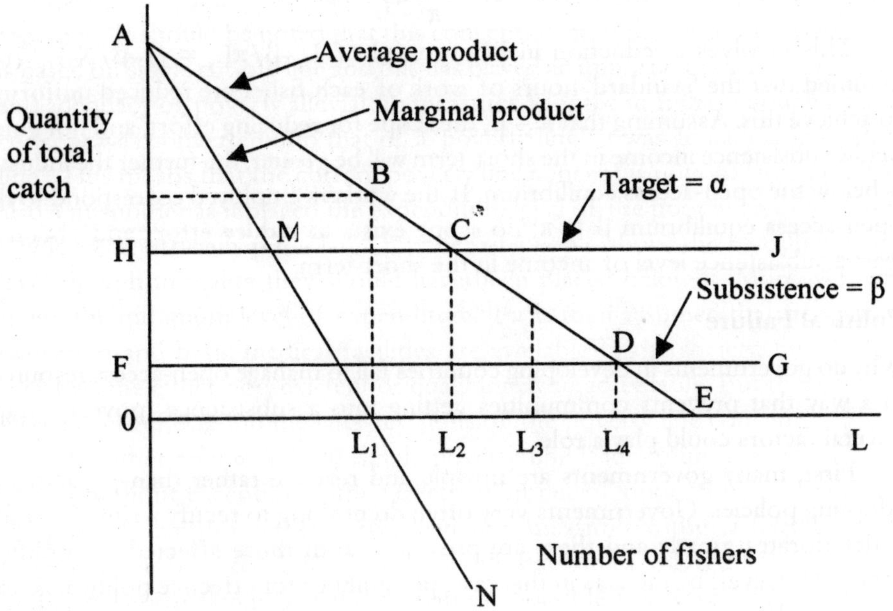

Now it can be observed that if the long-run open-access equilibrium, D, prevails that the government of a developing country has no leeway to extricate the community from this situation, for example to reduce effort so income per fisher rises from β to α. For example, given that fishers have no opportunity to earn a subsistence level of income elsewhere, any attempt to reduce the effort of each will initially depress their incomes below subsistence level. This is because initially their catch is likely to fall in proportion to the reduction in their effort. Only in the longer term will levels of the population of the fish increase. If fishers are already at or near the poverty level, reducing effort will initially force them below it; a situation that will be politically unacceptable. Because of limited finances available to governments in developing countries, they are likely to be unable to provide income support to fishers while the level of fishing stocks recover.

If π represents average income earned by fishers, then the higher is π in relation to β, the subsistence level of income, the greater is the scope for reducing effort in the open-access industry without reducing per capita income to a level below subsistence in the very short term. For example, if L_3 in Figure 4 represents the numbers employed in open-access and if π is their per capita income, a level of labour effort equivalent to that in the following equation is compatible with those in the industry obtaining a subsistence level of income in the very short term:

$$L = \frac{\beta}{\pi} L_3$$

This involves a reduction in labour used of $L_3 - \beta/\pi L_3 = (1-\beta/X)L_3$. It is assumed that the 'standard' hours of work of each fisher are reduced uniformly to achieve this. Assuming that $\pi = \beta$, the scope for reducing effort, and not going below subsistence income in the short-term will be greater, the further the industry is below the open-access equilibrium. If the workers employed correspond to the open-access equilibrium $\beta = \pi$, no scope exists to reduce effort and obtain at least a subsistence level of income in the short-term.

Political Failure

Why do governments in developing countries fail to manage open-access resources in a way that prevents communities getting into a subsistence (poverty) trap? Several factors could play a role.

First, many governments are myopic and reactive rather than proactive in adopting policies. Governments very often do nothing to rectify a situation until it deteriorates greatly and there are pressures from those affected for political action. However, by then, as in this case, possibilities for effective political action may have disappeared.

Secondly, the costs and difficulties faced by governments in developing countries in regulating resources used by those living in rural villages should not be underestimated. This is a barrier to the management of resource use and appears to be a more serious one than in developed economies.

Encouragement of the adoption of new more productive technologies is sometimes seen as a means to assist those in open-access industries to raise their income. This it can do. However, unless it is accompanied by appropriate regulation of effort, in the long-run and given the model outlined here, income per head will sink back to subsistence level. For example, new technology may cause the productivity curves in Figure 4 to move upwards, and in the short-term, this will raise income per capita. However, higher incomes may increase entry or the level of the population depending on the industry, and a new equilibrium at the subsistence level of income will be established in the long-term.

Nevertheless, the above case is a relatively favourable one. Another possibility is that the productivity curves in Figure 4 move upwards on their left hand side but swing sharply left (clockwise) on their right hand side. This can occur because the new technology depresses the population of the fish stock at a faster rate in relation to effort than the previous technology. The new average product curve could, therefore, cut line AD to the left of D. A new open-access equilibrium might be established with less employment than with the previous technology but with the same level of subsistence income. This raises serious problems for those who are no longer able to earn a subsistence level of income in the industry due to the introduction of the new technology, that is those displaced by the new technology.

Concluding Comments

The governments of developing countries face formidable problems in managing their open-access resources in a manner that prevents over-exploitation of these resources, and which also stops those who rely for their livelihood on such resources falling into poverty. The problems faced in managing open-access resources in developing countries has been shown to be much more serious than in developed economies. Policies used to manage such resources in developed economies are difficult or impossible to apply in less developed economies.

A major problem for developing countries is that their open-access industries are likely to come into an equilibrium in which those engaged in those industries just earn a subsistence level of income at or near the poverty level. As demonstrated, once such an equilibrium emerges, governments in developing countries have no leeway to extricate themselves from it. This has implications for foreign aid. Governments of developing countries wishing to adopt policies to reduce harvesting in open-access industries need foreign aid to provide income support to those involved in the transition. Or, alternatively, they need foreign aid to develop industries that can provide alternative employment for those displaced by reduced effort in an open-access industry. In some cases, for example, fisheries, aquaculture development could provide an alternative. On the other hand, foreign aid designed to increase the productivity of the open-access harvesting may, as explained above, do more economic harm than good in the long run.

In conclusion, it should be observed that the standard economic theory of the use of open-access resources has limitations when applied to developing countries. This theory suggests that there is greater scope for public management of these resources than does exist in practice. Understandingly, this theory does not consider the possible poverty trap associated with the use of those resources in developing countries. This trap seriously limits the capacity of governments in developing countries to address the over-exploitation of open-access resources.

REFERENCES

Bromley, D.W. (1991), *Environment and Economy: Property Rights and Public Policy*. Addison-Wesley, Boston, USA.

Gordon, H.S. (1954), The Economic Theory of a Common Property Resource: The Fishery. *Journal of Political Economy* 62, 123-162.

Ostrom, E. (1990), *Governing the Commons: The Evolution of Institutions for Collective Action*. Cambridge University Press, Cambridge, UK.

Plourde, C.G. (1971), Exploitation of Common-property Replenishible Natural Resources. *Western Economic Journal* 9, 256-266.

Tietenberg, T. (2003), *Environmental and Natural Resource Economics.* Addison-Wesley, Boston, USA.

Tisdell, C.A. (2002), *The Economics of Conserving Wildlife and Natural Resources.* Edward Elgar, Cheltenham, UK and Northampton, MA, USA.

Tisdell, C.A. (2005), *The Economics of Environmental Conservation: Second Edition*, Edward Elgar, Cheltenham, UK and Northampton, MA, USA.

13

THE 'STABILISATION TRAP' AND POVERTY REDUCTION—WHAT CAN MONETARY POLICY DO?

Anis Chowdhury

Introduction

Burdened with the stagflation of the 1970s in the wake of two oil price shocks and the debt crises of the early 1980s, the profession of development economics was preoccupied with stabilisation in the last two decades. This was also the period of aid-fatigue and the rise of conditionality based lending by international financial institutions such as the International Monetary Fund (IMF) and the World Bank (WB). One major component of conditionality has been macroeconomic stabilisation. However, under the weight of the IMF and WB, stabilisation was solely meant to be nominal stabilisation a configuration of a low inflation (targeted at less than 5% in the medium term) and a low budget deficit (targeted at near zero primary deficit). Thus, the balanced budget principle has become a new orthodoxy, which has been captured in the following words:

> ... 'deficit financing' can lead to a very unsustainable economy. Bolivia in the 1980s is an extreme example: its deficit rose to 28% of GNP–leading to hyperinflation and a serious economic crisis. So, each country should aim at roughly balancing its budget..." (Human Development Report, 1991, p. 42)

The root of the developing countries' debt crises was identified to be high budget deficits that caused inflation, which in turn was responsible for their loss of competitiveness and growth stagnation.[1] Therefore, adherence to a balanced budget principle and a low inflation target wasz expected to accelerate much desired growth needed for poverty reduction. However, two decades of such policies have failed to produce expected results. For example, the weighted average inflation rate in low-income countries (excluding China and India) fell from 19.2% during 1965-80 to 14.9% in the 1980s. Instead of the expected rise in their growth rate,

---

Note: Chapter marked with will be reprints from the special issue of the Indian Development Review.

the weighted average GDP growth in these countries fell from 4.6% (1965-80) to 3.4% (1980-89). More specifically, 14 countries with average inflation rates between 15% and 3% during 1965-80 had a drop in the inflation rate in the 1980s. Except two (Bangladesh and Pakistan), all experienced a decline in their growth rate. Interestingly, Indonesia whose average inflation rate dropped from 35.5% during 1965-80 to 8.3% in the 1980s, also experienced a growth recession from 7% to 5.3%. A comparison of the inflation and growth figures in the 1980s and the 1990s reveals a similar picture. The countries that grew faster in the 1990s were the ones which could beat hyperinflation in excess of 40-45%.

The picture becomes even worse when one looks at the growth of per capita income. The weighted average per capita GNP growth in low-income countries (excluding China and India) during 1985-95 was a dismal–1.4.%[2] Thus, it is no wonder that after two decades of severe austerity and the pursuit of macroeconomic stabilisation goals, poverty in most developing countries has gone up.[3] In sombre words, the recently retired President of the World Bank, James Wolfensohn acknowledges, "… if we take a closer look, we see something else–something alarming. In developing countries, excluding China, at least 100 million more people are living in poverty today than a decade ago. And the gap between rich and poor yawns wider."[4]

Thus, we can see a renewed interest in poverty reduction as reflected in the ambitious Millennium Development Goals (MDGs) to halve world poverty by 2015. This is a paradigm shift from nominal targeting to real targeting. This, therefore, requires a re-examination of the role of macroeconomic policies. In a recent UN commissioned report, Sachs and his associates argued that the macroeconomic framework of the IMF and WB is incompatible with the requirements of MDGs. They also advocated a supportive monetary policy framework to accommodate public sector led investment programs in employment intensive infrastructure and social sectors. (See, UN, 2005).

Based on a survey of the macroeconomic performance of developing countries, this paper argues that while there is a danger that persistent high budget deficits and consequent high inflation can damage an economy, fear of such a situation cannot be the basis of public policy. Too low an inflation target and zero budget deficits can be an over-kill and create a 'stabilisation trap'–a situation characterised by low inflation and insufficient growth for poverty reduction.[5] This conclusion is based on the following observations:

1. The relationship between inflation and economic growth is non-linear. That is, both too low and too high inflation can be harmful for economic growth; but moderate inflation and economic growth are positively related.
2. The effect of inflation on the poor is not straightforward. It depends on the sum of employment and real wage (income distribution) effects. Both too high and too low inflation can harm the poor.

3. Both average income of the poor and income distribution are adversely affected by aggregate demand variability. The average income of the poor falls and income distribution widens during the downswing of the economy.
4. The probability of moderate inflation to slip into a hyper-inflationary situation is extremely low. The upper limit of 'moderate' inflation can be as high as 40%.
5. Countries with unsustainable budget deficits and hyper-inflation are outliers and experienced breakdowns of their political system and institutions as a result of a civil or external war or revolution. Examples include Iran and Nicaragua.

This paper thus argues that monetary policy should aim at both price and output stabilisation, instead of solely targeting low inflation. In other words, for the purpose of poverty reduction it should have two objectives–price stabilisation and employment generation. This may mean tolerating 'moderate' inflation in the range of 10-12%. When the monetary policy is entrusted with two goals, it needs at least two independent instruments. While the central banks can use their traditional instrument of interest rate or monetary aggregates to achieve a moderate inflation target, directed (specialised) credits for employment-intensive sectors (e.g agriculture and SMEs) can be used for the employment target.

Cross-country evidence on inflation, growth and income distribution is presented in the next two sections. The subsequent section discusses the political economy of central bank independence. This is essential not only because the argument for central bank independence depends on the strength of inflation-growth relationships in the short- and long-run, but, more importantly, due to potential contradiction between democratic governance and the technocratic insulation of an institution in charge of monetary policy. This also raises important political economy issues concerning the choice of weights in the social welfare function.

Does Inflation Harm Economic Growth?

Milton Friedman (1973, p. 41) highlighted the uncertainty about the inflation-growth relationship when he observed, "Historically, all possible combinations have occurred: inflation with and without [economic] development, no inflation with and without [economic] development." The historical evidence shows that many countries grew at respectable rates even when the inflation rates ranged between 15% and 20%. For example, one of the dynamic East Asian economies, the Republic of Korea, grew by more than 8% during the 1960s and 1970s when the average inflation rates were 17.5% and 16.5%, respectively.

Figure 1 presents the scatter plots of average annual inflation rates and average annual growth rates in 141 developing countries during 1980-1998. As can be seen, the negative relationship between inflation and growth is influenced by extreme values or outlying countries having exceptionally high inflation rates.

Figure 1
Scatter Plots Inflation and Growth

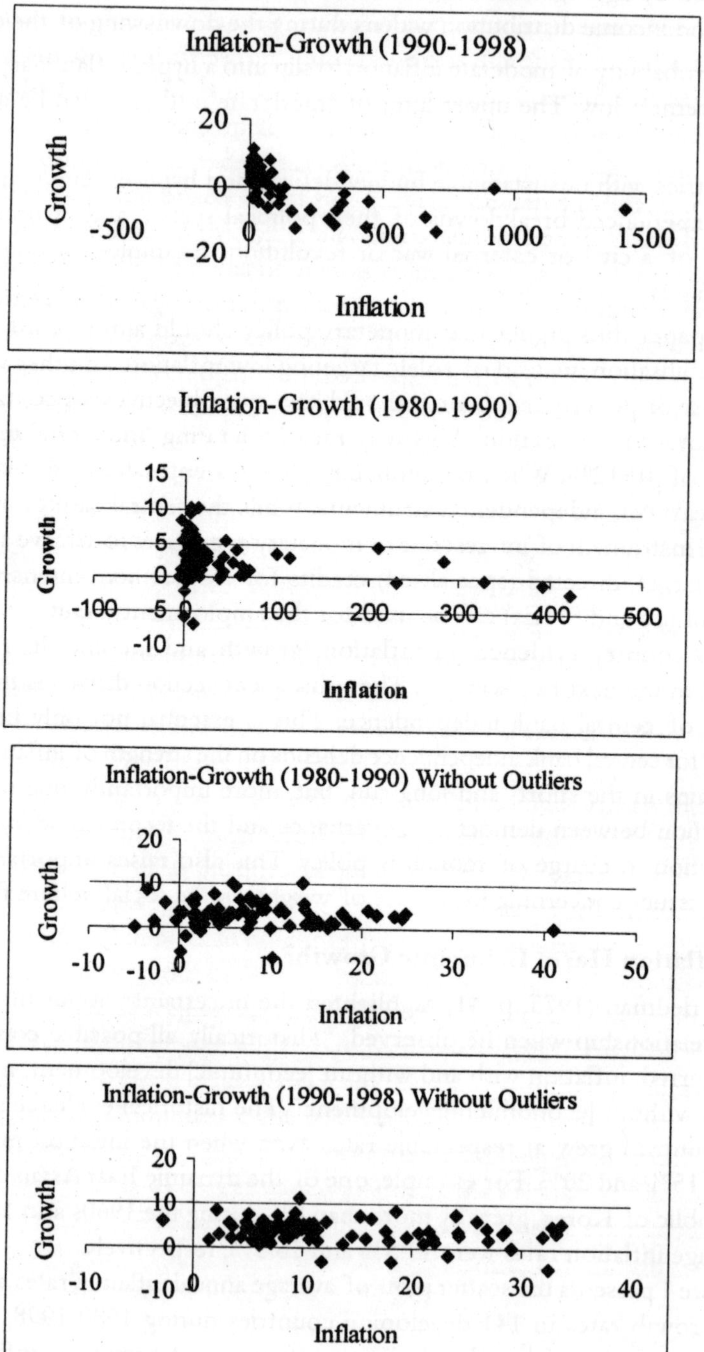

Source:

The overall picture depicted in Figure 1 is consistent with the findings of Bruno and Easterly (1998), who examined inflation-growth data for the period 1961-1994. After extensive empirical research, they concluded, "the correlation loses significance with the omission of a single observation–Nicaragua, which had hyper-inflation and negative growth in the 1980s ... More generally, significance and sign of the cross-section correlation depends on the inclusion of the countries with high inflation crises–the above 40% episodes...".[6] They also observed, "the significance of the negative growth during 20-40% inflation vanishes if a single extreme annual observation is omitted – Iran in 1980" (Bruno and Easterly, 1998, p. 15). Bruno and Easterly (1998) did not find any significant evidence of a negative association between inflation and growth during the episodes of 20-40% inflation. Thus, "moderate" inflation does not seem to harm economic growth.[7] Easterly (2003) reported similar findings and regarded inflation rates below 35% as "moderate".

A more recent study of modern hyper- and high inflations by Fischer, Sahay and Vegh (2002) reported similar findings. This study categorised inflation rates over 100% as "very high", between 50% and 100% as "high" and between 25% and 50% as "moderate to high". It found that real GDP per capita fell on average by 1.6% per annum during very high inflation episodes (average 739%), but rose by 1.4% during years of low inflation (average 22.4%). A similar pattern was found for private consumption per capita and investment growth per capita. They also found that current account and fiscal deficits worsened during high inflation.[8]

Figure 2 plots average inflation and growth rates over four decades (1960-2000) for 141 countries. Two interesting features emerge. First, the inflation-growth relationship was negative in the period 1960-1979. One, however, needs to bear in mind that the1970s was an exceptional period characterised by stagflation caused by two oil price shocks.[9] We can get a better understanding of the inflation-growth relationship from the figures in the later periods when the relationship became non-linear–first positive and then negative in the later period of 1980-2000. This

Figure 2
Average GDP Growth & Inflation Rates (1960-2000) for 141 Countries

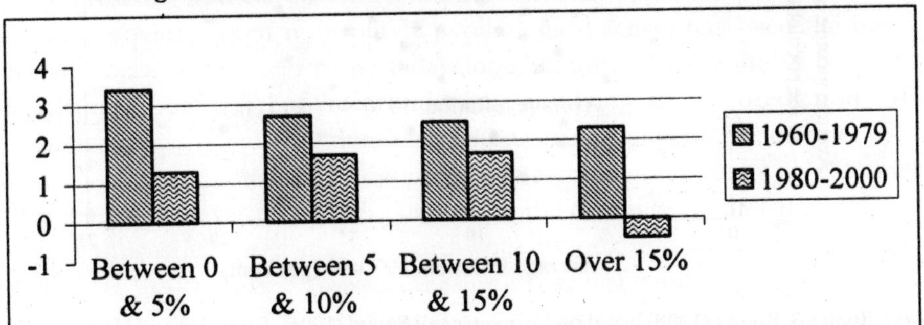

Source: Islam, 2003.

confirms the uncertain nature of the inflation-growth relationship. Second, the variation in growth rates between the two time periods is much larger at both low and high inflation. That is, both high and low inflation rates can be destabilising, and hence, harmful to the poor.

Figure 3a
Income of the Poor and Average Inflation

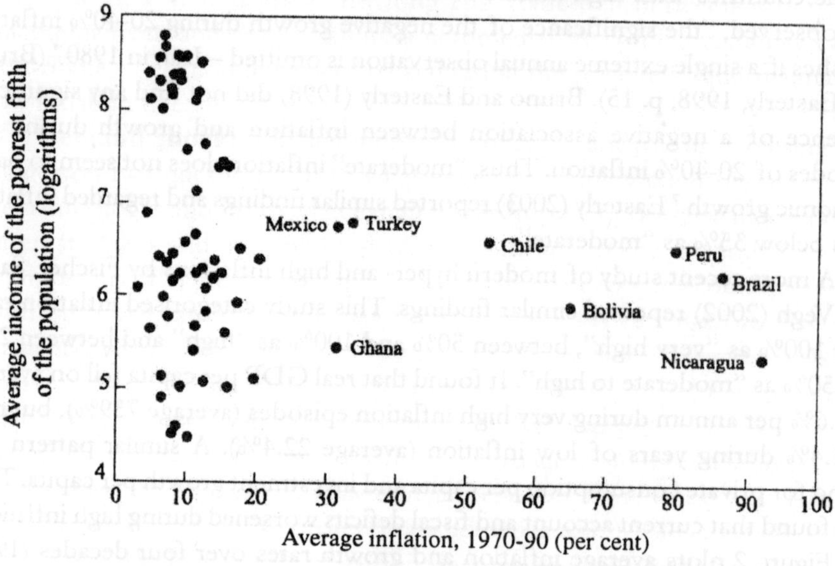

Figure 3b
Income of the Poor and Average Inflation Excluding Outliers

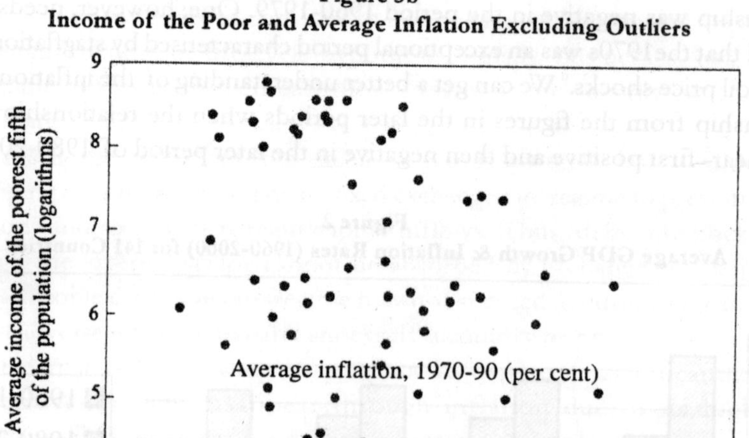

Source: Romer & Romer (1998) based on Deininger and Squire (1996), Summers and Heston (1991) & World Bank's World Data CD-ROM (1995 edition).

Finally, we present cross-country scatter plots of average inflation and income of the poor (Figure 3). Clearly the claim of the orthodox school that inflation harms the poor breaks down when one considers an inflation rate in the range of 5-15%. Consistent with the aggregate inflation-growth relationship, the negative relationship between inflation and the income of the poor is based on a few cases of extreme inflation.

Thus, one may conclude that while policy makers should guard against high inflation, a country may need 'moderate' inflation to sustain economic growth. This understanding is essential when there is an excess capacity and persistently high unemployment or underemployment. The over-fixation with a single digit inflation target cannot be justified based on the fear of inflation getting out of control once it is allowed to go beyond, say, the 10% level. Dornbusch and Fischer (1993) found that an inflation rate in the moderate range of 15-30% does not usually accelerate to extreme levels. Similarly Bruno and Easterly (1998) found the threshold inflation rate of 40% at which the probability of the inflation rate accelerating rises significantly. Furthermore, there are only a handful of cases where inflation rates did accelerate and output stagnated or declined in the past, and these cases could be attributed to unusual circumstances (e.g. Iran or Nicaragua in the 1980s following dramatic fall of the regimes).

Fischer, Sahay and Vegh (2002, p. 841) noted that the episodes of hyper-inflations are "quite rare ... still relatively rare [are] episodes of very high inflation, defined as inflations in excess of 100 per cent per annum." They also found that when the inflation rate is less than 25% it is highly likely (a probability of 95.4%) that it will stay in that range in the following years, and until inflation reaches the 200% level, it is more likely to fall than rise. Fischer, Sahay and Vegh (2002, p. 845) concluded, "... most of the time, in most countries, inflation is low..."

Interestingly, Fischer *et al.* found that despite a very high association between money growth and inflation, the causality (in a Granger sense) in most cases does not run from money growzzth to inflation. Instead inflation was found to 'Granger cause' money growth. Although they identified a budget deficit as a trigger factor for inflation (which causes money growth), "the relationship between the fiscal balance and inflation becomes significant for the high-inflation countries but does not for the low-inflation countries" (p. 854). According to them, "... no obvious long- or short-run relationship between inflation and fiscal balance is found for the low-inflation countries or during the low-inflation episodes in the high-inflation countries" (p. 855). (Note that low inflation is defined as less than 25%).

In sum, there is no empirical basis to fear that a moderately expansionary monetary policy required to support fiscal expansion for poverty reduction and to break the stabilisation trap will lead to high inflation. More importantly, 'fear' of excesses cannot be a basis for sound public policy.

Money in the Short-run: Is There any Output Stabilisation Role?

Having examined the inflation-growth relationship, we now examine the neo-liberal position on money's role in short-run stabilisation in response to demand and supply shocks. The orthodox school, following Milton Friedman, holds the view that monetary policy should not be used to stabilise output. Rather, monetary policy should seek to stabilise the price level. This is consistent with the new classical view that there is no long-run trade-off between inflation and unemployment, and that inflation is detrimental. Accordingly, money can best contribute to economic growth by stabilising the price level and maintaining a low inflation rate.

Demand Shock: Whether monetary policy has any role in stabilising output hinges on two questions–(a) to what extent developing countries are prone to demand shocks and (b) to what extent prices (product prices, exchange rates and interest rates) and wages are flexible. Contrary to the orthodox view, the components of aggregate demand are less stable in developing countries. To begin with, since the export base of developing countries is very narrow, their export demand remains vulnerable to instability in the international market. This is true even for the newly industrialising economies as is evident from the growth slow-down in Singapore due to the recent decline in the world electronic market. Secondly, in developing countries with a high incidence of absolute poverty, current income plays a dominant role in determining consumption expenditure. This makes consumption expenditure pro-cyclical and hence exacerbates the effects of any exogenous shock. The role of current income becomes more significant when underdeveloped credit markets create a liquidity constraint, which causes the short-run marginal propensity to consume to become larger than what is implied by the permanent income or life-cycle hypothesis. Finally, businesses, too, are more vulnerable to shocks to their cash-flow streams as they mainly depend on their own finance.

Among the key prices, the exchange rate is generally less flexible as most developing countries follow a quasi-fixed exchange rate regime to prevent imported inflation, and to attract foreign capital inflows. Thus, demand shocks coming through the external sector cannot be absorbed by exchange rate adjustments. Even a flexible exchange rate regime may not succeed in cushioning an economy against adverse external demand shocks. If a country responds to a sudden fall in export demands by allowing its currency to depreciate significantly, soon its competitiveness will disappear through inflation due to its high import dependence.[10] Moreover, if the decline in external demand is widespread, affecting most countries, then depreciating currencies are likely to create a "beggar-thy-neighbour" like situation with no benefit for anyone, but high inflation.

Therefore, adjustment to demand shocks has to happen by either output cuts or declines in prices and wages (or some combinations of both). As can be seen from Figure 4, the decline in output is larger in the case when price is rigid than when price falls in response to an adverse demand shock. It is generally believed that industrial product prices and wages are inflexible or sluggish downward. This follows from the less competitive nature of the industrial product market and more unionisation in the urban/industrial sector vis-à-vis the agricultural and informal sectors. Therefore, adjustment in the industrial or formal sector happens through output cuts. This can have an adverse effect on employment and hence on the income of the low skilled poor workers.[11]

Figure 4
Adjustments to Demand Shocks

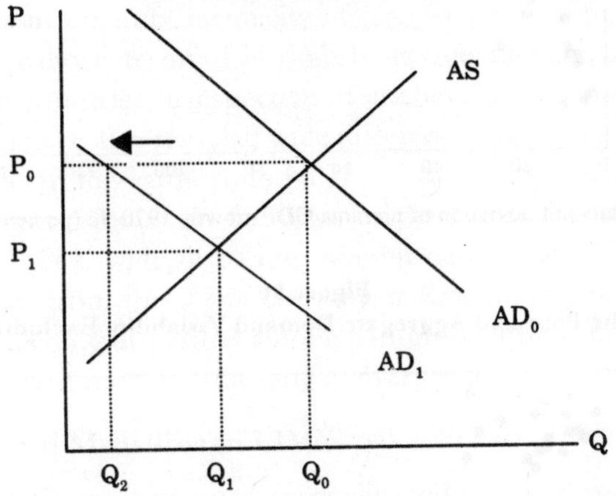

If the unemployed seek employment in the more competitive agriculture and informal sectors, then wages in these sectors will decline. This may push wages below the subsistence level with devastating effects on the material well-being of unskilled poor workers.

Therefore, regardless of whether the adjustment happens through output or prices, falling aggregate demand will have serious implications for the poor. If the adjustment happens through cuts in output and employment, the first to lose their jobs are the unskilled and unorganised workers. On the other hand, if the adjustment happens through declines in wages, again the unorganised and unskilled workers would be forced to accept lower wages. Thus, the poor, unorganised workers are forced to choose between jobs and lower real wages. In either case, the average income of the poor is likely to drop when the nominal GDP growth drops from its trend. Cross-country evidence (Figure 5) shows that the average income of the poor is negatively related to the aggregate demand variability. This negative relationship does not break down even when the outliers are omitted. Therefore, from the point of view of protecting the poor, monetary policy needs to stabilise output in the face of an *adverse* demand shock.

Supply Shock: It is generally accepted that developing countries are more prone to supply shocks than demand shocks. This is due to their heavy dependence

Figure 5a

Income of the Poor and Aggregate Demand Variability

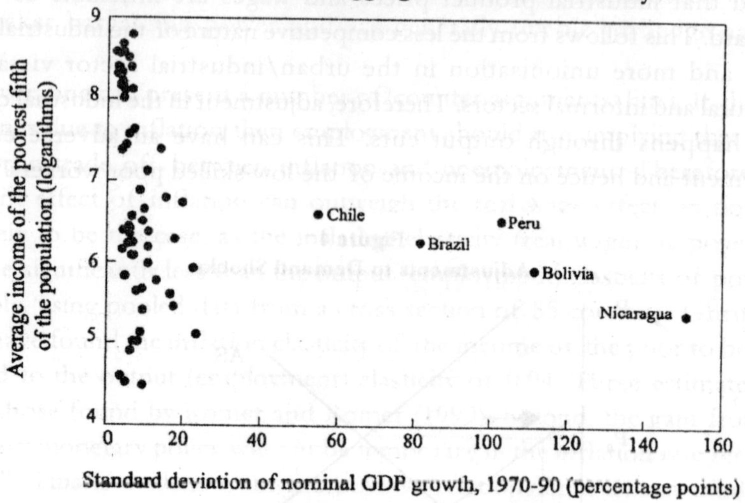

Figure 5b

Income of the Poor and Aggregate Demand Variability Excluding Outliers

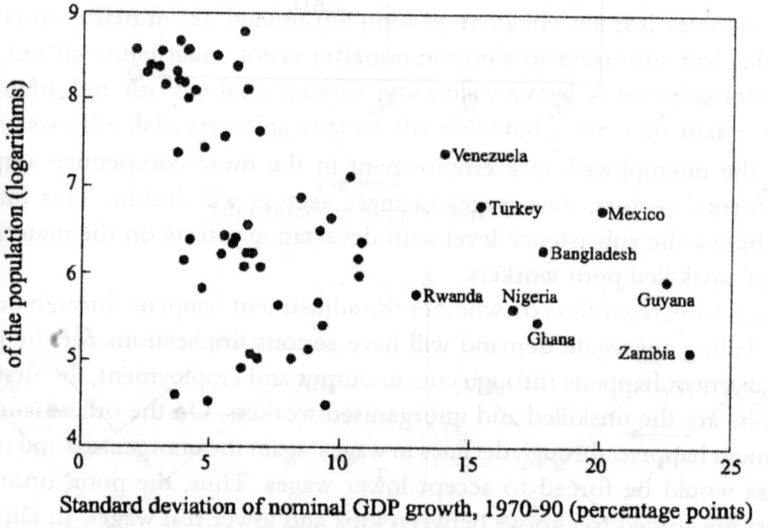

on agriculture and imported raw materials, and energy (oil). While alternating floods and drought are almost regular phenomena affecting agriculture, a declining terms-of-trade due to the rising prices of imported raw materials and energy adversely affects the industrial sector. Siregar and Ward (2001) have found that Indonesia is more prone to supply shocks than demand shocks. Hossain and Chowdhury (1996) documented Bangladesh's episodes of supply shocks due to repeated floods.

The choice between output and price stabilisation becomes starker in the case of a supply shock. This can be shown diagrammatically as below:

In panel A, the response to an adverse supply shock is an expansionary monetary policy to stabilise output at Q_0, whereas in panel B, the response is a contractionary monetary policy to stabilise the price level at P_0. When the response is an expansionary policy, the price level rises further to P_2, causing higher inflation. On the other hand, when the objective is price stabilisation with a contractionary monetary policy, output declines further to Q_2. Beddies (1999) has demonstrated that inflation-targeting monetary policy does not lead to optimal output stabilisation of aggregate supply shocks. That is, a price-stabilisation target leads to greater output variability.

Furthermore, using the Malaysian data, Domac (2001) has found that monetary tightening has a larger impact on small and medium enterprises (SMEs) than it does on larger firms both in terms of persistence and variability of output.[12] That is, the output of the SME sector declines much more and SMEs remain depressed for a longer period following a monetary contraction than is the case for larger industries. The interest cost of servicing debts rises in the face of a declining demand caused by monetary contraction. Since SMEs are more dependent on bank lending for their working capital than the large enterprises, which can rely on internal financing or raise funds from the capital market, tighter monetary policy causes disproportionate cash-flow problems for the SMEs. The cash-flow problem of SMEs is exacerbated as their access to bank lending declines due to the decline in the value of marketable collateral with rising interest rates when the supply of bank loan is reduced.[13] Given the labour-intensive nature of SMEs, this is likely to have an adverse effect on the income of the poor and low skill workers. Thus, it is not a surprise that the cross-country evidence cited earlier (Figure 5), shows adverse impacts of output variability on the average income of the poor.

In sum, when the concept of poverty is widened to include 'vulnerability', monetary policy needs to stabilise the employment of the poor, regardless of the sources of the shocks. The policy makers must accept 'moderate' inflation as a trade-off. As the findings reported earlier (Figure 5) show, moderate inflation is more likely to protect the income of the poor than adversely harm them. In other words, moderately expansionary policies in the wake of a shock can prevent the vulnerable from becoming unemployed and falling into a poverty trap.

Inflation and Income Distribution

It is alleged that inflation disproportionately hurts the poor. There are at least two channels through which it can happen. First, since wage adjustments typically fall behind price rises, inflation reduces the real wage. Since most of the poor are wages earners, the share of the income of the poor in the national income declines vis-à-vis that of profit earners. Second, if there are any savings, the poor mostly hold it in money. Inflation reduces the real value of money holdings. If inflation is unanticipated, the poor will be harmed even more disproportionately as they have a weaker bargaining power and are generally unable to hedge against inflation.[14]

However, one can present a number of counter arguments. First, if the real wage declines due to inflation then employment should rise, implying that there is a short-run trade off between inflation and unemployment. Therefore, the employment effect of inflation can outweigh the real wage effect on poverty. This is likely to be the case, as the inflation elasticity (real wage) of poverty is found to be significantly less than the output (employment) elasticity of poverty. For example, using pooled data from a cross section of 85 countries Ghruha et al. (2002) have found the inflation elasticity of the income of the poor to be 0.03 as opposed to the output (employment) elasticity of 0.94. These estimates are similar to those found by Romer and Romer (1999). Second, the gain from an expansionary monetary policy will not be temporary if the inflation rate remains "moderate". This is evident from the positive relationship between moderate inflation and economic growth as demonstrated earlier. These findings are consistent with the evidence presented in Figures 3 and 5.

Third, the poor have very limited financial assets; they are largely net financial debtors. Thus, inflation can benefit the poor by reducing the real value of their net debt. On the other hand, lower inflation not only increases the real value of financial debt, but also the high interest rate policy aimed at bringing inflation down increases the debt servicing cost of the indebted poor. This makes them

Figure 6
Adjustment to Supply Shocks

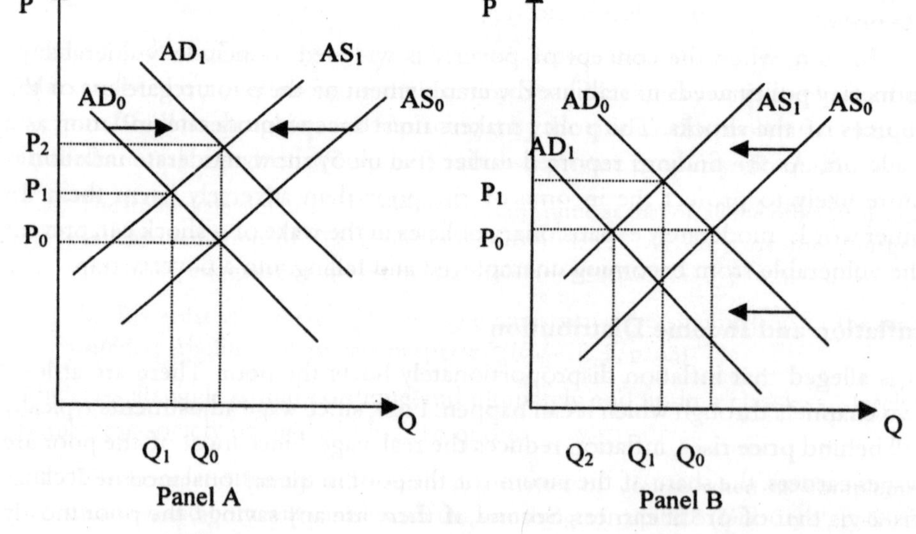

doubly disadvantaged. As a matter of fact, studies have found that income distribution narrows during the expansionary phase and widens during the contractionary phase of a business cycle. Figure 7 presents the scatter plots of average inflation and inequality (measured by the Gini coefficient). Once again,

Figure 7a
Inequality and Average Inflation

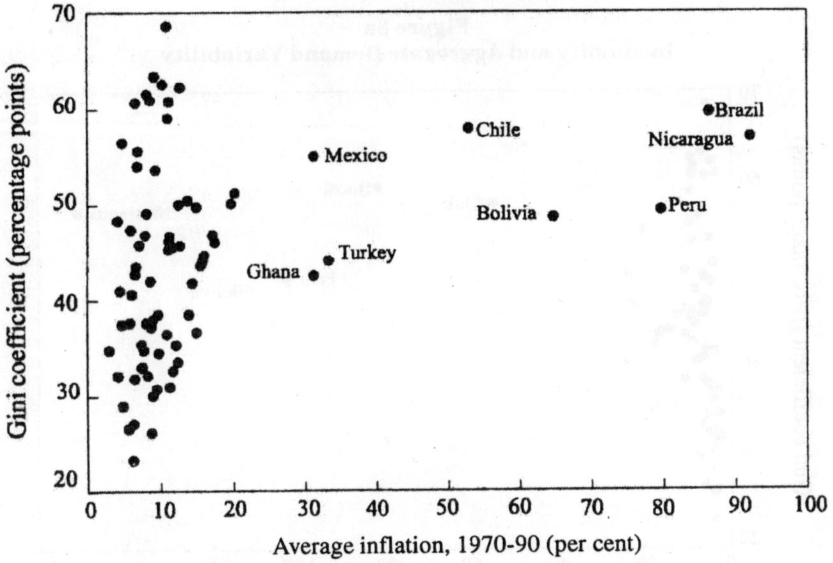

Figure 7b
Inequality and Average Inflation Excluding Outliners

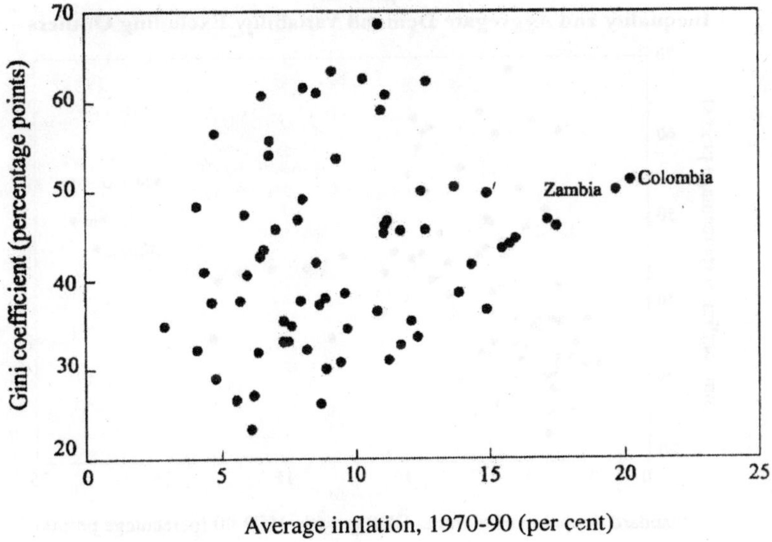

we find that the claim of the adverse distributional effect of inflation is based on extreme inflationary cases. There seems to be no relation between inequality and inflation when the inflation rate ranges between 5 and 15%. On the other hand, inequality rises with the variability of nominal GDP growth even when outliers are excluded (Figure 8). The evidence presented in Figures 7 and 8 vindicates the need for an output-stabilising monetary policy stance that allows for 'moderate' inflation.

Figure 8a
Inequality and Aggregate Demand Variability

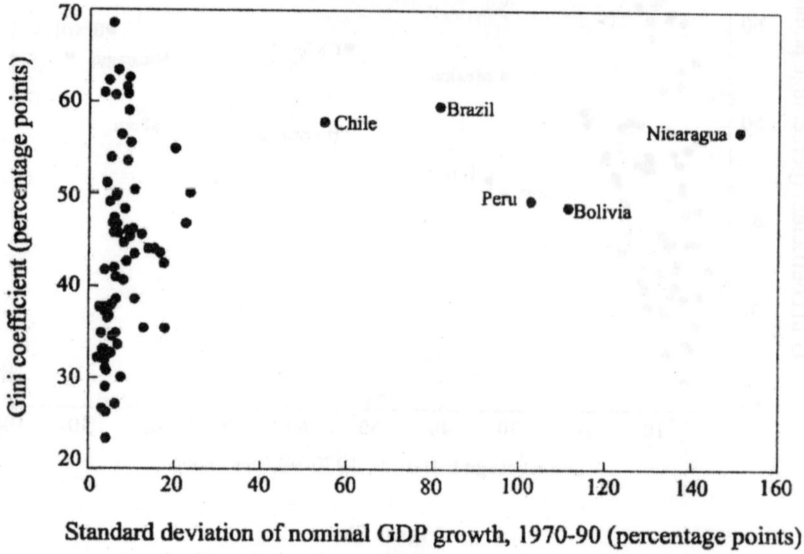

Figure 8b
Inequality and Aggregate Demand Variability Excluding Outliers

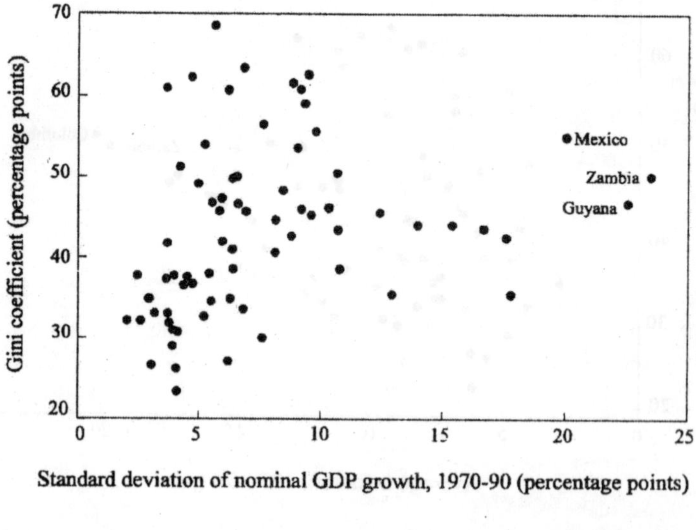

Summary: Does Inflation Affect the Poor?

The above survey of empirical evidence and past studies shows that only extreme inflation adversely affects the poor. The average income of the poor declines when the inflation rate is either very low and very high; but moderate inflation was not found to affect the poor. However, the average can be misleading; the average inflation rate can be moderate, yet the inflation rate of particular items that feature prominently in the consumption basket of the poor, may be quite high. Therefore, from the poverty reduction point of view, policy makers should monitor not only average inflation but also its components. Of particular importance is the price of food. The poor are vulnerable to food price rises even when overall inflation remains moderate. As the experience of Indonesia shows, food price stabilisation contributes significantly to rapid poverty reduction (see Timmer, 2005).

Food price inflation is generally caused by supply shortages, due to either supply shocks and/or market manipulation by unscrupulous traders. Monetary policy is not a very good instrument for controlling it. If the average inflation rate rises due to food price inflation then the application of a restrictive monetary policy can only worsen the condition of the poor by inducing the contraction of other sectors.

Food price stabilisation is a complex task. It requires a combination of subsidies and market regulation through government procurement and legislations against hoardings and manipulations. Subsidies and government procurement of food will have implications for fiscal balance, requiring support from monetary policy.

The Political Economy of Central Bank Independence and Inflation-targeting

Despite its seemingly settled nature, the orthodox position remains a subject of debate. To begin with, as the preceding discussion has demonstrated, too low an inflation target may be harmful for both economic growth and poverty reduction. Furthermore, the empirical evidence on the performance of independent central banks is still mixed. The conditions required for the success of an inflation-targeting approach include the lack of fiscal dominance and the absence of any other objectives. None of these conditions appear to hold in most developing countries. The revenue base of these countries is very low and their capital market is underdeveloped. This forces most developing countries to borrow from the central bank. These countries also have some sort of quasi-fixed exchange rate systems that are needed to prevent imported inflation and to attract short-term portfolio foreign capital. Thus, money supply responds to developments in the balance of payments.

Leaving aside the technical argument, the performance of an independent central bank and the desirability of a very low inflation target, there is a broader issue of democratic governance and technocratic insulation of institutions. It is pertinent at this juncture to quote Milton Friedman, who is on record for voicing the concern that '… money is too important to be left to the central bankers'. His concerns are elaborated in the following quote:

> The political objections are perhaps more obvious than the economic ones. Is it really tolerable in a democracy to have so much power concentrated in a body free from any direct political control? … One economic defect of an independent central bank … is that it almost invariably involves dispersal of responsibility… Another defect … is the extent to which policy is … made highly dependent on personalities… A third technical defect is that an independent central bank will almost invariably give undue emphasis to the point of view of bankers… The defects I have outlined constitute a strong technical argument against an independent central bank.
>
> (Friedman, 1985, p 8)

Stern and Stiglitz (1996) have made the point more succinctly:

> The degree of independence of the central bank is an issue of the balance of power in a democratic society. The variables controlled by the central bank are of great importance and thus require democratic accountability. At the same time the central bank can act as a check on government irresponsibility. The most successful economies have developed institutional arrangements that afford the central bank considerable autonomy; but in which there is a check provided by public oversight, an oversight that ensures the broader national interest is taken into account in the final decisions.

In this respect, it is worth highlighting the distinction between 'goal independence' and 'instrument independence'.[15] The former refers to the central bank's ability to set the inflation target independently of the government and the latter is its independence in the choice of instruments, and hence relates to the central bank's day-to-day operations. No central bank can be entirely independent of a democratic government although it can be entirely free in choosing its instruments. Several authors (e.g. Auerbach, 1985; Frey and Schneider 1981) have pointed out that even the Federal Reserve System and the Bundesbank, which are considered highly independent in practice, follow the monetary policy of their governments. "In general, central banks with inflation targets are directly accountable to the government. Regular testimony to the parliament and the publication of annual reports have been the main vehicles of this accountability" (Debelle et al, 1998, p. 6).

However, most developing countries are new democracies. In such a situation, a central bank with both goal and instrument independence may choose a very low inflation target which can undermine a nascent democracy by delaying economic recovery. Furthermore, the very argument that an elected government cannot be trusted with the responsibility of managing the economy goes against the very principle of a representative democracy.

The above issues have become more prominent in Indonesia as the new central bank law (enacted in 1999) grants the Bank Indonesia (BI) both goal and instrument independence. This has been responsible for open disputes between the BI and the Parliament on a number of occasions on the appropriateness of BI's monetary policy stance. The national planning agency (BAPPENAS) has also expressed concerns about the mismatch between the monetary policy stance of the BI and fiscal policy.[16]

It is rather strange that under the provision of the current legislation of BI independence, neither the president nor the parliament can remove the governor of BI before the expiry of his/her tenure. This led to the much publicised stand-off when President Wahid wanted to remove the Governor after he was indicted in a corruption case. The Governor refused to resign even when the court found him guilty.

In sum, inflation targeting and central bank independence are not merely technical matters, as the orthodoxy tends to believe. It is pertinent at this juncture to point to the observation made by a central bank insider, Guy Debelle (1996, p. 1).

> An increase in the inflation aversion of the central bank, while always reducing the inflation rate, may reduce welfare because of its adverse effects on output and government spending. The net welfare effect is shown to depend on the weights in the welfare functions of the fiscal authority and society. Thus, increasing the central bank's inflation aversion is not necessarily a free lunch.

Thus, the essence of inflation targeting is embedded in the so-called social welfare function that includes both inflation and economic growth. As the preceding discussion shows, the high unemployment that is required to bring the inflation rate to a single digit level or to keep the inflation rate in the range of 3-5% has significant and systematically regressive effects on the distribution of income. The poor fare worse when unemployment rises and persists, especially when there is no adequate safety-net or social security system. At the same time, the real value of their net debt rises with falling inflation. Hence, the poor have reasons to be more averse to unemployment and less averse to inflation than the elite in society. As the poor lack a voice and representation, the choice of weights for inflation and unemployment in the social welfare function raises an important issue of conflicts and the political economy of public policy (see Hibbs, 1976; Gramlich and Lauren, 1984 and Bowles, 1994).

Concluding Remarks

Monetary policy can play an important role in poverty reduction. However, the link between monetary policy and poverty reduction is a complex one. This is because money and inflation are positively correlated, but inflation can either promote or retard economic growth, which is essential for poverty reduction. Empirical evidence shows that very low and very high inflation is harmful for economic growth, but moderate inflation positively correlates with respectable growth rates. What constitutes 'moderate' inflation can vary across time and countries. Cross-country studies indicate that moderate inflation lies in the range of 10-30%. Thus, a conservative monetary policy aimed at an inflation rate between 3-5% may run the danger of deflation, leading to a situation that can be described as a 'stabilisation trap'. On the other hand, too lax an expansionary monetary policy may cause inflation to accelerate and harm economic growth. Thus, monetary policy can be an 'Okum's razor' as far as poverty reduction is concerned. Fortunately, however, the upper range of 'moderate' inflation and the threshold inflation rate beyond which it can become harmful to poor is quite high, 35-40%.

There are further complications. First, the poverty reducing effect of growth depends on the nature of growth. If growth is capital or skill intensive and hence causes inequality to rise, its impact on poverty reduction will be less than if growth is employment intensive and inequality reducing. The experience of 'miracle' economies of East and Southeast Asia shows that poverty can be reduced rapidly through employment intensive growth that reduces inequality.

Second, the impact of inflation on poverty and inequality can be either negative or positive. Inflation not only erodes the purchasing power of current income, it also reduces the real value of financial debt. Thus, the net affect of inflation on poverty depends on the relative strength of income and wealth effect (i.e, reduced real value of financial debt). Cross country evidence reveals that inflation in the range of 10-15% does not adversely affect the average income of the poor. Moderate inflation is also found to stabilise employment. The employment and wealth effects on the average income of the poor are found to be pro-cyclical. Thus, excessive emphasis on a very low inflation target even in the face of negative output shocks implies the poor's lack of voice in the policy making process.

In sum, the net effect of monetary policy on poverty reduction depends on a number of elasticities. The precise value of these elasticities is likely to vary from country to country and over time. However, the following four general principles for poverty reducing monetary policy can be laid down:

1. Recognise both price and output stabilisation roles. That is, avoid both too conservative and too expansionary monetary policies. Inflation in the range of 10-15% can be regarded as safe both from the point of view of avoiding a stabilisation trap and the harmful affects of expansionary monetary policy. In other words, monetary policy should have the twin objectives of employment creation and keeping inflation at a moderate level.

   Even when the inflation rate remains moderate, policy makers should monitor the inflation rates of items (in particular, food), which dominate the consumption basket of the poor. Monetary policy should support the fiscal authority in stabilising the prices of food and essential items.

2. Achieve consistency with the fiscal policy stance. Safe expansionary monetary policy within the above guidelines will allow governments to borrow from

the central bank to finance employment-intensive public infrastructure investment programs. This can create and stabilise employment without putting pressure on interest rates. Thus private investment is unlikely to be crowded out; rather, both domestic and foreign investment will be encouraged by demand growth and externality benefits from improved physical infrastructure. This means demand expansions will be matched by expansions of supply. Thus, well-coordinated expansionary monetary and fiscal policies can keep inflation within the safe limit and promote growth.[17]

3. Develop directed credit programs for employment-intensive small and medium enterprises, agriculture and rural industries. This is essential because they are more dependent on bank credits than larger enterprises, who have better access to capital markets. Therefore, even when overall credit growth needs to be restrained, directed credit to SMEs and rural-agricultural sectors must be maintained to avoid an asymmetric adverse impact on employment. This will protect the income of the poor and offset likely adverse impacts of cyclical downturns on inequality.

4. Central banks should be given autonomy to choose and implement the instruments of monetary policy within the overall economic objectives dictated by the poverty reduction strategy of the government. This means a participatory policy making process so that the trade-off parameter between inflation and unemployment reflects the concerns of the poor, and not of the elite or multilateral agencies.

The above policies are internally consistent. For example, when monetary policy is assigned to two objectives–employment creation and maintaining moderate inflation–it needs at least two independent instruments according to the well-known Tinbergen rule. While the central banks can still have their traditional instrument of interest rate (or such instruments as reserve requirements) assigned to keep inflation at a moderate level, specialised credit regulation can be the second instrument directed to employment creation. Critics have often pointed out the distortionary effects of directed credit policies, and associated inefficiency and rent seeking activities that harm the economy. However, these need to be weighed against the cost of imperfection in the financial and credit markets. One recent study (Jaramillo and Schiantarelli, 1996) of Ecuador finds that directed credit programs accounted for approximately 50% of the total credit in the economy in 1984 and thus substantially compensated the inability of the financial system to generate funds for investment. This explained why total credit in the economy rose during the 1970s and early 1980s, and peaked (reaching 23% of GDP) in 1983 despite financial repression.[18]

In order to improve the operational efficiency, the central banks can consider a number of options in designing specialised credit programs. For example, in India, all banks (public and private) are required to lend at least 40 per cent of their net credit to the 'priority sector'. If banks fail to meet this requirement, they are required to lend money to specific government agencies at a very low interest as a penalty. Studies by Banerjee and Duflo (2004) found that most banks complied with the regulation and the program contributed significantly to the expansion of the agriculture and small scale industries.

Alternatively, the central banks can use some *carrot and stick* measures by combining the Indian type system of penalty for failure with incentive based measures such as asset-based reserve requirements, support for pooling and underwriting small loans, utilising the discount window in support of employment generating investments (see Pollin, 1993, 1995, 1998). As Epstein (2002) observed, asset based reserve requirements are an effective tool for creating incentives for banks to invest in socially productive assets. For example, based on well-researched findings of employment elasticities, the central banks would list a set of employment generating investment, and a lower reserve requirement would apply for the deposits invested in these activities than the deposits invested in speculation or Treasury Bills. The central banks can also take steps to create liquidity and risk sharing institutions for loans to small businesses which have promise to generate employment, but do not have adequate access to the credit market. For example, the central banks can provide financial and administrative support for asset backed securities, which would take loans to small businesses and other employment intensive activities, bundle these investments and sell them as securities on the open market. Finally, the central banks can open a special discount window facility to offer credit, guarantee or discount facilities to institutions that are on-lending to firms and co-operatives engaged in employment intensive activities.

NOTES

1. Governments can finance deficits by printing money (borrowing from the central bank), borrowing at home from the non-bank public, or borrowing from abroad. Easterly and Schmidt-Hebbel (1993, p. 213) highlighted the macroeconomic implications of fiscal deficits in the following words:

   [E]ach type of financing, *if used excessively*, results in a specific macroeconomic imbalance. Money creation leads to inflation. Domestic borrowing leads to a credit squeeze... and the crowding out of private investment and consumption. External borrowing leads to a current account deficit and the appreciation of the real exchange rate and sometimes to a balance of payments crisis ... or an external debt crisis. (Emphasis added).
2. Figures quoted here and the preceding paragraph are from *World Development Reports*, 1991, 1997, 2000.
3. See Rodrik (1998), Easterly (2001). Easterly (2001) termed the period of 1980s and 1990s as "the lost decades".
4. Foreword to Thomas et al (2000), *The Quality of Growth*, Oxford University Press, New York for the World Bank.

5. Argentina is an extreme example of an economy in a stabilisation trap. Throughout the 1980s, Argentina suffered from hyper-inflation when the average annual inflation rate was around 391% and the economy contracted by an average annual rate of nearly 1%. The orthodox IMF stabilisation package succeeded in bringing the inflation rate down to a single-digit level averaging 1.5% annually, and the economy grew by an average annual rate of 6.7% during 1991-1997. However, the continuation of severe restrictive macroeconomic policies forced the economy into a deflationary spiral–the inflation rate dropped to–0.9% and–1.3% in 2000 and 2001 respectively. The economy contracted by–3.4% in 1999 and by–2.1% in 2000. The "stabilisation trap" caused the unemployment rate to rise from 6.5% in 1991 to 17.5% in 1996. Consequently, the poverty rate (head-count ratio) rose from 21.8% in 1993 to 34.3% in 2002, and the Gini coefficient from 0.45 to 0.49. Tobin (1987) highlighted the danger of too much emphasis on inflation control long before the Argentine collapse.
6. This is consistent with Levine and Zervos (1993) who found that the inflation-growth relationship disappeared when two extreme cases of Nicaragua and Uganda were omitted. Surveying the past studies and based on his own research Stanners (1993, 106) concluded, "No evidence has been found to support the notion that a low rate of inflation has in the past and in various countries been associated with improved growth rate…"
7. On the question, "Is inflation harmful to growth?", Bruno and Easterly (1998, p. 3) concluded, "The ratio of fervent beliefs to tangible evidence seems unusually high on this topic."
8. This is consistent with Levine and Zervos (1993) who found that the inflation-growth relationship disappeared when two extreme cases of Nicaragua and Uganda were omitted. Surveying the past studies and based on his own research Stanners (1993, 106) concluded, "No evidence has been found to support the notion that a low rate of inflation has in the past and in various countries been associated with improved growth rate…"Fischer, Sahay and Vegh (1996) put the figure beyond which inflation can be harmful at 50% for transition economies. However, works within the IMF by Sarel (1996) and by Khan & Senhadji (2000) found that inflation rate above 7-11% can be harmful for growth.
9. Bruno and Easterly (1998, p. 10) found that the growth-inflation association were sensitive to changes in the sample period.
10. Most countries are forced to adjust nominal wages upward following a large depreciation as the workers demand protection of their real wages from imported inflation. This phenomenon is known as "real wage resistance" which offsets the effects of depreciation.
11. If nominal wages are sticky downward due to either institutional reasons (e.g. minimum wage or union power) or their subsistence nature, the insistence on price stability or a very low inflation target is likely to raise real wages. See Akerlof et al (1996).
12. Similar findings are also reported from Tanzania. See Hellinger *et al* (2001). The Indonesia country report highlighted how monetary tightening exacerbated the crisis by causing cash-flow problems even for sound enterprises.

13. See Stiglitz (2002) on how high interest rate policy can cause corporate distress.
14. These are the two channels of forced savings, highlighted by the early development economists. However, the difference between the early development economists and the neo-liberal orthodoxy is that the early development economists believed that inflationary financing would promote economic growth whereas the neo-liberal school believes that inflation is harmful for growth. Thus, according to the neo-liberal school inflation hurts poor doubly–by reducing their average income and by making the income distribution more unequal.
15. One influential early work on central bank independence is that of Cukierman, Webb and Neypal (1992). This study covered 72 countries (21 industrial and 51 developing countries), and the period of study extends to the 1950s if a central bank existed then. It used a much wider range of information on central bank independence. From this study, one cannot detect a clear systematic relationship between the index of legal independence and the average rate of inflation. For example, countries like Belgium, France, Japan and Norway which are at the bottom of the scale ranked in terms of the index of legal independence have average annual inflation rates which are comparable with Canada, Denmark and the United States which are ranked at the top. Since actual independence in practice diverge from legal or formal independence, the study also included the frequency of turnover of central bank governors and the specialists' perception of actual independence. Spain was found to have the highest turnover rate during 1950-89 (an average tenure of 5 years) and the lowest turnover rate was found in Iceland (only one change in 29 years). Yet Iceland had the highest average annual inflation rate (32% in the 1980s). The average inflation rates in countries such as France, Ireland, Luxembourg and the UK whose central banks were perceived to have less actual independence were comparable with those in Australia, Denmark and Finland, which were ranked high in terms of perceived actual independence of their central banks. Italy, which was ranked 4th in terms of the perceived actual independence of its central bank, had a double-digit inflation rate. Their cross-country regression reflected this lack of a clear systematic relationship when the apparent outlying case of Iceland is dropped from the sample.
16. A more recent review by Debelle et al. (1998, p. 6) of performance of seven industrial countries that have granted their central banks independence to pursue a pre-announced inflation target (or a band) concludes in the following words:

    Still, it is probably too early to declare that the inflation-targeting approach has succeeded in delivering lower inflation, given that inflation has also generally declined in many industrial countries that have not adopted inflation targeting. ...Comparing unemployment in the inflation-targeting countries with that in other major industrial countries shows that the average unemployment rate rose significantly in the early 1990s in the inflation-targeting countries.
17. Friedman, (1962, p. 219).
18. Debelle and Fischer, (1994).
19. BAPPENAS (2001, p. 27) observes:

    Monetary policy aimed at lower interest rates... lower domestic debt servicing costs is now attractive for... budgetary reasons... Higher interest rates increase the interest cost on the large, outstanding stock of [debt]... This significantly complicates the task of implementing monetary policy.

One recent study of Indonesia (Mckinley *et al.*, 2003 p. 19) notes:

It is difficult to ease monetary policy and achieve some consistency between fiscal and monetary policies when the Bank of Indonesia (BI) remains relatively autonomous–and wedded to tight monetary policies. While BI should have autonomy in determining its policy instruments, its objectives should be subject to public discussion and oversight. By setting low inflation as its overriding objective, BI can compromise the achievement of other objectives, such as growth of income and employment generation, which most people value highly, in addition to price stability.

20. McKinley *et al.* (2003, p. 18) conclude, "Public investment can help create a coordinated rise in investment (positively affecting both aggregate demand and profit expectations), which can trigger further private investment. Without such a stimulus, private domestic investors are faced with coordination failure, in which each one is reluctant to invest because others are also reluctant."

21. Beginning in 1984, Ecuador eliminated or scaled down directed credit programs and removed administrative controls on interest rate as part of financial sector liberalisation programs. Since then the supply of credit declined drastically with the contraction of government provided loanable funds and reached as low as 9% of GDP in 1990. The firm level debt structure data show that together with the decline in total credit, the share of long term loan fell from 12% in the early 1980s to 8% in 1992. The growth rate of real long term credit was negative for most years. The firm level data also show that the percentage of directed credit was much higher for longer term maturities prior to liberalisation reforms. This percentage declined from 59.3% in 1985 to 35.9% in 1990. The percentage of directed short-term credit declined from 31.1% in 1985 to 3.3% in 1992. The decline in the access to long-term credit had negatively affected firms' performance, especially in terms of productivity. In particular, the lack of access to long-term credit adversely affected firms' ability to acquire improved technology.

REFERENCES

Auerbach, R. (1985), 'Politics and the Federal Reserve', *Contemporary Policy Issues,* Vol. 3, No. 5.

Baer, W. (1967), "The Inflation Controversy in Latin America: A Survey", *Latin American Research Review*, February, pp. 3-25.

Banerjee, A.V. and E. Duflo (2004), "Do Firms Want to Borrow More? Testing Credit Constraints Using a Directed Lending Program", MIT working paper.

Bank Indonesia (2000), *Economic, Monetary and Banking Developments,* 2nd quarter.

Bank Indonesia (2002), *Evaluation of the Implementation of Bank Indonesia's Policies in 2001 and Policy Direction of 2002*, BI website.

BAPPENAS (2001), *The Indonesian Economy in the Year 2001: Prospects and Policies,* Jakarta: BAPPENAS.

Beddies, C. (1999), 'Monetary Policy and Public Finances: Inflation Targets in a New Perspective', *IMF Working Paper*, WP/99/26.

Blank, R.M. and, A.S. Blinder, (1986), "Macroeconomics, Income Distribution, and Poverty", in Sheldon, H. D. and D. H. Weinberg (eds), *Fighting Poverty: What Works and What Doesn't*, Cambridge: Harvard U. Press, pp. 180-208.

Blank, R.M. and D. Card (1993), "Poverty, Income Distribution, and Growth: Are They Still Connected?, *Brookings Papers on Economic Activity*, 2, pp. 285-229.

Bowles, P. and G. White (1994), "Central Bank Independence: A Political Economy Approach", *Journal of Development Studies*, Vol. 31 (2), pp. 235-264.

Bruno, M. and W. Easterly (1998), "Inflation crises and Long-run Growth", *Journal of Monetary Economics*, 41, pp. 3-26.

Cukierman, A., S. Webb, and B. Neyapti. (1992), 'Measuring the Independence of Central Banks and its Effect on Policy Outcomes', *World Bank Economic Review*, Vol.6, No.3, pp. 353-398.

Cutler, D.M. and L.F. Katz (1991), "Macroeconomic Performance and Disadvantaged", *Brookings Papers on Economic Activity*, 2, pp. 1-74.

Debelle, G. (1996), 'Central Bank Independence: A Free Lunch?', Working paper No.1-EA, International Monetary Fund.

Debelle, G. and S. Fischer. (1994), 'How Independent Should a Central Bank Be?' in J.C. Fuhrer (ed.), *Goals, Guidelines, and Constraints Facing Monetary Policy*, Conference Series No. 38, Federal Reserve Bank of Boston, 195-221.

Debelle, G., *et.al.* (1998), 'Inflation Targeting as a Framework for Monetary Policy', *Economic Issues*, No. 15, IMF, Washington, DC.

Domac, I. (2001), "The Distributional Consequences of Monetary Policy: Evidence from Malaysia", World Bank Working Paper.

Dornbusch, R. and S. Fischer (1993), "Moderate Inflation", *World Bank Economic Review*, 7, pp. 1-44.

Dornbusch, R. and A. Reynoso (1989), "Financial Factors in Economic Development", *American Economic Review Papers and Proceedings*, 79 (2), pp. 204-209.

Easterly, W. (2001), "The Lost Decades: Developing Countries Stagnation in Spite of Policy Reform 1980-98", *Journal of Economic Growth.*

Easterly, W. (2003), "National Policies and Economic Growth: A Reappraisal", *Working Paper*, No. 27, Center for Global Development, New York University.

Epstein, G. (2002), "Employment-Oriented Central Bank Policy in an Integrated World Economy: A Reform Proposal for South Africa", Working Paper, Political Economy Research Institute, University of Massachusetts, Amherst.

Easterly, W. and K. Schmidt-Hebbel (1993), "Fiscal Deficits and Macroeconomic Performance in Developing Countries". *World Bank Research Observer* 8(2): 211-239.

Findlay, R. (1984), "Growth and Development in Trade Models", in Jones, R. and P. Kennen (eds.), *Handbook of International Economics*, Vol. 1, Amsterdam: North-Holland.

Fischer, S., R. Sahay, and C.A. Végh. (1996), "Stabilization and Growth in Transition Economies: The Early Experience", *Journal of Economic Perspectives*, 10, pp. 45-66.

Fischer, S., R. Sahay, and C.A. Végh. (2002), "Modern Hyper- and High Inflations", *Journal of Economic Literature*, Vol. 40 (September 2002), pp. 837-880.

Friedman, M. (1962), 'Should there be an Independent Monetary Authority?' in L.B. Yeager (ed.), *In Search of a Monetary Constitution*, Cambridge, Mass.: Harvard University. Press, pp. 219-43.

Friedman, M. (1968), 'The Role of Monetary Policy', *American Economic Review*, Vol. 78, B1-17.

Friedman, M. (1973), *Money and Economic Development*, Toronto: Lexington Books.

Friedman, M. (1985), 'The Case for Overhauling the Federal Reserve', *Challenge*, July-August, 4-12.

Ghura, D., C.A. Leite and C. Tsangarides (2002), "Is Growth Enough? Macroeconomic Policy and Poverty Reduction", *IMF Working Paper*, WP/02/118.

Gramlich, E.M. and D.S. Lauren (1984), "How Widespread Are Income Losses in a Recession?", in the D.L. Bawden (ed), *The Social Contract Revisited*, Washington DC: Urban Institute Press.

Hellinger, D., K. Hansen-Kuhn and A. Fehling, (2001), "Stripping Adjustment Policies of Their Poverty-Reduction Clothing: A New Convergence in the Challenge to Current Global Economic Management", *The Development Gap*, June 2001.

Hibbs, A. (1976), "Economic Interest and the Politics of Macroeconomic Policy", Department of Economics, MIT.

Hossain, A. and A. Chowdhury (1996), *Monetary and Financial Policies in Developing Countries: Growth and Stabilisation*, London: Routledge.

Islam, I. (2003), "Avoiding the Stabilisation Trap: Towards a Macroeconomic Policy Framework for Growth, Employment and Poverty Reduction", processed, Griffith University.

Jaramillo, F. and Schiantarelli, F. (1996), "Access to Long Term debt and Effects on Firms' Performance: Lessons from Ecuador", paper presented to the conference "Term Finance: Theory and Evidence", Policy Research Department, the World Bank, Washington, DC, June 14, 1996.

Johnson, O. (1984), "On Growth and Inflation in Developing Countries", *IMF Staff Papers*, 31, pp. 636-660.

Kaldor, N. (1955-6), "Alternative Theories of Distribution", *Review of Economic Studies*, 23, pp. 83-100.

Kalecki, M. (1976), *Essays on Economic Development*, Brighton, Sussex: Harvester Press.

Khan, M. S. and S. S. Abdelhak (2000) "Threshold Effects in the Relationship between Inflation and Growth", IMF Working Paper 00/110.

Levine, R. and S. Zervos (1993), "What Have We Learned About Policy and Growth from Cross-country Regressions?", *American Economic Review Papers and Proceedings*, 83, pp. 426-430.

McKinley, *et al.* (2003), *Pro-Poor Macroeconomic Policies in Indonesia*, Country Report, Macroeconomics of Poverty Reduction, UNDP.

McKinnon, R. (1964), "Foreign Exchange Constraints in Economic Development and Efficient Aid Allocation", *Economic Journal*, 74, pp. 388-409.

McNelis, P.D., Joseph, C.P., Dewandaru, J., Ari, H.D. (2001), 'Inflation targeting in a Dynamic General Equilibrium Model: the case of Indonesia', *Mimeo.*

Mundell, R. (1965), "Growth, Stability and Inflationary Finance", *Journal of Political Economy*, 73, pp. 97-109.

Mundell, R. (1971), *Monetary Theory*, San Francisco: Goodyear Publishing.

Pollin, R. N. (1993), "Public Credit Allocation Through the Federal Reserve: Why it is Needed; How it Should be Done", in D. Baker, G. Epstein and R. Pollin (eds), *Transforming the US Financial System.*

Pollin, R.N. (1995), "Financial Structures and Egalitarian Economic Policy", *New Left Review*, December, pp. 26-61.

Pollin, R.N. (1998), "Can Domestic Expansionary Policy Succeed in a Globally Integrated Environment? An Examination of Alternatives", in D. Baker, G. Epstein and R. Pollin (eds), *Globalization and Progressive Economic Policy*, Cambridge: Cambridge University Press.

Robinson, J. (1962), "A Model of Accumulation", in *Essays on the Theory of Economic Growth*, London: Macmillan.

Rodrik, D. (1998), "Where Did all the Growth Go? External Shocks, Social Conflict and Growth Collapse", *National Bureaus of Economic Research Working Paper*, No. 6350.

Romer, C. and D. Romer (1999), "Monetary Policy and the Well-Being of the Poor", *Federal Reserve Bank of Kansas City Economic Review*, 1st Quarter, pp. 21-49.

Sarel, M. (1996), "Nonlinear Effects of Inflation on Economic Growth", *IMF Staff Papers* 43, pp. 199-215.

Siregar, H. and Ward, B. (2002), 'Were Aggregate Demand Shocks Important in Explaining Indonesian Macro-economic Fluctuations?', *Journal of the Asia Pacific Economy*. 7(1).

Srinivasan, T.N. (2001), "Growth and Poverty Alleviation: Lessons from Development Experience", processed, New Haven, Connecticut: Yale University.

Stanners, W. (1993), "Is Low Inflation an Important Condition for High Growth?", *Cambridge Journal of Economics*, 17, pp. 79-107.

Stern, N. and J. Stiglitz (1996), 'A Framework for a Development Strategy in a Market Economy: Objectives, Scope, Institutions and Instruments', *Working paper* #20, European Bank for Reconstruction and Development.

Stiglitz, J. (2002), "Macro-Policy Issue: Dealing with an Economic Downturn" The Task Force on Macroeconomic Policy, Initiative for Policy Dialogue, Columbia University.

Swinburne, M. and M. Castello-Branco (1991), "Central Bank Independence and Central Bank Functions", in P. Downes and R. Vaez-Zadeh (eds.), *The Evolving Role of Central Banks*, Washington D.C.: IMF.

Thirwall, A. (1989), *Growth and Development with Special Reference to Developing Countries*, London: Macmillan.

Timmer, C.P. (2005), "Food Security and Economic Growth", *Asian-Pacific Economic Literature*, 19(1), pp. 1–17.

Tobin, J. (1965), "Money and Economic Growth", *Econometrica*, 33, pp. 671-684.

Tobin, J. (1987), *Policies for Prosperity: Essays in Keynesian Mode*, Brighton, Sussex: Wheatsheaf.

UNSFIR (2002), "Indonesia's Monetary Policy Dilemma–Constraints of Inflation Targeting", by Chowdhury, A. and H. Siregar, Jakarta.

PART - II
India: Broad Features and Trends

14

INDIAN PERCEPTION OF HUMAN DEVELOPMENT: AN ASSESSMENT OF ITS QUALITATIVE DIMENSION

S.A.R. Bilgrami

Humanisation of the Development Process

The human-centered development approach envisages the process of growth as "enlarging people's choices and expanding their capabilities". The accomplishment of this task has been visualized in the expansion of knowledge and awareness, leading a long and healthy life, productivity enhancement and increasing real per capita income. Reduction in human poverty, improvement in gender empowerment, guaranteed human rights, and increased respect for and the dignity of the poor have been added later on. The wide range of indicators covers all the essential dimensions of human life required to assess human development. But one should realise that these variables are not independent and absolute. They are influenced and even controlled by different socio-cultural variables to which insufficient attention has been paid so far.

The Indian socio-cultural life-style is surrounded by age-old traditions, conventions, practices, beliefs and even superstitions. They play a decisive role in determining perceptions, opinions and a level of acceptability of the aforesaid variables. In the Indian context, the.understanding and assessment of human development without giving proper consideration to socio-cultural variables, will remain incomplete, imperfect and narrow.

Unfortunately, these socio-cultural variables—folklores, rituals, traditions and conventions, practices and beliefs—are treated merely a tool of entertainment; an unproductive and valueless exercise to shape a style of living. If we pay little attention, these simple tools of entertainment may prove to be a genuine source of varied information and a means of determining the level of awareness of people about various socio-economic, political and environmental issues. This cultural canvas is so wide and multi-dimensional that no part of life is left untouched by it.

These socio-cultural sources show high participation rates of the people, maximum transparency and utmost freedom of expression. Hence, with this medium the exposure of the realities of life is frankly open. These features are of special significance for the female community, especially for the rural folk. There are various complex and sensitive areas where the feelings, inspirations, emotions and opinions of rural women cannot be expressed frankly and boldly before the male community due to cultural taboos, family and community traditions, compulsions and hesitations. These are the only means through which the suppressed feelings, sentiments and emotions of the females are being expressed frankly. To them they serve as a tool of communication, education, awareness, motivation, persuasion, mobilization and organization besides entertainment.

Our surveys based on exhaustive structured questionnaires, despite modifications and improvements, are incapable of capturing the in-depth realities of life especially of women folk. Even the gathered information, especially of sensitive and complex social and cultural situations, always remains doubtful. They create more controversies than solutions. Information gathered by the conventional surveys will become richer if it is supplemented by greater cultural awareness.

Human development cannot be assessed only by the few selected variables. It is more social, value-based and humane rather than merely economic and materialistic. Even economic goals cannot be attained without taking account of social and cultural considerations. One of the reasons for the failure of our various economic schemes is negligence of the social sector. Our traditions, practices, rituals and beliefs flash-out valuable messages which should not be by-passed on the pretext that they are merely a means of entertainment. They are powerful means of communication and an effective source of expression. If human development is to be visualized in India in terms of expanding opportunities and enlarging choices, this can be done by expanding education, improving health and ensuring more income and employment prospects but it also requires adequate consideration of social and cultural variables. The question of acceptability will always remain doubtful if we do not pay attention on social and cultural dimensions of the selected variables.

Some Qualitative Dimensions of India's Human Development Folklore

This section investigates folklores, practices and rituals as a basic source of information and of levels of social awareness. The section is divided into two parts. Part one deals with the folklores and the other one presents some practices and rituals specifically related to health and hygiene of the pregnant women of the rural and semi-urban/town areas. Here our focus is on the northern parts of India, namely the Awadh region.

Indian folklores of every region and state are the reservoir of human values. They adopt a family-centered promotional approach to human values and present a broad spectrum of our socio-cultural, economic, ethical and religious life-style. They are the oral poetic mode of communication employing vocal, musical and visual arts to express indepth feelings, inspirations, emotions and motivations of the people frankly. Since the feelings came from the bottom of their heart disbanding all the hesitations and inhibitions, the language of communication is always found to be simple, plain and spontaneous and based on colloquial words and phrases. A deliberate and cautious effort of delivering ideas beautifully by choosing suitable words and phrases is seldom found.

They show flexibility and in-built capacity to adjust to changing needs. If the prevailing contents do not suit the socio-economic needs, people on their own put fresh content into them without distorting their basic structure. "Allah", a famous classical ballad of Uttar Pradesh and Madhya Pradesh, for example, is now forcefully used as an effective means of communication for family planning programme, immunization campaigns, AIDS awareness, and health and hygiene, consciousness etc. Even political parties and sales promotion agencies are using it to get their message popularized. This story of warriors and its style of recitation attracts the masses most and hence without distorting its original style, it has now been used as a most effective mode of communication for our present needs.

Folklores encompass deep socio-economic issues of human life. They cover injustice, discrimination, exploitation, migration, health and hygiene, environment, political awareness, corruption, impacts of scientific innovation, contributions of the service-class and local needs and requirements. In all these areas, they expose the negative and adverse impacts as well as the positive and healthy aspects and thus present a rational assessment of the issues.

The favourite themes of folklores are exposing injustice, discrimination, exploitation and corruption of the society. They capture all forms of injustice, discrimination and exploitation. Here they appear as a "vehicle of social protest". Man and environment, health and hygiene and the role of those providing services are some other areas that have been widely explored. Some examples can be given to illustrate this.

In one folklore, a bonded female labourer expresses her anguish and utter unwillingness to continue further her assigned work of cleaning grains for meagre wages in kind because her master, who is a high class farmer, wishes to send his son to school and expects her son to look after his cattle in the field. The victim's revolt against discrimination is for a healthy cause. She can tolerate every excess, but not the discrimination against education, which she realizes, is the basic source for breaking all the barriers to backwardness and deprivation.

Migration-related problems faced by rural female have always been an area of serious research for the social scientist. Migration of males for a job within the country and abroad brings prosperity. Various folklores acknowledge these positive aspects of migration. In one folklore, a clear exposition of the relationship between income and prosperity is found in this way. "As our husband got employment, we began to construct our house, arrange our garments and purchase ornaments. But as his job is lost, our house began to fall-down, clothes become old and shabby and ornaments began to be mortgaged."

The cost of the migration of males in Indian social and cultural milieu is high. Indian rural women left behind face a major crisis in the family and society. They become more socially vulnerable at home as well as in the society. Development of sour relations with in-laws, disintegration of family, non-cooperation of family members, extra liabilities and responsibilities, and mismanagement of resources are the usual consequences which such women bear. The agony is that despite realising every misdeed, a wife cannot express her feelings and experiences openly due to social and cultural taboos. Here folk-lore is the only media whereby she can express her feelings. See how a women expresses the unsupportive attitude of her in laws while she is alone: "My hut is breaking and water is seeping in drop by drop. Who will take care of me? My husband's elder brother [Jetha] has thatched his big house, and younger brother [Devar] his choupal. Who will thatch my hut whose husband is away for a job."

The absence of male members for a long period gradually shatters the peace and integrity of the family. Females bear the sting most. During the Mughal Period in India when King Aurangzeb decided to besiege Daccin, he recruited hundred of males into his army from the capital Delhi and around. Years passed but he could not succeeded in his mission. The waiting women uttered with despair: "Our thatched roof has become old and rubbed and its bamboo structure has started cracking. He had promised to come back, but the whole year has passed away and he has not returned". Obviously, the arrangement of the required material for roof is the responsibility of a male family member. The prolonged absence of the husband has started leaving negative impressions. The disheartened lone woman at home has started taunting.

"Delhi is no doubt prosperous in every respect. But what I got out of it? Nothing. Alamgeer [The King Aurangzeb] has taken away the males who were the source of our peace and prosperity". And in the last moment of utter disappointment, they sigh: "my husband went to earn gold (wealth) and left the house dissolute. He found nothing, neither gold nor returned back home. What I got, in return, is the grey hair, the sign of my old age." This scenario is not changed much even today despite having fast, efficient and reliable communication links worldwide. The migration of males in foreign countries, especially in the Middle-East for a long duration brings prosperity but its human cost for females still persists.

The excess burden of physical work from adolescence, their ill-treatment by in-laws and atrocities against women hamper their health, efficiencies and capabilities. This area has been extensively studied, surveyed and empirically assessed. Our structural questionnaire technique of gathering information on this sensitive area usually fails to touch the realities. Folklores boldly depict the facts and reveal the severity of the situation. In one song a brother reveals that "my sister who was once as beautiful as the sun and the moon is now burning like a coal in a furnace of a blacksmith in her husband's house [Sasural]". Her brother observed the facts but she tries to conceal misdeeds in order to safeguard the honour and dignity of Sasural. Girl retaliates: "forget all misdeeds what you have observed my brother by throwing them away in the river."

This has been an accepted fact that the improvement of skill leads to the expansion of opportunities and capabilities. This also provides respect and status in family and community. A girl's life becomes miserable at home and in her husband's house [*Sasural*] if her skill status is low. Folksongs highlight this aspect in different ways. In one song a girl is complaining to her mother that neither she learns any skill, not even cooking and consequently her mother-in-law and sister-in-law are cursing her badly. This is intolerable to her. Her mother advises her that she should concentrate on learning domestic work and improving skills gradually. Even after that if somebody curses me, let him do that. I am confident that if you follow my instructions the misbehaviour of your in-laws will change into support and respect.

In Indian social milieu the girls are being trained on the basis of a tough model of "Sasural" Training is given in such a way that could boost the harmonious relations in two different families—girl's house [*Maika*] and husband's house [Sasural]. She carries forward the values and the traditions of her family and also prepares herself to learn new values and traditions of the Sasural. Divergencies and clashes are inevitable. To defuse these folklores educate the girl for silent observation, flexibility and acceptability, minimum retaliation and for developing affectionate relationships. At the time of departure [*Bidai*] a girl is advised by her mother to foster peaceful and harmonious relations with everybody in Sasural. She promises to her grieved mother that do not be disheartened on my leaving the house. I will address my mother-in-law as mother so that your absence could not disturb me. I will address my father-in-law as father so that his love and affection could not distract me. And I will call my husband's younger brother [*Devar*] as my brother so that his immense love could not grieve for any more.

The socio-cultural fabrics of Indian rural life is closely and deeply associated with the elements of nature. Our farmers can forecast climatic changes, and natural disasters accurately with the help of the direction, intensity and humidity of wind, observing sudden change in the behaviour of bird's, animal's and insects and realising sudden changes in their voices and behaviour. In rural life, the birds, animals, trees, river, ponds, clouds and wind all are the trusty companions and messengers before whom secrets are disclosed and sentiments and feelings are expressed. This association of man with nature provides a base for the advancement of science and technology and the exploration of the mysteries of space and the universe. The air and gases found in the space establish the links between earth and space. Here they are the messengers and are a means of communication. Today, animals especially dogs are considered not only a reliable investigators, but a powerful means of diagnosing diseases.

We today educate people about the significance of protecting trees, vegetation and forestry wealth in order to safeguard ecological balance. We educate urban people to love animals and birds and treat them as companions. We today feel proud to develop "farm-house" culture, "hat-bazaar"and "holiday resorts" with rural and village attributes. All such conscious efforts are in fact, reactions to deviating from our roots. The 'U'-turn of urban society towards the rural roots is an acknowledgement of man's association with the element of nature. If a man deviates from this root, as our urban society shows, the disastrous consequences tend to follow him firmly. Numerous folklores, dohey, riddles and proverbs are a rich treasure for describing the varied relationship of man with nature.

Folklores are the mirror of our socio-cultural life. They are the unexplored treasure of information and of a level of awareness. They promote human-values relating to every aspect of human life and I consider them superior to merely the materialistic values. The assessment of human development in India will remain narrow, incomplete and imperfect if such a treasure of information is over looked. This area needs proper attention so that the assessment of Indian human development in terms of enlarging choices/opportunities and expanding capabilities could be more meaningful and in accordance with our own social needs.

Observation of Practices and Rituals in Relation to Health and Hygiene of Women

The health of women has a profound impact on the overall health and the well-being of the community. This is more so in rural, semi-urban, urban-poor and town communities than in cities because in these areas women bear more physical and mental strain and share more family responsibilities than men. Hence, for promoting the health of the community as a whole, a woman must enjoy the highest attainable standard of physical and mental health.

Rural female health and hygiene especially during pre-and post-pregnancy period is deeply influenced by numerous age-old practices, rituals, beliefs and superstitions.

Practices

In almost all towns and villages as well as in the middle-class urban families of the northern parts of India, the old ladies of the families are found to be quite concerned and vigilant about the physical movements, the workload and dietary schedule of pregnant women in the family. Constant instructions can be heard about the style of body movements during work and rest, casual sitting, bending and sleeping. In most of the poor and small families such practices are found to be absent while in well to do large families these are the common feature.

The tradition of preparing some special nutritious food and drink, paste and massage at home is also a common feature of all such families. Suitable garments, cushions and other essential items of daily use are also prepared, both for the mother and her expected child, well in advance. Locally experienced ladies and Dais are engaged for daily massage and exercises. This work is also done by the adult ladies of the families. In all such activities, the economic status plays a significant role in determining the variety, quality and the duration of the use of the items. But every family whether it is economically well off or poor follows these practices according to their permissible resources.

The important ingredients or items are food, medicated water for bathing and drinking, some special medicines, massage oil, pastes and powders, prepared from time-tested herbs such as mint leaves, turmeric, herbal roots. Apart from this, oil of specific seeds, dried-fruits, gum, milk and pure ghee are readily used for preparing such items. Most of the items are locally available. The process of preparation passes through boiling, grinding, evaporating, mincing and extracting. The work is usually performed by the family members and neighbours jointly under the supervision of old ladies. The work atmosphere is enriched by the folk-songs known as "Sohar" and "Zach-Cha-Geerian".

Old ladies reveal that these food and drinks supplement deficiencies, preserve strength and vigour, remove constipation, maintain blood-pressure and promote over-all well-being. They also improve the digestive system, strengthen the nerves and metabolism and supplement the blood-loss during delivery. The massage oil, special medicines used during pre- and post-delivery period, uptan-powder, pastes, and medicated luke-warm boiled water for drinking and bathing strengthens the joints and organs, tone-up the tissues and skin and remove wrinkles on face, belly and thigh besides maintaining hygiene.

The practice of burning wood logs/cow-dung mixed with specific leaves and roots for producing medicated smoke in and around the room of a pregnant woman is, as a popular belief reveals, for keeping the evil souls away from the house. But the practice, in fact, unconsciously maintains a hygienic environment. This superstition should not be criticized and discouraged at this stage of ignorance. At least it fulfills a healthy cause on the pretext of keeping away the evil souls. The expansion of education, market, transport, business and movement of resources not only improve and modify these practices but also convert them into a discipline for keeping the environment clean.

These practices with a festive zeal subside the mental tensions, stress and strains, anxieties of a pregnant woman and leave a soothing impact on her nerves and mind. She feels more secure, strong and confident with such cooperation and support. This is, in fact, psychotherapy for a pregnant woman as well as for her expected baby. The observation of these practices confirm a level of awareness in relation to required food-in-take, supplementary diet, body care, needed precaution and hygiene. Though the process of preparation and the method of application of these items may be crude, unhygienic and unscientific, yet their medical and nutritional values can not be denied. Improvement and modification can be introduced by our unani and ayurveda system, social workers, women organization and NGOs.

Rituals

"Pachmasa", "Satmasa" and "Naumasa" are the popular pregnancy related rituals of the Northern parts of India specially of Awadh-region. These rituals are concerned with specific month of pregnancy which signify the specific importance of the month. The performance of the rituals and the related songs provide valuable information and awareness.

"Pachmasa" is celebrated in the end of the fourth and the beginning of the fifth month of the pregnancy. Our medical science reveals that these are the months when life in the foetus accelerates and body structure, muscles, bones and organs start building up. These are the months when high doses of calcium, iron and rich calories based diet are recommended by the doctors. The ritual acknowledges these requirements. The related folksongs express the awareness about the significance of these months by revealing biological changes and the needed precautions. Songs inform the pregnant women to be aware, as the fourth month starts, the baby in your womb starts moving. The pregnant women with the mode of songs inform her husband that her appetite for a normal diet is reducing and inclination towards spicy food is increasing. She also informs her husband that most of the time she feels nausea and her shin is paining. These songs educate the pregnant women as well as the whole community about various biological changes, changes in behaviour and temperament and about needed precautions.

Usually some dried-fruits, fruits, green leafy vegetables along with celebratory items such as mehendi leaves/powder, perfumes, garments, sweets etc. come from women's house [*maika*] in a decorative manner. Vegetables, fruits and dried-fruits are kept in women's lap accompanied by group songs. Apparently the ritual gives a festive impression, an entertainment and family enjoyment, but in fact it is an acknowledgement of the most needed nutritious diet.

"Satmasa" and "Naumasa" are the other relevant rituals which are related to seventh and the ninth months of the pregnancy. In these months, the baby starts sharp movements up to the ninth month when the baby takes its final position for delivery. Medical science reveals that these months are crucial and sensitive too. A slight carelessness may create fatal complications for both the mother as well as the child. Utmost care is, therefore, needed in the body movements, body posture, physical labour and even rest.

Folksongs of these months are full of instructions and education. These songs are the welcome songs where the beautiful features of the expected baby are being described focusing on the description of the childhood of Lord Krishna.

They also educate the women how to hold the baby during feeding, bathing and sleeping. Songs also give instruction about minimizing physical exertion and mental stress. In one song, a full description of the preparations is narrated in this way: "I shall arrange low level of cot with puffy cushions, smooth matting and soft pillows and mirror all around you Zach-Cha-Rani so that when you go to sleep you could take a sound sleep with beautiful dreams." This is an acknowledgement of the required physical comfort and mental peace for pregnant women.

The room where the delivery is expected is usually decorated with beautiful photographs of children and religious places. Children's clothes and other essential items are displayed among the close relatives accompanied by songs and the distribution of sweets.

The practices and rituals described here provide a level of awareness about health-related matters of pregnant women. This level of awareness is comfortably matched by the medical instructions. In almost all hospitals, nursing homes, primary health centers, pregnancy-related instructions and precautions hanging in the doctor's room, corridors and other appropriate places read like this:

(i) Well balanced diet composed of leafy vegetables, fruits, meat, eggs, pulses, wholesome grains and milk-products.

(ii) Right posture during sleeping, sitting and bending is essential throughout pregnancy.

(iii) Exercise as advised by doctors to control stress, blood-pressure, low back pain and improving well-being.

(iv) Lifting of heavy objects, climbing and bending in straight legs should be avoided.

(v) Sleeping flat and waking up with jerks must be avoided.

(vi) Wearing tight fitting clothes and high heels should be avoided.

[Holy-Family Hospital]

Conclusion

The understanding and assessment of human development in India is complex and multi-dimensional. The established variables—education, health and environment—are not enough to conceptualise it perfectly. Our social and cultural values, traditions, practices and beliefs influence these variables and shape the Indian perception of human development. Cultural closeness is, therefore, essential for understanding the Indian perception of human development. Expansion of education and awareness will certainly increase the opportunities and enlarge choices. But the level of acceptability will be influenced by the social and cultural variables. Hence, we cannot avoid, by-pass, or underestimate those variables. These are yet unexplored areas and need sincere efforts to use them as an important source of information and awareness.

The UNDPs Human Development Reports are now paying more attention to cultural factors. Various NGOs are also engaged in examining the impacts of social and cultural variables in expanding capabilities, enlarging choices and determining a level of acceptability. (See the Bibliography). In the absence of consideration of these variables, the Indian concept of human development will remain incomplete and imperfect. Such an approach can help identify aspects of social disadvantage that are unlikely to be discovered by more formal methods of investigation and can signal the depth of feeling about such disadvantage, such as in the case of the bonded female labourer mentioned above. Cultural traditions and practices can also help to educate the disadvantaged, for example, women in relation to health and hygiene. Consequently, folklore, cultural practices and rituals can be a rich source of knowledge about the qualitative dimensions of human development and social disadvantages.

REFERENCES

Azhar Ali Farooqui (1981), *Uttar Pradesh Key Lok Geet.* Urdu, Tarqqui Urdu Bureau.

Barli Development Institute For Rural Women, Indore [various issues] of the magazine "Kokila".

Basue A.M. (1992), *Culture, The Status of Women and Demographic Behaviour.* Oxford University Press, New York.

Centre For Operational Research and Training (2002), *Quality of Family Welfare Services in Madhya Pradesh: A Case Study of Vidisha.* Vadodara, Gujarat.

Centre For Research in Development and Change (2002), *Impact of Gender-based Violence on the Health of Women.* Vadodara, Gujarat.

Deva, Indira (1989), *Folk-culture and Peasant Society in India.* Rawat Publication, Jaipur.

Gopalan Dr. S. (1991), "Women's Health" In Health and Family *Welfare Development in Independent India: A Critique and Future Directions,* Vol II. National Institute of Health and Family Welfare, New Delhi.

Haq, Mahibubul (1996), *Reflections on Human Development,* Oxford University Press, Delhi.

Islam Mazharul (1984), *Folk-lore; The Pulse of the People.* Concept Publishers, Delhi.

Pandey S.P. and Singh A.K. (2005), *Folk-culture in India.* Serials Publications, New Delhi.

Ready P. Channa, Babu M. Sarat (2004), *Folk-Lore in the New Millennium.* Research India Press, New Delhi.

Saha N. (1978), "Customs and Economy". In S.M. Dubey [ed]: *North-East India A Sociological Study* [ed] Rawat Publication, Jaipur.

Shayam P. (1994), *Traditional Folk-Media in India.* Research Press, New Delhi.

UNDP Human Development Report [various issues since 1990] Oxford University Press, New York.

15

MAPPING UNEMPLOYMENT AND POVERTY ACROSS DIFFERENT SOCIAL GROUPS IN RURAL INDIA

Suchitra Krishna Kumar and B.P. Vani

Introduction

Poverty amidst plenty is the greatest challenge faced by most of the countries of the world. Of the total 6 billion people, 2.8 billion (almost half) live on less than $2 a day and 1.2 billion (one fifth) live on less than $1 a day with 44% living in South Asia. The average income of the top 20 richest countries is 37 times the average of the bottom 20 poorest countries-a gap that has doubled in the past 40 years. Independent India has earned prosperity, power, and landmark achievements especially in the field of science and technology. However, we still face problems of poverty, hunger, violence, discrimination, casteism, unemployment and communalism, which have been persisting for decades. This has been compounded by the problem of inequities and inequalities. India is considered to be the home of 22% of the world's poor. Such a high incidence of poverty is a matter of great concern. Eradication of poverty is considered to be an integral part of humanity's quest for sustainable development. Poverty and unemployment are the critical twin problems faced by Indians.

This study analyses unemployment and poverty across different states and maps it across social groups in India. Unemployment and poverty rates across different social groups reveal great disparity. Extreme poverty or ultra poverty, defined as consisting of individuals having an income of less than the 80% of official poverty line, also indicates that the poverty among social groups of lower strata is of a much deeper sort. The sources of this can be institutional and individual.

Even after six decades of independence, poverty still persists in Indian society. Poverty being a multidimensional factor, the search for the causes of poverty has led to many answers. One view relates it to social structure. Indian society has a long history of hierarchy of different communities and caste groups. The low caste and tribals were discriminated against and were considered as untouchables.

Even though Indian constitution prohibits against such discrimination and has abolished untouchability, it is still practised in certain ways.

The 50th round of NSSO distinguished two socially disadvantaged groups. Those belonging to Scheduled Castes (SC) and Scheduled Tribes (ST) have been specifically mentioned in the Constitution of India for affirmative state action. The scheduled castes are at the lowest end of the Hindu caste hierarchy based on birth. Over long periods in the past, the social system ascribed occupations to this group which were not only low in social order but were also characterised by very low productivity. This system did not permit occupational mobility. Consequently, this group remained at the lowest end of the economic hierarchy as well. While the intensity of caste-based discriminatory social practices varied in different parts of the country and was partially moderated with the penetration of the impersonal market forces in varying degrees, this group remained on the fringe of the traditional village society and rural economy practising lowly occupations with little social exposure and educational opportunities.

STs in contrast were not part of the Hindu social hierarchy and their social and economic backwardness arises from their long habitation in geographically isolated areas with difficult terrain and their practice of shifting cultivation. Lack of exposure to education and isolation from the social mainstream made them vulnerable to exploitation by non-tribals and to exclusion from their traditional lands and occupations. Hence, they were relegated to the lowest end of the economic hierarchy.

The residual omnibus social group of 'others' consisted of castes other than SC in the Hindu social hierarchy and non-ST members of other religious communities. In the 55th round this residual (non SC/STs) group has been further subdivided into other backward castes in the Hindu social hierarchy announced by the state government as being socially backward and eligible for state-initiated programmes of affirmative action. Comparable poverty indicators for both 50th (1993/94) and the 55th (1999-2000) rounds can be computed for three social groups SC/ST and others. We have aggregated by computing population weighted averages of the Other Backward Classes (OBC) and others in the 55th round to make it comparable with others in the 50th round. Such discrimination in the past has led to poverty in people belonging to such groups. The government is taking enormous care to uplift these people from poverty. Several anti-poverty programmes are designed especially for these groups. In spite of all these measures, poverty is still dominant among these households. Sundaram and Tendulkar (2002) find that SC households are more vulnerable to poverty than other social groups followed by ST. In this context, we would like to look at poverty across social groups at the state level and map in relation to unemployment rates.

Social Groups

The social groups considered for the analysis are dictated by the availability of the data. The National Sample Survey (NSS) 55th (1999-2000) round, consumer expenditure survey, provides data for four different social groups viz.. Scheduled Tribes (ST), Scheduled Castes (SC), Other Backward Classes (OBC) and Others. Other Backward Classes are the dominant category constituting 38% of the total rural population. SCs constitute 20% of total rural population and STs constitute 11%. Scheduled Castes and Scheduled Tribes are the most socially disadvantaged groups and together account for 31% of India's rural population.

Figure 1
The Relative Sizes of Social Groups in Indian Rural Society:

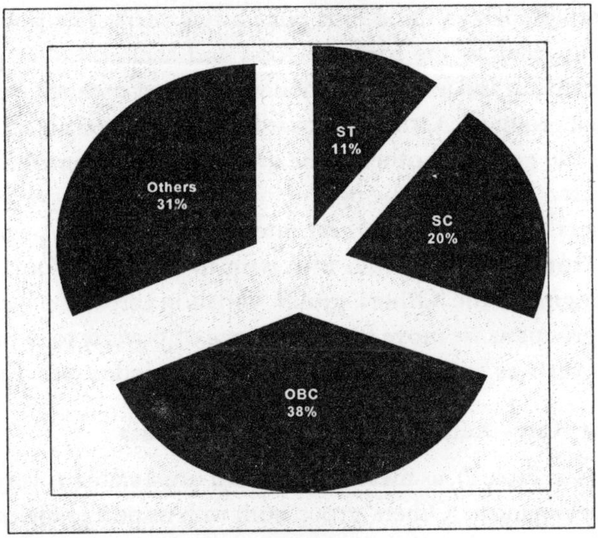

Source: Based on Indian National Census 2001 data

Poverty across Social Groups

Table 1 presents the incidence of poverty across social groups at the All India level and their contribution to total numbers considered to be in poverty in India.

Table 1
Poverty Across Social Groups in India, 1999-2000

Social Group	*Head Count Ratio*	*% Contribution to Total Poverty*
Schedule Tribe	45.03	17.26
Schedule Caste	35.85	26.75
Other Backward Classes	27.54	37.76
Others	15.88	18.23
All Classes	27.65	100

Source: Based on 55th NSS round data.

From Table 1, it is clear that the incidence of poverty among Schedule Tribes is the highest followed by Schedule Castes. These two groups, even though they constitute only 31% of the total rural population, account for nearly 44% of the rural poor at the All India level. Even at the State level poverty is the highest among the ST and SC households (see appendix Table, A1). States like Bihar, Madhya Pradesh and Orissa have more than 50% of their households below the poverty line. The picture is the same even if one views the other measures of poverty which look at the depth and severity of poverty. Among the 15 major States, Orissa witnesses the highest poverty among STs (i.e., 74% of households are below poverty line) and Bihar among SCs (59%) (Appendix Table A1). This may be due to the fact that these two states i.e Orissa and Bihar, were devastated by natural calamities such as floods for quite a few years. The political concern was for providing relief in the form of food and shelter. Other priorities like education, employment, and industrialisation were not given much weight. Coming to the other social group i.e., Other Backward Classes, poverty is moderate and it is lowest among the group of others. The group 'Others' contributes only 18% of those in poverty. In spite of being the lowest in terms of poverty estimates the group, 'Others' showed the highest inter-state disparity. Across the States poverty ranged from as high as 40% in Assam to 1.66% in Punjab among the households belonging to the 'Others' group. Variation across the States increased for all the social groups as we move from incidence of poverty to depth of poverty or severity of poverty as indicated by the poverty gap index (see Table A2).

Unemployment Rates Across Social Groups in India

Unemployment (see Table 2), as measured through usual status, is very high among the households belonging to 'Others' group both with respect to males and females. Unemployment rates are found to be least among the households belonging to Schedule Tribes. Unemployment rates are high among males compared to females. Comparing unemployment rates with the educational level, we see that unemployment rates are the lowest among those who are not literate. Among all social groups unemployment rates for females who are not literate are zero. As one moves higher on the education ladder, unemployment rates starts increasing and are highest among those who are graduates and above, across all social groups. After middle school level, unemployment is more among females than males across all social groups.

One of the reasons for unemployment being high among the females could be due to the fact that more women are illiterates, have fewer opportunities to develop their skills and so on. The unemployment among graduates and above could be higher as they do not possess any technical skills. Very often education, including the syllabi that students study, does not help them to get jobs. The resultant effect is that large numbers of graduates remain unemployed.

The unemployment picture is more or less the same across all the states with a wide variation in unemployment rates (see Table A3). Kerala is the state with the highest unemployment rate. Contrary to other states, the unemployment rate is higher among females compared to males. Kerala's unemployment rate was 55 (i.e., 55 unemployed per 1000 persons in the labour force) for males and 107 for females. Unemployment rates among females were zero in Haryana and Gujarat across all social groups. Among the socially backward groups, unemployment is high in Punjab, Tamil Nadu, West Bengal, Assam and Karnataka states.

Table 2
Unemployment Level Across Education Levels in India

Level of Education	*Scheduled Tribe*		*Scheduled Caste*		*Other Backward Classes*		*Others*	
	Male	*Female*	*Male*	*Female*	*Male*	*Female*	*Male*	*Female*
Not literate	2.13	1.39	3.32	0.00	1.12	0.00	4.62	0.00
Literate & up to primary	4.37	3.24	11.22	6.90	7.85	4.54	10.27	9.40
Middle	27.20	18.31	33.55	41.67	20.05	31.95	21.82	34.75
Secondary	48.49	53.44	72.21	96.03	37.42	104.38	39.11	106.46
Higher secondary	54.31	91.89	98.12	106.90	59.49	164.79	59.22	142.24
Graduate & above	64.34	130.31	115.97	278.37	84.69	400.84	81.23	265.09
Total	10.11	2.97	18.52	9.17	13.95	10.85	22.95	20.65

Source: Based on NSS 55th round data.

Mapping Poverty with Unemployment across Social Groups

Poverty and unemployment rates are mapped in Table 3 for each social group based on the estimates of poverty rates and unemployment rates. Poverty rates and unemployment rates are classified into low or high by taking the All India figures as the demarcation point. Thus all the states with poverty and unemployment estimates lower than the All India estimates are treated as the ones with low poverty and low unemployment. Other states are treated as high poverty and high unemployment states. Thus based on this classification, the mapping shows the picture presented in Table 3.

Table 3
Relationship between Unemployment and Poverty Rates for Scheduled Tribes by Indian States

Scheduled Tribes		*Poverty rate*	
		Low	*High*
Unemployment Rates	Low	Andhra Pradesh Gujarat Haryana Karnataka Maharashtra Rajasthan	Assam Himachal Pradesh Kerala Punjab Tamil Nadu Uttar Pradesh
	High	Madhya Pradesh Orissa	Bihar West Bengal

States like Bihar and West Bengal figure in both the high poverty and the high unemployment rates category. In these states, the schedule tribe population is small. Scheduled tribes constitute only 8% and 6% respectively of their population. The high ST population dominated states are Madhya Pradesh (30%) and Orissa (27%), these are placed in the high unemployment and the low poverty categories.

Table 4 maps unemployment rates and poverty incidence for scheduled castes by Indian states. States where the SC population constitutes nearly 30% are Tamil Nadu, West Bengal and Uttar Pradesh, They fall either into the high poverty–low employment rates region or the low poverty–high unemployment regions. Assam and Orissa fall into the high unemployment and high poverty category. Assam has only 10% of its population belonging to SC category, but Orissa has a reasonably large proportion of its population in the SC category.

Table 4
Relationship between Unemployment Rates and Poverty Incidence of Scheduled Castes by Indian States

Scheduled Castes		*Poverty rate*	
		Low	*High*
Unemployment Rates	Low	Andhra Pradesh	Himachal Pradesh
		Gujarat	Karnataka
		Haryana	Kerala
		Maharashtra	Punjab
		Rajasthan	Tamil Nadu
	High	Bihar	West Bengal
		Madhya Pradesh	Assam
		Uttar Pradesh	Orissa

Table 5
Relationship between Unemployment Rates and Poverty Incidence of Other Backward Castes by Indian State

Other Castes Backward		*Poverty rate*	
		Low	*High*
Unemployment Rates	Low	Andhra Pradesh	Himachal Pradesh
		Gujarat	Kerala
		Haryana	Punjab
		Karnataka	Tamil Nadu
		Maharashtra	West Bengal
		Rajasthan	Assam
	High	Madhya Pradesh	Bihar
		Uttar Pradesh	Orissa

Table 5 provides data on unemployment rates and the incidence of poverty for other backward classes according to Indian states. The states of Assam, Bihar and Orissa belong to the high poverty and high unemployment category. Here again Bihar and Orissa have high levels of backward populations. Other regions where, either poverty or unemployment is high include Tamil Nadu and Kerala.

For the other classes (see Table 6), the states of Assam, Bihar, Orissa and West Bengal appear in the high poverty and high unemployment category.

Table 6
Relationship between Unemployment Rates and Poverty Incidence of Other Classes by Indian states

Others		*Poverty rate*	
		Low	*High*
Unemployment Rates	Low	Andhra Pradesh Gujarat Haryana Himachal Pradesh Karnataka Madhya Pradesh Rajasthan	Kerala Maharashtra Tamil Nadu
	High	Uttar Pradesh	Assam Bihar Orissa West Bengal

Taking the overall picture, most social groups appear to fall in the high unemployment and high poverty category in the states of Assam, Bihar, Orissa and West Bengal. However, as will be seen in the next section these states receive the lowest levels of per capita government expenditure on poverty relief programmes.

Indian Public Policy and Poverty Alleviation Programmes

Per capita expenditure on poverty alleviation programmes by states in India is poorly linked with the incidence of poverty in Indian states. This is evident from Figure 2. The per capita allocation of funds to states where the incidence of poverty is high tends to be less than in states where the incidence of poverty is low. Thus, states such as Orissa, Bihar, Assam, Madhya Pradesh and West Bengal fare poorly in the distribution of public funding for poverty reduction compared to states like Haryana.

Figure 2 clearly indicates the extent of that poverty and expenditure under poverty alleviation programme do not go hand in hand. Thus bias exists in allocating funds for poverty alleviation programmes across Indian states. There is a wide disparity in the allocation of funds. The developed states are given more funding as compared to the backward states.

The causes of poverty amongst India's social groups are varied. The SC and STs have been made to do menial jobs. They have been underpaid and have been exploited to a large extent, for centuries. It is only with the intervention of the father of the Indian nation, Mahatma Gandhi, that they were given better opportunities. Prior to this, they were treated as Untouchables and were not allowed to share a common well for water also. They were not allowed to touch a person of upper caste. If, by mistake, a child belonging to the Untouchables touched a member of a higher caste, the person would go home and bathe and pray to God. Such was the extent of discrimination.

Figure 2

Per Capita Expenditure on Poverty Alleviation Programmes in India by States Compared to their Poverty Incidence, 1999-2000.

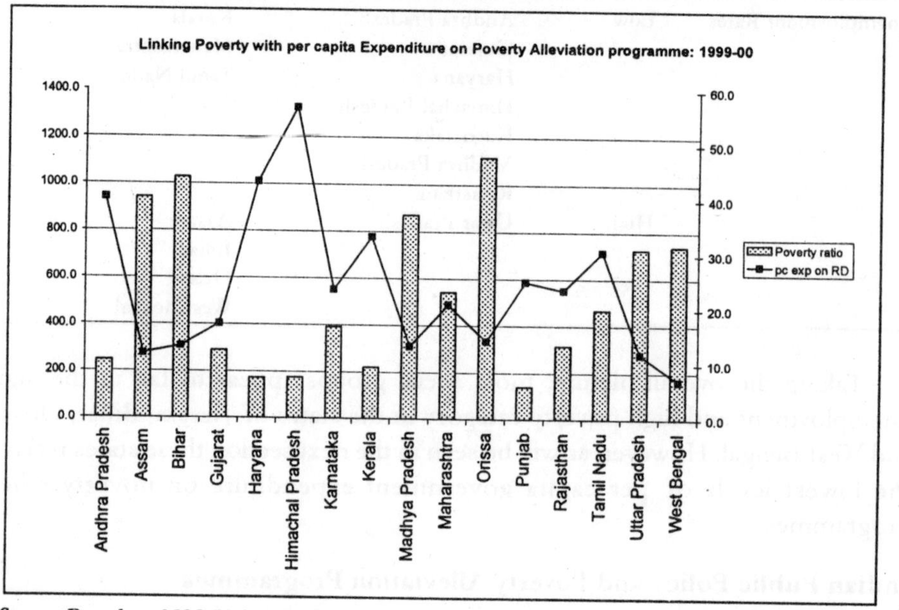

Source: Based on NSS 50th round data.

Over the years, the Indian Government has made steps to uplift these people. They are given free education and are provided with scholarships. They are given relaxation regarding both age and merit when applying for educational institutions as well as jobs. But still a lot of backwardness persists among these groups, especially in the rural areas. These people are often not aware of the facilities available to them. Free housing is available in various cases to them yet very often, due to corruption, the rich make use of these facilities under the guise of the poor SC and STs. The benefits do not reach the right persons.

A possible solution is to create awareness camps, to punish the corrupt people, and to try to create more literate people by providing educational facilities in every village. The Government should also provide more job-oriented courses. The rural-urban divide, the rich and poor and upper and lower caste divides should be eliminated. Policies should be implemented and not remain as words in documents.

Various anti-poverty measures exist at present intended to uplift the low castes and backward people. Indira Awas Yojana is meant to provide free housing for SC and STs. Other programmes in this regard are:

- Food for work program
- Sampurna gramin rozgar yojana
- Samagra awas yojana
- Million wells scheme
- Self help group scheme
- Integrated rural development scheme
- Social security programmes

Nevertheless, it is not enough to allocate funds for the upliftment. It is most important to see that their benefit reaches all the targeted groups.

APPENDIX TABLES

Table A1

The Incidence of Poverty (%) in Indian States and All India by Social Groups. Head-count ratio, 1999-2000

States	*ST*	*SC*	*OBC*	*Others*	*ALL*
Andhra Pradesh	24.47	17.99	11.38	4.34	12.17
Assam	38.01	42.74	39.26	39.84	39.69
Bihar	58.99	59.23	42.28	27.29	43.36
Gujarat	29.01	18.06	12.19	4.47	13.16
Haryana	0.00	18.17	11.80	1.95	8.29
Himachal Pradesh	5.77	14.93	7.51	6.48	8.42
Karnataka	25.07	26.87	16.09	12.58	18.08
Kerala	19.94	15.09	11.15	6.09	9.75
Madhya Pradesh	55.20	40.79	32.64	12.21	36.58
Maharashtra	42.49	32.86	22.51	13.51	24.43
Orissa	74.35	51.42	39.57	25.01	47.98
Punjab	21.51	12.41	8.06	1.66	6.42
Rajasthan	25.40	19.76	10.62	5.93	14.08
Tamil Nadu	43.09	32.96	15.11	12.63	20.93
Uttar Pradesh	36.51	42.44	32.92	18.58	31.45
West Bengal	49.30	34.52	22.52	30.68	32.28
All India	45.03	35.85	27.54	15.88	27.65

Source: Based on 55th NSS.

Table A2
Size of the Poverty Gap Index in Indian States and All India by Social Groups

States	*ST*	*SC*	*OBC*	*Others*	*ALL*
Andhra Pradesh	4.63	3.04	1.72	0.73	1.98
Assam	7.23	8.51	9.07	9.21	8.82
Bihar	13.90	13.87	8.48	5.06	9.25
Gujarat	5.91	2.81	2.20	0.60	2.33
Haryana	0.00	3.01	1.91	0.31	1.33
Himachal Pradesh	0.70	1.88	0.78	0.86	1.06
Karnataka	3.83	4.90	2.78	1.86	3.04
Kerala	4.48	2.72	1.76	0.84	1.55
Madhya Pradesh	12.96	9.02	6.83	1.94	8.10
Maharashtra	10.15	6.48	4.18	2.21	4.86
Orissa	21.45	12.49	9.11	4.32	12.20
Punjab	2.69	1.59	0.94	0.07	0.78
Rajasthan	4.86	3.42	1.24	0.70	2.16
Tamil Nadu	12.70	6.54	2.67	2.76	4.02
Uttar Pradesh	8.17	9.20	6.30	3.35	6.35
West Bengal	10.25	7.40	4.96	6.11	6.68
All India	10.93	7.70	5.40	2.83	5.70

Source: Based on NSS 55th round data.

Table A3
Unemployment Rates in Indian States and All India by Social Groups.
(Number of Unemployed Persons per 1000 Persons in the Labour Force)

Rural	*ST*		*SC*		*OBC*		*OTHER*	
States	*Male*	*Female*	*Male*	*Female*	*Male*	*Female*	*Male*	*Female*
Andhra Pradesh	3.29	0.00	8.21	3.72	9.90	4.04	16.16	8.11
Assam	29.04	13.95	17.76	37.84	31.30	51.72	39.47	104.00
Bihar	17.01	13.29	16.79	0.00	18.33	6.62	38.05	10.87
Gujarat	0.00	0.00	12.57	0.00	3.38	0.00	15.49	0.00
Haryana	0.00	0.00	9.69	0.00	8.66	0.00	14.58	0.00
Jammu & Kashmir	0.00	0.00	5.02	4.91	3.27	3.86	12.96	12.35
Karnataka	0.00	4.57	28.96	2.35	8.13	2.69	6.72	5.67
Kerala	37.38	51.16	66.02	118.60	67.14	124.03	54.55	166.04
Madhya Pradesh	5.33	0.00	3.82	0.00	5.59	2.72	13.38	9.57
Maharashtra	11.21	4.07	15.47	0.00	11.24	4.34	30.41	13.12
Orissa	10.20	0.00	23.81	9.32	27.92	24.10	39.25	43.80
Punjab	93.53	211.38	31.78	3.91	36.00	17.30	15.90	9.58
Rajasthan	5.69	0.00	9.90	2.81	5.99	0.00	6.15	3.28
Tamil Nadu	15.02	31.69	37.61	2.18	19.32	11.99	23.97	50.23
Uttar Pradesh	29.66	0.00	8.16	3.86	6.12	0.00	16.74	6.58
West Bengal	18.87	11.36	34.97	34.68	56.90	7.63	25.88	32.52
All India	10.64	4.55	18.48	6.12	14.81	9.84	22.56	21.93

16

TRENDS AND INFLUENCES ON THE INCIDENCE OF POVERTY IN INDIA, PARTICULARLY SOCIAL INFLUENCES

M. Ramanjaneyulu

Introduction

"Who are India's Poor?–The agricultural workers, many of whom are small scale farmers or casual labourers. The people of Scheduled Caste and Scheduled Tribes are far more likely to be poor, than those of other social groups, as low Caste status, and gender barriers still operate as social obstacles that block or exclude them from opportunity"–World Bank Development Policy Review (2003).

The Indian economy has a dual character comprised of capital freedom for the rich and because of socio-economic inequality little freedom for the poor. Poverty is a multi-dimensional phenomenon and a significant issue for economic development. Large sections of the population do not have resources for their survival because the government is in the hands of the rich class and therefore, equal resource allocation has not taken place in India since Independence.

India is not an egalitarian society, but it is pretending to be egalitarian. It is a society divided by caste and social groupings. Large segments of the poor in society are striving hard to get food, clothes and shelter. The small group of the rich class can easily exploit the poor and break them into different sub-groups and try in such a way as to prevent them from having peasant associations, solidarity and unity. This involves a policy of divide and rule. It is a society of the rich at the cost of the peasantry who are really the source of national productivity.

The policies of the government are not trying to reduce the gap between the rich and the poor. This is the strategy of the rich class in India. In addition to this the caste upper community is treating them as very low and maintaining their distance from the Scheduled Caste due to brahmanical ideology. system prevails, and a large proportion of the population has been treated as Scheduled Caste untouchables. Untouchability is also widely practiced in India. An untouchable person cannot become a vendor or seller of tea, coffee and any eatables to the public.

The Brahmins created the caste system in India. The caste system is a curse and plague for the lower strata of Scheduled Caste untouchables. This results in social poverty and consequently economic inequality (of property, income, living standards etc) and generates social inferiority, dependence and exploitation of the lower castes. In other words, a low level in the social stratum is associated with lack of wealth, among other things. The social category of the poor arises in stratified societies in which the upper and lower strata have direct experience and knowledge of each other. Poverty identifies those belonging to the lower the strata. A German proverb says, "Poverty is the rich man's cow" and poverty is the hand and foot of wealth. Poverty always involves weakness and a low position in the social hierarchy or personal inferiority for the poor.

Hunger is actually the worst of all weapons of mass destruction claiming millions of victims every year. Fighting hunger and poverty is a truly sustainable way to achieve world peace. The Brazilian President Lula Da Silva said that "There will be no peace without development and there will be neither peace nor development without social justice." The growing divide between the wealthy and poor, between opportunity and misery, are both a source of political and social instability.

There has been remarkable progress in reducing poverty since 1990. Extreme poverty in developing countries has fallen from 28 per cent in 1990 to 21 per cent in 2001. If the current projections of economic growth are met, global poverty will fall to 10 per cent by 2015. And while poverty would not be eradicated, that would bring us, much closer to the day when we can say that all the world's people have at least the bare minimum to meet their daily needs. Hunger and malnutrition go with poverty. Even where poverty rates are falling, hundreds of millions of people do not obtain enough food to meet their daily needs. Poverty and hunger will remain wherever poor health and lack of education deprive people of productive employment, where environmental resources have been depleted or spoiled, and where corruption, conflict and mis-governance occur.

The benefit from economic development must go to the less privileged classes of society, not the wealthy and those with economic power. In India poverty is basically a phenomenon occurring amongst Scheduled Castes and Tribes who get little from economic development.

The Indian Seventh Five-Year Plan inaugurated the augmented poverty line on the basis of the norm of monthly private consumer expenditure. The norm is added to by the per capita monthly public expenditure by each State Government on social overheads such as: 1. health and family welfare; 2. water supply and sanitation; 3. education; 4. administration of police, jails and courts; 5. roads; and 6. social welfare.

The WTO during its first multilateral trade negotiations declared that "international trade can play a major role in the promotion of economic development and poverty alleviation". Although all our people may benefit from the increased opportunities and welfare gains that the multilateral trading system generates, multilateral trade liberalization is a challenging assignment. Agricultural trade ensures food security which in turn can also reduce the poverty. Nearly 52 per cent of India's population is concentrated in agriculture and 58 per cent of its economically active population is in agriculture. The development of trade in agriculture can play a major role in the reduction of poverty. The numbers experiencing food insecurity and nutritional under-nourishment has increased from 215.8 millions in 1990-92 to 221.1 million in 2000-02. The proportion of the under-nourished in the total population has declined from 25 per cent to 21 per cent. The dietary energy supply also increased from 2366 calories to 2420 calories per person per day and its annual growth rate registered a 0.19 per cent increase during the period 1990-2002. The poverty headcount for the national population was also at 28.6 per cent in 2003.

The World Bank has conducted a study of 193 countries to estimate the development of human capabilities through better education, health and nutrition which can help the transformation of the society and create prospects for a higher rate of economic growth in low human development countries. The study concluded that only 16 per cent of the growth takes place due to physical capital (machinery, buildings and physical infrastructure) whereas 20 per cent arises from natural capital. The most important part is that 64 per cent of the growth is achieved from human and social capital. Both human and social capital have been positively influencing economic growth as well as reducing the poverty levels of nations.

Objectives

The objectives of this paper taking into account the above factors, are as follows:

1. To study the trickle-down effect on poverty of increased social sector expenditure and the economic development of India during the period 1980-81 to 2004-05.
2. To study the behaviour of poverty in relation to the state NDP of different states in India.
3. To study rainfall and agricultural production as determinants in reducing poverty.
4. To assess the role of human capital and employment in contributing to a reduction in poverty in India.
5. To study the income levels of Scheduled Castes and Scheduled Tribes in India.

Hypotheses:

The hypotheses framed to test the above objectives are as follows:

1. Increasing the level of social expenditure positively influences the economic growth of the nation.
2. The fluctuation in the state net domestic product is causing to oscillate of poverty in different states of the nation.
3. Rainfall and agricultural production are contributors to the level of poverty in India.
4. Human capital and employment generation are responsible for reducing poverty in India.
5. The level of income of Scheduled Castes and Scheduled Tribes is low in India.

Methodology and Data Sources: Quantitative Results

Multiple regression analysis has been used for the period from 1980-81 to 2004-05 in social sector expenditure as sub-variables known as independent variables and GDP of the nation as a dependent variable. The cross-sectional data on the percentage of poverty in rural, urban and combined across the states for seven periods from (1973-74 to 2006-07) have been used for the analysis. National Sample Survey data on different levels of income have also been used for Scheduled Caste and Scheduled Tribes. The model of multiple regression analysis is as follows:

$$GDP = \beta 0 + \beta_1(EDUC) + \beta_2\ (SSR) + \beta_3\ (M\&PH) + \beta_4\ (FAMWEL) + \beta_5\ (HOUSE) + \beta_6\ (URBAND) + \beta_7\ (BRORCO) + \beta_8\ (LABOREM) + \beta_9\ (RELIEFNC) + \beta_{10}\ (SOSEWEL) + u \ldots \ldots 1$$

Dependent Variable = GDP Gross Domestic Product

Independent Variables:

1. EDUC = Education, Arts and Culture
2. SSR = Scientific Services and Research
3. M&PH = Medical and Public Health and water supply & sanitation
4. FAMWEL = Family Welfare
5. HOUSE = Housing
6. URBAND = Urban Development
7. BRORCO = Broadcasting,
8. LABOREM = Labour & Employment
9. RELIEFNC = Relief on Natural Calamities
10. SOSEWEL = Social Security Welfare

Results 1:

The influence of the variables of the social sector on economic growth:

GDP = 365407.7 + 12.631(EDUC) + 110.145 (SSR) –4.480 (M&PH) -313.353 (FAMWEL)

t =	(15.037)	(1.781)**	(4.146)	(–.197)	(–3.079)
sig	0.000	0.092	0.001	0.847	0.008

–143.564 (HOUSE) +25.457 (URBAND) + 52.891 (BRORCO)

(-4.112)	(0.948)***	(2.909)
0.001	0.359	0.011

+336.982 (LABOREM) + 245.780 (RELIEFNC) +44.166 (SOSEWEL) + u

(2.790)*	(4.795)	(1.695)**
0.014	0.000	0.112

R^2 = .998 Adj R^2 = .997 F = 722.782 D.W = 1.843

Note: *indicates 1% level, ** shows 5% level and *** reveals 10% level of significance.

The GDP of the nation and the elasticity coefficients of social sector expenditure have been analyzed with the help of linear multiple regression analysis. The values of the positive coefficients are education (12.631), scientific services and research (110.145), urban development (25.457), broadcasting (52.891), labour and employment (336.982), relief of natural calamities (245.780) and social and community services (44.166) contributing to the growth of GDP of the nation which in turn reduces the poverty levels of the nation. The R^2 shows 0.998 of variation explained by the independent variables. The Durbin-Watson test statistic is around 2, so it is a goodness of fit, implying a functional relationship. The null hypothesis is rejected in the case of many variables which are at the 1 per cent level and 5 per cent levels of significance. Thus, the increasing level of social sector expenditure has a positive association with increasing economic growth and it has trickle-down effect on poverty reduction.

Results 2:

Rural Poverty: Cross sectional data of all states of India during 1973-74 to 2006-0:

a. *Rural Poverty* = 23.285 – 0.338 (1973-74) – 0.281 (1977-78) + 0.495 (1983-84)

t =	(3.427)*	(1.110)	(–.740)	(2.147)*
Sig	0.002	0.278	0.466	0.042

+ 0.235 (1987-88) + 0.006 (1993-94) + 0.282 (1999-2000) -0.362 (2006-2007)

(0 .971)	(0 .023)	(0 .668)	(–0.970)
0.341	0.982	0.571	0.342

R^2 = .326

Note: * indicates 1% level, ** shows 5% level and *** reveals 10% level of significance.

The constant value of rural poverty is estimated at 23.28 per cent and its t value is 3.427 showing a high significance level. Coefficient values of 1973-74, 1977-78 and 2006-07 are exhibiting negative values and could not contribute to an increase rural poverty. The coefficient values of 1983-84, 1987-88, 1993-94 and 1999-2000 show a positive influence, but the 1983-84 value of the coefficient was 0.495 which means that the 0.5 per cent increase is more significant at the 1 per cent level. Overall the R^2 reveals a 32.6 per cent goodness of fit of the test with regard to rural poverty.

Urban Poverty: Cross-sectional data of all states of India during 1973-74 to 2006-07

b. Urban Poverty: = 13.128 – 0.791 (1973-74) + 0.675 (1977-78) + 0.400 (1983-84)

t =	(1.906)**	(–2.012)	(1.337)***	(1.750)**
Sig	0.069	0.056	0.197	0.093

–0.323 (1987-88) + 0.044 (1993-94) + 0.823 (1999-2000) –0.809 (2006-2007)

(–1.538)***	(0 .124)	(0 .821)	(–1.215)***
0.137	0.902	.420	0.236

R^2 = .299 F = 1.463

Note: * indicates 1% level, ** shows 5% level and *** reveals 10% level of significance.

The constant value of urban poverty is estimated at 13.128 per cent and its t value is 1.906 which is significant at the 5 per cent level. Coefficient values of 1973-74, 1987-88 and 2006-07 are showing negative values and therefore could not influence an increase in urban poverty. The coefficient values of 1977-78, 1983-84, 1993-94 and 1999-2000 show a positive influence, but the 1983-84 value of the coefficient was the 0.400 which means that the 0.4 per cent increase is more significant at the 5 per cent level of significance. Overall the R^2 reveals 29.9 per cent of the goodness of fit of the test with regard to urban poverty.

Poverty Combined: Cross-sectional data of all states of India during 1973-74 to 2006-07

C. Combined Rural + Urban:

36.179 – 1.014 (1973-74) + 0.073 (1977-78) + 0.452 (1983-84)

t =	(4.131)	(-2.676)*	(0.195)	(1.623)**
Sig	0.000	0.013	0.847	0.118

+ 0.882 (1987-88) –0.818(1993-94) + 0.539(1999-2000) –0.347(2006-2007)

(0.562)	(–1.781)**	(0 .752)	(–0.766)
0.017	0.088	0 .459	0.457

R^2 = .224 F = 2.282

Note: * indicates 1% level, ** shows 5% level and *** reveals 10% level of significance.

Overall poverty, including rural and urban, has a constant value of 36.179 per cent with a high level significance of the t value. In the year 1983-84 its coefficient value is 0.452 which is significant at the 5 per cent level. Even in the year 1993-94 its coefficient value is negative but significant at the 5 per cent level. Its R^2 and F-values are 22.4 per cent and 2.282 showing appropriateness of the model. Thus, all the results given above indicate a downward linear trend of poverty in India.

The Progress of Social Indicators

Social indicators like education, health and sanitation have, it seems, been contributing enormously to reducing poverty levels of India. There is an inverse relation between poverty incidence and social indicators. The incidence of poverty has declined from 44.5 per cent in 1980 and again declined to 36.00 per cent in 1990 declining further to 28.6 per cent by 2000. The literacy rate increased from 44 per cent in 1980, to 52 per cent in 1990 and 71 per cent by 2000. Female literacy also increased from 53 per cent to 71 per cent and life expectancy increased from 55 per cent to 61 per cent while infant mortality also decreased considerably. Moreover, sanitation facilities improved during this period. The progress social indicators can be seen from the Table 1.

Table 1
Progress of Social Indicators in India 1980-2000

	1980	*1990*	*2000*
Poverty Incidence %	44.50	36.00	28.60
Education Literacy Rate	44	52	65
Female literacy rate	53	61	71
Health Life Expectancy	55	60	61
Infant Mortality	115	79	68
Sanitation			
Water Resources	n.a.	68	78
HHs Toilet facility	n.a.	30	36

Source: Economic Survey of India 2005-06.

Comparison of Poverty with other Regions

Extreme poverty in India at less than a $ 1 a day has declined from 41 per cent in 1990 to 35 per cent 2001. However, the incidence of poverty in India is higher than in China, East Asia and the Pacific, as well as South Asia, Eastern Europe, Central Asia, and Latin America and the Caribbean (See Table 2). On the other hand, India's incidence of poverty is lower than in the Middle East and North Africa. As Table 2 reveals the extent of the decline in the incidence of poverty between 1990 and 2001 was much less in China than in South China.

Table 2
Population Below Extreme Poverty Line
(% people living one less than $ 1 a day PPP)

	1990	*2001*
Latine America & Caribbean	11	10
Eastern Europe & Central Asia	1	4
Middle East & North Africa	45	46
South Asia	31	30
East Asia & Pacific	30	15
China	33	17
India	41	35

Source: World Development Indicators-2005 Washington DC.

Table 3
Percentage of population Below Poverty Line in India
1970-71 to 2001-2007

Year	*Rural*	*Urban*	*Total*
1970-71	53.00	51.00	52.30
1974	56.40	49.00	54.90
1977-78	53.14	45.20	51.30
1979-80	50.70	40.00	48.40
1983 (38 Round)	45.65	40.79	44.48
1987-88 (43 Round)	39.09	38.20	38.86
1989-90 (45 Round)	33.70	36.00	34.28
1990-91 (46 Round)	35.04	35.29	35.11
1992 (48 Round)	41.70	37.80	40.70
1993-94 (50 Round)	37.27	32.36	35.97
1994-95 (51 Round)	38.03	34.24	36.98
1995-96 (52 Round)	38.46	33.97	36.08
1997 (53 Round)	45.25	34.58	43.01
2000	30.20	24.70	28.60
1999-2000 (55 Round) 30 Days	27.10	23.60	26.10
7 Days	24.00	21. 60	23.30
2007	21.07	15.06	19.34

Source: Central Statistical Organisation, Statistical Hand Book,1999.

Percentage of the Population below the Poverty Line in India

Table 3 shows the percentage of the population below the poverty line in India during the period of 1970-71 to 2007. During the period 1970-71 to 1979-80, rural poverty has prevailed to the extent of more than 51 per cent, particularly in 1974 when it was 56.4 per cent. In the case of urban poverty it has declined from 51 per cent to 40 per cent. In this period the country had suffered severe poverty. During the period of 1990-91, rural and urban poverty came down to 35 per cent. Again in 1992, it increased to 42 per cent in rural areas and 39 per cent in urban areas. By 2000 it had declined to 30 per cent and 25 per cent in both areas respectively and it has been forecast to decline to 21 per cent in rural areas and 15 per cent in urban areas by 2007. Both declining rural and trends in poverty can be seen in Figure 1 which represents a marginal decreasing trend in rural poverty of minus 1.798 and in urban poverty trend of minus 1.787. It shows a continuous fall in the poverty levels of the nation due to the positive contribution of several social and economic factors.

Figure 1
Trends in the Incidence of Rural and Urban Poverty in India 1970-71 to 2007

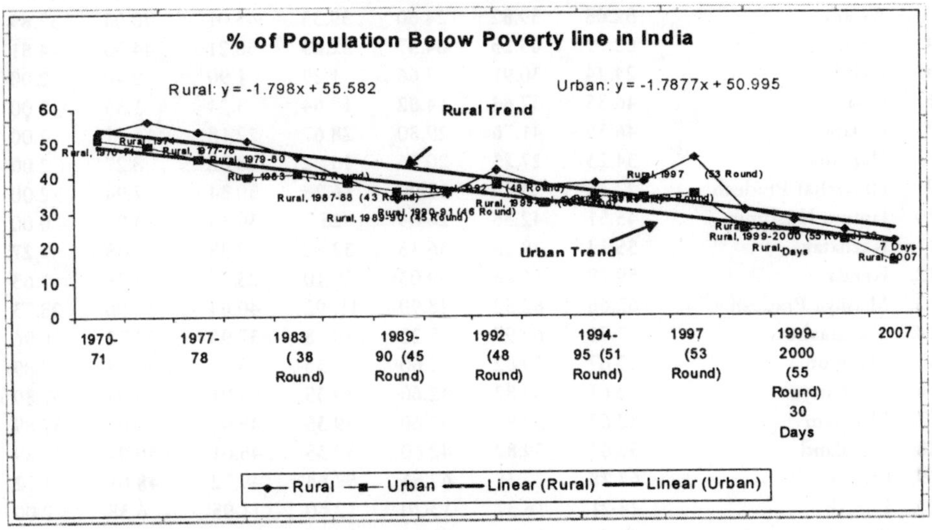

Rural Poverty

Rural poverty as estimated by Planning Commission of India shows a declining trend from 56.44 per cent to 21.07 per cent. In the case of Bihar and Orissa rural poverty is estimated to remain at 44.81 per cent and 41.72 per cent respectively by 2006-07. In all the study periods these two states were not able to reduce poverty to the levels of the national average. States like Arunachal Pradesh, Assam, Manipur, Meghalaya, Mizoram and Nagaland stood at 37.89 per cent, and West Bengal has been maintaining he rural poverty equal or little above the national rural poverty level. During the period of 1973-74 and 1977-78, the rural areas had suffered to the extent of 56.44 per cent and 53.07 per cent of population below the poverty line. During 1970's, the rural population has suffered severely due to low rainfall and low agricultural production in the country.

Social sector expenditure has been contributing directly to reduce poverty in rural areas. The states which have been estimated to be below 5 per cent of rural poverty by 2006-07 comprised of Andhra Pradesh, Delhi, Goa, Gujarat , Haryana, Himachal Pradesh, Jammu and Kashmir, Kerala, Punjab, Tamil Nadu, Andaman

Nicobar Islands, Chandigarh, Dadra and Nagar Haveli, Daman and Diu and Lakshadweep.

Table 4
Percentage of the Rural Population Below Poverty Line by States and UTs 1973-74 and 2006-07

States/ UTs		*Rural*						
		1973-74	*1977-78*	*1983-84*	*1987-88*	*1993-94*	*1999-2001*	*2006-07*
1.	Andhra Pradesh	48.41	38.11	26.53	20.92	15.92	11.05	4.58
2.	Arunachal Pradesh	52.68	59.82	42.60	39.35	45.01	40.04	37.89
3.	Assam	52.68	59.82	24.60	39.35	45.01	40.04	37.89
4.	Bihar	62.99	63.25	64.37	52.63	58.21	44.30	44.81
5.	Delhi	24.44	30.91	7.66	1.29	1.90	0.40	2.00
6.	Goa	46.85	37.64	14.82	17.64	5.34	1.35	2.00
7.	Gujarat	46.35	41.76	29.80	28.67	22.18	13.17	2.00
8.	Haryana	34.23	27.73	20.56	16.22	28.02	8.27	2.00
9.	Himachal Pradesh	27.42	33.49	17.00	16.28	30.34	7.94	2.00
10.	Jammu Kashmir	45.51	42.86	26.04	25.7	30.34	3.97	0.00
11.	Karnataka	55.14	48.18	36.33	32.82	29.88	17.38	7.27
12.	Kerala	59.19	51.48	39.03	29.10	25.76	9.38	1.63
13.	Madhya Pradesh	62.66	62.52	48.90	41. 92	40.64	37.06	28.73
14.	Maharashtra	57.71	62.97	45.23	40.78	37.93	23.72	16.96
15.	Manipur	52.67	59.82	42.60	39.35	45.01	40.04	37.89
16.	Meghalaya	52.67	59.82	42.60	39.35	45.01	40.04	37.89
17.	Mizoram	52.67	59.82	42.60	39.35	45.01	40.04	37.89
18.	Nagaland	52.67	59.82	42.60	39.35	45.01	40.04	37.89
19.	Orissa	67.28	72.38	67.53	57.64	49.72	48.01	41.72
20.	Punjab	28.21	16.37	13.20	12.60	11.95	6.38	2.00
21.	Rajasthan	44.76	35.89	33.50	33.21	26.46	37.40	11.09
22.	Sikkim	52.67	59.82	42.60	39.35	45.01	40.40	37.89
23.	Tamil Nadu	57.23	57.68	53.99	45.80	32.48	20.55	3.68
24.	Tripura	52.67	59.82	42.60	39.35	45.01	40.04	37.89
25.	Uttar Pradesh	56.53	47.60	46.45	14.10	42.28	31.22	24.25
26.	West Bengal	73.16	68.34	63.05	48.30	40.8	31.85	21.98
27.	Andaman & Nicobar	57.43	57.68	53.99	45.80	23.84	20.55	3.68
28.	Chandigarh	27.96	27.32	23.79	14.67	11.35	5.75	2.00
29.	Dadra & Nagar Haveli	46.85	37.64	14.81	67.11	51.95	17.57	2.00
30.	Daman and Diu	0.00	0.00	0.00	0.00	5.34	1.35	2.00
31.	Lakshadweep	59.19	51.48	39.03	29.10	25.76	9.38	1.63
32.	Pondicherry	57.43	57.68	53.99	45.80	32.48	20.55	3.68
	All India	56.44	53.07	45.65	39.09	37.27	27.09	21.07

Source: 1. Planning Commission, Government of India, 2. Indian Year Book 2004, Manpower Profile, Directo

Urban Poverty

Urban poverty in India was very high during 1973-74 and 1977-78. The states of Andhra Pradesh, Bihar, Delhi, Gujarat, Karnataka, Kerala, Madhya Pradesh, Orissa, Rajasthan, Uttar Pradesh, and Lakshadweep registered more than a 50 per cent incidence of urban poverty during 1970-74 (see Table 5). States such as Karnataka, Kerala, Madhya Pradesh, Orissa and Lakshadweep registered above 50 per cent urban poverty during 1977-78. During 1983-84, only Madhya Pradesh had an incidence of 53 per cent of urban poverty. From then onwards all states registered a very low rate of urban poverty. It has also been estimated that for 2006-07 of states like Bihar, Madhya Pradesh, and Orissa will still experiencing an incidence

Table 5

Percentage of the Urban Population Below Poverty Line by States and UTs 1973-74 and 2006-07, India

States/ UTs	*Urban*						
	1973-74	*1977-78*	*1983-84*	*1987-88*	*1993-94*	*1999-2001*	*2006-07*
1. Andhra Pradesh	50.61	43.55	36.30	40.11	38.33	26.63	18.99
2. Arunachal Pradesh	36.92	32.71	21.73	9.94	7.73	7.47	4.48
3. Assam	36.92	32.71	21.73	9.94	7.73	7.47	4.48
4. Bihar	52.96	48.76	47.33	48.73	35.5	32.91	32.69
5. Delhi	52.23	33.51	27.89	13.56	16.03	9.42	2.00
6. Goa	37.69	36.31	27.00	35.48	27.03	7.52	2.00
7. Gujarat	52.57	40.02	39.14	37.26	27.89	15.59	2.00
8. Haryana	40.18	36.57	24.15	17.99	16.38	9.99	2.00
9. Himachal Pradesh	13.17	1 9.44	9.43	6.29	9.18	4.63	2.00
10. Jammu Kashmir	21.32	23.71	17.76	17.47	9.18	1.98	0.00
11. Karnataka	52.53	50.36	4.82	48.42	40.14	25.25	8.00
12. Kerala	62.74	55.36	45.68	40.33	24.55	20.27	9.34
13. Madya Pradesh	57.65	58.66	53.06	47.09	48.38	38.44	31.77
14. Maharashtra	43.87	40.09	40.26	39.78	35.15	26.81	15.20
15. Manipur	36.92	32.71	21.73	9.94	7.73	7.47	4.48
16. Meghalaya	36.92	32.71	21.73	9.94	7.73	7.47	4.48
17. Mizoram	36.92	32.71	21.73	9.94	7.73	7.47	4.48
18. Nagaland	36.92	32.71	21.73	9.94	7.73	7.47	4.48
19. Orissa	55.62	50.92	49.15	41.63	41. 64	42.83	37.46
20. Punjab	27.96	27.32	23.79	14.67	11.35	5.75	2.00
21. Rajasthan	52.13	43.53	37.94	41. 92	30.49	19.85	15.42
22. Sikkim	36.92	32.71	21.73	9.94	7.73	7.47	4.48
23. Tamil Nadu	49.40	48.69	46.96	38.64	39.77	22.11	9.64
24. Tripura	36.92	32.71	21.73	9.94	7.73	7.47	4.48
25. Uttar Pradesh	60.09	56.23	49.82	42.96	35.39	30.89	26.17
26. West Bengal	34.67	38.20	32.32	35.08	22.41	14.86	8.98
27. Andaman & Nicobar	49.40	48.69	46.96	38.64	39.77	22.11	9.64
28. Chandigarh	27.96	27.32	23.79	14.67	11.35	5.75	2.00
29. Dadra & Nagar Haveli	37.69	36.31	27.00	0.00	39.93	13.52	2.00
30. Daman and Diu	0.00	0.00	0.00	0.00	27.03	7.52	2.00
31. Lakshadweep	62.74	55.62	45.68	40.33	24.55	20.27	9.34
32. Pondicherry.	49.40	48.69	46.96	38.64	39.77	22.11	9.64
All India	49.01	45.24	40.79	38.20	32.36	-23.62	15.06

Source: 1. Planning Commission, Government of India.
2. Indian Year Book 2004, Manpower Profile, Directorate General of Employment and Training.

of poverty at a high level of 32.61 per cent, 31.77 per cent and 37.46 per cent respectively. However, overall, urban poverty in India has also declined from 49.01 per cent to 15.06 per cent during the period 1973-74 to 2006-07.

Table 6

Percentage of the Overall Population Below Poverty Line by States and UTs 1973-74 and 2006-07, India

States/ UTs	*Combined*						
	1973-74	*1977-78*	*1983-84*	*1987-88*	*1993-94*	*1999-2001*	*2006-07*
1. Andhra Pradesh	48.86	39.31	28.91	25.90	22.19	15.77	8.49
2. Arunachal Pradesh	51.93	58.32	40.88	36.20	39.35	33.47	29.33
3. Assam	51.21	57.15	40.47	36.20	40.86	36.09	33.33
4. Bihar	61.91	61.55	62.22	52.10	54.96	42.60	43.18
5. Delhi	49.61	33.23	26.22	12.40	14.69	8.23	2.00
6. Goa	44.26	37.23	18.90	24.50	14.92	4.40	2.00
7. Gujarat	48.15	41.23	32.79	31.50	24.21	14.07	2.00
8. Haryana	35.36	29.55	21.37	16.60	25.05	8.74	2.00
9. Himachal Pradesh	26.39	32.45	16.40	15.50	28.44	7.63	2.00
10. Jammu Kashmir	40.83	38.97	24.24	23.80	25.17	3.48	0.00
11. Karnataka	54.47	48.78	38.24	37.50	33.16	20.04	7.85
12. Kerala	59.79	52.22	40.42	31.80	25.43	12.72	3.61
13. Madhya Pradesh	61.78	61.78	49.78	43.70	42.52	37.43	29.52
14. Maharashtra	53.24	55.88	43.44	40.10	36.86	25.02	16.18
15. Manipur	49.96	53.72	37.02	31.40	33.78	28.54	30.52
16. Meghalaya	50.20	55.19	38.81	33.90	37.92	33.87	31.14
17. Mizoram	50.32	54.38	36.00	27.50	25.66	19.47	20.76
18. Nagaland	50.81	56.04	39.25	34.40	37.92	32.67	3 1. 86
19. Orissa	66.18	70.70	65.29	55.60	48.56	47.15	41.04
20. Punjab	28.15	19.27	16.18	13.20	11.77	6.16	2.00
21. Rajasthan	46.14	37.42	34.46	35.20	27.41	15.28	12.11
22. Sikkim	50.86	55.89	39.71	36.10	41.43	36.55	33.78
23. Tamil Nadu	54.94	54.79	51. 66	43.40	35.03	21.12	6.61
24. Tripura	51.00	56.88	40.03	35.20	39.01	34.44	31.88
25. Uttar Pradesh	57.07	49.05	47.07	41.50	40.85	31.15	24.67
26. West Bengal	63.43	60.52	54.85	44.70	35.66	27.02	18.30
27. Andaman & Nicobar	55.56	55.42	52.13	43.90	34.47	20.99	5.82
28. Chandigarh	27.96	27.32	23.79	14.70	11.35	5.75	2.00
29. Dadra & Nagar Haveli	46.55	37.20	15.67	67.10	50.84	17.14	2.00
30. Daman and Diu	0.00	0.00	0.00	0.00	15.8	4.44	2.00
31. Lakshadweep	59.68	52.79	42.36	35.00	25.04	15.60	4.59
32. Pondicherry	53.82	53.25	50.06	41.50	37.4	21.67	7.72
All India	54.88	51.32	44.48	38.90	35.97	26.10	19.34

Source: 1. Planning Commission, Government of India,
2. Indian Year Book 2004, Manpower Profile, Directorate General of Employment and Training Employment Review for various years, Institute of Applied Manpower Research New Delhi.

Combined Rural and Urban Poverty

Combined rural and urban poverty during 1973-74 to 2000 declined from 54.86 per cent to 26.1 per cent which implied that 50 per cent of the reduction took place in 25 years. States like Bihar and Orissa have been estimated to still have 43.18 per cent and 40.04 per cent of their population below the poverty line. Some states are still have an incidence of poverty above 30 per cent, for example, Arunachal Pradesh, Assam, Bihar, Manipur, Meghalaya, Madhya Pradesh, Nagaland, Orissa, Sikkim and Tripura. Bihar and Orissa are estimated for 2006-07 to have an incidence of poverty of 43.18 per cent and 41.04 per cent respectively, the highest in the states of India.

Table 7

Grovrth Rate (GR) of State NDP of High Poverty States in India

Year	*Bihar*	*Gr*	*MP*	*Gr*	*Orissa*	*Gr*
1980-81	14156	–	19442	–	10875	–
1981-82	14947	5.59	19938	2.55	10856	–0.17
1982-83	15086	0.92	20825	4.45	10209	–5.96
1983-84	16548	9.70	21901	5.17	12271	20.20
1984-85	18098	9.36	20839	–4.85	11687	–4.76
1985-86	18490	2.17	22658	8.73	13036	11.54
1986-87	19955	7.92	21651	–4.44	13216	1.38
1987-88	18851	–5.53	24610	13.66	12805	–3.11
1988-89	21233	12.63	26415	7.33	15500	21.04
1989-90	20880	–1. 66	26964	2.08	16532	6.66
1990-91	22860	9.48	30796	14.21	13724	–16.99
1991-92	21567	–5.66	28575	–7.21	15468	12.70
1992-93	20289	–5.92	30671	7.34	15206	–1.69
1993-94	20780	2.42	33937	10.65	16185	6.44
1994-95	23163	11.47	34529	1.74	16974	4.87
1995-96	19582	–15.46	36601	6.00	17749	4.57
1996-97	24569	25.47	39057	6.71	16524	–6.90
1997-98	23404	–4.74	41101	5.23	18902	14.39
1998-99	24879	6.30	43815	6.60	19482	3.07
1999-00	26130	5.03	48415	10.50	20693	6.22
2000-01	31760	21.55	42773	–11.65	20691	–0.01
2001-02	29944	–5.72	47037	9.97	22573	9.10
2002-03	34553	15.39	43923	–6.62	21862	–3.15
2003-04	39162	13.34	40809	–7.09	21151	–3.25
2004-05	43771	11.77	37695	–7.63	20440	–3.36

Source: Central Statistical Organisation, New Delhi.

Net Domestic Product and High Poverty States

The states of Bihar, Madhya Pradesh and Orissa have the highest recorded occurrence of poverty-stricken periods and in these states, the low rate of NDP growth is responsible for the high rate of poverty. In the state of Bihar, NDP growth was satisfactory in 1983-84 at 9.36 per cent, and it was 12.63 per cent in

1988-89, about 25 per cent in 1996-97 and 21.55 per cent in 2000-01. Several years recorded a negative rate of growth of NDP in the state of Bihar. In the case of Madhya Pradesh, NDP growth was positive in the years of 1983-84 at a growth rate of 5.17 per cent, and in 1987-1988, it was 13.66 per cent, in 1990-91 14.21 per cent, 1993-94 10.65 per cent. In 1999-2000, it was 10.05 per cent and in 2001-02 it was 9.97 per cent. The maximum number of years with a negative rate of growth of NDP was in Madhya Pradesh. Even in the state of Orissa, the negative growth years of NDP are higher. Therefore, high poverty in these states is accompanied by low NDP growth and high variability of NDP growth associated with considerable fluctuations in rainfall. These states depend heavily on agriculture for their NDP. The fluctuations of NDP of these poverty-stricken states is evident from Figure 2, derived from Table 7.

Figure 2
Fluctuations in Rate of Growth of NDP and Trends in Growth of NDP in the three most Poverty Severe states in India (Source: Table 7)

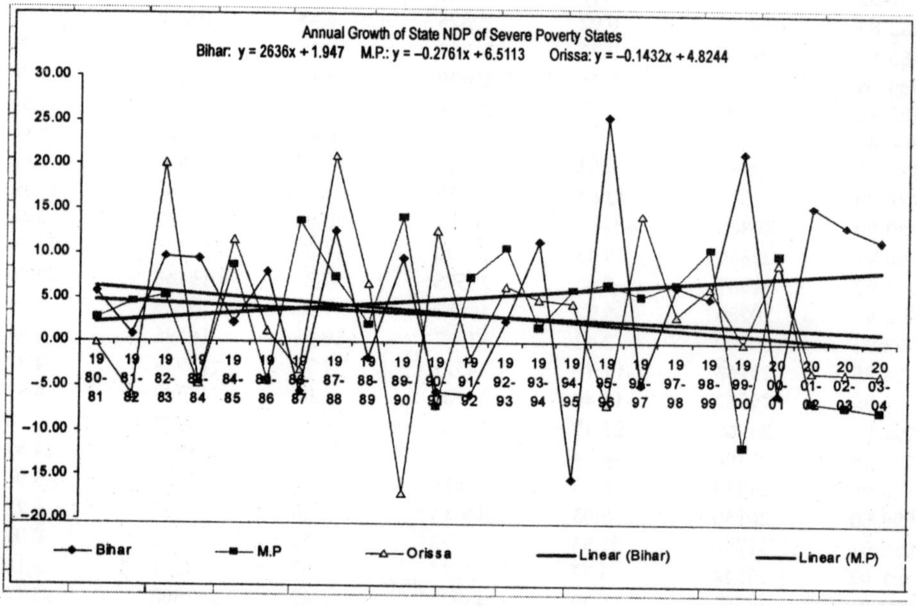

Net Domestic Product and Lower Poverty States

The states of Andhra Pradesh, Maharashtra, Uttar Pradesh and West Bengal registered a very low level of poverty due to the less adverse effects of NDP growth in those states during the period of 1980-81 and 2004-05. In this period very few years show negative growth of NDP in the states. Andhra Pradesh has four years of negative growth of NDP, two years in Maharashtra and only one year of negative growth in Utter Pradesh and West Bengal during 25 years. Therefore, less fluctuation and continuous growth of NDP result in low poverty levels in these states. Their situation is represented in Figure-3 which is derived partly from Table 8.

Table 8
Annual Growth Rate of State NDP of Low Poverty States in India

Year	*AP*	*Guj.*	*Mah.*	*Guj.*	*Orissa*	*Guj.*
1980-81	24340	–	44485	–	41953	–
1981-82	28282	16.19	45529	2.35	42959	2.40
1982-83	28780	1.76	47281	3.85	46315	7.81
1983-84	29983	4.18	50250	6.28	48132	3.92
1984-85	29076	–3.03	50895	1.28	48896	1.59
1985-86	30917	6.33	54903	7.87	50812	3.92
1986-87	30076	–2.72	55651	1.36	53013	4.33
1987-88	34144	13.52	59403	6.74	55408	4.52
1988-89	39977	17.08	65605	10.44	62633	13.04
1989-90	43157	7.96	76428	16.50	64375	2.78
1990-91	45131	4.57	79869	4.50	68204	5.95
1991-92	47664	5.61	79620	–0.31	68483	0.41
1992-93	46377	–2.70	91660	15.12	69219	1.08
1993-94	51655	11.38	101767	11.03	70935	2.48
1994-95	54564	5.63	103743	1.94	74635	5.22
1995-96	57951	6.21	115188	11.03	77046	3.23
1996-97	61955	6.91	119732	3.94	85563	11.05
1997-98	60321	–2.64	126339	5.52	84340	–1.43
1998-99	68036	12.79	130744	3.49	85113	0.92
1999-00	70904	4.22	143201	9.53	91803	7.86
2000-01	77077	8.71	137991	–3.64	93865	2.25
2001-02	80490	4.43	145620	5.53	99050	5.52
2002-03	82034	1.92	154466	6.07	102811	3.80
2003-04	83578	1.88	163312	5.73	106572	3.66
2004-05	85122	1.85	172158	5.42	110333	3.53

Source: Central Statistical Organisation, New Delhi.

Rainfall, Irrigation Performance and Poverty Alleviation

According to the World Bank (1998), a significant inverse relationship exists between the incidence of poverty and the extent of irrigation. This conclusion based on analysis of both districts and agro-climatic zones. It is claimed that while the incidence of poverty is as high as 69 per cent in the districts comprising less than 10 per cent cropped area under irrigation, the incidence of poverty is as high as 26 per cent in the districts with more than 50 per cent cropped area under irrigation, and poverty is as low as 10 per cent in the districts of Punjab and Haryana having 70 per cent of their cropped area under irrigation. State agricultural production is predominantly based on irrigation facilities and the amount of rainfall. Changes in the level of poverty are caused by the amount of rainfall and irrigation facilities.

Figure 3
Trends and Fluctuation in NDP of some states of India Registering Low Poverty Rates and Results for West Bengal (Source: Table 8)

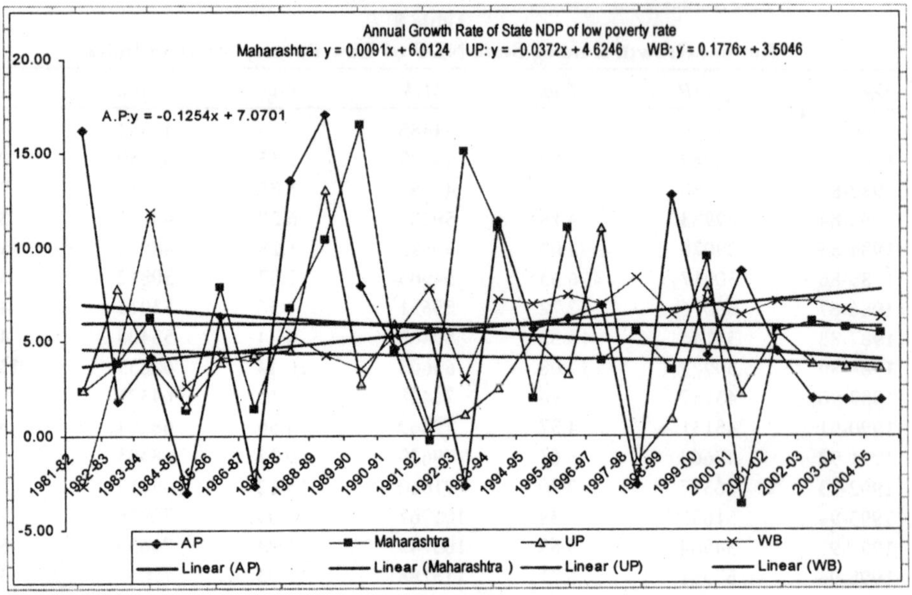

Monthly Per Capita Expenditure (MCPE) of Scheduled Castes and Scheduled Tribes in Rural Areas of India

The expenditure level of Scheduled Castes and Scheduled Tribes is very low due to their low level of income. Those with a per capita expenditure of Rs. 225 per month.are comprised of 25 per cent of Scheduled Tribes, 28 per cent of Scheduled Castes and 27 per cent of Other Backward Classes. The majority of the weaker sections are in this bottom level of expenditure in India. Nearly 4.4 per cent of STs and 8.5 per cent of SCs and 30.8 per cent of OBCs (Other Backward Classes) are in the monthly expenditure level of Rs. 950 and above. Poverty and illiteracy are more than 50 per cent and 60 per cent respectively in the two groups of Scheduled Castes and Scheduled Tribes. This indicates that social sector expenditure has not been extended fully to these weaker sections of the society.

Table 9 reveals the comparatively wretched situation of Scheduled Tribes and Scheduled Castes in India, particularly that of Tribes. Scheduled tribal households account for 10.1 per cent of rural households but 25.2 per cent are in the lowest monthly per capita expenditure category. The situation is somewhat better for the SCs; they account for 21.6 per cent of of the rural population and 28.1 per cent are in the lowest expenditure category. The situation is better for OBCs; they account for 38.5 per cent of the rural population but only 27 per cent are in the lowest expenditure category. For others the situation is even better.

They account for 30.3 per cent of the rural population but only 19.6 per cent are in the lowest expenditure category. The social bias in income distribution based on tribal and and caste division in India is apparent.

Table 9

Per 1000 Distribution of Rural Households by Social Groups for each MPCE Class, Rural Areas, India

Rural MPCE (Rs)	*Number per 1000 HHs with MPCE Class*						
	ST	*%*	*SC*	*%*	*OBC*	*%*	*Others*
000-225	252	25.2	281	28.1	270	27.0	196
225-255	152	15.2	433	43.3	292	29.2	123
255-300	148	14.8	204	20.4	486	48.6	162
300-340	133	13.3	245	24.5	435	43.5	186
340-380	143	14.3	255	25.5	362	36.2	239
380-420	103	10.3	229	22.9	395	39.5	273
420-470	86	8.6	295	29.5	364	36.4	256
470-525	88	8.8	209	20.9	441	44.1	262
525-615	68	6.8	210	21.0	354	35.4	368
615-775	61	6.1	146	14.6	407	40.7	386
775-950	51	5.1	123	12.3	336	33.6	490
950-Above	44	4.4	85	8.5	308	30.8	464
ALL classes	101	10.1	216	21.6	381	38.1	303
average MPCE	408		426		478		589

Source: (NSSO) Household Consumer Expenditure and Employment and Unemployment situation in India, 2000-01, September, 2002, Govt. of India.

Monthly Per Capita Expenditure (MPCE) of Scheduled Castes and Scheduled Tribes in Urban Areas of India

Table 10 reveals also that in urban areas the expenditures (incomes) of the Scheduled Tribal households and Scheduled Castes households are low as well as those of Other Backward Classes in comparison to those not belonging to these groups. For example, although the householders of Scheduled Tribes constitutes 3.7 per cent of urban households, they account for 7.8 per cent of urban households with a monthly expenditure of less than 300 Rs. Scheduled Caste households make up 14.3 per cent of urban households and contribute 24.8 per cent of those in the lower expenditure category and, for OBC households the respective figures are 29.6 per cent and 39.3 per cent. By contrast, others not in these groups account for 52.4 per cent of households but only 28.6 per cent of these households are in the lowest monthly expenditure category. They are also comparatively over represented in the higher income category. It seems that there has been little trickle-down of the benefits of economic growth to those belonging to Scheduled Castes and Tribes.

Table 10
Per 1000 Distribution of Urban Households by Social Groups for each MPCE Class, India

Urban MPCE (Rs)	*Number per 1000 HHs with MPCE Class*						
	ST	%	*SC*	%	*OBC*	%	*Others*
000-300	73	7.3	248	24.8	393	39.3	286
300-350	79	7.9	244	24.4	371	37.1	306
350-425	46	4.6	214	21.4	426	42.6	315
425-500	39	3.9	218	21.8	379	37.9	365
500-575	47	4.7	166	16.6	382	38.2	404
575-665	49	4.9	198	19.8	305	30.5	451
665- 775	41	4.1	197	19.7	322	32.2	439
775-915	27	2.7	143	14.3	327	32.7	502
915-1120	37	3.7	118	11.8	267	26.7	577
1120-1500	24	2.4	61	6.1	240	24.0	673
1500-1925	27	2.7	75	7.5	207	20.7	692
1925- Above	19	1.9	39	3.9	140	14.0	801
ALLCLASS	37	3.7	143	14.3	296	29.6	524
averageMPCE (RS)	749		670		745		1096

Source: (NSSO) Household Consumer Expenditure and Employment and Unemployment situation in India, 2000-2001, September, 2002, Govt. of India.

Concluding Comments

The World Bank has proposed the Millennium Development Goals to be implemented and achieved by 2015 in all developing and poor countries to minimize the severity of poverty among the poor. These include, in comparison to the situation in 1990:

1. Reduction of extreme poverty (those living below US $ 1 per day) by half.
2. Ensuring that all children are enrolled in primary schools and universal primary education in all countries by 2015.
3. Eliminating gender gap and empowerment of women by eliminating gender inequality in all levels of education by 2015.
4. Reducing by two-thirds the infant mortality rates and children under 5 by three fourths, the mortality rates for mothers by 2015.
5. Ensuring all women have access to reproductive health services by 2015.

It will be very challenging for India to achieve all these goals but it is making progress towards their achievements.

Evidence has been provided that growth in GDP has been positively associated with social sector expenditure which in turn has been correlated with a declining incidence of poverty in India since 1980-91. However, in India, the trickle-down effect seems to depend on social groupings; it appears to be slight for those belonging to Scheduled Tribes and 'backward' Castes.

The incidence of poverty in India is clearly associated with social groups. It is particularly high amongst the household of Scheduled Tribes in both rural and urban areas. A somewhat similar situation exists for household belonging to Scheduled Castes, but the incidence of poverty is not quite as marked. Household income and expenditure is highly skewed in favour of households not consisting of members from the Scheduled Tribes or 'backward' classes. As pointed out in the introduction to this paper, egalitarianism in India still has along way to go before it is approached in India.

REFERENCES

Central Statistical Organization, *Statistical Hand Book* (1999), Planning Commission, Government of India, Manpower Planning 2003-04.

Economic Survey of India (2005-06), Ministry of Finance, New Delhi.

Food and Agricultural Organization (2005), *The State of Food and Agriculture, Agricultural Trade and Poverty: Can trade work for the poor?* FAO, Agricultural series No. 36, UN, Rome.

Government of India, *Tenth Five-Year Plan*, Planning Commission, New Delhi.

Government of India (2004-05) *Public Finance Statistics*, Ministry of Finance, Department of Economic Affairs, New Delhi.

Indian Year Book (2004), Manpower Profile, Directorate General of Employment and Training employment review, Institute of Applied Manpower Research, New Delhi.

National Sample Survey Organization (2002), *Household Consumer Expenditure and Employment and Unemployment Situation in India 2000-2001*, September.

Reserve Bank of India (2004) *Hand Book of Statistics of the Indian Economy 2003-04*, Mumbai.

World Development Indicators (2006) Washington DC New York.

World Bank Development Policy Review (2003), "India Sustaining Reform Reducing Poverty", July, 14.

World Bank Report (2006), *Poverty Reduction and Growth: Virtuous and Vicious Circles*, Washington DC.

17

POPULATION, POVERTY AND HUMAN DEVELOPMENT IN INDIA

M.S. Gupta

Introduction

Population, poverty and human development are closely related because people and poverty are the common factors for hindering the economic development of India. Again due to increase of population, poverty created obstacles for human development. This is evident from widespread poverty, poor protectivity, huge size of unemployment and low per capita income. Mass poverty and chronic under utilization of the vast human and natural potential are recognized as our most pressing problems.

So, it is reflected in human development increase in population and mass poverty, hinder the human development in India. Hence, an attempt is made to analyze the relationship of human development with poverty and population.

Extent of Population

India is the second most populous country in the world and is accounts for 16 per cent of global population. She runs the risk of achieving the dubious distinction of being the most populous country in the world by about the year 2050. One of the advantages though that India will continue to enjoy for some years is what is termed as a 'demographic dividend', namely a young population and a declining dependency ratio (GOI, Economic Survey, 2005-06). Table 1 shows India's population projections in millions from the year 2001 to 2026.

Extent of Poverty in India

Mass poverty is one of the major problems in India confronting planners and policy makers in India. The extent of incidence of absolute poverty has significantly declined over the years. The decline in the incidence of poverty in urban areas is depicted in Table 2, which shows the percentage of population below the poverty line between 1973-2000 and the target for 2007.

Table 1
Estimates of Population in Millions (In millions)

Year	*2001*	*2006*	*2011*	*2016*	*2021*	*2026*
Total	1027	1114	1197	1275	1347	1411
Below 15 Years	363	360	351	343	337	328
15-64 Years	622	702	780	854	916	967
65 Years and above	42	52	66	78	94	116

Source: GOI, Economic Survey, Ministry of Finance, 2005-06, p. 215.

Table 2
Estimates of Poverty (In per cent)

Year	*Rural*	*Urban*	*All-India*
1973-1974	56.4	49.0	54.9
1977-1978	53.1	45.2	51.3
1983	45.7	40.8	44.5
1987-1988	39.1	38.2	38.9
1993-1994	37.3	32.4	36.0
1999-2000	27.1	23.8	26.1
2007	21.1	15.1	19.3

Source: Tittham, (*Tamil Yojana*), January 2005, Vol. 36, No. 5.

Although reduction of the overall poverty ratio in India from 55 per cent to 26 per cent during a period of three decades is significant, India's performance in poverty reduction has been weak as compared with some of the East Asian countries. Poverty is closely linked with unemployment and underemployment. Even urban poverty is a reflection, in most cases, of a lack of employment opportunities in rural areas. India continues to be a predominantly agriculturally oriented economy and over 70 per cent of its population is dependent on agriculture for their livelihood (Kamalakannan, 2005).

Poverty in the Human Development Perspective

The UNDP Human Development Report 1990 has defined human development as the process of enlarging people's choices. The most critical ones are to lead a long and healthy life, to be educated and to enjoy a decent standard of living. Additional choices include political freedom, other guaranteed human rights and various ingredients of self-respect–including what Adam Smith called the ability to mix with others without being "ashamed to appear in public". These are among the essential choices, the absence of which can block many other opportunities. Human development is thus a process of widening people's choices as well as raising the level of well-being achieved. If human development is about enlarging choices, poverty means that opportunities and choices most basic to human development are denied–to lead a long, healthy, creative life and to enjoy a decent standard of living, freedom, dignity, self-respect and the respect of others.

The contrast between human development and human poverty reflects two different ways of evaluating development. One way, the "conglomerative perspective", focuses on the advances made by all groups in each community, from the rich to the poor. This contrasts with an alternative viewpoint, the "derivation perspective", in which development is judged by the way the poor and the deprived fare in each community. Lack of progress in reducing the disadvantages of the deprived cannot be "washed away" by large advances–no matter how large–made by the better-off people.

Interest in the process of development concerns both perspectives. At a very basic level, the lives and success of everyone should count, and it would be a mistake to make our understanding of the process of development completely insensitive to the gains and losses of those who happen to fare better than others. It would go against the rights of each citizen to be counted and also clash with the comprehensive concerns of universalist ethics. Yet a part–a big part–of the general interest in the progress of a nation concentrates specifically on the state of the disadvantaged.

Status of Human Poverty

In addition to the indicators that have been identified and used in building the core set of composite indices for a country like India, there are always issues and concerns that have direct bearing on the well-being of people at local level and therefore, need to be included in any meaningful framework for evaluating development. The compilation of indicators in UNDP (1990) covers such aspects of social environment that influence individual and collective well-being. This includes indicators on the state of the elderly, the working children, the disabled; and violence and crime against women. Besides, physical environment also has a bearing on the quality of life. Accordingly, selective environment indicators have also been included.

Dimensions of Poverty

Concerns with identifying people affected by poverty and the desire to measure it have obscured the fact that poverty is too complex to be reduced to a single dimension of human life. It has become common for communities to establish an income-based or consumption-based poverty line. Although income focuses on an important dimension of poverty, it gives only a partial picture of the many ways human lives can be blighted. Someone can enjoy good health and live quite long but be illiterate and thus cut off from learning, from communication and from interactions with others. Another person may be literate and quite well educated but prone to premature death because of epidemiological characteristics or physical disposition. Yet a third may be excluded from participating in the important decision-making processes affecting her life. The deprivation of none of them can be fully captured by the level of their income.

Also, people perceive deprivation in different ways–and each person and community defines the deprivation and disadvantages that affect their lives. Poverty of lives and opportunities–or human poverty–is multidimensional in character and diverse rather than uniform to content.

Different Perspectives on Human Poverty

Over the years, the concept of poverty has been defined from different perspectives (GOI, 2001) as follows:

- *Income Perspective:* A person is poor if, and only if; his income level is below the defined poverty line. Many countries have adopted income poverty lines to monitor progress in reducing poverty incidence. Often the cutoff poverty line is defined in terms of having enough income for a specified amount of food.
- *Basic Needs Perspective:* Poverty is deprivation of material requirements for minimally acceptable fulfillment of human needs, including food. This concept of deprivation goes well beyond the lack of private income: it includes the need for basic health and education and essential services that have to be provided by the community to prevent people from falling into poverty. It also recognizes the need for employment and participation.
- *Capability Perspective:* Poverty represents the absence of some basic capabilities to function–a person lacking the opportunity to achieve some minimally acceptable levels of these functionings relevant to this analysis can vary from such physical ones as being well nourished, being adequately clothed and sheltered, and avoiding preventable morbidity to more complex social achievements such as partaking in the life of the community. The capability approach reconciles the notions of absolute and relative poverty since relative deprivation of incomes and commodities and lead to an absolute deprivation in minimum capabilities. Poverty in the human development approach draws on each of these perspectives but draws particularly on the capability perspective.

In the capability concept, the focus is on the functioning that person can or cannot achieve, given the opportunities one has. Functioning refer to the various valuable things person can do or be, such as living long, being healthy, being well nourished, mixing well with others in the community and so on.

The capability approach concentrates on functioning information, supplemented by considering, where possible, the options a person had but did not choose to use. For example, a rich and healthy person who becomes ill nourished through fasting can be distinguished from a person who is forced into malnutrition through a lack of means or as a result of suffering from a parasitic disease. In practice such discrimination is difficult when dealing with aggregate statistics (as opposed to detailed micro studies of individuals), and the practical uses of the capability concept in poverty analysis have been mainly with simple functioning data. The *Human Development Report* too presents information that is essentially about living conditions and functionings.

In choosing particular aspects of living for special investigation in a poverty study, there is need for public discussion. There is an inescapable element of judgement in any such selection. In constructing any index of poverty (such as the Human Poverty Index. HPI-1, presented in UNDP *Human Development Report 1997),* the selections and the weights have to be explicitly stated and clarified so that public scrutiny can occur. It is very important that the standards to be used are not determined on top-down basis, but are open to–it possible, emerge form–a participatory, democratic process. One of the purposes of the Human Development Report has been precisely to facilitate such a process and this applies to poverty analysis as well.

The "sustainable livelihood approach" to the study of poverty has particularly emphasized the need for local participation. In this approach, each community can define criteria of well-being and the key elements of deprivation as they appear in the local context. This process brings out the concerns and worries of vulnerable people that are persistently neglected in national statistics and in many studies of poverty. The following criteria drawn from various participatory studies were used by local people in Asia and Sub-Saharan Africa for defining poverty and ill-being (GOI, 2001):

- Being disabled (for example: blind, crippled, mentally impaired, chronically sick).
- Lacking land, livestock, farm equipment, a grinding mill.
- Being unable to decently bury their dead.
- Being unable to send their children to school.
- Having more mouths to feed, fewer hands to help.
- Lacking able-bodied family members who can feed their families in a crisis.
- Having bad housing.
- Suffering the effects of destructive behaviours (for example: alcoholism).
- Being "poor in people", lacking social support.
- Having to put children in employment.
- Being single parents.
- Having to accept demeaning or low-status work.
- Having food security for only a few months each year.
- Being dependent on common property resources.

In the 1970s, the concept of social exclusion came into the literature to analyse the condition of those who are not necessarily income-poor–though many are that too–but who are kept out of the mainstream of society even if not income-poor. The inadequacy of traditional definitions of poverty based on income and consumption, was widely acknowledged to explain these new concerns.

Measurement of Poverty and The Human Poverty Index

Can the concept of human poverty be targeted and monitored? Can an overall measure of poverty be developed that can inform as well as be used for policy? Can an internationally comparable measure be defined?

Human Development Report 1997 introduces a Human Poverty Index (HPI-1 for developing countries) in an attempt to bring together in a composite index the different features of deprivation in the quality of life to arrive at an aggregate judgement on the extent of poverty in a community. Human Development Report 1996 attempted this through a particular version of the 'capability poverty measure'. The HPI pursues the same approach, focusing on a broader and more representative set of variables, in a consistent relationship to the Human Development Index (HDI).

Like many other concepts human poverty is not fully captured by any particular measure including the HPI. As concept, human poverty includes many aspects that cannot be measured–or are not being measured. It is difficult to reflect them in a composite measure of human poverty. Critical dimensions of human poverty excluded from the HPI for these reasons are lack of political freedom, inability to participate in decision-making, lack of personal security, inability to participate in the life of community and threats to sustainability and intergenerational equity.

The Human Development Index and the Human Poverty Index

While human development focuses on progress in a community as a whole, human poverty focuses on the situation and progress of the most deprived people in the community. The distinction between the two is analogous to the distinction between GNP and the income-based poverty index. In the income-based perspective, poverty incidence is needed to monitor progress in eliminating poverty. In the same way, the HPI is needed to judge the extent of human poverty in a country and to monitor its progress.

The growth rate of GNP per person gives an account of progress seen in the aggregative perspective–everyone's income counts in the GNP total. In contrast, the reduction of an income based poverty index–such as the decline in the proportion of people below the poverty-line income–uses the derivational perspective, concentrating only on the incomes of the poor. In this income-based perspective, it would make little sense to argue that since GNP is already based on income information, any income-based poverty measure must be a substitute for GNP. Nor would it be sensible to suggest that the availability of GNP as an indicator makes it redundant to seek a measure of income poverty. GNP and the income poverty measures use the income information in different perspectives–

with GNP taking a conglomerative view and the income poverty measures focusing specifically on people poor in income.

The relationship between the HDI and the HPI has to be seen in a similar way. Both have to use the rich categories of information associated with human development–characteristics of human lives and quality of living that go far beyond what income information can provide. But while the HDI uses these characteristics in the aggregative, the HPI must use them in the derivational perspective. The availability of GNP measures does not obviate the need for an income-based poverty indicator, nor does the HDI measure eliminate the need for a HPI (GOI, 2001).

Human Development Index

$$HDIj = 1/3 * \Sigma_i (X_i)$$

Where, HDI is for the jth state, i goes from 1 to 3; and

$$X_i = (X_{ij} - X_i^*) / (X_i^{**} - X_i^*)$$

Where, Xij refers to attainment of the jth state on the ith indicator; Xi** and Xi* are the scaling maximum and minimum norms, such that:

X_1: Inflation and inequality adjusted per capita consumption expenditure;

X_2: Composite indicator on educational attainment;

X_3: Composite indicator on health attainment.

$$X_2 = [(e_1 * 0.35) + (e_2 * 0.65)]$$

Where, e_1 is literacy rate for the age group 7 years and above, and e_2 is adjusted intensity of formal education.

$$X_3 = [(h_1 * 0.65) + (h_2 * 0.35)]$$

Where, h_1 is life expectancy at age one, and h_2 is infant mortality rate. In case of IMR, the reciprocal of the indicator has been used (GOI, 2001).

Human Poverty Index

As in the case of HDI, for constructing the HPI deprivation in health, educational and economic dimensions have been equally weighted. However, within the composite derivational measures on education, as well as on economic aspects, based on a sensitivity analysis, indicators with somewhat distinct attributes have been clubbed using unequal weights so as to reflect appropriately the country's context, development priorities and the desired policy focus.

$$HPI_j = [1/3 * (P_1^3 + P_2^3 + P_3^3)]^{1/3}$$

Where, HPI is for the jth State and P_i, i goes from 1 to 3 refers to the deprivation in the three identified dimensions, such that:

P_1: Longevity deprivation captured by the indicator persons not expected to survive beyond age 40 years;

P_2: Composite indicator on educational deprivation;

P_3: Composite indicator on economic deprivation.

$$P_2 = (ed_1 * 0.35) + (ed_2 * 0.65)$$

Where ed_1 is illiteracy rate for the population in the age group 7 years and above, and ed_2 is proportion of children in the age group 6-18 years not enrolled in the schools.

$$P_3 = 1/4 * \Sigma_i (P_{3i})$$

Where, i goes from 1 to 4, such that:

P_{31}: Proportion of population below the poverty line;

P_{32}: Proportion of population not receiving medical attention at birth. This indicator has been substituted in the alternate HPI for 1991 by proportion of children in the age group 12 to 23 months, not fully vaccinated;

P_{33}: Proportion of population living in kutcha houses;

P_{34}: Proportion of population without access to basic amenities, including the access to safe drinking water, sanitation and electricity. For 1981, a simple average has been of the population not having access to any of these amenities individually. Whereas for 1991 in the alternate HPI, the cross tabulation of population not having access to any of these amenities has been used (GOI, 2001).

Human Development through Poverty Alleviation Programmes in India and Employment Generation

Human development is a goal and economic development is only a means to reach that goal. Economic development is not a goal or aim in itself. We can reach the target of human development only though the source of economic growth. So, the aim of economic development should be of the life of people.

The experience of the various countries shows that there is no automatic relationship between economic growth and human development. This latter concept was developed by the UNDP in the "Human Development Report" in 1990.

It is desirable to have an ideal relationship between economic progress and human development. In some countries the human resource is more developed in spite of per capita income being less, because such countries have invested certainly more in human development sector. In some countries, the per capita income is comparatively very high, but the human resource is in undeveloped position due to negligence of the sectors like health and education. Such is the position of different states also within India.

It becomes important to know that what factors are essential for human development. Providing productive jobs, ending poverty, empowerment of weaker section of the society and women, maximum co-operation and participation of the maximum number in the development process, problem of long-term sustainability of development etc, are the factors, which decide human development. Growth, equity and democracy are the main three aims for human development.

In India, as a result of the development process, economic inequality has increased as is revealed in "Human Development Report" 1996. The increase in income during the plan periods has become concentrated in the few hands and the other persons having a low income and the poor remain struggling for their survival.

In India, the inequality of economic growth and human development consists of the following kinds: (a) High human development and low income as in Kerala; (b) Low human development and high income as in Haryana; (c) Accelerated economic growth and slow human development as in Rajasthan; (d) Slow economic development and slow human development as in West Bengal; (e) Economic development and human development occurring together all in Punjab, Gujarat, Tamil Nadu, Maharashtra; and (f) Economic development and human development, pressing slow effect on each other like Andhra Pradesh, Madhya Pradesh, Uttar Pradesh, Orissa and Bihar (Thakur, 2003).

The Indian government has also started several vocational training centres for handicapped persons. With the aid of the Indian Red Cross Society, assistance is provided to the physically handicapped. In addition to the above, the government has launched several welfare schemes and programmes to help the poorer/weaker sections of society to develop the infrastructure in rural areas, to provide employment and to eradicate poverty among the rural masses. The entire programme can be divided into three broad categories: (i) assistance to the people for raising their income above the poverty line of Rs. 6400 by providing infrastructure for self-employment; (ii) provision of infrastructure assets and training for self-employment in rural areas to speed up the process of development; and (iii) implementing labour-intensive schemes in rural areas to generate wage-based employment and create of durable assets.

The schemes being implemented by the Department of Rural Development are outlined below:

Integrated Rural Development Programme (IRDP)

The IRDP was started in 1980-81 in all blocks of the country and continued as a major self-employment scheme up to March 31, 1999. IRDP had several sub-programmes such as Training of Rural Youth for Self-Employment (TRYSEM), Development of Women and Children in Rural Areas (DWCRA), Ganga Kalyan Yojana (GKY), Million Wells Scheme (MWS) and Supply of Improved Toolkits to Rural Artisans (SITRA). Later on it was restructured as the Swarnajayanti Gram Swarozgar Yojana (SGSY) in April 1999. It aimed at self-employment of the rural poor. The objective was to enable sought to be achieved through acquisition of productive assets or appropriate skills that would generate an additional income on a sustained basis to enable them to cross the poverty line. The IRDP and SGSY are credit-cum-subsidy programmes. Since the introduction of the programme till 1998-99, 54.39 million families were covered under IRDP at an expenditure of Rs. 13,708 crore leading to an investment of over Rs. 33,964 crore. During the first two years of the Ninth Plan (1997-1999) about 3.38 million families were reported to have been covered of which 46 per cent were Scheduled Castes/Scheduled Tribes and 35 per cent women. Details can be seen from Table 3 below.

Table 3
Overview of Achievements under Self-Employment Programme (IRDP/SGSY) since Introduction

Particulars	*1980-85 VI Plan*	*1985-90 VII Plan*	*1990-92 Annual Plans*	*1992-97 VIII Plan*	*1997-99 Part of IX Plan*	*1999-2000 (SGSY) Part of IX Plan*
1	2	3	4	5	6	7
1. Physical Progress (lakh families assisted)	165.61 (33.12)	181.8 (36.36)	54.35 (27.18)	108.4 (21.68)	33.84 (16.92)	29.02 (9.67)
(a) % of SCs/STs covered	39.30	45.10	50.49	50.03	46.35	44.78
(b) % of Women covered	NA	18.89	32.02	33.58	34.4	42.26
2. Total Expenditure (Rs. in crore)	1661.2	3315.8	1582.6	4876.7	2271.8	2045.9
3. Credit Disbursed (Rs. in crore)	3101.6	5372.5	2337.4	7566.3	4170.7	3831.5
4. Total Investment (Rs. in crore)	4762.8 (952.56)	8080.6 (1616.12)	3663.3 (1831.65)	11542.3 (2308.46)	5915.4 (2957.7)	5734.4 (1911.47)
5. Credit Subsidy ratio	1.87	1.98	1.76	1.90	2.39	2.01

Notes: Total expenditure includes subsidy plus administrative expenditure.
Total investment includes credit plus subsidy.
Figures in brackets indicate average annual figure.

IRDP has been widely assessed by researchers and different national institutions and international organizations. These studies have pointed out several conceptual and administrative problems with it.

Jawahar Rozgar Yojana (JRY)

JRY was launched as a Centrally Sponsored Scheme (CSS) on 1.1.1989 by merging National Rural Employment Programme (NREP) and Rural Landless Employment Guarantee Programme (RLEGP). Its main objective was generation of additional gainful employment for the unemployed and under employed people in rural areas through the creation of rural economic infrastructure, community and social assets with the aim of improving the quality of life of the poor.

The JRY has been recast as the Jawahar Gram Smridhi Yojana (JGSY) with effect from 1.4.1999 to impart a thrust to creation of rural infrastructure. While JRY resulted in creation of durable assets, the overriding priority of the programme was the creation of wage employment. It was felt that a stage had come when rural infrastructure needed to be taken up in a planned manner and given priority. The Gram Panchayats can effectively determine their infrastructure needs and the responsibility of implementing the programme has been entrusted to them. The funds are directly released to the Gram panchayats by the DRDA/Zila Parishad. The JGSY is implemented as a CSS with funding in the ratio of 75:25 between the centre and the states.

The progress of implementation of JRY/JGSY in terms of expenditure and maydays of employment generated is presented in Tables 4 and 5:

Table 4
State-wise Utilization of Funds under JRY/JGSY During the Plan Periods
(Amount Rs. in lakhs)

Sl. No.	*States/UTs*	*Seventh Plan (1985-90)*		*Two Annual Plans (1999-92)*	*Eighth Plan (1992-97)*	*Ninth Plan (1997-2002)*	
		*NREP+ RLEGP (1985-89)**	*JRY (1989-90)*	*JRY (1990-92)*	*JRY (1992-97)*	*JRY (1987-99)*	*JRY (1999-2002)*
1	2	3	4	5	6	7	8
1.	Andhra Pradesh		18415.55	38382.87	140991.40	33455.92	33640.74
2.	Arunachal Pradesh		165.40	444.92	1204.07	567.94	1623.42
3.	Assam		4801.66	10649.01	36459.48	16514.28	20373.02
4.	Bihar		31690.69	80163.06	253358.55	78101.87	79610.98
5.	Goa		292.35	641.68	1666.16	322.57	517.97
6.	Gujarat		8076.28	17552.34	53314.69	12958.05	13949.03
7.	Haryana		1970.95	4438.47	11436.67	4274.36	9054.15
8.	Himachal Pradesh		987.48	2456.83	5250.04	1777.60	3630.08
9.	Jammu & Kashmir		1767.50	4016.29	10867.56	2964.79	3929.53
10.	Karnataka		10942.81	21974.94	92461.67	23867.04	29126.09
11.	Kerala		6587.35	140.72.71	35213.31	7745.03	11961.61
12.	Madhya Pradesh		20562.93	55916.00	182110.90	47334.71	54384.41
13.	Maharashtra		21059.06	37379.03	140889.28	42219.00	54626.33
14.	Manipur		440.01	696.83	1657.17	545.58	489.39
15.	Meghalaya		172.29	820.82	1746.05	596.70	2274.65
16.	Mizoram		188.07	1093.92	1323.17	442.55	849.15
17.	Nagaland		504.99	1351.30	2466.21	1232.93	1423.31
18.	Orissa		10445.27	2678.85	103201.86	30292.35	45496.38
19.	Punjab		1720.68	2276.52	7400.64	2691.49	4024.34

Sl. No.	*States/UTs*	*Seventh Plan (1985-90)*		*Two Annual Plans (1999-92)*	*Eighth Plan (1992-97)*	*Ninth Plan (1997-2002)*	
		*NREP+ RLEGP (1985-89)**	*JRY (1989-90)*	*JRY (1990-92)*	*JRY (1992-97)*	*JRY (1987-99)*	*JRY (1999-2002)*
1	2	3	4	5	6	7	8
20.	Rajasthan		10648.94	30293.90	75002.09	20111.43	26673.53
21.	Sikkim		155.85	526.40	1551.93	597.38	735.17
22.	Tamil Nadu		20162.77	40795.67	138856.44	35674.40	36494.06
23.	Tripura		542.26	1128.39	3810.81	2648.34	4888.14
24.	Uttar Pradesh		52950.57	93920.81	324060.69	103629.31	112410.59
25.	West Bengal		19975.36	36361.25	120515.44	24777.18	42509.49
26.	Andaman & Nicobar Islands		95.59	188.75	552.17	51.43	123.71
27.	Chandigarh		27.00	12.29	—	—	—
28.	D & N Haveli		89.01	169.84	331.33	61.46	0.85
29.	Daman & Diu		32.28	42.69	141.26	36.32	—
30.	Delhi		90.39	56.84	—	—	—
31.	Lakshadweep		52.12	113.87	305.59	108.27	46.22
32.	Pondicherry		194.20	357.75	704.94	139.38	143.49
33.	Chhattisgarh		–	–	–	–	11214.58
34.	Jharkhand		–	–	–	–	30937.29
35.	Uttaranchal		–	–	–	–	
	Total	535185.00	245807.66	525174.84	1748751.37	495739.66	643185.15

*State-wise data for the period 1985-89 are not available.

Source: Union Ministry of Rural Development, New Delhi.

Table 5

State-wise Mandays of Employment Generated under JRY/JGSY During the Plan Periods (Mandays in lakhs)

Sl. No.	*States/UTs*	*Seventh Plan (1985-90)*		*Two Annual Plans (1999-92)*	*Eighth Plan (1992-97)*	*Ninth Plan (1997-2002)*	
		*NREP+ RLEGP (1985-89)**	*JRY (1989-90)*	*JRY (1990-92)*	*JRY (1992-97)*	*JRY (1987-99)*	*JRY (1999-2002)*
1	2	3	4	5	6	7	8
1.	Andhra Pradesh		727.43	1491.07	3546.40	535.66	434.20
2.	Arunachal Pradesh		7.25	15.01	27.98	6.84	21.08
3.	Assam		122.51	250.04	921.87	314.10	361.95
4.	Bihar		907.31	1977.31	5154.34	1117.95	907.95
5.	Goa		8.62	18.44	36.78	4.25	5.75
6.	Gujarat		202.93	442.95	1040.77	141.99	130.79
7.	Haryana		34.13	72.52	146.46	34.96	92.06
8.	Himachal Pradesh		37.86	70.02	121.64	25.50	42.22
9.	Jammu & Kashmir		52.19	114.64	229.80	44.64	47.49

Contd...

Sl. No.	States/UTs	Seventh Plan (1985-90)		Two Annual Plans (1999-92)	Eighth Plan (1992-97)	Ninth Plan (1997-2002)	
		NREP+ RLEGP (1985-89)*	JRY (1989-90)	JRY (1990-92)	JRY (1992-97)	JRY (1987-99)	JRY (1999-2002)
1	2	3	4	5	6	7	8
10.	Karnataka		407.56	888.20	2345.09	488.07	445.23
11.	Kerala		231.79	358.04	539.18	81.21	96.81
12.	Madhya Pradesh		932.24	1903.96	3742.63	666.49	716.23
13.	Maharashtra		795.93	1621.86	4582.31	931.55	887.37
14.	Manipur		10.50	17.27	31.90	7.75	6.64
15.	Meghalaya		4.02	19.90	38.77	10.45	31.22
16.	Mizoram		4.79	25.64	34.48	6.27	10.42
17.	Nagaland		20.29	46.90	57.37	31.44	25.41
18.	Orissa		517.63	690.83	2446.36	596.66	696.82
19.	Punjab		34.23	41.57	109.00	26.72	27.68
20.	Rajasthan		443.77	893.64	1864.68	330.33	273.90
21.	Sikkim		6.28	22.42	52.49	7.79	10.08
22.	Tamil Nadu		910.81	1586.94	4234.97	593.53	446.82
23.	Tripura		19.53	39.77	95.18	40.63	69.03
24.	Uttar Pradesh		1624.93	3190.41	6874.03	1253.10	1246.13
25.	West Bengal		558.81	1008.84	2253.68	341.03	341.44
26.	Andaman & Nicobar Islands		3.08	5.15	9.52	1.42	1.05
27.	Dadra & Nagar Haveli		3.04	4.78	8.77	1.16	0.01
28.	Daman & Diu		1.08	1.51	2.87	1.83	—
29.	Lakshadweep		2.53	4.46	8.73	1.88	0.65
30.	Pondicherry		8.08	10.09	18.81	0.66	0.47
31.	Chandigarh		0.42	0.11	—	—	—
32.	Delhi		2.30	0.89	—	—	—
33.	Chhattisgarh		—	—	—	—	145.05
34.	Jharkhand		—	—	—	—	321.51
35.	Uttaranchal		—	—	—	—	66.81
	Total	26319.17	8643.87	16837.60	40561.06	7715.54	7910.26

Note: *State-wise data for the period 1985-89 are not available.
Source: Union Ministry of Rural Development, New Delhi.

Employment Assurance Scheme (EAS)

The EAS was launched on 2nd October 1993 in 1772 identified backward blocks of 257 districts situated in drought prone desert, tribal and hill areas where the Revamped Public Distribution System (RPDS) was in operation. The programme was subsequently extended to more blocks and thereafter was universalized and implemented in all the 5448 rural blocks of the country. As its primary objective, EAS was set to create additional wage employment opportunities during a period of acute shortage through manual work for the rural poor living below the poverty line. The secondary objective is the creation of durable community, social and economic assets for sustained employment and development. In September 2001, both JGSY and EAS were merged and a new scheme named Sampoorna Grameen Rozgar Yojana (SGRY), had come into force with an annual outlay of Rs. 10,000 crore. Under the scheme 50 lakh tonnes of food grains amounting to Rs. 5,000 crore (half the outlay) will be provided every year free of cost to state governments and union territory administrations. The progress of state-wise utilization of funds under EAS/SGRY and mandays generated during the plan periods is presented in Tables 6 and 7 respectively.

National Rural Employment Guarantee Scheme (NREGS)

The National Rural Employment Guarantee Scheme Act was notified on September 7, 2005 and the scheme launched on February 2, 2006. The on-going programmes of Sampoorna Grameen Rozgar Yojana (SGRY) and National Food for Work Programme (NFFWP) will be subsumed within the 200 districts identified in the initial stage. All the districts in the country will be covered under the scheme within five years (GOI, Economic Survey, 2005-06).

The objective of the Act is to enhance the livelihood security of the people in rural areas by generating wage employment through works that develop the infrastructure base of that area. The choice of work suggested addresses the causes of chronic poverty like drought, deforestation and soil erosion. The objective behind suggesting certain key activities/works is to rejuvenate the natural resources of the area to stimulate the local economy enabling those who work for wage employment in creating an asset to take advantage of it to engage in productive wage of self-employment and augment the income.

Implementation of the Act calls for the formulation of NREGSs by the State Governments. Section 4 of the Act provides that within six months from the date of commencement of the Act, every State Government shall, by notification, make a scheme for providing not less than 100 days of guaranteed employment in a financial year to every household in the rural areas covered under the scheme and whose adult members volunteer to do unskilled manual work subject to the conditions laid down in the Act (GOI, Economic Survey, 2005-06).

However, some experts believe that after the passing of the bill, struggle should now be on better implementation of this rural job scheme *via* right to information and social audit (Dev, 2005) and it is also said that employment guarantee scheme, unless seen in an overall context of policy and institutional reform, will be just a poverty alleviation scheme (Virmani, 2005).

Thus, poverty reduction has been an important goal of development policy since the inception of planning in India. Several anti-poverty and employment generation programmes have been launched by centre with the help of state governments for development of rural areas and industries for decades in India. Some of them are as follows:

Table 6
State-wise Utilization of Funds under EAS/SGRY during the Plan Periods (Amount Rupees in lakhs)

Sl. No.	*States/UTs*	*Eighth Plan (1992-97)*	*Ninth Plan (1997-2002)*	
		EAS 1993-97	*EAS 1997-2001*	*SGRY 2001-2002*
1	2	3	4	5
1.	Andhra Pradesh	54112.60	77346.58	14199.86
2.	Arunachal Pradesh	5010.47	6509.95	298.20
3.	Assam	23691.44	38317.08	12103.40
4.	Bihar	45017.20	108466.03	12422.60
5.	Goa	—	666.57	24.69
6.	Gujarat	15278.69	24273.02	3156.86
7.	Haryana	10157.66	12565.26	3100.12
8.	Himachal Pradesh	1734.27	9201.51	1123.64
9.	Jammu & Kashmir	14506.47	16047.58	1276.32
10.	Karnataka	35154.77	47484.56	10196.66
11.	Kerala	6377.92	17943.45	4987.47
12.	Madhya Pradesh	67644.11	93687.13	15143.97
13.	Maharashtra	30218.87	52835.27	17451.63
14.	Manipur	3913.39	3127.16	—
15.	Meghalaya	934.08	1983.78	974.54
16.	Mizoram	6210.67	2934.43	475.54
17.	Nagaland	7060.20	6737.58	413.22
18.	Orissa	45848.43	57167.89	16357.80
19.	Punjab	—	8464.79	1355.85
20.	Rajasthan	39182.68	45507.46	8988.03
21.	Sikkim	1364.02	2119.81	170.00
22.	Tamil Nadu	29324.24	77900.24	11993.08
23.	Tripura	7115.86	7689.20	2396.72
24.	Uttar Pradesh	46120.97	17364.90	30622.31
25.	West Bengal	33714.74	46221.36	9269.79
26.	Andaman & Nicobar Islands	80.03	124.36	13.75
27.	Dadra & Nagar Haveli	75.89	93.73	3.86
28.	Daman & Diu	17.49	21.51	—
29.	Lakshadweep	155.63	240.73	8.57
30.	Pondicherry	—	801.86	20.54
31.	Chhattisgarh	—	7242.62	8722.80
32.	Jharkhand	—	8804.19	12657.03
33.	Uttaranchal	—	1890.83	2155.66
	Total	530022.79	964418.01	202084.53

Source: Union Ministry of Rural Development, New Delhi.

Table 7
State-wise Mandays of Employment Generated under EAS/SGRY During the Plan Periods (Mandays in lakhs)

Sl. No.	*States/UTs*	*Eighth Plan (1992-97)*	*Ninth Plan (1997-2002)*	
		EAS 1993-97	*EAS 1997-2001*	*SGRY 2001-2002*
1	2	3	4	5
1.	Andhra Pradesh	1029.43	1162.68	159.45
2.	Arunachal Pradesh	114.20	113.22	4.84
3.	Assam	471.45	627.95	200.66
4.	Bihar	804.09	1417.61	138.13
5.	Goa	—	7.44	0.11
6.	Gujarat	257.44	284.27	30.42
7.	Haryana	126.05	79.31	57.94
8.	Himachal Pradesh	23.55	108.26	11.91
9.	Jammu & Kashmir	284.91	212.23	11.34
10.	Karnataka	792.48	931.33	142.40
11.	Kerala	91.47	176.44	33.11
12.	Madhya Pradesh	1182.28	1206.41	225.82
13.	Maharashtra	868.37	1018.35	217.08
14.	Manipur	79.59	44.39	—
15.	Meghalaya	15.59	33.69	12.86
16.	Mizoram	123.40	48.36	5.77
17.	Nagaland	184.38	169.11	8.05
18.	Orissa	1063.09	1132.90	244.16
19.	Punjab	—	56.82	9.75
20.	Rajasthan	823.78	727.94	82.56
21.	Sikkim	29.78	30.10	2.01
22.	Tamil Nadu	832.02	1292.54	132.51
23.	Tripura	164.42	132.76	43.52
24.	Uttar Pradesh	818.80	2095.82	313.63
25.	West Bengal	543.16	488.94	84.22
26.	Andaman & Nicobar Islands	1.10	1.41	0.13
27.	Dadra & Nagar Haveli	0.84	0.87	0.03
28.	Daman & Diu	0.50	0.37	—
29.	Lakshadweep	3.42	3.95	0.15
30.	Pondicherry	—	1.57	0.23
31.	Chhattisgarh	—	83.32	299.00
32.	Jharkhand	—	100.31	121.37
33.	Uttaranchal	—	11.07	12.38
	Total	10731.59	13704.21	2605.54

Source: Union Ministry of Rural Development, New Delhi.

1. *Prime Minister's Rozgar Yojana (PMRY):* The PMRY was launched on 2nd October 1993 with the objective of providing employment opportunities to educated unemployed youth through setting up of small-scale enterprises in rural and

urban areas. The loans under the scheme are available to all educated unemployed youth between 18-35 years for men and 18-45 years for women who have passed the 8th standard examination for undertaking all economically viable activities including agriculture and allied activities. This scheme also provides for preference to weaker sections and women. The PMRY has been allocated Rs. 196.65 crore in 2005-06 budget. It has a Tenth Plan target of setting up 11 lakh micro enterprises providing employment to 16.5 lakh persons (Kamalakannan, 2006).

2. *Training of Rural Youth for Self-Employment (TRYSEM):* Training of Rural Youth for Self-Employment (TRYSEM) aims at providing basic technical and entrepreneurial skills to the rural poor in the age group of 18 to 35 years to enable them to the take up income generating activities. This plan had announced in nineties. During the Eighth Plan, 15.28 lakh youth were trained under TRYSEM, of self-employment and remaining unemployed (Kapila, 2003).

3. *National Food for Work Programme (NFFWP):* National Food for Work Programme was launched on November 14, 2004 in 150 most backward districts of the country to generate additional supplementary wage employment with food security. Under this programme, states receive foodgrains free of cost. The focus of this programme is on works relating to water conservation, drought proofing, land development, flood control/ protection and rural connectivity in terms of all-weather roads. In 2004-05, allocation of Rs. 2,020 crore and 20 lakh tonnes of foodgrains generated 7.85 crore persondays of employment. In 2005-06, of the allocation of Rs. 4,500 crores and 15 lakh tonnes of foodgrains, Rs. 2,219 crore and 11.58 lakh metric tonnes of foodgrains had been released up to January 27, 2006. About 17.03 lakh persondays were generated up to December 2005 (GOI, Economic Survey, 2005-06).

4. *Development of Women and Children in Rural Areas (DWCRA):* The special scheme for development of women and children in rural areas (DWCRA) was started in 1982-83 on a pilot basis in 50 districts and has now been extended to all the districts of the country. It aims at improving the living conditions of women and thereby children through the provisions of opportunities for self-employment. DWCRA also provide more income generating activities for supplementing their incomes. It also encourages the habit of thrift and credit among the poor rural women to make them self-reliant. This programme also takes care of family welfare, health care, nutrition, education, childcare, safe drinking water, sanitation and shelter to improve the quality of life of the family and community. This programme was successfully implemented in Andhra Pradesh, Kerala, Tripura and Gujurat. But in other states the performance was not so well (Kapila, 2003).

5. *Swarnjayanti Gram Swarozgar Yojana (SGSY):* SSGY, launched in April 1999 after restructuring the Integrated Rural Development Programme and allied schemes is the only self-employment programme for the rural poor. The objective is to bring the self-employed above the poverty line by providing them income-generating assets through bank credit and government subsidy. Up to November 2005, the centre and the states, sharing the costs on 75:25 basis had allocated Rs. 8,067 crore, of which Rs. 6,980 crore had been utilized to assist 62.75 lakh self-employed (GOI, Economic Survey, 2005-06).
6. *Sampoorna Grameen Rozgar Yojana (SGRY):* SGRY, launched on September 2001 to provide additional wage employment in the rural areas, has a cash and food grains component and the centre bears 75 per cent and 100 per cent of the cost of the two with the balance borne by the States/Union Territories. In 2005-06, the number of persondays generated under SGRY was 48.75 crore upto November, 2005, while the Centre's contributions in terms of cash and foodgrains components up to January 2006 were Rs. 4,651 crore and 35 lakh tonnes respectively. Under the special component, about 11.65 lakh of foodgrains have been released to the 11 calamity-hit states in the current year, 2005-06 (GOI, Economic Survey, 2005-06).
7. *Indira Awaas Yojana (IAY):* Indira Awaas Yojana (IAY) aims to provide dwelling units, free of cost to the Schedule Castes (SCs), Scheduled Tribes (STs) and free bonded labourers and also to non-SC/ST BPL families in rural areas. It is funded on a cost-sharing basis in the ratio of 75:25 between the centre and the states. Under IAY, the ceiling on construction assistance is Rs. 25,000 per unit in the plains and Rs. 27,500 for hilly and difficult areas and Rs. 12,500 on upgradation of unserviceable kutcha house to pucca/semi-pucca for all areas. Up to January 30, 2006, about 138 lakh houses had been constructed or upgraded with an expenditure of Rs. 25,208 crore (GOI, Economic Survey, 2005-2006).
8. *Swarna Jayanti Sahari Rozgar Yojana (SJSRY):* Launched in December 1997, the Urban Self Employment Programme and the Urban Wage Employment Programme, which were the two special components of SJSRY, substituted for various programmes operated earlier for urban poverty alleviation. The SJSRY is funded on a 75:25 basis between the centre and the states. In 2003-04, the central allocation of Rs. 94.5 crore plus Rs. 10.5 crore for North-Eastern Region including Sikkim was fully utilized. Even the 2004-05 saw the release of the entire budgetary allocation of Rs. 122 crore. In 2005-06, out of an allocation of Rs. 160 crore, Rs. 84.52 crore had been utilized till November 2005 (GOI, Economic Survey, 2005-06).
9. *Valmiki Ambedkar Awas Yojana (VAMBAY):* Launched in December 2001, VAMBAY facilitates the construction and upgradation of dwelling units for the slum dwellers and provides a healthy and enabling urban environment

through community toilets under Nirmal Bharat Abhiyan, a component of the scheme. The Central Government provides a subsidy of 50 per cent with the balance provided by the State Government. Since its inception and upto 31st December 2005, Rs. 866.16 crore had been released as central subsidy for the construction and upgradation of 4,11,478 dwelling units and 64,247 toilet seats under the scheme. For 2005-06, out of the tentative central allocation of Rs. 249 crore upto 31 December 2005, an amount of Rs. 96.4 crore had been released covering 60,335 dwelling units and 381 toilet seats (GOI, Economic Survey, 2005-06).

10. *Pradhan Mantri Gram Sadak Yojana (PMGSY):* Launched in December 2000 as a 100 per cent centrally sponsored scheme, PMGSY aims to provide all-weather connectivity to all the eligible unconnected rural inhabitation. Bharat Nirman, envisages connectivity by 2009 to all the habitations with a population of 1000 or more in the plains and of 500 or more in the hilly, desert and tribal areas. The systematic upgradation of the existing rural road network also is an integral component of the scheme, funded mainly from the accruals of diesel cess in the Central Road Fund with support of the multilateral funding agencies and the domestic financial institutions. Upto December 2005, with an expenditure of Rs. 12,049 crore, a total length of 82,718 km of road works had been completed (GOI, Economic Survey, 2005-06).

The on-going reforms attach great importance to removal of poverty and addressing specifically the wide variation across states and the rural-urban divide. Anti-poverty strategy has three broad components: promotion of economic growth; promotion of human development; and targeted programmes of poverty alleviation address multi-dimensional nature of poverty. The various programmes targeted at the poor have been streamlined and strengthened in recent years including through the NREGS (GOI, Economic Survey, 2005-06).

Failures of Poverty Eradication Programmes

Self-employment is a major form of employment in the rural areas. However, dependence on wage employment alone to tackle the problem of poverty will lead to total dependence of the poor on employers. Though, there are several programmes but they face various problems which lead to their failure.

The failures of these programmes are:

(i) The financial allocations and physical targets under the IRDP were determined on a uniform basis without any consideration being given to the size of population and the incidence of poverty. This resulted in the selection of ineligible families.

(ii) The selection of IRDP schemes was often done without any consideration to ability of beneficiaries, differences in infrastructural support, backward and forward linkages, etc. In fact, in the selection of activities overwhelming bias was shown in favour of animal husbandry.

(iii) The rural youth trained under TRYSEM were only interested in the stipends; in most cases, they had not used the knowledge for further self-employment prospects.

(iv) Training under TRYSEM was not related to the capacity or aptitude of trainers.

(v) It was not possible for trained rural youth under TRYSEM to run a self-employment enterprise, given the poor technological base and uncertainty over availability of credit.

(vi) DWCRA failed due to lack of homogeneity among the group members, selection of non-viable activities, poor backward and forward linkages, lack of institutional financial support, inadequate training and motivation of the staff.

(vii) From a three-year study (1999-2002), it was revealed that credit-subsidy ratio of SGSY had declined as compared to IRDP.

(viii) Inadequate technical and other support at the district level for micro-planning and technical aspects (markets, technology transfer, etc.) has also hampered meaningful progress under SGSY.

(ix) Employment generated through NREP/RLEGP was too inadequate to bring about any meaningful increase in the earning of the beneficiaries.

(x) Project selected bear no relationship to the local needs or agricultural development strategy. Neither the location of such works nor their timing was in accordance with the spirit of the programme. The timing of works coincided with the peak agricultural season.

(xi) The works undertaken involved high material cost and were not particularly labour intensive.

(xii) Large number of works could not be completed in time on account of shortage of funds, administrative constraints and weaknesses.

(xiii) The share of women in employment generated under the programme was only 17 per cent.

(xiv) There were instances of different wages paid to male and female workers.

(xv) JRY and similar rural work programmes also tended to breed corruption both at political and administrative level.

(xvi) SGSY that aimed at creation of demand-driven community/village infrastructure for sustained employment also failed to achieve its target.

(xvii) The objective of providing 100 mandays of employment per person under EAS was a far cry.

In the matter of asset creation, it is found that central norms have not been followed under EAS. It created incomes for the rural poor but left no assets behind at individual level. Once such programmes are withdrawn, the poor might again fall below the poverty line in the absence of family-based assets.

Conclusion

The combined effects of economic growth and measures for direct interventions for poverty alleviation have resulted in an impressive decline in the incidence of poverty in the recent past years. This trend will continue in future with sustained economic growth and the launching of the major initiative for creation of rural employment in the form of NREGS. Further, other effective implementations along with transparency through the Right to Information Act and accountability through decentralized Panchayati Raj Institutions (PRIs) are expected to make a permanent dent on the incidence of unemployment and poverty in India.

Regarding the human population, there is a greater stress on improvement in the quality of elementary education being imparted, quality of primary health care being delivered, quality of water supply and creation of productive assets through wage employment programmes. These ultimately result in tangible human development, which will enhance the capacity of the people and improve the opportunity for their productive participation in the growth process.

Apart from above, a focused intervention by the government is required at all times for improving the level of human development. There is a need to target the disadvantaged regions as well as the people. Enhanced productivity of human capital may help in providing the missing link between the resource richness and the socio-economic backwardness of India.

REFERENCES

Dev, S. Mahendra (2005), "Should EGS be Universalised" *The Economic Times*, Kolkata, August 23.

GOI, (2005-06), *Economic Survey*, Ministry of Finance, Economic Division, New Delhi.

GOI, (2001), *National Human Development Report*, Planning Commission, Oxford University Press, New Delhi.

Kamalakannan, K. (2006), "Rural Industrialisation and Poverty Alleviation", *Kurukshetra*, Vol. 54, No. 7, May.

Kapila, Uma (2003), *India Economic Issues in Development and Planning and Sectoral Aspects*, Academic Foundation, New Delhi.

Thakur, R.N. (2003), "Human Development, Economic Growth and Poverty", In the Indian Economic Association, 86th Conference Volume, Kolhapur (Maharashtra).

UNDP (various issues), *Human Development Report.*

Virmani, A. (2005), "Should EGS be Universalised", *The Economic Times*, Kolkata, August 23.

18

POVERTY ALLEVIATION PROGRAMMES IN INDIA: ISSUES AND CHALLENGES

S.K. Dhage

Introduction

Poverty is the biggest challenge to development in India. Of all the major problems, which India is facing today, the problem of poverty is perhaps the most fundamental. All the political parties in India in one form or the another have adopted poverty eradication as an important goal. Various schemes and programmes have been launched to achieve these objectives. But the problem of poverty continues to persist in India. In order to have a better understanding of poverty, its meaning, extent, causes and measures taken in the recent year to alleviate the problem in India need to be studied in detail and shelter, they are said to be living below the subsistence level and suffering from poverty. When a large number of people in a country live in such miserable conditions there is mass poverty in that nation.

The Concept of Poverty

Poverty is a social phenomenon in which a section of the society is unable to maintain its minimum standard of living. It is a situation in which people do not have the basic minimum necessities of life. When people do not get basic needs like food, clothing and shelter, they are said to be living below the subsistence level and suffering from poverty. When a large number of people in a country live in such miserable conditions there is mass poverty in that nation.

The concepts of poverty differ from country to country depending upon the country's stages of economic development. While poverty is defined with reference to a reasonable standard of living in developed countries, it is defined with reference to a minimum lower standard living in developing countries like India.

According to the Government of India, Economic Survey 2001-02, a high poverty level is characterized by a poor quality of life, deprivation of minimum needs, malnutrition, illiteracy and low human-resource development.

Incidence of Poverty

Widespread poverty in India has attracted the attention of a number of economists and organizations. Dandekar and Rath, B.S. Minhas, P.K. Bardhan, the World Bank and the Planning Commission of India have conducted leading studies on poverty.

A. *Estimates of Dandekar and Rath:* In their article "*Poverty in India*" (1971), Dandekar and Rath made a path-breaking study of the poverty phenomenon in India. Using the NSS data on consumption, they concluded that in 1960-61, about 40 per cent of the rural population and about 50 per cent of the urban population lived below the poverty line in India.

B. *Estimates of the Planning Commission:* The Ninth Five-Year Plan (1997-2002) gave estimates of incidence of poverty for the year 1993-94. These were based on the National Sample Survey (NSS) consumer expenditure data of 50th Round (July 1993 to June 1994). Table 1 presents poverty ratios and the number of poor at the all-India level for different years. With reference to Table 1, the Ninth Plan remarked, "The incidence of poverty expressed as a percentage of people below the poverty line is observed to have declined from 56.4 per cent in 1973-74 to 37.3 per cent in 1993-94 in rural areas and from 49.0 per cent in 1973-74 to 32.4 per cent in 1993-94 in urban areas. For the country as whole, the percentage of people below the poverty line declined from 54.9 per cent in 1973-74 to 36 per cent in 1993-94. However, the number of poor in the country remained more or less stable at around 320 million due to the rise in population. This fact should not over shadow the 300 million persons who joined the non-poor group during the twenty year period between 1973-74 and 1993-94, but underlines the need for the containment of the growth rate of population".

Table 1
Percentage and the Number of Poor in India

Year	*Poverty ratio*			*Number of poor (in million)*		
	Rural	*Urban*	*Combined*	*Rural*	*Urban*	*Combined*
1973-74	56.4	49.0	54.9	261.3	60.0	321.3
1977-78	53.1	45.2	51.3	264.3	64.6	328.9
1983	45.7	40.8	44.5	252.0	70.9	322.9
1987-88	39.1	38.2	38.9	231.9	75.2	307.1
1993-94	37.3	32.4	36.0	244.0	76.3	320.3

Note: The estimates are based on the methodology recommended by the Expert Group on Estimation of Proportion and Number of poor as adopted by the Planning Commission.

Source: Government of India, Planning Commission, Ninth Five-Year Plan, 1997-2002, Vol. I, P. 27, Table 1-9.

The latest estimates of the poverty incidence in India are available in *Economic Survey*, 2002-03. These are reproduced in Table 2, to quote, "The success of the anti-poverty strategy is reflected in the combined poverty ratio from 54.9 per cent in1973-74 to 36.0 per cent in 1993-94. The poverty ratio declined by nearly 10 percentage points and in the proportion of poor in the rural areas declined from 56.4 per cent in 1973-73 to 27.1 per cent in 1999-2000. The decline in urban areas has been from 49 per cent to 23.6 per cent during this period. The poverty reduction target set by the Planning Commission for the Tenth Five-Year Plan aims at achieving a poverty ratio of 19.3 per cent for the country as a whole by 2007, 21.1 per cent for the rural and 15.1 per cent for the urban areas".

Table 2
Estimates of Incidence of Poverty in India

Year	*Poverty ratio (%)*		
	Rural	*Urban*	*Combined*
1973-74	56.4	49.0	54.9
1993-94	37.3	32.4	36.0
1999-00	27.1	23.6	26.1
2007*	21.1	15.1	19.3

*Projection

Source: Government of India, *Economic Survey*, 2002-03, P. 213, Table 10.6.

The conclusions of various studies are different because they have adopted different methodologies to arrive at their estimates. However, there is a consensus on some points. Firstly, poverty in urban areas is largely the result of the overflow of the rural poor into the urban areas. Secondly, the incidence of poverty is the greatest among small farmers and landless workers in rural areas.

Poverty Alleviation Programmes

Poverty alleviation programmes in India can be divided into two-time periods:

1. Poverty Alleviation Programmes up to 1990.
2. Poverty Alleviation Programmes in the Reform Period.

1. Poverty Alleviation Programmes up to 1990

In order to tackle poverty, various target-based schemes were introduced after independence. However, it was during the Fifth Five-Year Plan that a sustained and direct attack on poverty was evolved as a key plan strategy. It was noted that the elimination of abject poverty could not be attained as a corollary to an acceleration in the rate of growth of the economy alone. Major poverty alleviation programmes introduced during 1950-1990 were the following:

1. Community Development Programme (CDP) in 1952.
2. Crash Scheme for Rural Employment (CSRE) in 1972.
3. Drought-prone Area Programme (DPAP) in 1973.

4. Marginal Farmer and Agricultural labour agency (MFALA) in 1973.
5. Small Farmer Development Agency (SFDA) in 1974.
6. Twenty-Point Programmes (TPP) in 1975.
7. Food for Work Programme (FWP) in 1977.
8. Training Rural Youth for Self-Employment (TRYSEM) in 1979.
9. Integration Rural Development Programme (IRDP) in 1980.
10. National Rural Employment Programme (NREP) in 1980.
11. Development of Women and Children in Rural Areas (DWCRA) in 1982.
12. Jawahar Rozgar Yojana (JRY) in 1989.
13. Nehru Rozgar Yojana (NRY) in 1989.

Most of these programmes were conceived and founded by the Central Government, which determined the criteria for allocation between the states. Actual implementation was left to the State Government agencies subject to guidelines regarding the scope and content of schemes, and their targeting and implementation procedures. Only a few have been taken up entirely on the initiative of states. However, up to the 1970s none of these programmes comprehensively covered the whole country, though in certain parts of the country some of these programmes operated simultaneously for the same target group. Apart from this territorial overlap, the major limitation of these programmes was that they were reduced to mere subsidy-giving programmes, lacking any planned approach to enable the rural poor to achieve a higher level of income. The element of adhocism in these programmes further reduced their effectiveness from the point of view of poverty alleviation. Hence, the need was felt for undertaking programmes, which were not only far more comprehensive in coverage but could also make a direct assault on rural poverty.

In view of the above IRDP, NREP and RLEGP were conceived during the 1980s, aimed at achieving the objective of poverty alleviation. Initially, the IRDP was started only in 2300 development blocks as a programme of development. But later on during the Sixth Plan it was extended to the entire country. However, the IRDP concerned as anti-poverty programmes aimed at helping the small and marginal farmers, landless labors and artisans. It was thought by the planners that these people were poor, because they possessed neither any productive assets nor any special skills. Therefore, IRDP was designed to help the poor by creating new assets for them. The basic strategy was self-employment of the poor with the help of these assets so that they could manage to earn enough to rise above the poverty line.

2. *Poverty Alleviation Programmes in the Reform Period*

For the purpose of poverty alleviation, several special programmes for employment generation are being implemented both in rural and urban areas during the reforms period. These programmes provide employment to targeted poor, enhance their income and generate assets for poor families. The following are the major programmes which have been adopted during the reform period.

(i) Employment Assurance Scheme (EAS)

The EAS was launched from 2nd October 1993 in 1778 development blocks in the rural areas of 261 districts. The main objective of this scheme is to provide profitable employment of not less than 100 days to every desirous person aged between 18 years and 60 years during the lean agricultural season. Also, to create economic infrastructures and community projects in order to supply sufficient employment and development activities. EAS is a demand-driven programmes.

(ii) Prime Minister's Rozgar Yojana (PMRY)

PMRY was also introduced on 2nd October 1993 in 1993. Under this scheme every selected educated unemployed youth in the group of 18-40 years and having a family income below Rs. 40, 000 is provided a loan up to Rs. 1 lakh for opening his own enterprise and Rs. 2 lakh for other activities. During 1993-94, this scheme was implemented only in urban areas but since April 1994 it has been implemented both in urban and rural areas.

(iii) National Social Assistance Programme (NSAP)

The NSAP was launched in August 1995. It has three components:

- National Old Age Pension Scheme (NOAPS),
- National Family Benefit Scheme (NFBS), and
- National Maternity Benefit Scheme (NMBS).

The NSAP is a centrally sponsored programme that aims at ensuring a minimum national standard of social assistance over and above the assistance that the states provide from their own resources. The NOAPS provides a monthly pension of Rs. 75 to destitute BPL persons over the age of 65. The NFBS is a scheme for BPL families who are given Rs. 10,000 in the event of the death of the breadwinner. The NMBS provides Rs. 500 to support the nutritional intake for pregnant women.

(iv) Swarnajayanti Shahri Rozgar Yojana (SJSRY)

SJSRY has been operational since December 1997. This scheme provides gainful employment to the urban unemployed and underemployed poor by encouraging the setting up of self-employment ventures and provision wage employment.

(v) Swarnajayanti Gram Swarozgar Yojana (SGSY)

SGSY was launched in April 1999 after the restructuring of the erstwhile IRDP and an allied scheme. It is the only self-employment programme currently being implemented. It is conceived as a holistic programme for micro-enterprises covering all aspects of self-employment. Its objective is to bring the assisted swarozgaris above the poverty line by providing them with income-generating assets through bank credit and Government subsidies. Since its inception, and up to April 2004, a total allocation of Rs.6734 crore was made available by the Center and States. Out of this Rs. 4980 crore have been utilized up to April 2004, hence benefiting 45.67 lakh swarozgaris. However, SGSY is funded by the center and states in the ratio of 75:25.

(vi) Pradhan Mantri Gramodaya Yojana (PMGY)

PMGY was launched in 2000-01 in all states and union territories in order to achieve the objective of sustainable human development at the village level. PMGY initially had five components viz. primary health, primary education, rural shelter, rural drinking water and nutrition. Rural electrification was added as an additional component in 2001-02. The Planning Commission is carrying out both financial and physical monitoring of this programme.

(vii) Antyodaya Anna Yojana (AAY)

AAY was launched in 2000. The scheme aims at providing food security to poor families. Under this scheme 1 crore of the poorest of the BPL (below poverty line) families covered under the targeted PDS (Public Distribution System) are identified and 25 kgs of food grains was made available to each of the eligible families at a highly subsidized rate of Rs. 2 per kg for wheat and Rs. 3 per kg for rice. The quantity has been increased from 25 to 35 kg since April, 2000. The scheme was further expanded in June 2003 by adding another 50 lakh to BPL families.

(viii) Pradhan Mantri Gram Sadak Yojana (PMGSY)

The PMGSY was launched in December 2000 to provide road connectivity to 1.6 lakh of unconnected habitation with a population of 500 persons more in the rural areas by the end of Tenth Plan period. It is being executed in all the states and UTs of India.

(ix) Valmiki Ambedkar Awas Yojana (VAMBAY)

The VAMBAY was launched in December 2001 to ameliorate the conditions of the urban slum-dwellers living below the poverty line without adequate shelter. The scheme has the primary objective of facilitating the construction and upgrading of dwelling units for slum dwellers and providing a healthy and enabling urban environment.

(x) Sampoorna Grameen Rozgar Yojana (SGRY)

SGRY was launched in September 2001 by merging the ongoing scheme of Jawahar Gram Samridhi Yojana (JGSY) and the Employment Assurance Scheme (EAS). The objective of this programme is to provide additional wage employment in the rural areas and also food security, along with the creation of durable community, social and economic infrastructure in rural areas. This programme is open to all rural poor who are in the need of wage employment and desire to do manual and unskilled work in and around the village. The scheme is implemented through Panchayat Raj Institutions. The scheme envisages the generation of 100 crore man-days of employment in a year.

At present, the Government of India has several programmes and scheme to reduce urban as well as rural poverty. Old schemes are reviewed, new scheme are implemented and new strategies are being evolved to accelerate growth and reduce poverty.

Table 3

Percentage of People Below the Poverty Line in India, 1973-74 to 1999-2000

Years	*1973-74*		*1993-1994*		*1999-2000*	
All India Average	*54.88%*		*35.97%*		*26.10%*	
Region	*Poverty Ratio*	*Rank*	*Poverty Ratio*	*Poverty Ratio*	*Poverty Ratio*	*Rank*
Orissa	66.18	1	48.56	3	47.15	1
Bihar	61.91	3	54.96	1	42.60	2
Madhya Pradesh	61.78	4	42.52	4	37.43	3
Sikkim	50.86	16	41.43	5	36.55	4
Assam	51.21	14	40.86	6	36.09	5
Tripura	51.00	15	39.01	9	34.44	6
Meghalaya	50.20	19	37.92	10	33.87	7
Arunachal Pradesh	51.93	13	39.35	8	33.47	8
Nagaland	50.81	17	37.92	11	32.67	9
Uttar Pradesh	57.07	7	40.85	7	31.15	10
Manipur	49.96	20	33.78	17	28.54	11
West Bengal	63.43	2	35.66	14	27.02	12
Maharashtra	53.24	12	36.86	13	25.02	13
Pondicherry	53.82	11	37.40	12	21.67	14
Tamil Nadu	54.94	9	35.03	15	21.12	15
A & N Islands	55.56	8	34.47	16	20.99	16
Karnataka	54.47	10	33.16	18	20.04	17
Mizoram	50.32	18	25.66	21	19.47	18
Dadra & Nagar Haveli	46.55	24	50.84	2	17.14	19
Andhra Pradesh	48.86	22	22.19	27	15.77	20
Lakshadweep	59.68	6	25.05	24	15.60	21
Rajasthan	46.14	25	27.41	20	15.28	22
Gujarat	48.15	23	24.21	26	14.07	23
Kerala	59.79	5	25.43	22	12.72	24
Haryana	35.36	28	25.05	25	8.74	25
Delhi	49.61	21	14.69	30	8.23	26
Himachal Pradesh	26.39	31	28.44	19	7.63	27
Punjab	28.15	29	11.77	31	6.16	28
Chandigarh	27.96	30	11.35	32	5.75	29
Daman & Diu	NA	32	15.80	28	4.44	30
Goa	44.26	26	14.92	29	4.40	31
Jammu & Kashmir	40.83	27	25.17	23	3.48	32

Source: Based on Economic Survey 2000-01 Ministry of Finance, India, Table 10.5 complied from data of the Planning Commission *Website*: WWW.indiabudget.nic.in

Table 3 ranks the state and main administrative regions in India by their officially estimated poverty incidence (ratios) in 1999-2000, and provides comparisons for 1973-74 and 1993-94. It can be seen from that Table 3 the highest incidence of poverty occurs in the northeastern segment of India. At all all-India level, poverty level was as high as 54.88 in 1973-74, which came down to 38.86 in 1987-88 and to just 26.10 in 1999-2000. Thus the extent of poverty has been reduced by more than 50 per cent. The rate of decline in poverty has been increasing: 1.7 per cent during 1973-77, 3.4 per cent during 1983-87 and 5.3 per cent during 1998-99 per year.

The poverty level has declined in almost all the states in India with some exceptional cases over time. But the rate of decline has varied among the states . The highest declining growth rates are observed in Goa, Haryana Himachal Pradesh, Jammu and Kashmir, Kerala, Punjab, Dadra and Pondicherry. During the reform periods (1993/94-1999/2000), poverty has remarkably reduced in the states of Goa, Gujarat, Haryana, Himachal Pradesh, Jammu and Kashmir, Karnataka, Kerala, Punjab, Rajasthan, Tamil Nadu, Chandigarh, Dadra and Nagar Haveli, Daman & Diu, Delhi, Lakshadweep and Pondicherry. Thus poverty is relatively low in the northern states compared to other states in India possibly due to the proper implementation of poverty alleviation programmes.

Changing Scenario of the Regional Dimension of Poverty

Table 4 provides details regarding the physical and financial performance of the various Indian poverty alleviation schemes during Eighth and Ninth Five Year Plan. It can be seen from this table that the total expenditure on IRDP, SGRY reduced to 4716.17 crore in the Ninth plan from Rs. 4867.68 crore in the Eighth plan. The number of beneficiaries in terms of swarozgaris was also significantly dropped to 56.92 lakh from 108.36 lakh during these two periods. (1992-1993 to 2001-2002). The allocation by both the center and states under JRY went down from Rs. 18691 crore in the Eighth Plan to Rs. 11688 crore in the Ninth Plan. The employment generation went down to Rs. 666.27 lakh mandays from Rs. 4717.74 lakh mandays during the Ninth Plan period. The allocation was also reduced to Rs. 530.92 crore from 2914.97 crore during the same period.

Conclusion

Poverty alleviation programmes do not ensure that the poor can really manage to get adequate food all the year round for their family. This is because the value of their supplements depend on the price, supply care and time-distribution of income. These programmes are basically relief-oriented and are not creating durable assets. They do not recognize the importance of an increased flow of social inputs through family welfare, nutrition, social security and minimum needs programmes in alleviating the conditions of poverty on a long-term basis. Likewise, there is also some consensus among researchers that the present form of public

Table 4

Financial & Physical Performance by years of Poverty Alleviation Programmes IRDP SGRY, JRY JGRY and EAS during Eighth and Ninth Plan

	Total Allocation Center + State	*Total expenditure*	*Lakh families swarozgaries*	*Total allocation center+State*	*Total expenditure*	*Employment in lakhs Mandays*	*Total allocation Center+State*	*Total expenditure*	*Employment in lakhs Mandays*
1	2	3	4	5	6	7	8	9	10
Eighth Plan									
1992-1993	662.22	693.88	20.69	3169.05	2709.59	7821.02	0		
1993-1994	1093.43	956.65	25.39	4059.42	3878.71	10258.4	0	183.75	494.74
1994-1995	1098.22	1008.31	22.15	4376.92	4268.33	9517.07	0	1235.45	2729.56
1995-1996	1097.21	1077.16	20.89	4848.7	4466.91	8958.25	0	1720.61	3465.27
1996-1997	1097.21	1131.68	19.24	2236.79	2163.98	4006.32	0	2160.41	4030.02
Total	5048.29	4867.68	108.36	18690.88	17487.52	40561.06	0	5300.22	10719.6
Ninth Plan									
1997-1998	1133.51	1109.54	17.07	2499.21	2439.38	3955.89	2460.48	2904.97	4717.74
1998-1999	1456.28	1162.28	16.77	2597.03	2525.48	3766.41	2485.15	2882.18	4279.36
1999-2000	1472.34	959.86	9.34	2205.58	2032.45	2683.08	2431.46	2182.61	2786.17
2000-2001	1332.5	1116.27	10.3	2192.96	1929.23	2683.17	2082.27	1861.11	2183.92
2001-2002	774.5	555.15	6.25	2493.01	699.07	860.79	1730.92	530.92	666.27
Total	6169.13	4716.17	56.92	11687.93	9625.61	13949.34	11190.28	10361.7	14633.5

Note: 2001-2002-SGRY-up to January, 2002, 2001-2002 JGRY-up to October, 2001, 2001-2002 EAS-up to September, 2001.

system is not helping the poor and it is not a cost-effective anti-poverty programmes. Hence, there is a need for restructuring the existing method of public distribution. The major criticism of the government-based anti-poverty programmes relates to a lack of people's participation. The government approach seems to be technocratic and top-down in implementing these programmes. In order to overcome these limitations, the anti-poverty strategies need to be firmly grounded on two key strategies. First, expanded capabilities to provide education, income health, nutrition, and skills so as to better address the problems encountered by poor. Second, it is necessary to have adequately functioning Panchayat Raj Institutions (PRIs), NGOs, self-help groups and community-based organizations in the rural areas capable of formulating and implementing development programmes and for strengthening government programmes. Such an approach can ensure more efficient use of resources and efforts aimed towards the elimination of poverty.

BIBLIOGRAPHY AND REFERENCES

Journal Articles

Dandekar V.M. and Rath N. (Jan. 1971), "Poverty in India" *Economic and Political Weekly*, pp. 25–45. EPW Research Foundation, Mumbai-01.

Dhage S.K. (2006), "International Incidence of Poverty and Poverty Situation in India", *Asian Quarterly*, pp. 83-103, Volume No. 3, Issue No. 1-2, Forum for Cultural Studies, Pune-7.

Kamalakannan K. (May, 2006), "Rural Industrialization and Poverty Alleviation" *Kurukshetra*, pp. 3-8, Ministry of Rural Development, New Delhi-11.

Popli G., Parikh A. Palmer-Jones R. (Oct. 2005), "Are the 2000 Poverty Estimates For India a Myth, Artifact or Real?" *Economic and Political Weekly*, pp. 4619-4623, EPW Research Foundation, Mumbai-01.

Sen A. and Himanshu, (Sept. 2004), "Poverty & Inequality in India" *Economic & Political* Weekly, pp. 47-62, EPW Research Foundation, Mumbai-01.

Books and Book Articles

Agarwal A.N. (2005), "Underdevelopment" in *Indian Economy*, 35th Edition, Wishwa Prakashan, New Delhi-02.

Agarwal H.S. (1985), "Poverty In India" in *Simple Indian Economy*, Lakshmi Narayan Agarwal, Education Publication, Agra-03.

Dhage S.K. (2003), "Causes, Trends and Allevation of Poverty in India" IEA 86th Conference Volume, Kolhapur 2003, pp. 117-125, Published by the Indian Economic Association.

Jain T.R. (2001-2002), "Vicious Circle of Poverty" in *Indian Economy*, pp. 56-67, V.K. Publication, New Delhi-02.

Kapila Uma (2002-03), "Poverty in India" in *Indian Economy*, pp.164-184, 3rd Edition, Academic Foundation, New Delhi-02.

Lekhi R.K. (1999), "Inequality of Income Poverty and Alleviation Programmes" *The Economics of Development and Planning*, Kalyani Publishers, Ludhiyana.

Misra S.K. and Puri V.K. (2005), "Poverty and Income Inequalities in the Developing Countries" in *Economics of Development and Planning*, pp. 283-310, 11th Edition, Himalaya Publishing House, Mumbai-04.

Radhakrishna R. and Ray S. (2005), "Poverty Trends in India" in Oxford *Handbook of Poverty in India*, pp. 1-34, Oxford University Press, New Delhi-1.

Rao M. Govinda (2002), "Poverty in India–Trends, Macro Policies and Direct Programmes" *Development Poverty and Fiscal Policy*, Oxford University Press, New Delhi.

Ray Debraj (2004), "Poverty and Under Nutrition". *Development of Economics*, pp. 249-294, 7th Edition, Oxford University Press, New Delhi–01.

Sinha A.K. and Sen R.K. (2003), "Amartya Sen on Poverty, Inequality and Famine". pp. 193-209, Deep & Deep Publications Pvt. Ltd., New Delhi-27.

Sury M.M. (2004), "Economic Reforms & Social Sectors" in *Indian Economy in the 21st Century*, pp. 273–277, 1st Edn, Indian Tax foundation, New Delhi-02.

Reports

Asian Development Review (1998), Vol. 16, No. 2 Asian Development Bank, Manila, Philippines.

Economic Survey (2000-2001) Ministry of Finance and Company Affairs, Economic Division, Government of India, New Delhi-02.

Economic Survey (2001-2002), Ministry of Finance and Company Affairs, Economic Division, Government of India, New Delhi-02.

Economic Survey (2002-2003), Ministry of Finance and Company Affairs, Economic Division, Government of India, New Delhi-02.

Economic Survey (2004-2005), Ministry of Finance and Company Affairs, Economic Division, Government of India, New Delhi-02.

*Human Development Report (*1999), *UNDP,* Oxford University Press, New York.

Human Development Report (2000), *UNDP* Oxford University Press, New York.

Human Development in South Asia (2002) *UNDP* Oxford University Press, New York.

Planning Commission (2002-2007) *Five-Year Plan*, Volume-1, Government Of India, New Delhi.

World Bank (2001) *World Development Report 2000-01: Attacking poverty*, Oxford University Press, New York.

World Bank (2005), *World Development Report 2004-05: A Better Investment Climate, Growth and Poverty,* Oxford University Press, New York.

19

REDUCTION OF POVERTY IN INDIA: FURTHER PERSPECTIVES

S.K. Dhage

Introduction

Even after more than 50 years of independence from almost two centuries of British rule, large-scale poverty remains the most shameful blot on the face of India. Poverty is a social phenomenon having economic consequences. It is a great curse for mankind. It is often said that, India is a rich country inherited by the poor. It means that nature has endowed India with vast natural resources, but we have not been able to tap all the resources to the fullest extent and to our advantage. This has resulted in low production, low income levels and a low standard of living leading to poverty. In other words poverty generates poverty and sustains itself.

The Indian economy is trapped in a vicious circle of poverty. Poverty generates a dreadful feeling-a feeling of misery, fear and distress, it is associated with disease, starvation, desperation and even death. It degrades and demoralizes the individuals facing poverty. In fact, is not only affects the 'have-nots' but it also arouses sympathy among the 'haves'. Poverty is the result of the interaction of many economic and social factors.

Estimates of Poverty in India

The incidence of poverty is measured in terms of the percentage of total population living below the poverty line. It shows how many are poor and brings out the extent of poverty in the country. Several economists and organizations have conducted studies about the extent of poverty in India. Some of the important studies have been undertaken by V.M. Dandekar and N. Rath, P.D. Ojha, B.S. Minhas, S.D. Tendulkar, the Planning Commision of India, World Bank and others.

Planning Commission's Estimates

Poverty Projection for 2007. The Planning Commission of India adopted the nutritional criteria to measure poverty. In 1979, the calorie requirement according to it was 2400 per person in rural areas and 2100 in urban areas. The monthly expenditure required to have the necessary calorie intake according to 1979-80 prices was Rs. 76 in rural areas and Rs. 88 in urban areas. Those who could not incur that expenditure lived below the poverty line. The Seventh Plan has drawn the poverty line on the basis of annual income per family of 4 to 5 persons. This involves a minimum annual income per family in the rural area is Rs. 6,400 and Rs. 7,300 for the urban families. Families with less than this income are said to be absolutely poor. The estimates of incidence of poverty at national level is given the Table 1.

Table 1
Planning Commission's Estimate of Poverty in India

Year	*Poverty Ratios (per cent)*			*Number of poor (million)*		
	Rural	*Urban*	*Combined*	*Rural*	*Urban*	*Combined*
1977-78	53.1	45.2	51.3	264.3	64.6	328.9
1983-84	37.3	32.4	36.0	244.0	76.3	320.3
1999-00	27.1	23.6	26.1	193.2	67.1	260.3
2007 *	21.1	15.1	19.3	170.5	49.6	220.1

Note: Poverty Projection for 2007.
Source: Economic Survey 2003-04.

The Planning Commission's figures on poverty, given in Table 1, brings out of the following facts about poverty in India.

1. A steady decline in poverty. The incidence of poverty has witnessed a steady decline from 51.3 per cent in 1997-78 to 36 per cent in 1983-84 and 26 per cent in 1999-2000. It is projected to decline to 19.3 per cent in 2007.
2. The number of poor. Though the poverty ratio has declined, the number of poor in the country has remained at around 320 million for a long period due to India's growth of population. But the latest estimates of poverty for 1999-2000 reveal a significantly reduced number of poor to about 260 million out of a total population of 997 million. The number of poor in India is projected to fall to 220 million in 2007.
3. Poverty rate in 1999-2000. The poverty ratio is estimated to be 27.1 per cent in rural areas 23.6 per cent in urban areas and 26.1 per cent for the country as a whole in 1999-2000. The Planning Commission projects the poverty rate to fall to 21.1 per cent and 15.1 per cent respectively in rural and urban areas in 2007.
4. Wide disparities between rural and urban areas. Wide disparities are visible in the poverty ratios between rural and urban areas. Poverty ratios are higher in rural areas compared to urban areas.

World Bank's Estimates of Poverty in India

The World Bank brings out two types of data on poverty viz. the first is based on international poverty line and the second on national poverty line.

World Bank's Estimates of Poverty Based on International Poverty Line

World Bank's concept of international poverty line is based on a composite measure of the total household consumption per member. Poor people are the defined as those living in households below this measure of consumption such as below $1 or $ 2 per day. The population living in India below $1 a day was 44.2 per cent in 1997.

World Bank's Estimates of Poverty Based on National Poverty Line

The World Bank in its study on Indian poverty, employment and social services estimated India's poverty line along similar lines to that of the Planning Commission. The poverty line is in terms of monthly per capita consumption expenditure at 1993-94 prices. The people below this expenditure are considered to be poor . These expenditures are sufficient to provide 2400 calories per person per day in rural areas and 2100 calories daily per person in urban areas. The World Bank's estimates of poverty is give in Table 2.

Table 2
India's Population Below Poverty Line (in per cent) as Estimated by the World Book

Year	*Rural*	*Urban*	*All India*
1974	55.92	47.96	54.10
1987	38.81	34.29	37.69
1994	36.66	30.51	35.04
1997	35.60	29.99	34.40

Source : The World Bank, India Reducing Poverty Accelerating. Development Oxford University Press, New York 2000 p. 141.

Important findings of the World Bank's 2000 study are as follows:

1. Steady decline in the incidence of poverty. The incidence of poverty declined steadily from 54 per cent in 1979 to 34 per cent in 1997.
2. Poverty in India is predominantly rural. Poverty in India remains a predominantly rural phenomenon. Three out of every four poor Indians live in rural areas. The incidence of poverty is highest among agricultural labourers.

Estimates of Poverty from the National Sample Survey

According to the latest large sample survey data on consumption expenditure made available by the National Sample Survey Organization. (NSSO) from its

Table 3
India's Planning Commission's Estimates of Population of below the Poverty Line by States

	No. of persons in lakhs			*Poverty Ration (% of Population)*			*Poverty Reduction*	
	1987-88	*1993-94*	*1999-00*	*1987-88*	*1993-94*	*1999-00*	*87-88 to 93-94*	*93-94 to 99-00*
1. Delhi	10.3	15.5	11.5	12.4	14.7	8.2	-2.3	6.5
2. Punjab	25.2	25.1	14.5	13.2	11.8	6.2	1.4	5.6
3. Chandigarh	0.8	0.8	0.5	14.7	11.4	5.7	3.3	5.7
4. Himachal Pradesh	7.5	15.9	5.1	15.5	28.4	7.6	-12.9	20.8
5. Daman & Diu	–	0.2	0.1	–	15.8	4.4	–	11.4
6. Haryana	25.4	43.9	17.3	16.6	25.1	8.7	-8.5	16.4
7. Jammu & Kashmir	17.0	20.9	3.5	23.8	25.2	3.5	-1.4	21.7
8. Goa	3.0	1.9	0.7	24.5	14.9	4.4	9.6	10.5
9. Andhra Pradesh	160.4	154.0	119.0	25.9	22.2	15.8	–	–
10. Kerala	88.5	76.6	41.0	31.8	25.4	12.7	6.4	6.3
11. Mizoram	1.7	1.9	1.8	27.5	25.7	19.5	1.8	6.2
12. Manipur	5.3	6.8	7.2	31.4	33.8	28.5	-2.4	5.3
13. Gujarat	122.4	105.2	67.9	31.5	24.2	40.1	7.2	6.8
14. Meghalaya	5.5	7.4	8.2	33.9	37.9	33.9	-4.0	4.0
15. Nagaland	3.7	5.1	5.5	34.4	37.9	32.7	-3.5	5..2
16. Lakshadweep	0.2	0.1	0.1	35.0	25.0	15.6	10.0	9.4
17. Rajasthan	142.9	128.5	81.8	35.2	27.4	15.3	7.8	7.5
18. Sikkim	1.4	1.8	2.1	36.1	41.4	36.6	-5.3	4.8
19. Tripura	8.8	11.8	13.0	35.2	39.1	34.4	-3.9	4.7
20. Assam	75.8	96.4	94.6	36.2	40.9	36.1	-4.7	4.9
21. Arunachal Pradesh	2.8	3.7	4.0	36.2	39.4	33.5	-3.2	3.3
22. Karnataka	158.6	156.5	104.4	37.5	33.2	20.0	4.2	13.2
23. Maharashtra	296.3	305.2	228.0	40.4	36.9	25.0	3.5	11.9
24. Uttar Pradesh	563.5	604.5	529.9	41.5	40.9	31.2	0.6	9.7
25. Pondicherry	3.1	3.3	2.4	41.5	37.4	21.7	4.1	15.7
26. Madhya Pradesh	264.3	298.5	298.5	43.1	42.5	37.4	0.6	5.1
27. Andaman & Nicobar	1.1	1.1	0.8	43.9	34.5	21.0	9.4	13.5
28. Tamil Nadu	231.1	202.1	130.5	43.4	35.0	31.1	8.4	13.9
29. West Bengal	283.6	254.6	213.5	44.7	35.7	27.0	9.0	8.7
30. Bihar	420.9	493.4	425.6	52.1	55.0	42.6	-2.9	12.4
31. Orissa	165.9	166.6	169.1	55.6	48.6	47.1	7.0	1.5
32. Dadra & Nagar Haveli	0.8	0.8	0.3	67.1	50.8	17.1	16.3	33.7
All India	3070.5	3203.7	2602.5	38.9	36.0	26.1	2.9	9.9

Note: States have been arranged in the ascending order on the basis of poverty ratio 1987-88.

Source: Planning Commission (1998) Ninth Five-Year Plan (1997-2002), Vol. 1 & Press release of the Planning Commission dtd. 22nd Feb. 2001 regarding poverty Estimates for 1999-2000.

55th round survey (July, 1999-June, 2000), the poverty ratio is estimated at 27.09 per cent in rural areas, 23.62 per cent in urban areas and 26.10 per cent for the country as a whole.

Table 3 shows that the state-level data present a mixed and, in a sense, a very disturbing picture. A number of states exhibited increases in their poverty ratios. Himachal Pradesh, Haryana and Bihar are among the major states in this group. However, the entire North-Eastern region including Mizoram, Manipur, Meghalaya, Sikkim, Nagaland, Assam, Tripura and Arunachal Pradesh did likewise. Obviously, this underlines the need for promoting growth in the North-Eastern region if insurgency and terrorism are to be seriously controlled. States which have shown better record of poverty reduction are West Bengal, Gujarat, Kerala, Karnataka, Maharashtra, Tamil Nadu and Orissa. Though some of these exhibit a high proportion, their population below the poverty lines are more than 40 per cent.

A very disturbing feature of the poverty scenario is that seven major states, viz., Maharashtra, Uttar Pradesh, Madhya Pradesh, West Bengal, Tamil Nadu, Bihar and Orissa accounted for 2319 lakh poor in 1993-94 i.e., 72.4 per cent of the total poor in the country. This shows a high concentration of India's poor in these seven states.

Economic Reforms and Reduction of Poverty

A natural question arises: what has been the impact of economic reforms initiated since 1991 on poverty reduction ? A research study has been conducted by Dr. Gaurav Datt and another by Dr. S.P. Gupta. We summarise below the results of these studies:

Dr. Gaurav Datt of the World Bank in his article "Has Poverty Declined since Economic Reforms ?" (see Table 4) has drawn the following conclusions:

1. While there was a marked decline in both rural and urban poverty rates in India between 1973-74 and 1986-87, there is no sign of anything comparable thereafter.
2. For the rural sector, for the period 1973-74 and 1990-91, the headcount index of poverty declined at the annual rate of 2.7 per cent, but the rate of decline since then (i.e. in the post reform period) is not significantly different from zero.
3. For the urban sector, during 1973-74 and 1990-91, the headcount index of poverty declined at the annual rate of 2.2 per cent and the same trend continued in the post–reform period (1990-91 to 1996-97) at the annual average rate of 2.2 per cent.
4. While the urban sector seems to have continued its march of poverty reduction in the process of growth, rural poverty reduction was choked off by lack of rural growth. (Table 4).

Table 4
Poverty in India , 1973-97

		Head count Index		*Poverty Gap Index*		*Squared Poverty Gap Index*	
Nss Round	*Survey Period*	*Rural*	*Urban*	*Rural*	*Urban*	*Rural*	*Urban*
28	Oct 73-Jun 74	55.72	47.96	17.175	13.602	7.128	5.219
32	Jul 77-Jun 78	50.60	40.50	15.205	11.687	6.057	4.526
38	Jan 83-Dec 83	45.31	35.65	12.649	9.517	4.841	3.557
42	Jul 86-Jun 87	38.81	34.29	10.013	9.100	3.700	3.395
43	Jul 87-Jun 88	39.23	36.20	9.275	9.125	2.982	3.056
44	Jul 88-Jun 89	39.06	36.60	9.504	9.537	3.291	3.293
45	Jul 89-Jun 90	34.30	33.40	7.799	8.505	2.575	3.038
46	Jul 90-Jun 91	36.43	32.76	8.644	8.509	2.926	3.121
Pre-reform	Jul 89-Jun 91	35.37	33.08	8.222	8.507	2.751	3.080
47	Jul 91-Dec 91	37.42	33.23	8.288	8.244	2.680	2.902
48	Jan 92-Dec 92	43.47	33.73	10.881	8.824	3.810	3.191
50	Jul 93-Jun 94	36.66	30.51	8.387	7.405	2.792	2.417
51	Jul 94-Jun 95	41.02	33.50	9.285	8.382	2.995	2.799
52	Jul 95-Jun 96	37.15	28.04	8.098	6.781	2.527	2.222
53	Jan 97-Dec 97	35.78	29.99	8.312	7.762	2.757	2.725
Post-reform	Jul 95-Dec 97	36.47	29.02	8.205	7.273	2.642	2.474

Source: Gaurav Datt, Has Poverty Declined since Economic Reforms, *Economic and Political Weekly*, December 11-17, 1999.

Causes of Failure in Reducing Poverty

Now the question arises: Why did the plans in India fail to reduce poverty as much as hoped for, not to speak of removing poverty? This was due to the fact that the planners assumed that the growth strategy aiming at an increase of national income, supplemented by policies of progressive taxation and public expenditure, would lead to a rise in the level of living of the poor. The production-oriented approach of planning without altering the mode of production could not but result in the appropriation of the gains of development by the owners of instruments of production. Admitting this fact, the Fifth Plan in its earlier draft stated: "In elaborating our strategy of development–in earlier plan documents, we seem to have assumed that a fast rate of growth of national income will by itself create more and fuller employment and produce higher living standards of the poor. We also seem to have assumed that, for reduction of disparities in income and wealth, the scope of redistribute policies is severely limited." The philosophy of automatic transmission of the benefits arising from an increase in production to the bulk of the small farmers, landless labourers or factory workers without transferring the property or tenurial rights either to the State or the peasantry was destined to be a failure.

The planners, therefore, missed the inescapable fact that growth and a reduction in inequality are both indispensable to a successful attack on mass poverty. Emphasizing this point Mrs. Kamla Suri and S. Gangadharan write: "All these show that poverty in India also emerges out of a long established malaise in the economic structure-skewed distribution of the ownership of income-yielding assets. The institutional malady needs to be rectified to completely eradicate poverty in the long run. The effect of an initial unequal distribution of income yielding assets has been cumulative, resulting in the continuance and intensification of this skewness, that is, we find two inter-connected vicious circles, one of affluence and the other of poverty. Thus, any attempt to break the vicious circle of poverty without tampering with the vicious circle of affluence will not affect the cumulative process or halt the widening gap between the rich and the poor. It is in this context that *Garibi Hatao* (removal of poverty) is incomplete as a drive in the eradication of poverty. In other words, it must be complemented *Amiri Hatao* (removal of affluence)."

The record of both Congress party and Janata party rule indicate that production and distribution were being treated separately. However, the forces of production determine the distribution pattern and thus there is no justification for treating productive efficiency and distributive justice as two independent variables of growth. Production and distribution are interlinked in a more fundamental sense that the pattern of income distribution determines the pattern of production. Unless the pattern of income distribution is altered, the objective of increasing the production of wage goods sufficiently to remove poverty will be distorted. And for this purpose an attack on correcting the maldistribution of assets, both in the rural and urban sectors is a *sine qua non.* This is a decision, which more appropriately belongs to the domain of politics than of economics. A strong political will to bring about institutional changes leading to redistribution of income-yielding assets either through land reform or ceiling on urban property has not been indicated so far. Consequently, removal of poverty continues to be an elusive goal, and thus progress in achieving objective is rather halting.

Conclusion

The allevation of poverty has been a major objective of India's Development Plans. The *"Garibi Hatao"* slogan given by Indira Gandhi in the early 1970s marked the beginning of an intensified approach to help the poor as reflected in a wide range of programmes for direct intervention to benefit the backward and poor sections of the society. These programmes have had some notable achievements to their credit, such as a public distribution system with a wide rural coverage, notable achievements to their credit, employment programmes with significant impact on the rural poor, and improvement in rural amenties and infrastructure like roads, schools, health centres, banks, communication facilities. A good indicator of the impact of the anti-poverty programmes in India is the reduction in the extent of poverty. The percentage of population living below the poverty line declined from 55 per cent during 1973-74 to 36 per cent during 1993-94 and further to 26.1 per cent during 1999-2000 for India as a whole. However, it may be noted that the whole of the decline in the poverty cannot be attributed to anti-poverty programmes alone but there appears to be a consensus among the researchers that these programmes have been an important factor in the reduction in India's poverty over the last three decades.

The policy-makers should take a careful look at past Indian experiences to see how India's anti-poverty strategy could be strengthened to meet the objective of eradication of poverty. The reduction in poverty is not the same thing as eradication of poverty. A person/household above the poverty line may still be subject to severe deprivation along other dimensions of well-being. Eradication of poverty should mean reduction of deprivation along all the major and important dimensions of well-being including but not confined to food deprivation. Raising the poor above the presently defined poverty line needs no more than a delivery system for the poor capable of providing unskilled employment, subsidized food and free education and health facilities on a sufficiently large scale.

BIBLIOGRAPHY AND REFERENCES

Journal Articles

Dandekar V.M. and Rath N. (Jan, 1971), "Poverty in India" *Economic and Political Weekly*, pp. 25-45.EPW Research Foundation, Mumbai-01.

Datt Gourav, (1999), "Has Poverty Declined since Economic Reforms", *Economic and Political Weekly*, December 11-17, 1999.

Dhage S.K. (2006), "International Incidence of Poverty and Poverty Situation in India", *Asian Quarterly*, pp.83-103, Volume No. 3, Issue No. 1-2, Forum for Cultural Studies, Pune-7.

Kamalakannan K. (May, 2006), "Rural Industrialization and Poverty Alleviation" *Kurukshetra*, pp. 3-8, Ministry of Rural Development, New Delhi-11.

Books

Agarwal A.N. (2005) "Underdevelopment" in *Indian Economy*, pp. 1-12, 35th Edition, Wishwa Prakashan, New Delhi-02.

Dhage S.K. (2003), "Causes, Trendes and Allevation of Poverty in India" IEA 86th Conference Volume Kolhapur 2003, pp. 117-125, published by the Indian Economic Association.

Kapila Uma (2002-03), "Poverty in India" in *Indian Economy*, pp. 164-184, 3rd Edition, Academic Foundation, New Delhi-02.

Lekhi R.K. (1999), "Inequality of Income Poverty and Alleviation Programmes" in *The Economics of Development and Planning*, Kalyani Publishers, Ludhiyana.

Misra S.K. and Puri V.K. (2005), "Poverty and Income Inequalities in the Developing Countries" in *Economics of Development and Planning*, pp. 283-310, 11th Edition, Himalaya Publishing House, Mumbai-04.

Ray Debraj (2004), "Poverty and Under Nutrition" in *Development of Economics*, pp. 249-294, 7th Edition, Oxford University Press, New Delhi–01.

Sury M.M. (2004), "Economic Reforms & Social Sectors" in *Indian Economy in the 21st Century*, pp. 273–277, 1st Edn, Indian Tax Foundation, New Delhi-02.

Reports

Economic Survey (2003-2004) Ministry of Finance and Company Affairs, Economic Division, Government of India, New Delhi-02.

Economic Survey (2004-2005) Ministry of Finance and Company Affairs, Economic Division, Government of India, New Delhi-02.

Planning Commission (1998), *Ninth Five-Year Plan* (1997-2002), Vol. I., Govt. of India.

Planning Commission (2002-2007) *Tenth Five-Year Plan*, Volume-1, Government Of India, New Delhi.

The World Bank (2000), *India Reducing Poverty Accelerating Development* Oxford University Press, New York.

20

NUTRITIONAL INTAKE AND DYNAMICS OF UNDERNOURISHMENT OF FARM HOUSEHOLDS IN RURAL INDIA

Praduman Kumar and Madan M. Dey

Introduction

The key challenge in the new Millennium is food and nutritional security for the growing global population. The available estimates show that about 800 million people in the world are chronically undernourished and food insecure (IFPRI 1995). In the Indian context, about 55% of its population was categorized as poor and undernourished in 1973. Increased agricultural productivity and rapid industrial growth in the country in recent years have contributed to a significant reduction in the poverty level, to 26% of the population in 1999. Despite these impressive achievements, India is the home of about 251 million people below the poverty lines adopted by the Planning Commission of the Government of India. Of these, two-thirds live in the rural areas and one-third in the urban areas of India (Table 1). Under-nourishment is largely a rural phenomenon and these vulnerable people must be targeted in food and nutritional security and poverty alleviation programs throughout the country.

Table 1
Number and Percentage of Population below Poverty line in India

Year	*Rural*		*Urban*		*All India*	
	No. of persons (million)	*% of persons*	*No. of persons (million)*	*% of persons*	*No. of persons (million)*	*% of persons*
1973	261	56	60	49	321	55
1983	254	46	74	41	328	45
1993	213	33	75	32	288	32
1999	170	24	81	30	251	26

Source: Computed from various NSS rounds consumer household expenditure survey, New Delhi, India: Government of India.

Note: Chapter marked with will be reprints from the special issue of the Indian Development Review.

Landless agricultural households and small farm households (< 1 ha landholding) constitute more than 50% of India's population and account for more than half of the poor people (148 million out of 251 million) in India. Some of the fundamental questions that may be raised are: Is it the small farm-size of the majority of these households which is the main cause of perpetuating poverty and undernourishment? Is there any prospect of liberating these farm households from undernourishment and poverty? How can the role of these small farm households be enhanced in fighting poverty? What are the socio-economic policies that are required? All these questions have been addressed in this paper along with a diagnosis of the nutritional status and identification of the technological and socioeconomic factors influencing nutritional security of the farm households in rural India.

Data used for the study

The paper has used Indian household data on dietary patterns and consumer expenditure collected by NSSO at the national level by survey method and is based on various rounds of the National Sample Survey (NSS) and pertains to the period 1983 (January to December) to 1999-00 (July–June). The data for the year 1983 in the analysis were included to compare the change process before economic reforms, as observed from the data for years 1983 and 1987-88 with the change process during reforms, as revealed by comparing 1987-88 situation with that during 1993-94 and 1999-00. For the analysis, sample rural households were grouped into landless agricultural households and farm households were divided into sub-marginal farms (< 0.5 ha land), marginal farms (0.5-1.0 ha land), small farms (1.0-2.0 ha land), medium farms (2.0-4.0 ha land) and large farms (> 4 ha land).

The calorie and protein intake in the study refers to their respective consumption from different food items, calculated using the conversion factors provided by NSSO (Report No. 405, 1996). The minimum (threshold) food-energy requirements were taken as 1800 kcal/person/day for the rural households (Sukhatme, 1977). It represented 75% of the recommended energy requirement, viz. 2400 kcal/person/day for the rural households. An intake below this threshold is regarded as not sufficient to maintain health and body mass, or to support light physical activity. The threshold level of food-protein intake is used as 48 gram/person/day (which is also 75% of the recommended level of protein for the average Indian). The households whose average intake of calories and protein were below these threshold levels were categorised as undernourished and malnourished, respectively. The poverty line adopted by the Planning Commission of the Government of India for rural households by provinces (States of India) for the years 1983 to 1999 was used to assess the sample households under poverty.

Results and discussion

Household nutrition and food security

The average per capita calorie intake in farm households in India was 2289 kcal/day in the year 1983 which increased to 2423 kcal/day during 1987-88. With the beginning of economic reforms, calorie intake declined to 2277 kcal/day and remained at this level during the period up to 1999-2000 (Table 2). The protein intake increased between 1983 and 1987-88 and declined thereafter. Among different farm-size groups, calorie intake showed a decline in the beginning of the reforms and an increase thereafter, except in the case of large farm-size groups, which recorded a decline. In all the survey years, per capita calorie intake increased with the increase in farm-size.

Calorie intake in landless agricultural households dropped sharply at the beginning of the reforms and recovered subsequently. In 1999-00, it was slightly higher than its value in 1983 but was lower than that in 1987-88. There was a sharp reduction in the percentage of agricultural households consuming less than the recommended minimum level of calories between 1983 and 1987-88, but this, however, was reversed in the beginning of economic reforms. With further progress in reforms, there was an increase in the percentage of undernourished (i.e. deficit in calories) farm households but there was a sharp decline in the case of landless households.

The incidence of malnourishment (i.e. deficit in protein) in farm households showed a sharp decline before the economic reforms but with the beginning of them, these exhibited a slight increase. Intensification of reforms with trade liberalization, however, was accompanied by a sharp increase in the malnourishment of farm households. The situation was found to be somewhat different in the case of landless households; their protein-deficit population increased substantially in the beginning of reforms but dropped subsequently. According to the estimates for the year 1999-2000, more than 26% of farm households and more than 45% of landless households were suffering from energy and protein deficiencies.

As seen in Table 2, the decline in poverty before the reforms was associated with a sharp reduction in undernourishment and malnourishment. However, after 1987-88, the decline in poverty did not reduce undernourishment. No significant reduction in poverty was observed between 1987-88 and 1993-94 but between 1993-94 and 1999-00, a decline from 30.1% to 21.0 % for farm households and from 54.6% to 39.6% for landless households was observed. In a sharp contrast to the reduction in poverty, the incidence of undernourishment depicted a small increase and malnourishment showed a large increase in farm households. However, in landless households, the reduction in poverty between 1993-94 and 1999-00 lowered undernourishment to a considerable extent, even though the undernourished population was higher in 1999-00 than in 1987-88.

Table 2
Undernourishment, Malnourishment and Poverty among Agricultural Labour Households and Farm Households of Various Farm-Size Groups in Rural India

Aspect/Year	*Agricultural labour households*	*Farm-size groups*					
		Sub-marginal (<0.5 ha)	*Marginal (0.5-1 ha)*	*Small (1-2 ha)*	*Medium (2-4 ha)*	*Large> 4ha*	*All farms*
Population below poverty line, %							
1983	64.6	53.4	46.0	41.3	33.5	24.2	42.6
1987-88	55.3	42.8	38.1	32.4	25.4	16.1	31.6
1993-94	54.6	43.1	34.9	29.8	21.9	14.1	30.1
1999-00	39.7	28.9	23.5	19.9	13.3	7.4	21.0
Undernourished population, %							
1983	48.6	42.3	30.1	25.1	19.6	15.0	29.0
1987-88	41.2	33.3	25.2	20.7	16.0	11.1	21.9
1993-94	53.6	34.5	26.7	22.8	18.6	12.1	24.0
1999-00	45.5	33.0	26.7	25.7	19.6	16.2	26.2
Malnourished population, %							
1983	44.1	41.2	28.6	24.8	17.7	11.8	27.7
1987-88	38.0	33.0	25.0	20.7	14.6	8.6	21.1
1993-94	50.0	33.7	26.7	20.9	15.9	8.3	22.3
1999-00	48.7	36.5	30.1	27.2	20.7	14.1	28.2
Calorie intake/person/day, kcal							
1983	1908	2018	2252	2327	2496	2673	2289
1987-88	2010	2142	2298	2404	2539	2822	2423
1993-94	1819	2058	2183	2270	2377	2616	2277
1999-00	1948	2147	2221	2274	2409	2561	2278
Protein intake/person/day, gram							
1983	54.0	56.2	63.2	65.5	71.5	78.2	64.7
1987-88	56.9	60.1	64.7	68.1	72.9	83.1	69.2
1993-94	50.7	57.7	61.6	64.7	69.2	77.9	65.3
1999-00	51.9	58.1	60.2	62.4	67.8	73.1	62.7
Sample households, No.							
1983	11074	15868	9920	11171	6408	4215	47582
1987-88	4909	15095	10134	11213	8845	7658	52945
1993-94	9013	12255	8208	8578	5986	5391	40418
1999-00	10627	15236	8541	7651	5190	3993	40611

Source: Computed from various NSS rounds consumer household expenditure survey, New Delhi, India: Government of India

The distribution of the poor and undernourished rural population in various groups revealed that 60% of poor and 55% of undernourished persons in rural areas belonged to the marginal farm category (Table 3). Landless agricultural labourers accounted for 23% of poor and 19% of the undernourished rural population. One-tenth of the rural poor and 13% of the undernourished households were from the small landholding category. There were some poor (2%) and undernourished (4.9%) households even in the large-size land holdings category. The results revealed that the agricultural landless labour and marginal farm-size constituted more than 82% of the total poor and 73% of the undernourished population in the year 1999-2000, and alarmingly, their number has been growing with time. If India were to meet the target of the World Food Summit in 1996 of reducing, by half, the number of poor people in the world by 2015, and the Indian Prime Minister's call for doubling food production and making India hunger-free in 10 years, highest priority must be accorded to the landless agricultural labour and marginal farm households in raising their income and employment levels. These households are net buyers and need hard cash to buy food from the market; their only economic resource is their 'labour' and/or the undertaking of diverse farm activities.

Table 3
Proportion of Poor and of Undernourished Persons in Different Farm-size Groups, Rural India, 1999-2000

Category	*Agricultural labour households*	*Marginal farms (< 1 ha)*	*Small farms (1-2 ha)*	*Medium farms (2-4 ha)*	*Large farms (>4 ha)*	*Total persons (million)*
% share of each group in total poor persons	22.8	59.6	10.3	5.3	2.0	159.8
% share of each group in total under-nourished persons	19.1	54.6	12.9	8.4	4.9	223.2

Source: Computed from 55th NSS rounds on consumer household expenditure survey, New Delhi, India: Government of India.

A question that may be raised is whether a landholding of less than one hectare (marginal farm households) can provide enough income to meet the minimum calorie requirements of the whole household? The reply to this question must be "Yes". Now the query that arises is how to do it? Although several factors influence the extent and depth of undernourishment and poverty, some of them have depicted overwhelming impacts under the Indian scenario. These are discussed in the next section.

Factors Influencing Poverty and Nutritional Security

This section examines the major socio-economic factors which may diversify the food basket for meeting the energy requirements of the farm households in rural India. These include: (i) cropping systems, (ii) irrigation, (iii) livestock, (iv) aquaculture, (v) education, and (vi) societal structure. Only the 50th NSS round data, pertaining to the year 1993-94, provided the information on these socio-economic factors and these were used to establish the relationships between various dimensions, as discussed ahead and to identify factors impacting on poverty and undernourishment of sample households.

Cropping systems

Diverse cropping systems prevail in various agro-eco-regions of India. In the present study, four major cereal-based cropping systems were evaluated in the context of calorie intake. These were delineated based on the extent of the area under specific production activity. These included coarse cereals, rice, wheat, and rice-wheat-based cropping systems. Table 4 contains data on undernourished farm households in different cropping systems. It is interesting to note that only 20% of farm-households in the rice-wheat and 21% in the wheat-based cropping systems were undernourished. The proportion of undernourished farm-households in rice and coarse cereals-based cropping systems was quite large, 35% and 41%, respectively. The most vulnerable categories were the sub-marginal (50%) and marginal (43%) farm-households in the coarse cereals-based cropping systems. The higher calorie intake ratio of non-cereals to total calories intake per capita suggests the presence of more diversified food baskets in the rice-wheat and wheat-based cropping systems than in the rice and coarse cereals. Such a phenomenon suggests that the higher production of rice and wheat could not only improve the calorie intake of farm households but could also diversify their food basket due to a rise in the income level.

Table 4
Impact of Cropping System on Calorie Intake and Undernourishment in Different Farm-size Groups in Rural India

Cropping system	*Sub-marginal farms*	*Marginal farms*	*Small farms*	*Medium farms*	*Large farms*	*All farms*
Daily per caput calorie intake, kcal						
Coarse cereals	2418	2558	2696	2976	3148	2595
Rice	2523	2682	2844	3029	3173	2642
Wheat	2801	2944	3154	3332	3444	3021
Rice-wheat	2760	2986	3198	3382	3473	2979
Share of non-cereals in total calorie intake, %						
Coarse cereals	26	28	31	34	37	29
Rice	22	23	26	27	28	23
Wheat	31	33	36	37	37	34
Rice-wheat	27	31	36	37	39	31
Undernourished population, %						
Coarse cereals	50	43	35	21	17	41
Rice	41	31	24	19	20	35
Wheat	28	23	17	11	10	21
Rice-wheat	27	18	13	9	10	20

Source: Computed from the 50th NSS rounds 1993-94 data on consumer household expenditure survey, New Delhi, India: Government of India.

This analysis has further substantiated the need for improved agricultural technologies in overcoming the problem of undernourishment in rural India. Use of improved technologies for rice and wheat crops in the northern and of wheat in the central parts of India have been credited with raising the production and calorie intake levels in these areas. The coarse cereals system in the southern and western regions, and the rice system in the eastern and northeastern regions have been found to be lagging far behind those of the rice-wheat and wheat-based cropping systems (Kumar, 2001). Concerted efforts are needed to develop demand-driven technologies for the coarse cereals. Targeting these cropping systems would mean covering about 50% of the total farm households in rural India.

Table 5
Impact of Irrigation on Calorie Intake and Undernourishment in Different Farm-Size Groups in Rural India

Irrigated area (%)	*Sub–marginal farms*	*Marginal farms*	*Small farms*	*Medium farms*	*Large farms*	*All farms*
Daily per caput calorie intake, kcal						
Rainfed	2495	2614	2724	2954	3274	2589
< 20	2797	2782	2961	3137	3312	2976
20-50	2698	2778	2906	3218	3318	2909
50-80	2682	2957	3120	3286	3259	2961
>80	2730	3003	3292	3438	3601	2965
Share of non-cereals in total calories, %						
Rainfed	23	24	26	29	33	24
<20	26	26	29	32	34	29
20-50	25	27	30	33	33	29
50-80	26	28	31	34	34	30
>80	28	33	38	40	43	32
Undernourished population, %						
Rainfed	43	35	30	20	13	38
<20	25	27	23	21	15	23
20-50	32	30	24	12	15	25
50-80	35	20	16	9	10	22
>80	30	19	11	9	10	22

Source: Computed from the 50th NSS rounds 1993-94 data on consumer household expenditure survey, New Delhi, India: Government of India.

Availability of Irrigation Facilities

To understand the role of irrigation in influencing the calorie intake, the sample households were classified according to the extent of their irrigated areas. The results revealed that about 38% of the farm households were undernourished where there was no source of irrigation (Table 5). With the availability of some irrigation water (only up to 20% of the cultivated area), the number of undernourished farm households dropped to about 23%. Further increases in the irrigated area, however, did not show a substantial change in the calorie intake. This indicates that the introduction of irrigation, however small it may be, can meet the challenge of nutritional security in the rural areas of India. A more diversified food basket was observed in the irrigated areas than in the rainfed farms. In this context, the role of watershed and water-saving technologies (e.g. drip and sprinkler systems) in the rainfed areas was found to be very crucial. Access to even some irrigation water may help overcome the drought conditions during the critical crop growth periods and this would substantially raise production and income levels, and improve the calorie intake. The Government of India has already extended high priority to the watershed development programs in the rainfed areas. Similarly, water-saving technologies are offered high subsidies to expand micro-irrigated areas in the rainfed regions. In this context micro-level studies may be initiated to study the contribution of watershed programs and water-saving technologies in raising the nutritional security of the poor farm-households in the rainfed areas.

Indian farmers cultivate 63 million hectares of irrigated gross cropped area and 107 million hectares unirrigated (rainfed) area. As per the agricultural census, the marginal and smallholdings have relatively better access to irrigation input. This has important implications for modernising their farm activities and the adoption of modern technology, leading to higher economic growth, equity and food security at both national and household levels. Generally, there is a higher concentration of the poor and undernourished households in the rainfed areas, which are not only fragile and risk-prone but are also low in productivity.

Livestock

Livestock is another important area which can improve the living standards of the rural poor households in India. To assess the contribution of livestock to nutritional security, the study focused on the number of dairy and draught animals in the area. To evaluate the role of dairy animals, the sample households were divided into four categories as possessing (i) no dairy animal, (ii) cow only, (iii) buffalo only, and (iv) both cow and buffalo. The results revealed that about 27% of farm households were undernourished when both cow and buffalo were possessed by them (Table 6). The corresponding number for those who did not have any dairy animal was 56%. The calorie intake was about 23% more for those possessing both cows and buffaloes (3139 kcal per caput) as compared to those having no milch animal (2552 kcal per caput). Diversity in the food basket for energy was also witnessed for those who had both cows and buffaloes in contrast to those who had no animal.

Draught animals are important for land preparation and other farm activities in India. Their availability with the farm households can substantially increase

Table 6
Impact of Livestock on Calorie Intake and Undernourishment in Different Farm-Size Groups in Rural India

Livestock for milking purpose	*Sub-marginal farms*	*Marginal farms*	*Small farms*	*Medium farms*	*Large farms*	*All farms*
Daily per caput calorie intake, kcal						
No animal	2474	2626	2811	2992	3200	2552
Cow only	2620	2764	2880	3025	3057	2738
Buffalo only	2844	3004	3239	3378	3520	3053
Both cow & buffalo	2855	2997	3182	3370	3438	3139
Others	2518	2522	2578	2935	3166	2572
Share of non-cereals in total calorie intake, %						
No animal	22	23	27	29	29	23
Cow only	25	25	28	29	32	26
Buffalo only	31	34	37	39	39	35
Cow & buffalo	31	33	36	37	37	35
Others	22	23	24	29	35	24
Undernourished population, %						
No animal	61	51	42	31	26	56
Cow only	52	41	37	32	36	45
Buffalo	40	32	24	18	16	31
Cow & buffalo	38	30	27	18	17	27
Others	56	54	50	37	30	53

Source: Computed from the 50th NSS rounds 1993-94 data on consumer household expenditure survey, New Delhi, India: Government of India.

resource-use efficiency. The sample households were classified according to their access to draught animals, viz. (i) no draught animal, (ii) one bullock, and (iii) more than one bullock. It may be cautioned that the category of 'no draught animal' under medium and large farm households may be different from that of the sub-marginal and marginal farm households (Table 7). The medium and large farm households, categorized under 'no draught animal' may possess tractors, while the sub-marginal and marginal farm households could be highly dependent only on draught animals for land preparation and other farm operations, who need special attention. Since a majority of sub-marginal or marginal farm household do not possess any draught animal, they have to depend on medium and large farm households for their farm operations. It delays their farm operations and is a major obstacle in enhancing their agricultural productivity. In this context, the custom-hire service may play a significant role in increasing agricultural production and meeting the nutritional needs of poor farm households. Besides the quantity, the nutritional balance and quality of the households possessing livestock was better than that of those without livestock. Moreover, the growth rate of total factor productivity (TFP) of the livestock sector (1.79z%, Birthal *et al.* 1999) was higher than that of the crop sector (about 1%, Dholakia and Dholakia

1993, Kumar 2001 and Kumar *et al.* 2004a). Thus, livestock should be encouraged as a major strategic option for the eradication of poverty and undernourishment and improvement of nutritional intake in rural India. Research and technology development efforts should be directed to further improving the productivity of the livestock sector by removing constraints related to genetics, health and nutrition.

Table 7
Impact of Draught Animals on Calorie Intake and Undernourishment in Different Farm-Size Groups in Rural India

Number of draught animals	*Sub-marginal farms*	*Marginal farms*	*Small farms*	*Medium farms*	*Large farms*	*All farms*
Daily per caput calories, kcal						
No animal	2588	2809	3086	3376	3579	2748
	(64)	(44)	(36)	(30)	(24)	(50)
One animal	2602	2777	3032	3417	3447	2801
	(11)	(11)	(11)	(11)	(10)	(11)
More than one animal	2652	2801	2994	3132	3272	2860
	(25)	(45)	(53)	(59)	(66)	(39)
Share of non-cereals in total calories, %						
No animal	26	30	35	38	40	29
One bullock	24	29	35	39	42	29
More than one animal	33	38	48	55	61	42
Undernourished population, %						
No animal	38	28	18	10	9	32
One animal	36	27	22	13	10	29
More than one animal	33	26	20	15	14	25

Note: Figures within the parentheses are the percentages of total farmers in the farm-size category.
Source: Computed from the 50th NSS rounds 1993-94 data on consumer household expenditure survey, New Delhi, India: Government of India.

Aquaculture

To study the implications of aquaculture on the nutritional status, the sample households were classified as: (i) crop cultivation only, (ii) crop cultivation and aquaculture, and (iii) crop cultivation and wage earnings (Table 8). The group that depended on wage earnings showed the maximum proportion (37%) of undernourished households compared to other classes. It was also noted that farm households who supplemented their income by aquaculture had diversified their food basket and had improved their average calorie intake by 10.9% (285 kcal/caput/day) as compared to wage earners and by 3.1% (88 kcal/caput/day) in comparison to households without aquaculture activity. The aquaculture activity provided additional income to the farm households and reduced the undernourished population by about 10% among marginal and small farm households. Aquaculture being a labour-intensive activity provided higher employment and income-earning opportunities to the farm households and could add fish to their food basket. Promotion of aquaculture activities can make a large contribution to the alleviation of malnutrition in the country.

Table 8
Impact of Aquaculture on Calorie Intake in Different Farm-Size Groups in Rural India

Source of income	*Sub-marginal farms*	*Marginal farms*	*Small farms*	*Medium farms*	*Large farms*	*All farms*
Daily per caput calorie intake, kcal						
Crop cultivation only	2614	2804	3034	3240	3367	2806
Crop cultivation and aquaculture	2687	2895	3101	3277	3409	2894
Crop cultivation & wage earner	2508	2673	2874	3050	3175	2609
Share of non-cereals in total calorie intake, %						
Crop cultivation only	25	28	33	35	36	28
Crop cultivation and aquaculture	28	30	34	37	37	31
Crop cultivation and wage earner	24	26	30	32	35	25
Undernourished population, %						
Crop cultivation only	36	27	20	13	12	29
Crop cultivation and aquaculture	33	24	15	13	11	25
Crop cultivation and wage earner	42	34	25	16	16	37

Source: Computed from the 50th NSS rounds 1993-94 data on consumer household expenditure survey, New Delhi, India: Government of India.

Technology and policy changes have made a significant contribution to the growth of fish production in India and the inland fisheries have emerged as one of the fastest growing sectors in the Indian economy with an annual growth rate of more than 6.5% since 1980. Aquaculture is becoming a principal source of livelihood for a large section of the economically underprivileged households of rural India. The annual growth in total factor productivity (TFP) has been much higher for the inland fisheries sector (4.1%) than the crop sector (1-2%). This has contributed towards higher availability of fish at a lower price to the consumers while producers get higher income and more nutritional security (Kumar *et al.* 2004b).

Education and research

To study the role of education in meeting nutritional security, the sample households were divided into four classes based on the level of education of the head of a household as: (i) illiterate, (ii) schooling below primary level, (iii) schooling above primary level, and (iv) technical education. Education depicted a conspicuous effect on the calorie intake. Only 13% of farm households were undernourished where the head of households had received technical education, in contrast to 33% of households where the head was illiterate (Table 9). The share of cereals in the total calorie intake was 74% for the illiterate and 64% for the technical education class. It may be due to better employment opportunities for the head of households and easy access to information about prices and new innovations in the former category. The results of this analysis clearly demonstrate the role of literacy in attacking poverty and nutritional and food insecurity in the rural India. Some recent studies (Fan, *et al.* 1999; Mittal and Kumar 2000) have shown literacy as the main influence on the adoption of technology, TFP growth and the reduction in poverty. Recognising that in India there were serious yield gaps, it is highly pertinent to maintain a desirable growth rate in TFP for food security and equity at the household and national levels. Thus, the educational policy of the country must be geared up to removing illiteracy as quickly as possible since more than 50% of farm households are still illiterate in India.

Table 9
Impact of Education on Calorie Intake and Undernourishment in Different Farm-Size Group in Rural India

Education of head	*Sub–marginal farms*	*Marginal farms*	*Small farms*	*Medium farms*	*Large farms*	*All farms*
Daily per caput calories, kcal						
Illiterate	2560	2730	2904	3145	3221	2706
Below primary	2565	2781	3015	3158	3370	2772
Above primary	2679	2875	3137	3341	3449	2900
Graduate & technical	2944	3095	3377	3402	3690	3169
Share of non-cereals in total calories, %						
Illiterate	23	26	31	33	35	26
Below primary	25	27	31	32	35	27
Above primary	27	30	33	36	37	31
Graduate & technical	33	34	38	40	41	36
Undernourished population, %						
Illiterate	40	31	25	15	14	33
Below primary	38	27	17	18	16	29
Above primary	32	24	17	10	10	24
Graduate & technical	19	15	7	6	8	13

Source: Computed from the 50th NSS rounds 1993-94 data on consumer household expenditure survey, New Delhi, India: Government of India.

In the face of shrinking natural resources and ever increasing demands for more food and higher agricultural production arising due to high population and income growths, agricultural intensification is the main course for the future growth of agriculture in India. Research for product diversification could be another important area. Besides developing technologies for promoting intensification, the country must give greater attention to the development of technologies that will facilitate agricultural diversification, particularly towards the intensive production of fruits, vegetables, flowers and other high-value crops that are expected to increase income levels. The per capita availability of arable land is quite low in India and it is declining over time. Diversification towards high-value and labour-intensive food commodities can provide adequate income and employment opportunities to small farm households. Due importance should also be accorded to the quality and nutritional aspects of these commodities. Post-harvest losses range from 5% to 10% for non-perishables and about 30% for perishables in the country. These losses could be and must be minimized. Let us remember, 'a grain saved is a grain produced'. High attention should be focused on developing post-harvest processing and value-addition technologies not only to reduce heavy post-harvest losses but also to improve the quality of food commodities through proper storage, packaging, handling and transport. The agro-processing facilities should be located close to the points of production to generate off-farm employment opportunities in the rural areas.

Table 10
Calorie Intake and Undernourishment in Different Farm-Size Groups by Societal Structure in Rural India

Societal Structure	*Sub-marginal farms*	*Marginal farms*	*Small farms*	*Medium farms*	*Large farms*	*All farms*
Daily per caput calorie intake, kcal						
Schedule tribes	2402	2517	2596	2824	2825	2494
	(17)	(20)	(13)	(10)	(9)	(16)
Schedule castes	2552	2741	2811	3210	3361	2639
	(19)	(10)	(7)	(5)	(2)	(13)
Others	2674	2893	3122	3291	3418	2898
	(64)	(70)	(80)	(85)	(89)	(71)
Share of non-cereals in total calorie intake, %						
Schedule tribes	20	21	22	24	25	21
Schedule castes	23	25	28	30	33	24
Others	27	30	34	36	37	31
Undernourished population, %						
Schedule tribes	65	56	52	37	44	59
Schedule castes	56	44	40	28	35	51
Others	49	36	28	21	19	38

Note: Figures within the parentheses are the percentages of total population in the farm-size group.

Source: Computed from the 50th NSS rounds 1993-94 data on consumer household expenditure survey, New Delhi, India: Government of India.

Societal structure

In the Indian Constitution, certain castes have been identified as 'Scheduled Castes' and certain castes as 'Scheduled Tribes' and so on. The level of poverty, educational status, social status varies substantially across different castes. The societal structure, including castes and religions, was found to be critical in determining the income status and nutrition level of farm households. The analysis revealed that scheduled tribes (see Table 10) were least able to meet their nutritional needs. The undernourished people were recorded as maximum in the tribal households (59%), followed by scheduled castes (51%), and other castes (38%.). The share of cereals in total calorie intake was at a maximum for scheduled tribes (80%), followed by scheduled castes (76%) and other castes (67%). This indicates that the consumption of non-cereals was more by the 'other castes' category than by scheduled tribes and scheduled castes. Among different religious groups, undernourishment was least in the Sikhs (7%), followed by the Muslims (32%), and Hindus (28%). The Sikhs also topped in consuming the most diversified calorie sources (Table 11). The results of this analysis suggest that the welfare schemes should be focused more in the tribal areas of the country.

Table 11

Calorie Intake and Undernourishment by Religions in Rural India

Religion	*Sub–marginal farms*	*Marginal farms*	*Small farms*	*Medium farms*	*Large farms*	*All farms*
Daily per caput calorie intake, kcal						
Hinduism	2624	2815	3028	3224	3355	2813
Islam	2535	2800	3081	3207	3223	2707
Christianity	2469	2541	2668	2729	2082	2508
Sikhism	3097	3261	3501	3713	3876	3472
Share of non-cereals in total calories, %						
Hinduism	25	28	32	34	35	28
Islam	24	26	32	31	35	26
Christianity	24	22	26	24	23	23
Sikhism	48	50	52	53	53	51
Undernourished population, %						
Hinduism	36	27	20	13	12	28
Islam	41	25	13	13	24	32
Christianity	45	36	25	27	NA	41
Sikhism	17	10	5	3	2	7

Source: Computed from the 50th NSS rounds 1993-94 data on consumer household expenditure survey, New Delhi, India: Government of India.

Identifying the Target Population

In the context of equity dimensions and social welfare, it is quite important to identify the target population and prioritize target domains for improving the nutritional status of farm households in rural India. The sample households were divided into four classes based on the incidence of undernourishment in each farm-size class. The results revealed that 59% of the total undernourished households belonged to the sub-marginal and 28% to the marginal farm household categories (Table 12). Of all the undernourished sub-marginal farm households, more than three-quarters were highly undernourished and about 74% of marginal farm households were moderately undernourished. The incidence of undernourishment among small, medium and large farm households was negligible. Therefore, under the limited resource scenario in India, the target population to meet the challenge of undernourishment should be sub-marginal farm households in the first instance, and the marginal farm households subsequently. This can be done through the diversification of agriculture and by the targeting of welfare activities for sub-marginal and marginal farm households. Identification of need-based productive programs is highly critical and could be explored through characterization of the production environment in the country. Addressing the nutritional needs of this group means targeting about 87% of the undernourished farm households in the rural areas of India. Similarly, the target regions for the sub-marginal farm households in each state of India have been prioritized based on the presence of poor households in the region (Table 13). It is highly desirable to develop demand-driven and location-specific programs to meet the nutritional and food security of the most vulnerable households in the rural areas.

Table 12
Distribution of Undernourished Population in Rural India

Incidence of undernourished population	*Sub-marginal farms*	*Marginal farms*	*Small farms*	*Medium farms*	*Large farms*	*All farms*
Low	0.2	1.3	0.6	2.3	1.3	5.6
Moderate	4.5	20.6	6.9	0.4	0.2	32.5
High	45.1	2.9	0.7	0.2	0.1	48.9
Severe	9.1	3.2	0.6	0.2	0.1	13.1
Total	58.8	27.9	8.7	3.0	1.6	100

Source: Computed from the 50th NSS rounds 1993-94 data on household expenditure survey, New Delhi, India: Government of India.

Conclusions

The nutritional status of the rural farm households has been studied and about 26% of them have been found to be undernourished. Small farm households with less than one hectare of land constitute more than half of the number of undernourished and poor households in India. Education, skill development, livestock, aquaculture, irrigation, diversification and institutional policy support have been identified as the major factors having tremendous impact on reduction of undernourishment, malnourishment and food insecurity. Efficient resource management and science and technology-led productivity growth have been suggested for rationally and effectively addressing the interrelated and complex problems of small landholders. The development of livestock and aquaculture should be accorded high priority with multiple objectives of diversifying agriculture, raising income levels and meeting the nutritional security of the undernourished farm households. The study has suggested targeting the small-holders in the first instance for uplifting the nutritional status, which would cover a large proportion of the population of the country. Similarly, tribal areas and northeastern parts of India have been identified that need priority attention for providing nutrition and food security.

Table 13
Priority Allocation to States and Zones of India for Planning Undernourishment Removal in Sub-Marginal Farm Households in Rural India

States	*Zones*
Andaman & Nicobar	Andaman & Nicobar (38)
Andhra Pradesh	Inland Northern (51), Inland Southern (45),Coastal (47), South-western (39)
Arunachal Pradesh	Arunachal Pradesh (46)
Assam	Hills (63), Plains Eastern (50), Plains Western (51)
Bihar	Southern (47), Northern (30)
Dadra & Nagar Haveli	Dadra & Nagar Haveli (84)
Daman & Diu	Daman & Diu (67)
Goa	Goa North (66)
Gujarat	Eastern (62), Plains Southern (56), Saurashtra (45), Plains Northern (42), Dry areas (34),
Karnataka	Coastal Ghats (52), Inland (49), Inland Southern (47)
Kerala	Northern(57), Southern (34)
Madhya Pradesh	South-Western (60), Central (63), South (49), Malwa (46), Vindhya (36), Chhattisgarh (40)
Maharashtra	Inland Northern (69), Inland Central (65), Coastal (50), Inland Eastern (52), Inland Western (46), Eastern (35)
Mizoram	Mizoram (42)
Orissa	Southern (51), Northern (32)
Sikkim	Sikkim (58)
Tamil Nadu	Coastal North (67), Southern (56), Inland (58), Coastal (43)
Tripura	Tripura (45)
Uttar Pradesh	Eastern (32)
West Bengal	Himalayan (45)

Note: Figures within the parentheses are undernourished population in percentages to the total population in each zone.

Source: Computed from the 50th NSS rounds 1993-94 data on consumer household expenditure survey, New Delhi, India: Government of India.

REFERENCES

Birthal, P. S., A. Kumar, A. Ravishankar and U.K. Pandey (1999), *Sources of Growth in the Livestock Sector.* Policy Paper No. 9. New Delhi, India: National Centre for Agricultural Economics and Policy Research (ICAR).

Dholakia, R.H. and B.H. Dholakia (1993), Growth of Total Factor Productivity in Indian Agriculture. *Indian Economic Review,* 28 (1): 25-40.

Fan, S., P.B.R. Hazell and S. Thorat (1999), *Linkages between Government Spending, Growth, and Poverty in Rural India.* Research Report No 110. Washington, D.C., USA: International Food Policy Research Institute

IFPRI (1995), *A 2020 Vision for Food, Agriculture, and the Environment.* Washington, D.C.: USA: International Food Policy Research Institute.

NSSO (1996), *Nutritional Intake in India: Five Quinquennial Survey on Consumer Expenditure.* Government of India, Report No. 405. New Delhi, India:National Sample Survey Organization.

Kumar, P. (2001), Agricultural Performance and Productivity. In: *Indian Agricultural Policy atthe Crossroads,* edited by S.S. Acharya and D.P. Chaudhri. Jaipur India: Rawat Publications. pp. 353-476.

Kumar, P., A. Kumar and S. Mittal (2004a), Total Factor Productivity of Crop Sector in the Indo-Gangetic Plain of India: Sustainability issues revisited. *Indian Economic Review,* 39 (1): 169-201.

Kumar, P., A. Kumar and C.P. Shiji (2004b), Total Factor Productivity and Socio-economic Impact of Fisheries Technology in India. *Agricultural Economics Research Review.* 17 (Conference No.): 131-144.

Mittal, S. and P. Kumar (2000), Literacy, Technology Adoption, Factor Demand and Productivity: An Econometric Analysis. *Indian Journal of Agricultural Economics,* 55 (3): 490-499.

Sukhatme, P.V. (1977), Incidence of undernutrition. *Indian Journal of Agricultural Economics,* 32 (3): 1-7.

21

CHANGING STRUCTURE AND ORGANISATION OF AGRICULTURE AND DIFFICULTIES FACING SMALL FARMERS IN INDIA

Sukhpal Singh

Introduction

Agriculture in India still engages about 58% of the work force and contributes about a quarter of its GDP. A very large majority of the farmers/cultivators belong to the category of small and marginal holders. The number and proportion of such holdings have been growing over time. They constituted 68.15% of the total operational holdings in 1971-72 but their proportion increased to 80.59% in 1991-92. The area cultivated by them grew from 24.01% of the total in 1971-72 to 34.3% in 1991-92 (Singh, 2005). The share of marginal and small holdings increased to 61.6% and 18.7% respectively by 1995-96, altogether accounting for 80.3% of all holdings. On the other hand, the number of farms in the largest category declined and the average size of the largest category has fallen. Further, large holdings (>4 ha) were estimated to decline to only 7% by 2000-2001 and are predicted 5% by 2010-2011 and account for only 36% and 28% of the area respectively (Jha, 2001). Given this general picture, it is not surprising that the average size of operational holding has been declining since the 1960s when it was only 1.37 hectares and average size of ownership holding only 1.14 hectares in 1992. Small farmers (with holdings of <2 ha) accounted for 83.9% of all operational holdings by 2003 (Singh, 2005) Also, small farmers (including landless) had higher livestock ownership (60-80% of all the livestock population) including cross-bred cattle whereas 12-20% small farm and landless households owned these animals compared with only 8-15% in case of larger farm households (Jha, 2001).

Small farms produce 41% of India's total grain (49% of rice, 40% of wheat, 29% of coarse cereals and 27% of pulses), and over half of total fruits and vegetables despite being in rain fed areas, resource constrained, and assuming that they are only as productive as large farms (Singh, et al, 2002; Muller and Patel, 2004). Their contribution to incremental wheat and rice production during

1971-91 was even higher (62% and 48% respectively). The marginal holdings also had higher cropping intensity (143) compared with that of the small, medium and large farmers (129.9, 119.6, and 111.6 respectively) in the mid-1980s and higher irrigated area as percentage of net sown area with more of it being irrigated by tubewells and canals (1/3rd each) and even that with tanks being quite important (8-11%) (Agrawal, 2000; Singh, et al, 2002).

Dairying accounts for more than 50% of the household income of the landless and 30% of that of the marginal and small landholders. In fact, at the lower end of marginal and small farmer category are those who are 'near landless' i.e. they owned land between 0.002 and 0.200 ha only and accounted for more than 31% of rural households in 1991-92. These are households besides the landless (owning <0.002 ha) who accounted for 11.3% of the total rural households. The 'near landless' category has shown a steady increase since the late 1960s. Thus, more than 42% of the rural households were landless or near landless (Rao and Hanumappa, 1999).

This discussion paper examines the nature, problems and potential of contract farming (CF) in India from the perspective of small and marginal farmers, under commercialized and globalised agriculture. It profiles the difficulties of dealing with commercial and diversified farming by small farmers, and the concept and rationale for contract farming and its practice in India so far is examined. Section 6 focuses on important policy, legal, and institutional mechanisms for promotion of CF in India and for facilitating small farmer participation in CF in India. The paper concludes by emphasizing that CF is context specific and only a means of agricultural development, not an end in itself.

Profile and Problems of Small Farmers

The average size of the operational marginal holdings was only 0.35 hectares and those of the small holdings 1.41 hectares in 1992 compared with 2.69 and 5.79 hectares respectively of the semi- medium and medium-category holdings and 15.41 hectares in the case of large category holdings. The ownership holding averages for these categories were even smaller with the exception only of large category holdings which was slightly larger (Singh, 2005). In the case of rural labour households which are landless or near landless, the average size of holding varied from 0.04 hectares in Punjab to 0.74 hectares in Rajasthan in 1993-94 (ETKS, 2003). Further, small farms are highly fragmented. Land transactions lead to further fragmentation making them non-viable in terms of resource use as well as family sustenance (Mani and Pandey, 1995). A study of a Tamil Nadu village found that of all the farmers in the village, small farmers (60% of all) who owned less than three hectares of land each, 35% had 3-5 plots and 25% had 5-10 plots and the remaining less than three plots. On the other hand, of all the farmers in the village, only 20% farmers had more than 5 plots, another 40% had 3-5 plots each and remaining less than three plots each. Thus, small farms were more fragmented. (Parikh and Nagarajan, 2004). On the other hand, in Punjab, where the average size of the operational holding was 37 and 22 acres respectively for contract and non-contract growers, compared with the state average size of operational holding of the order of about 9 acres, each holding had, on an average, 4.45 plots in case of contract growers and 2.67 plots in case of non-contract growers. The number of plots ranged from 1.36 for small farmers to 5.15 for larger farmers in CF households and 1.46 and 5.13 respectively in case of non-CF households. The larger number of plots per holding was also partly due to leased in land due to the practice of reverse tenancy in the state, especially by the contract growers (Kumar, 2005).

In India, the cropping pattern on small farms is dominated by food grains (75%) compared with that on the large farms (67%) and on medium farms (72%). But, the small farms devote more area for fruit and vegetable production (3.7%) compared to only 1.7% by large farmers and 2.4% by medium farmers, as these crops are more labour intensive (Jha, 2001). Even diversification option in terms of change of crop sequence was exercised more by small holders than that by large holders both in irrigated and non-irrigated areas (Singh, *et al,* 2002). Also, relatively more of the marginal and small holdings were irrigated than those of the medium or large holdings, and they used higher amount of inputs like fertilizers and farm yard manure (Singh, et al, 2002; ETKS, 2003), human labour, bullock power (Reddy, 1993; Sharma 2000), pump sets, and tractor power though the last two were not owned (Sharma and Sharma, 2000; Singh et al, 2002).

The extent of interlocking of markets was more prevalent in case of marginal and small farmers and more so in irrigated areas as irrigated agriculture has higher needs of modern inputs (Swain, 2000). The input market constraints include lack of information about markets, lack of business and negotiating experience and lack of a collective organization which deprive small farmers from interacting on equal terms with the other market participants or market intermediaries. On the other hand, prices they receive are lower than those obtained by larger farmers due to their weak bargaining power and holding capacity (Agrawal, 2000). Major problems of small and marginal farmers in India include spurious input supply, inadequate and costly institutional credit, lack of irrigation water and costly access to it, lack of extension services for commercial crops, exploitation in the marketing of their produce, high health expenditures, and lack of alternative (non-farm) sources of income. The small and marginal farmers account for the bulk (more than half) of the rural poor and the under nourished (Vyas, 1996; Agrawal, 2000; Singh, *et al.* 2002; Muller and Patel, 2004). The employment which is the only way to raise these farmers' incomes, is low on these fields because of the low employment elasticity of output due to increasing mechanisation and the kind of crops being grown (Muller and Patel, 2004).

In Punjab, a green revolution region, a small farmer's average land holding is 0.9 hectares. In this state, there is a crisis of sustainability (economic and environmental) of farming since the late 1980s due to higher costs of cultivation. Tractors were being underutilized on a much larger scale in small farms (77%) as against only by 50% and 32% in medium and large farms respectively with the overall idle tractor power being 43% for the region (Bathinda district). This indicates overcapitalisation of small farms in the state which has led to higher costs of cultivation due to fixed cost component. Even electric motors and diesel pumps which number more than 11 lakh in the state (GoP, 2005), were being grossly underutilized on small farms (16% and 84% respectively) as against overuse of the electric motors to the extent of 11% on both medium and large farms and underutilization of diesel pumps to the extent of 67% and 38% respectively (Singh and Sharma, 2004). Also, the machinery costs accounted for as much as 23% of all operating costs in 1991-92 and were no different from those on large farms (Jha, 2001). In Punjab, the benefits of input subsidies are also skewed towards larger farmers. Small and marginal farmers constitute 36% of the farmers in the state and cultivate 9% of the land, but they receive only 6% of the power subsidy, 7% of the fertilizer subsidy, and 5% of the canal water subsidy. Politically, continuation of these subsidies is often justified on the inability of small and marginal farmers to pay higher user charges, but it is really the larger farmers who are obtaining most of the subsidy benefits (World Bank, 2003).

However, small farmers are certainly going to stay for long time in India though they are going to face a number of challenges. Therefore, what happens to small and marginal farmers has implications for the entire economy and people's livelihoods. But, they can adequately respond to these challenges only if there is right policy environment. Otherwise, they will only be losers in the process of globalization and liberalization. It is here that we need to examine the relevance of CF for small farmers in the context of commercialization and globalisation of Indian agriculture.

Commercial Agriculture, Diversification and Small Farmers

Commercial farming means risks, additional to the natural phenomena which are intrinsic risks of farming everywhere: the risk of output prices that fluctuate, of input prices that may not be commensurate with increased output, of increased vulnerability to pests and so forth (Payer, 1980). A sudden drop in international prices can drive already poor and indebted farmers off the land over the short term. So, small farmers not only lose in terms of lower price realization but also pay higher prices for inputs due to opening up of the domestic economies, in the presence of declining public investment in agriculture and high interest private sector credit (Muller and Patel, 2004). Instead of an access to lucrative markets, they end up without proper mechanisms, losing their domestic markets to imported goods. Thus, the cost of adjustment, due to globalisation and trade liberalization, to poor people becomes substantial when markets do not work very well. Market failure can happen for many reasons like lack of basic information, dominance of the markets by a few key players, weak economic governance or poor enforcement of the law. Thus, declining viability of small farms in such situations leads small farmers to sell or lease out land to larger farmers (Payer, 1980) which is known as 'reverse tenancy' in India. CF practice has increased the incidence of reverse tenancy in India recently (Singh, 2002). The leased in area in Punjab was 19% and in Haryana, as high as 34% of the total area cultivated in 1992. In India as a whole, marginal and small farmers leased in only 35% of the total leased in area, the rest being with large farmers (43%) and medium farmers (22%). Though reverse tenancy seems to be win-win situation for both the small farmers leasing out and the large farmers leasing in as they maximize their incomes, but in agriculturally backward areas, this practice may alienate the marginal and small farmers from land altogether without alternative sources of employment (Haque, 2000). In fact, due to reverse tenancy, the number of operational holdings in Punjab declined from 13.75 lakhs in 1970-71 to 10.88 lakh in 1985-86 and were 10.93 lakh in 1995-96 (GoP, 2005). This decline in number of holdings came largely from the category of small land marginal holdings which declined by over two lakh between 1990-91 and 2000-01 and accounted for only 29.66% of the total in 2000-01 compared with 44.74 in 1990-91 (Gill, 2005).

There is plenty of distress among farmers both in agriculturally strong as well as backward regions manifested in farmer suicides. A large number of suicide cases are reported from marginal and small category of farmers. Most of the suicide cases have been reported from Andhra Pradesh, Karnataka, Maharashtra, Haryana and Punjab (Shiva *et al.* 2000; Iyer and Manick, 2000; Mohanty, 2001; Deshpande, 2002; Ahlawat, 2002). The areas which have achieved a greater level of modernisation and commercialisation of agriculture have also witnessed suicides by farmers and agricultural labourers (Gill, 2004). In the absence of any support, the coping costs of commercial modern farming are too high for marginal and small farmers. For example, motor burnout costs for marginal farmers were 10% of their gross farm income in Haryana and 7.7% in Andhra Pradesh This figure for large farmers was only 1.6% and 2.3% in the two states respectively (World Bank, 2004). Further, since marginal farm households are net buyers of food, the increasing and fluctuating prices can hit them hard (Singh, *et al.* 2002).

The viability of the small holdings is an important issue and promoting agricultural diversification towards high value crops is argued to be one of the means through which this can be achieved (Vyas, 1996; Sen and Raju, 2005). Also, the seasonality of employment that is induced by specialization could, to a large extent, be mitigated by introducing a larger number of crops in the cropping pattern that would offer fuller employment to agricultural labour round the year (Sen and Raju, 2005). Small farmers in irrigated areas tend to specialize in few crops which is more of a forced specialization and the larger farmers in dry regions (water scarce regions) are found to be more diversified in their crop and livestock patterns. Thus, there is a positive relationship between farm size and crop or livestock diversification but negative relationship so far as employment and income diversification are concerned (Saleth, 1997).

Crop diversification can be viewed as a strategy for profit maximisation or risk minimization. The profitability would depend on yield, price and cost of cultivation (Sen and Raju, 2005). Farmers adopt or do not adopt a technology/ crop depending on the economic sense it makes and other risks and environmental factors associated with it, besides awareness and persuasion which do help. But, farmers do not easily switch from field crops to horticultural or other high value crops as these are much more labour and other input intensive and require more post-harvest handling. Further, profitability is much more dependent on meeting market requirements of freshness and quality. Thus, while farmers can expect to earn more from these crops, they are required to work harder, learn new skills, and risk more capital (Benziger, 1996). Therefore, to adopt a new crop or technology, farmers need more than just the technology. Diversification towards high value crops would involve a higher level of investment per unit area, both direct and indirect. The former is in terms of higher cost of production, and the latter due to infrastructural and institutional changes required for producing and marketing many of these products that are mostly perishable or semi-perishable. Many of the high value products such as fruits, vegetables and flowers are characterized by highly volatile and speculative pricing structure due to the 'small volume' of trade. Diversification and risk are, thus, closely linked as diversification exposes producers to the greater volatility of both domestic and world prices. Risk aversion has been identified as a significant impediment to what would otherwise seem to be a rational diversification on the basis of average profitability of alternative crops which is affected by attitudes of the farmer and the nature of technology (Sen and Raju, 2005).

However, concerns have been raised about certain in-built constraints the marginal and small farmers are faced with, in particular while diversifying towards high value profitable crops. The primary constraints to successful diversification by small farmers include non-availability of sufficient and timely irrigation, relatively higher costs of cultivation, lack of capital and credit availability, lack of knowledge about markets, lack of access to new technologies, relatively shorter shelf life of produce, price fluctuations, pests and disease proneness of improved varieties of these commodities (fruits and vegetables) and high risk (Pingali and Khwaja, 2004; Sen and Raju, 2005). However, the nature of the product/crop in favour of which diversification is taking place would to a large extent influence the motivation for diversification for small farmers. Diversification by its very nature favours large farmers (Pingali and Khwaja, 2004). Even those small farmers who can be encouraged to go for the crop switch cannot be immune from the problem of 'double exploitation; where they receive lower prices for their horticultural output but pay higher prices for food grains obtained from the open market. In fact, it is this phenomenon emerging from the existing system of agricultural marketing that explains why small farmers do not have the incentive to switch that easily to non-food crops (Sen and Raju, 2005). A study of cut flowers for Delhi market by growers in an U.P. village revealed that the net returns from flower cultivation were many times higher than those from traditional crops of sugarcane or wheat. Further, flower cultivation was dominated by large farmers, and small farmers did not take to flower cultivation as readily. Not only that, the small farmers were relatively late entrants to this crop and it seemed they could not stay in it for long due to high risk and cost of cultivation involved (Sen and Raju, 2005).

CF and Small Farmers

Among the various institutional mechanisms available for agricultural development, so far India has mainly relied on the state and public sector-led growth and development of the farm sector with micro-level operations i.e. farming per se (with or without control) being with the individual farmers. But, since most of the operators have been small and marginal farmers, the growth in farm sector was mainly determined by the role of the state–both in capital financing as well as in regulation of the activities in terms of the incentive structure created. With the liberalisation of the farm sector policy, the other two modes, of private industrial capital directly entering into the farm sector with large resources (corporate farming) which is still not legalized (for details of debate on the issue, see Singh, 1998), and the industrial capital aligning with the farming interests to bring about improvement in productivity and value addition (CF), are evolving in almost all parts of the country, especially CF, in more developed regions. In fact, CF has been seen as an institutional innovation for agricultural development in the developing world since the 1980s (Glover, 1987).

CF can be defined as a system for the production and supply of agricultural and horticultural produce by farmers/primary producers under advance contracts, the essence of such arrangements being a commitment to provide an agricultural commodity of a type, at a specified time, price, and in specified quantity to a known buyer. In fact, CF can be described as a halfway house between independent farm production and corporate/captive farming and can be a case of a step towards complete vertical integration or disintegration depending on the given context. Due to the efficiency (co-ordination and quality control in a vertical system) and equity (smallholder inclusion) benefits of this hybrid system, it has been promoted aggressively in the developing world by various agencies (Glover, 1987). It basically involves four things—pre-agreed price, quality, quantity or acreage (minimum/maximum) and time (Singh, 2002).

CF is known by different variants like the centralised model which is company-farmer arrangement, outgrower scheme which is run by government/public sector/joint venture, nucleus-outgrower scheme involving both captive farming and CF by the contracting agency, multi-partite arrangement involving many types of agencies, intermediary model where middlemen are involved between the company and the farmer, and satellite farming referring to any of the above models (Eaton and Shepherd, 2001; GoI, 2003). In fact, CF varies depending on the nature and type of contracting agency, technology, nature of crop/produce, and the local and national context.

The contracts can be of three types: (i) procurement contracts under which only sale and purchase conditions are specified; (ii) partial contracts wherein only some of the inputs are supplied by the contracting firm and produce is bought at pre-agreed prices; and (iii) total contracts under which the contracting firm supplies and manages all the inputs on the farm and the farmer becomes just a supplier of land and labour. The relevance and importance of each type varies from product to product and over time and these types are not mutually exclusive (Hill and Ingersent, 1987; Key and Runsten, 1999). Whereas the first type is generally referred to as marketing contracts, the other two are types of production contracts (Scott, 1984; Welsh, 1997). But, there is a systematic link between product and factor markets under the contract arrangement as contracts require definite quality of produce and, therefore, specific inputs (Scott, 1984; Little, 1994). Also, different types of production contracts allocate production and market risks between the producer and the processor in different ways. The price of the contracted produce can be growers' fixed price, residual (profit/loss) sharing by sponsor and grower, open market-based price, spot market price, consignment based, two part split price, tournament price (fixed plus variable based on relative performance), base price plus quality based incentive price, or administered price.

For different reasons, both farmers and farm product processors/distributors may prefer contracts to complete vertical integration. A farmer may prefer a contract which can be terminated at reasonably short notice. Also, contracting gives access to additional sources of capital, and a more certain price by shifting part of the risk of adverse price movement to the buyer (Hill and Ingersent, 1987). Farmers also get access to new technology and inputs, including credit, through contracts which otherwise may be outside their reach (Glover, 1987; Eaton and Shepherd, 2001). For a processor or distributor, contracts are more flexible in the face of market uncertainty, make smaller demands on scarce capital resources, and impose less of an additional burden of labour relations, ownership of land, and production activities, on management (Buch-Hansen and Marcussen, 1982; Kirk, 1987). The firm even gets access to unpaid family labour (White, 1997) and can make use of state funds indirectly through agricultural production sector which are directed at farmers by development agencies (Clapp, 1988). Also, food processors can minimise their overhead costs per unit of production by operating their plants at or near fully capacity as contracting gives assured and stable raw material supplies from farms. The firm can also project an image of working with local producers as a partner when it undertakes CF and may even obtain statal and international agency incentives for its activities as developmental projects, instead of corporate farming (Kirk, 1987). Contracts also help improve product quality by directly introducing incentives and penalties as there are problems of adverse selection and moral hazard in any contractual arrangement resulting in underinvestment or shirking by any of the parties (Wolf *et al.* 2001).

At more macro-economic level, contracting can help to remove market imperfections in produce, capital (credit), land, labor, information and insurance markets; facilitate better co-ordination of local production activities which often involve initial investment in processing, extension etc.; and can help in reducing transaction costs (Grosh, 1994; Key and Runsten, 1999). It has also been used in many situations as a policy step by the state to bring about crop diversification for improving farm incomes and employment (Benziger 1996; Singh, 2000). CF is also seen as a way to reduce costs of cultivation as it can provide access to better inputs and more efficient production methods. The increasing cost of cultivation was the reason for the emergence of CF in Japan and Spain in the 1950s (Asano-Tamanoi, 1988) and in the Indian Punjab in the early 1990s (Singh, 2000).

From an institutional economics perspective, the logic for CF could also come from the creation of positive externalities like employment, market development or infrastructure, if agribusiness firms create them better than the open market or the state (Key and Runsten, 1999). In other words, can CF help people other than those who have direct stakes and pay for it? CF figures as an institutional arrangement for agricultural development in the fields of inputs, product exchange, and product upgrading, the last referring to research and innovations (Christensen, 1992).

Some others recommend CF as the only way to make small-scale farming competitive as the services provided by contracting agencies can not be provided by any other agencies (Eaton and Shepherd, 2001). Contract faming also lowers transaction costs for the farmers as many of the transactions are internalised by the procuring firm (IFPRI, 2005). CF is also an alternative to corporate farming which may be costly, risky, and difficult to manage and still not viable (Payer, 1980). Furthermore, in India, supermarket chain growth including FDI in retail, international trade and quality issues like SPS, organic trade, fair trade, and ethical trade, promotion by the central and state agencies, banking and input industry push for CF, farming crisis and reverse tenancy, and failure of traditional cooperatives, will help spread of CF across crops and regions as they provide new space to this arrangement in the context of withdrawal of state from agricultural space. Even new International Property Rights (IPR) regime which encourages protection and exploitation of proprietary genetics is likely to accelerate contract farming practice (Wolf *et al.* 2001).

But, generally, contracting agencies especially private, tend to prefer large farmers for CF because of their capacity to produce better quality crops due to the efficient and business-oriented farming methods, large volumes of produce which reduces the cost of collection for the firm, their capacity to bear risk in case of crop failure, and various services provided by these large producers like transport, storage, etc. (Wilson, 1986; Winson, 1990; Burch and Pritchard, 1996; Fulton and Clark, 1996; Key and Runsten, 1999). On the other hand, small farmers are picked up by firms for contracts only when the area is dominated by them, there is government directive to do so or they are found to be low cost producers in certain areas and crops (CDC, 1989). Further, firms may work with small farmers to make use of the state support (financial and technical) to these producers under various development programmes (Glover and Kusterer, 1990) and to benefit from lower cost production on these farms as these farmers have access to cheaper family labour, and being residual claimants of their labour, work more conscientiously than hired labour (Key and Runsten, 1999). In fact, some of them even use large growers, rural elite, and local small processors as sub-contractors to procure from the small growers for the company (Kirk, 1987). The seed companies in India use small companies as subcontractors to procure seeds produced under contracts (Shiva and Crompton, 1998). In Canada, small tomato growers were preferred as the crop required hand-picking which only small farmers do as the large ones do mechanical harvesting, especially when weather limits the use of mechanical harvesters (Winson, 1990). Similarly, in India, gherkin CF is carried out by small and marginal farmers as the crop requires plenty of labour inputs which these farming families can provide from within (Dev and Rao, 2004). Also, working with many small farmers in the case of small processors gives the required flexibility in procurement schedule helping to extend the processing season and use the equipment efficiently; and helps spread risk of supply failure as compared to working with a few large farmers.

Status and Experience of CF in India

CF has various models/variants being practiced in India at present (Figures 1, 2, 3, 4, 5, 6 and 7). There have been some studies of the CF system in India more recently. But, most of them look at the economics of the CF system in specific crops, compared with that of the non-contract situation and/or competing traditional crops of a given region, e.g. in gherkins (hybrid cucumber) in Tamil Nadu (Chidambaram, 1997) and Andhra Pradesh (Haque, 2000; Dev and Rao, 2004) tomato in Punjab (Bhalla and Singh, 1996; Haque, 2000; Rangi and Sidhu, 2000) and Haryana (Dileep et. al., 2002) and cotton in Tamil Nadu (Agarwal *et al.* 2005). It is found that contract production gave much higher (almost three times) gross returns compared with that from the traditional crops of wheat, paddy and potato in case of tomato (Bhalla and Singh, 1996; Rangi and Sidhu, 2000), tomato and onion in the case of gherkin (Chidambaram, 1997) and cotton (Agarwal *et al.* 2005) due to higher yield and assured price under contracts. The studies of tomato contract production in Punjab and Haryana (Haque, 2000; Dileep *et al.* 2002), of cucumber in Andhra Pradesh (Haque, 2000) and cotton in Tamil Nadu (Agarwal

Figure 1
Bi-partite CF model

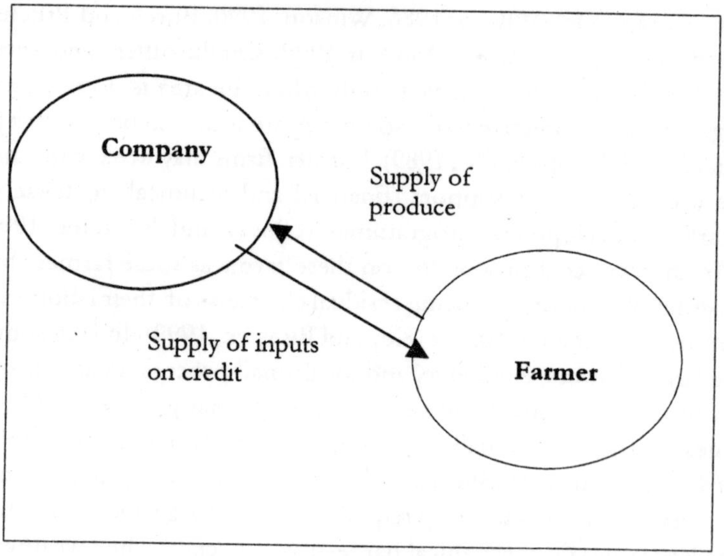

Figure 2
Tri-partite CF model

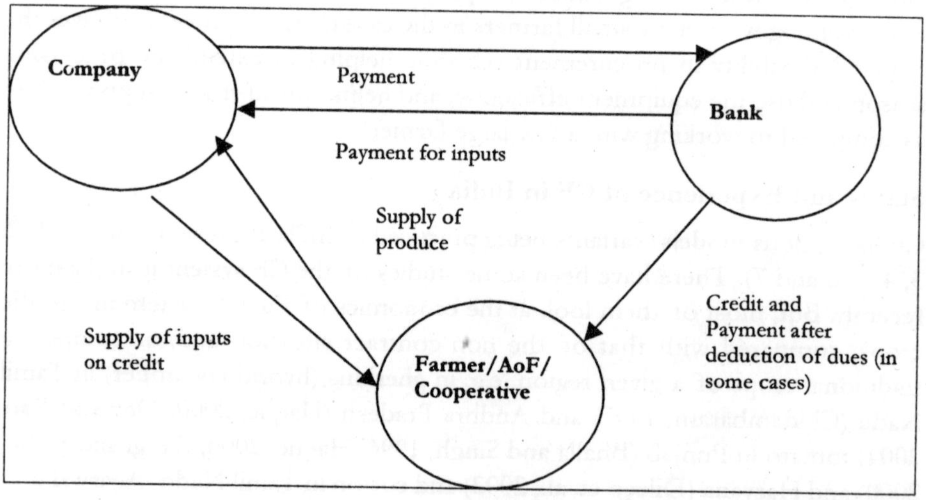

et al. 2005) also found the net returns from these crops under contracts being much higher than those under non-contract situations though production cost in tomato was higher under the contract system (Dileep *et al.* 2002). A more recent study across crops, companies and locations in Punjab also confirms this (Kumar, 2005). In case of cotton in Tamil Nadu, the contract growers had lower input cost, lower interest loans, faster payment for produce, and the crop insurance facility (Agarwal *et al.* 2005). The studies in the states of Punjab and Haryana also reveal that contract growers faced many problems like undue quality cut on produce by firms, delayed deliveries at the factory, delayed payments, low price and pest attack on the crop (Bhalla and Singh, 1996; Singh, 2002; Rangi and Sidhu, 2000;

Figure 3
State-led Contract Farming System in Punjab (Original Model)

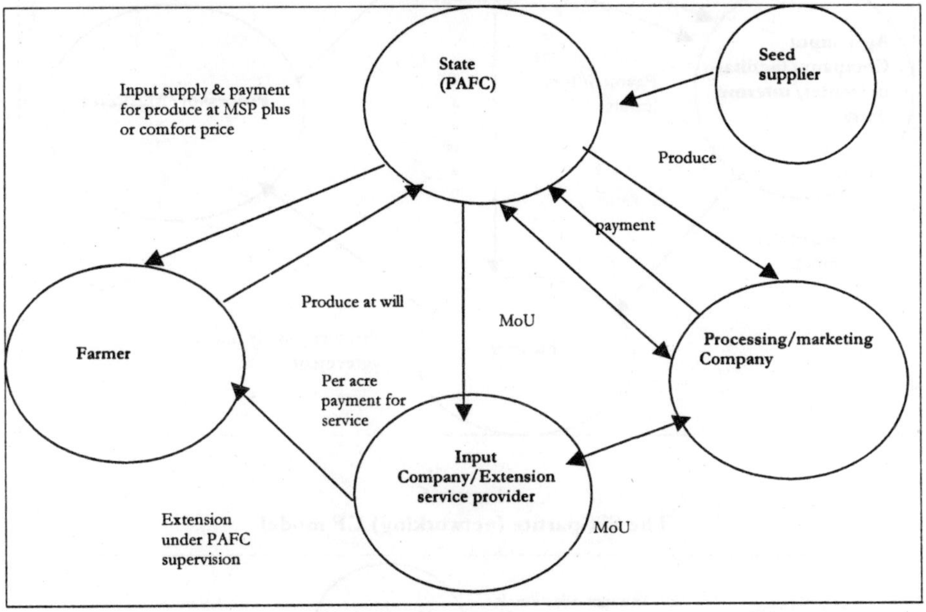

Figure 4
State-led Contract Farming System in Punjab (Revised Model)

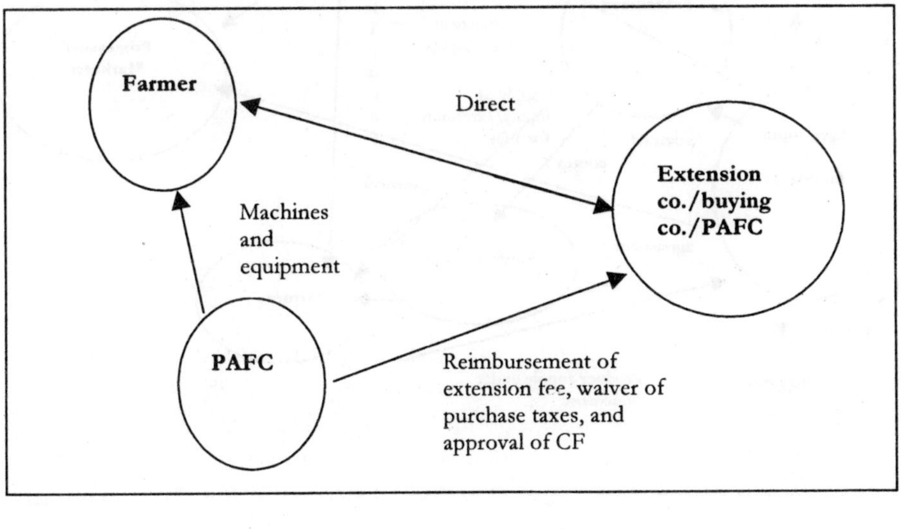

Figure 5
The Quad-partite CF model

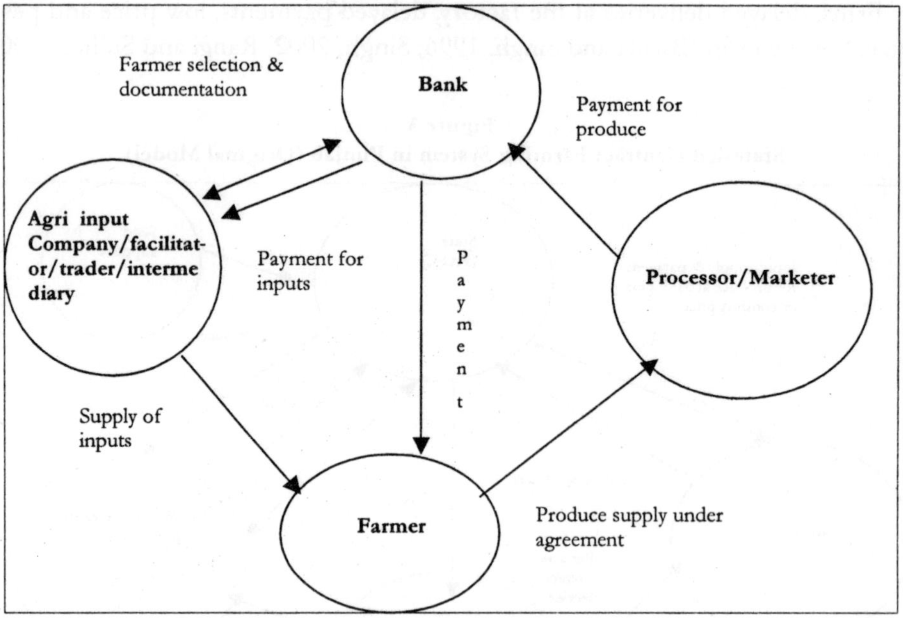

Figure 6
The Six-partite (networking) CF model

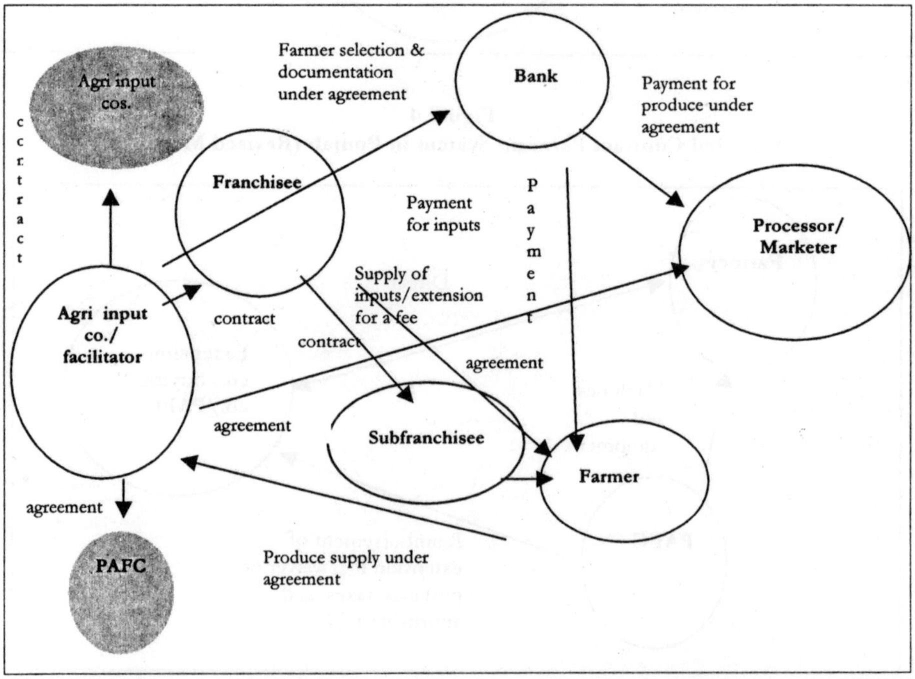

Figure 7
Tri-partite (Intermediary) model of contract

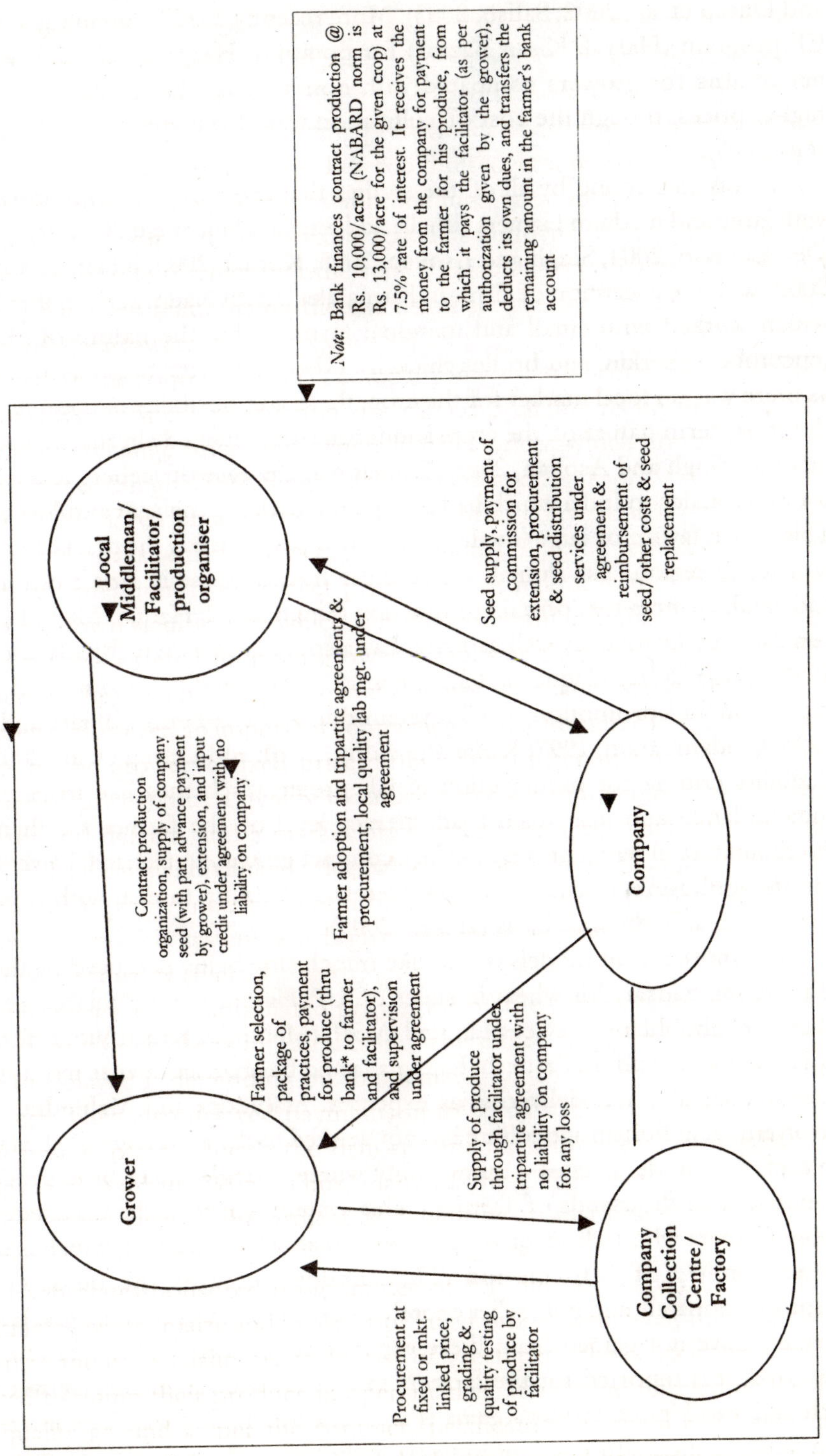

and Dileep et. al., 2002; Satish, 2003). More recently, DSCL run input supply and CF program (Haryali Kisan Bazaar) for potato in Haryana also showed higher net returns for growers compared with non-growers due to higher yields and higher prices, though the cost of cultivation was also higher (17-24%) (Tripathi *et al.* 2005).

It was also found by all of the studies that most of the firms work mostly with large and medium farmers (Bhalla and Singh, 1996; Singh 2002; Haque, 2003; Dev and Rao, 2004; Singh and Asokan, 2005; Kumar, 2005; Khairnar and Yeleti, 2005) with the exception of firms in Karnataka, Tamil Nadu, and Andhra Pradesh which worked with small and marginal farmers due the nature of the crops (cucumber/gherkin, and broiler chicken). Gherkin contracting was also smooth as there was no local market for the crop, there was flexibility in contracts due to the short-term nature of the crop, and farmers maintained alternative sources of income (Singh and Asokan, 2005). Similar was the case of iceberg lettuce grown for McDonalds in India which had a very thin market (Khairnar and Yeleti, 2005). This bias in favour of large/medium farmers is perpetuating the practice of reverse tenancy in regions like Punjab where these farmers lease in land from marginal and small farmers for contract production (Singh, 2002; Haque, 2003). Breach of contracts by farmers as well as firms has also been reported (Bhalla and Singh, 1996; Singh 2002; Haque, 2003). Some of these studies recommend further expansion and promotion of CF system due to its benefits (Bhalla and Singh, 1996; Chidambaram, 1997; Rangi and Sidhu, 2000; and Dileep et. al., 2002). The eligibility criteria for participation in CF projects/schemes like irrigated land, suitable land, land near main road, literacy level of the farmer are themselves discriminatory in terms of who can be a contract grower. In fact, in CF everywhere, private agribusiness firms have less interest and ability to deal with small scale farmers on an individual basis (Hazell, 2005).

The more recent models of CF like franchising being practiced by the Tatas (Tata Kisan Sansar) for wheat in states of UP, Haryana and Punjab; and by the Mahindra Shubhlabh Services Limited (MSP) (Mahindra Krishi Vihar) for paddy in Tamil Nadu, Andhra Pradesh, Karnataka and basmati and maize in Punjab and Haryana are also not delivering as expected. Mahindra and Mahindra's recent involvement in Punjab agriculture has not worked to the advantage of the farmers. In fact, this model creates a monopsony where a single buyer buys produce of hundreds and thousands of farmers. This system works to the disadvantage of those farmers who lack adequate information about the market, which is termed as asymmetry of information. This model increases the buyer's power disproportionately and puts seller entirely at the buyer's mercy. Small and marginal farmers have not gained from these experiments. Wherever any gain has been reported, it is reported for the farmers in general and distinction between big/rich and small/poor farmer's gains is not reflected in any way. The interests of the poor farmers are not synonymous with those of large/rich farmers (Gill,

2004). One of the limiting factors in performance of the contract scheme in Punjab seems to be the MSP which introduces price rigidity and acts unfavourably for the buyers and exporters. On the other hand, because Basmati is out of the purview of the MSP, its contracting performance has been quite favourable for the processors and exporters as they could discover a market price. Also, being an export crop, it enjoys a well established high value market which in turn has created a lot of comfort for the exporters. The performance of CF in Punjab has been tardy despite the fact that the state Punjab Agro Foodgrains Corporation (PAFC) has been reimbursing the extension service fees to the companies, on behalf of the growers.

Further, the contracts protect company interest at all costs to the farmer and do not cover farmer's production risk e.g. crop failure, retain the right of the company to change price, and generally offer prices which are based on open market prices (Singh, 2002; Singh, 2005a; Singh and Asokan, 2005; Khairnar and Yeleti, 2005). Even organic produce buyers offer conventional produce market price based prices to their growers (Singh, 2006a). This is a serious issue as even a significant premium over market price may not help a farmer if open market prices go down significantly which is not uncommon in India. The market price based price is offered to avoid grower defaults as they can, otherwise, sell the produce in the open market due to availability of alternative market due to product symmetry. However, an important contracting agency in India offers two alternative prices to the grower: a fixed price different for different times of the season (staggered prices) plus a quality incentive based on produce quality in terms of content and defects, and a market price (preceding three days' average market price in the local mandi) linked price (which is slightly lower than prevailing market price) and a quality incentive again based on content and defects. This is quite innovative and fair system which gives the flexibility and choice to the grower and rewards quality (Fig. 7).

The firms also manipulated provisions of the contracts in practice, e.g. in case of broiler chickens in Tamil Nadu where they picked up birds before due date or delayed it depending on the demand which meant losses for contract growers. They also delayed payments upto 60 days. But, growers were locked into these contracts due to the firm specific fixed investments they had made (Singh and Asokan, 2005). Thus, many of the CF projects also failed due to either poor design of the project or default by at least one of the contracting parties.

Even state-sponsored programmes of CF did not deliver in Punjab. The contracted winter maize and hyola crops failed almost completely due to inclement weather and poor quality seeds. In case of green peas, the contract growers were forced to dump their produce in open market, after being rejected by the PAIC on quality ground as per the contract specification, as there had been fungus infection due to inclement weather which was marked by heavy rains in winter season and then sudden rise in temperature. An area of 500 acres under contract production of green peas in Patiala and Fatehgarh Sahib districts had been affected. Some farmers found fault with the fungicide supplied by the contracted company in this regard. The dumping of contract-produced crop in open market led to fall in local market prices and it was being sold at Rs. 3 per kg. now as against a promised price of Rs. 5 per kg. by the PAIC (Singh, 2003; Rangi and Sidhu, 2003). In general, across crops and regions, the CF program could not achieve the stated area goal. Not only it fell short in terms of contracted area being less than that stated by the agency, but also the farmers did not plant the entire contracted area with the contract crops. The gap was much larger in latter case and even as high as 50% in winter maize in Ludhiana and 20% in hyola in both Ludhiana and Patiala. There was a different private seed company for each crop and they only provided seed and no other extension service. Finally, none of the companies procured the produce and advised the farmers to sell in open market either because open market prices were higher than contract price or quality was not as desired. Except the oilseed crops (hyola and sunflower), the net returns from contract crops were found be lower than what farmers would have got from wheat crop. Most of the problems farmers faced related to production and quality (like quality of seed and extension) and not marketing of produce (except peas) as open market could take care of contract produce. Due to this experience, a large majority (60%) were not willing to enter into CF arrangement again (Dhaliwal *et al.* 2003). There have also been instances of corruption and malpractice in the PAFC run CF program due to conflicts of interest among implementing agencies and lack of monitoring (Ramachandran and Dogra, 2006; Singh, 2006).

The recent World Bank reports also point to the deficiencies in the CF program launched by the State Government of Punjab. It states that for the programme of CF to be successful, it should take into account the aspects of selection of crops for contracting, development of quick and effective contract enforcement and dispute resolution system, limiting fiscal risks to the state government, limiting the number of parties in a contractual arrangement, and developing farmers' organizations capable of contracting with sponsors, with a view to reduce transaction costs, increasing information flow, and improving farmers' negotiation position (World Bank, 2003; WB, 2004).

It is not incidental that most of the CF projects are in the states of Punjab, Haryana, Gujarat, Maharashtra, Karnataka and Tamil Nadu which are agriculturally developed states. On the other hand, vast areas of the country such as Bihar, Jharkhand, Chhattisgarh, Orissa, West Bengal, the entire north-east India and areas of Uttaranchal, Himachal Pradesh, Kerala and Jammu and Kashmir have been bypassed by CF projects. Does it mean that these areas and farmers would not benefit from commercialization and vertical integration of agriculture? These are areas with highest concentration of small and marginal farmers (Gill, 2004). This essentially means that contracting companies do not encourage the participation of those who need to be helped to participate as risk preference and innovativeness require not just attitude but also resources and risk-taking capability to undertake risky crops and ventures (Glover, 1987). The aspects of contracting which contribute to CF excluding small producers are: enforcement of contracts, high transaction costs, quality standards, business attitudes and ethics like non/delayed/reduced payment and high rate of product rejection, and weak bargaining power of the small growers (Kirsten and Sartorius, 2002). CF also reinforces reverse tenancy where in small and marginal farmers lease out land to large and medium farmers who are often contract growers for the companies as was the case in the Indian Punjab (Singh, 2002).

Making CF Work for Small Farmers

There have been warning notes since the 1980s about the widespread applicability of CF as a development tool (Goldsmith, 1985; Glover, 1987). Further, the hybrid nature of CF, and the often conflicting objectives it is supposed to meet, makes it difficult to either design effective public policy interventions or to organise growers (Glover, 1987). Viewed in the light of experience, the potential problems of CF point to the policy steps which are required to reduce the ill-effects of such a system like regulation and monitoring of contracts and to facilitate its smooth functioning in small farmer contexts.

Legal Framework and State Support

It is difficult to police contracts due to the multiple variables involved in a farming contract like output price, input prices and supply, payments, and quality standards (Glover, 1987; Wolf *et al.* 2001). Therefore, if the firm really wants to manipulate/ sabotage a contract, there are dozen ways to do it. A Government can not really do much to police a contract, and it should not impose contract on an unwilling firm or in an inappropriate situation. Further, the State Government may not always stand by the small growers due to the pressure from the agribusiness interests, and may suffer from the conflicting objectives of its various agencies. Since policy interventions can not really change the outcome of a fundamentally unworkable situation and the relevance of CF for small farmer development, it is better to have more realistic expectations about the policy intervention effect and define an appropriate niche for small holder CF in terms of crops and markets. It is better to plan carefully *ex ante* for CF based on earlier experiences elsewhere (Glover, 1987). But, still, the State Government can play both regulatory and enabling/developmental role in CF. Legal protection to contract growers as a group must be considered to protect them from ill effects of contracting practiced by supply chain drivers. There are cases of legal protection given to subcontracting industries in Japan in their relations with large firms. These laws specify the duties (to have a written and clear terms contract with the subcontractor) and forbidden acts for the large parent firm. The latter include refusal to receive delivery of commissioned goods, delaying the payment beyond agreed period, discounting of payment, returning commissioned goods without good reason, forced price reduction, compulsory purchase by subcontractors of parental firm's products, and forcing subcontractors to pay in advance for materials supplied by the parent firm. These provisions are monitored by the Fair Trade Commission. Interestingly, most of the violations by parent firms were on the written form and clear terms of the contracts (Sako, 1992). If CF is only the flexible production systems prevalent in industry applied to farm production, then it is only logical to extend such legal provisions with necessary modifications to farming contracts. In farming sector per se, there is the Model Producer Protection Act, 2000 of Iowa State in the USA which requires contracts to be in plain language and disclose material risks, provides a three days' cancellation period for the producer to review and discuss production contracts with their advisors, provides for producers to be first priority lien for payments due under a contracts in case of contracting company bankruptcy, protects against undue cancellation of contracts by companies and prohibits 'tournaments' (contracts where compensation to grower is determined by his performance relative to others) (*www.flaginc.org/pubs/poultry/poultrypts*).

In India, the legal reform process is already under way with the Union Government enacting the Model Act for the state Agricultural Produce Marketing (Development and Regulation) Act, 2003 and many states (8 as suggested, and 10 partially like Gujarat, Haryana, Karnataka, Maharashtra, U.P. Delhi and Chandigarh permitting only direct marketing/CF or private/co-operative markets (only Karnataka)) carrying out the amendment in their Acts. This amended act deals with setting up of private markets, selling of produce by growers outside the Agricultural Produce Market Committees (APMCs) (regulated markets), setting up of direct markets, specialized commodity specific markets, regulation and promotion of CF, provision for agencies and measures to promote quality, standards, and alternative markets, and public-private partnerships to facilitate more and better linkage between firms and farmers (GoI, 2004). The amended APMC Act has certain mandatory and optional provisions regarding CF wherein mandatory ones include aspects like who can undertake CF (type of sponsor and of contract grower), details about the land under contract, duration of contract, description of farm produce, other contract specifications like quantity i.e. acreage, entire crop, or fixed quantity, produce quality specifications and penalties for lower quality like rejection, or lower price, crop delivery arrangements i.e. at farm/factory gate/collection centre and transport arrangements, pricing and credit mechanisms, farmer asset/land indemnity, compulsory registration of contracts with the local authority and the procedure for dispute resolution. On the other hand, the optional features include those relating to farm practices, joint crop insurance, support services to be provided, farmer-management forum for monitoring of contract system performance, and monitoring of quality and yields.

The model contract agreement is quite fair in terms of sharing of costs and risks between the sponsor and the grower (GoI, 2003). But, it leaves out many aspects of farmer interest protection like delayed payments and deliveries, contract cancellation damages if a producer made firm-specific heavy investments, inducement/force/intimidation to enter a contract, disclosure of material risks, competitive performance based payments, and sharing production risks. Also, there are state level variations in the amended Acts and the spirit has been diluted. For example, in Gujarat, the amended Act makes the APMC as a party in the tripartite contract stating the logic that APMCs have a useful role as facilitator as they have long standing relationship with farmers and can disseminate the CF concept and practice besides monitoring its practice. It makes the Gujarat State Agricultural Marketing Board (GSAMB) and the local APMC as the registering authority for contracts. The Managing Director of GSAMB will examine the contract for its fairness to the farmers and can refuse to register the same if it is found inadequate in the protection of the farmer's interest. It is also the arbitrator in case of disputes. The registration costs Rs. 200 for the sponsor. Though the Central Model Act exempts contract procurement from market fee, the Gujarat Act makes it mandatory to pay the prescribed cess to the concerned APMC or in case of multi-location operations, to the GSAMB which will apportion it to the concerned APMCs. Though the monitoring role of APMC is desirable, but making it a party to the contract is totally unnecessary and undesirable as that is not the best way to protect the farmer interest, if that, at all, is the logic for giving the role of a party to the contract to the APMC in contracts between sponsors and the growers. Further, it is not known how far the model contract agreement will be adopted by the agencies unless it is conditionality to avail certain other incentives or policies. In Thailand, even after three years of its notification, the standard agreement was used only by two companies (Singh, 2005d).

Role of the State

CF will work for agricultural diversification only if the current system of procurement based on Minimum Support Price (MSP) is changed in favour of new crops because it provides a powerful economic incentive to prolong the wheat paddy rotation. The Government of Punjab through PAFC has been reimbursing extension cost to the CF agencies/facilitators at the rate of Rs. 100 per acre. But, doing it irrespective of the size of holding of the contract growers defeats the purpose as it does not ensure that small and marginal farmers who can not afford to pay for extension and need to be brought into the contract system are included. Similarly, the Ministry of Food Processing industries has been providing an incentive since the beginning of the 9th Plan in the form of a reimbursement of five per cent of the value of raw materials procured through CF with farmers with a maximum ceiling of Rs. 10 lakh per year for a maximum of three years with the condition that any organization (private/public/co-operative/non-government organization (NGO)/joint venture/assisted) should work with at least 25 farmers under contract for at least three years (MFPI, 1998).

In Thailand, the state not only provided coordination and support of local authorities such as agricultural extension agents, local administration officers, and the Bank of Agriculture and Agricultural Cooperatives (BAAC), it also reallocated 250 million Baht deposit in BAAC. The interest compensation for the farmer participants in the program (3.5% p.a.) was made available to encourage more farmer participation and to reduce production cost. But, later, farmers could obtain only low interest rate (5% p.a.) loan instead of getting compensation for interest charge. The Ministry of Agriculture and Cooperatives (MOAC) through its Department of Agricultural Extention (DOAE) still carries out training in CF for farmers and local officials which includes aspects like guidelines for CF implementation, i.e. types of products suitable for certain kind of contracting arrangement, familiarity with the system of CF, supervision of contract arrangements, special financial assistance to companies undertaking CF, and process of implementation of the CF project in terms of co-ordination between public and private sectors and choice of relevant area and farmers. It even specifies requirements before a CF projects is undertaken which are: farmer willingness and exposure to the concept of CF, feasible standards of quality of produce, price flexibility, and production and marketing plan. Discussing factors in success of CF project, it emphasizes on clear understanding of the concept of CF and a felt need for it among project participants, besides physical proximity between producing and processing areas, strict adherence to quality standards and honesty and sincerity of all parties involved. It assigns specific roles and responsibilities to farmers, farmer groups, companies, and government agencies in terms of dealing with each other for the project. It finally recommends suitable types of systems of CF for different types of commodities and advocates CF with farmer organisations instead of individual farmers. It even goes on to advise having multiple outlets for produce, both contract and non-contract, for different grades of produce from the same group of farmers (MOAC, 2002). The state intervention helped the farm sector and its farmers only to the extent that it has promoted competition that has been beneficial for growers like in potato in northern Thailand, and also led to pumping of capital in farm sector through the Bank of Agriculture and Agricultural Co-operatives (BAAC) loans for contract growers. But, on most other counts, like making the system fair for farmers in terms of nature of contracts, or helping farmer organizations in processing or marketing or even in collective selling to companies, it has not really been effective. The role of the government should be enabling and developmental in nature. That credit support to contract farming projects by the state is crucial has been emphasized earlier as well in other contexts (Goldsmith, 1985).

The state and development agencies need to internalize the fact that increasingly product markets will mean supermarkets. Therefore, market-oriented programmes and policies will indeed be supermarket oriented. If, in a given country, a few chains command majority of the food sector, then development policies and programmes need to learn how to deal with this handful of big companies. The development agencies also need to realize that small farmers and entrepreneurs have to gear up quickly to compete in the new markets that are spreading over most of the food economy. The local market niches are disappearing and the distinction between global and domestic market is getting blurred. The government and the donors will have to focus their programmes not just on exports but also on the growing market of the local supermarkets. It is important to promote good business practices that optimize retailer-supplier relations, protecting both sides. This can be initiated by establishing or improving contract regulations and business rules of practice some of which are already available in the form of legal acts in the US and Argentina. These practices can also be forced by private sector codes of practice. Regulation of supermarket chains to control or mitigate their market power can be a potential tool to ensure the presence of small growers in value chains as seen in the case of banana trade regime in pre-WTO period in the EU policy, single channel (monopoly) exports by producer bodies in some exporting countries like South Africa, and regulation of domestic import markets in France (Gibbon, 2003). However, regulations do not ultimately change the economic forces under which the supermarkets operate and the changes in procurement systems are driven by these forces. These changes and the basic requirements they impose on growers are conditions which will have to be met if the growers are to be able to tap the powerful market of the supermarkets. Therefore, it is crucial that government and donor agencies help small farmers and entrepreneurs to make the investments in equipment, management, technology, commercial practice and the development of strong and efficient organizations to meet those requirements. There have been such attempts in Brazil and Guatemala (Reardon and Berdegue, 2002). In organic produce chains as well, group certification by public or development agencies can provide a chance for small farmers to take up organic cultivation.

Contracts and Farmer/Civil Society Organisations

Contracts need to be transparent and require frequent and independent scrutiny so that they remain competitive both with similar contracts and with open market transactions. Wide publicity of contract terms can help to stimulate competition. Secondly, vigorous bargaining co-operatives, or other agricultural producer organisations are needed to negotiate equitable contracts (Goldsmith, 1985; Key and Runsten, 2003). These types of organisations have been able to secure the standardisation of contracts and their scrutiny by a government agency in the USA (Wilson, 1986) and the bargaining groups have negotiated input purchase and output sale collectively (Welsh, 1990). In Japan as well, farmers have managed their relationships with companies well through co-operatives (Asano-Tamanoi,

1988). Producers' organizations amplify the political voice of small holder producers, reduce the costs of marketing of inputs and outputs, and provide a forum for members to share information, co-ordinate activities and make collective decisions. Producers' organizations create opportunities for producers to get more involved in value adding activities such as input supply, credit, processing, marketing and distribution. On the other hand, they also lower the transaction costs for the processing/marketing agencies working with growers under contracts. Collective action through cooperatives or associations is important not only to be able to buy and sell at a better price but also to help small farmers adapt to new patterns and much greater levels of competition (Farina, 2002). There is also need to strengthen small farmer organizations and provide them technical assistance to increase productivity for the cost competitive market, provide help in improving quality of produce, and to encourage them to participate more actively in the marketing of their produce in order to capture value added in the supply chain. Finally, the problem of financing the small producers needs to be tackled by finding innovative ways to provide finance (Schwentesius and Gomez, 2002).

There have been cases of success when public or private assistance to the small growers in terms of technical assistance and supply of input credit was made available. In some places in Brazil, small farmers have gone in for collective tanks to meet the scale requirement though the large farmers will have an advantage as they do not face the transaction cost involved in collective use of physical assets. The dairy companies and cooperatives encourage the use of collective tanks, even by financing or facilitating credit for milk producers in some cases (Farina, 2002). Many attempts including offering differentiated contracts under CF schemes to include small farmers failed in Mexico though firms had no option but to contract with small vegetable growers. A few firms succeeded in including small farmers in their CF projects only when they also employed the farmers' family members in their processing units, used local intermediaries to supervise small growers, and/or limited the small grower contracts only to areas close to the highway, besides the other reasons like the small growers having lower cost and being more efficient than the firm's own farms, their poor access to alternative outlets for produce and source of credit, and having low labour and land opportunity cost. These measures reduced the information asymmetry between the growers and the firm and the transaction cost of dealing with small growers (Warning *et al.* 2003). Thus, there is need to promote/encourage farmer groups for CF as was the case in Thailand where besides contract grower groups, the potato growers' co-operative also dealt with a multinational contracting company on behalf of its members. Group CF proves benefits for both growers and companies (Singh, 2005e) through there may be difficulties in enforcing collective actions due to group heterogeneity, agency resistance to such actions, and making members adhere to group norms in the absence of any legal authority in such collectivities (Glover, 1987).

Besides the resources and technology which determine CF performance, it is the relationship among state, companies, and farmers, which shapes formal and informal institutions and gets mediated by them, that matters (Ornberg, 2003). The practice of contracts needs to be monitored by farmer organisations or NGOs. In fact, the companies should proactively involve NGOs into their CF operations and even organise farmer co-operatives or groups for more sustainable CF programs (Mayers and Vermeulen, 2002; Pingali and Khwaja, 2004). The groups or farmers' organisations like co-operatives not only lower transaction costs of the firms but also lower input costs for the farmers and give them better bargaining power as was the case of a potato growers' co-operative in north Thailand which acted as a link between the growers and the company (Ornberg, 2003). In contract arrangements with small producers in west African countries, the cotton companies started transferring some of the operational or functional responsibilities like distribution of inputs, equipment orders, and credit repayment management, to the village associations in the 1970s itself. They provided these associations with management skills for these tasks. The companies relied on traditional village authority structures for organising the associations but limited the associations to one per village to simplify company purchasing, delivery and marketing procedures. This arrangement accounted for a significant part of each cotton company's success (Bingen *et al.* 2003). But, unfortunately, contracting companies have not been very keen to organise or support co-operatives in India.

Farmers and CF Agencies

In CF, both companies and growers try to improve their own positions as a negotiation which change over time (Vellema, 2004). Further, contract design is a complex task given that there is always a problem of incomplete contracts due to bounded rationality of the contracting parties (Lorenz, 1999; Tirole, 1999). Companies generally use some of the four policing mechanisms: input control, monitoring of farms/production activity, quality measurement, and revenue sharing as residual claimancy to tackle grower opportunism or 'blind spots' which arise due to information asymmetry and consequent moral hazard involved in contracting. Whereas input control can be exercised by supplying specific inputs, monitoring can be done by field staff or by new techniques like remote sensing, electronic data interchange, and precision farming which are cost effective and transparent methods. The latter two mechanisms (quality measurement and residual claimancy) are more difficult to use (Wolf *et al.* 2001). Therefore, it is important to consider contract design as a multi-criterion decision problem. Some basic rules of contract design include (i) co-ordinating to minimize production costs which means using price signals or instructions or both, (ii) balancing decentralization and centralisation in farm decisions which impacts problems like moral hazard and hold up, (iii) minimizing or sharing risk and uncertainty, (iv) reducing the costs of pre- and post contractual opportunism (adverse selection and moral hazard) by various mechanism of allocating contracts and monitoring them, (v) encouraging group or co-operative action among producers to lower costs and ensure better compliance, (vi) long-term contracts to reduce hold up problem, (vii) balancing pros and cons of renegotiation of contracts over time, (viii) reducing direct costs of contracting, and (ix) using transparent contracts (Bogetoft and Olesen, 2002).

Finally, it is the trust between farmers and processors that is important for the realignment of the chain (Heron, 2003). Trust has been defined as the willingness to rely on an exchange partner in whom one has confidence. Trust is the function of relationship specific investments, satisfaction with product quality, prior experience, and importance of input. Trust is developed by a constant and detailed exchange of information which reduces the uncertainty of performance. In the case of farmers, a reciprocal purchase agreement has positive relationship with the farmer's trust in the buyer. Commitment is thought to be closely related to mutuality, loyalty, and the forsaking of alternatives (Batt and Rexha, 1999). Earning the farmer's trust is fundamental to success. This comes from mutuality of benefits. A host of small, timely, and regular steps help build trust. Some examples are prompt payments, being available on site, and sharing and updating best practices. The best catalyst is increasing demand from the company which improves farmers' profitability. Employing locals for extension and procurement related functions helps in facilitating better communication with growers. Growers should be allowed and encouraged to grow diversified set of crops so that risk of crop failure or contract failure can be minimised (Datta, 1996).

Developing successful backward linkages is not a short-term target. The experiences show that it requires commitment, patience and perseverance. The farmer must be convinced of new technologies. Continuous demonstration is thus essential. The most successful vehicle for change is to show the benefits to farmers through demonstrations in nurseries or on the field. Upfront investment in processing is the surest way of showing the farmers the commitment of the company. If farmers can see the processing plants coming up in their area, it acts as confidence builder for them in adopting new crops and methods (Datta, 1996). Giving farmers equity shares can make them feel that they are part of the arrangement and realise that failing the firm would be failing themselves (Mishra, 1997). In fact, in Karnataka, a Belgaum based public limited private sugar company (Shree Renuka Sugars) has more than 9000 of its sugarcane contract growers as its shareholders owning 30% equity (Srinivas, 2005a). Establishing exacting quality standards right from the inception at every stage of the operation is an important aspect of the relationship. No effort is too great especially in the initial period, to highlight the importance of quality. The farmer will understand that process quality is key to product quality and adopt necessary practices.

It is often desirable to plan and provide inputs across a wide range of activities and not just for the raw material needed. Given small land holdings, it is all the more important that the farmer benefits on a scale that motivates him to do better. This is achieved through a combination of technology, service and networking. Technology involves providing the best inputs and proper harvest and post-harvest conditions. Service ensures that the resources are made available in time and the post-harvest offtake is efficient. Networking assures government support, infrastructure, banking facilities, etc. (Datta, 1996). In some situations, it is not possible and easy to build immediate partnerships. Therefore, there can be a quasi-judicial system at the local level (panchayat, district administration) to monitor the contracts and resolve any conflict with appropriate penalties to any of the defaulting parties. There has to be a general code of conduct for both the parties in order to avoid conflicts and the breaking down of contracts (Datta, 1996). Partnerships with government or its agencies can help in building relations with the producers. Working with farmer co-operatives for better and more sustainable contract procurement also seems to work. This is being tried out by Marico Industries in Maharashtra in sunflower oilseeds. The company provides working capital, infrastructural facilities, managerial inputs, and job work to the co-operatives which helps these oilseed milling co-operatives to become viable.

Conclusions

Though there are concerns about the ability of the small farms and firms to survive in the changing environment of agribusiness, still there are opportunities for them to exploit niches in product differentiation with origin of product or organic products and other niche markets. But, the major route has to be through exploitation of other factors like external economies of scale through networking or clustering and such other alliances like CF (Kirsten and Sartorius, 2002). The experience of CF across the globe suggests that it is not the contract per se which is harmful as a system but how it is practised in a given context. If there are enough mechanisms to monitor and use the contract for developmental purposes, it can certainly lead to a betterment of all the parties involved, especially small and marginal farmers.

It is important to remember that there cannot be a single blue print or CF model for all situations so far as the role and nature of CF is concerned. Even for individual farmers, it is not contract per se but the relationship it represents which is crucial as the divergence between the two may prove crucial in determining the development of CF as an institution (Clapp, 1988; White, 1997). Further, it is the context of the contract which can make a whole lot of difference as there are many actors and factors in the environment which influence the working and outcome of contracts and lead to a culture of contracting which is location and community specific. The way farmers perceive CF, i.e. define their relationship with the companies, differs in each cultural context (Asano-Tamanoi, 1988; White, 1997; Ornberg, 2003). In fact, there is so much diversity in the type of firms, farmers, nature of contracts, crops, and socio-economic environment that it is better to focus on specific situation than the generic institution of CF (Little, 1994; White, 1997).

Major conditions for successful interlocking between agribusiness firms and small producers include increased competition for procurement instead of monopsony, guaranteed market for farmer produce, effective repayment mechanism, market information for farmers to effectively bargain with companies, large volumes of transactions through groups of farmers, for lowering transaction costs, co-operation among genuine agribusiness firms in the area, and no alternative source of raw material for firms (Kirsten and Sartorius, 2002). Further, for the sustainability of company-farmer partnership schemes, it is important that the company is able to successfully market its products so that farmers do not suffer from lack of market (Baumann, 2000; Haque, 2000). Building of relationships of trust with farmers through company reputation rather than marketing gimmicks is crucial. This requires mutual respect, fair and transparent negotiation process, realistic assessment of benefits, long term commitment, equitable sharing of risk, and sound business plans (Mayers and Vermeulen, 2002). Innovative pricing mechanisms like bonus at the end of the processing cycle, shares in company equity, dividends, producer's fixed price, and quality based pricing, which reward performance can help contract performance.

There are a large number of institutional arrangements to co-ordinate the small producers which should be assessed for their relevance and effectiveness in a given context, though a priori, it seems the co-operative and other similar forms of farmer organization are more relevant and sustainable, especially the New Generation Co-operatives (NGCs) which are voluntary, more market-oriented, member responsive, self-governed, and avoid free riding and horizon problems as they have contractual equity based transaction with grower members (Singh, 2004; Hazell, 2005). It is also important to note that farm sector problems like high cost of farming, lower returns, environmental sustainability require different kind of institutions (collectivities instead of individual enterprise) for which institutional innovations are a must. The legal system made available the new organizational option i.e. the Producer Companies (co-operative companies) under the Companies Act which farmers in many states have gone ahead with in various existing and new projects.

There have been a large number of institutional innovations in agriculture in India at the local level recently. These include the Non-Pesticidal Management (NPM) of crops especially cotton in Punnukula village in Andhra Pradesh (CSA, 2004), producer companies for organic produce in Kerala, regulation of private tubewell water prices by village council in West Bengal as a non-market based local level institution managing a local private market driven resource (groundwater), second hand tractor markets in Punjab (Singh, 1999) and co-operative tubewells by small and marginal farmers in West Bengal which have improved efficiency (lower cost) and equity in water access, and reduced reverse tenancy (Rawal, 2002. These experiments point to the hidden local potential to create robust local institutions in such a crucial area of economy i.e. marketing. There is a need to allow and encourage such informal arrangements provided there are no irregularities and practices detrimental to the interest of the market participants. The role of the state in such situations should be supportive and somewhat supervisory in order to ensure the efficient functioning of these institutions which can deliver objectives of growth, equity, and sustainability. Another important aspect of these institutions is that they function fairly competitively, which is beneficial to the users of these markets as they get fair deal in their transactions. Some of the coping strategies/innovations adopted by farmers in CF situations include labour- water exchange, share cropping, and group leasing of land by marginal and landless farmers (Deshingkar, et. al., 2003; Singh, 2002).

Given the nature of modern farming involving tremendous amount of technological input and market orientation which require capital resources, it is but inevitable to involve private corporate business interests in agricultural development through CF system. Therefore, what is required is marketing extension in terms of better product planning at the farmer level, provision of market information, securing/accessing markets for farmers, provision of alternative markets and market orientation in terms of improved marketing practices at the farmer level (Patnaik, 2003).

Though there has been plenty of successful intermediation in primary production by state and NGOs, much more of it is needed in agro-processing, credit, market access, information, and technology to enable small farmers to reap enhanced competitive benefits offered by freer market. Land reforms alone will not help make a dent on poverty, if not accompanied by marketing links for small farmers who are more efficient and more valuable as they are labour intensive. Intermediation is required for small farmers to link them up with global markets in processing and marketing (Goldsmith, 1985; Lipton, 2002). In India, due to the small farm domination of agricultural sector, the delivery systems are to be attuned to the demands and needs of small farmers which are small in scale and of sporadic nature (Vyas, 1996). Therefore, new institutional mechanism like groups, associations, co-operatives, New Generation Co-operatives (NGCs) and other collectivities or networks are needed to reach small and marginal producers more effectively. There is a role for the state agencies and the NGOs to intervene in contract situations as intermediaries to protect the farmer and broader local community interests. The NGOs can also play a role in information provision, and in monitoring and regulating the working of contracts. Better co-operation and co-ordination between companies and co-operatives for agricultural development also needs to be encouraged.

Further, both companies and state should promote group contracts with the intermediation of local NGOs and other organisations and institutions so that contractual relationships are more durable, enforceable, and fair. An insurance component in farming interventions is must to protect the farmer interest and it is noted that some companies are already doing it. But, the most important thing is to ensure market for the farmer produce at better price under these agribusiness projects. Government should also play an enabling role by legal provisions and institutional mechanisms, like helping farmer co-operatives and groups, to facilitate smooth functioning of contract system, and not intervene in CF directly as seen in the case of Punjab where the experiment field (Kumar, 2005). On the other hand, the success and smooth functioning of the CF system in mint by A.M. Todd in the state of Punjab with no involvement of the state government, due to the nature of the crop, clear terms of the contract, ensured returns to growers by competitive prices and the commitment of the company, corroborates the point that CF is best left to the company and the growers (Singh, 2005c). This was also the case in Thailand where the state facilitated it from outside with credit and extension (Singh, 2005d).

Also, it is important to ensure competition in CF so that farmers have choice of options. For example, CF in gherkins in Karnataka was also successful, besides the reason of lack of local market for produce, due to the fact that more than two dozen companies operated in the state. This also helps reduce exploitation of the small growers. Further, since farmers did not put their entire land under contract and cultivated only 0.5 acres under gherkin contracts on an average, they were not subject to any major risk of contract failure.

Though contract farming is receiving a push from many stakeholders as discussed above, there are many factors like the APMC regulation including Gujarat's tri-partite arrangement, improving open market efficiency, MSP policy, corporate farming including leasing of wastelands, and an overwhelming presence and interest of NGOs in farming sector, which will act as dampeners to the growth of CF. However, corporate farming can also work favourably if corporate agencies resort to leasing of these lands to contract growers or provide contractual access to these lands to small and marginal farmers and landless labour, as corporate farming is unlikely to be viable. In fact, corporate farming is a double-edged weapon. It can help small farmers in better access to technology, but can also weaken their bargaining power with the company (Glover, 1987). Most likely, the more widespread model of CF is likely to be the intermediary model due to the transactions cost logic and competitive national and international food/fibre markets where cost and quality will determine success. It is already being practiced in different forms by many CF agencies. But, the exclusion of small farmers will remain an important issue.

Finally, there is no need to look for permanence in CF arrangements though short or medium term sustainability is desired for availing of its effects on growers and local economy. But, as market conditions for a crop/commodity change, CF can wither away as market becomes efficient. CF as a vertical co-ordination mechanism is only a response to a situation of market failure and depends on commodity/crop/sector dynamics which are liable to change anytime, especially in globalised and liberalised world. But, there are many indications that CF can continue even in the presence of competitive markets as in the developed countries or even Thailand (Ornberg, 2003). CF is only an instrument/means for agricultural and rural development, not an end in itself.

REFERENCES

Ahlawat, S.R. (2002), "Political Economy and the Peasant Suicide–A Case of Haryana State", *Guru Nanak Journal of Sociology,* 23 (1), 1-17.

Agarwal, I., S. Priya and S. Bhuvaneswai (2005), "Contract Farming Venture in Cotton: A Case Study in Tamilnadu", *Indian Journal of Agricultural Marketing,* 19(2)153-161.

Agrawal, R.C. (2000), "Perspectives for Small Farmers in Developing Countries: Do They have a Future?", Forum zur Gartenkonferenz 2000 (http://userpage.fu.berlin/~garten/Buch/Agrawal(englisch).htm. (downloaded April 6, 2005).

Asano-Tamanoi, M. (1988), "Farmers, Industries, and the State: The Culture of Contract Farming in Spain and Japan", *Comparative Studies in Society and History,* 30(3), 432-452.

Batt, J.P. and N. Rexha (1999), "Building Trust in Agribusiness Supply Chains: A Conceptual Model of Buyer-Seller Relationships in the Seed Potato Industry in Asia", *Journal of International Food and Agribusiness Marketing,* 11 (1), 1-17.

Baumann, P. (2000), Equity and Efficiency in Contract Farming Schemes: The Experience of Agricultural Tree Crops, ODI Working Paper No. 139, Overseas Development Institute (ODI), London, October.

Benziger, V. (1996), "Small Fields, Big Money: Two Successful Programs in Helping Small Farmers Make the Transition to High Value-Added Crops", *World Development,* 24 (11), 1681-1693.

Bhalla, G.S. and G. Singh (1996), *Impact of GATT on Punjab Agriculture,* Ajanta Publications, Delhi.

Bingen, J., A. Serrano and J. Howard (2003), "Linking Farmers to Markets: Different Approaches to Human Capital Development", *Food Policy,* 28, 405-419.

Bissell, S.L., S.G. Chadha and A.K. Shiva Kumar (2002), "Elimination of Child Labour: Corporate Options and Public Actions" *The Indian Journal of Labour Economics,* 45 (3), 633-640.

Bogetoft, P. and H.B. Olesen (2002), "Ten Rules of Thumb in Contract Design: Lessons from Danish Agriculture", *European Review of Agricultural Economics,* 29(2), 185-204.

Buch-Hansen M. and H.S. Marcussen (1982), "Contract Farming and the Peasantry: Cases from Western Kenya", *Review of African Political Economy,* Number 23, 9-36.

Burch, D. and B. Pritchard (1996), "The uneasy Transition to Globalisation: Restructuring of the Australian Tomato Processing Industry" in D. Burch, R.E. Rickson and G. Lawrence (eds.): *Globalisation and Agri-Food Restructuring–Perspectives from the Australasia Region,* Brookfield (USA), Avebury, 107-126.

Chengappa, P.G., L. Achoth, K.K.P. Rashmi, V. Degga, B.M.R. Reddy and P.K. Joshi (2005), "Emergence of Organised Retail Chains in India during Post Liberalisation Era", paper presented at the South Asia Regional Conference "Globalisation of Agriculture in South Asia: Has it made Difference to Rural Livelihoods?" Hyderabad, India by CESS/IFPRI/IAAE/ISAE/ISAM/ANGRAU, March 23-25.

Chidambaram, M. (1997), A Study of Export Potentials for Gherkins (Hybrid Cucumber) in Tamil Nadu, Department of Agricultural Economics, Centre for Agriculture and Rural Development Studies, TAU, Coimbatore (unpublished).

Christensen, S.R. (1992), *Between the Farmer and the State: Towards A Policy Analysis of the Role of Agribusiness in Thai Agriculture*, Thailand Development Research Institute (TDRI) Background Report to the 1992 Conference on Thailand's Economic Structure: Towards Balanced Development?, Chon Buri, Thailand.

Clapp, R.A.J. (1988), "Representing Reciprocity, Reproducing Domination: Ideology and the Labour Process in Latin American Contract Farming", *The Journal of Peasant Studies*, 16(1), 5-39.

CDC (Commonwealth Development Corporation) (1989), *Review of Smallholder Agricultural Programmes, Final Report*, Vols. 1 (Analysis, Conclusions and Proposals) and 2 (case studies), London, CDC, April.

CSA (Centre for Sustainable Agriculture) (2004), *No Pesticides, No Pests*–The Remarkable Story of how a Village in AP Rid Itself of Pesticides, CSA, Hyderabad, October.

Datta, S.M. (1996), "Linkages with Agriculture–The Experience of the Food Processing Industry", *The Economic Times*, June 26, Ahmedabad.

Deshingkar, P., U. Kulkarni, L. Rao and S. Rao (2003), "Changing Food Systems in India: Resource Sharing and Marketing Arrangements for Vegetable Production in Andhra Pradesh," *Development Policy Review*, 21(5-6), 627-639.

Deshpande, R.S. (2002), "Suicide by Farmers in Karnataka: Agrarian Distress and Possible Alleviatory Steps", *Economic and Political Weekly*, 37(26), 2601-2610.

Dev, S.M. and N.C. Rao (2004), "Food Processing in Andhra Pradesh–Opportunities and Challenges", CESS Working Paper No. 57, Centre for Economic and Social Studies (CESS), Hyderabad, June.

Dhaliwal, H.S., M. Kaur, and J. Singh (2003), Evaluation of Contact Farming Scheme in the Punjab State, Department of Economics, Punjab Agricultural University (PAU), Ludhiana.

Dileep, B.K., R.K. Grover, and K.N. Rai (2002), Contract Farming in Tomato: An Economic Analysis", *Indian Journal of Agricultural Economics*, 57(2), 197-210.

Eaton, C. and A.W. Shepherd (2001), *Contract Farming: Partnerships for Growth*, Food and Agriculture Organisation (FAO), Rome.

Elson, D. (1999), "Labour Markets as Gendered Institutions: Equality, Efficiency and Empowerment Issues", *World Development*, 27(3), 611-627.

ETKS (The Economic Times Knowledge Series) (2003), *Rural Economy 2002-2003*, The Economic Times, Mumbai.

Farina, E.M.M.Q. (2002), "Consolidation, Multinationalisation, and Competition in Brazil: Impacts on Horticulture and Dairy Products Systems", *Development Policy Review*, 20 (4), 441-457.

Frenkel, S.J. and D. Scott (2002), "Compliance, Collaborations and Codes of Labour Practice: The Adidas Connection", *California Management Review*, 45 (1), 29-49.

Fulton, A.L.A. and R.J. Clark (1996), "Farmer Decision making under Contract Farming in Northern Tasmania" in D. Burch, R.E. Rickson and G. Lawrence (eds.): *Globalisation and Agri-Food Restructuring–Perspectives from the Australasia Region,* Brookfield (USA), Avebury, 219-237.

Gibbon, P. (2003), "Value Chain Governance, Public Regulation and Entry Barriers in the Global Fresh Fruit and Vegetable Chain into the EU", *Development Policy Review*, 21(5-6), 615-625.

Gill, S.S. (2004), "Small farmers and Markets" (a book review), *Economic and Political Weekly*, 39(23), 2356-2358.

Gill, S.S. (2005), "Diversification of Punjab Agriculture: A Faulty Design and Bureaucratic Apathy", an unpublished paper.

Glover, D. (1987), "Increasing the Benefits to Small holders from Contract Farming: Problems for Farmers' Organisations and Policy Makers", *World Development*, 15(4), 441-448.

Glover, D. and K. Kusterer (eds.) (1990), *Small Farmers, Big Business-Contract Farming and Rural Development*, Macmillan, London.

GoI (Govt. of India) (2003), *Contract Farming Agreement and its Model Specifications*, Ministry of Agriculture, Department of Agriculture and Co-operation, Krishi Bhawan, New Delhi, September 17.

GoI (Govt. of India) (2004), *Economic Survey 2003-04,* Ministry of Finance, GoI, New Delhi.

Goldsmith, A. (1985), "The Private Sector and Rural Development: Can Agribusiness help the small farmer?", *World Development*, 13(11/12), 1125-1138.

GoP (Govt. of Punjab) (2005), *Statistical Abstract of Punjab, 2004*, Economic Adviser to Govt. of Punjab, Economic and Statistical Organisation (ESO), Publication No. 905, Chandigarh, February.

Grosh, B. (1994), "Contract Farming in Africa: an Application of the New Institutional Economics", *Journal of African Economies*, 3(2), 231-261.

Haque, T. (2000), "Contractual Arrangements in Land and Labour Markets in Rural India", *Indian Journal of Agricultural Economics*, 55(3), 233-252.

Haque, T. (2003), "Land Reforms and Agricultural Development: Retrospect and Prospect", in S. Pal et al (eds.): *Institutional Change in Indian Agriculture*, National Centre for Agricultural Economics and Policy (NCAP), New Delhi, 267-284.

Hazell, P.B.R. (2005), "Is there a future for small farms?", in D. Colman and N. Vink (eds.): *Reshaping Agriculture's Contributions to Society*, Proceedings of the 25th Intl. Conference of Agricultural Economists (ICAE), August, 16-22, Blackwell, USA, 93-101.

Heron, L.R. (2003), "Creating Food Futures: Reflections on Food Governance Issues in New Zealand's Agri-food Sector", *Journal of Rural Studies*, 19 (1), 111-125.

Hill, B.E. and K.A. Ingersent (1987), *An Economic Analysis of Agriculture*, Heinemann, London.

IFPRI (2005), High Value Agriculture and Vertical Co-ordination in India–Will the Smallholders Participate?, A draft research report, International Food Policy Research Institute (IFPRI), Washington.

Iyer, K. Gopal and M.S. Manick (2000), *Indebtedness, Impoverishment and Suicides in Rural Punjab*, Indian Publishers and Distributors, Delhi.

Jha, D. (2001), "Agricultural Research and Small Farms", Presidential Address at the 60th Annual Convocation of the ISAE, Kalyani (WB), January 22-24.

Kar, J. (2002), "The Issue of Child Labour in Orissa: A Developmental Approach", Indian *Social Science Review*, 4 (1), 117-131.

Key, N. and D. Runsten (1999), "Contract Farming, Smallholders, and Rural Development in Latin America: The Organisation of Agroprocessing Firms and the Scale of Outgrower Production", *World Development*, 27 (2), 381-401.

Khairnar, S. and V. Yeleti (2005), "Contract Farming in India: Impact and Implications", in Ramesh Chand (ed.): *India's Agricultural Challenges-Reflections on Policy, Technology and Other Issues*, Centre for Trade and Development (CENTAD), New Delhi, 105-128.

Kirk, C. (1987), "Contracting Out: Plantations, Smallholders and Transnational Enterprise", *IDS Bulletin*, 18 (2), April, 45-51.

Kirsten, J. and K. Sartorius (2002), "Linking Agribusiness and small-scale farmers in Developing Countries: is there a new role for contract farming?", *Development Southern Africa*, 19(4), 503-529.

Kumar, P. (2005), "Commercialisation of Indian Agriculture and its Implications for Small and Large Farmers: A case study of Punjab", a paper presented at the FAO Symposium on Agricultural Commercialisation and the Small Farmer, Rome, May 4-5.

Lipton, M. (2002), "Access to Assets and Land in the Context of Poverty Reduction and Economic Development in Asia" Paper presented at the Global Distance Learning Course *'Reaching the Rural Poor: Strategies for Rural Development for the East Asia Region'*, Bangkok, June 3-6.

Little, P.D. and M.J. Watts (eds.) (1994), (eds.): *Living Under Contract-Contract Farming and Agrarian Transformation in Sub-Saharan Africa*, University of Wisconsin Press, Madison, 216-247.

Lorenz, E. (1999), "Trust, Contract and Economic co-operation", *Cambridge Journal of Economics*, 23, 301-315.

Mani G. and V.K. Pandey (1995), "Agrarian Structure under the New Economic Policy", *Indian Journal of Agricultural Economics*, 50(3), 524-530.

Mayers J. and S. Vermeulen (2002), *Company–community forestry partnerships: From raw deals to mutual gains?*, International Institute for Environment and Development (IIED), London.

MFPI (1998), *Food Processing Industries*, outline of Assistance under schemes of the Ninth Plan 1997/2002, Ministry of Food Processing Industries (MFPI), Govt. of India, November.

Mishra, S.N. (1997), "Agricultural Liberalisation and Development Strategy in Ninth Plan", *Economic and Political Weekly*, 32 (13), A19-A25, March 29.

MOAC (Ministry of Agriculture and Co-operatives) (2002), Approach paper for the Workshop 'Linking Production and Marketing under Contracts' (Contract Farming) held on February 8, MOAC (translated from Thai).

Mohanty, B.B. (2001), "Suicides of Farmers in Maharashtra: A Socio-economic Analysis", *Review of Development and Change*, 6(2), 146-189.

Muller A.R. and R. Patel (2004), Shining India? Economic Liberalisaiton and Rural Poverty in the 1990s, Food First Policy Brief No. 10, Food First/Institute for Food and Development Policy, Oakland, May.

Ornberg, L. (2003), "Farmers' Choice: Contract Farming, Agricultural Change and Modernisation in Northern Thailand", paper presented at the 3rd International Convention of Asia Scholars (ICAS3), Singapore, August 19-22.

Page, S. and R. Slater (2003), "Small Producer Participation in Global Food Systems: Policy Opportunities and Constraints", *Development Policy Review*, 21(5-6): 641-654.

Parikh, K. and H.K. Nagarajan (2004), How Important is Land Consolidation? Land Fragmentation and Implications for Productivity: Case Study of Village Nelpathur in Tamil Nadu, National Bank for Agricultural and Rural Development (NABARD) Occasional Paper No. 31, NABARD, Mumbai.

Patnaik, G. (2003), "Marketing, Storage, and Extension Services: State of Agriculture in India" in B. Debroy and A.U. Khan (eds.): *Enabling Agricultural Markets for the Small Indian Farmer*, Bookwell, New Delhi, 81-120.

Payer, C. (1980), "The World Bank and the Small Farmer", *Monthly Review*, 32 (6), 30-46.

Pingali, P. and Y. Khwaja (2004), "Globalisation of Indian Diets and the Transformation of Food Supply Systems", *Indian Journal of Agricultural Marketing*, 18(1), 2004, 26-49.

Ramachandran, R. and C.S. Dogra (2006), "Punjab-Caught in A Con Tract", *Outlook*, January 23, 24-26.

Rangi, P.S. and M.S. Sidhu (2000), "A Study on Contract Farming of Tomato in Punjab", *Agricultural Marketing*, 42(4), 15-23.

Rangi, P.S. and M.S. Sidhu (2003), "Contract Farming in Punjab", *Productivity*, 44(3), 484-491.

Rao, V.M. and H.G. Hanumappa (1999), "Marginalisation Process in Agriculture–Indicators, Outlook and Policy Implications", *Economic and Political Weekly*, 34(52), A133-A138.

Rawal, V. (2002), "Non-Market Interventions in Water-Sharing: Case Studies from West Bengal, India" *Journal of Agrarian Change*, 2(4), 545-569.

Raynolds, L.T. (2004), "The Globalisation of Organic Agro-Food Networks", *World Development*, 32(5): 725-743.

Reardon, T. and J.A. Berdegue (2002), "The Rapid Rise of Supermarkets in Latin America: Challenges and Opportunities for Development", *Development Policy Review*, 20 (4): 371-388.

Rustagi, P. (2002), "Girl Child Labour: Regional Dimensions and Motivations", *The Indian Journal of Labour Economics*, 45 (3), 465-477.

Sako, M. (1992), *Prices, Quality and Trust : Inter-firm Relations in Britain and Japan*, Cambridge University Press, Cambridge.

Saleth, R.M. (1997), "Diversification Strategy for Small farmers and Landless: Some Evidence from Tamil Nadu", *Indian Journal of Agricultural Economics*, 52(1), 73-86.

Satish, P. (2003), "Contract Farming as a Backward Linkage for Agro Processing–Experiences from Punjab", paper presented at the 63rd Annual Conference of the ISAE held at Bhubaneswar.

Schwentesium, R. and M.A. Gomez (2002), "Supermarkets in Mexico: Impacts on Horticulture Systems", *Development Policy Review*, 20 (4): 487-502.

Scott, C.D. (1984), "Transnational Corporations and Asymmetries in the Latin American Food System", *Bulletin of Latin American Research*, 3(1), 63-80, January.

Sen, S. and S. Raju (2005), "Globalisation and Expanding Markets for Cut-Flowers: Who Benefits?", paper presented at the South Asia Regional Conference "Globalisation of Agriculture in South Asia: Has it made Difference to Rural Livelihoods?"Organised at Hyderabad, India by CESS/IFPRI/IAAE/ISAE/ISAM/ANGRAU, March 23-25, 2005.

Shiva, V. and T. Crompton (1998), "Monopoly and Monoculture-Trends in Indian Seed Industry", *Economic and Political Weekly*, 33(39), A137-A151.

Shiva, V., A.H. Jafri, A. Emani and M. Pande (2000), *Seeds of Suicide: The Ecological and Human Costs of Globalisation of Agriculture*, Research Foundation for Science Technology and Ecology, New Delhi.

Singh, G. and S.R. Asokan (2005), *Contract Farming in India-Text and Cases*, Oxford & IBH, New Delhi.

Singh, G. (2005c), "Contract Farming of Mint in Punjab", *Indian Journal of Agricultural Marketing*, 19(2), 121-129.

Singh, J. (2003), "Contracted Green Peas Dumped in open Market", *The Tribune*, Chandigarh, March 28, 15.

Singh, J.P. (2005), "Changing Agrarian Relations in Rural India", a Keynote Paper presented at the 65th Annual Conference of the ISAE held at PAU, Ludhiana, November 24-26.

Singh, M.P. (2006), Shifting Patterns of Agricultural Space: Evolution of Contract Farming in Punjab, an unpublished manuscript.

Singh, R.B., P. Kumar and T. Woodhead (2002), *Smallholder Farmers in India: Food Security and Agricultural Policy*, FAO, ROAP, Bangkok, March.

Singh, S. (1998), "Should Indian Farming Go Corporate?", *Business India*, August 24-September 6, 122-123.

Singh, S. (1999), "Institutional Innovations in Indian Agriculture: A Case of Input Markets", *Institutional Development*, 6(2), 3-10.

Singh, S. (2000), "Contract Farming for Agricultural Diversification in the Indian Punjab: A Study of Performance and Problems" *Indian Journal of Agricultural Economics*, 56 (3), 283-294.

Singh, S. (2002), "Contracting Out Solutions: Political Economy of Contract Farming in the Indian Punjab", *World Development*, 30(9), 1621-1638.

Singh, S. (2004), "The New Generation Co-operative: Theory, Practice and Relevance", *The Co-operator*, 42(5): 229-230.

Singh, S. (2005a), *Political Economy of Contract Farming in India*, Allied, New Delhi.

Singh, S. (2006a), Organic Produce Supply Chains in India, Draft Report, CMA, IIM, Ahmedabad.

Singh, S. (2005d), "Role of the State in Contract Farming in Thailand: Experience and Lessons", *ASEAN Economic Bulletin*, 22(2), August, 217-228.

Singh, S. (2005e), "Contract Farming System in Thailand", *Economic and Political Weekly*, 40 (53), December 31, 5578-5586.

Singh, T. and V.K. Sharma (2004), "Employment of Farm Resources in Punjab Agriculture", *Productivity*, 45(1), 140-144.

Srinivas, N.N. (2005), "Field Test: You Reap What You Sow", *The Economic Times*, Ahmedabad, March 30, 1.

Srinivas, N.N. (2005a), "Rural Folks Convert to Equity Cult", *The Economic Times*, Ahmedabad, August 6, 1.

Swain, M. (2000), "Agricultural Development and Interlocked Markets", *Indian Journal of Agricultural Economics*, 55(3), 308-3316.

Tirole, J. (1999), "Incomplete Contracts: Where Do We Stand?", *Econometrica*, 67(4), July, 741-781.

Tripathi, R.S., R. Singh and S. Singh (2005), "Contract Farming in Potato Production: An Alternative for Managing Risk and Uncertainty", *Agricultural Economics Research Review*, 18, 47-60.

Vellema, S. (2004), "*Institutional Modalities in Contract Farming: The Case of Fresh Asparagus in the Philippines*", paper presented at the mini-conference on Northern Consumption/ Southern Production, Copenhagen, Denmark, October 10-12. (The revised version Published as "Regional Cultures and Global sourcing of Fresh Asparagus" in Fold N. and B. Pritchard (eds.) (2005): *Cross-continental Food Chains: Structures, Actors and Dynamics in Global Food Systems*, Routledge, London, 124-136.

Vyas, V.S. (1996), "Diversification in Agriculture: Concept, Rationale and Approaches", *Indian Journal of Agricultural Economics*, 51 (4), 636-643.

Warning, M., N. Key and W.S. Hoo (2003), Small Farmer Participation in Contract Farming, a draft paper.

Welsh, R. (1997), "Vertical Co-ordination, Producer Response, and the Locus of Control over Agricultural Production Decisions", *Rural Sociology*, 62(4), Winter, 491-507.

White, B. (1997), "Agro-industry and Contract Farming in Upland Java", *The Journal of Peasant Studies*, 24(3), 100-136.

Wilson, J. (1986), "The Political Economy of Contract Farming", *Review of Radical Political Economics,* 18(4), 47-70.

Winson, A. (1990), "Capitalist Coordination of Agriculture: Food Processing Firms and Farming in Central Canada", *Rural Sociology*, 55(3), Fall, 376-394.

Wolf, S., B. Hueth, and E. Ligon (2001), "Policing Mechanisms in Agricultural Contracts", *Rural Sociology*, 66(3), 359-381.

World Bank (2003), India: *Revitalising Punjab's Agriculture*, Rural Development Unit, South Asia Region, The World Bank, Washington.

World Bank (2004), *Resuming Punjab's Prosperity—The Opportunities and Challenges Ahead*, The World Bank, Washington and New Delhi.

22

CORPORATE FARMING IN INDIA: IS IT THE ANSWER TO OVERCOMING COMPETITIVE DISADVANTAGE?

Sukhpal Singh

Introduction

Now that the new economic policy has already made significant progress in the trade and industrial sectors, the focus is now shifting towards bringing about structural reforms in other sectors especially agriculture in terms of mode of organisation of production. This is being attempted in order to bring greater efficiency to input and output markets and promote the growth performance of the sector. Corporate farming is one such initiative in many states alongside contract farming. Corporate farming refers to direct ownership or leasing in of farmland by business organisations in order to produce for their captive processing requirements or for the open market. When it is done for captive purposes, it is referred to as captive farming as well, though most of the time, the two terms are interchangeably used. Though, at present, corporate farming is not allowed in India, there have been loud voices in the recent years to get the legal constraint removed so that agribusiness firms could acquire and cultivate land for their raw material requirements. The most vocal demand has been that by the corporate businesses and business associations. Since this kind of arrangement is not legal at present, the agribusiness firms are increasingly choosing contract farming as a way out of the situation wherein they work with independent growers or their groups under contracts for production and procurement of required quality raw materials at pre-agreed price and volume or acreage.

Since agriculture is basically a state subject, many state governments in India have attempted liberalisation of land laws, especially land ceiling laws. The states of Gujarat, Madhya Pradesh, Karnataka, and Maharashtra have recently allowed agribusiness firms to buy and operate large landholdings for R&D, and export-oriented production purposes. And, even states like Punjab are planning to raise the ceiling on holdings in order to encourage large-scale farming for making farming a viable proposition in the state. The farmer organisations and political parties representing larger farmers in Punjab are also lobbying for the removal or relaxation of the *Ceiling on Land Holdings Act* in Punjab (Dhaliwal, 2005). The states of Maharashtra and Gujarat have also enacted laws to allow corporate farming on government wastelands by providing large tracts of these lands (upto 2000 acres each) to agribusiness companies on a long term (20 year) lease (Bharwada and Mahajan, 2006). Earlier, the government of Andhra Pradesh had attempted corporate farming under a project in Kuppam in Chittor district during 1997-2002 where the purpose was to test the feasibility of large-scale farming through contract farming on lands leased by an agribusiness company (BHC Agro India Private Limited—an Israeli consultancy firm). The focus was on precision farming, drip irrigation and quality standards (Dash, 2004). In fact, these changes in land laws can be viewed as a part of the global process of new internationalisation of agriculture wherein new production mechanisms (technology and other inputs) and the new actors (global capital and trading interests) are setting new rules of the game (Raynolds et al, 1993).

There were 21.22 million hectares of barren and uncultivable land (7% of total reported area), 11.8 million hectares of permanent pastures and grazing land (3.9% of total reported area), 15 million hectares of cultivatable waste land (4.9% of total reported area) and 23 million hectares of fallow land (7.7% of total reported area) in India in 1990-91. Overtime, most of these categories of wasteland have declined in area terms, except current fallows, at the All India level as well as across states. Gujarat and Rajasthan have a large area of cultivatable wasteland as percentage of total reported area (10% and 16% respectively) compared with all India average of 4.9%. They account for 12% and 35% of the total wasteland in India respectively. They also account for 15% and 16% respectively of total barren and unculturable land in India. There have been many initiatives of the NWDB, Department of Wasteland Development, MoAC, MoEF, and the Planning Commission for the development of wastelands, besides the Tree Growers' Co-operatives (TGCs) of the NDDB (FES, n.d.). But, the overall performance of these schemes has been slow and inadequate due to reasons like lack of finance, non-transfer of land to communities, poor design of public-private partnership schemes, and land-ceiling laws at the state level (Chadha, 1996). The development of wastelands still remains a challenge, and there are issues of gender and equity in the development programmes (Chadha, 2002; FES, n.d.). Therefore, there is a renewed interest in handing over wastelands to private companies on a long-term lease basis more recently as part of the overall liberalisation and privatisation process in the rural sector. The Government of Gujarat has recently offered wastelands up to 2000 acres for horticulture and biofuels for 20-year lease to big corporate houses and resourceful farmers at the rate of Rs. 500 per acre interest free security deposit. If project does not take off in five years, the leased land will be taken back and the deposit forfeited. There will be no rent for the first five years. For the years 6-10, annual rent will be Rs. 40

per acre and for years 11-20, annual rent will be Rs.100 per acre. There will be a 50% increase in rent if any value addition activity is taken up on the land. The leasee will use micro-irrigation technology which is being supported by the Gujarat Green Revolution Company with an initial capital of Rs. 1500 crore. The mortgage of land for loan purposes is allowed. No 'non-agricultural' permission will be required for processing activity (Bharwada and Mahajan, 2006).

Practice of Corporate Farming in India

Ion Exchange Enviro Farms Limited (IEEFL), Pune is a subsidiary of the Ion Exchange India which has been into water treatment equipment and waste disposal for the last 50 years and is a pioneer in water business in India. It is originally a British company and the present chairman was an employee of the erstwhile British company.

In 1995, the company objectives got extended to clean food and it entered the horticulture business with a Collective Investment Scheme (CIS). At that time, there were hundreds of companies in plantation schemes, mainly teak, like Maxworth Orchids and Anubhav plantations. IEEFL formed in 1995 is the only company to transfer land titles to the investors as it was to only manage the farms on behalf of the investors. The sharing of profits from this plantation was to be on 80:20 basis with 80% going to the investors after meeting all expenses. It has 12 farms with four in Tamil Nadu, seven in Maharashtra and one in Goa. A total of 1500 acres is made up by about 650 acres in Tamil Nadu, 750 acres in Maharashtra and 100 acres in Goa. The land put to CIS was bought from farmers and was cultivable wasteland. Each farm is in a compact zone in each State and mostly in Konkan region. The land was bought at the rate of Rs. 25-30,000 per acre. There were about 800 participants in the CIS with the largest and the only one with 150 acres and the smallest with 0.5 acres which was the minimum needed as per the company policy. The land was marked with stones and boundaries for the purpose of ownership for each investor. There is a formal agreement with shareholders which is renewed every 5 years. The company is only managing the farms on behalf of the owners who number 900.

Mainly horticultural crops are grown on these farms besides some intercrops. The organic bananas were sold to the National Dairy Development Board (NDDB) during 1998-2003 for processing into banana puree for export which was of the order of 400 MT tonnes. There were advance orders with 50% advance payment and a premium of 30% on market price for conventional bananas in Jalgaon market in Maharashtra. Besides, a commission of Rs. one per kg. was paid as transport cost for delivery to the NDDB factory at Goregaon in Mumbai. The NDDB factory was also certified organic as part of IEEFL's chain of custody with the cost of certification being born by the NDDB. Other than selling to the NDDB, the organic produce was sold in the local market as the company was not involved in exports or domestic market in organic produce. Even now, there are no direct exports by the company. The supplies to NDDB have been stopped now due to crash of international prices for banana puree. The CIS still continues though no returns have been given to the investors so far. There is a farm manager for each farm and one assistant for 50 acres each. The labour supply comes from those who sold land to the company. They work as casual labourers. The manager and the assistant, besides a watchman, stay on the farm.

The farms have been levelled and provided with drip and lift irrigation implemented by Excel and Netafim. All these farms are now totally organic and certified by EcoCert since 1997. The cost of drip installation was Rs. 12,000/- per acre at that time (1995-96). The certification cost for all the farms is Rs. seven lakh per annum. The farms were bought in the name of the directors of the company as agriculturist who were so to begin with, and some employees of the company who were also agriculturists, to avoid the *Land Ceilings Act.* There was a ceiling of 12 acres for irrigated land and 54 acres for wasteland. The other shareholders in the scheme to whom the land was to be transferred were made agriculturists by buying 100 acres of wasteland in M.P. as it was already permitted there. This land was bought by the company in the name of investors. The titles of the farms bought in Maharashtra were transferred to these so called agriculturists. In Tamil Nadu and Goa, there is no condition of only agriculturists being eligible to purchase land. Though the share price varies across farms and farmers in Maharashtra, it was Rs. 1,30,000/- per acre per share of which Rs. 30,000/- were spent on land development and registration besides maintenance of the land. The gestation period has just got over and now the 80:20 sharing will take place. However, the land appreciation has already taken place for the investors. The company also gives gifts of farm or any other organic produce to the investors.

The farm managers of the company have been trained in organic farming by experts. The present supply chain manager is a former employee of Excel Industries. Since its own farms were in wasteland, it got certification in first year itself. It also provides consultancy for organic farms at the rate of 15% of project cost except land and infrastructure or including them in some cases, so that it has larger base to procure from. It has provided such services to 12 farms in India already and one in Oman. So far as corporate farming is concerned, the cost of production is very high due to the high overheads. Here the company is continuing as its only managing the farms in the name of shareholders who are land owners (Singh, 2006).

Since 2004, Field Fresh as an equal partnership venture between Bharti Enterprises (Airtel group) and Rothschild, two large and respected business entities in India and globally, respectively. Field Fresh has planned an outlay of $50 million in the first phase. These funds are being used to create state-of-the-art infrastructure for research & development, climate controlled processing facilities and cold stores. For the purpose, the company has acquired 300 acres of land from the Government of Punjab for its flagship operations and first R&D farm called the Field Fresh Agri Centre of Excellence which is the model R&D Farm in Ludhiana, Punjab. The primary focus is on crop and varietals trials, progressive farming techniques, and identification and adoption of appropriate technologies. The farm includes 42 acres of state-of-the-art protected cultivation including, poly-houses, glass and green houses and net houses. The company aims to engage directly or indirectly over 100 thousand people in its operations. FieldFresh has also partnered with one of India's leading Agricultural University, the Punjab Agricultural University (PAU) at Ludhiana, Punjab to share existing manpower resources, employ PAU graduates and conduct periodic joint training and development programmes. Field Fresh has partnered with SGS, a world leader in quality control. All Field Fresh farms are HACCP, Eurep Gap, BRC and AVA accredited. The initial marketing focus is on the distribution of fresh fruits and vegetables in European Union, Eastern Europe, South East Asia, Middle East & the CIS Countries. It has partnerships with Plastro Irrigation Systems (P) Ltd which is a world leader in the manufacture and supply of irrigation equipments and systems, and ACM China, an industry leader in building green houses (www.fieldfresh.in). Besides this, In Punjab, Field Fresh has leased in hundreds of acres and is using those former owner cultivators as labourers on these leased farms and claims that their livelihoods have improved compared to when they were cultivator owners (personal communication with Mr. Mittal).

Similarly, Reliance Industries through its subsidiary–Jamnagar Farms Pvt. Ltd. based in Gujarat has also got into export-oriented corporate farming with its 7500 acres of farm land which has agro-forestry, and horticultural crops, with mango occupying 450 acres making it the largest mango orchard in Asia. The farm was originally set up as an environmental protection measure near its refinery. Now, it is being seen as a profitable venture in itself. The company has invested Rs. 10 crore on the farm during the last 3-4 years and plans to have such farms in other states like Andhra Pradesh, Maharashtra and Karnataka. The projects are expected to take seven years for breakeven and give 30% return after that. It is also planning to sell the farm produce in domestic market through Reliance Retail outlets (Bose, 2006). There are two other companies–Agri-gold based in Hyderabad and SYP Agro based in Ahmedabad which are practicing corporate farming to some extent in India.

More recently, Vimal Dairy with a capacity to process 2.5 lakh litres of milk (a part of the Rs. 900 crore Vimal Group) has set up the first contract cattle farm in India on 1000 acres of land in the Narmada canal area in north Gujarat with an investment of Rs. 30 crore. Vimal is a multi-product group dealing in engineering, resin, micrones, oils, crude and dairy products. This land (1000 acres) will be leased on contract to landless and marginal farmers with each getting 6-12 acres for 10 years. They will also be provided with water, electricity, and milch animals along with land. It will also have veterinary and milk-chilling facilities. The milk produced on these farms will be procured by Vimal Dairy and after deducting all the payments due for water, electricity and animals, the farmers will be paid for their milk. The young calves of the animals will belong to farmers. The contract will be renewable with mutual understanding and the project is focused on women dairy farmers. It is expected to provide livelihoods to 70-100 families. The Vimal Group is also undertaking a project in potato chips and fried and wet-fried snacks at Mehsana (Patel, 2006).

The Anil Dhirubhai Ambani Group (formerly part of the Reliance Industries Limited) has recently got approval to set up a 5,000 acre Special Economic Zone (SEZ) in Punjab. The proposal, made by one of the group companies–Reliance One World–intends to set up the SEZ in the Mansa-Bathinda area which is considered an industrially backward-belt of the state. This entails an investment of nearly Rs. 5,000 crore. The group has reportedly purchased about 3,500 acres of land from farmers for the project. This would be a multi-product SEZ that would have separate units dealing in food and agricultural produce, the automobile, industry and garments and apparel, among other items. By locating the SEZ in Mansa, the company intends to cater to Haryana and Rajasthan and also be closer to the National Capital Region when approached via Hisar (*The Tribune*, June 8, 2006, Chandigarh.

This paper examines the rationale for corporate farming in the Indian context in and then goes on to examine the validity of the various arguments in favour of corporate farming. It concludes with some alternatives to the corporate farming model.

Rationale for Corporate Farming

It is argued that large-scale corporate agriculture is more efficient than peasant farming prevalent in India. It leads to better allocative efficiency, induces higher private investment in agriculture, and results in higher output, income and exports (Mishra, 1997). In fact, it has been argued that the small and marginal farms even in states like Punjab are not viable for sustaining a family and need larger holdings (Johl, 1995). They should get out of farming if they are not able to move on to more export-oriented and commercial crops like fruit and vegetables as it will not be viable to grow food crops on small holdings. Even some farmer leaders like Sharad Joshi of Shetkari Sanghatana argue that the state should facilitate the exit of small and marginal farmers from farming by buying their land at market prices and provide them capital and training to go for non-farm occupations. Only those who have the mindset, technology, management, and financial resources to face the challenge of the Second Green Revolution should be permitted to do farming as an agribusiness (Joshi, 2006). Further, small farms are highly fragmented. Land transactions have led to further fragmentation making them non-viable in terms of resource-use as well as family sustenance. The costs of fragmentation included increased travel time between farms and hence lower labour productivity, higher transportation costs of inputs and outputs, negative externalities for land quality improvement like irrigation, loss of land on boundaries and greater potential for disputes (Mani and Pandey, 1995). A study of a Tamil Nadu village found that of all the farmers in the village, small farmers (60% of all) who owned less than three hectares of land each, 35% had 3-5 plots and 25% had 5-10 plots and the remaining less than three plots. On the other hand, of all the farmers in the village, only 20% farmers had more than five plots each, another 40% had 3-5 plots each and remaining less than three plots each. Thus, small farms were more fragmented. Further, the study showed that fragmentation had adverse impact on the technical efficiency and the production of most of the crops, and consolidation led to large gains in technical efficiency. But, still markets have not even led farmers to consolidate their operational holding, if not owned holdings (Parikh and Nagarajan, 2004).

Further, export-oriented agriculture requires large investments which only big agri-business enterprises can afford (Rangswamy, 1993). It is argued that India has been exporting some agricultural products which are available for exports after meeting domestic requirements. It is alleged that she has never produced for export. This not only leads to instability of supplies in domestic markets, but also a failure to meet export commitments, which results in the loss of the established markets. Besides, India ends up going to the world market for importing for domestic consumption as well. It is here, that corporate farming is a must for stable production and export performance (Singh, 1994). It is also said that allowing foreign companies to buy and operate land would open the doors to their technology in horticulture, food processing, etc. Further, if there is no ceiling on the assets of a firm, why should there be such a restriction on the farm firms or agribusiness enterprises? (Johl, 1995).

The argument for corporate agriculture is also made in terms of the new economic policies wherein industry has been liberalised to a large extent. The argument is that liberalisation of industry is going to help only about 10% of the people in the country. On the other hand, if agriculture is liberalised, it will help the population at large. It is only logical that when industry has been liberalised, agriculture should also be given the same policy treatment. In fact, some people argue that liberalisation of agriculture should precede that of industry because agriculture forms the basis of industrial production and performance, to a large extent (Singh, 1994). Further, if there is no ceiling on the assets of a firm, why should there be such a restriction on the farm firms or agribusiness enterprises? (Johl, 1995).

The Case Against and Implications

The opponents of corporate farming argue that allowing companies to buy land will make farmers landless since the companies would offer prices which may be too tempting for the poor farmers to resist. Land owners, therefore, would run the risk of becoming landless (Vyas, 2001). To avoid such a situation, it is proposed to allow only leasing in of land by the companies and to share the company profits with the farmers who will lease out land to the companies. On both these fronts, the chances of agriculturists being taken for a ride by the companies are quite high. The key issue is how to protect the farmers, while allowing the companies to use their land where the farmers work as labour and suffer from the monopolistic contracts with the companies? (Dash, 2004). Also, in a country where the population pressure on agricultural land is already high, it is debatable whether captive or corporate farming results in the optimal use of agricultural or even degraded land.

Also, investing capital in land purchase per se does not yield profit, irrespective of the existence or absence of ceilings on land ownership. Such an investment by a business enterprise is solely for the purpose of rent-seeking and/or for unearned speculative capital gain in a situation of fast rising land prices. Corporate demand for removal of ceilings makes sense only in the presence of such a motivation. But, this is contrary to the nature of a corporate, capitalist enterprise driven by profit seeking. Such an investment is also socially wasteful of capital, even otherwise a scarce social resource. It merely leads to the transfer of land from one hand to another (Mishra, 1997). In fact, it is known from experiences of other developing countries, and of India where contract farming is now widespread, that agribusiness firms producing for export tend to undermine the local food production systems as they go in for export-oriented non-food crops by displacing area under basic food crops which is so crucial for local and national food security (Patnaik, 1996) and exploit farmers (Dash, 2004).

So far as giving away wasteland is concerned, it is not known whether any corporate house would come forward to buy such land if they are not allowed to purchase irrigated or cultivable land. Even if fallow land is given to them on a platter, who will make the provision of water for the crops to be grown? Besides, the provision of water for this kind of land has implications for the already deteriorated ground water table (Singh, 1994). In the past also, many attempts to allow captive farming on degraded land under the agro-forestry programmes have become controversial over such issues as the definition of degraded land and the displacement of those holding grazing or other common rights to such land as the 'so-called wasteland' is not really wasteland for those who depend on it for their livelihoods (food, fuel, and fodder needs) as a common property resource (Singh, 2002; FES, n.d.) as is the case of Maldharis in Gujarat. Further, classification of wastelands is also questionable as e.g. in Gujarat 'common lands' and 'uncultivable' land have been classified as wastelands (Bharwada and Mahajan, 2006).

So far as efficiency is concerned, there is no conclusive evidence of farm productivity rising with increasing farm size. In fact, land reforms drew their logic from the evidence which pointed to the inverse relationship between farm size and productivity (Lipton, 1993). Also, economies of scale are important not at the production level but at the processing stage which can be availed of under contract farming or co-operative processing arrangements (Vyas, 2001). If the argument of efficiency of large holding has any logic at all, it can still be practised by increasing the size of operational holdings even under the existing land laws by way of consolidation. Ownership of land is not a necessary condition for corporate agriculture. Since agricultural sector in India, quite in contrast to the industrial sector, has functioned in a competitive environment-with very large number of producers and consumers in the market-there is no evidence to suggest that under the present system of peasant farming, allocation of resources is inefficient (Rao, 1995). If a proof is needed, it should be seen in the growth rate of agricultural production and changes in the efficiency of capital use. Agricultural production has grown at an average rate of 3–3.5% per annum since the late 1960s and the marginal efficiency of capital in Indian agriculture more than doubled, from 0.150 in the 1960s to 0.414 in the 1980s (Mishra, 1997).

Further, the experiment of corporate farming in many developed and developing country situations did not succeed largely due to the internal problems of the agribusiness firms. For example, in Iran, most of the firms failed, when they were given large chunks of land for cultivation, due to the mismanagement which resulted from the lack of relevant experience. The main reasons were managerial in nature, like neglect of field improvement, no contingency planning, under-capitalisation, managerial inflexibility, and poor labour relations (Strohl, 1985; Johnson and Ruttan, 1994)). The external reasons included diseconomies of scale which suggested that there were limits to farm size growth worldwide (Johnson and Ruttan, 1994). Large-scale corporate farms failed in UK, Venezuela, Brazil, and Philippines besides Iran despite the presence of significant 'external economies of scale' in terms of subsidised inputs including land, low interest credit, and tax and duty benefits (Johnson and Ruttan, 1994). On the other hand, there have been many cases of success when the firms worked with local farmers under the contract system or leased in their land (Johnson, 1985).

The argument of parity with the industrial sector for removal of ceilings (Johl, 1995) too does not stand ground on closer examination. It is well known that the assets of a private, corporate industrial firm are not exclusively owned by those who control and manage it or by the business house in whose name the firm is run. The assets are owned by hundreds, and in cases where the firm is large, by tens of thousands of shareholders, financial institutions, and trust funds. When such a pattern of asset ownership is transplanted to agriculture, it implies widespread ownership of land and also capital assets of an agri-business firm. This condition is met when hundreds of landowners in various size-classes lease out their land to the firm and become shareholders in its capital investment, if the firm's goal is direct agricultural production. Alternatively, if the firm's goal is agro-processing, then the above condition is met by vertical co-ordination of production, processing and marketing. In this case, hundreds of owner-farmers engage in required type of production under a contractual arrangement, and the agro-processing enterprise processes the produce. However, under such an arrangement, transaction costs of the enterprise are high and when the open market price of the produce is high, delivery of the produce becomes uncertain as the producers divert the produce to the open market. The solution to such problems lies in making the producers shareholders in the enterprise in such a way that they not only share the transaction costs but also lose on the dividend earnings for failure to deliver more than the expected gains from open market sales. In brief, they are made to have a stake in the processing enterprise (Mishra, 1997).

Conclusion

There is no case for removal of ceilings on land holdings for corporate business to operate in agricultural production sector or for farmers to reap economies of scale, on grounds of size limitation, provided there exists a freer land-lease market (Vyas, 2001; Dogra, 2002). Even in Punjab, it should be resisted as it is neither necessary nor desirable for resolving the present crisis. If operational holdings are to be enlarged for more viable operations, that can be achieved by making the land lease market more efficient or by pooling land together under some co-operative enterprises. If agricultural growth is to be shared in order to realise the virtuous circle of growth and distribution, only a peasant farming system using modern technology of production can achieve it, as the East-Asian experience has shown. Not only it is more competitive compared to the capitalist/corporate farming system, but also peasants do respond and adopt new technologies of production whenever opportunity arises. The experience of the Green Revolution in Punjab is an excellent example of this. Secondly, it is able to employ more labour as the peasant farmers substitute labour for capital much better, than the capitalist farming can ever do, given its normal motive to maximise profit (Mishra, 1997).

There is, however, a case for increasing the holding size at the lower end to make the holdings viable (Mani and Pandey, 1995). This can be done by provision of term credit through Land Development Banks to the small/marginal farmers below the poverty line, so that those willing could purchase land and increase the size of their ownership holdings (Rao, 1995). But, it may not help solve the problem of viability as it leaves no room for those at the lowest end who want to move out of it. The best course seems to be to have a free land market within the limits of land ceilings, with provision of land purchase credit facility for the small/ marginal farmers. But, given the population pressure, family divisions, equal inheritance law, and deep-rooted attachment to land, even this policy may not wholly succeed in eliminating the unviable marginal holdings. About 15 years ago, a working group of agricultural economists under the chairmanship of late Sukhmoy Chakravarty, had come to the conclusion that introduction of a floor to the ownership holdings would be necessary to tackle the issue. The UP *Zamindari Abolition and Land Reforms Act* of 1950 accordingly has a clause fixing the floor limit at 1.26 hectare. It is another matter that this provision has never been implemented. Of course, it goes without saying that the floor limit will have to be different in different states just as the ceiling limits are different (Mani and Pandey, 1995; Mishra, 1997).

Finally, there is a need to look at contract farming alternative as it meets the needs of both corporate agribusinesses as well as small producers. It has been in practice for quite some time with mixed results. There is need to bring partnership into contract farming where companies not only offer contractual terms for working with farmers but also share their business risk and profits with producers as shareholders. It is being done successfully by a sugar company in Karnataka in South India.

REFERENCES

Bharwada, C. and V. Mahajan (2006), "Gujarat: Quiet Transfer of Commons", *Economic and Political Weekly*, 41(4), January 28, 313-315.

Bose, P.R. (2006), 'Reliance Ind. Plans to Enter Agri. Sector', *The Hindu Business Line*, Mumbai, March 19, p. 2.

Chadha, G.K. (1996), *Wastelands in Rural India: Policy Initiatives and Programmes for their Development*, National bank for Agricultural and Rural Development (NABARD) Occasional Paper No. 2, NABARD, Mumbai.

Dash, M. (2004), "Political Economy of Contract Farming", *Mainstream*, 42(52), December.

Dhaliwal, S. (2005), "Political, Farmers' Bodies Propose Agri. Policy to Centre', *The Tribune*, March 13, Chandigarh.

Dogra, B. (2002), "Land Reforms, Productivity and Farm Size", *Economic and Political Weekly*, 37(6), 532-533.

FES (Foundation for Ecological Security) (n.d.), *Spaces for the Poor-Working with Communities and Commonlands in Central Aravalis, Rajasthan*, FES, Anand.

Johl, S.S. (1995), "Agricultural Sector and New Economic Policy", *Indian Journal of Agricultural Economics*, 50(3), 473-487.

Johnson, D.A. (1985), "Sabritas' Backward Integration into Agricultural Production", in J. Freivalds (ed.): *Successful Agribusiness Management*, Gower, Vermont, 108-115.

Johnson, N.L. and V.W. Ruttan (1994), "Why Are Farms So Small?", *World Development*, 22(5), 691-706.

Joshi, S. (2006), "Give Farmers a real way out", *The Hindu Business Line*, March 22, p. 10.

Lipton, M. (1993), "Land Reform as Commenced Business-The Evidence Against Stopping", *World Development*, 21 (4), 641-657.

Mani G. and V.K. Pandey (1995), "Agrarian Structure undet the New Economic Policy", *Indian Journal of Agricultural Economics*, 50(3), 524-530.

Mishra, S.N. (1997), "Agricultural Liberalisation and Development Strategy in Ninth Plan", *Economic and Political Weekly*, 32 (13), March 29, A19-A25.

Parikh, K. and H.K. Nagarajan (2004), How Important is Land Consolidation? Land Fragmentation and Implications for Productivity: Case Study of Village Nelpathur in Tamil Nadu, National Bank for Agricultural and Rural Development (NABARD) Occasional Paper No. 31, NABARD, Mumbai.

Patel, A. (2006), "Gujarat's first 'Contract Cattle farm'", *Divya Bhaskar*, May 6, Ahmedabad (in Gujarati).

Patnaik, U. (1996), "Export-Oriented Agriculture and Food Security in Developing Countries and India", *Economic and Political Weekly*, Special Number, September.

Rangswamy, G. (1993), "Corporate Agriculture: The Key to Poverty Eradication", Guide on *Food Products (GFP) Year Book*, 114-116.

Rao, C.H.H. (1995), "Liberalisation of Agriculture in India-Some Major Issues" *Indian Journal of Agricultural Economics*, 50 (3), 468-472.

Raynolds, L.T., D. Myhre, P. McMichael, V. Carro-Figueroa and F. Buttel (1993), "The "New" Internationalisation of Agriculture-A Reformulation", *World Development*, 21 (7), 1101-1121.

Strohl, R.J. (1985), "Farming Failures: The Fate of Large-scale Agribusiness in Iran", in J. Freivalds (ed.): *Successful Agribusiness Management*, Gower, Vermont, 133-146.

Singh, R.V. (2002), *Forests and Wastelands: Participation and Management*, The Ford Foundation, New Delhi.

Singh, S. (1994), "Corporate Farming: Risky step?" *Financial Express*, February 16, Mumbai.

Singh, S. (2006), Organic Produce Supply Chains in India, a Research Report, Centre for Management in Agriculture (CMA), Indian Institute of Management (IIM), Ahmedabad.

Vyas, V.S. (2001), "Agriculture: Second Round of Economic Reforms", *Economic and Political Weekly*, 36 (10), 829-836.

23

DEMOGRAPHY AND THE WELFARE OF WOMEN AND CHILDREN IN SOUTH ASIA: AN INDIAN FOCUS

J. Nirmala and Dhulasi Birundha

Poverty

Poverty is a situation that usually gives rise to a feeling of a substantial discrepancy between what one has and what one "should have". What one should have is an internal construct; hence each person's feeling and experience of poverty is individual and unique. But the feeling of 'powerlessness' and 'resourcelessness' is possessed by all poor people. It is associated with "lack of livelihood strategies, inaccessibility to resources (money, land, credit), feelings of insecurity and frustration, inability to maintain and develop social relations with others as a consequence of lack of resources", according to Henry Berstein as quoted in Ahuja (1997; p. 27).

The poverty of a given society is often associated with inferior resources, low national income, low per capita income, a high disparity in income distribution, weak defence, and the like.

Inadequate development has been identified as a contributor to poverty. Lack of capital prevents industrial growth. Human capital deficiencies or a lack of skills and abilities in workers prevents them from finding good employment and thereby increasing their income. Achieving skills and abilities depends more on the availability and accessibility of opportunities than on genetic endowments or natural ability. Since the poor belong to a social environment where they fail to get the required opportunities, they remain unskilled, which in turn affects industrial growth.

High rates of unemployment in a country too add to poverty. Poverty is related to health also. If a large number of people in the country suffer from chronic malnutrition or live in an unsanitary environment, they suffer from many diseases which make them incapable of working and earning. If they earn income, their medical expenses are high.

Poverty is often correlated with an increase in family size as well. Frequently, the larger the family, the lower the per capita income and the lower the standard of living. The educational level of the people in the country also contributes to poverty. Discrimination, prejudices, 'casteism', communalism and parochialism also affect employment opportunities and income. Population growth is the most important contributing factor to poverty, in our view.

There is a relationship between poverty and the age structure of the country's population too. The poverty of the old people is forced and inevitable.

Man is a social animal, living in a group, called the family. Groups of families form a society and many groups of a society successfully form an economy. The basic structure of life in the world is the family that consists of three different individuals–*men, women and children.* "It is not good for the man to be alone" and so God has given him a family to live in. The companionship of women and children gives meaning to life. Throughout the world, the way in which people make a living varies greatly. Hence issues on status of living should concern the three groups of people:–Men, Women and Children. Of the three, if any one is marginalised, the other two cannot survive well or if any two suffer, the remainder is seriously affected.

Humankind is blessed with many riches to enjoy. But not all individuals are able to enjoy these riches. A great curse on humanity is inequality that leads to poverty. Poverty is nothing but a status of inadequacy in the standard of living of some. A state of being very poor called poverty is a dangerous signal for prosperity everywhere. The poverty trap is a common feature in an under developed country i.e. leaving the people no better off even after an increase in income. To make the problem less severe, the governments of these less developed countries go for many remedial measures. The efficacy of such measures depends mainly on the part of the government in identifying the socially unfavourable or disadvantaged group who are less wealthy and have fewer opportunities than most people.

To eradicate poverty, we need to rethink fundamentally, the very objectives of development. It should be assessed no longer simply in quantitative terms of financial and economic growth, resulting in a better standard of living. Rather, we need to measure it qualitatively, in terms of people's participation, human rights, gender equality and ecological sustainability. In other words, the standard of life.

Any development-oriented action of the government should focus mainly on the three groups of individuals. The outcome of development policies and principles should be equitable and just in order to avoid the existence of marginalised and handicapped groups within them. Otherwise, the disadvantaged group will become a burden. In several countries the status of women has been inferior to that of men and as has been that of children. Respect for the human rights is vital to any society's future health and prosperity. There is enough evidence to show that women and children need empowerment and support. Let our children have the chance to grow to a full and satisfying adulthood, and assume a constructive role in society and let our women enjoy a fair and decent status in society in order to have overall development.

The next part of the paper deals with the demographic position of women and children in the countries of South Asia with special reference to India.

South Asia

South Asia is a land of many contrasts. Its landscape ranges from the mighty peaks of the Himalayas in the north, through to vast plains and arid desert, to tropical forests and palm-fringed beaches in the South. More than one-fifth of the world's people live here, and a long history of foreign invasions has left a mosaic of hugely different cultures, religions and traditions and thousands of languages and dialects.

Nearly 85 per cent of the world's population lives in Asia and Africa. Of these two major areas, nearly 63 per cent of their population is accounted by Asia, mainly from the two countries–China and India.

Most South Asia's people live in villages scattered across the fertile river floodplains, in mountain valleys or along the coasts, but increasing numbers are migrating to the cities in search of work. Overcrowding is a serious problem in both rural and urban areas. In many cities, thousands of people are forced to live in slums or on the streets.

A massive, towering wall of snow-capped mountains stretches in an arc across the north, isolating South Asia from the rest of the continent. The huge floodplains and deltas of the Indus, Ganges and Brahmaputra rivers separate the mountains from the rest of the Peninsula: A great rolling plateau is bordered on either side by coastal hills called the Eastern and Western Ghats. Deforestation is a problem in the tropical south as well as in the Himalayas, where trees are being felled for fuelwood, causing soil erosion. Many of the large cities suffer from poor air quality. Over 60 per cent of the population is involved in agriculture, but most farms are small, and produce only enough food to feed one family. Grains are the staple food crops.

The Position of Women in South Asia

In 1960, 2.1 billion of the world's 3 billion people i.e., 70 per cent of the global population lived in less developed regions. By late 1999, the population of less developed regions had grown to 4.8 billion i.e., 80 per cent, and 98 per cent of the projected growth of the world's population by 2025 will occur in these regions. It is interesting to note that out of every 100 humans, 57 are Asian, 51 are females, 6 individuals control 50 % of the world's wealth, 70 are unable to read, 50 suffer from malnutrition, 1 is near death and 1 is about to be born and only 1 has a college education.

In early 2001, nearly one-third of the world's population was living in just two countries, with a population in excess of one billion i.e., China and India. Of the world's 1.3 billion poor people, it is estimated that nearly 70 per cent are women. Between 75 and 80 per cent of the world's 27 million refugees are women and children. Of the world's nearly one billion illiterate adults, two-thirds are women. In most countries, women do approximately twice the unpaid work that men do.

Women are an integral and vital force in the development process and they are a key to socio–economic progress. Particularly rural women, form the backbone of the agricultural labour force across much of the developing world and produce 35–45 per cent of GDP and well–over 50 per cent of the developing world's food. Yet, half a billion rural women are poor and lack access to resources and markets (Geneva Declaration, 1992). An estimated 20 million unsafe abortions are performed worldwide every year, resulting in the deaths of 70,000 women. Approximately 6,00,000 women die every year, over 1600 every day, from causes related to pregnancy and child birth.

In Asia, women perform over 50 per cent of the labour involved in intensive rice cultivation. In the case of most of the South Asian (SAARC) countries, except Bhutan, the percentage increase of the female population exceeds the percentage increase of the male population. (See Table 1) In Bhutan, the percentage is more or less equal.

Table 1
Percentage Increase in Men and Women in South Asian Countries (1990 – 2010)

Country	*Women*	*Men*
Bangladesh	88	77
Bhutan	62	63
India	81	70
Nepal	81	64
Pakistan	95	84
Sri Lanka	102	67

Source: The Sex and Age Distribution of the World Population, United Nations, 1999.

In most South Asian countries, elderly females exceed the number of elderly males (Table 2). Table 3 indicates that, globally, amongst the very elderly (80 years of age and over) females outnumber males. However, the ratio of very elderly women compared to man is lower in South Asia than it is in the world as a whole. The bulk of the world's elderly population is in less developed countries. Asia alone contains around 52% of the world's senior citizens.

More than 120 parliamentarians, ministers and observers from 30 countries in Asia and the Pacific, as well as Central Asian, African, Arab and European countries, gathered at the 3rd Asian Women Parliamentarians and Ministers

Conference-Engendering MDGs:A Challenge, held in Colombo, Sri Lanka on the 2-3 August, 2005.

Table 2
Elderly Population-Women and Men in South Asia by Country

Country	*60+ as % in population*		*70+ as % in population*	
	Women	*Men*	*Women*	*Men*
Bangaladesh	9.1	8.4	57.1	56.9
Bhutan	11.5	9.5	51.5	44.8
India	13.3	11.7	59.4	56.8
Pakistan	9.6	8.8	54.2	56.7
Sri Lanka	14.3	14.1	66.9	68.5
Nepal	11.7	10.2	50.2	51.3

Source: As for Table 1.

Table 3
Absolute (in'000) and Relative Frequencies of Women and Men 80 Years and Over, World and South Asia

Region	1995		2025	
	Women	Men	Women	Men
WORLD	40,006 (13.3)	21,519 (8.9)	84,896 (13.4)	51,027 (9.4)
SOUTH ASIA	3,824 (8.1)	3,539 (7.9)	13,369 (10.6)	10,525 (8.9)

Source: As for Table 1.

The Conference brought parliamentarians and women ministers together to review the current situation of women in the region and worked to improve the status of women and implement legislation to empower women. Also discussed was the impact of the Millennium Development Goals in promoting gender equality and the empowerment of women. The Hon. Minister of Information of Namibia, Mrs. Netumbo Nandi Ndaiwah, and Dr. Fatna El K'heli, Deputy Speaker of the Moroccan Parliament represented the Forum of African and Arab Parliamentarians on Population and Development (FAAPPD) while eight European MPs represented the Inter-European Parliamentarians Forum on Population and Development (IEPFPD). A number of observers from different International NGOs, youth representatives and UNFPA officials also took part in the conference. A one-year Plan of Action was adopted to further involve male and female parliamentarians in effort to achieve the goals of better women's participation in public life, legislation on the elimination of violence against women, and a special programme to involve male parliamentarians in women's empowerment.

A top United Nations' expert said in July, 2005: "Violence against women remains dramatic in Afghanistan in its intensity and pervasiveness, in public and private spheres of life. At least 6.5 million people out of a population of between 21 and 26 million are dependent on food aid, and there is a very real risk of famine. Afghanistan has one of the lowest life expectancies in the world - just 44.5 years. A fifth of its children die before they reach the age of five. About two million Afghans are now living abroad, most of them in Iran and Pakistan. In Kabul, an estimated 500,000 people are homeless or living in makeshift accommodation. Only 40% of children are vaccinated against major diseases, and barely 25 % of the population has access to safe drinking water and adequate sanitation. There is just one doctor per 6,000 people, and one nurse per 2,500 people. Some 72,000 new cases of tuberculosis are reported every year. Women account for most TB deaths. Up to 100 people are killed or wounded by mines and unexploded ordnances every month. Every year, an estimated 400,000 are affected by natural disasters."

Obviously, there is a high percentage of South Asian women in the world's population. But have they been sufficiently recognized?

The Position of Children in South Asia

In South Asia, children make up over 40 per cent of the population–around 539 million with more than 1.2 billion people under 18 years old and 13.3 per cent of the total number being under five. Together they constitute a quarter of the children in the world. Their status is not just an important measure of the human rights situation in South Asian countries, but of the state of children in the world at large. The promotion and protection of their rights is vital to the future development in the region and to that of humanity as a whole.

According to UNICEF, each year 4.7 million children die in South Asia under the age of five. Throughout South Asia, many individuals and NGOs are working to promote and protect children's rights. The protection of children in the community and in the privacy of family life poses enormous challenges for Governments in South Asia. Children are found crushing bricks in Bangladesh. Young children may be seen asleep on the streets in Nepal. The experience of poor and disadvantaged children in South Asia serves as a powerful reminder of inequalities in human rights. The child's enjoyment of civil and political rights is fundamentally compromised by a lack of economic, social and cultural rights and the economic, social and cultural development of the child cannot be advanced effectively without civil and political freedoms and protection.

Out of each 100 of the world's children, 55 are in Asia, including 19 in India and 18 in China. The births of 33 of these children went unregistered. As a result, they have no official existence, no recognition of nationality. Some of them have no access to health facilities or education without this official proof of their age and identity. Thirty-two of them suffered from malnutrition before the age of five and 27 were not immunized against any diseases. Nine died before the age of five. Eighteen do not attend school of whom 11 are girls. Eighteen of them have no access to safe drinking water and 39 live without sanitation.

Recognising the position of their children, the SAARC countries have agreed on the period 2001 to 2010 as the Decade of the Rights of the Child. The year 2010 has been set as the deadline for eradicating all child labour.

Table 4 indicates the proportion of girls and boys in the population of South Asian countries. In each case, the number of girls exceeds the number of boys. However, the girl-boy ratios vary and are lowest for Pakistan.

Table 4
Percentage of the Population of South Asian Countries

Country	*Girls*	*Boys*
Bangladesh	12.7	12
Bhutan	15.1	12.4
India	21.7	19.2
Nepal	13.5	12.2
Pakistan	10.7	10.4
Sri Lanka	29.5	26.9

Source: As for Table 1.

Many children in South Asia suffer abuse when they are put into the care of institutions that are supposed to look after their needs. Even when the abuses become widely known, the authorities appear unwilling to take decisive action to protect the children. Children in bonded or in exploitative employment are extremely vulnerable to ill-treatment. Some are ruthlessly beaten or even raped by their employees. UNICEF said that the trauma experienced by many Kabul children was chronic and the psychological impact would be long–lasting. Most of them were suffering from nightmares, anxiety and concentration problems, which have affected their appetite and their ability to play.

The Welfare of Women and Children–A Remedy to Eradicate Poverty

Since a considerable percentage of the population consists of children, they cannot be ignored. No doubt, children and women are the two groups in any economy, who need empowerment. Even though they are strong in numbers, they need more recognition. Their status in society is not secure and certain. There is no guarantee for their standard of living or their standard of life.

Women as a group may be relatively invisible but they belong to society and society needs to take care of them. It becomes the responsibility of the government. "In no society are women secure or treated as equal to men. Personal insecurity shadows them from cradle to grave . . . from childhood through adulthood; they are abused because of their gender."

The World Summit for Children seemed in itself a sign that the world had moved into a new and brighter phase in which its policy-makers and politicians could gather to consider how to guarantee children a better life rather than deal with the implications of superpower rivalry. Children's survival, development, protection and education were no longer matters of charitable concern but of legal obligation. The declaration to which the world leaders signed their name was bold and unequivocal: "The well–being of children requires political action at the highest level". The cause of children, for perhaps the first time in human history, was at the top of the world's agenda. The rights of children are not negotiable and paramount and society should be satisfied until the rights of all are guaranteed and respected. Investing in children is, quite simply, the best investment a government can make. No country has made the leap into meaningful and sustained development without investing significantly in its children.

The world should be under no illusion. Despite all extraordinary developments in the world, and all its wealth and skills, these have not been fully harnessed to deliver a world fit for children to live in. This is the result of misguided leadership and a dereliction of duty.

The UN Secretary General in his report at the time of the Millennium Summit stated: "No shift in the way we think or act can be more critical than this: we must put people at the centre of everything we do. No calling is more noble and no responsibility greater, than that of enabling them, women and children, in cities and villages around the world, to make their lives better."

Indian Social Issues and Policies Involving Females and Children

Admitting its failure to prevent the increasing incidence of female foeticide in India, the Government announced a Special Task Force, to tackle the problem. "The two major areas in the health sector where India failed are containing the spread of HIV/AIDS and bringing down the number of female foeticides in the country. New technologies like ultrasound and sex-determining blood tests are abused as they are used to abort female foetuses in several states leading to adverse sex ratios. Every girl has a right to be born and unless the status of the woman is improved in society, female foeticide and infanticide will continue." Amendments to the *Medical Termination of Pregnancy* Act have been sent to the Government, as stricter laws were needed to protect the girl child: The sharp decline in the number of girls being born will not only have demographic effects like no brides for men but also lead to an increased number of sexual crimes against women. Delhi today has 865 girls to a 1000 boys while Chandigarh has 845 girls to 1000 boys. The statistics also show that the problem is worse in the educated upper class, which has more access to latest technology. This is why awareness campaigns and improvements in the economic status of women is the key to preventing these murders.

The governments of South Asia have recognized their important responsibility towards children. They have reinforced this commitment collectively, making children a priority area.

Even in the developed countries, the women's share of managerial jobs is below 40%. While law, medicine and engineering have sufficient female representation, their participation in decision-making remains low. The gender gap is omnipresent. There are abundant women in low status jobs but few women own businesses and employ others. There are only 20 countries in the world which have 30% or more women in parliament. The leaders are Rwanda (48%) followed by Sweden (45.3%), Norway (37.9%) and Finland (37.5%). In all parliaments across the globe, taken together, women's participation is only an average 16.3%. In Arab countries, the rate is 8.2%. In India, the attempt to pass the Bill for 33% Reservation for Women in Parliament has failed to get acceptance due to the stubbom opposition of certain political parties. However, at Panchayat level such a reservation for women has been highly successful with more and more women heading the local Panchayats. It is good to mention that Bangladesh, Mozambique, New Zealand, S. Korea and Sao Tome have women Prime Ministers while Chile, Finland, Latvia, Liberia and Phillippines have women Presidents and Germany has a woman Chancellor.

In the world of media, the number of women journalists and communicators is increasing especially in the press, radio, television and the electronic media. However, the percentage of senior media executives and decision-makers is limited to 3%. In academia, a traditional stronghold of women, the number of women teachers is higher, but at the highest level, such as Chancellors or Vice-Chancellors of universities, their representation is very low. It may take many years before women attain their rightful position of at least 50% of decision-making positions. The key in this process has been the education of girls and women from primary to university-level studies. Sexual harassment in the workplace whether on the farm or in executive chambers or in factories or shops is rampant. Framing appropriate policies, laws and protecting women's rights and the strict enforcement of laws will help ensure a safe and secure environment for women to achieve their destined goal of empowerment.

India's Budget for 2006-07 contained the following policy proposals and information.

- *Surva Siksha Abhiyan:* 93 per cent of children in the age group 6-14 years are in school. The number of children not in school has fallen by about one crore to a 10,041 crore in 2006-07; 500,000 additional classrooms well be constructed and 150,000 more teachers are to be appointed;
- *Mid-day Meal Scheme:* There are now 12 crore of children covered. Funding for this scheme is to be increased from Rs. 3,010 crore to Rs. 4,813 crore.
- *Drinking Water and Sanitation:* 56,270 dwellings and 140,000 schools are to be covered in the current financial year; non-recurrent assistance of Rs. 213

crore to be provided in 2006-07 for setting up district-level water testing laboratories and field-level water testing kits; provision for Rajiv Gandhi National Drinking Water Missing to be increased from Rs. 3,645 crore to Rs. 4,680 crore and for the Rural Sanitation Campaign from Rs. 630 crore to Rs. 720 crore.

- *National Rural Health Mission:* More than 200,000 Associated Social Health Activists (ASHA) to be fully functional and over 1,000 block level community health centres to provide round the clock services; their allocation is increased from Rs. 6,553 to Rs. 8,207 crore.
- *Integrated Child Development Services*: An additional 188,168 centres are to be created to assist the States to the extent of 50 per cent of the actual expenditure incurred for supplementary nutrition or 50 per cent of the cost norms, whichever is the lesser cost estimated at Rs. 1,500 crore and this assistance to increase to Rs. 1,700 crore; total allocation for ICDS is to be increased from Rs. 3,315 crore to Rs. 4,087 crore.
- *National Rural Employment Guarantee Scheme:* An allocation of Rs. 14,300 crore for rural employment in 2006-07 with Rs. 11,300 crore under NREO Act and Rs. 3000 crore under SGRY, more funds are to be provided according to need.
- *Jawaharlal Nehru National Urban Renewal Mission:* For urban renewal, the Indian Government will make an estimated outlay of Rs. 6,250 crore for 2006-07 with a grant of Rs. 4,595 crore; the Government is to promote the establishment of new towns, preferably focussed on a specific industry, for example information technology, or a specific theme, for example education or health.
- *National Social Assistance Programme:* Old age pension to destitutes over the age of 65 years to increase from Rs. 75 per month to Rs. 200 per month; Rs. 1,430 crore provided for 2006-07; State Governments are urged to make an equal contribution. A system is to be established, for this purpose, within two years, for pensions to be credited directly to the account of the beneficiary at a post office or a bank.
- *Women and Children:* Gender sensitivities in the budgetary allocations highlighted through an enlarged statement on gender. Budgeting includes schemes whereby 100 per cent of the allocation is for the benefit of women as well as schemes where at least 30 per cent of the allocation is targeted towards women; The statement covers 24 demands for grants in 18 Ministries-Departments and five. Union Territories and schemes with an outlay of Rs. 28,737 crore; 32 Ministries and Departments have set up Gender Budgeting Cells.
- *Scheduled Castes and Scheduled Tribes:* A statement on schemes for the welfare and development of SCs and STs is included in Budget ; allocations for

schemes benefiting only SCs and ST is enhanced by 14.5 per cent to Rs. 2,902 crore and for schemes with at least a 20 per cent allocation for SCs and STs is enhanced by 13.9 per cent to Rs. 9,690 crore ; equity contributions to the National SC Finance and Development Corporation increased to Rs. 37 crore and to the National Safai Karamchari Finance and Development Corporation to Rs. 80 crore.

- *Minorities: Corpus of Maulana Azad Educational Foundation* to be doubled to 200 crore; Rs. 16.47 crore to be contributed to strengthen the equity base of the National Minorities Development and Finance Corporation; The Corporation's to intensify efforts to reach a artisans and weavers in urban and semi-urban centres especially in districts with a concentration of minorities; programme to focus on skill enhancement, credit and techno-managerial support; The allocation to the National Council for Promotion of the Urdu Language is increased from Rs. 10 crore to Rs. 13 crore; Government to finance 20,000 merit-cum-means based scholarships to encourage students to pursue higher studies.
- *Kasturba Gandhi Balika Vidyalaya Scheme:* 1,000 new residential schools for girls from SC, ST, OBC and minority communities to be opened in 2006-07; Rs. 128 crore is provided and an additional sum of Rs. 172 crore is to be provided during the year; as a further incentive to a girl who passes the VIII Standard Examination and enrols in a secondary school, a sum of Rs. 3,000 is to be deposited in her name, to be withdrawn by her on reaching 18 years of age.

Enhanced women's participation in decision-making at the higher level will be possible only when women achieve leadership positions. This will not be possible automatically because male-leaders will hardly surrender their chairs to women on their own. A sustained and planned campaign is required to equip women leaders to occupy positions of power by creating quotas for important positions, by the committing political parties to fixed quotas for women in parliaments and other agencies and creating monitoring mechanisms to audit progress in women's movements from the insignificant level to the pinnacles of authority. The glass ceiling is not so brittle, there is a steel coating above it!

Is India's Large Population an Asset?

India's billion plus population is slated to overtake that of China by the middle of this century. It is regarded by policy-planners not as a liability but as an asset that could drive economic growth. With just 2.4% of the global land mass housing 16% of the global population, successive Indian governments have been faced with the problem of how to reduce ever increasing pressure on ever-dwindling resources. Now India's massive workforce is being seen as the country's greatest resource. This change has been aided by the revolution in the information technology sector. Over the last decade, India has emerged as a major back office to the world, with global firms outsourcing work ranging from credit card processing to air ticketing to take advantage of the country's less expensive, educated, English-speaking workforce.

India produces 2.5 million information technology (IT), engineering and life sciences graduates a year, besides about 650,000 post-graduates in science and IT related subjects. The IT sector alone employs about 850,000 graduates and professionals while the pharmaceutical and biotechnology sectors are snapping up others. The government says 402 million Indians are aged between 15 and 59, the working age, and that this number will grow to 820 million by 2020.

Economists such as Jayati Ghosh, of the Jawaharlal Nehru University, advocate increased investment in areas like health infrastructure, education and sanitation if India wants to take advantage of its workforce opportunities. India will also need to improve the lot of the 20 or 30% of its population which is currently below the poverty line. The population growth rate has been declining. India will achieve population stabilization by 2015 to 2020 when its fertility rate declines to 2.1, the level required to replenish the existing population.

Conclusion

Political commitment at the highest levels, matched with resources and sustained over time, is crucial for the success of democracy in bringing the desired end i.e. the welfare of the society.

In a real democracy, young people and women should be involved in all decisions that affect their lives. There should be shadow youth and women's council for all government departments so that youth and women can review and have an input in what goes on in their area. Let the corrupt powerful persons in the poor countries care more about their own people.

BIBLIOGRAPHY AND REFERENCES

Books

R. Ahuja *Social Problems in India*, Rawat Publications, Jaipur and New Delhi, 1997.

Bible, "Genesis"–Chapter 2, Verse 18.

J.C. Johari, *Indian Politics*, Vishal Publication, Jalandhar, 2001.

V.D. Mahajan, *Political Theory*', S. Chand & Company Ltd., New Delhi-2000.

Ragini Sen, '*Ave the Billion*'–*A Social Psychological Perspective on India's Population*-2005.

Mary Eming Young. *Early Child Development: Investing in the Future*, World Bank, Washington.

Journals and Magazines

Economic and Social Commission for Asia and the Pacific–ESCAP, 1991, *Status of Elderly Women in the Asia and Pacific Region* Bangkok.

M.V. Pylee, Former Vice-Chancellor, University of Cochin, "Constitution of India", *Competition Success Review*, 2002.

M.C. Paul, 'Persuasive Policy Option for Checking Population Explosion, *Yojana*, June 1998.

H.R. Uma, "The Ageing Population" *Yojana, A Development Monthly*, Vol. 49, October 2005.

Publications Division, Ministry of Information and Broadcasting, Government of India, 2002, *India 2002*, A Reference Annual.

Reports

Women's World Summit Foundation, 1211, Geneva 1, Switzerland, 2003.

Report of the Geneva Declaration for Rural Women, 1992.

Human Development Report, United Nations Development Programme, 1995.

Library of Congress, Regional Political Parties in India, 1995.

Report of the Secretary General, 'United Nations Development for Economic and Social Information and Policy Analysis, Population Division. E/CN (9) 1997/9.

Reports of the United Nations–1999, 2000.

Reports of the Department of Human Resources Development, 1995.

Report of the United National Population Fund–UNFPA, (a) State of World Population Report. Integrated Population and Development Project, November, 1999.

Report of the UNICER, 'The State of the World's Children 2003'.

National Population Policy, India, 2000.

'Report of the Government of India–Demographic Scenario' Compiled by Mr. Manmohan Singh–Secretary, Ministry of Health and Family Welfare.

Economic Survey of India–2003-04.

A. Kofi Annan, Secretary–General of the UN, "We the peoples" The Role of the UN in the 21st Century, UN Department of Public Information, New York, 2000, page 7.

Carol Bellamy, Executive Director of UNICEF, United Nations Children's Fund, UNICEF, 2004.

3rd Asian Women Parliamentarians' and Ministers' Conference–"Engendering MDGs: Challenge",–Colombo, Srilanka, 23rd Aug., 2005.

Daily Newspapers

"Bad Economics", *The Hindu*, 18 October 2005.

"Population Policy–2000", Editorial in *The Hindu*, 18 February 2000.

"Population Policy: Nostrums Revisited", S. Swaminathan, *The Hindu*, 15 March 2000.

Websites

www.indiachild.com

www.postcolonialweb.org

http://www.censusindia.net/results/population.html

http://www.woman.ch/-WWSF Report of Women's World Summit Foundation, 121 Geneva 1, Switzerland, 2003.

24

POVERTY, ENERGY CRISIS AND SOCIAL DISADVANTAGE: AN INDIAN FOCUS

Siddhartha Sarkar

Introduction

Poverty is one of the most fundamental issues, and urgently needs to be addressed. Moving people out of poverty forms a basis of much international development policy (Sarkar 2005a). In almost all of the South Asian countries there exist absolute poverty. There are high rates of poverty among rural people, indigenous South Asians and some groups of immigrants. It negatively affects the life chances and opportunities of women and children. Children are vulnerable and dependent, and the effects and impacts of poverty can so easily stultify and distort the future lives of women and children by robbing them of opportunities to develop their potential.

Poverty can be measured in different ways. It is often expressed in relation to a poverty line, a defined income level that is updated regularly. Each measure has advantages and disadvantages, and slightly different methods of estimation and updating may fabricate somewhat different results. As well as measuring family incomes, it is useful to consider the distribution of assets or wealth, which might offer some protection in the event of an income crunch, such as hasty unemployment or prolonged illness. People living on low incomes report poor health and the incidence of illness at much higher rates than people on high incomes. This can be due to stress, crowded housing and poor nutrition. Poverty can also lead to homelessness. Both the shortage of low-cost private rental accommodation and continuing high levels of unemployment affect people's ability to pay rent. Members of families with low incomes often have limited educational opportunities, leading to much narrower employment options. It can also contribute to poor self-esteem and less participation in society. In this way, poverty and social exclusion can affect successive generations.

According to the World Energy Assessment, energy services are indispensable for human survival and development. They play a critical role across the whole spectrum of development activities. Of the three billion people living in rural areas in developing countries today, nearly 2 billion still have neither access to nor can pay for modern energy carriers, such as electricity and/or liquid or gaseous fuels. These energy carriers provide essential energy services such as heating for cooking, motive power, lighting and cooling (refrigeration). Their absence seriously reducing income opportunities and the quality of life. Access to electricity and other modern energy sources is a necessary, but not a sufficient, requirement for economic and social development. The escape from poverty also requires, among other things, clean water, adequate sanitation and health services, a good education system and a communication network. Yet cheap and available energy is indispensable. Electricity provides the best and most efficient form of lighting; most household appliances require it. Kerosene and Liquefied Petroleum Gas (LPG) are more energy-efficient cooking fuels than traditional biomass.

The concentration of indoor air pollutants coming out from combustion of biofuels such as wood, agriculture crops and dung cake used by rural households in developing countries cause severe health problems, especially for women and children under five years of age. Mothers and their children spend an average of six hours per day in highly polluted indoor areas. It has been estimated that approximately half the global population and up to 90 per cent of rural households in developing countries still rely on biomass fuels and about 75 per cent of Indian households use biofuels for cooking purposes. (Sarkar 2005b). Typically cooked indoors in open fires or poorly functioning stoves, leads to levels of air pollution that are among the highest ever measured. Therefore, indoor air pollution with biofuels is an issue that requires to be addressed through gender, energy, environment and health policy.

Some of highest concentrations of pollutants come about due to the use of biofuels for cooking in rural indoor environments (Sarkar 2004). In developed countries transformation has without exception come with by a shift from biofuels to petroleum products (kerosene, LPG) and electricity. In developing countries even where cleaner more sophisticated fuels are available, households often continue to use biomass (Smith 1987). Although the portion of global energy derived from biofuel has fallen substantially there is evidence that biofuels use is increasing among the poor. Poverty is one of the main hurdles to the adoption of cleaner fuels and slow pace of development in many countries implies that biofuels will continue to be used by the poor for many years. Poor people frequently lack access to affordable, reliable, safe and environmentally benign sources of energy. This hinders their efforts to move out of poverty and seriously constrains their ability to improve their living situations. People without modern energy services must spend more of their time and physical energy on survival and, therefore, have fewer opportunities to pursue educational and income-generating activities.

Limited access to energy is also a problem that has a disproportionate effect on women, especially in rural areas. Rural women spend up to 25 per cent of their time carrying heavy loads of fuel over increasingly long distances, at great risk to their health and safety.

In most ethnicity, women and men have differing roles and responsibilities according to socially defined division of labour based on gender. This gender inequity is reflected in a variety of social and economic dimensions. In terms of reproductive activities, women generally have primary responsibility for the care and feeding of children and families, as well as health care and education. In many developing countries, it is the women who perform most of the work related to subsistence agriculture, plus gathering and managing fuel and water as a part of the household responsibility. Their productive activities are often unpaid and labour-intensive. When women in rural areas do generate income, it tends to be within the informal sector, and not adequately reflected in national accounting systems. This serves to under-represent the importance of energy as an input to women's economic activities. Because they operate mostly in the informal and unpaid sectors, poor women have less access to financial resources, credit and equipment than do men, and less of a voice in household, or community-level, decision making.

Gender-poverty is a problem that has a disproportionate effect on women and girls, especially in rural areas. The most obvious factors relate to time and physical effort. Many women in developing countries have to spend long hours gathering fuel and hauling water, using their own labour to carry heavy loads over long distances in addition to other informal work. When women are overburdened, they are more likely to keep their daughters home from school to assist with own household activities, including fuel and water collection, thereby limiting opportunities for girls to move forward through education, and rising the likelihood that their families will remain in poverty.

Energy and Vulnerability

In South Asia, millions of women spend hours each day carrying fuel and water, taking away valuable time for other activities. Women in rural areas in South Asia are at the bottom rung of the so-called energy ladder, which associates users of progressively cleaner, more efficient fuels with corresponding higher levels of income. It is a situation that is both a determinant and a manifestation of poverty and inequitable gender relations. Traditional biomass (dung, agriculture residues and fuel wood) is at the bottom rung of the ladder for cooking, with charcoal, then kerosene and finally Liquid Petroleum Gas (LPG) and electricity are towards the top. Traditional rural energy systems are characterized by the use of biomass, in the form of wood, plant residues, dung for heating and cooking, and human energy and or animal energy for motive power.

Human energy, measured in energy units, constitutes a small proportion of energy resources consumed compared to other sources. But the labour of women and children are indispensable in making the energy chain work such as the extraction/collection of biomass to its transformation into an energy service such as heat for cooking. The extraction, transport, processing, conversion and distribution are the responsibility and the work of women, girls and boys primarily, according to the social norms which prescribe which activities are the obligations of women and which are those of men. Women are also at the bottom rung of another energy ladder for motive force. They depend entirely on their own motive force and are normally without any other resources such as animal power, mechanical or electrical devices for such energy transformations. Even where animal power and/or mechanical equipment are available in the household, gender norms, relations of power and division of labour tend to exclude women from use and certainly ownership and control of these assets.

This energy situation has tremendous survival and developmental implications since the tasks associated with food preparation are critical to the prevailing agricultural systems. Small landowners engaged in agricultural production make up about three quarters of the rural population. Their production, the main source of rural livelihood and income, is primarily based on human and animal energy that is on muscle power. This motive power requires the biological conversion and storage of food into useful energy. Food intake, crucial for the daily reproduction of human energy for agricultural labour, in turn depends on processing and preparing the food harvested or gathered. The frequent, repetitive tasks associated with post-harvest food preparation, such as provisioning for water, firewood, grinding grain, pressing cooking oil and processing other ingredients are women's responsibilities and obligations. These are in addition to women's other labour inputs in agricultural production and in gathering the wild resources used in food preparation, oil and soap making and other household provisioning needs. Dependence on such traditional energy systems leads to multiple social and economic costs, which are overwhelmingly borne by poor women. Linked to the lower energy efficiency of fuel wood combustion are its higher emissions of sulphur, carbon dioxide and particulates, pollutants resulting from incomplete combustion. The occupational hazards for women and for their young children from exposure to indoor air pollution, smoke and particulates when cooking are the negative impacts in terms of health of burns, acute respiratory infections, lung disease, internal disorders and eye problems. Load carrying of fuel and other materials, for example in palm oil processing takes a health toll in terms of injury, miscarriages, and fatigue. Poor women in particular pay a disproportionate price for energy services not only because of the inefficiency and associated health costs. Long hours are spent collecting water and firewood for food preparation and agro-processing, as well as the multiple other tasks that sustain rural livelihoods.

The arduous and time-consuming nature of women's activities in such energy systems has significant opportunity costs in terms of other activities. These are agricultural production and other productive and income generating uses of time and energy, as well as time and energy for child care, health, education, rest, social and cultural activities, recreation and personal maintenance. As traditional fuel wood sources and water get increasingly scarce, the costs in terms of women's time and energy become more severe. This can also mean that they need to generate cash to buy firewood that is no longer possible to collect individually and this cash generation in its turn takes time and energy, including marketing time. Widening access to modern energy services can be a catalyst for sustainable human development, given these patterns of energy uses. But increased income is necessary to be able to afford to climb another rung of the energy ladder and release human time and energy for human development purposes. However, this increased income is not possible without spending further time and human energy, when usage levels are already very high. Such is the energy-poverty trap which women in South Asia, in particular are struggling to get out of.

The relationship between gender and poverty is a complex and controversial issue that is now being discussed more than ever before. Although much policymaking has been informed by the idea of feminization of poverty, the precise nature of the nexus between gender and poverty needs to be better understood and operationalized in policymaking. The difficulty originates from the different shapes and forms gender inequalities and poverty take depending on the economic, social and ideological context.

Yet another difficulty involves the scarcity of gender disaggregated data for a number of South Asian countries. For the last three decades, many women's advocates have been arguing that women are poorer than men. The most common empirical expression of this idea is the concept of feminization of poverty. This idea has become popular both in shaping analyses of poverty and poverty alleviation strategies. Thus, targeting women has become one means for gender-sensitive poverty alleviation. Poor women have become the explicit focus of policymaking, for example, in the areas of micro credit programmes and income generation activities. However, the universal validity of the feminization of poverty is being empirically challenged. Although the idea that there are gender differences in experiences of poverty is not abandoned, a more nuance and complex analysis of poverty and gender inequalities is emerging. This, in turn, is giving rise to a more gender-aware approach to poverty elimination strategies.

In the literature on poverty, one frequently posed question is: are women poorer than men? In these discussions, the concept of feminization of poverty is used as a short hand for a variety of ideas. It can mean either one or a combination of the following.

- Women compared to men have a higher incidence of poverty.
- Women's poverty is more severe than men's.
- Over time, the incidence of poverty among women is increasing compared to men.

In addressing women's poverty, many studies measure the incidence of income or consumption poverty among female-headed households and compare it to that of male-headed counterparts.

On a priori grounds, there are reasons to be concerned about the welfare of female-headed households, since women are subject to discrimination in labour, credit and a variety of other markets and they own less property compared to men. In some societies, widows, divorced or abandoned women may be subject to social exclusion, isolation and harassment, making it very difficult for them to maintain a livelihood for themselves or their children. Women heads of households with young children may face great time constraints and may have to limit their work hours. Even though female-headed households are a relatively small proportion of households. This has been seen as evidence that women are becoming poorer over time relative to men. The comparative poverty of female-headed households vis-à-vis male-headed counterparts is not universal. It has also been argued that it may be more meaningful to study female-maintained households as opposed to those headed by women. Female-maintained households are those in which women are the primary providers of the family. What is also necessary to understand is the process through which households become women-headed or female-maintained rather than viewing headship as a static indicator. When programmes targeting female-headed households analyze the reasons for the rise, nature and vulnerability of such households, it has been possible to design effective anti-poverty programmes that target female headship.

Engendering Poverty

The household-headship approach in the studies of gender inequalities and poverty resulted from the fact that the household has been the unit of analysis for studying poverty and female headship was the only gender-transparent factor in this approach. This line of research has been very useful in revealing characteristics of households associated with the gender of household heads, such as differences in dependency ratios and time constraints. However, it also had the effect of disguising other types of linkages between gender and poverty. For example, it failed to address the poverty experienced by women in non-poor households resulting from gender bias in the distribution of resources within households. Thus, gendered analyses of poverty need to go beyond household-headship approach. At the microeconomic level, there is a need to understand the gender and age based power relations within households, the mechanisms of cooperation and conflict as well as the dynamics of bargaining that shape the distribution of work, income and assets. Such processes of bargaining do not take place in a social vacuum, however. They are affected by social norms as well as the differential access to opportunities and resources men and women have outside the household. Therefore, the analysis also needs to be extended to the meso level, where the interaction of households and household members with a variety of other economic and social institutions such as the state or markets is studied. Often institutions, which are not inherently gender biased, are nonetheless bearers of gender bias. In a similar vein, engendering the macroeconomic level of analysis is equally important since the economic, social, political and ecological environments in which households maintain themselves or fall into destitution are shaped by macroeconomic policies (Sen 1990).

Poverty has been traditionally understood to mean a lack of access to resources, productive assets and income resulting in a state of material deprivation. Emphasizing deficiency in private consumption, poverty has been defined as private consumption per person falling below a particular level. In this approach, absolute rather than relative poverty has been the focus of attention. Recently, the concept of poverty and the discussion of its causal explanations have been broadened. As the consumption/income approach to defining poverty has come under increased criticism, it has been suggested that in the analysis of poverty common property resources and state-provision of commodities should be taken into account and the concept of poverty should be broadened to include lack of dignity and autonomy. The inclusion of the latter in the meaning of poverty draws from the insight that being non-poor implies a freedom from the necessity to perform activities that are regarded as subservient and (their) ability to choose self-fulfilling and rewarding life styles. In these increasingly multidimensional conceptualizations, poverty is being viewed as a process, rather than as a static concept. For example, the poor, rather than being viewed as passive victims of society in need of handouts, are viewed as agents who struggle to cope with poverty with whatever assets they may posses. The emphasis is on the assets they own and resources they can access rather than on what they lack. Along these lines, in the literature that focuses on the coping mechanisms of the poor, the concept of assets has been extended to include social capital and household relations (Moser 1996).

Furthermore, new qualitative, as opposed to quantitative, approaches to poverty assessment have emphasized the poor own criteria of poverty as well as their own solutions (Chambers 1996). The policy implications of this new approach have emphasized programmes that enable the poor to exercise their agency, their own solutions and creativity by creating an enabling environment as well as making available critical external resources such as credit. Empowerment of the poor is viewed as critical to the success of poverty elimination. Another recent approach, the social exclusion approach, emphasizes the importance of institutions and norms that exclude certain groups from a variety of social networks and the importance of social solidarity in sustaining livelihoods. These new insights on poverty have far reaching implications for analyzing the gendered nature of poverty as well as the relationship between gender inequalities and overall poverty levels.

The UNDP has contributed to these efforts both by broadening the discussions around the conceptualizations and measurements/assessments of poverty as well as by introducing new approaches to poverty elimination policies. Particularly, the capabilities/entitlements approach spearheaded by Sen, which constitutes the analytical basis of UNDP's Human Development Reports and the concept of Sustainable Human Development have helped broaden the understanding of poverty and vulnerability. According to this perspective, poverty represents the absence of some basic capabilities to function. Functioning, in turn, represent the doings and beings of a person. Thus, the capability approach reconciles the notions of absolute and relative poverty, since relative deprivation in incomes and commodities can lead to an absolute deprivation in minimum capabilities (UNDP 1997). UNDP bases the concept of human poverty, which was introduced in the 1997 Human Development Report, on the capabilities approach. As distinct from income poverty, human poverty refers to the denial of opportunities and choices for living a most basic or tolerable human life. It therefore, takes into account more than the minimum necessities for material well-being and views poverty as multidimensional. The Human Poverty Index (HPI), also introduced in the same report, measures deprivation in basic human development i.e., a short life, lack of basic education and lack of access to public and private resources.

Although human poverty is related to income poverty, the two concepts are not the same. Measurements of income poverty, such as the head-count ratio (HCR), focus on levels of absolute income poverty, while the HPI focuses on capabilities such as access to clean water, health services and the level of literacy. Focusing on the concept of human poverty helps us see the causes of poverty, not merely its symptoms. Quantitative measures such as the HCR implicitly treat households as harmonious units and limit our understanding of gender and poverty. Just as growth based approaches to poverty alleviation assume that the benefits of growth automatically trickle down to poor households, consumption/income approaches to poverty assessment assume that the benefits of an income increase in poor households trickle down to all members equally. However, households exhibit conflict and inequality as well as cooperation and sharing. Thus, the concept of human poverty has been helpful in shedding light on the relationship between gender inequalities and poverty. Although households are still very important as units of poverty analysis, the human poverty concept makes it possible to disaggregate the household and analyze the relative poverty or well being of household members. Such an approach focuses the discussion on gender differences in deprivation in basic education (illiteracy) health services and life expectancy (short lives) and the socially constructed constraints on the choices of various groups such as women or lower castes. Poverty eradication is an aspect of human development, which is defined as a process of enlarging people's choices (UNDP 1990).

From a human poverty or capabilities perspective, it can be seen that women are indeed poorer in most societies in many dimensions of capabilities such as education and health, but not necessarily in terms of life expectancy, although there are also societies in which women's life expectancy is shorter than men's due to maternal mortality or child mortality that may result from biases against girls' health and nutrition needs. Resource allocation within households is often biased against girls and women. In addition, it is harder for women to transform their capabilities into incomes or well being. Gender inequalities in the distribution of income, access to productive inputs such as credit, command over property or control over earned income, as well as gender biases in labour markets and social exclusion that women experience in a variety of economic and political institutions form the basis for the greater vulnerability of women to chronic poverty.

Across a wide range of cultures and levels of economic development, women tend to specialize more in unpaid reproductive or caring labour compared to men, who tend to specialize in paid production activities. Women's combined paid and unpaid labour time is greater than men's (UNDP 1997). Although it is often stated that labour is the poor's most abundant asset, women are relatively time-poor and much of their work is socially unrecognized since it is unpaid. Furthermore, when women are in paid work, the return to their labour is lower than the return to men's labour. Thus, women on average work more, but have less command over income as well as assets. Nor do they always have control or command over their own labour. In some cases, men may prohibit their wives from working outside the household and seclude them. In other cases, men may extract labour from women with the threat or actuality of violence, as for instance, in the case of unpaid women family labourers. Men tend to have more command over women's labour than vice versa so that in crisis situations, men may be able to mobilize the labour of women, while women generally do not have the reciprocal right or ability to mobilize men's labour.

Women's responsibilities for reproductive labour limit the range of paid economic activities they can undertake. Women are less mobile than men because of their reproductive/caring labour activities and because of social norms that restrict their mobility in public. In the paid sphere, they tend to be concentrated in informal labour activities (such as home working), since such activities allow them to combine paid work with unpaid reproductive labour. However, these are also insecure forms of work. It is hard for such workers to get organized for collective action. The gender-based division of labour between unpaid (and often reproductive labour) and paid labour renders women economically and socially more insecure and vulnerable to not only chronic poverty but also to transient poverty that can result from familial, personal or social and economic crises, including those that arise from macroeconomic policies, political and ethnic conflict situations or health-related crises such as the HIV/AIDS epidemics. Yet, in such crises, as in the case of structural adjustment policies and macroeconomic crises, women work harder compared to men and increase their paid and unpaid labour activities to maintain their households (Moser 1996).

This is not to argue that the stake is always loaded against women in general and poor women, in particular. For example, the feminization of labour in paid work associated with structural adjustment policies implies that women potentially can have greater control over income within the household. This can lead to an increased bargaining power for women within the household and is therefore potentially empowering. However, this comes at the expense of increased time-poverty. The concept of multidimensionality of poverty makes it clear that poor people often face trade-offs between different dimensions of poverty in their struggle with deprivation. However, women face many more such trade-offs compared to men as their economic choices are more socially constrained and as their work burden is almost universally higher. Although it is clear that poor women should not be viewed as passive victims and their agency should be recognized, gender relations and inequalities cause women and men to experience poverty differently within households.

Thus, the new approaches to the conceptualization of poverty and the recent popularity of participatory approaches to poverty assessment have helped us recognize how women are poorer in a multiplicity of dimensions of poverty and how they experience poverty differently to men. This does not mean that quantitative methods are useless or necessarily gender biased. Both the qualitative and the quantitative methods are as gender biased as the user of the methods (Kabeer 1996). While the quantitative methods have their limitations from a gender perspective as pointed out above, qualitative methods such as Participatory Poverty Assessments (PPAs), which is an approach that defines poverty through the eyes of the poor using the criteria that poor people themselves put forth, must also be carefully designed. Such assessments must be gender aware in the sense of including women's and men's views, without assuming that the needs of poor men and poor women coincide or that the assessments of poor women and poor men about poverty and their needs about poverty elimination are the same. There may also be reasons for participatory approaches to be gender biased since sometimes it may be more difficult for women to voice their views publicly or the local patriarchal ideology may be held similarly by men and women shaping views of both groups about study of poor urban communities in the developing countries.

Moser (1996) found that the principle coping response to economic crisis in developing countries is the mobilization of women's and children's labour. In three of the communities women and men performed the same amount of paid labour, but women did much more unpaid labour compared to men. In all four cases women's combined labour burden was higher than men's. Women increased their paid work often in the informal sector. Girls tended to take over the domestic work responsibilities of mothers, while boys tended to be mobilized into paid labour. Thus, girls' labour was also less visible. The gender-based earnings differentials in the informal sector are greater than those in the formal sector and feminization of the labour force under crisis conditions can lead to further deterioration of women's position in labour markets. The economic empowerment of women and capacity building for transformatory change has been emphasized in South Asia Poverty Alleviation Programme (SAPAP) supported by United Nations Development Programme (UNDP).

SAPAP started in 1994 as UNDP's effort to support South Asian countries in eradicating poverty. Bangladesh, India and Nepal were chosen as pilot areas for a programme of social mobilization through participatory community organizations of the poor. In 1996, a larger programme was formulated to include pro-poor macro-policy initiatives and participatory poverty-monitoring components in its framework, and it was expanded to include Sri Lanka, Pakistan and Maldives in its implementation area. The social mobilization component is the most critical element of the SAPAP and the synergy among the three components makes it a unique project. UNDP's contribution to social mobilization has been the promotion of experiential learning to demonstrate the effectiveness of appropriate models of social mobilization for scaling-up poverty alleviation efforts and improved participatory development planning.

In India, since 1994, the project has been implemented in three districts of Andhra Pradesh, which are characterized by high level of social stratification with high levels of poverty, caste differentiation, severe ecological degradation, landlessness and landlordism, poor transport infrastructure, high prevalence of child labour, child marriage, high underemployment due to droughts, low wages, high infant mortality and recurring epidemics like measles. According to participatory poverty assessments, households with female heads, single parents and elderly with no support mechanisms are extremely poor. More than 50 per cent of the households covered by the project are below poverty line.

The approach taken in India views the poor as agents and partners in the effort to reduce poverty, recognizing the creativity of the poor and their capacity for enterprise and accords them respect and dignity as partners in development. Based on these premises, the project has been building associations and groups to help unite the poor at both intra-and inter-village levels. The groups at the village level are called Self Help Hroups (SHGs), averaging around 16 members. The SHGs federate into Village Development Organizations (VDOs). The VDOs in turn unite into mandal level organizations. As of August 1997 there were 2,458 SHGs with 40,720 members and almost all (98 per cent) were women's associations. Most groups are caste-based.

The main focus of activity of the SHGs is to generate savings for income-generating projects in the village. The seed capital is provided by the UNDP. With its focus on the landless poor and small farmers, the seed capital is intended to increase the resource-base of the poor and gradually enable them to cross the poverty line. At the end of August 1997, the total amount of seed capital was Rs. 10 million, the total amount of savings accumulated through the SHGs was

Rs. 21.43 million and another Rs. 5.1 million was provided by the government and NGOs. Thus, the total amount of loans given out was Rs 36.5 million. More than a half of the total amount of loans (52 per cent) were given for health, education and consumption; areas which women are in need of the most, the rest were used for directly productive purposes.

The project has pioneered a unique participatory method for the identification of projects as well as beneficiaries at the grassroots level in the true sprit of planning from below. Although the entry point of the project is mainly credits and savings, the SHGs benefit the people in every aspect of life in a village community. The groups are instrumental, first in collectively identifying problems and the people or groups mostly affected by them, second in coming up with different alternatives i.e., projects as possible solutions, and finally in selecting the most suitable projects from those possible alternatives. The groups have shown enormous sensitivity to those extremely poor in the selection of female-headed households, deserted women, landless labourers, and families facing health or other problems. Thus, SHGs differ from the more traditional micro-credit programmes in that it is the group members who identify the problems, the possible solutions and projects and the allocation of loans according to criteria set by themselves.

The activities of the SHGs generated considerable advances in women's empowerment both quantitatively and qualitatively. The provision and redistribution of funds created a great support for the most vulnerable groups, the majority of which are poor women. However, the SHGs, and hence the overall project, is more beneficial in its qualitative and long-term capacity building effect on women's empowerment. The project helped women demonstrate their very high level of awareness. The collective activities under the roof of SHGs set in motion the extraordinary leadership and management skills of women. The women members report that the opportunity to save provided them with a sense of security and access to consumption and emergency loans, which has released them from subservience to money lenders, who charge extremely high interest rates. This, they point out, has given them back their self-dignity. They have gained new recognition and a new status in the community as they attended the SHG meetings and voiced their opinions on economic issues. The collaborative and positive relationships among the women members have contributed to the emergence of mutual trust and a sense of security among them. They have also gained respect in the eyes of their husbands and in-laws as they brought tangible benefits to the entire family. Men have started to appreciate the collective power of women in tackling issues of poverty. They have also begun to adopt a similar attitude in their SHGs, with women's SHGs setting an example for the entire community.

Cooperative activities of SHGs have also benefited the community in more tangible ways. These activities included construction of approach roads to bring public transport to the village, construction and operation of day care centres, local school classrooms and cleaning of irrigation tanks and canals. The dynamism of the SHGs, reflected in these community-wide activities has helped defuse social conflict as the women's groups are seen to be bringing benefits to the entire community. The empowered scheduled castes have started to question, though mildly, caste differentiation.

The SHGs not only alleviate poverty in a temporary way, but also have the potential to eradicate it by tackling the root causes and processes that reproduce poverty intergenerational. Along these lines, the women members of SHGs have formed separate young-girls SHGs to mobilize their daughters, started night education and skill training classes for child labourers, or in some instances stopped child labour, used some of the loans for reproductive health and fertility control, (in some areas) formed agricultural unions to secure the legal minimum wages and challenged gender gaps in wages, and have begun resisting child marriages that they identify as one of the root causes of destitution and women's social subordination. In this sense, SHGs rather than being coping mechanisms represent a transformatory potential for the eradication of poverty.

The benefits of the project for women, indicated above, can be summarized as follows:

- The formation of groups has provided the women with confidence and a network of solidarity to tackle issues of poverty and (gender, class and caste-based) social discrimination that confront them.
- The SHGs, through the generation of savings habit in the community, mobilized community savings and made for easy availability of loans, facilities that did not exist earlier.
- The availability of consumption and emergency loans from their own savings has released the women from subservience to moneylenders and gave them back their self-dignity.
- The project created opportunities for women for income generation through access to credit and skill formation, by contributing to family welfare and increasing their status in the family.
- Group activities by the women for social action and community infrastructure have enhanced their status and respect in the community.

Concluding Remarks

The challenge is how to enable poor women particularly, as well as men, to get out of the energy-poverty trap, and have affordable and sustainable modern energy services. The main lesson is that for energy services to be affordable by poor women and men, it has to be for end-uses, which are directly productive and income-generating. It is this chain of conversion of energy for income, which can facilitate the transition over time to cleaner, more efficient fuels, and more opportunities for enhancing productive and welfare uses of human time and energy. However, the following outlook should facilitate in integrating gender-energy-poverty concerns in developing economies:

- Some 1.6 billion people, one-quarter of the world population have no access to electricity. In the absence of vigorous new policies, 1.4 billion people will still lack electricity in 2030.
- Four out of five people without electricity live in rural areas of the developing world, mainly in South Asia and sub-Saharan Africa. But the pattern of electricity deprivation is set to change, because 95 per cent of the increase in population in the next three decades will occur in urban areas.
- Some 2.4 billion people rely on traditional biomass namely, wood, agricultural residues and dung for cooking and heating. That number will increase to 2.6 billion by 2030. In developing countries, biomass use will still represent over half of residential energy consumption at the end of the outlook period.
- Lack of electricity and heavy reliance on traditional biomass are hallmarks of poverty in developing countries. Lack of electricity exacerbates poverty and contributes to its perpetuation, as it precludes most industrial activities and the jobs they create.
- Investment will need to focus on various energy sources, including biomass, for thermal and mechanical applications to bring productive, income-generating activities to developing countries. Electrification and access to modern energy services do not *per se* guarantee poverty alleviation.
- Renewable energy technologies such as solar, wind and biomass may be cost-effective options for specific off-grid applications, while conventional fuels and established technologies are likely to be preferred for on-grid capacity expansion.

REFERENCES

Chambers, R. (1996), *Whose Reality Counts?* IT Publications, London.

Kabeer, N. (1996), Agency, Well-being and Inequality: Reflections on Gender Dimensions of Poverty. *IDS Bulletin.* 27 (1): 11–21.

Moser, C.O.M. (1996), *Confronting Crisis: A Comparative Study of Household Responses to Poverty and Vulnerability in Four Poor Urban Communities.* Environmentally Sustainable Development Series and Monograph Series No. 8. The World Bank, Washington, DC.

Sarkar, S. (2004), Air Pollution: Its Perilous Chronic Hygienic Impacts. *J Hum Ecol,* 16(2): 129-132.

Sarkar, S. (2005a), Poverty and Girl Child Labour: A Study in Brick Kilns. *South Asian Journal of Human Rights,* 1(1-2): 173-183.

Sarkar, S. (2005b), Economic Valuation and Health Linkages to Air Pollution. *International Journal of Environment and Development,* 2(2): 141-151.

Smith, K.R. (1987), *Biofuels, Air pollution and Health: A Global Review.* Plenum Press, New York.

Sen, A. (1990), Gender and Cooperative Conflict. In: Irene Tinker (ed.). *Persistent Inequalities.* Oxford University Press, Oxford.

UNDP (1990), *Human Development Report.* Oxford University Press, New York.

UNDP (1997), *Human Development Report.* Oxford University Press, New York.

INDEX